Retail Advertising

Management and Technique

William Haight

General Learning Press
250 James Street
Morristown, New Jersey 07960

Manufactured in the United States of America

Published simultaneously in Canada

Library of Congress Catalog Card Number 75-46173

ISBN 0-382-19046-7

Preface

Most people, when they think of advertising, call to mind the ads they see and hear every day. They visualize the big two-page newspaper spreads full of food items and prices, enticing fashion ads that show and tell what people are wearing and where to get it for how much, or perhaps busy little classifieds that offer jobs, find lost articles, or tell who has a used canoe for sale or a spare room for rent. Others remember the lively, colorful commercials that came with the popular television show last night, depicting happy people enjoying all sorts of new products—or old ones—in their daily activities. Still others think of gigantic billboards that introduce a splash of color to an otherwise dreary roadside, or of sparkling illustrated messages in a favorite magazine.

Business people think of these things, too, because they themselves often play the role of customers who want information about what to buy. But they think of ads primarily as tools with which they can fashion persuasive sales messages to draw customers and help make profits. Retail business people, in particular, look to advertising to assist them in selling particular products, to create traffic through their aisles, and to promote services and stimulate feelings and attitudes toward their businesses among nearby folks who are, or hopefully may become, customers.

Students who set out to study advertising are likely to think of it in terms of a future job, or a means of doing a better job in store management if they plan to enter the retail field and want to get ahead. Some students may have heard a bit about retail advertising from others, or they may have taken a peek at some facets of it by reading books or articles. A few may have had a brief introduction to retail advertising as part of a course previously taken in school or college. They will perhaps think of it in terms of layouts and copywriting, storyboards and sound effects, budgets and campaign themes and copy platforms. They may know it has much to do with *media,* the vehicles through which messages are delivered to an audience, and with other sales-stimulating activities with which it is integrated.

But our plan for this book is to hold off on examining technical things. Advertising has to do especially with *people*: the people to whom it is directed and the people and institutions (in this case, stores) who originate ads. So our Part 1 will deal with the people of America and the fast-changing, dynamic society they have created (with running comments on the implications of this society for retail advertising). It will deal, too, with the different kinds of retail stores, how they are evolving to match the fast-paced changes occurring in the society they serve, and how the people who run them work and carry on their business. It will look at the researching of markets and how this affects advertising.

Because the management and planning of advertising must precede its implementation if the latter is to have any hope of success, Part 2 will focus on what has to happen before any advertising is put into concrete form: the budgeting of funds for advertising; planning its distribution over seasons, months, weeks, and even days; and its allotment to the various departments, product lines, and services a store offers. Here also we shall consider the implications of image-building advertising as opposed to the immediate-sell ads traditionally emphasized in retailing. All these areas involve decisions so fundamental that a store's top management, not just its advertising specialists, participate in them.

Part 3 will focus on the increasingly complex problems of media selection, beginning with general guidelines for choosing channels of communication to the consumer. Each commonly used retail medium —newspapers, broadcast media, direct advertising, and others—will be examined in detail, with emphasis on its special strengths and limitations. We shall also see how a store's ads can be integrated with other means of promotion.

Part 4 will cover the work involved in creating and producing advertisements, starting with the selection of their contents and the kinds of appeals and approaches that motivate readers, listeners, and viewers. Techniques for writing advertising copy, designing and illustrating ads, and creating broadcast commercials and ads to be sent through the mail or posted on signs will be treated. Then the restraints placed on the persuasive power of advertising by legal and ethical considerations will be investigated. Finally, our book will conclude with suggestions for following through to make sure that ads do what they are supposed to do.

We realize that our readers will have varied interests, motivations, talents, and career intentions. Many will be students of retailing and/or advertising, and some will make a career of retail or local service advertising. Others will enter such fields as merchandising, display, public relations, or retail management, where they will need to know how advertising works and how to work with and through it. Still others will already be active practitioners of retailing or advertising, seeking to upgrade their own professionalism. As you read this volume, it will help, at times, to imagine that you are one of the decision-makers in advertising or management in a not-too-large retail or service establishment, and that you are looking for ways in which it can use its advertising to give better service to its customers and increase its profits. This kind of viewpoint will provide a *learning framework* from which to observe the promotional process as a whole and to see the role that technique plays in accomplishing goals.

The suggested questions and projects at the end of each chapter are intended not just as assignments for those taking formal classes, but also as learning aids for lone readers who want to review their own understanding of the salient points in each chapter and investigate their own advertising environment as well. It is often interesting to see how local situations compare to the national norms that must form the core of a book intended for use in many different geographical areas. Many of the questions and projects have this "localizing" end in view.

The bibliography contains suggested readings that will flesh out and add depth and breadth to your view of advertising. These extra readings will expose you to different points of view and make the reading of this book, too, more enjoyable and rewarding. The reading lists also point out recent volumes that are narrower and deeper in scope; these can intensify your knowledge of those areas of retail advertising that appeal most to you.

The glossary defines and explains unfamiliar words and expressions found both in this book and in trade magazines, other texts, and the everyday verbal language of advertising people and retailers.

Many of the ideas discussed in this book, especially in Chapters 5 and 6, were originally formulated by Charles M. Edwards, Jr., and William H. Howard in *Retail Advertising and Sales Promotion* (Englewood Cliffs, N.J.: Prentice-Hall, 1930) and, later, in the third edition, in which Russell A. Brown replaced Mr. Howard as co-author. Although these ideas have been modified and expanded by myself and others over the years, I would like to acknowledge these original authors.

WILLIAM HAIGHT

Contents

PART 1

The Context of Contemporary Advertising: People-Oriented Retailing

Understanding retail advertising in its contemporary context begins with appreciating the sweeping changes taking place in today's society, and the even more sweeping changes expected in tomorrow's society. This is no simple task, since our world is changing at a pace unprecedented in any past era. The ordinary, everyday living patterns of twentieth-century individuals undergo more alterations than the lifestyles of human beings did in centuries in the past.

These changes are taking place at an ever-accelerating rate; they affect you and me more than they did our older brothers and sisters and will affect our younger siblings and our children more drastically than most of us dare to contemplate. This whirring, stirring, and churning up of the old and its replacement with the new have an impact on our family life, our homes, our communities, our jobs, and everything about us. And among the things that are changing are many time-honored ideas once thought to be fixed and immutable.

In this decade and the next, we are told, a revolution is taking place and will go on. The days of the industrial era are ebbing, and signs of a services-oriented society are appearing everywhere. Over the horizon lies the postindustrial or superindustrial age. We will examine the transformation taking place in the world's markets only briefly in this volume, touching on a few highlights that have a particular impact on retail businesses and how they advertise. We shall take a closer look at the vast revolution modern retailing itself is undergoing to meet the changes in its markets, at how stores today operate, and at the research they do on customers and hoped-for customers to guide them in the performance of their merchandising and promotional functions.

Preview

Modern retailing encompasses far more than the original function of a merchant: to sell tangible merchandise to a largely homogeneous population hungry for personal possessions. Present-day stores are in the business of pleasing people by catering to their many and diverse needs, both physical and psychological. Customers must be cultivated with the utmost sophistication, and advertising, as the store's chief means of reaching out to influence customers, must communicate with them in terms consonant with their needs and values.

Foremost among recent changes in the market of retail stores have been *changes in the size of various age groups* and *changes in the geographic distribution of the population.* The proportion of young adults in the population is growing fastest, as is the buying power of this group. The elderly are also gaining rapidly in relative numbers and purchasing ability. The proportion of middle-aged persons and children, especially young children, has declined. Vast migrations have altered the geographic balance of the market place, bringing huge growth to suburban areas while the "core" cities they surround have stagnated and rural areas have been largely depopulated. The newest trend is an upsurge of growth in small and medium-sized communities, many of them isolated, as people seek to escape the pressures of life in the megalopolises.

Other shifts in the retail market are related to modern customers' mobility, preference for smaller homes (apartments, townhouses, and mobile homes), educational level, affluence and the widespread dispersion of discretionary income, new spending patterns, and shorter working times and working lives, with a consequent expansion of leisure time. A new branch of social science, *psychographics,* is arising to help marketers pinpoint the changing needs, wants, aspirations, attitudes, and values of the customers of today and tomorrow. Understanding these customers and directing both the merchandising and advertising policies of a store along paths consonant with their needs is vital to successful retailing.

Learning Goals

Chapter 1 is designed to provide an overview of the trends in American society as a whole that force changes in the structure, management philosophy, operations, and advertising policies of retail business. Only by becoming familiar with the basic sources of change can the retailer discern and evaluate changes to come and apply this knowledge to the management of retail operations in general and advertising in particular.

1

The Customers
of Today
and Tomorrow

Stores grow and prosper to the extent that they promptly sense, and correctly adjust to, *changes* in their social and economic environment. They shrivel and die to the degree that they hang on to outworn methods, obsolete techniques, and attitudes inherited from bygone eras.

Selling, in its narrowest sense, was the primary function of "storekeepers" (and other businesspersons) in the past. Now *marketing* has taken its place. Theodore Levitt cogently explains the difference between the two in a study of innovations in marketing:

> Selling is preoccupied with the seller's need to convert [a] product or service into cash; marketing with the idea of satisfying the needs of the customer by means of the product or service and by the whole cluster of customer-getting value satisfactions associated with creating, delivering and finally consuming it.[1]

Merchants used to be *goods-oriented;* those who succeed are now *people-oriented.* Stanley Goodman, president of the May Company department store group, has this to say:

> We must see that retailing is people-business and understanding people in all their variety. . . . Too often we sell the wrong thing, the item we bought, rather then the subjective value it will bring the customer.[2]

Faced with these definitions of marketing and retailing, we dare not simply jump into the study of retail advertising *techniques.* Those responsible for the advertising of a store must be even more aware of, and responsive to, the attitudes, ambitions, whims, fancies, goals, and aspirations of customers than are their colleagues in other departments. For *retail advertising* is the mechanism by which the store reaches out to communicate, inform, and influence people in *their own environment,* long before other store personnel have an opportunity to contact them on the store's premises, in *its* environment.

As the world grows more complex, it becomes harder to advertise effectively, to know where to advertise and how. Once it was possible for marketers to assume that their countrymen had a distinctive national character, a unity of needs, habits, and states of mind. But the beliefs and modes of living that unified people in the past have altered. The once-touted "mass market" has exploded into hundreds of market segments, and the focus today is on catering to individuals rather than to masses.

Consumers today live in a world where sameness is viewed as blandness, and many people want to express their individuality by making choices among a variety of offerings. The marketer's number one problem is to recognize, understand, and define segmented markets;

after that, effective merchandising, promotion, and advertising can follow.

1 WHO the Customers of Today and Tomorrow Are, and WHERE They Live

The U.S. population edged past the 213 million mark in 1975. The annual growth rates in the early seventies approximated only three-fourths of 1 percent, scarcely half what they were in the 1960s. And the sixties themselves were years of population-growth slowdown. The 13-percent increase in population in that decade was the lowest ten-year gain since the depression thirties. After nearly 200 years of virtually uninterrupted rapid growth, the nation's population may reach a static level within the lifetime of the children, or even the younger adults, alive today.[3]

5

Although population growth is slowing down, the number of households continues to rise. This seeming paradox is explained by a decrease in the average number of persons in each household, which slid from a peak of 3.7 in 1940 to slightly below 3.0 in 1974. If the number of households, now over 70 million, reaches the projected level of 90 million in 1990, their average size will probably be below 2.5 persons, with fewer than half consisting of traditional husband-and-wife families. The key to this situation is the rapid decline in the number of children per married couple and the rapid rise in the number of households maintained by "singles" or by groups of unrelated individuals.

By 1974, only two-thirds of U.S. households were "primary family groups" including a husband and wife. In almost an eighth of these households, the head of the house had no spouse. (These were chiefly households headed by females, far more often black than white.) More than a fifth of the households consisted of "primary individuals." This latter group (singles and unrelated persons) accounted for a whopping 46 percent of the increase in the number of households since 1970, while the number of "traditional" households increased by less than 6 percent.

All these trends have profound implications for marketing. Sales of goods consumed on a *per person* basis face a declining growth rate, and those consumed on a *per child* basis face a marked decline. Goods called *nondurables,* like clothing, cosmetics, food, and jewelry, will be affected in this way. But items bought on a *per household* basis enjoy brighter prospects: Sales of appliances, furniture, and entertainment units, for example, will probably rise. Most of these goods are what are termed *durables.*

SHIFTING AGE GROUPINGS
IN THE 1970S AND 1980S

Changes in the number and proportion of persons in various age groups have a resounding impact on all aspects of marketing, retailing, and advertising. Two-thirds of the U.S. population growth during the 1970s is occurring in the young-adult age group, whose members are 20 through 39. The number of young adults, which was 54 million in 1970, will swell to 72 million by 1980. (This 34 percent increase is taking place during a decade when the total population will grow by less than 10 percent!) The numbers of heads of households aged 25 to 34 will grow by 50 percent as the products of the post-World War II "baby boom" mature.

This growth in the young adult population creates a unique marketing opportunity for retailers. Few stores will prosper, few ads will "pull," that fail to capture their share of this population segment. Two characteristics of the young adults of today and tomorrow are particularly relevant: their *affluence* and their *small families.* The personal income of this group is expected to nearly double while that of the nation as a whole rises but 50 percent. It has been calculated that half of all income *gains* to 1985 will be among persons under 35. In addition, increasing numbers of young adults are opting for only one or two children, or none at all; others are staying single and childless. People with few or no children have more money to spend on nonessential, "discretionary"

Millions of people

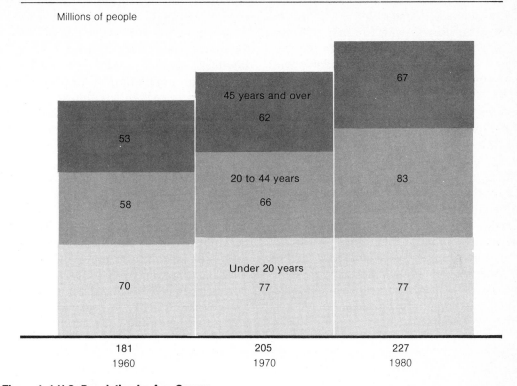

Figure 1–1 U.S. Population by Age Groups

Figure 1–1 U.S. Population by Age Groups
   Merchandisers and advertisers must keep their eyes on statistics such as these to know what to sell and how to promote it to an ever-changing "mix" in the marketplace. Note how the big growth in the 1970s is occurring in the young adult age brackets with moderate growth in the older group and very little in the youngest segment of the population. The early years of the 1970s saw continuing steep decline in the birth rate, and it is probable that the growth of the young will not even reach the modest levels projected here.
   Source: U.S. Bureau of the Census.

goods and services. They have more mobility and fewer responsibilities. Another factor that affects marketers is the generation gap. Today's young adults do not and will not think, act, live, work, play, *or buy merchandise* in the same ways as their parents and grandparents. They favor smaller cars and homes (often apartments), more travel, and a greater investment of time and money in leisure and cultural pursuits. They want more self-satisfying jobs and individualistic lifestyles. Better educated than any past generation, they are prepared to assert their rights as consumers, and they are fatally critical of merchants (and advertising) that fail to play fair, ring true, and offer rational values.

   At the opposite end of the life-cycle progression is a second group whose importance to marketers is increasing significantly: the elderly. The number of people over 60 climbed to 28 million in 1970 and will increase to 33 million by 1980. The growth rate for this segment in the 1970s is twice that of the population as a whole. By 1990, the elderly will have increased in number by a third over the 1972 level, a gain even outpacing the growth rate of the young adults. Reasons for this gain include the high birth rate of the World War I period, a greater rural population before World War I (more children are born per 1,000 people in rural areas than in cities, a worldwide phenomenon that has held true for centuries), and better health and medical care. The elderly today are healthier, wealthier, longer-lived, and more active spenders than any past group of "oldsters," and they have needs, habits, and attitudes that differ sharply from those of young adults.

The number of middle-aged persons has actually been shrinking during the 1970s, but this group still controls far more than its proportionate share of disposable income. After 1980, the middle-aged segment will slowly increase in size, and this, together with the more rapid increase in the numbers of the elderly, will bring the median age of the U.S. population up to 33 years by 1990, from 28 in 1972.

Census officials point out that the composition of the younger age groups by 1990 is anybody's guess; it all depends on trends in the birth rate between now and that date. Current indicators point to a lower percentage of youngsters in the U.S. population in the future. The number of teenagers (the rear guard of the "baby boom"), which peaked in 1975, is now beginning to decline; youngsters aged 5 to 13 will have decreased their total by 4 million by the

end of the 1970s; and preschoolers (children under five) have been steadily dropping in number since 1960. People below 18 could constitute anywhere from a low of 26 percent to a high of 34 percent of the total population by 1990. The one thing that is certain for the near future is that children will not dominate the marketplace as they have in the recent past.

The most dramatic signal that the population composition of the near future will be drastically different from that of any period in the historic past came in the years after 1957, with the precipitous crash of the national birth rate. The absolute number of children born has dropped from a high of 4.3 million in that year to about 3.1 million in 1974 despite greatly increased total population and an unprecedented number of women of child-bearing age in the latter year. The crude birth rate—the number of children born per thousand persons—reached 25.3 in 1957 and slid to 14.9 in 1974, the lowest in U.S. history. The total fertility rate had sunk to 1.8 by 1974, and it takes a 2.1 rate to keep a population on an even level over a period of a generation. Unless the fertility rate begins to climb, U.S. population could cease all growth and even begin to decline sometime after the year 2000.

A HODGEPODGE
OF GEOGRAPHICAL PATTERNS:
THE ERA OF THE SUBURB AND EXURB

Retailers have to go where the people are—and so must the newspapers, broadcast signals, and other media that carry their advertising messages. The messages themselves must be adjusted to take into account the new ways of living that come with migrations to different kinds of communities and the adoption of new lifestyles.

Regionally, in the period just ended, the West Coast was the leader in population gains. The population in the Far West swelled by an average of nearly 3 percent annually from 1950 to 1969, almost double the national growth rate for that period. Projections now indicate that the southeastern states will be the big growth area of the near future, with a growth rate of 1.2 percent per year from 1969 to 1990 versus a rate for the total United States of 0.9 percent or less.

Everywhere, it has been the *suburbs* where the most growth has occurred, and this trend is continuing. During the sixties, U.S. suburbs grew by 28 percent, the old "core" cities grew by a mere 1 percent (with the biggest ones generally losing population), and the rest of the country by only 7 percent. By 1973, the suburbs contained 37 percent of the total population, and the Census Bureau predicts that over half the nation will be

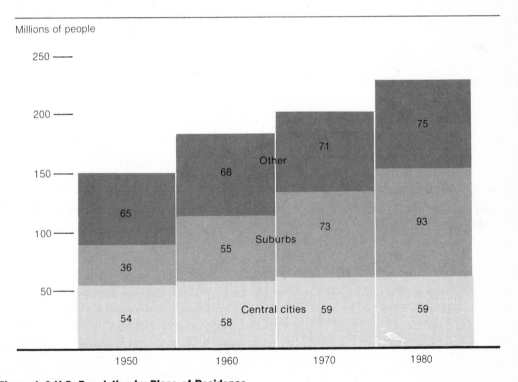

Figure 1–2 U.S. Population by Place of Residence
Knowing the communities in which the population lives is as important to the retailer as knowing the size of age groups. This graph shows that population has been concentrating in the suburbs for two decades, while growth of the central cities slowed down. Annual changes in the first half of the 1970 decade indicated that the cities are suffering a net loss of residents and that the suburbs will not continue to experience the uninterrupted growth that is projected here. The outlying communities or "other places" may show greater attraction than was forecast early in the decade.
Source: U.S. Department of Commerce.

suburbanites by the mid-1980s. It is the young and the affluent who migrate to the suburbs, leaving behind in the big cities the old, the poor, and the under-privileged—most of whom are poor customers for retailers and poor "targets" for stores' ads.

Industry and offices have followed population migration out of the old downtowns to the suburbs. The image of the suburbs as "commuter" towns is already becoming obsolete, with over half the suburban residents finding employment, as well as homes, in the suburban areas. The suburbs now more closely resemble the older cities themselves. Residents complain of high taxes, over-crowding, traffic congestion, and pollution, and the demand for apartment houses is growing.

The terms *strip city* and *exurb* have been coined as a result of the ever-widening expansion of population around metropolitan areas. One city's suburbs stretch out to meet the next city's, forming a long strip of urbanization. Distant smaller cities and rural villages, the *exurbs*, come to life as people commute longer distances. *Outcommuting* is another new development; people live in a big city's suburbs but drive farther out to work on a booming industry in a smaller town surrounded by open spaces, not back downtown as in the past. Later they will probably make their homes there, too.

More rapid increases in manufacturing and service jobs in smaller cities and towns, new communication technology, improved transportation, and citizens' frustration with urban crime and pollution appear to be making such communities the growth focus of the future. Since 1970, all growth has been in such places rather than in large metropolitan areas, where the shrinkage of the core cities has canceled out the continuing gains of the suburbs. (Nearly 6 million people moved out of metropolitan areas while more than 4 million moved in, for a net out-migration of 1.8 million.) By the early 1970s, nonmetropolitan areas were gaining population at a rate nearly twice that of metropolitan areas. Much of this gain in nonurban regions and smaller cities has been due to changes in residence by young adults in their 20s, those most likely to produce families that will further accelerate the growth of the hinterlands at the expense of the big cities. Another factor to be considered is the construction of "new cities" like Columbia, Maryland, and Reston, Virginia. Such communities are underway or planned in at least 100 other places.

2 HOW the Customers of Today and Tomorrow Live, and WHAT They Ask from Life

The mere statistics cited above are not enough to provide an understanding of today and tomorrow's customers. Stores will fail and ads will fall on fallow ground unless the people behind them are also aware of the attitudes and emotions of their customers. Going blindly forward as if things are as they used to be will not work. As society changes, new kinds of retailing and advertising must emerge.

THE MOBILE CUSTOMER

The Census Bureau tells us that nearly 19 percent of the people in this country change their residence every year, two-thirds going to a new home in the same county, a sixth to another county in the same state, and another sixth to a different state. More than 40 million people move each year, and the average American moves 14 times in his lifetime. This mobility is most pronounced among the fast-growing population of young adults, among people with above-average present and potential earning power and disposable income, and among those with the most education. People quickly need new sources of retail goods and services after a move, and advertising is a key factor in helping them make choices among stores at that crucial point in time.

People today also travel far and wide to shop, though not as far as they sometimes did in the sixties when modern shopping complexes were less evenly spread throughout metropolitan areas and smaller communities. Studies show that people will spend up to 20 minutes traveling from home to a store, and with modern roads this gives them a big geographical area in which to shop.

THE MODERN RESIDENCE: THE "FAMILY HOME" ERA ENDS

For two centuries most Americans shared a common dream: to own a home of their own with a nice yard and garden, preferably a big, beautiful house in "the right neighborhood." A house was the symbol of "having arrived," of the sought-after "middle class" status. Federal mortgage financing stimulated the building of single-family homes during the 1950s and well into the 1960s. Private homes were practical for the large families then in style and fit in with the migration to the "wide open spaces" in suburbia.

But counterforces that began to be felt in the 1960s are already altering typical residential patterns. Big, expensive houses are less practical for people who want to be mobile, to have smaller families, to travel, to pursue hobbies, and to enjoy life in other ways without the work and expense of keeping up a home. Houses are impractical, too, for the growing numbers of "empty-nesters," elderly persons whose children have grown up and often moved far away from the family homestead. As tight money and high interest rates on mortgages discourage financing, private individuals turn increasingly to rented apartments or lower-cost mobile homes. In the mid-1950s, 88 percent of permanent residential units being built were single-family houses, but by the 1969–1974 period only 56 percent of new living units were constructed for one-family use. Soon traditional single-family houses may account for only about a third of the new housing.

This historic turnaround brings with it marked changes in the market for home furnishings (which now tend to be smaller, to be built in, in some cases, and to be rented rather than owned in other cases), for yard and maintenance items, and for other things that homeowners need. The drop in popularity of private homes frees cash for other *intangible* things like babysitting services and air travel and tennis court time. Most recently the same trend has been appearing even in isolated small cities and country towns.

THE BOOM IN EDUCATION

A short 20 years ago marketers (who were presumed to have had some education) dealt with customers who were, on the whole, more poorly educated than themselves. Only four out of ten adults in the 1950s had finished high school, and not quite one in six had been to college. Fewer still were college graduates. Nowadays the consumer is not at such a disadvantage, thanks to the education boom of the past 20 years. Six out of ten adults are high school graduates, and a quarter have been to college. Of

those in the key young adult age group, three-fourths are high school graduates, and a sixth hold diplomas from four-year colleges.

Increasing years of education translate into a heightened consumer sophistication—an inclination to buy better merchandise, seek more value, exhibit more taste, and respond to more rational sales and advertising appeals. Perhaps

Figure 1–3 The Trend in Housing: Toward Apartments and Mobile Homes

Far more popular today than the traditional family home are apartments and mobile homes, which allow people to be more mobile and to be free of heavy financial responsibilities. The trend toward these residences brings with it changes in buying patterns. There is a decreased need for yard and maintenance items and for home furnishings and appliances, which are included in the mobile home by the manufacturer and which may be provided by the apartment owner. There is an increased demand for intangibles. Retail advertisers must take these changes into account in cultivating their markets.

Source: Photo at left courtesy of Marlette Homes, Inc., Marlette, Michigan.

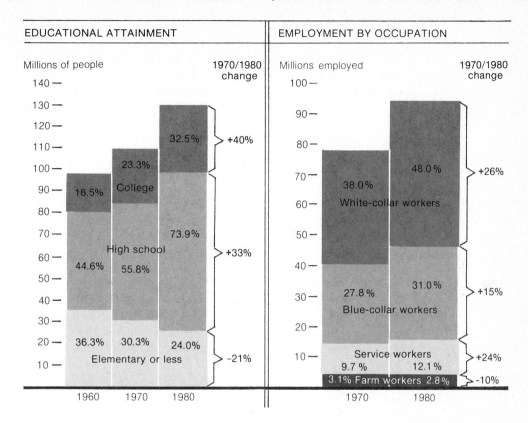

Figure 1–4 Trends in Educational Attainment and Employment of the U.S. Population

Marketing is greatly affected by the level of educational achievement and the types of jobs of customers. More education brings preferences for various kinds of products and services. People with different occupational ties have contrasting needs and habits that affect how, where, when, and why they shop. These graphs, which are based on government reports for the past and estimates to 1980, show great growth in relative numbers of high school and college graduates, while the early 1970s brought forth evidence that the projections for college level of educational attainment may have been overstated. The figures remain firm for the burgeoning majority who have a high school education and the shrinking minority who have not gone to high school.

Employment trends for this decade are turning out to be about as had been expected. Shrinkage in farm laborers' numbers and a relatively slow growth rate for "blue collar" workers reflect continuing automation of farm and factory. Of the two occupational groups that are expected to have the greatest growth, many believe the increase in service workers will outpace that of "white collar" employees in the 1980s.

Sources: "Educational Attainment" from U.S. Department of Commerce; "Employment by Occupation" from U.S. Department of Labor.

more significant yet, education increases earning power. In a special study released in 1974, the Census Bureau reports that in 1972 college graduates earned an average of $14,351. Those with high school diplomas averaged $9,996, while those who quit after eight grades averaged only $7,133 and elementary-school dropouts averaged a mere $6,310.

During the 1960s, the median family income increased by 72 percent while the consumer price index went up only 33 percent. Gains in income continued to outstrip inflation rates through 1972 so that "real" purchasing power kept rising. However, starting in 1973 and continuing through 1974, the economy of the United States, along with that of the rest of the industrialized world, went into an inflationary spiral. Real purchasing power dropped as inflation more than ate up dollar gains in income.

In 1972, which might be considered the last "normal" economic year, 30 percent of U.S. families enjoyed incomes above $15,000 while 56 percent had incomes of greater than $10,000. A relatively small 17 percent were pinched by below-$5,000 incomes. Blacks continued to be disadvantaged, though the income gap between blacks and whites narrowed in the 1960s. Over 14 percent of American blacks had above-$15,000 family incomes in 1972, compared to 1 percent as recently as 1959. About one-third topped $10,000. Overall, however, black family incomes did not quite equal 60 percent of what white families received. The country's young adults were relatively affluent; 58 percent had incomes above $10,000, compared with 56 percent of the total population. The middle-aged (those 45–54) still had more buying power, however; one out of eight had family incomes of more than $25,000, and 45 percent topped the $15,000 figure. Multiple wage-earners were the source of much of this prosperity; in the most affluent family groups, both husbands and wives tended to work. There continued to be wide disparities in income, with salaries varying according to the occupational group, the geographical region, and the educational level required of the job.

Forecasts point to a family income of $25,000 for nearly 40 percent of all Americans by 1980 and to that figure as the national median by 1985. However, only time will tell whether these figures will mean anything in terms of actual increases in purchasing power.

ALTERED SPENDING PATTERNS

How people spend their money is almost as important to retailers as how much of it they have to spend. And here great shifts have been taking place. In the early fifties, about 70 percent of the public's effective buying income (i.e., income after taxes) was spent for tangible merchandise in retail outlets; in 1970, only 53 percent of it was spent in this way. For the first time, in 1971 spending for *services* exceeded spending for nondurable goods. (Consumer spending for services and nondurables had long ago surpassed consumer spending for durable goods.) However, inflationary increases in the cost of food and fuel and a rise in housing costs, together with the preponderance of young-adult families in the goods-acquiring stage of the life cycle, brought spending for tangible goods back up to 58 percent in 1973.

Nevertheless, most economists believe the long-range trend will be toward the purchase of services as opposed to physical possessions. Older families already have most of the physical possessions they need, and younger ones are rapidly acquiring them. Moreover, the value the younger age group places on such goods is declining. People are inclined to spend more on such items as medical services, education, recreation, personal care, financial services, legal services, insurance, communications, and travel.

LEISURE TIME AND ITS USES: A STIMULUS FOR MARKETERS

The one great area of consumption said to be destined to experience the greatest boom ever (once the cost of essentials stops skyrocketing) is the great cluster of goods and services related to *leisure time* and its uses. The work week has been growing shorter, vacations have been growing longer, and retirement age has been coming earlier for a long time. A four-day work week was in effect at some 1,000 companies in the early 1970s, and there is talk of an eventual split-shift, three-day work week.

This trend has fueled the boom in travel, outdoor sports, spectator sports, at-home recreation, and the "culture kick." People need something to do with their free time, and they do everything from building model airplanes and riding bikes to building second homes and trekking across Europe. The exact nature of these activities will be affected by the economic situation. For instance, the combination of fuel shortage, inflation, and unemployment that occurred between 1973 and 1975 caused people to abandon expensive travel plans and purchases of recreational vehicles and forced them to stay close to home. At-home leisure activity went on the rise,

with people turning to reading, music listening, hobbies and handicrafts, and tennis, golf, and other sports. Alert retailers are cashing in on the trend to more leisure time by keeping track of current popular activities and stocking and promoting merchandise that fills consumers' needs.

THE INNER CONSUMER: MOTIVATIONAL AND PSYCHOLOGICAL FACTORS

Dividing the consumer population into segments according to its age, location, occupation, education, race, type of residence, and even its hobbies and recreational preferences is a useful type of market analysis. It is the beginning of understanding the new kind of *targeted* merchandising and advertising that has replaced the old notion of the mass market (a concept that was always a myth, even when it was popular). Knowing the *demographics* of a market—the groups it can be divided into—helps a merchant to understand who is most likely to buy certain products or services, where these people are, and how to reach them with advertising messages.

But modern marketing goes deeper than this, into the *psychographics* of the consumer.[4] The term psychographics was coined in 1968 to describe analyses of *why* people buy things. Retailers today study people's emotional attitudes, their images of themselves, their psychological reasons for behaving as they do in the marketplace. There are personality types that differ markedly regardless of demographic characteristics. There are value standards and styles of living that affect why, what, and how people buy. These standards and lifestyles are in a constant state of change, but some

Figure 1–5 Retail Advertising at the Dawn of the "Services Society"

As increasing numbers of Americans tend to reject a goods-oriented way of life and to enjoy more leisure time, many retailers are edging toward emphasis on services rather than on sales of tangible merchandise. These ads reflect this trend. The ad on the left, by a store that sells fabrics and sewing materials, does not even mention its product (although its other ads will assuredly do so!). It seeks to attract customers by offering instruction in crafts, hobbies, and money-saving at-home skills. The ad above, at left, which suggests renting, not buying, furniture for one's apartment, is an ad from a store that for many years has earned its way by *selling* furniture. More and more people now prefer to rent, not buy, a wide range of goods, including furniture, hobby and sports goods, home-care equipment, and autos. The ad at right is by a noted musical-goods store, which has long marketed its own brand of piano. Yet not a single word in this ad refers to the product—only to lessons that will permit children to acquire a skill that leads to *enjoyment* of the product. Nowadays the emphasis is more often on the pleasure the use of an item will bring to its owner than on the merchandise itself.

broad, general trends can be discerned.

One key factor is social class. Business people tend to oversimplify the concept of social class, to see it as dependent solely on a person's income. Social classes and income brackets are not the same, though they are interrelated to a degree. Consider, for example, the following profiles of three men with the same income who exhibit behavioral differences based on their class status:

John Smith is a carpenter. He earns a high hourly rate, but his employment depends as much on the weather as on the business cycle. He earns approximately $12,000 a year and regards himself and is regarded by others as upper working class. If he and his wife were so inclined, their income would be sufficient for a lower-middle class lifestyle, but they prefer the familiarity of their workingclass neighborhood where they can be "big fishes in a small pond." The Smith home is comfortable and well furnished, and stands out in the neighborhood. His car is relatively new, big and loaded with "extras" and his color television set is the envy of the block.

Since he has more than enough money to live on a par with his neighbors, Mr. Smith is an "overprivileged" member of his class. He can afford to indulge in "conspicuous consumption" and does so to remind himself, his family and his neighbors that he is not "just another working man." For recreation, he hunts and fishes in season, displaying in the process much expensive paraphernalia. He bowls the year around with a custom-made bowling ball. He is also devoted to spectator sports and regards his newspaper and his TV set principally as a means of enjoying them.

John Jones is a school teacher, now enjoying an income of $12,000 a year. He still cannot forget the poverty years when he had to hold odd jobs on Saturday and at night to supplement his slim paycheck. As a member of one of the low-pay professions, he has lower-middle class status. Having no love for administrative duties, he expects to spend the rest of his work career as a classroom teacher. Consequently, he expects his salary to rise but modestly from year to year, and he plans his expenditures accordingly. His home is in a lower-middle class neighborhood. It is minimal: three bedrooms, one bath and a playroom which doubles as a study. (Smith, the carpenter, has more space.) Jones has a large-screen black-and-white TV set in his playroom and a portable in his bedroom. His car is one of the low-priced three and several years old. But unlike Smith, he does not service or repair his own car. Like Smith, he paints his own house, but he does so reluctantly, complaining about house painters who feel they should be better paid than college-trained professional people. His life is insured for three times as much as Smith's, and, also unlike Smith, his auto liability policy is for far more than the minimum required by law. He, not Smith, is saving money for the college education of his children.

Jones reads a good deal, especially in summer when his temporary job as a recreation director allows him considerable free time compared to the 60-hour work week a conscientious teacher puts in during the school year. He also has a respectable collection of phonograph records and tapes, and occasionally the Jones take in a concert or ballet.

John Brown, M.D., is serving his residency at All Saints' Hospital where he is paid $11,000 a year. A little "moonlighting" for an insurance company brings in an additional thousand dollars. Dr. and Mrs. Brown are painfully aware that their income is insufficient for the upper-middle class life style which society expects of the practitioners of the more lucrative professions. But there is the consolation that within a year or two his private practice will provide them with a much higher income, so they now make the best of a bad situation. Their income, as far as it will go, must be spent on items which denote their status. No doubt a disproportionately large share will go for housing "on the right side of town." Furniture will be sparse but of good quality and in good taste. And the hands that hold the stethoscope must never touch a paint brush; the professional painter will be paid his atrocious price with quiet resignation and a resolution to retaliate when the opportunity presents itself.

Dr. Brown would normally work and study longer hours than the teacher; he would have less time for recreation. (Ironically, higher status people usually work longer hours.) Perhaps he might borrow against future earnings to join an appropriate (upper-middle class) country club, and try to think up excuses to avoid the poker games in the locker room.[5]

Many social scientists and marketing executives believe that traditional social class distinctions are becoming blurred. They are therefore less useful than the aspirations, self-images, and values that characterize new, emerging lifestyles in determining merchandising and advertising strategies.

Affluence has made possible the co-existence of different lifestyles not based on income. The publisher of *Harper's Magazine,* William S. Blair, identifies

two emerging lifestyles and contrasts their characteristics in psychographic terms:

1. *The affluent blue-collar worker,* so recently the beneficiary of major redistribution of income away from college-educated middle-management and to unionized production workers, is more likely to watch TV than to read a newspaper, more apt to put more money into a home and its furnishings, more apt to buy a new car than take a trip to Europe, and more likely to prefer a big car to a small one.

2. *The youth culture* is sharply critical of the present economic and political systems and also of other areas of established society. No one knows for sure whether these attitudes will be modified as today's young people mature, or whether they will upset a lot of past marketing predictions by carrying these views into their middle years.[6]

Other social science professors, research specialists who serve the world of industry and communications, and business leaders have discussed market segmentation in psychographic terms, focusing on different aspects of consumer behavior. Some of these people see two distinct behavior patterns based largely on age. They cite the generation gap and construct scales of old and new values: productivity (old) versus pleasure (new), achievement (old) versus experience (new), aggression (old) versus passivity (new), past and future time value (old) versus the present (new), and intellectualism (old) versus mysticism (new).

Probing for underlying, unspoken motivations of individuals and groups reveals great differences that arise from varied lifetime experiences. There are many persons in today's society who feel free at last from the fear of poverty; they look now for personal fulfillment, not just money and the things it will buy. Others yearn for excitement, stimulation, and challenge as opposed to more practical goals. Still others are motivated by a reaction against the complexities of modern living. They want a simpler life, a return to nature, a chance to be alone and to go their own way. Although young people have always tended to be idealistic, great numbers of today's youths have strongly rejected traditional social values in favor of more liberal, relaxed attitudes, an emphasis on pleasure as an end in itself, and a rejection of hypocrisy.

Investigation of these elements of human nature used to be largely the province of psychologists and sociologists. When blended, their work came to be termed social psychology. As marketers became increasingly aware of the contribution this knowledge could make to the moving of merchandise in the practical world of business, terms like motivational research and psychographics became popular. Now some marketers suggest further specialization, perhaps breaking psychographics down into a trio of new social sciences: *egographics* to deal with the customer's personality, *life-graphics* to probe lifestyles, and *value-graphics* to measure needs and values.

Whatever one may call the emerging subsciences, they are key dimensions in modern selling and advertising. People are not all alike inside, and stores' appeals to move merchandise or sell services must be based on a knowledge of the forces motivating customers. These consumers' attitudes, values, and lifestyles bear mightily on what can be sold today in the stores, how it is sold, and how it can best be advertised. These factors have changed the outlook and the advertising approach of every successful businessperson—even, in a way, the structure of retailing itself.

The established institutions of society have been under attack in recent years for preserving old ways and for being unresponsive to the needs of a changing society. Business, like the family, the church, and government, is suspect. And because retailing is the most visible, universal, and conspicuous facet of business, merchants and their stores come in for a disproportionate share of the assault on "things as they were." Their advertising can either add fuel to the fire or help build new images of business that consumers can respect.

Understanding these evolving attitudes, none of them shared equally by all segments of the populace, is the key to the future. Each group in our society expects something different of the merchandise it buys, the stores it patronizes, the people it meets at the sales counter. Many of the social changes we have briefly traced have drastically altered time-honored ideas about trade areas, customer loyalty, and the basic reasons for buying. The very act of "going shopping" has for many people meanings that are different from what they were in the past.

Few retailers, if any, can please all these diverse groups; fewer still of their advertisements can motivate all (or even several) of them. Thus, narrowly targeted advertising is the wave of the future that is fast replacing the mass appeals of the past.

Questions for Discussion

1. Why has retailing, which was formerly thought to be essentially a business focused on merchandise, now become an enterprise centered on people?

2. A dramatic change in the birth rate like that since the middle 1950s has an obvious impact on expansion plans for a toy store or children's wear shop. What effects does it have on the kinds and sizes of homes built, the furniture and household appliance businesses, and travel bureaus? Does it also have a relationship to the models of automobiles sold?

3. What are the opportunities for selling merchandise and services to the "leisure market"? In particular, how does this relate to the two fastest-growing age groups in today's society?

4. Since 1970, some 25-year-old trends in our society have played out or even showed signs of reversing. What kinds of cities are growing the fastest today? What proportion of their income are consumers spending through retail-store channels? Discuss other trends that you believe have the greatest effect on retail selling and advertising.

5. What are some of the main differences in values between the "older generation" and the "youth culture"? How would a knowledge of these differences affect your work if you were responsible for selecting mer-

chandise and developing basic advertising appeals for two stores, one in a neighborhood where the median age of the head of the household was 45 and one where it was 30?

Suggested Projects

1. At a session in your school library or the nearest major reference library, determine (with the help of the reference librarian) how your community's population has increased (or decreased) between 1960 and 1970 and since the 1970 census. How does its growth compare with that of the Standard Metropolitan Statistical Area of which it is a part (if it is part of an SMSA), with that of the state as a whole, and with that of the United States as a whole for the same periods? How does central-city growth in your area compare with suburban-area growth? What age groups have shown the most growth (or shrinkage) in your area?

2. Find out from the area planning commission and/or the building permits officer of your city or county what kinds of residential structures have been built there in recent years (single-family homes or apartment units). How does this compare with the state and national distribution of new residential building?

3. Check up on the influx, if any, of new families into your commuity. A local utility company may be able to give you some figures on recent meter connections, and the board of education office may have information on students transferred into your district. Compare what you find with national trends. Would you

say that your community has a relatively "mobile" population? How will this affect retailing and advertising for local stores?

4. Go out and look at several new houses built in your neighborhood within the past year or two. Then look at a like number that have been there since you can first remember. Compare and contrast the two groups of houses, overall, with respect to their size, architectural style, the kinds of yards and gardens they have, and other features. What trends do you find in home construction in your area, and how will these trends affect the kinds of goods and services stores sell?

Notes

1. Theodore Levitt, *Innovation in Marketing* (New York: McGraw-Hill, 1962), p. v.

2. Reported by *Fairchild News Service*.

3. Figures cited here and elsewhere throughout this chapter have been derived from current population reports of the Bureau of the Census.

4. The word *psychographics* is as yet so new that there is no consensus among scholars on a universally acceptable standard definition. A simple one might be *the measurement of markets in terms of the personality traits of individuals who make up those markets.* Another could be *the science of measuring consumer lifestyles, motivations, attitudes, and unfulfilled product needs* [Alan R. Nelson, "New psychographics: action-creating ideas, not lifeless statistics," *Advertising Age* (June 29, 1971), p. 1].

5. Vincent V. Mott, *The American Consumer: A Sociological Analysis* (Florham Park, N.J.: Florham Park Press, 1972), pp. 56–57.

6. "Emerging Life Styles Make for Hazy Prediction of Future, Blair Asserts," *Advertising Age* (December 7, 1970), p. 30.

Preview

American retailing evolved over a period of more than a century from an untidy web of peddlers' wagons and general stores into a complex and orderly marketing mechanism. Reacting to the new social forces defined in Chapter 1, stores met the challenge of a transformed society and drastically altered their physical nature, operational methods, management techniques, and the scope of their activities. The department stores, specialty shops, and chain stores of today stand well prepared to serve the diverse and demanding consumers of this new era. Several key trends in retailing have emerged in recent years:

1. The number of retail outlets and their sales volume have greatly increased.

2. Diversification, or *scrambled merchandising,* has all but knocked out the limited-line specialty shop.

3. Chain stores have enjoyed a growth rate far surpassing that of independents in many trade lines, while in other merchandise categories smaller organizations have remained the norm.

4. Low-margin, self-service selling has spread from food and drugs into the general merchandise field and some specialty lines, giving rise to the so-called "discount houses." Discounters have not been uniformly successful, but they have precipitated vast changes in other forms of retailing, which have adjusted to meet the discounters' challenge.

5. The geographical dimensions of retailing have been transformed by the development of shopping centers that have become the "new downtowns" for fast-growing suburban communities, replacing the central business districts of older cities. Meanwhile, older retail districts in some places have been successfully revitalized by borrowing techniques from the shopping centers.

6. Though smaller independent stores have become less important in some areas of retailing, they have held firm in other segments of the industry, usually as a result of various degrees and forms of cooperation among themselves.

Learning Goals

Chapter 2 is designed to show the changes that have occurred and are occurring in retailing. It should provide a perspective on the major trends of the "retail revolution" and on the relative importance of various aspects of the transformation the industry is undergoing. Understanding the position of any given store or store group (such as other tenants in a mall) in the complex mass of retailing as a whole forms the basis for using advertising to carve out a suitable "target market" in this highly competitive industry.

2

Merchants' Responses to Change: The Retail Revolution

1 The Retail Industry Today

Nineteenth-century history shows how modern retailing grew from its early roots. It entered successive stages as vast spaces of land became populated, towns grew, and transportation and communication improved. The original Yankee peddler carried merchandise to the customer's door on his back or in his wagon, and the wilderness trading post swapped the necessities of life for raw materials. The Industrial Revolution multiplied the variety and nature of merchandise available, raising standards of living. Later the general store became a fixture of each town and village, supplying all the basic needs, plus a few luxuries, to those within its trading area, which was usually defined by the distance a horse-drawn vehicle could travel in a day.

As towns grew larger, there were enough people to support shops that stocked only a few lines of merchandise but a wider selection. These early dry goods, food, hardware, and drug stores were the ancestors of the specialty stores of today. Following the Civil War, the general stores in major cities evolved into department stores—large aggregations of shops under one roof, situated at the focal points of the mass transportation of that era. As postal facilities expanded, mail-order houses also appeared on the scene. Competition among retailers and an increasing variety of goods resulted in *retail advertising* in much the same form that we know today.

The early twentieth century saw the rise of department stores to dominance in urban areas, the further refinement and multiplication of specialized shops to serve the increasingly complex needs of consumers, and the birth of nationwide and regional chains. The economies of mass production were matched by economies of mass distribution that lowered the price of goods as demand and personal income grew. The big stores and chains gained an economic power that balanced and even exceeded that of the large manufacturers. Advertising by retailers came to dominate first newspapers and then radio, serving both to reinforce and to counterbalance the manufacturers' national advertising that largely sustained magazines earlier in the century and television later on.

Since World War II, many new forms of retailing have evolved, and some of the older forms have experienced rapid transformations. Supermarkets have profoundly altered the nature of the "grocery-store" business with their self-service and low-margin techniques. "Discount houses" have had a massive impact both on the general merchandise field and on certain specialty lines, forcing traditional merchants into new paths. Big downtown stores have thrust branches out into the suburbs—branches that, in the aggregate, outsell the parent stores. And now those same downtown giants are reaching out to invade distant cities and transform themselves into regional chains. Telephone selling, a revival of in-home sales, automated selling through vending machines, warehouse-to-consumer marketing, and direct marketing by manufacturers are among the new twists and turns that have made retailing in the 1970s a dynamic industry.

There are endless variations of store types today. Among them are promotional, semipromotional, and nonpromotional stores; chain stores and independents, plus two kinds of "in-betweens," the affiliated independents belonging to voluntary associations that give them the appearance and many of the characteristics of chain stores, and the franchised dealers of national or regional merchandising firms. Each has a different approach to its advertising and promotion.

THE INCREASE IN STORE NUMBERS

There are today about 1.8 million retail stores in the United States, or about one store for every 118 persons. Table 2–1 shows the numbers and types of retail enterprises counted in the 1963 and 1972 Censuses of Retail Trade.

Automotive dealers, apparel and accessory stores, and furniture, home furnishings, and equipment stores have led all other categories of stores in recent gains in numbers. The great increase in the numbers of department stores, shown in the general merchandise group, is especially significant because of their very great sales volume per store. Much of the increase in that category has been due to the discount store boom and the building of suburban branches. However, nonstore retailers (such as Avon) as a whole are increasing much more rapidly than any type of retail store proper.

Most dramatic losses in numbers of stores occurred among the food stores as giant supermarkets displaced smaller neighborhood groceries, and in the building materials, hardware, and farm equipment group as the decline of family-sized farms closed down many farm-related businesses. There are now fewer drug stores, but more large ones, often in shopping centers.

THE INCREASE IN SALES VOLUME

Let us turn now to the number of consumers' dollars each of these types of retailers attracts. Table 2–2 shows that three broad categories of stores account for well over half of all retail sales: the food, automotive, and general merchandise groups. If gas stations are added to the automotive group and restaurants and bars to the food category, these groups account for 71.4 percent of all retail sales. Nearly three-fourths of all retail expenditures, then, have to do with food (eaten at home or on the premises where it is sold), with autos (buying, adorning, or maintaining them or "feeding" them gas and oil), or with goods purchased from department stores and other general merchandisers. Almost 55 percent of all retail sales have to do with food or cars.

Sales figures for the apparel group may seem small, but the amount actually spent for clothing is vastly greater because of the large proportion of the general merchandise sales that are actually sales of wearing apparel. In fact, 55 percent of the gross sales of traditional department stores are made in their apparel divisions, and both discount and variety stores do a huge volume in these "soft lines."

For projections of sales to 1980 for selected store types, see Table 2–3. It shows that department stores and eating and drinking places are expected to grow in sales volume faster than the retail industry as a whole, while variety stores and drug stores will probably fall substantially behind average growth rates.

It should be noted that these tables reflect traditional reports of sales by *types of stores.* Such statistics are not as useful as they were in the heyday of the specialty merchant. Diversification has dimmed the distinctions between store types, and future statistics will increasingly be reported according to the lines of merchandise sold rather than by types of stores.

Economists divide all consumer goods into two broad types: *durables*

Table 2–1

Numbers of Retail Establishments in the United States

Categories of Establishments	1963	1972	Gain or Loss 1963–1972	
			Numbers	Percentage
Eating and Drinking Places	**334,500**	**359,500**	+ 25,000	+ 7.5%
Eating places	223,900	253,100		
Drinking places (alcoholic beverages)	110,600	106,400		
Food Stores	**319,400**	**267,400**	− 62,100	− 16.3
Grocery stores	244,800	194,300		
Meat and fish (seafood) markets	20,100	16,600		
Fruit stores and vegetable markets	8,900	8,400		
Candy, nut, and confectionary stores	15,000	12,900		
Retail bakeries	18,600	19,200		
Other food stores	12,000	16,000		
Gasoline Service Stations	**211,500**	**226,500**	+ 15,000	+ 7.1
Automotive Dealers	**98,500**	**131,800**	+ 33,800	+ 33.8
Motor vehicle dealers	61,300	64,200		
Tires, battery, and accessory dealers	25,900	37,500		
Miscellaneous automotive dealers	11,300	30,100		
Apparel and Accessory Stores	**116,200**	**129,200**	+ 13,000	+ 11.2
Women's ready-to-wear stores	29,700	38,800		
Women's accessory and specialty stores	12,500	8,900		
Furriers and fur shops	2,300	2,000		
Other apparel and accessory stores	71,800	79,600		
Furniture, Home Furnishings, and Equipment Stores	**93,600**	**116,900**	+ 23,200	+ 24.8
Furniture stores	37,200	38,700		
Home furnishings stores	17,700	28,000		
Household appliance stores	20,300	20,300		
Radio, television, and music stores	18,400	29,900		
Building Materials, Hardware, and Farm Equipment Dealers	**92,700**	**76,800**	− 15,900	− 17.2
Building materials and supply stores	46,700	40,900		
Hardware stores	29,600	26,400		
Farm equipment dealers	16,400	9,600		
General Merchandise Group Stores	**62,100**	**76,000**	+ 14,800	+ 23.8
Department stores	4,300	7,700		
Variety stores	22,400	21,900		
Miscellaneous general merchandise stores	35,400	46,400		
Drug Stores and Proprietary Stores	**54,700**	**51,500**	− 3,200	− 5.9
Miscellaneous Retail Stores	**244,900**	**336,700**	+ 91,900	+ 37.6
Total Retail Stores	*1,628,100*	*1,772,300*	+144,200	+ 8.8
Nonstore Retailers	**79,800**	**162,100**	+ 82,300	+103.2
Total Stores and Nonstore Retailers	*1,707,900*	*1,934,500*	+226,500	+ 13.2

Source: 1963 figures—U.S. Bureau of the Census, Census of Business 1963, *Retail Trade United States Summary, BC67-RA1* (Washington, D.C.: U.S. Government Printing Office, 1970), pp. 1–5; 1972 figures—U.S. Bureau of the Census, *Census of Retail Trade 1972, Area Series United States, RC72-A-52* (Washington, D.C.: U.S. Government Printing Office, 1975), pp. 70, 71.

Table 2–2

Retail Sales, 1969–1974

Type of Store (primary merchandise line)	Sales in Billions		Increase (1969–1974)		Percentage of Total	
	1969	1974	Dollars (in billions)	Percentage	1969	1974
Food Group	**$ 78.3**	**$119.8**	**$ 41.5**	53.0	21.9	22.3
Grocery stores	72.9	111.3	38.4	52.7		
Other	5.4	8.5	3.1	57.4		
Automotive Group	**68.2**	**93.1**	**24.9**	36.5	19.1	17.3
Car dealers	63.1	84.8	21.7	34.4		
Tire, battery, & accessory stores	5.1	8.3	3.2	62.7		
General Merchandise Group	**57.6**	**89.3**	**31.7**	55.0	16.1	16.6
Department stores	35.7	55.9	20.2	56.6		
Mail order houses (dept. store merchandise)	3.5	5.8	2.3	65.7		
Variety stores	6.4	8.7	2.3	35.9		
Other	12.0	18.9	6.9	57.5		
Eating & Drinking Places	**27.0**	**41.8**	**14.8**	54.8	7.5	7.8
Gasoline Service Stations	**25.9**	**39.9**	**14.0**	54.1	7.2	7.4
Apparel Group	**19.9**	**24.9**	**5.0**	25.1	5.6	4.6
Men's & boys' wear stores	4.6	5.7	1.1	23.9		
Women's apparel & accessories stores	7.5	9.6	2.1	28.0		
Shoe stores	3.6	4.0	0.4	11.1		
Other	4.2	5.6	1.4	33.3		
Furniture & Appliance Group	**17.3**	**25.5**	**8.2**	47.4	4.8	4.7
Furniture & home furnishings stores	10.5	15.4	4.9	46.7		
Household appliance & TV-radio stores	5.7	8.0	2.3	40.4		
Other	1.1	2.1	1.0	90.9		
Lumber, Building, & Hardware Group	**15.0**	**23.5**	**8.5**	56.7	4.2	4.4
Lumber & bldg. materials dealers	11.6	18.3	6.7	57.8		
Hardware stores	3.4	5.2	1.8	52.9		
Drug & Proprietary Stores	**12.2**	**16.8**	**4.6**	37.7	3.4	3.1
Liquor Stores	**7.4**	**10.3**	**2.9**	39.2	2.1	1.9
All Other Stores	**29.1**	**52.9**	**23.8**	81.8	8.1	9.9
All Retail Stores	**$357.9**	**$537.8**	**$179.9**	50.3	**100.0**	**100.0**

Note: The largest-volume store categories not listed (included in "All Other Stores") are fuel and ice dealers, jewelry stores, sporting goods outlets, and florists, each of which accounts for substantially more than $1 billion in annual sales.

Source: Figures for 1969 are from *Survey of Current Business* (Washington, D.C.: U.S. Department of Commerce, February 1972), p. S–11. Figures for 1974 are from *Survey of Current Business* (March 1975), p. S–12.

Table 2–3

Projected 1980 Sales for Selected Store Categories

Types of Stores	Projected 1980 Sales (in billions)	Projected Increase 1973–1980 (compound annual growth rate)
Grocery stores	$166.0	7.8
Department stores	97.0	9.7 *
Variety stores	13.3	7.0
Eating & drinking places	65.0	7.9
Men's & boys' wear stores	9.5	7.5
Women's apparel & accessory stores	15.4	7.5
Furniture stores	17.2	7.5
Household appliance stores	8.4	7.5
Drug stores	25.0	7.0
All Retail Stores	**$849.0**	7.8

* Note how department stores are expected to outpace their competitors in growth to 1980.

Source: *U.S. Industrial Outlook—1975* (Washington, D.C.: U.S. Department of Commerce, 1974), p. 173.

(those expected to last more than three years) and *nondurables.* Sales of durables tend to decline much more rapidly during recessions because people can postpone replacing them until times are better. Sales of nondurables slip less rapidly when money is scarce because so many (like food) are necessities. Statisticians include cars, furniture and appliances, and lumber, building materials, and hardware in the durables category. Clothing, drugs, food, gasoline, general merchandise, liquor, and miscellaneous merchandise are classified as nondurables. Consumers spent about $167 billion in durable goods stores in 1974 and $370 billion in nondurable goods stores.

2 Major Trends in Retailing

Certain clear-cut trends are reshaping retailing and distribution. Each of these trends is generating new challenges for retailers and advertisers, forcing them to develop new approaches and fresh ways of thinking.

GETTING INTO THE OTHER FELLOW'S ACT: DIVERSIFICATION

Diversification is a keynote in all industries these days, among manufacturers as well as stores, but it has special significance in the retail sector. A century ago the local general store sold kerosene, rope, yard goods, pants, and soda crackers. In the early years of this century, the limited-line stores and specialty shops came into their own. Now history has gone full circle; the rush is back to the general store as nearly all retailers move in the direction of becoming "department" stores.

This trend started with the chain drug stores of the 1920s, which offered the public spark plugs, restaurant service, watches, jewelry, and cameras. Today's "druggist" often handles lamps, liquor, hosiery, lawn furniture, small appliances, and leather goods. In fact, less than half of a drug store's sales volume is derived from prescriptions and proprietary drugs. Meanwhile, over at the supermarket, people spend billions on "health and beauty aids"—the items once thought to be the mainstay of the drug store. (Food stores' HBA sales, which doubled during the sixties, are expected to double again, to nearly $7 billion, in the seventies.) In addition to selling "scrambled merchandise" in the same store, national chains (and even local store groups) diversify into each other's territory by operating whole strings of outlets for merchandise unrelated to their original, "normal" trade lines. The Walgreen "drug" company, for example, operates a chain of 50 general merchandise stores selling an estimated $250 million worth of items in no way related to drugs. At the same time, J. C. Penney, noted as the world's greatest soft-line department-store chain, is busy operating the Thrift Drug Company chain!

The supermarkets now account for one-sixth of ladies' hosiery sales and are making inroads into sales of other apparel items (especially casual shoes),

Figure 2–1 Is This an Ad for a Home Furnishings Store?

No, hardly! It is a typical ad for a chain drug store that offers a vast variety of merchandise unrelated to traditional drug-store items. "We're a drug store and a whole lot more!" is the campaign slogan featured under the company name at the top of the ad. The entire content of the ad is devoted to lamps and associated electrical products. Drug chains are said to have started the trend to diversification in retailing back in the 1920s, and they are still in the forefront. Meanwhile, food stores have become strong in drug-store products, and department stores and discount houses have fought back by establishing pharmacies. All other lines of retail business are now greatly affected by the rush to "scrambled merchandising," and it poses many problems for those who handle their advertising.

housewares, linens, toys, small appliances, and records. Virtually every type of former "specialty" shop is joining this trend. Ladies' apparel stores are adding men's sections (and vice versa); gift shops are appearing in hardware stores, florist shops, and liquor stores. Hardware stores, lumber yards, and other building-supply dealers are merging into new stores called "home centers." Department stores, which had the diversification idea a century ago, are growing at nearly twice the pace of the rest of the retail industry. And they are adding still further to the diversity of their offerings, especially in the area of *services*.

CHAIN STORES: THE GROWTH LEADERS

The "chain" concept was pioneered by several large retail corporations early in this century. The concept worked, and it worked well. Because of the chains, more people could get more merchandise, usually for less money. By 1960, 22 percent of the total dollar volume of retail business was done by organizations with 11 or more stores; by 1974, they controlled 31½ percent of all retail sales. (See Figure 2–2.)

Many different forms of chains have evolved: the great national corporate chains that handle general merchandise and many specialty lines, regional and local chains, chains that operate department stores as autonomous units (without the public being generally aware that they are in fact chains), voluntary and cooperative chains of small specialty merchants who own their own shops, and franchised chains with local ownership but strong central control.

The great nationwide general mer-chandise chains are Sears, Roebuck & Co., with 1974 sales of $13.1 billion; The J. C. Penney Company, $6.9 billion; S. S. Kresge (now considered a "discounter" by many), $5.6 billion; Montgomery Ward (a division of Marcor Corp., which was acquired by Mobil Oil in 1974), $4.7 billion; and F. W. Woolworth, $4.2 billion. Other chains with sales above $1 billion in 1973 were the W. T. Grant and Gamble-Skogmo stores.[1]

Sears' leading position is underscored by the fact that its sales volume is almost a seventh of all general merchandise sales, which amounts to over 1 percent of the gross national product, and twice the sales volume of its nearest competitor. With almost 900 big stores plus nearly 3,000 catalog, retail, and telephone offices and independent catalog franchisees, it serves virtually the entire United States and dominates the market for a number of categories of consumer goods with its famed Sears-brand merchandise.

J. C. Penney has recently challenged Sears by moving into both hard lines (it was originally essentially a soft-goods chain) and the catalog business. At the same time it has been edging away from its Midwestern small-town base and invading large urban areas, primarily in big shopping centers. Kresge was first of the big stores to recognize the meaning of the "discount" stores' popularity. Its sales and profits grew at a fantastic rate in the 1960s and early 1970s as it converted from the variety to the low-margin general merchandise field and moved from urban to suburban sites. Montgomery Ward and Woolworth, whose growth a few years ago lagged behind that of the other massive chains, have since woken up and become newly aggressive; they are successfully playing a catch-up game in the 1970s.

In the food field, Safeway Stores, strongly entrenched in fast-growing California and a leader in establishing very large stores with maximum local autonomy for the management, recently caught up in sales volume with the long-time leader, the Great Atlantic & Pacific Tea Company. In 1974, Safeway reported $8.2 billion in sales as against $6.9 billion for A & P, which had too many stores, too many of them small, and had failed to capture a West Coast foothold. The Kroger Grocery & Baking Company ranked third among the food giants in 1974, with a sales volume of $4.8 billion. It was followed by Lucky Stores, with sales of $2.7 billion, and Jewel Stores (a highly innovative and rapidly diversifying company), with sales of $2.6 billion.

There are a number of chains of department and specialty stores that do not *look* like chains because each store operates independently, as it did before its acquisition by a chain, under local, usually one-family, management. The largest of these chains is the Federated Department Stores chain, whose stores had a combined sales volume of $3.3 billion in 1974. Federated is the country's ninth-largest retailer and ranks sixth in general merchandise sales. Other store groups of this nature are the Allied Stores Company, May Department Store, Dayton-Hudson, Associated Dry Goods, R. H. Macy, and Carter-Hawley-Hale, all of which had sales of over $1 billion in 1974.

"Chains" of locally owned stores, linked through cooperatively owned and managed headquarters or by an affiliation with a sponsoring wholesaler, are prominent in the food, variety store, hardware, and drug store fields. Franchised chains dominate the automotive field and are strong in convenience food stores, fast-food restaurants, and other lines.

An offshoot of the chain-store boom has been development of *house brands*. These are brands of merchandise made for a retailer and sold in competition with manufacturers' branded products (usually, but not necessarily, at a lower price). Virtually all the big chains have store brands, and in some cases they sell nothing else. Sears uses its own name on 90 percent of its merchandise and rigidly specifies how it is to be manufactured, often in factories where the retail giant itself is a stockholder. Many stores, especially department stores and supermarkets, sell their own brands right along with national brands.

Figure 2–2 Degree of Large Chain Store Dominance, by Tradelines
This graph compares the growth in sales volume of two categories of retail stores. "Big stores," called "Group II" by the Bureau of the Census, are those retail chains with 11 or more units; "small stores" are single stores or chains with under 10 units. Note that large chains dominate department and variety store sales and hold a slight edge among grocery stores, while small stores retain dominance for all other categories shown. In annual growth rates, however, big stores are outpacing the "smalls" in all categories of retailing except variety stores.
Source: Graph based on figures from *U.S. Industrial Outlook—1972* (Washington, D.C.: U.S. Department of Commerce, 1971), p. 357.

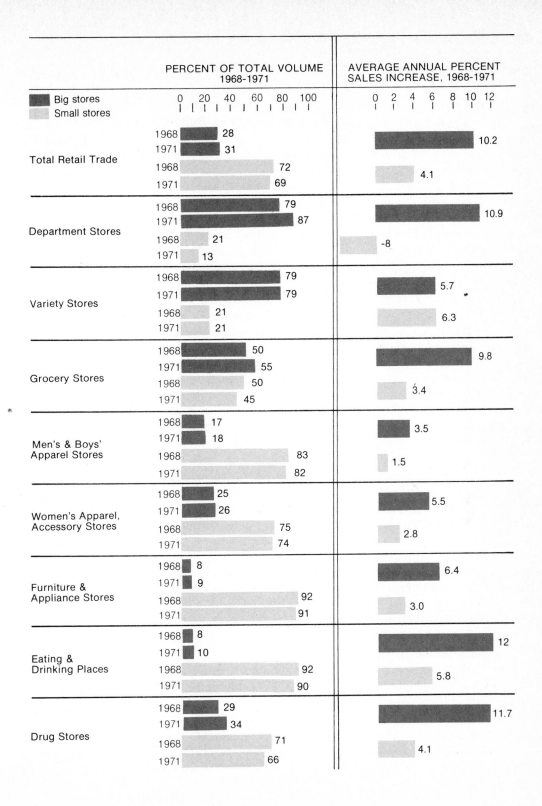

	PERCENT OF TOTAL VOLUME 1968-1971	AVERAGE ANNUAL PERCENT SALES INCREASE, 1968-1971
Big stores / Small stores	0 20 40 60 80 100	0 2 4 6 8 10 12
Total Retail Trade	1968 — 28 / 1971 — 31 / 1968 — 72 / 1971 — 69	10.2 / 4.1
Department Stores	1968 — 79 / 1971 — 87 / 1968 — 21 / 1971 — 13	10.9 / -8
Variety Stores	1968 — 79 / 1971 — 79 / 1968 — 21 / 1971 — 21	5.7 / 6.3
Grocery Stores	1968 — 50 / 1971 — 55 / 1968 — 50 / 1971 — 45	9.8 / 3.4
Men's & Boys' Apparel Stores	1968 — 17 / 1971 — 18 / 1968 — 83 / 1971 — 82	3.5 / 1.5
Women's Apparel, Accessory Stores	1968 — 25 / 1971 — 26 / 1968 — 75 / 1971 — 74	5.5 / 2.8
Furniture & Appliance Stores	1968 — 8 / 1971 — 9 / 1968 — 92 / 1971 — 91	6.4 / 3.0
Eating & Drinking Places	1968 — 8 / 1971 — 10 / 1968 — 92 / 1971 — 90	12 / 5.8
Drug Stores	1968 — 29 / 1971 — 34 / 1968 — 71 / 1971 — 66	11.7 / 4.1

DISCOUNTING: REVOLUTION
OR EVOLUTION?

Experiments with the discount idea were conducted in New England in the 1930s, but the first modern discount store is said to have been established in Rhode Island in 1953. The name derives from the early practice of offering merchandise *discounted* from manufacturers' list prices. Although "fair-trade" laws once upheld a manufacturer's right to enforce pricing policies on dealers, these laws were reinterpreted and then repealed, and the way was left open for retailers to set their own price on any product—which the discount stores did *en masse.* The word *discount* has lost much of its original meaning now that all stores can (and often do) set their own prices, and it is being dropped from the names and advertising of "discount" stores even as other low-margin stores begin to use it to describe their own merchandising.

Because no firm definition of a discount store exists and official figures fail to segregate this type of store from others, it is hard to pin down their aggregate sales volume. Trade association and trade magazine estimates of their gross annual sales in the early 1970s range from $28 to $38 billion. The number of discounters grew from about 2,000 to over 6,000 from 1960 to the early seventies, and their total sales volume went up by roughly 400 percent during that period (while general merchandising sales as a whole grew only by about 40 percent, or only one-tenth as much).

Much of this increase in sales volume, however, must be attributed to Kresge's brilliantly successful K-marts, which have been established nationwide.

Many of the discount stores in local or regional chains have faltered, failed, merged, or consolidated. Zayre reported over $1 billion in 1974 sales, but only one other approached that figure—Vornado, with $927 million. In an attempt to be more successful, many of the discount stores, which now prefer to call themselves mass retailers or merchandisers, have edged away from their original austere operating methods. Yesterday's stark, bare-bones merchandising is being abandoned as they begin to upgrade their images by diversifying their product lines, improving shoppers' conveniences, selling services as well as goods, adopting house brands, and otherwise merging with the mainstream of chain-store merchandising.

Even more significant than the discounters' rapid growth has been their impact on the retail industry as a whole. Other stores met the "discounter threat" of the sixties by rebuilding an image of quality and service, by revitalizing their own basement or other low-priced departments, and, most interestingly, by going into discount operations themselves through subsidiaries with different names from the parent stores. For example, in addition to precipitating Kresge's metamorphosis from variety chain to discount leader, the mass retailers forced traditional department stores, in self-defense, to imitate them: Federated established its Gold Circle and Gold Triangle units, Allied its Almart and Hunter stores, and the May Company its Venture marts.

Essentially, there has been a narrowing of the gap between the discounters and conventional stores. Each has learned from the other, and the competition has been fierce, both among the discounters themselves and between them and the traditional retailers. Originally an urban phenomenon, many discount stores are now moving into smaller towns to tap new markets. At first barred from shopping centers by landlords and key tenants, many are now being welcomed to help draw traffic.

The newest concept in retailing is the *warehouse-catalog showroom*. This idea was pioneered by the Levitz Company, a furniture store group based in Pennsylvania that has now gone nationwide. In the 1970s, showrooms have replaced the discount houses as the focus of attention, and both ex-discounters and traditional stores have followed Levitz's lead. Huge stocks of merchandise are maintained in massive warehouses close to traffic arteries; display models on the floor may be inspected, or the stores' catalogs may be consulted at home. The shopper who has a suitable vehicle can cart away a purchase, or the store will deliver at an extra charge. The warehouse idea spread rapidly from the furniture field to other merchandise lines, and at least 1,000 such "stores" were operating in 1972. Further expansion was nipped in the bud by the recession of 1973–1975, which plunged many of these operations into financial distress, so the future of this concept remains an open question.

Similar in some respects and newer yet is the gigantic *hypermarche*, a European innovation in which a store selling food and general merchandise is adjacent to a massive warehouse. The French prototype may have as much as 250,000 square feet of sales floor and may do $50 million a year in sales. The hypermarche was being introduced to American shoppers in a few places by the mid-1970s.

One of the first, near Detroit, offered 100,000 items with 59 checkout lanes and merchandise stacked high in bins, special containers, or original cartons.

OTHER INNOVATIVE RESPONSES TO ALTERED CUSTOMER NEEDS AND LIFESTYLES

In-home selling today is thriving, led by a resurgence of catalog merchandising. Half of the nearly $6 billion in catalog sales made annually is accounted for by Sears, and 90 percent by five leading firms. Another $4 billion in sales are made each year by knocking on doors; this kind of in-home retailing doubled in volume from 1965 to 1970, with Avon Products leading the pack. Avon's half a million salespersons approached $1.3 billion in volume in 1974. Telephone selling, often in direct response to ads, is also gaining in popularity. All these methods of selling are used to some degree by many conventional stores.

New technologies are also having an impact on retailing. Vending machines are becoming more sophisticated and are being used to sell products other than chewing gum, candy bars, and soft drinks. Some firms are experimenting with automated stores, reducing the stores' staffs to a minimum and relying instead on computers and machinery to do the job. Some observers predict that the telephone, the TV set, and the warehouse showroom will eventually link up to create nonstore retailing on a scale that will make many present forms of merchandising obsolete. With two-way audio and visual communication, perhaps a catalog, some code numbers, and push buttons, all shopping could be done at home.

Rental and leasing services are thriving as more people buy the use of specialty products just for the period when they are needed. Factory outlets are bypassing normal retail channels and in some lines are growing into manufacturer-operated chains. In the contract market that is being cultivated by many stores, sales are made not to the ultimate owner, but to builders, mobile-home makers, developers, and others who in turn sell completely equipped "packaged" homes.

ADVERTISING IMPLICATIONS

All these trends in retailing affect the ways stores advertise. Diversification of merchandise calls for changing the image of the former specialty shop and exposing its broader product lines to the public, and it demands more knowledgeable, versatile advertising personnel. Chain stores (including the voluntary independent groups and franchisers) get professional advertising support from national or regional headquarters or advertising agencies, so that little need be done at the store level. Those stores that put a strong emphasis on house brands must promote their brands as well as their stores, and the biggest chains are now doing this through national advertising just like the manufacturers. A trend has developed, however, of delegating some advertising decision-making authority to local groups or stores where fragmented markets make a uniform local ad policy unwise.

The department-store chains continue to maintain large independent advertising staffs in each store since the big appeal of the chains is the local orientation of each store and its suburban branches. The discounters forced a return to strictly price-oriented ads, not just for themselves but for others competing with them; but as this segment of the industry matured, it, too, sought to differentiate store from store and to build store personalities and images. New methods of marketing rely in large measure on some form of advertising to explain, introduce, and pave the way for their general acceptance.

3 Where's the Action These Days? The "New Downtown" (the Shopping Center) versus the Old Downtown

The early waves of suburban expansion created incomplete, unbalanced "bedroom communities," lacking adequate retail and service facilities. Suburbanites found it equally unsatisfactory to fight traffic by going back to the old core cities to shop or to make do with what nearby rural villages had to offer. Into this void came the shopping center.

In 1949, at the start of the shopping center boom, there were only 75 nationwide; this number grew to 4,500 by 1960 and to 17,725 by 1975. Some estimates predict as many as 25,000 shopping centers by 1985. By the early seventies, shopping-center-based stores accounted for 46 percent of retail sales (other than car and gasoline sales), and 80 percent of all new retail construction is now in such locations.

The centers are of three types: (1) *neighborhood centers*, with 10 to 15 stores serving from a few thousand to perhaps 40,000 people; (2) *community centers* anchored to a supermarket or junior department store, where a variety of merchants serve indistinctly defined markets of from 40,000 to 150,000 people; and (3) *regional centers,* with two or more major department stores and from 50 to 100 smaller shops, which draw customers from 10 to 15 miles away and need a minimum market population of 100,000 to succeed. There were nearly 500 of these big centers in the mid-seventies.

Shopping centers have evolved through three distinct phases. In the fifties they were conceived and operated purely as concentrations of *retail* stores. People who shopped there for tangible merchandise had to go elsewhere for the vast variety of services they also needed. The next decade witnessed the evolution of the regional centers (and, to a degree, the community centers) into aggregations of stores *plus* service facilities of all kinds. These expanded centers could compete in every way with the long-established city cores and nearby smaller-town business-service districts. In effect, the *old downtowns were simply replaced* by new "downtowns" closer to the homes of those they served. The third phase of center development is upon us now: totally planned *new communities,* in which one gigantic development firm (often working with real-estate subsidiaries of the major retailers) creates a complete and balanced community embracing not only retail and service facilities, but living quarters, recreational and cultural facilities, and business enterprises as well.

Nearly all the branch stores of downtown conventional retailers are in shopping centers, and the big stores themselves have been among the leaders in developing the centers. Nearly all new construction by the regional and national chains has also been in centers, and they, too, invest in development of whole centers.

Independent specialty shops, particularly the smaller ones, tend to be underrepresented in centers because landlords need tenants with an AAA credit rating to secure financing. Women's apparel shops are more heavily represented in the centers than other specialty stores and have proven more profitable in terms of sales per square foot than any other tenants.

The newest centers are gigantic, climate-controlled covered malls financed jointly by huge corporations and major financial institutions. They have an unprecedented variety of nonretail functions and facilities; they include mass retailers in the store "mix"; they put a greater emphasis on shoppers' pleasure and convenience; and they tend toward vertical construction as land costs keep going up. Some centers specialize in particular types of tenants and have particular "target" customers. They are spreading from suburbia into the old central cities as well as into the hinterlands to serve small-town consumers.

WHAT NEXT? NEW TOWNS
ON THE HORIZON!

The creation of superregional shopping centers is one aspect of retail development; another is the creation of *new towns,* first satellites of existing cities, then whole new cities in areas now thinly populated. Planners today know that retail business may be the heart of a community, but it is not the whole body. Controlling just one facet of area development, the retail-trade center, leaves the gate wide open for the subsequent erection of indiscriminate clusters of facilities, creating the same ugliness and confusion typical of the played-out city cores. The new towns are planned with each facet of community, family, and personal life in mind, with due regard for incremental growth.

For retailers, there is an essential difference between a giant shopping center and a whole new town. The former, though based on a well-planned internal operation and developed after considerable market research, must draw trade from subdivisions, communities, and apartment complexes built by someone else. A new town, in contrast, is an integrated whole, with preplanned residential facilities for many, if not most, of the people who will shop (and be employed) in its stores. Thus it has, from the start, more of a captive market.

New towns make geographic mobility less necessary, releasing people from dependence on the private automobile. The big parking lots that now characterize shopping centers may become obsolete in these cities as people once again shop near their homes. Six new towns now being developed with assistance from the federal government will have a total population of 400,000 when they are completed, and each of these towns will have an integral retail area. Some new cities will be designed as retirement or recreational towns, but most will not. All, however, will have built-in leisure-time facilities, and the market for related merchandise will be enormous. By their nature, they will call for more emphasis on the service aspects of marketing, and

retailers there may be the innovators in the new services-oriented society.

Through the early 1970s new towns appeared to be the wave of the future. Then recession and inflation brought second thoughts to planners and developers. Enormous funds are needed for such new towns, and the supply of money from either government or private lenders dried up. Population growth slowed down, and existing smaller cities revitalized themselves, causing further downward reassessment of the new-town idea. Time only will tell how soon and on what scale these plans will be revived.

HAVE THE OLD DOWNTOWNS REALLY HAD IT?

The downtown areas are literally committing suicide. They are killing themselves with problems such as the erosion of the central cities, parking limitations, law and order difficulties, high cost and scarcity of land and distance from population centers.

This is the way Albert Sussman, executive vice president of the International Council of Shopping Centers, described the old downtowns as long ago as 1969 at a management institute on the campus of Michigan State University. Others have echoed this dismal viewpoint in later years.

But to balance the gloomy evidence of retailers abandoning core cities, and to suggest that by now the process may well have bottomed out, comes news of many stores strengthening their downtown operations and investing huge sums in new or remodeled stores in reviving central districts. Not everyone sees central cities as doomed. Government, commerce and industry, educational institutions, and community organizations have joined with leading retailers to establish and implement survival plans, and some observers foresee an eventual polarization of retail trade into two areas: (1) bigger-than-ever suburban malls and new towns and (2) revitalized, rebuilt downtowns better suited to late–twentieth-century trade than the nineteenth-century anachronisms that are literally being bulldozed out of existence to make way for modernization.

Certain basic socioeconomic factors seem to favor the survival, if not outright growth, of old downtowns. Office buildings continue to go up in the core cities, increasing the white-collar workforce there on business days and thus the number of customers for stores that cater to noon-hour and after-work shoppers. Visitors, tourists, and other transients still tend to concentrate in downtown areas, and many can be coaxed to spend money there. New expressways, revitalized (if subsidized) rapid transit, and massive municipal parking facilities make it increasingly feasible for affluent suburbanites to travel quickly and pleasantly into downtown areas, at least for occasional sprees.

Action programs to stimulate these trends, capitalize on these changes, and build defenses against the further deterioration of downtowns abound. Downtown shopping centers have been created, modeled after the suburban plazas and malls but adapted to the urban environment. Buildings like the Marina Towers or the John Hancock building in Chicago are actually combined office-apartment-services-amusement complexes, with entire floors devoted to retail shops.

To survive, downtown retailers must cultivate specific market segments: minority groups whose needs, desires, and aspirations differ markedly from those of the urban middle class of two decades ago, and also from those of the suburban shoppers with which the branch store of today is familiar; the daytime white-collar population of downtown office structures; tourists and business travelers; and the new breed of high-rise–apartment dwellers. In addition, efforts must be made to draw suburban shoppers back downtown.

It should be noted that downtown decay is not an exclusive problem of large metropolitan cities, nor is urban renewal their private domain. Many medium-sized and small towns, feeling a loss of trade to nearby city shopping centers (or new centers on their own outskirts) have "saved" their downtown areas by prompt, aggressive action. In some cases retailers, civic leaders, and municipal authorities have worked together to transform dingy, unattractive "Main Streets" into lovely, flower-bedecked pedestrian malls. This happened in Kalamazoo, Michigan, and again in Decatur, Illinois. Even very small towns have licked the problem, sometimes by simply wiping out their old business districts and replacing them with sparkling new enclosed malls.

ADVERTISING IMPLICATIONS

Each new major shopping center has its own promotion and advertising staff that carries on a continuous sequence of promotions and events to keep

Figure 2–3 Department Stores of the Seventies: Two Patterns

These contrasting new stores, both opened in 1972, exemplify a trend and a countertrend characteristic of major-store site location and construction concepts of this decade. The bottom photo shows the 176,000 square-foot Gimbels store in the Northridge shopping center, a massive regional mall in the outer suburban fringe of Milwaukee. The store is on two levels, and of its five entrances two open to upper level parking areas.

The Yorktown community on Manhattan's East Side in New York City, which is presently undergoing a dramatic expansion in high-rise apartment house development, is the setting for Gimbels East, at left. Considered a prototype of things to come in revitalizing urban areas, this store was the first high-rise department store erected in Manhattan in half a century. This 12-story structure built on a 35,000 square-foot lot contains a huge 440,000 feet of floor space, including two floors below ground level. Vertical transportation within the store is provided by 24 escalators and 5 high-speed passenger elevators, and the store has a direct connecting passage with an intermediate platform built by the store to facilitate shoppers' use of the nearby subway station. This free-standing unit provides many of the services and conveniences that are found in a suburban shopping mall, including a full floor devoted to customer services, a twin theater, a community room for use by civic groups, restaurants, and a cocktail lounge.

Like Gimbels, other big retailers who have expanded primarily in the suburbs and the malls for decades are now taking a second look at big-city "rebirth" and reevaluating what modern apartment developments and mass transit can mean to merchandisers who do not neglect the market potential of cities themselves.

Sources: Gimbels Northridge, photo courtesy of R. L. Meyer Advertising & Promotions, Inc., Milwaukee; Gimbels East, photo courtesy of Abbott Merkt & Company, Inc., Architects and Engineers.

Figure 2–4 Transformation of a Downtown Retail District

Prior to 1959, the main downtown shopping district of Kalamazoo, Michigan (pop. 96,000), appeared as in photo at left and offered little to appeal to shoppers. The country's first open-air downtown pedestrian mall was then opened (photo on right) with the street closed to cars, but with massive municipal parking facilities close by. With the revitalization of the area, merchants on that mall enjoyed an average annual sales growth of 10 percent.

Still later, the downtown merchants, working with their city government, moved on to another phase: complete modernization and addition of many shopper's amenities on the mall. Many other cities have followed a similar pattern, which has kept a major share of retail business in their central business districts. Others have thrown in the sponge and allowed suburban retail development to drain trade and stores away until downtown areas have become hollow shells. Characteristic of all successful downtown retail efforts has been aggressive joint advertising to keep the public aware of the downtown, matching the consistent promotion of the suburban shopping centers.

Sources: Photo at left courtesy of the City of Kalamazoo, Michigan; photo at right courtesy of the *Kalamazoo Gazette.*

traffic lively for the benefit of all the tenants. All the stores contribute proportionally to sustain this effort. A whole new specialty within the retail advertising field has grown up around this function, that of the shopping center promotion manager. The International Council of Shopping Centers conducts annual training seminars for these people, and for those centers too small to have large professional staffs, specialty firms have arisen to give counsel, plan promotion schedules, and supply materials (sometimes in a handy, easy-to-use "package"). Each store must allot some of its budget to this kind of advertising and adjust its own promotion to mesh with its neighbors'.

Downtowns that have successfully revived have stolen this idea from the suburban centers: They have organized solid merchants' associations and set up joint promotions of their own to draw and hold downtown trade. Often, the downtown areas are better favored by media patterns than the outlying centers, which sometimes have to devise their own media to reach a desired trading area effectively. The new towns, at least the larger ones, have local newspapers, cable TV, and FM radio stations designed specifically to suit residents' and merchants' needs.

4 The Independent Merchant: A Vanishing or Thriving Species?

Must *all* future retailing be by large chains, departmentalized general-merchandise giants, discounters, and shopping-center–based stores? Maybe. In some segments of the industry, most

probably. But maybe not. In certain other areas of the vast and diverse retail field, there are signs that progressive, innovative, and well-conceived small retail enterprises will not merely survive but multiply and prosper in the years ahead. The less-than-gigantic store or shop, after all, has certain fundamental advantages:

1. The increased recognition of the diverse interest groups, age groups, and lifestyles in modern society makes it easier for smaller shops boldly targeted at a specific market to develop.

2. Flexibility of decision-making, always a great equalizer when the small are matched against the big, may prove an ever greater advantage in the future than it has in the past. As the pace of living quickens, the multi-unit chain or very large store with sacrosanct management programs may lag behind the alert small merchant in its reaction to change.

3. In the past, sheer mismanagement caused many small-store failures. The proprietor-manager of today is likely to have had a much better business education than his predecessors. He will have adult continuing-education classes available almost everywhere and numerous seminars and short courses to keep him sharp and his thinking viable.

4. The government, particularly through the Small Business Administration and also via the Federal Trade Commission, is actively committed to helping smaller business. Its fundamental policy is to encourage competition by legislation and administrative action, as well as legal intervention, to protect independent retail operations. Retail

advertising, in particular, comes under the scrutiny of FTC, which bares its teeth if a manufacturer favors large over small merchants in allotting cooperative advertising money or if newspapers and broadcast stations too heavily favor big advertisers in their sliding-scale rate cards.

5. The revolt of the young adult generation against depersonalization and "bigness" may stimulate a flow of dollars back toward smaller shops that provide individualized service and an unhurried, friendly, intimate shopping atmosphere. The phenomenal success of many boutiques in the late sixties is an indication of this trend.

6. The cooperative and voluntary chains and related types of organized independents such as franchised ventures provide a way for smaller, proprietor-managed stores to gain many of the advantages of the big merchandisers without losing local control.

7. Shopping center locations, at least in community and neighborhood sizes, may come easier for small shops as a result of recent court action by the FTC against "exclusivity clauses" in leases. Even in major regional malls, big retailers are coming to recognize that a healthy mix of different kinds and sizes of stores attracts customer traffic.

8. In many lines of trade, wholesalers and manufacturers back up the small retailer with credit, management training aids, research, and advertising-promotional reinforcement on a cost-sharing basis. Many big manufacturers and producers recognize the value of independent, services-oriented distributors for their products and even view them as a balancing factor to reinforce their own position vis-à-vis the retail giants in the struggle for marketing power.

9. Certain technological innovations, such as the development of smaller computers for inventory control and customer billing and the spread of computer service bureaus to handle these tasks for shops too small to own and operate internal EDP systems, are helping smaller stores to hold their own. Improved transportation and communication make it possible to do business with a smaller inventory.

10. The fundamental advantage of the small operation is management's close contact with store personnel and customers. When "the boss" is personally on the scene most of the time, things often get done more efficiently. Management policies are more easily understood and more likely to be adhered to when management is close at hand than when it is 1,000 miles from the sales counter. When a disgruntled customer storms in the door, the owner is there to hear the complaint and to placate him or her in person, perhaps turning that customer into a lifelong booster once the fracas is over.

WHAT THE STATISTICS SHOW ABOUT INDEPENDENT RETAILING

There were about 10,500 stores in the United States that had more than 100 employees when the Census Bureau made a head count in 1971. This may sound like a lot of stores, but it is only one-sixth of 1 percent of all the stores in the country. The U.S. Census of Business turned up half a million stores with *no paid employees* (i.e., those operated by the proprietors and perhaps a helpful spouse, daughter, or son). This was an increase in numbers of 15 percent since 1963, and in the same period of time larger stores with payroll had increased by less than 7 percent. In 1972, these small family-operated shops constituted more than a quarter of all stores—including nearly two-thirds of fruit markets and antique shops, nearly half of fur stores, confectioneries, and sporting goods stores, and many home furnishings, jewelry, and auto goods outlets. The average sales of $33,500 they brought in in 1972 was a 42 percent gain since 1963.

It is a fact that American retailing continues to be dominated by small shops. Only in the general merchandise field and in particular among department stores have large chains reached a position of overwhelming dominance; the small department store has indeed "had it." But most of the many lines of specialty shops have not. In apparel, furniture, appliances, restaurants, and drugs, the smaller retailer holds the upper hand. In fact, two successive Censuses of Business taken during the sixties (in 1963 and 1967) showed single-unit independents in some trade lines—appliance dealers in the above-$300,000 volume bracket, all hardware stores, and all radio-TV shops, for example—to have *increased* their share of the market.

Retailing is a rewarding field for young entrepreneurs who want to create their own lifestyles and succeed by their own efforts. Retailers can handle the products and services that interest them if their interest is shared by a wide enough market. They can deal in rock music or camping equipment, in auto repairs or hairstyling, in paperback books or oil paintings, in faded jeans or high fashion or Italian food. Not every type of enterprise will flourish everywhere, but the independent merchant who is clever enough to identify a need then move quickly and work hard to fill it still has many opportunities to succeed.

Standing in the historical shadows behind every one of the great retail concerns of our day are the independent retailers of yesterday. Sebastian S. Kresge started with a "dime store" in Detroit. James Cash Penney was a small-town merchant in sparsely populated western Wyoming. Joseph L. Hudson was an Ionia, Michigan, haberdasher before he moved his stock across the state to found J. L. Hudson's, now the second-largest department store in the United States. Richard Sears was a 19-year-old railroad agent in tiny North Redwood, Minnesota, when he bailed out a C.O.D. shipment of watches intended for a defunct jeweler and sold them by telegraph and mail, mostly to fellow railroad men along the line.

In our own times, other retail businesses have grown from small beginnings. Hendrik Meijer of Greenville, Michigan, was a barber in the depression year of 1934 when the tenant in the other half of his modest building went broke. To keep himself afloat, he turned the empty store into a low-margin consignment-goods food store, the forerunner of the huge one-stop shopping marts called Meijer's Thrifty Acres. Melvin Landow made a million in appliance shops, then retired at 37 after a career that began with lugging TV sets to customers' homes as a salesman's assistant. He made one fortune in Pittsburgh and another in Florida. (His retirement didn't

Figure 2–5 The Specialty Shop and Its Imitators

Pictured at left is the interior of an unusually attractive specialty shop, The Crown House of Gifts in the Somerset Mall, Troy, Michigan (an upper-income Detroit suburb). Shops of this kind have personalities all their own, each featuring a special atmosphere of intimacy that sets them apart from other stores. Dramatic merchandise groupings set off by unusual display and lighting techniques es-

tablish a mood and stimulate psychological impulses to browse, to buy, or to chat with the affable sales personnel. This store won the Gift and Decorative Accessories Association of America award as the "Best Designed Gift Shop" in 1970. Advertising for such shops concentrates on a single image and must be created with the utmost care to insure that it properly projects the personality and atmosphere of the store, its merchandise, and its personnel, thus attracting the particular type of customer it is designed to serve.

The strength and vitality of small boutiques or specialty shops such as this one is best proven by the thousands of such shops that major retailers have set up in recent years to compete with them. Shown below is the Gourmet Cookware, a shop within a huge full-line department store operated by The Boston Store in the Northridge Mall near Milwaukee. This shop is designed and decorated to give the feeling of a tiny, intimate "country kitchen." By dividing their space into specialized shops like this, large stores capture much of the charm and attractiveness that characterizes the small specialty store. Advertising for big stores becomes complex when these special-image shops must be promoted along with the store as a whole.

Sources: Picture at left, photography by The Crown House of Gifts; photo at right by courtesy of The Boston Store, Milwaukee.

last long!) He shared his experience with others in his famous book, *How to Make a Million in Retailing.*

ADVERTISING AND THE
SMALLER MERCHANT

Problems relating to advertising and promotion, the particular concern of this book, are high on the list of management challenges to the smaller store operator today. The small retailer obviously cannot maintain a staff of specialists to handle advertising and promotion. Much of the work must be done by the retailer alone or with outside help. In the chapters that follow, we shall consider problems facing the smaller merchant: how to squeeze the most out of a limited advertising budget, what to learn from the way "the big fellows" do things, and how to utilize the various outside services available to upgrade messages to customers and give those messages a professional touch.

Questions for Discussion

1. What types of retail stores are the most numerous? What types of stores have been declining in numbers in recent years? Why has this been happening? What types of retail outlets do the greatest gross dollar volume annually? What kinds of stores have been increasing their sales volume most rapidly, and why?

2. What is meant by the diversification of merchandise lines in modern retailing? In what types of stores has this trend been most pronounced? Give some examples of this in your own area.

3. Mention several types of retail chains, and explain how they differ from one another.

4. How have the so-called "discount" stores changed over the years? What have been the primary reactions of traditional retailers to the emergence of the "discount" concept? What is the latest trend in the continued evolution of this type of retail outlet?

5. How are shopping centers classified? What three phases have been noted in the development of the shopping center system as a whole?

6. What have older retail districts in central cities been doing to combat losses of trade to suburban shopping centers? Is anything of this nature being done in your area?

7. What facts and trends indicate the continued viability of relatively small independent stores?

Suggested Projects

1. Survey the numbers of different kinds of retail establishments in your community. Count the number of general merchandise, hardware, shoe, apparel, and other stores in the Yellow Pages; then compare the proportion of each with the national proportions given in Table 2–1. Is your community perhaps oversupplied with stores in some categories and undersupplied with stores in other categories, compared with the United States as a whole? Walk down some main business streets and into major shopping malls, and make notes on the kinds of stores most recently built or expanded. Also check vacant stores and note what kinds of retail outlets have recently closed down. What kinds of

outlets are growing, and which are declining? Why?

2. Check the regional and national chain outlets in your community. Are they relatively new or mostly long-established? For what kinds of merchandise do you, your family, and your friends habitually shop in these chain stores? For what kinds of goods are locally owned independent shops preferred? Why, in your opinion, do people seem to prefer chains for some kinds of purchases and independents for others?

3. Go into several supermarkets near your home or school, walk through the aisles with a notebook, and list the product lines *other than food* on the shelves. Then go into several women's wear shops and note how many men's apparel items are sold. Go into a men's store and check for women's items. Why, in your opinion, are some or all of these stores diversifying their merchandise?

4. Collect retail ads from the nearest daily newspaper over a period of several days or a week. Make a list of nationally sold branded merchandise that is advertised during the period and another list of store brands or "private label" goods. Which predominates? How many stores advertise both manufacturers' brands and their own brands? Which do you buy most often? Which do your family and friends buy?

5. Go to the nearest large "discount" store and make a list of the prices of 20 specific items selected at random. Include as many well-known national brands as possible. Now go to several local independent stores (specialty shops or department stores), and check their prices for the same or comparable products. Do the same at the nearest national chain outlet (Sears, Penney's, Ward, or Woolco, for example). List those items that could be obtained in all three kinds of stores. How much difference was there in their prices? Can you find any reasons other than price to explain why local shoppers buy these products in one store or another?

6. Visit the shopping centers in your community (or the nearest larger city). How many are covered and how many are open-air centers? How many are multi-storied? Which would you classify as regional, community, or neighborhood centers? How many stores in the centers are branches of downtown stores? How many are chain outlets? What non-retail activities and enterprises are there in the shopping centers? What are downtown merchants in your community doing, individually or as a group, to meet competition from these centers?

Notes

1. These and other estimates of stores' 1974 sales are from "The Fifty Largest Retailing Companies (ranked by sales)," *Fortune* (July 1975), p. 122. Reprinted from the 1975 Fortune Directory by permission.

Preview

The management of any retail establishment entails a number of vital functions. In a large store, the advertising staff must coordinate its activities with those of many other persons. In a smaller operation, the top manager handles many functions alone, so that coordination is often easier.

Retailers are involved in the management of three types of resources:

1. human resources (personnel),
2. physical resources (buildings, fixtures, and stock), and
3. financial resources.

Management information systems based on electronic data processing have become a prime factor in retail decision-making, as well as in reduction of the time and money spent on clerical chores. Though it is now used chiefly for inventory control and to handle accounts receivable and payrolls, EDP is destined to play an increasingly direct role in the management of advertising.

Learning Goals

The mission of Chapter 3 is to provide a general picture of retail management, of the problems it involves, and of how some of these problems relate to the store's advertising effort. It is intended to introduce the student, briefly, to financial reports such as profit and loss statements and balance sheets and to various types of productivity ratios. It should also provide a general understanding of the functions of EDP and its potential for improving the effectiveness of advertising.

3

Retailing from the Inside: Managing the Store

1 How Retail Stores Operate

The basic functions of any retail business are *merchandising, publicity* (including *advertising*), *store operation,* and *accounting and control.* In the very smallest of stores, the proprietor-manager has to perform all these functions alone. As the enterprise grows, its personnel may fall into two groups: those responsible for merchandising and for store operations; later the accounting and control staff may become a separate unit. The very large store develops a lengthy roster of specialized departments; the basic *functions* performed, however, remain the same.

There is a growing tendency to separate the buying function from selling. Whereas formerly it was normal for a buyer also to supervise the sales force, more stores are now moving toward a system in which a department manager (who is not a buyer) is responsible for the sales force. Another trend is toward upgrading the status of the personnel

director, in recognition of the importance of the selection, training, and motivation of personnel. There are also a movement toward long-range management planning, a movement away from one-man rule, and an increased emphasis on research.

A typical medium-sized or large store may have a *general manager* with two staff assistants, the *treasurer-controller,* and the *personnel director,* as shown in Figure 3–1. Under the manager may be two major executives, a *director of store operations* and a *director of merchandising and sales promotion.* The operations executive supervises a *store superintendent,* and his division is responsible for maintenance, workrooms, adjustments, deliveries, receiving, stockrooms, protection, service, purchasing, and supervision of the expense budget. The merchandising/sales promotion executive, who may have the title of vice president, controls the buying and selling functions that are the reason the store exists in the first place. Working under this executive are two others—the *merchandise manager* and then the *manager of publicity* (or promotion, or advertising—the title may vary)—upon whose abilities the success of the entire enterprise very largely depends.

The merchandise manager, with whom the advertising/promotion people work very closely, is involved in merchandise management, buying, selling, personal shopping, comparison shopping, unit control, and supervision of the merchandise budget. The publicity manager (whose various roles are the focus of most of the rest of this volume) handles advertising, display, special-purpose publicity, press releases, and institutional promotions. The advertising manager, who is subordinate to the publicity director, has a staff of copywriters, artists, production specialists, broadcast coordinators, and others. The size of this staff depends on the size of the operation and the degree to which various functions are handled by outside personnel.

Multi-unit organizations (i.e., chains), modify this standard organizational structure. Some functions are tightly centralized at national or regional headquarters, leaving individual store managers fewer areas of responsibility—perhaps only store management and selling. There is a trend among the largest chains to delegate authority downward to zone or district offices, but the local manager still has no say in the buying function (except to adjust orders to emphasize merchandise that will sell well in a particular locality), and a weak voice, if any, in promotion and advertising. However, the big corporate chains put together by acquisition of family-owned, conventional, local stores normally allow maximum local autonomy.

Common to both large and small companies is a trend toward manage-

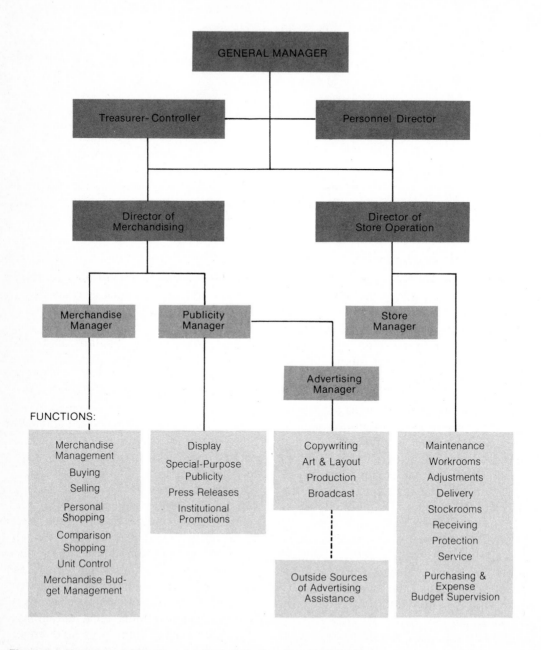

Figure 3–1 Management Structure of a Typical Medium-Sized Retail Store

ment *by objectives* (long-range planning). This involves several steps: (1) designating the planning period; (2) setting objectives and establishing quantitative and qualitative goals; (3) defining, in detail, the tasks to be undertaken to attain the objectives; (4) preparing a summary of the actual requirements that the planned actions impose on the company; (5) assigning the responsibility for each segment of the plan to a specific executive and setting up a schedule for its accomplishment; and (6) pinning down sales and profit projections for each planned action (so that it can be reevaluated in view of these anticipated results). Advertising people are often deeply involved in this all-important planning, and the best type of advertising emerges when a store's forward-thinking management incorporates promotional plans into its overall strategy to attain its stated objectives. In fact, *the best advertising plans are themselves based on a long-range objective-and-task approach.*

There once was a day when retail advertising people were mere technicians. If they could draw sketches, write descriptions of items to be promoted, and rough out acceptable layouts for printers, little more was expected of them. Today, ad people tend to become involved in all phases of store management. The advertising they create is viewed as part of an *overall* marketing strategy. They are consulted in the preparation of long-range objectives and are involved at every stage in the achievement of these goals. They are called on to share their expertise with specialists in other areas (buyers, personnel managers, controllers, branch-store managers) and to integrate the advertising

plans with all other phases of store activity.

RETAILING RESOURCES

Today's retail executives manage human resources, physical resources, and financial resources. *Advertising management is related to all three.*

Managing Human Resources Finding competent people to staff the store —in all departments and at all levels— is often viewed as *the* fundamental problem of retail management, and it affects stores of all sizes. Employee productivity in retailing has been nothing to brag about. Figures derived from government statistics reveal that from 1958 to 1968 output per operating employee in major industries increased at these annual rates: in agriculture, by 7.2 percent; in manufacturing, by 4.9 percent; in service industries, by 3.1 percent; and in *retailing, by only 2.8 percent.*

At the same time, payroll costs have been increasing faster than retail sales. Between 1963 and 1972, retail income increased by 88 percent while retail payrolls increased by 100 percent. In some trade lines, the disparity was more pronounced. For example, in the groceries field (the mainstay of self-service retailing) volume rose by 78 percent while payrolls rose by 112 percent. Sales of auto dealerships rose by 81 percent while their payrolls rose by 95 percent. In the general merchandise field, where spectacular dollar gains were made by the self-service discount houses, an increase in sales volume of 117 percent was matched by a payroll increase of 116 percent.[1]

Payroll costs can be controlled to

some extent by careful decisions about the optimum staff size for the store. A manager must consider the *customer: staff ratio* (C:S)—the ratio of the number of customers (or would-be customers) to the number of salespersons on duty per hour (or per some other unit of time). This ratio is particularly crucial in these days of split shifts, part-time workers, and extended shopping hours and days. It is a waste of time for the advertising staff to draw throngs of people to the store if they then become "walkouts" and go away without buying because of poor service or no service. Equally alarming to cost-conscious management is the sight of people sitting around twiddling their thumbs during slack periods because the selling floor is over-staffed.

Determining the optimum number of salespeople is not the only problem retailers have in managing human resources. Store executives are virtually unanimous in defining their most serious problems as problems with the quality of personnel available. Employees too seldom "give a damn" about customers, sales, or service, don't try hard enough to prevent shoplifting or employee thefts, don't respond to training programs, don't show up for work, quit their jobs before they become productive, and even bring drug abuse problems into the store.

Edith Lynch, vice president of the Personnel Division of the National Retail Merchants Association, offers these suggestions, equally applicable to large or small organizations, for better handling of the personnel function:

1. Take inventory of your people. Do you really know their shortcomings and their strengths? . . . What about motivating the young person with brains? . . . Try your people at different jobs.

2. If you need new blood or replacements, be careful whom you hire.

3. Take suggestions from your people on how they think they can do the job better. They are often closer to it than you.

4. If you buy machinery of any kind . . . be sure the employees who know how to operate it do so.

5. Know how you stand competitively on payroll costs, and keep your policies in line if you want to keep good employees.

6. Handle grievances swiftly and justly.

7. No matter how distasteful the subject, face the possibility that employee theft may be cutting down on your productivity.

8. Keep good records. Sloppiness in records is almost as bad as no records at all.

9. Take a look at the results of some of the behavioral science techniques that have proved so helpful in the bigger stores—they may work for you.

10. And finally, communicate all the time. Let your employees know how they are doing. Set a good example.[2]

The Role of Middle Management Retailing, by its nature, is an industry that relies on vast numbers of part-time and temporary employees, particularly for "entry-level" sales positions. It is simply not financially feasible to invest great sums of money or extensive periods of time in their training. This places a crucial burden on the hard-core front-line supervisors and middle-level managers—those who see the salespeople every day and work with them.

It is at this level that many of a store's future higher-level executives get their initial baptism of fire and learn the fundamentals of the business. Their know-how and their morale brush off on those working beneath them, and it is their day-by-day interpretation of company policy that determines what customers come to think of the whole organization. Small retailers, too, have to think in terms of developing a back-up person to deal with management tasks in their absence and of having people who can handle branch-store management when the time arrives to expand.

Care in selecting and training these executives is one of the keys to retailing success. Seminars, evening classes, and correspondence courses provided by trade associations and colleges are helping personnel people do a better job in training and motivating future executives. The trend toward early retirement by senior executives and the mushrooming of branch stores and new departments open up realistic opportunities for reasonably quick advancement, too.

There are more supervisory and executive positions per 1,000 employees in retailing than in any other industry—a fact that, when publicized, helps interest many bright young men and women in training programs for retail careers. Opportunities for women and for blacks are better in retailing than in most other career fields.

Managing Physical Resources A second major area of concern for retail executives is management of the tangible assets of the company: the structures in which the merchandise is displayed and sold and those where reserve stock is held; the ordering, transportation, unpacking, inspection, and pricing of that merchandise; and the control mechanism established to keep track of it. This logistical function of management was once practically its sole function, and it remains a vital one—made increasingly complex by the sheer variety of products today and the speed of changes in customer preferences.

The basic *physical structure of retail buildings* changes slowly through the years. This is because the vast construction costs make it necessary to utilize a building over a long period.

Most good stores built in recent years were designed from the inside out (rather than vice versa, as was once the case), after a study of the functions to be performed in the structures. A few have round shapes and other design features that are exotic departures from the ordinary. Many chains use the same design nationwide, such as the early-American facades on A & P markets, to establish an identity and a consistent image. Stores without windows and others that are "all windows" are seen. Modern stores employ a minimum number of fixed interior walls and a maximum number of easily moved dividers or partitions below ceiling height, so departments can expand or contract to reflect the seasons or to match shifts in customer lifestyles. Often each department is identified by its own "mood color" for ceiling, carpeting, lights, displays, and advertising. Departmental definitions are thus dramatized, and customers soon learn the "color code" that leads them to the area they seek on each shopping excursion. The impact of the code is designed to be psychological rather than merely physical and rational: Soft pink may signal infants' wear; deep brown can identify men's clothing. Vinyl, plexiglas, chrome, and other new materials add excitement. Theatrical effects are produced by the use of contemporary art, graphic wall designs, cinematographic and movable displays resembling stylized "trees," and modular cubical capsules.

An intimate, homelike atmosphere characterizes many stores of the seventies, in sharp contrast to the stark businesslike expanses of older stores. One comes upon easy-chairs grouped around a fireplace. Electronically amplified music, strobe lights, videotapes, and subtly dimmed lights with changing hues to fit specific moods make shopping a psychological experience, not a chore.

Today's *merchandise buyer* must be more knowledgeable and flexible than the buyers of yesteryear, taking into account the rapid changes in fashion trends, consumer lifestyles, and competitors' actions. Merchandise assortment planning is a science in itself, truly the key to retail profits. Assortments must be matched to the taste of the store's clearly defined segment of the consuming public. Relations must be maintained with resource firms, not too many and not too few. Often a resident buying office offers advantages not only in buying but in collateral areas of merchandising—fashion reports, operations, even store planning and advertising. The buying office represents the store in negotiations with suppliers every day of the year and is an important and useful extension of its own buying staff.

Inventory control plays a vital role in pleasing customers and, hence, in strengthening profits. The way this function is handled determines whether the store has sufficient quantities of the right merchandise at the correct time to satisfy all its customers' needs or whether, conversely, sales and profits will be lost (and customers driven into the welcoming arms of competitors) because desired products are out of stock when the customers are in the mood to buy. Good inventory control means maintaining adequate, predetermined minimum levels of stock and not tying up large sums of capital in goods lying idle at the warehouse. An open-to-buy budgeting system uses the velocity of actual sales as a guide in buying additional stock. A nationwide *Standard Merchandise Classification System,* in which items and merchandise lines have a *Universal Product Code* number that is the same for all retailers and manufacturers, is now under development. It is useful in both manual and computerized inventory control systems and is in fact quite essential for the latter to reach its full potential. A store's advertising should be integrated with its inventory control policies to capitalize on seasonal peaks in demand and to clear out marked-down merchandise at the season's end.

Managing Financial Resources Like all businesses, retailers need certain *basic financial records* to tell management where it stands, how things have changed over a given period, and where trends are taking the business in the future. A *profit and loss statement* (sometimes called an income statement or operating statement) summarizes the results of the company's operations over a period of time such as a month or a year. The company's *balance sheet* reveals where it stands at a given moment and what its net worth is at that time.

Table 3–1 is a hypothetical profit and loss statement for "Smith's Clothiers," a small shop doing $100,000 in annual sales. This greatly simplified statement includes an *operating ratio* column at the far right in which all expenses (and the firm's profit) are expressed as *percentages of net sales*. Thus the manager can compare one year's operations with another year's, even though the sales figures are quite different. He can also compare the store's

Table 3–1
Hypothetical Profit and Loss Statement for Smith's Clothiers, Year Ended December 31, 1974

			Operating Ratio (percentage of net sales)
Income from Sales			
Sales	$100,000		
Less returns	−3,000		
Net income from sales		$97,000	100.0
Cost of Goods Sold			
Purchases	$ 75,000		
Less returns	−1,500		
Net purchases	73,500		
Less inventory on Dec. 31	−14,000		
Cost of goods sold		−$59,500	61.3
Gross Profit or Margin on Sales		**$37,500**	38.7
Operating Expenses (variable)			
Outside labor	500		0.5
Supplies	1,500		1.5
Wages & salaries	10,000		10.3
Repair & maintenance	500		0.5
Advertising & promotion	2,000		2.1
Car & delivery	500		0.5
Bad debts	300		0.3
Administrative & legal	500		0.5
Miscellaneous	500		0.5
Total variable expenses		$16,300	(16.8)
Fixed Expenses			
Rent	3,600		3.7
Utilities	1,800		1.9
Insurance	700		0.7
Taxes & licenses	800		0.8
Interest	300		0.3
Depreciation of equipment	700		0.7
Total fixed expenses		$7,900	(8.2)
Total Expenses		**$24,200**	25.0
Net Profit for the Year (Before taxes & including proprietor's salary)		**$13,300**	13.7

performance with that of another store or a group of stores. Operating ratios vary widely depending on the type of merchandise carried, the nature of the market, and the objectives of management. The amount spent on advertising is one of the variable (or *controllable*) operating expenses. How *large* this item is and *how wisely the money is used* can have a great impact on the size of the top line of the profit and loss statement (gross sales) and, much more importantly, on the bottom line (net profit). (At this point it may be helpful to skip forward to Table 5–1 and Table 5–2 in Chapter 5, where we demonstrate how a balance sheet can change favorably as the result of management decisions to increase advertising.)

The *balance sheet* is another standard and vital accounting tool. It shows a firm's assets and liabilities, which together determine its *net worth*. Table 3–2 shows a simplified balance sheet that might be used by a small shop.

Retail managers use a *cash flow* budget to forecast the flow of cash through the store. This is usually set up a year in advance, showing the estimated cash on hand at the beginning of each month, the anticipated income and expenses for each month, and the resulting excess cash on hand or deficit (which may necessitate short-term borrowing) at the end of each month. A cash-flow budget enables management to plan intelligently to handle recurring "ups and downs" in liquid cash due to the timing of expenses and income.

Many managers use *break-even analysis* to help plan ahead for maximum profits. Figure 3–2 shows why a store with $10,000 in fixed expenses (per year, per month, or for any given period) must obviously attain more than $10,000 in sales before it can even think of making a profit or staying in business. However, as its income rises *beyond that point,* its other expenses—its variable expenses—*do not increase as rapidly as its sales volume.* Once the store's volume equals its fixed *plus* its variable expenses, it has reached the *break-even point* (BEP on the chart).

Table 3–2

A Hypothetical Balance Sheet for Jones Hardware Sales, Inc., December 31, 1974, and June 30, 1975

	Dec. 31 '74	June 30 '75
Assets		
Cash	$ 20,000	$ 24,000
Accounts receivable from customers (less bad debts)	16,000	16,000
Inventory (current or actual cost, whichever is lower)	77,000	84,000
Fixtures & equipment (after depreciation)	31,200	30,000
	$144,200	$154,000
Liabilities		
Accounts payable	$ 54,000	$ 56,000
Loan from First National Bank	12,000	14,000
Net Worth of the Business	78,200	84,000
	$144,200	$154,000

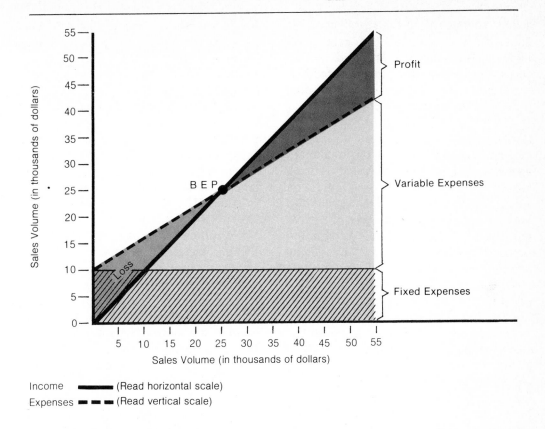

Figure 3–2 Break-Even Analysis Chart

BEP is the *break-even point,* the point at which income equals expenses.

Variable expenses include the cost of merchandise for resale; part-time or seasonal help; delivery and shipping costs; promotion and advertising costs; wrapping and packaging costs; sales and income taxes; and payroll above the minimum necessary to operate.

Fixed expenses include the interest on invested capital; rent, or depreciation on owned buildings and fixtures; property taxes; basic full-time payroll (the minimum necessary to operate); and utilities.

As sales continue to grow beyond that BEP, profits increase *more rapidly* than sales volume, since fixed expenses have long been covered and variable expenses increase at a *declining* rate with each added increment of sales. *Here is where advertising can be used to make a push for extra income,* beyond that amount needed to *pay for itself.* Suc- cessful advertising, especially for the store that is at or near the BEP, can make the difference between just breaking even or making a profit.

Actually, there are just three things that can be done to increase profits. Fixed expenses, by definition, cannot be reduced, whether sales are $1 or $10 million. Management can, however, (1) reduce some or all of the store's variable expenses (the controllable costs), (2) increase the sales volume, and (3) improve the store's gross margin (the difference between the cost and the selling price of merchandise).

Advertising can figure in all three strategies. In its eagerness to reduce variable expenses, a shortsighted management can order cuts in advertising that have a counterproductive impact on sales. A better way to effect economies may be by more efficient use of media, more effective control of production costs, or acquisition of increasing amounts of manufacturers' cooperative advertising aid. Used constructively as a profit-generating tool, advertising's most obvious job is to increase sales volume. Less obviously, but just as importantly, it can be employed to increase a store's average gross margin, even on the same sales volume—either through a more judicious selection of high-profit items to be pushed in ads or by more effective timing in capitalizing on seasonal demand peaks so that merchandise does not have to be marked down later in order to sell it. Merchandising and advertising people must work as a team both in controlling costs and in increasing sales and profits.

One significant criterion for gauging a store's efficiency is the sales volume *per square foot* of sales-floor space. This is especially important in view of rising land and construction costs and the vast sums of capital retailers have tied up in their property or committed to rent. This measure of profitability permits a rapid calculation of the relative efficiency of different stores selling similar kinds of products, such as the many outlets of a chain or the different branches of a downtown store. One big general merchandise chain, for example, *averages* $87 per square foot over its many hundreds of units; but *some* of its best-managed stores make over $200 per square foot. It is not unusual for well-managed small specialty shops to exceed the $200-per-square-foot mark, too. A European chain of new hypermarche stores (superstores selling foods and general merchandise, now being copied by some U.S. retail firms) average *over $300* per square foot.

Another critical factor in merchandising is the *stock-turnover rate* ("stockturn"), or the number of times per year merchandise bought by the store is sold to the public and replaced by new merchandise. If the store does a $500,000 volume in a year and its average inventory is $125,000, the stock-turnover ratio is four; if a like sales volume could be maintained with an average inventory of only $100,000, the stockturn would rise to five and profits would improve. Stockturn ratios differ greatly among various kinds of retailers. Those with costly and slow-moving inventories (such as jewelers) have low stock-turnover ratios, while supermarkets, which sell a great many low-priced goods quickly, have very high ratios of sales to inventory. *It is a primary function of promotion to accelerate turnover of merchandise.* When the turnover is too slow, there are little or no profits. A store's balance sheet may show that it has a considerable net worth, but if too many of its assets are tied up in inventory, it may still be unprofitable.

Retailers are continually sharpening their ability to control their enterprises through better financial management. Some of the tactics they use are

1. The *retail method of accounting,* basing figures on the retail price of inventories, rather than on their wholesale cost.

2. The *return on investment (ROI)* system, first developed by the du Pont company for its own use and later adapted for use by other concerns, including retailers. The ROI is the investor's actual return on his capital. It is computed by dividing the net profit after taxes of an enterprise by its tangible net worth. It can vary greatly not only for individual stores but for types of stores.

3. The use of *leverage*—that is, the borrowing of additional funds for current operations and/or leasing and renting (rather than buying) real estate, equipment, and fixtures—to keep capital free for expansion and reinvestment in profit-making opportunities.

All retail accounting activities are aimed at assembling data for tax returns and other government-required reports in a convenient form and at producing guidelines for improving the company's operations. *Ratios* are often far more meaningful than dollar figures, since they permit easy comparisons of one period to another and one store to another. Especially critical are

1. The *current ratio*—current assets divided by current liabilities.

2. The *stock-turnover ratio*—cost of goods sold divided by average inventory at cost.

3. The *gross margin percentage*—gross margin (difference between cost and selling price) divided by net sales. This should be calculated by departments and by brands or merchandise lines.

4. *Expenses percentage to sales*—operating expenses (the total of all expenses and also each particular expense category) divided by net sales.

5. The *working capital turnover ratio*—net sales divided by working capital for a given year or other time period.

6. The ratio of *working capital to sales*—working capital divided by net sales.

7. The ratio of *working capital to inventory*—year-end inventory in dollars divided by year-end working capital in dollars.

8. The firm's *return on investment*—net profit before taxes and after owner's salary divided by the tangible net worth.

A study by the National Cash Register Company produced some revealing statistics on crucial operating ratios for several types of retail corporations. The results of this study are shown in Table 3–3.

CUSTOMER CREDIT

Customer credit is an area of rapid change and considerable current ferment. Traditional department stores and quality specialty shops long ago carried customers' accounts as a matter of course, oriented as they were to a stable, affluent, upper-middle-class trade. The extension of credit to all classes of society has been a major trend of the past quarter-century. The big stores began issuing credit cards for identification and prestige, and they continue to look on their charge-card holders as a loyal hard core of big-spending, repeat customers. The big national chains, and many smaller specialty shops as well, have established their own credit services.

Table 3–3

Examples of Productivity Ratios

	1964	1969
Composite Rates of Return on Net Worth		
27 leading department store companies	11.2%	10.0%
12 leading discount firms	17.3	12.2
4 leading general merchandise/mail-order concerns	13.2	12.6

	1956	1968	Percentage Change
Accounts Receivable Productivity Ratios—Department Stores			
Net sales per dollar invested in accounts receivable	$ 6.67	$ 5.50	−17.5
Accounts receivable as a percentage of total current assets	44.2	50.0	+13.1
Accounts receivable as a percentage of net working capital	60.5	88.5	+46.3
Inventory Productivity Ratios—Department Stores			
Sales per dollar invested in inventory	$ 6.86	$ 5.55	−19.1
Gross margins per dollar invested in inventory	2.50	2.13	−14.8
Controllable margins per dollar invested in inventory	1.75	1.50	−14.3
Net profits per dollar invested in inventory	.21	.15	−28.6
Space Productivity Ratios—Department Stores			
Sales per square foot of selling area	$92.00	$81.03	−11.9
Gross margins per square foot of selling space	33.49	31.10	−7.1
Controllable margins per square foot of selling space	23.41	21.85	−6.7
Net profits per square foot of selling space	2.85	2.22	−22.1

Source: From *The Changing Economics of General Merchandise Retailing.* Copyright 1970, The National Cash Register Company. Reproduced with permission of the copyright owner.

During the sixties, everyone got into the act: oil companies, travel-entertainment charge-card "clubs," and then the banks, with two nationwide credit-card systems, BankAmericard and Master Charge. Small merchants have been the backbone of the bank-card networks, but many discounters have joined them in recent years. Even the conventional department stores, which have been wooed but seldom won by the bankers, and supermarkets are showing stirrings of interest.

An estimated one-third of all retail sales are on credit. In traditional department stores charges account for about 60 percent of all sales; among the major general merchandise chains, just over half are charges. Among specialty merchants the percentage of credit sales ranges from as much as two-thirds (for jewelry, appliance, and furniture stores) to virtually zero (for groceries). The credit volume of discounters, handled mostly through banks, is about 23 percent. Young people constitute a disproportionately large share of users of retail credit, especially of long-term installment sales credit for big-ticket household items, automobiles, and the like. Stores that have done research on the subject believe that credit customers spend more than cash customers and remain more loyal to the store. Thus retailers have devoted a considerable share of their promotional efforts to coaxing people to become charge customers.

MANAGING THE SMALL STORE

There is much temptation to focus on the complex management problems of major retailers to the exclusion of problems of the small store. One finds drama in the actions of the top management of big retailing operations, dealing with dollars by the billions, customers by the millions, and employees by the tens of thousands. As this kind of retailing has expanded physically and financially, it has necessarily institutionalized its management, separated it from personal contact with individual customers, insulated its decision-makers from one-to-one human relationships. Bureaucratic walls surround the head office, shutting out the din and the throb of the marketplace.

The small-store operator, who must make do without sophisticated gadgetry and a battalion of specialized staff personnel, does have some advantages: no institutionalization, no insulation, no walls! Knowledge of front-line conditions comes to this manager through personal observations of customer satisfaction and employee morale. Decisions can be made quickly and independently by the operator alone.

No magic formula for retail success exists, but some very useful guideposts have been pointed out by those who have succeeded. The following management checklist for small-store proprietors is adapted from one prepared by William Burston, recently retired from the vice presidency of the National Retail Merchants Association. Basically, Burston encourages the small merchant to capitalize on the many special advantages of a small operation:

Know your competitors, with whom you vie for patronage, and *decide to be different* in one or more ways: in your merchandise, service, or customer contacts.

Know yourself and your limitations, and decide *what you want to be* as a store. Review your *written statement* of policy every year. *Analyze* your store, its strong points, its limitations; then play up the strong points, correct the weaknesses, and review your progress.

Develop *repeat business* with the same people; go after new business, but not to the point of neglecting your regulars.

Intensify your *personal contacts* with customers—your *unique advantage.*

The fact that you have no invisible walls between departments and categories permits more *interselling* and a great deal more *suggestion selling.* You can make *swifter decisions* and *quicker changes,* and you and your salespeople must *know more about the merchandise* than those in a big store.

Buy to a plan. Take a middle road in selecting sizes and restrict your lines, but *keep in stock* everything you decide to stock. Be *important* to a *few* manufacturers, and buy *items,* not lines. Manufacturers will backstop you from stock ready for delivery, and *the special-order customer* will wait if he knows you can satisfy him. Know the *best sellers* and *always have them in stock.*

You shouldn't have too much to clear at seasonal clearance time; the secret of *good turnover* is to know what merchandise you have on hand that can *substitute* for what you've sold out.

Take the *cash discounts* offered by suppliers, even if you have to borrow money to pay them by the date specified.

Join a buying office; belong to your retail organization and come to meetings.[3]

2 The Computer and EDP

Electronic data processing came late to the retail industry. Others had been using the computer for some time when, in the early sixties, a few large stores began adapting it to retail use. Later in that decade, manufacturers of computer equipment turned to making special systems for retailers. Now, the use of computers and associated equipment is nearly universal among large department and discount stores and major chains, and is spreading fast among medium-level stores and a few forward-looking small shops. The applications of EDP in the stores are growing apace, but the full potential has yet to be tapped.

Computers, of course, cannot actually "think." They work with *numbers,* and the information fed into them through their *input terminals* must be reduced to numbers, or *encoded.* They can add and subtract, multiply and divide, store up numbers for future retrieval in virtually unlimited quantities, and establish relationships between specified numbers converted to percentage terms. They can accept *input* in several different forms and spew back *output* on demand, through several different visual and auditory reporting devices. They work at incredible *speeds,* taking mere seconds to accomplish tasks that might take weeks to do manually. And

they are versatile. They can be programmed to do an almost endless variety of tasks and to work on many different jobs at the same time.

EDP in stores helps retailers manage three essential assets: *inventory, accounts receivable,* and *personnel.* The information fed into the computer is obtained from four primary *data bases:* (1) a *merchandise data base* (including data on inventory and accounts payable), (2) a *financial data base* (including data from the firm's general ledger), (3) a *customer data base* (data on accounts receivable and credit authorizations), and (4) a *personnel data base* (data on the payroll and on employees). An input mechanism is set up to "capture" and send to the computer's memory bank certain kinds of information from each of these four sources. This data must be encoded into computer language, that is, into numerical expressions.

Computer input can be transmitted via typewriter keyboards, punched cards, punched tape, magnetic tape, or printed or hand-lettered figures and symbols to be read by an optical scanner (a device like a miniature television camera that "looks" at the figures and "recognizes" their form). *On-line* input devices feed facts to the central computer through wires, provided the computer itself is running continuously, or operating on a *real-time basis.*

Information can also be stored at or near the point of "capture" and later transmitted electronically to the central processing unit. In some cases, data on tape or cards may be physically carried or mailed to the central EDP unit. When small stores contract with computer service bureaus to process their data, or when larger stores "share time" with other users of a computer (such as local banks), the latter system is most often used. Sometimes, this creates a time-lag that reduces the value of the information.

Information generally comes out of the computer on printed sheets or rolls of paper or is flashed on a closed-circuit TV screen. Output can be transmitted over wires to distant points and to computers in other cities that are programmed to accept and act on such messages.

The retail applications of EDP are focused on increasing the ease of operation and improving the accuracy of *input devices at the point of sale.* Inputting information that originates in the store's office and programming and operating the computer itself have become pretty much of a routine thing. When a new customer opens a charge account, a new employee is added to the payroll, or a new firm is added to the roster of suppliers, this data is fed into the computer at the central office of the retail firm. When merchandise arrives, the warehouse and stockroom feed in data on the supplier, the general classification of the merchandise, and each kind of product in the shipment. Each department in the store has its own code.

When customer A buys for $30 two units of product B, which the store bought from manufacturer C for $10 each, and the sale is rung up by salesperson D in department E, the computer, at the point of sale, relates this transaction to a dozen or more different things it is programmed to keep track of and report. It (1) increases the amount customer A owes the store by $30; (2) adds $30 to the store's overall accounts receivable figure; (3) reduces the retail value of the store's inventory by $30 and its value at cost by $20; (4) deducts two units from the inventory of product B on hand (possibly flashing a special warning to the buyer—or even direct to the supplier who may be in another city —to reorder if B is a critical product and the sale reduces the inventory of it below a predetermined reorder point); (5) records the fact that manufacturer C has just contributed $10 to the store's gross margin, and that this $10 is 33 percent of the retail price and/or 50 percent of the wholesale price of product B; (6) remembers that salesperson D processed the sale and that the amount of the sales equals a certain percentage of D's salary; and (7) digests the fact that department E has just completed one charge transaction involving merchandise from vendor C, adding $30 to the store's gross sales. These actions are performed instantaneously in a real-time setup or overnight if a direct hookup is not used.

Data on the transaction can be extracted from the computer on call and combined with data on ten thousand other transactions, none of them precisely similar, to show management, buyers, advertising people, and others what is happening on the sales floor and how it is affecting the store's operation and profits. Each store programs its computers to generate the information it wants and the kind of data it chooses to monitor.

All systems that tabulate the movement and sale of merchandise require the tagging of each item or the printing of a symbol on the package in a form that computer input terminals can accept. When the Standard Merchandise Classification Code comes into general use by the retail industry as a whole, the same code will be used for the same item everywhere, and the tags will be affixed or the symbols imprinted by the supplier before shipment to wholesalers and retailers. Some tags use punch-hole combinations to activate the recording devices, while others employ color codes or printed numbers, but the bar code may become the system of the future. This Universal Product Code, devised in 1973 by an ad hoc committee of retailers, manufacturers, and trade associations, has a 10-digit identification number readable to the human eye. The first five digits identify the manufacturer, the second five digits the product; its parallel lines translate the number into machine-language to render it "scannable." Store checkout personnel pass each item through a laser scanning beam, and from the symbol it "sees" it sends various information electronically to be stored in the computer's memory bank. Two scanning methods are available: the wand system, a hand-held stylus that casts the laser beam from one end, and the slot method, which requires passing the product over a center slot or window containing the beam.

A study by the Mass Retailing Institute based on reports from 3,300 stores and 800 leased departments revealed that the only application of EDP common to *all* of the self-service mass retailers in the sample was the handling of customer accounts receivable billings and payments. Among *large* firms (those with over $100 million in sales), EDP was universally employed for the payroll function, too. The large companies also used or planned to use EDP for profit and loss reports from individual stores, while both large and small chains could

apply it to analyzing the turnover of merchandise by categories.

Very nearly all the firms in the study were using or would soon be using EDP for the dollar analysis of cash sales, for updating book inventory records, for keeping track of the movement of soft goods, for warehouse inventory control, and for controlling and reporting the expense budget. The under-$100 million group reported a high interest in automating profit-and-loss reports for individual stores, and the larger units were interested in EDP for individual store billing, reports to buyers and merchandisers (merchandise managers who supervise buyers) for detection of sales trends, unit control of soft goods, and order picking lists (used to select merchandise in a warehouse for shipment to stores in a chain).[4]

Applications of EDP in conventional department and specialty stores include all those referred to in the MRI survey, and then some. EDP is used to pinpoint slow- and fast-moving items and to segregate profitable from unprofitable sources of supply, to insure optimum staffing of departments at each hour of the selling day, to produce long-range sales forecasts for staple merchandise and determine inventory levels and lead-times for reordering that will maximize sales while reducing the total investment in inventory, and to test the effect of alternate courses of action on future sales and profits.

WHAT MERCHANTS GAIN FROM EDP

An evaluation of the results of a series of pilot computer installations during the 1960s, reported by IBM, indicated that lost sales ("walkouts") could be significantly decreased, stockturn rates greatly increased, and total sales volume substantially increased in stores using early versions of EDP machines. The IBM study established that for every sale lost through poor selling ability, 25 are lost through merchandise-related reasons, and that for every $100 spent by consumers in typical stores, another $90 would have been spent if consumer merchandise needs had been satisfied. Furthermore, IBM traced half this loss directly to the out-of-stock problem: Most stores had only from 65 to 90 percent of the items in stock that would-be customers asked for when they came to the stores. Use of EDP for inventory control eliminated most of these lost sales, as it resulted in computer-equipped stores having from 97 to 99 percent of the desired merchandise in stock when consumers asked for it. Based on its early surveys and test programs, IBM found that typical stores dealing with staple merchandise could use EDP to more perfectly balance inventory with consumer demand, thereby reducing lost sales by three-fourths without increasing inventory. As an alternative, store management could accept the same level of lost sales but maintain one quarter less inventory in stock. Either way, the EDP-equipped store would be more profitable.[5]

The National Retail Merchants Association (NRMA), which has had much experience helping smaller stores computerize their operations, reports stockturn improving by as much as 25 percent, markdowns being reduced by up to 35 percent, sales increasing by 30 percent in some stores and profits by as much as 20 percent.[6] Big stores report

that modern EDP credit-checking takes less than half the time it used to. This pleases customers and gives salespersons more time to actively sell merchandise.

An eight-unit department store chain in the South, typical of successful EDP users, credits its chainwide point-of-purchase terminals linked to a central computer with materially contributing to an improved stockturn rate. Before full automation, the company turned over its stock 2.7 times per year, but after the EDP system was completed, this rose to 3.2 times per year. The chain's management also believes EDP is vital to keeping up with exceptional sales growth, which in one major department increased 76 percent from 1972 to 1973 and rose again by 42 percent from 1973 to 1974 (despite the "soft" economy in that latter year).[7]

EDP FOR THE SMALL STORE

The cost of computers and associated point-of-sale electronic data-collecting devices prohibits their widespread use by smaller stores. However, several developments have combined to make many, if not all, of the advantages of EDP available to smaller merchants. For one thing, not all the great variety of highly sophisticated EDP applications are needed by, or suitable to the needs of, the smaller retailer. It is the sheer volume of work to be done in giant stores and sprawling multi-unit chains that makes computerization so attractive to them. Small stores use EDP mostly for inventory control, and they have several ways of securing EDP services at a price within their means.

Manufacturers of EDP equipment are developing for smaller businesses simpler, more compact units that cost less to lease, purchase, and keep up than the larger systems. Service bureaus in every city will take data in card or tape form and run it through their computers for a fee. Trade associations, such as the National Retail Merchants Association, National Radio-Television & Appliance Dealers, the Menswear Retailers of America, and the National Retail Hardware Association, have made arrangements for their members to use computer service bureaus under association-sponsored programs. Banks and other owners of computers that do not use them all the time are seeking clients to buy computer time, and some retailers find this service quite adequate.

INTEGRATING EDP INTO
THE RETAILING SYSTEM

A fundamental task that must be completed before retail computer systems can realize their full potential in the area of inventory management is the complete development of standard merchandise classification codes for all products and the standardization of tagging and labeling throughout the retail and manufacturing industries. When all makers and sellers of products use the same identification system and all makes of data-capturing devices can accept the same kind of input data, EDP operations will be more valuable, more economical, and doubtlessly universally accepted. The U.S. Bureau of Standards, along with the National Retail Merchants Association and various manufacturing and equipment makers, began moving in

this direction in 1972. By 1975, the system was operational in segments of the grocery field, and progress was being made in apparel as well as other general merchandise categories.

Personnel who resist or do not understand EDP operations and who will not or cannot learn to use the systems effectively present another (but decreasing) problem. EDP equipment is only as good as the people who feed in data.

Some stores have overdone the EDP idea, have tried to digest too much too quickly, and consequently are disillusioned. Often now, retailers will call in outside consultants to plan the modular development of computer-based information systems, starting out with only the most-needed and easiest-to-apply systems and moving gradually toward more complete automation of various functions.

EDP AND RETAIL ADVERTISING

Some stores have already moved to establish direct linkups between the new information technology and their advertising. Rapid reports to buyers on the movement of specific items of stock can signal a store to cease advertising slow movers (or to advertise clearance sales of the merchandise) and to restock and readvertise hot items.

EDP gives retailers the opportunity to monitor the movement of branded items and merchandise from different vendors. It can cue advertising writers as to which brands should be emphasized and point to whose cooperative advertising produces the most results. Customer data files, when matched with information on product movements and brand preferences, may open up a whole new era of effective "targeted" advertising. They can reveal specifically *what* to advertise to *whom*. Jack French, systems planning and development manager at Dayton's in Minneapolis, has this to say on the subject:

> The significance of the computer's customer data bank lies far beyond demographic detail. Future retail files will encompass the buying record of both cash and credit customers so that specific markets and demands can be exploited to the fullest.
>
> By maintaining demographic and sales history files by class for customers, buyers can exploit the computer in planning special promotions and strategy directed at their specific customers.[8]

By 1975 leaders in both the retailing and advertising industries were foreseeing the approach of a new era in which retail advertising would be immediately accountable for specific sales results. It was predicted that advanced application of EDP technology would soon be used to target advertising and promotion accurately to the best potential customers. Also it is expected to be able to furnish instant in-store evaluation of sales results by item and by medium, showing the effectiveness of both manufacturers' and retailers' advertising.

Questions for Discussion

1. If you were the owner or manager of a store employing from 20 to 30 persons, what job titles and duties might they have? Which persons would probably have dual functions, necessitating training and experience in more than one specific area? As manager in a store of this size, what would probably be your own primary tasks?

2. As manager of a small store just getting started, what kinds of financial records and reports would you and your accountant probably wish to set up to guide you in operating your business? What uses would you, as manager, find for each of them?

3. What two things could you do to increase the "profit area" on your break-even analysis chart (like Figure 3–2)? What things could you do to save your store if, after several years' operation, you had just reached the break-even point and your sales had leveled off, leaving you with no profit to justify your investment of capital and your hard work?

4. Why do many very large department stores and national chains prefer to have their own credit systems instead of using bank credit cards? What advantages do small- and medium-sized stores gain from using a bank credit card system?

5. What kind of information is now being reported by electronic data processing systems in large and medium-sized stores? What kind of data is most important to the stores' managements? Do you think that in the future the relative importance of the various kinds of information may change? Why?

6. What additional kind of information, not now widely used, could be drawn from store computers (or produced by computer service bureaus for small stores) to help the store's promotion and advertising people do a more efficient job?

Suggested Projects

1. Go to the largest independent department store in your community (or the nearest larger community where such a store exists). Ask the personnel manager for a copy of the store's employee handbook, which probably contains an organizational chart explaining the administrative structure of the store. If such information is not available in printed form, interview the personnel manager, training director, or public relations officer, find out the titles and duties of key executives, and from this construct such a chart. Do the same for the largest chain-operated general merchandise store in the community. Then compare the two stores' organizational structures and the titles and duties of the executives at comparable levels. See how each differs from the "typical" organizational structure shown in Figure 3–1.

2. Examine, inside and out, the newest retail store building in or near your community. Then look at a much older store building of comparable size. Note the differences in the two structures, in their general exterior form, in the construction materials used, in their shape, and so on. Observe contrasts in their interiors, in their layout, in departmental divisions, in facilities, in equipment and fixtures, and in decor. What could the older store do, at relatively little cost, to upgrade and modernize its building? Do you think the newer of the two stores you studied appeals significantly more to youthful shoppers? Why?

3. Visit the nearest major department store or large specialty store in or close by your community, and talk with the executive in charge of the store's internal computer operations. Compare the uses this store makes of EDP with the various uses explained in the text.

4. Visit the nearest computer service bureau in or near your community. (Addresses for these firms can be found in the Yellow Pages under "Data Processing.") Find out what small- and medium-sized stores without internal computers are doing in EDP through service agencies such as this one. Find out what services the data processing company can perform, if asked, beyond what it is doing for local stores. What do you think the future holds for these smaller retailers in terms of a greater use of EDP?

5. Visit the nearest branch office of IBM, the National Cash Register Company, Honeywell, the Univac Division of Sperry-Rand, or another computer manufacturer, and ask for a briefing on retail computer applications in your area. Also ask for booklets and literature the company makes available to prospective retail users of its equipment, and study them. Then prepare a report that amplifies the information in the text. Include a discussion of retail data terminals, or input devices, especially point-of-sale (cash register) equipment, and give examples of local EDP capabilities.

Notes

1. Figures are from U.S. Censuses of Business for 1963 and 1972.

2. Edith Lynch, "F.Y.I.: Ideas for Independents—Personnel," *Stores* (July 1971), p. 18.

3. William Burston, "The Merchant's Checklist for More Profitable Performance" (New York: National Retail Merchants Association), pp. 1–4.

4. *Data Processing in Mass Retailing—Application, Results, Trends* (New York: Mass Retailing Institute, 1971), pp. 6, 8, 11, 14.

5. *Retail IMPACT—Inventory Management Program and Control Techniques Application Description*, 6th ed. (White Plains, N.Y.: International Business Machines Corporation, 1970), pp. 1, 14, 15, 18, 19.

6. Figures are from "Is EDP for YOU?" (NRMA advertisement) *Stores* (November 1971), p. 38.

7. "Data Processing System Pays Off," *Stores* (May 1975), pp. 10–11. © 1975 NRMA.

8. Jack French, "POS, POR, Data Base and the Future," *Stores* (June 1972), p. 24.

Preview

I n former times merchants could make adequate studies of their customers, merchandise, and advertising on an informal basis. The great complexities and widening scope of modern retailing demands a more scientific approach. Formal research today is divided into four areas of inquiry:

1. marketing research to develop information about the store's customers;
2. merchandise research on the products the store sells;
3. operations research on methods of store management; and
4. advertising research to measure the effectiveness of ad messages, media, and timing.

Marketing and advertising research are the most important for students of retail advertising; the former will be discussed here and the latter in later chapters.

All types of research may be classified as secondary or primary.

1. Secondary research focuses on existing data that can be converted to the retailer's use. The data sources may be outside or within the local community, and perhaps in the store itself.
2. Primary research is conducted specifically by or for the store. It requires highly specialized skills, often provided by outsiders.

Research has certain capabilities and certain limitations; it can never substitute for judgment but can guide management in its decisions.

Learning Goals

C hapter 4 provides the student with an understanding of the several different kinds of research done by retailers and explains why research is more important today than ever before. The reader should learn the sources of existing data (secondary research) as well as the steps involved in a primary research project wherein the store seeks specific information for its own particular needs. The advantages and the limitations of each kind of research must be clearly appreciated. The student must also understand how to work with outside professionals when undertaking primary research and must learn how to evaluate research and use its findings as a guide to more rational decision-making in marketing and advertising.

4

Research
Points the Way

There used to be little need for retail research as we know it today. In the economy of scarcity that characterized the nineteenth century, almost anything a manufacturer offered through its wholesalers and jobbers could be resold by the storekeeper to his goods-hungry customers. The would-be merchant selected a location for his store using "common horse-sense" and a bit of intuition. People were generally very homogeneous within any given community, with virtually the same needs and tastes and much the same level of buying power.

The storekeeper of earlier times did some research, even if he didn't call it that. He dealt in a very limited variety of merchandise, there being few styles, brands, models, sizes, materials, colors, and price ranges to select from when a drummer came to town to pick up his order, or when he made his rare buying

trips. Since he dealt with a limited group of customers whom he saw nearly every day, his "research" could be literally carried on around a cracker-barrel. There he could swap pleasantries with the local shoppers and learn firsthand what they liked or didn't like about his store and his merchandise. Since travel was slow and difficult, he usually had a captive market anyway. Even if he didn't listen very carefully to customers' opinions, they would still have to buy from him out of necessity. He also learned very easily if customers saw an ad in the few media available.

Today's retailer selects stock from a vastly greater variety of available items from many more potential suppliers. The market for those items is a much larger customer group, infinitely more heterogeneous in its needs, wants, tastes, and buying power. Competition is intense, and the shopper has a free choice among dozens, if not hundreds, of competing outlets. Advertising media and options are numerous.

Consumer research for manufacturing corporations was pioneered in the early 1930s by men like George Gallup and Elmer Roper. Its accuracy and general acceptance among national marketers was greatly enhanced by improvements in techniques instituted in 1943 by Lester Frankel, who used *area probability samples* to insure that those polled were truly representative of the total *universe* of customers or prospective customers. No major consumer-goods maker today dares operate without market research, and all major agencies insist on adequate research before committing their clients' funds to an ad program.

Although retailers have benefited indirectly from manufacturers' efforts and can often use some of the information that spins off from such research, they have been slow to recognize its vital role in their own industry. The tradition that salespersons, buyers, managers, and advertising people develop a "feel" for the market sufficient to guide retailers' operations is an illusion in today's complex economy, but it is one that many store executives have supported. Management, in larger stores, operates at a distance from the sales counter and the cash register, so that the information it does receive often comes too late or in garbled form. Yet research being done outside the retail field that might be applied and adapted to retail decision-making is seldom fully exploited. And research being conducted by or for merchants themselves (except for a few large and progressive companies) is all too limited and piecemeal in scope.

The editors of Grey Advertising's

monthly newsletter, *Grey Matter,* have taken the pulse of retailers' research over the years. "Research as a basis for making retail management decisions is really *in its swaddling clothes,"* they declared in 1963. "As the retail organism becomes more complex . . . , it becomes necessary to rely on *facts* brought to light by *investigation,* rather than only on preconceived notions based on hunches or personal experience."[1]

Six years later a 1969 issue of the same publication reported that "many retail executives still cast a jaundiced eye on consumer research." However, there were then some signs that retailers were becoming interested in analyzing their customers and trying to anticipate their needs. Robert F. Hartley of George Washington University was quoted as follows:

> Contrary to the critics of retail practices, effective and worthwhile research efforts . . . are being done in some areas: trends in customer characteristics, buying habits and overall attitudes; consumer profiles for predicting what customers with certain characteristics are likely to buy; . . . [and] key departments and merchandise which influence consumer attitudes towards a store. . . .[2]

Eleven years after the first study quoted above, Grey warned,

> [T]he marketer and the retailer must take the pulse and measure the temperature of their customer, the consumer. Retail distribution, the place where the ultimate marketing action occurs, is at *the front of this marketing probing and not at the end,* as so many think.[3]

It was still necessary in 1974 to assert that

[C]reation and communication of store personality and positioning are areas of major weakness today. Although psychographic research and marketing aimed at *key target segments* have been used in a sophisticated manner for well over a decade by manufacturers, most retailers have *not begun* to exploit their potential. They know little of their market targets demographically, let alone of their customers' *psychographic characteristics.* . . . Too many retailers are also ignorant of the total personality they are projecting to the public. They often don't know who their best customers are —nor sometimes what their real competition is. . . . Information from *professional research* can help retailers develop their store and target customer profiles, and provide fodder for *new approaches* to every facet of doing business—from [the] *select[ion of] new locations* and *formulat[ion of] merchandise and pricing policies to the selection of media and tonality in ads.*[4]

1 What Retailers Need to Know

Virtually all types of research conducted for retailers, and much of that done by others (but adaptable to merchants' uses), are *interrelated.* The inside and the outside research, the informal and the formal, tend to overlap and reinforce each other. Authorities disagree among themselves on definitions of the various categories of retail research (or, as some prefer, "marketing research"). Nevertheless, it is possible to get a clearer view of the scope of the field by establishing four major categories of retail research, each with various subcategories:

1. *Marketing Research* (focused on the customer)

   (a) *Fundamental demographic research* that helps predict buying needs. This is a source of data on population; places and types of residences; age, income, occupational, and educational groups; ethnic, racial, and language elements; family and household size; and the number of women in the work force. Data for the present and for a base year in the recent past are needed to establish trends and make projections. Numerical breakdowns of data are often in *percentage* form to permit meaningful comparisons with national, regional, state, metropolitan-area, and county norms (to find out how "typical" a market area is). Percentage figures also make it possible to examine the differences between markets for two or more stores. It is useful, too, to segregate those in each demographic group who are customers of a store from those who are not.

   (b) *Psychographic and motivational research* on the "real" reasons for shoppers' decisions.

   (c) *Research on product preferences, product images, and the service desired by customers and noncustomers.*

   (d) *Site research,* to determine where a store with given characteristics will find the most customers, not just *now,* but over a long period. This type of research is crucial for expanding stores and chains.

   (e) *Research on the economy* in a given trading area, as a basis for estimating the *ability* of a store's customers to buy (as opposed to their *desire* to buy) over a stated timespan.

   (f) *Research on the competition,* to find out the proportion of the business other stores are getting and why, other methods of distribution (such as direct marketing and catalog selling), and even alternative products or services on which disposable income may be spent.

2. *Merchandise Research* (focused on products)

   (a) *Research on the physical characteristics of products and product lines,* that guides buyers in purchasing merchandise for resale and/or drawing up specifications for products to be made for the store. It also suggests promotional themes for advertising writers, since it reveals a product's strong and weak points.

   (b) *Research on fashion trends and style preferences.*

   (c) *Research on competing products* sold by other stores, useful in clarifying competitive selling and advertising strategies.

   (d) *Product-assortment research,* designed to assist the store in satisfying the maximum number of customer needs with a minimum of inventory.

3. *Operational Research* (focused on the store itself)

   (a) *Research on selling methods,* to determine which work best and which can be improved.

   (b) *Personnel research,* aimed at increasing the efficiency of the store's employees by more productive hiring and training practices.

   (c) *Pricing research,* to find optimum relationships among pricing policies, sales volume, advertising, and profits.

(d) *Sales projections,* to help forecast future volume and hence determine buying, stocking, staffing, and promotional plans.

(e) *Cost analysis,* including the analysis of promotional expenses to find out what beneficial sales results can be traced to them.

(f) *Management research,* to check on the effectiveness of the store's control and administration system.

(g) *Systems research,* to determine if internal information systems are being used with effectiveness.

(h) *Correspondence research,* to highlight facts that could result in better relationships with customers, suppliers, and others. This kind of research often produces tips for (or even the contents of) institutional ("image") ads.

4. *Advertising Research* (focused on the store's messages to its customers and the public)

(a) *Copy or message research,* aimed at guiding the advertising staff in choosing the most potent appeals.

(b) *Media research,* to measure the effectiveness of media through which the store's messages can be delivered to selected "target" audiences and to determine the media's relative usefulness for given messages at stated times.

(c) *Research on the most effective timing of advertising.*

(d) *Research on the advertising of the store's competitors.*

In addition to these four major areas of research, some stores also undertake (1) *weather research,* designed to improve sales forecasting and hence refine plans for inventory, staff utilization, and promotion; (2) *political research,* to guide management in assessing the prospects of changes in government policies and the legal aspects of operating a business; and (3) *basic research* for long-range management planning, including the whole sweep of societal relationships discussed in Chapter 1, any or all of which can have a bearing on the kinds of stores, services, and merchandise that will attract future shoppers.

All research has the same central goal: to present to managers facts (not hunches, opinion, or guesses) that answer the questions they must ask in making decisions. But the questions asked today are so numerous that finding *all* the answers through formal research would absorb much too much of a retailer's resources. Researching everything one wants to know would be impractical, even ruinous. So retail research in its formal sense is confined to seeking answers to those *few most vital questions* that concern management at any given point in time, for which adequate answers *cannot be found inexpensively by informal research.*

There are two main tracks to the attainment of research goals: *primary* research and *secondary* research. Primary research is far more costly and time-consuming and is undertaken only when secondary research fails to provide the information the store needs and adequate funds are available.

2 Locating and Using Existing Data

Tapping *secondary* sources of data and adapting it to their own needs is all most small- and medium-sized merchants do in the way of research. Even for giant merchandisers with impressive research budgets and their own research professionals, this is often all that need be done. Only a residue of *narrowly defined* and *extremely important* questions are answered through *primary* research financed by the retail company itself. A failure to understand the value and accessibility of secondary sources, to tap the great reservoir of research already accomplished, explains why so many retailers do no research at all, thinking it too expensive.

The problem is to *find* such information, *sort it out* in logical order, *reconcile* facts and figures from various sources, *reject* the irrelevant, and *refine the residue* into a form useful to a particular store in a specific market. For convenience, we may divide secondary sources of data into three groups: those *outside the local community,* those *within the community,* and unrecognized raw material available *in the store itself.*

SOURCES OUTSIDE
THE LOCAL COMMUNITY

The Federal Government By far the greatest source of retail market data is the Federal government, and in particular the Department of Commerce and the Small Business Administration. Keys to effective use of this information are several indexes and catalogs that enable the researcher to sort out what can and cannot be used effectively for a particular purpose. Many publications are free, and they are obtained from the issuing agency itself; others are sold, usually at very low prices, and *all* of these are purchased by making out checks payable

to "Superintendent of Documents," even if the order is sent to an issuing agency in Washington, to a field office in some other city, or to the Superintendent of Documents in Washington. Much data becomes obsolete even before it can be analyzed, edited, and printed for distribution to the public, so it is important to know how often any given publication is reprinted with more recent statistics and always to ask for the latest available edition. The Department of Commerce maintains 43 field offices and the Small Business Administration operates 74—in each major city and often also in state capitals—to expedite distribution of their publications locally. The document room or reference section of any major public educational library will have most of the Federal material needed, and indexes to all of it.

Start by studying catalogs, indexes, and checklists to determine what is available. From them, select the publications most useful for any given research task, and send for them or ask for them at the library.

Department of Commerce materials include the following:

1. *Retail Data Sources for Market Analysis,* published by the Bureau of Competitive Assessment and Business Policy, free for the asking. Its 14 easily understood, large-type pages describe 30 Department of Commerce publications, about half of which are "directly devoted to the retail industry"; the others are "related" to it. This simple, no-nonsense booklet tells what each publication contains, what it costs, and how often it is updated and reissued.

2. *Business Service Checklist,* a weekly guide to Department of Commerce

reports, books, and news releases, with a table of key business indicators, a convenient order blank, and a $5.50 annual subscription price. Typical issues contain from 55 to 75 titles with sources and prices (if any—many are free) immediately upon their publication by the many divisions of the Commerce Department. It is the sole effective substitute for the time-consuming chore of a *weekly* visit to a major reference library to keep oneself current on such research data. Economic and social trends, construction and housing activity, transportation, retail trade and distribution, environmental research, community development, population changes, employment, education, and management are among the topics covered on national, regional, state, and local levels.

3. *Bureau of Census Catalog,* available in three forms: annual, 4 quarterly issues cumulative to the annual volume, and monthly supplements. Cost is $2.75 for the annual or $6.50 for the quarterly and monthly issues. This is a key to the many Current Population Reports, Special Economic Reports, Construction Reports, Supplementary Reports, and other data sources offered continually by the Census Bureau.

4. Of the hundreds of sources indexed in the material described above, those of special interest to retail researchers are *Census Tract Studies* for each of the 241 Standard Statistical Metropolitan Areas, which dissect in massive detail the population characteristics of small areas, containing about 4,000 persons each, that constitute the immediate trading areas of small shops or branch stores; the annual *U.S. Industrial Outlook* with projections to future years (including retail trade categories and consumer services); *Current Retail Trade* reports on weekly, monthly, and annual bases; the monthly *Survey of Current Business* that includes data on retail inventories, sales, and credit; *Monthly Department Store Sales;* the annual *County Business Patterns* with employment and payroll data and retail trade statistics for every county in the United States (issued separately for each state); the annual *Statistical Abstract of the United States;* and the annual *County and City Data Book.*

The U.S. Small Business Administration is also a valuable source of data and of guides to statistics for retailers. Indexes of its free management assistance publications and for-sale booklets can be obtained from its Washington headquarters or its many field offices. Of particular value to retail researchers are SBA's *Discover and Use Your Public Library* (a management aid) and its bibliographies *Basic Library Reference Sources* and *Marketing Research Procedures,* all of which are free.

State Governments In each of the 50 state capitals are state departments of commerce, revenue or the treasury, highways, and labor, which issue reports, statistics, and tables useful in feeling the pulse of the local market and predicting future trends. Some states have bureaus of economic development and state libraries, which can find specific materials useful to retailers. A couple of telephone calls or a visit to the right department or agency may open up channels that will feed useful data into a store's research files for years to come. There is also a *Monthly Checklist of State Publications,* which is very useful for organizations with interests in several states, available for $4.50 a year from the Superintendent of Documents in Washington.

Advertising Media and Media Associations In most larger communities, newspapers and broadcast stations provide basic market research data as a service to their clients. In cities served by a radio station belonging to Westinghouse's "Group W," a retail information bank provides data to clients of the stations. The *Detroit News* will even provide computerized analyses of the market potential of any given present or proposed store location in the local metropolitan area.

In smaller towns, the research data available from local media may be rudimentary, if they offer any at all. But most newspapers and broadcasting stations belong to national associations that conduct research studies of value to advertisers in those media, certainly at the national level and perhaps at the local level too. These associations rarely work directly with stores, but their research is either on file locally or can be obtained through the research director, advertising manager, or sales director of the local paper or broadcasting station. The Newspaper Advertising Bureau, 485 Lexington Ave., New York, N.Y. 10017, serves 1,100 daily newspapers and is an especially prolific source of data. The Radio Advertising Bureau, 555 Madison Ave., New York, N.Y. 10022, which counts thousands of local stations among

its members, is another good source of information. Magazines, too, are always interested in helping to market locally the products advertised in them. Many do comprehensive research studies, as does the Magazine Publishers Association, 575 Lexington Ave., New York, N.Y. 10022. Other media associations that can be helpful include the Television Bureau of Advertising, 1 Rockefeller Plaza, New York, N.Y. 10020; the Outdoor Advertising Association of America, 625 Madison Ave., New York, N.Y. 10022; and the National Newspaper Association, 491 National Press Building, Washington, D.C. 20004.

Retail Trade Publications A prime source of information is the retail trade paper for a store's particular trade line. These papers are chock-full of news reports of research studies from various sources affecting the particular category of retailing to which they appeal. Usually they contain a summary of the findings and full particulars of where interested merchants can get copies of the full reports. Small Business Administration bibliographies for retail trade lines provide names, addresses, and subscription costs for such publications. Noteworthy among them are *Stores,* the monthly magazine of the National Retail Merchants Association (also available on a subscription basis to nonmembers); the commercial papers of Fairchild Publications, Inc., such as *Women's Wear Daily,* the *Daily News Record* (a menswear publication), *Home Furnishings Daily,* and others; *Progressive Grocer; Chain Store Age; The Merchandiser; The American Druggist; Sporting Goods Business* and other Bill Publications; and

DISCOUNT STORE SHOPPERS - - -
AND WHAT KIND OF STORE THEY LIKE

Do you prefer to have discount stores handle nationally advertised brands, private brands or both?

Nationally - 60.1%		Private - 4.3%		Both 24.4%	
Why?		Why?		Why?	
Familiarity	26.7%	Cheaper	71.4%	Choice	58.5%
Dependability	22.8	Quality	11.9	Price Comparison	30.5
Quality	17.7	Other Reasons	14.3	Other Reasons	10.6
Guarantee	15.0	Don't Know	2.4	Don't Know	.4
Greater Selection	4.0		100.0%		100.0%
Other Reasons	12.9				
Don't Know	.9				
	100.0%				

(No Opinion- 11.2%)

Do you prefer a discount store with long continuous aisles, or with departments separated by partions, like a department store?

Partioned	50.9%
Long Aisles	30.8
No Opinion	18.3
	100.0%

Would you rather shop in self-service discount stores, or be waited on by clerks?

Self-Service	71.1%
Clerks	25.4
No Opinion	3.5
	100.0%

Figure 4–1 Research Data Provided by Newspapers

These extracts from the 1973 "Discount Store Study" produced by the *Cleveland Press* provide information that is very useful to retailers. The above report reveals a strong preference for national brands that will adversely affect sales of private brands unless they are aggressively advertised to familiarize people with them and to convince customers of their quality and dependability. The discount store manager might wish to take advantage of the shoppers' choice of partitioned aisles and self-service by structuring a store in this way or by advertising that the store is so designed and arranged.

The profile of the discount store shopper (at right) gives data comparing them to "all families" in the metropolitan area. This information may surprise some who have failed to recognize that discounters appeal especially to all income groups above the $10,000 mark, to relatively high-status occupational groups, and to people under 50 years of age. Such knowledge is indispensable to store management in targeting its merchandising and advertising operations.

A PROFILE OF THE METROPOLITAN CLEVELAND
DISCOUNT STORE SHOPPER
1973

DAY OF WEEK SHOPPED*

	Sunday	Monday	Tuesday	Wednesday	Thursday	Friday	Saturday	No Special Day
1973	12.2%	2.5%	2.9%	3.8%	7.0%	10.1%	24.1%	49.1%

INCOME LEVELS

	Under $5000	$5000-7999	$8000-9999	$10,000-12,499	$12,500-14,999	$15,000 & Over
All Families	19.4%	10.7%	12.7%	19.8%	12.2%	25.2%
Discount Store Shoppers	10.9	7.7	11.5	23.8	15.5	30.6

OCCUPATIONAL LEVELS

	Owners, Managers & Professional	Clerical & Sales	Craftsmen & Operatives	Service & Laborers	Widow & Retired	Unemployed
All Families	23.4%	10.8%	34.4%	6.6%	19.2%	5.6%
Discount Store Shoppers	25.6	12.9	40.9	6.3	11.1	3.2

AGE CHARACTERISTICS

	Under 25	25-34	35-49	50-64	65 & Over
All Families	7.9%	24.2%	33.6%	22.6%	11.7%
Discount Store Shoppers	8.6	28.4	38.0	20.4	4.6

Based on discount store shopped most often

the *Hardware Retailer,* published by the National Retail Hardware Association.

Other Publications Scholarly research of direct interest to retailers is found in the quarterly *Journal of Retailing,* published by New York University and available for $10 per year, and in publications like the *Journal of Advertising Research,* the *Journal of Marketing,* and the *Journal of Marketing Research. The Marketing Information Guide,* an annotated bibliography of the constant flow of new literature on all phases of marketing from academic and governmental sources, trade associations, and periodicals is available monthly. Subscriptions can be obtained by writing to the publisher at 224 7th St., Garden City, N.Y. 11530. The annual cost is $10.

Two commercially produced magazines, each nearly indispensable for modern marketing and advertising people at the retail level, are *Sales and Marketing Management* (formerly *Sales Management*) and *Advertising Age. Sales and Marketing Management's* information-laden feature articles often include in-depth studies of just those facets of marketing that the alert retailer most needs to know about. Particularly valuable is its annual *Survey of Buying Power,* which appears in one of the July issues (available separately, but at more than the annual subscription rate). Many marketers regard this thick, timely reference work as the cornerstone of their reference library, large or small. It updates to December 31st of the preceding year basic economic and demographic data on each county, large or small; each city with 40,000 or more inhabitants (or less if it is a metropolitan area core city);

and each metropolitan area in the United States and Canada. A second big reference issue, published in October, contains three-year projections of the growth in population, households, income, and retail sales for metropolitan markets. The same issue surveys newspaper, TV, and radio markets.

Advertising Age is a must for the advertising people and useful for other executives as well. It contains, among other things, basic data on media investments, rundowns on ad agencies and major advertisers, in-depth features on copy and commercials, and the latest news on government restrictions on ads. It is a living textbook of the advertising business, full of reports on new research studies in marketing and advertising and on where and how to get copies of the data. Once a year an issue is devoted to a descriptive index of *more than 1,000 current research reports,* many on regional and local markets.

Much information of value to retail advertisers can be found in general business magazines too. Among the leaders are *Fortune* (whose July issue gives vital statistics of the 50 largest retail firms); *Forbes* (whose annual corporation data issue includes retail companies' financial data); *Time, Newsweek, U.S. News & World Report,* and newspapers like *The Wall Street Journal* and *The New York Times.*

Trade Associations The National Retail Merchants Association, with headquarters at 100 W. 31st St., New York, N.Y. 10001, publishes a whole library of materials on retail research and other retail management topics. The Mass Retailing Institute's comprehensive studies of shoppers' behavior and store operations are available at a modest cost, considering the quality of the material and its potential usefulness to merchants. MRI is at 579 7th Ave., New York, N.Y. 10018. The many great trade-line associations, such as the National Retail Hardware Association, the Menswear Retailers of America, the National Association of Retail Grocers, and the National Appliance & Radio-Television Dealers Association, are also good sources of research information.

Private Research Libraries These can provide some useful information. The library maintained by the Conference Board (845 3rd Ave., New York, N.Y. 10022) has cumulative and periodic indexes listing more than 400 CB studies. Membership in this organization may be well within the budget of larger retail firms, making this superior research matter available at a nominal cost. CB even provides tailored reports and services of 100 research specialists for specific members on request. Outsiders can get CB materials at a price of about five times what members pay. The McGraw-Hill Marketing Data Department, 1221 Avenue of the Americas, New York, N.Y. 10020, taps resources of 25,000 documents in 700 subject areas pertaining to marketing, advertising, and selling. A weekly bulletin, *McGraw-Hill Keys* ($40 per year) keeps subscribers posted on available materials and makes them eligible for low-cost individualized research reports. A 76-page index, or *Subject Headings Guide,* comes free with a subscription or can be bought separately for $5.

Suppliers and Manufacturers Manufacturers and wholesalers have a stake in their retailers' success, and their dealer-assistance programs increasingly include useful research on the retail market for their products. Some provide data through bulletins, pamphlets, or booklets; others sponsor dealer seminars at which their research experts explain the market. Many will supply extracts from national research applicable to a particular market area to retailers that ask for them. Manufacturers of equipment and supplies used in retailing also offer some significant studies, especially in the area of operational research. An example is the National Cash Register Company (Marketing Services Department), Dayton, Ohio 45409, or their nearest branch office.

Other Sources University bureaus of social and economic research and departments or schools of marketing and advertising often produce studies that local retailers can use. The research librarian at the nearest state, municipal, or university library can be very helpful in finding information on particular subjects. Some libraries will conduct limited research in response to a phone call or send out materials on loan. All have photocopy machines to facilitate extracting specific material.

SOURCES WITHIN
THE LOCAL COMMUNITY

Municipal and County Governments Local governments are loaded with information that stores can put to use in their research efforts. Various bureaus or offices can supply data on building permits, zoning and building code changes related to projected land uses,

Sporting and Field Activities

57% OF THE FAMILIES HAVE ONE OR MORE
MEMBERS WHO SWIM

ACTIVITY	% TOTAL FAMILIES PARTICIPATING	WHO PARTICIPATES		
		Wife	Husband	Children
Swimming	57%	69%	72%	70%
Fishing	47	57	92	46
Bowling	36	56	65	38
Camping	34	86	91	65
Hunting	27	30	92	33
Baseball	27	6	35	73
Ice Skating	24	38	34	76
Basketball	23	4	33	72
Golf	22	20	84	23
Football	20	3	32	74
Tennis	17	53	54	48
Skiing	14	44	57	54

Figure 4–2 Mass Retailing Institute Surveys Consumers' Personal Activities and Related Purchases
The information presented here is from a 1972 study, *Personal Activities and Related Purchases of Self-Service General Merchandise Shoppers,* by the Mass Retailing Institute and E. I. du Pont de Nemours & Co., Inc. To gather the data, personal interviews were conducted with 3,030 actual shoppers in 46 stores throughout the country. Through such studies, retail trade associations help their members (and others who buy their reports) to better understand their consumers, how and why they use the merchandise they buy, and why they choose the stores they do for their shopping.

SKIING PURCHASES

Where Majority of Items Purchased:

☐	Discount Store
▦	Other Type Store
■	Don't Buy or No Answer

27%   58%   15%

REASON FOR PURCHASE AT STORE INDICATED	Discount Store	Other Type Store
Good Price	61%	11%
Good Variety	10	9
Good Quality	8	42
Convenient Location	7	3
Loyalty to Store	3	1
Good Service	3	4
Preferred Brand	3	23
Good Adjustment Policies	1	-
Shopping Ease	1	-
This Store Does Not Carry	1*	3
Good Credit Policy	-	1
Employee Advice	-	2
No Answer	3	1

* *Reflects respondents going to a discount store other than the one where interviewed.*

birth and death records, marriage license statistics, road and street construction plans and related traffic patterns, and sewer and water-line extension plans. Municipal or regional planning commissions maintain projections on population trends and maps indicating areas of future development. This material is useful to most retailers and vital to merchants planning to open branch stores or relocate.

Nongovernmental Sources   Local libraries may have various data of interest to retailers. Public school systems often do surveys in order to forecast future enrollment trends, building needs, class sizes, and faculty requirements. The local chamber of commerce may have made surveys of retail trade for its members and may maintain files of survey material.

Local public utilities often have valuable information on current and projected population expansion on an area. Boards of realtors are another good source of data, as are major banks, many of which are rapidly moving to establish marketing-advisory services for their business clients. The personnel departments of major employers will sometimes release facts about their employees' places of residence, occupational classifications (the number of office and production workers), and other data convertible to useful retail information.

Stores in shopping centers can tap the research the center developer used in planning the project in the first place and any additional research it may do. Noncompeting merchants can profitably swap information, perhaps distilled from charge-account files. Local community-

college or high-school classes in distributive education may have collected retail trade studies or they may be willing to conduct them.

DIGGING USEFUL FACTS OUT OF THE STORE'S OWN FILES

Sometimes the information the retailer needs is so close he's lucky it hasn't bitten him! Much of what a merchant wants to know is stashed away in his own office, but since it is not labeled "research," he does not recognize it. Charge-customer records and delivery orders should be translated into pins in a large-scale map, showing clearly what the store's present real trading area is. (In the case of large stores, each pin can represent a cluster of 10, 50, or 100 customers.) Income data is on every credit application; information on shopping and paying habits is in the accounts receivable records. Stores using electronic data processing of customers' records can quickly, accurately, and inexpensively analyze such things as customers' brand preferences and service needs or changes in product preferences and shopping habits as its clientele ages through the life cycle. Target customers can be pinpointed by profiling their characteristics. All this can guide both buyers and advertising people to more productive operations. Small stores with manually handled files can also spade up facts, perhaps by taking every tenth or twentieth name in a file and determining customer characteristics and shopping habits through *sampling*.

Mail and telephone orders can be analyzed to suggest areas for branch-store expansion or revised media patterns for ads. Want slips and out-of-stock reports reflect how fads, fashions, and changing lifestyles are affecting consumer preferences. Daily and weekly sales analyses keep management aware of changes in favored days and hours for shopping. The new quick-action EDP inventory reports open up a whole new vista of inexpensive built-in research studies on trends in customer needs and preferences.

Stores equipped with the new *electronic cash registers* (point-of-sale terminals) that feed sales data to computers are probably destined to "open the door to revolutionary changes in the management of [national] brand advertising and the practice of advertising research," according to Paul E. J. Gerhold, president of the American Research Foundation. He foresees that when the sales information obtained by retailers' point-of-sale devices can be quickly consolidated and analyzed by national marketers, much of their present costly, and slow, research methods will become obsolete: "As the focus of advertising research moves toward the cash register, we may simply be able to research copy by using copy, to research media by using media, to research dollar expenditures by making dollar expenditures." [5]

3 The Steps to Success in Primary Research Projects

The retailer who cannot find adequate answers from the *secondary* sources suggested above may consider doing *primary research studies* to fill in the gaps. At some stage in the development plans and expansion programs of most progressive stores, the time will be ripe for one or a series of tailored surveys to help management make critical decisions.

When this point is reached, outside profesional help will surely be called for. Research advice from trained personnel knowledgeable about the store's trade line may be available from a state or national trade association. A nearby college or university may have on its staff a person who blends business know-how with academic competence in marketing and research fields and is glad to do some moonlighting, spend a vacation period with a store, or supervise some advanced students in a study that would be good for them and good for the merchant. Or, a commercial research firm may be the answer. Such a firm can be located by reference to "Market Research and Analysis" or "Research and Development Service" listings in the classified telephone directory in any sizable city. Also of help is the annual *Research Service Directory*, an official publication of the Marketing Research Association, 31 E. 28th St., New York, N.Y. 10016, which lists research companies and field services throughout the United States by state, city, and type of service.

A professional consultant will guide a merchant through the several stages of a primary (original) research project. This expert will help decide in what areas secondary data is adequate and where new spadework must be done to round out the picture. He or she will also determine, keeping in mind the retailer's budget, what (if anything) can be accomplished on a "do-it-yourself" basis and where specialists are called for to insure a satisfactory result.

WHAT IS INVOLVED IN AN
ORIGINAL RESEARCH STUDY

Definition of the Problem First off, management must define very precisely just what it wants to learn from the study—customers' attitudes toward the store, noncustomers' reasons for shopping elsewhere, the effect of several distinct types of advertising, the market potential of selected types of merchandise, or whatever. Seeking too much information results in fuzzy answers, inconclusive reports, and wasted money and time. It is essential to *leave out* a lot of peripheral topics and narrow down the field to the fewest possible number of questions. The project will have a firm base only when management can state *narrowly* what its intended purpose really is.

A sensible preliminary step is to list *all* the things you want to know. Then list the facts about which you are *already certain;* the facts that you *think you know* but need verification; and, finally, the areas about which you have *no information at all.* This will lead you to a crisp, precise statement of your goals. Declare *at the beginning* what you want to know *at the end.*

Exploitation of Secondary Sources Before launching into primary research, always review how much progress toward the research goals can be achieved through a shrewd analysis of existing data, and spend money only on the links that are still missing.

Establishment of a Research Design The basic plan of original research calls for decisions like these: (a) whether to do open-ended research, paired compar-

ison tests, or research with experimental models; (b) whether to do a highly structured inquiry to rigidly limit the types of responses or an unstructured inquiry to encourage free replies; (c) what type of sample to use, a *probability sample* scientifically drawn to insure that it closely resembles the total universe of people being studied or a sample based on storekeepers' knowledge of their markets or customers or even a sample of those persons most easily and inexpensively reached. Probability samples are virtually always preferred by professionals, and they alone can advise on means of obtaining such a sample to insure valid final results. One must also make choices, based on known mathematical laws, about how *large* a sample to use to stay within limits of error. The bigger the sample, the more accurate *and costly* will be the final result. The sponsor of the study must decide what limits of error are acceptable, bearing in mind the costs involved. The smaller the sample, the more skewed it may be and the more *misleading* the answers may be. A trained researcher can help determine, in advance, the point where still more numbers would add so little to the accuracy of the research as to make the extra expense a poor investment.

Selection of Interviewing Methods There are three basic kinds of interviews, each with advantages and disadvantages.

1. *Surveys conducted by mail.* Mail surveys are essentially inexpensive, can reach a large number of persons or households, and sometimes

bring in a large number of replies. They can include a large number of questions. But mail surveys can be badly skewed, simply because those who reply tend to be different from the *normal* person in the group to whom the mass of surveys are sent. Frequently, people with time on their hands will answer, and busy people will not. Those who enjoy filling out forms will answer, and others who hate to fill out questionnaires will not. In tests of opinions and attitudes, mailed-in replies tend to come largely from people with *strong opinions* either pro or con; the vast majority who have only mild opinions do not bother to reply.

2. *Telephone surveys.* Surveys conducted by telephone are inexpensive, get a large number of replies very quickly, and if properly controlled can produce a true probability sample with near-perfect scientific accuracy. But they must be confined to a very small number of very simple and easily understood questions, and they seldom stimulate voluntary additional comments by the persons interviewed.

3. *Personal interviews.* Interviews conducted in the home, office, or store or on the street are theoretically the best kind of survey. They can involve a great number of questions, even open-ended questions cleverly designed to probe psychological motivations. However, their cost is high because they are successful only if highly trained and well-paid interviewers are used. Also, they take a long time to accomplish and usually reach only a small sample.

Conduct of a Pilot Test Like a new-model car that may have bugs when it first comes off the assembly line, the tailormade survey planned to solve a retailer's special problem should be tested before it is put into full-scale production. A pilot test on a small segment of the sample is advisable as a trial run, which, after analysis, will suggest changes to smooth the way.

Design of the Questionnaire The exact choice of words and physical arrangement of the questionnaire form should be subject to editing by the research consultant, both before and especially after running the pilot test. Respondents must understand what they are being asked, and questions must be in *their* language and idiom (not the retailer's). It is necessary to weed out or alter items that people seem to rebel against, consistently misunderstand, or refuse to answer. Certain words are emotionally loaded, and synonyms should be found for them.

Don't get yourself into a situation like that of a well-intentioned "do-it-yourselfer" who, among other things, wanted to test how his store was attracting the "new people" in the community as opposed to the "old timers." One question read, "Length of residence in Central City? _____" The first return he opened had this scrawled in the answer space: "Exactly 38 feet, north to south, not counting attached garage." The professional research consultant would have emphasized that questions are less likely to be misinterpreted if they are very *precise.* "How long have you lived in Central City?" would have been an improvement, but this is better yet: "Please check *one* answer: I have lived in Central City (a) less than 1 year

Good morning afternoon, I'm from Special Surveys, a research company. We are doing a survey of consumer opinions and family shopping habits and we would like to have your ideas.

....

8a During the past seven days did you buy anything at any of the following discount stores?

1( )Gaylord's Giant Tiger   5( )Value City   11( )Clarkins
2( )Spartan-Atlantic   6( )Zayre's   12( )Grant City
3( )Topp's   8( )K Mart   (Berea Store)
4( )Uncle Bill's   9( )Gold Circle   10( )D.K.   **22**
   7( )None

....

IF "YES" ON QUESTION 8a, ASK:

8f Which two or three days during the week would you prefer to see discount stores advertise in the newspaper?

1( )Monday   4( )Thursday   7( )Sunday
2( )Tuesday   5( )Friday   8( )No choice   **28**
3( )Wednesday   6( )Saturday

8g Suppose you were in charge of a discount store's newspaper advertising---which do you think would bring more people into your store---ads showing many different kinds of items or ads showing a few related items?

1( )Many   2( )Few   3( )No Opinion   **29**

....

10g HAND RESPONDENT CARD

Here is a card showing different income groups. Will you please tell me the letter of the group ..not the amount, just the letter of the group which best represents the total annual income before taxes of your immediate family living in your household?

A( )Under $3,000   F( )$12,500 to $14,999
B( )$3,000 to $4,999   G( )$15,000 to $17,499
C( )$5,000 to $7,999   J( )$17,500 to $19,999
D( )$8,000 to $9,999   I( )$20,000 to $24,999
E( )$10,000 to $12,499   H( )$25,000 & Over

....

10i Which of these age groups does the woman in this household who does most of the buying fall into?

1( )Under 25   5( )40 to 44   9( )D.K.
2( )25 to 29   6( )45 to 49   0( )No Woman
3( )30 to 34   7( )50 to 64
4( )35 to 39   8( )65 & Over

....

( ); (b) more than 1 year but less than 5 ( ); (c) more than 5 years ( )."

Conversion of Raw Data into Meaningful Information Unless the numbers involved are exceptionally small, data collected in a survey will be tabulated by computer, perhaps at a service bureau, bank, or college if the store does not have suitable EDP equipment of its own. Recommendations from the technical people who will "run the survey" should be sought *in advance,* so that the questionnaire will fit the input capabilities of the machine to be used. Interpreting data, dealing with incomplete replies, and editing the results into plain language is the final stage. At this point the original hypothesis of the project is proven or disproven. Management's initial questions are answered, either conclusively or tentatively. And new and unforeseen problems may come to light that suggest further research.

THE LIMITATIONS OF RESEARCH

Research pays off if management actually uses the facts gathered, and uses them correctly, to *narrow the area of probable error* in decision-making. Much research is only partly accurate and leads to conclusions that are only partly right. A whole series of projects, conducted in a compatible fashion, and checked against one another, is more likely to be right and less likely to lead to wrong actions. In setting up a research program, it is wise to anticipate future studies that will verify or disprove the first one (as well as to measure changes over time, which give cues to trends).

A great many *variables* can enter into any situation, making it hard to *isolate* the one factor you are trying to research. For example, suppose you set out to define a store's trading area and resort to an old but valid method of finding out where the customers come from. You send out a crew to write down the license numbers of all the cars in the parking lot and adjacent streets, then, using a cross-referenced license directory, find out the home addresses of owners of those cars. However, your judgment tells you that a great many of the store's customers usually come from neighboring city X, and so does a quick spot-check of the charge-account files. Yet the survey shows extremely few city X residents' cars near the store. Why?

Figure 4–3 Questionnaire Form Used in Conducting Interviews
Shown here is a composite page of the questionnaire used in the survey that gathered the data in Figure 4–1. Special Surveys Company, an independent research organization in Cleveland, Ohio, handled the methodology of the survey, developed the questionnaire, and conducted the interviews for the *Cleveland Press.* Such surveys are taken monthly through personal interviews at 480 households in 159 interviewing blocks of the city; thus 5,760 households are included in a year. Trained interviewers are used who understand that there can be no deviation in form or sequence from the questionnaire that has been designed. The reliability of the results is ensured if (1) the questions are understood; (2) they are free from bias; (3) the people interviewed are representative of the total population; and (4) the sample size is large enough.

More than 100 questions in all are included in the survey. Some of the questions differ from month to month; others are the same throughout the year.

Investigation reveals that on the day you assembled your license-plate numbers, the merchants of city X were holding their annual townwide promotion, with free parking, free lunches, big bargains, and a famous band for dancing in Main Street. You chose a bad day to get a fair estimate of the store's normal trading area, and you need to repeat the survey. Taking two or three surveys a week or two apart is one way to level out variations caused by just such contingencies as city X promotions.

Or, suppose you want to test how product Y is selling, so you program the store's computer (or take a before-and-after inventory) to measure the movement of that product over a three-day span. Unbeknown to you, however, the store's major competitor is planning to promote that same product Y on those very days, with extra advertising and prices much below normal. Under such conditions, your test will mean nothing, because it will fail to measure the sales performance of the product under *normal* marketing conditions.

It is also very easy to survey the wrong audience. Suppose you make a telephone survey in January, and a large proportion of calls are not answered in one section of your survey area. In another section, almost everyone is at home. Your sample is badly skewed because the upper-class neighborhoods are empty at that season, their affluent residents busy sunning themselves in Florida or on Caribbean islands. At another season, you may hit factory shutdown periods for your community's major manufacturing plants. Then the telephones in working-class neighborhoods may not be answered because the residents are on *their* vacations to nearby fishing spots and cottage resorts.

A poor questionnaire design or incompetent interviewers can also throw off a survey and produce *misinformation*. People are influenced heavily by the way questions are phrased in print and by the tone of voice and facial expression of interviewers. They also tend to answer survey questions in a way that *they think makes them sound best,* not in a way that shows how things really are, to enhance their self-image. People who want to project an upper-class image may disavow shopping in discount stores, and yet in fact they patronize them frequently. People who wish to appear to be intelligent consumers may declare that they always shop three or four stores to compare prices before they buy major items, but the truth is they rush straight to their favorite store when they get an impulse to buy.

Two areas of secondary research that many marketers once assumed to be more or less infallible are now under suspicion. It has been revealed that blacks, Spanish-speaking people, and probably other underprivileged groups were substantially underrepresented in the 1970 census. It appears that the disadvantaged have been so disillusioned with "the establishment" that they resist any inquiries into their affairs (even the census-takers' calls), and they just disappear from what have been designed as valid samples of the public. Further, the Census Bureau dropped its studies of buying intentions after it was proven that few of them proved accurate. This evidently shows either that people change their minds very easily or that they simply do not choose to reveal their real plans when interviewers question them.

Emotions play a greater role in human behavior than was once thought to be the case, a primary reason why cheap or unscientific research can be worse than none at all. Three variables that influence a shopper's choice of a retail outlet have been pinpointed: (1) an evaluation by the shopper of the importance of such rational factors as price, convenience (location), the variety of merchandise, and store services; (2) the shopper's perceived rating of the store versus its competitors, on the basis of these same factors, as to whether or not the store really is or is not that low-priced, conveniently located, broadly stocked, or service-oriented; and (3) a continuing comparison process, wherein the customer keeps trying to justify the choice of stores by wanting to believe that the store to which he or she is emotionally attached does, in fact, offer those advantages. Thus the actual decision to go and shop in one store or another may depend on whether the customer's reason or emotions win out. This kind of decision can often be influenced by sophisticated, emotion-centered advertising.

Another place where emotion enters is in the attitudes of the store management that conducts the research. Some businessmen are sublime egotists, sure that they know all the answers. They call on "research" simply to endorse their own preconceived notions and to prove they were right in the first place. Results that suggest otherwise are ignored or a new research director is hired. This attitude makes money spent on research a waste. Unless research is pursued with a view to improving performance in some area, there is little point to it.

Questions for Discussion

1. Why has research become increasingly important for all stores?

2. Which of the many kinds of research retailers might do seems to you to be most important for an effective merchandising program? Which kinds of research are important to the more limited advertising function of the store? Why?

3. Before a merchant could wisely commit a great deal of capital to expanding a store or to establishing branches, what specific information should be sought through research?

4. What is the difference between primary and secondary research? Why do most smaller stores settle for doing secondary research? What are the sources of secondary data in your community, including within-store sources? What data might a store's EDP system produce?

5. What are the seven distinct steps in a primary research project? For which of these steps is a professional consultant most necessary, and why? Which steps do you think the store personnel itself could safely undertake to perform, if any? Why? How could EDP be helpful in this work?

Suggested Projects

1. Go to the nearest major library in or near your area (school, city, or governmental). Visit with the refer-

ence librarian, and ask for assistance in assembling statistical data (as much as you can in an hour or two) having a direct bearing on the market potential of the community in which your home, your school, or the library is located. Extract from that reference material pertinent data about the growth potential for retail trade in these lines: food, automobiles, ladies' apparel (fashion merchandise), home furnishings, children's wear and toys, and major household appliances. The focus of your research should be on *people* —their needs, interests, and ability to buy—not just on the merchandise available.

2. Pick out a medium-sized store in your community, and assume that the manager wants to know four things about the public's attitude toward the store as a guide to future merchandising, personnel, and advertising policies:

(a) whether the public believes that the store's merchandise is generally of good quality and worth the prices usually charged;

(b) whether it finds the store's personnel generally friendly, well-informed about merchandise, helpful, and courteous;

(c) whether it is satisfied or dissatisfied with the store's customer services, such as its credit system, refund system, delivery system, and handling of alterations and repairs; and

(d) whether it believes that the store's ads truthfully and adequately represent the merchandise and services it offers, are helpful to customers in deciding what and when to buy, and are noticed as frequently as those of competitors.

Design a questionnaire for telephone interviews with 50 known customers of the store (selected at random from the store's charge-account and delivery records) and 50 other persons in the same trading area selected at random from the telephone directory, none of whom are regular charge-account customers. Try out this questionnaire on 20 family members, neighbors, friends, teachers, and classmates (making it plain that it is not a real survey for the store). After this "pilot test," consider whether you should redesign your questionnaire in the light of what you learned from the 20 trial "respondents" and if so, in what ways.

3. Visit your nearest daily newspaper, radio station, and TV station. Ask for whatever market research, advertising research, and circulation or audience data they have available of particular interest to local retailers. Examine what they have to offer, and list any "missing links," that is, facts a store manager would like to know in order to do a good job of choosing among the media for his store's primary advertising and also for special "target" audience campaigns. How would you, if you were a store manager, rate the research material offered? How would you go about finding data the media could not supply? What would you recommend the management of these advertising media do to make their research more useful to merchants?

4. In the nearest business library, scan recent copies of *Advertising Age, Sales Management,* and *Stores.* Note the articles concerning marketing, advertising, and retail research you find there. Some will be brief sum-

maries of recent research projects, and others will deal with methods of research. Which areas of specific interest to retailers appear to be well represented, and which seem to be neglected? If you can, you might also check recent issues of a daily newspaper devoted to retailing: the *Daily News Record, Home Furnishings Daily,* or *Women's Wear Daily.* How could some of the information they contain be applied locally to stores' needs? How could local merchants obtain additional data particularly applicable to their own trading areas?

Notes

1. *Grey Matter* (May 1963).
2. *Grey Matter* (March 1969).
3. *Grey Matter* (October 1974).
4. *Ibid.*
5. Paul E. J. Gerhold, "Sweeping Changes Seen in Brand Ad Research," *Advertising Age* (July 15, 1974), p. 23.

Planning Promotion and Advertising for Profit— A Management Job

In Part 1 we examined the consumer population, the structure of the retail industry, the internal operation of retail stores, and the contributions of research to the solution of management's many-sided problems. Now we turn to the applications of advertising in the solution of problems arising out of the swift pace of change in today's markets, the nature of retail competition, methods of store management, and the knowledge being gained from research. We shall deal, in Part 2, primarily with the *advertising decision-making processes in which top management actively participates.*

Throughout U.S. industries, top management is increasingly taking a direct hand in determining the broad outlines of advertising policy. Retailing is no exception. Indeed, in the small retail store, one person or a very small group of family members or partners has always made all the significant decisions, including those pertaining to promotion and advertising, for obvious reasons. Among the retail giants advertising is the assigned responsibility of a major executive, and policy-making is a team effort in which that executive is deeply involved. It is basic policy decisions, wherein advertising is seen as one of the major functions of the store, to be integrated and coordinated with other major functions (such as buying, selling, and financing), that we must understand here.

Preview

Establishing the advertising appropriation for a retail operation is a top management task that merits deep thought and careful study, not just by the store's advertising professionals, but by its other executives as well. Advertising as a management tool can either help sell merchandise or create public awareness and acceptance of the store, its personnel, and its services. Better yet, it can accomplish both those objectives. The net long-range result of advertising should be to increase the store's profits, either directly or indirectly. However, it will be wasted unless these facts are understood: (1) advertising cannot sell unwanted merchandise; (2) there must be a commitment to consistent, regular advertising; and (3) the whole store must cooperate with its advertising program.

Among the many methods used for budgeting advertising funds, the percentage-of-sales method and the objective-and-task system prevail.

Progressive retail managers devise means of estimating the most profitable level of advertising expenditures and analyze "marginal sales" to determine the maximum amount that should be spent for advertising during a given period. Additional advertising expenditures are justifiable as long as they add to the store's profits.

The age of a store, the quality of its location, the nature of its market and trading area, the availability of effective media, the degree of manufacturer cooperation in paying advertising costs, the state of the economy, the amount and type of competition, and the store's basic philosophy of merchandising will determine whether, in a specified time period, it will need a relatively large advertising budget or can get by with a relatively small one. Nothing should be charged to advertising that should be charged to some other portion of a store's operating budget.

Learning Goals

This chapter should enable the reader to pinpoint why advertising is economically justified and to explain how good advertising increases a store's profits. Students should learn how to establish an advertising budget for a year (or some other period) using the percentage-of-sales method and the more complicated but superior objective-and-task method. They should come to an understanding of the significance of marginal sales and learn how to analyze increments in advertising in terms of the net profit derived from them. Simple rules of thumb for determining whether a given store requires a larger- or smaller-than-normal ad budget should be learned and remembered. And, finally, the reader should learn how to recognize which expense items belong in a retail advertising budget and which do not.

5

**Appropriating
Advertising Funds**

Effective retail advertising begins with top management's commitment to the proposition that promotion, properly conceived and skillfully executed, will produce a sufficient volume of additional sales to pay for itself, that it will generate more net profit than could be realized otherwise, and that advertising (as one means of promotion among several) is a more profitable use of the store's funds than alternate means of stimulating sales.

This commitment is expressed in dollar figures by an annual, seasonal, or monthly *appropriation* for the advertising function. The ad *budget,* often confused with the appropriation, directs *how* the appropriation is to be used.

1 Management Considerations in the Appropriation Decision

Determining the amount of money to be invested in advertising and estab-

lishing, broadly, how that money is to be used, is a high-priority management decision. Advertising specialists serve as staff assistants to management in reaching such decisions. They provide information, make recommendations, and submit tentative plans, but the chief executive gives the final word. In smaller stores without internal advertising staffs, the manager makes these decisions, often in a less formal manner and with or without the advice and counsel of his in-store assistants and outside specialists. These outside specialists may include media representatives, wholesalers, the promotional department of a chain with which the store is affiliated, an advertising agency, or trade association consultants.

Retail management is deeply and increasingly, concerned with advertising funding decisions for these reasons:

1. *The sheer magnitude of advertising costs*—Generally, a retailer's ad-

vertising costs are exceeded only by the cost of merchandise purchased for resale, payroll costs, and occupancy costs. Typically, the gross amount spent on promotion is as much or more than the net after-tax profits.

2. *The discretionary nature of promotional appropriations*—Other types of expenses are more rigidly fixed, more difficult to adjust upward or downward, than ad costs. And since other costs are less susceptible to change, advertising funds tend to attract special attention from those who want to do some overall cost-cutting or are looking for a rapid way to stimulate sales. In short, management *can* make more decisions concerning promotion than regarding most other operating expenses.

3. *The interrelationship of advertising with other facets of merchandising*—Buying, selling, pricing, branching out, selecting new-store locations, personnel policies, and financing are intertwined with promotion in one way or another. As a result, virtually all executives in a retail organization are affected by advertising and perform functions that may have an effect on the success of advertising. Some have strong opinions, pro and con, about advertising and the funds allotted to it. Only the firm's top decision-makers can reconcile conflicting views and interests and insure the proper correlation of promotion with other store activities.

4. *The increasing recognition of the power of advertising*—Past successful and unsuccessful promotions have built up an awareness that advertising can *make or break* a sale, a season, a year, or a firm. It is no longer left to chance, or delegated to underlings.

5. *The trend toward management by objectives*—Modern managers, many of them college-trained, are increasingly operating stores with a view to improving profits over the

long run by establishing *specific objectives* for each phase of the stores' operations (including promotion).

6. *The emergence of external and internal trends that force a heavier reliance on advertising*—The fragmented markets, increased mobility of shoppers, proliferation of merchandise and services, and greater sophistication of consumers in today's economy tend to force store managements to regard promotion more seriously than in past decades and to take a more active hand in determining both the amount and the nature of promotion. Concurrently, changes within the retail industry are encouraging a greater reliance on advertising. Sales forces are being diminished by self-service and vending machines, new merchandise lines and services are emerging as a result of the trend toward diversification, and stores are relocating to suburbs and shopping centers where competition is becoming more intense.

7. *The visibility of advertising*—By its very nature, advertising is the most visible part of the business structure. In this era of militant consumerism and heightened governmental scrutiny of business, any commercial enterprise tends to be judged increasingly by its advertising, simply because so many people who know little else about the firm see and hear it. Judgments formed as a result of advertising can set the stage for public and official acceptance of a retailer or a product or for a great deal of unofficial and official "trouble." Thus the retail manager who does not keep a tight rein on advertising may be courting disaster in more ways than one.

WHAT ADVERTISING CAN DO FOR THE STORE

Executives and stockholders have a right to ask just what advertising (*good* advertising) can *do* for a retail enterprise, for they have a vested interest in the answer. The answer to this question depends on the type of advertising that is employed.

Promotional advertising is expected to produce immediate, tangible results in the form of sales of specific items or visible traffic in a particular department on given days. It accounts for almost all the advertising of discounters, mass merchandising chains, supermarkets, and many other stores. The ad copy invariably includes prices and other facts, pictures tend to be largely of merchandise items, and the ads tend to be placed in newspapers. Fundamentally, promotional advertising is an alternative to and an extension of display cases, show windows, and personal selling ability.

Institutional advertising, in contrast, aims to create or reinforce a *store image,* to reach customers at an emotional as well as a rational level, and to make a favorable impression on them whether or not they buy anything from the store in the immediate future. Most institutional advertising does not even mention specific merchandise. It can be successfully delivered through a great variety of media. And it largely overlaps and reinforces the public-relations activities of the store. Results accrue slowly over a long period of time and are difficult to measure precisely. The amount of institutional advertising has been growing relative to the number of purely promotional ads in recent times, and much of the best and most expensive creative work in retail advertising has been in this area.

Combined promotional and institutional ads are becoming the rule rather than the exception, as some institutional "flavor" permeates almost all modern promotional ads. The best of the present-day sales-stimulating ("immediate-action") ads start with a careful selection of items that, by their very nature, tell something about the store. The format, background, illustrations, color, and (in broadcast commercials) the vocal or musical tone of the ad also convey a two- or three-dimensional message. This trend has been stimulated by a number of developments:

1. *Product differences have narrowed.* Both the *physical* differences in product characteristics and the *perceived* advantages of one product over another have become less pronounced. This forces the retailer to point to his *store—its atmosphere, its reputation, and its customer services*—as an attraction for shoppers. Psychologically speaking, *the store itself* becomes the "product" people buy.

2. As we move more and more toward a services-oriented society, *buying decisions increasingly hinge on intangible forces*—feelings, attitudes, aspirations, self-images—that can be appealed to by presenting the store as an institution that fills a consumer's psychological wants and needs rather than merely as a source for tangible possessions. Thus tangible goods are being sold more and more on the basis of related intangibles such as repair and maintenance services and shoppers' conveniences at the store. At the same time, intangibles like insurance, rentals,

and instruction make up an increasing proportion of the average store's product mix.

3. Finally, *service firms,* dealing in no physical products at all, *are more often being included in the definition of "a retail store."*

Business leaders today tend to consider a significant portion of their advertising as a *long-range investment.* Studies sponsored by both business and academic organizations have revealed that companies that habitually advertise (both institutionally *and* to sell specific products) over a long period of time tend to

1. lose a smaller share of their market in bad times,

2. regain a profitable level of sales more quickly at the end of such periods, and

3. realize higher ultimate profits during times of peak prosperity.

SPECIFIC REASONS FOR RETAIL ADVERTISING

All retail advertising has one or both of the *general* goals cited above: to stimulate immediate sales or to create goodwill. But specific promotional campaigns have more precise purposes, and individual ads have their assigned tasks.

To Insure Minimum Profit Every store would have *some* customers even without advertising. A *few* sales would come the easy way, from friends, relations, neighborhood residents, walk-in trade, or persons who hunted down the store because of an emergency that forced them to seek a source of supply for a particular item. Most stores will make a profit during the peak season for their particular merchandise lines, possibly with the aid of manufacturers' national advertising, but more probably because they get some of the spillover from more aggressive competitors whose ads create traffic. If it stays in business long enough, a nonadvertiser may even get an occasional customer as a result of word-of-mouth recommendations by satisfied customers.

But the odds are very greatly stacked against any substantial long-range profit for a store so managed. The history of nearly every successful modern business enterprise dealing in consumer goods starts with someone who believed in advertising, who kept it up consistently for a long time, and who was flexible enough to change the advertising approach to fit changing times.

The exceptions serve only to underscore the rule. Among national manufacturers and processors, the Hershey chocolate company long stood out as a successful concern that "did not believe in advertising." It depended instead on a quality product, a distinctive and highly visible wrapper, and a very efficient sales force.

During the 1960s, however, when Hershey sought to crack the Canadian market, it found an English candy bar (as good as its own, really) long heavily favored by the Canadian consumer. To meet its first real competition and speed up its penetration of the market north of the border, it turned to regular advertising media.

At about the same time, the company began to expand its product mix to include such things as chocolate syrup for cooking and an ice-cream topping. It had to fight for shelf space for these products, and again it turned to regular advertising. By 1973, it had an ad budget of $14 million.

In the retail industry, F. W. Woolworth was once a company that did virtually no media advertising. To compensate, it placed stores in prime traffic locations throughout the country, paying out in rent what it did not pay for advertising. Massive crowds passed its show windows, which were always expertly arranged. But by the early sixties traffic patterns were changing. Shopping habits were changing too, and the center of gravity of retailing was moving away from downtown locations to suburbs and shopping centers. Woolworth was then a slow-growth, low-profit company. Kresge and alert smaller competitors like G. C. Murphy were closing in, until, in the mid-sixties and early seventies, Woolworth awakened, drastically altered its merchandise offerings and store locations, and turned into one of the very largest retail advertisers!

Today's nonadvertiser is gambling dangerously, more so with each passing year. For the prudent retailer, advertising is an "insurance policy" against the loss of customers because of changing markets, changing neighborhoods, altered traffic patterns, new customer needs and attitudes, and unexpectedly tough competition.

To Increase Net Profits The nonadvertiser today is essentially an inactive factor in the marketplace. Such a store theoretically *could* succeed, at least in a modest way, if other factors happened to combine to compensate for its failure to use this management tool to full advantage. Given a most superior location, an exceptional line of products in high demand, an unusually stable trading area, an extraordinarily high-caliber personal selling effort, a superb public relations program—and a whole lot of *good luck*—a store just *might* continue for some time to reap satisfactory profits without the "expense" of advertising. But the vast majority of retailers find advertising necessary to carve out a profit-making territory for themselves in today's diversified markets. It offers a way for management to *do something* to get and hold customers and increase the store's short- and long-range profitability.

Suitable amounts of advertising used as part of an overall management strategy can increase a store's *sales revenues* and also its profits as its expenses become a *declining percentage of sales.*

Advertising can also increase a store's profitability by increasing its stock turnover rate. With a higher stockturn, it is possible *either* to increase profits by maintaining the same sales volume with a smaller investment in inventory *or* to increase sales without increasing the store's inventory.

Since there is a reciprocal relationship between increasing sales and an increasing turnover, the combined effect further increases net profits. More sales tend to speed up stockturn rates, and accelerating the stock turnover tends to further increase sales.

Table 5–1, a profit and loss statement for two successive years, demonstrates how a hypothetical store might significantly increase its net profits by *doubling its advertising appropriation.*

Table 5–1

Hypothetical Profit & Loss Statements for Two Years

	1st Year	Percentage of Sales	2nd Year	Percentage of Sales
Sales	$1,000,000	100.0	$1,250,000	100.0
Less **Cost of Goods Sold**	700,000	70.0	875,000	70.0
Gross Margin	**300,000**	**30.0**	**375,000**	**30.0**
Less **Expenses**				
Fixed	110,000	11.0	110,000	8.8
Variable				
Advertising	30,000	3.0	60,000	4.8
Other	125,000	12.5	140,625	11.2
Total variable expenses	155,000	15.5	200,625	16.0
Total expenses	**265,000**	**26.5**	**310,625**	**24.8**
Net Profit	**$ 35,000**	**3.5**	**$ 64,375**	**5.2**
Average Value of Stock at Retail	$ 250,000		$ 250,000	
Stock-turnover rate	4		5	

This table shows how, by *increasing* one of its variable (controllable) expenses, a store may actually *decrease* its total expenses as a percentage of sales (in this case, from 26.5 percent of sales to 24.8 percent, which saving is reflected in an increase in net profits [before taxes]). For purposes of this example, it was assumed that other variable expenses would increase at half the rate of increase in sales. (Sales increased by 25 percent, other variables by 12.5 percent.) Often the increase in other variable expenses is much less, especially when a small store enjoys a relatively modest increase in sales.

Even though advertising costs (one of the variable, or controllable, expenses) increase 100 percent from the first year to the second and account for a slightly larger percentage of sales, the store's total expenses are a smaller percentage of sales in the second year and its profits have greatly increased. A key factor is the fixed expenses, which do not increase at all, and the variable expenses other than advertising, which do not increase as rapidly as the sales volume.

It is also possible for increased advertising to improve profits *without* increasing sales. Table 5–2 uses the same figures we started with in column 1 of Table 5–1 and shows what can happen in the second year if advertising expenditures are increased by a mere $5,000. If the store's advertising *strategy* is to use

all the additional advertising funds and some of the original $30,000 to *promote fast-moving merchandise,* timing its ads to stimulate demand early in the season and avoid end-of-season clearances, the stock-turnover rate may increase, as it did in Table 5–1, to 5—even though the store's *sales* remain the same. This will create a crucial difference in the average stock the store must carry through the year, which will drop from $250,000 to $200,000.

Suppose now that none of the other variable expenses increase and some of them *decrease* because of the smaller inventory. The store saves $5,000 in interest because, in the past, it had to finance part of its excess inventory by borrowing $50,000 at 10 percent; it saves another $2,000 on end-of-season mark-

Table 5–2

Hypothetical Alternate Profit & Loss Statements for the Second Year

	Modest Advertising Increase to Improve Stockturn		Modest Advertising Increase to Improve Gross Margin	
		Percentage of Sales		Percentage of Sales
Sales	$1,000,000	100.0	$1,000,000	100.0
Less **Cost of Goods Sold**	700,000	70.0	690,000 *	69.0 *
Gross Margin	300,000	30.0	310,000 *	31.0 *
Less **Expenses**				
Fixed	110,000	11.0	110,000	11.0
Variable				
Advertising	35,000 *	3.5 *	35,000 *	3.5 *
Other	114,800 *	11.48 *	125,000	12.5
Total variable expenses	149,800 *	14.98 *	160,000 *	16.0 *
Total expenses	259,800 *	25.98 *	270,000 *	27.0 *
Net Profit	$ 40,200 *	4.02 *	$ 40,000 *	4.0 *
Average Value of Stock at Retail	$ 200,000 *		$ 250,000	
Stock-turnover rate	5 *		4	

* These figures differ from first-year figures in Table 5–1.

downs, since it now sells almost all its merchandise "in season"; it saves $2,000 more because with a smaller stock there is less damaged and stolen merchandise; it saves $600 on warehouse rentals, $350 in insurance, and $250 in personal property taxes. This results in a decrease in other variable expenses of $10,200. Thus, even with the $5,000 increase in advertising expenditures, the store's total variable expenses decrease from $155,000 to $149,800.

The $5,200 saved increases the most important figure of all, the store's net profits, to $40,200 (from $35,000). The store's percentage investment in advertising has increased from 3.0 to 3.5, its other variable expenses have declined from 12.5 percent of sales to 11.48 percent of sales, and its total expenses have been reduced from 26.5 percent of sales to 25.98 percent of sales. This may not seem like much of a drop, but it brings the store's net profits up to 4.02 percent of sales and means an extra $5,200 for the stockholders even though there was no increase in sales. In practice, an improved stockturn actually stimulates sales because people like fresh, in-season merchandise.

There is also another way that additional (and *improved*) advertising can increase profits *without increasing sales.* Let's again assume that the store adds only $5,000 to its original advertising appropriation and has only $35,000 to invest in ads the second year. But this time it focuses on increasing its gross margin and uses all the added $5,000 plus some of the original $30,000 of advertising funds to promote merchandise lines that marginal analysis has proven to be *most profitable.* It simultaneously retrains its sales force to do a better job of "suggestion selling" of brands that

yield the highest gross margins for the store, and it instructs the display department to concentrate on displays of merchandise lines known to have high profit margins.

When this second year is over, as Table 5–2 shows, the store's total sales still have not increased, but customers have been coaxed to buy products for which there is a greater "spread" between the wholesale cost and the retail selling price. The store's gross margin has been raised from 30 percent of sales to 31 percent, the cost of merchandise sold has declined from 70 percent of sales to 69 percent. None of the expenses (except advertising) have changed at all. But look what has happened to the bottom line. Because customers have been motivated to buy products that cost *them* no more but give the retailer a little wider margin of profit, the cost of goods sold has fallen to $690,000 and the gross margin has risen to $310,000. Total expenses have been increased by the extra $5,000 of advertising to $270,000. Deducting the slightly larger total expenses of $270,000 from the somewhat increased gross margin of $310,000 yields a net profit of $40,000. The store has gained $5,000, partly because it increased its advertising outlays by $5,000 and partly because it used the money more efficiently by planning for profits.

To Seek New Customers, by

1. attracting new target groups to the store;

2. expanding the geographical trading area of the store;

3. introducing the store's new branches to the people of their respective communities;

4. introducing new departments, merchandise lines, brand-name products, and services to customers and others in the trading area as the store diversifies operations;

5. reaching out to stimulate new sales via mail and telephone orders; and

6. exploiting the "leverage" effect of new customers who become regular customers and recommend the store to others.

To Sell More Merchandise and Service to Present Customers, by

1. increasing their pride in being a customer of the store and reinforcing a feeling of "oneness" with the store and its personnel;

2. continuously reestablishing customers' confidence in the store and building their self-image by reassuring them of their good judgment in being a regular patron; and

3. keeping customers aware of improvements in and additions to the store's merchandise, services, personnel, and policies.

To Increase the Stability of Store Operations, by

1. leveling out fluctuations in sales volume over time, enabling the store to minimize expenses associated with peak-season overloads and slack-season dearths or business, and

2. stabilizing the merchandise and service demands of customers, prices, and operating procedures so that the store can operate in the most economical way.

To Perform a Service for Customers and Prospective Customers, by

1. providing information that saves them time, effort, confusion, and

money (and ultimately creates goodwill that benefits the store) and

2. providing information on the use, maintenance, and repair of merchandise sold. This serves both to create goodwill, which benefits the store's future sales, and to generate business for service departments and/or replacement or tie-in sales.

To Make the Store a Community Personality, by

1. explaining candidly store policies that affect the community as a whole;

2. providing information on civic affairs;

3. performing various public services; and

4. taking notice of popular holidays and important local and national events.

To Influence the Morale and Effectiveness of Employees, by

1. building pride, understanding, and empathy among employees, management, stockholders, customers, and the community at large;

2. saving employees' time and energy by informing shoppers about merchandise and store policies; and

3. increasing total customer traffic through the store, enabling more salespersons to personally reach more customers and prospective customers.

To Reinforce the Impact of Other Promotional Efforts, by

1. paving the way for acceptance of sales solicitation by mail or telephone;

2. obtaining a list of prospects for mail, telephone, or personal selling;

3. following up locally on customer demand created by manufacturers' advertising;

4. capitalizing on the opportunities offered by manufacturers' cooperative advertising;

5. enabling the store to benefit from a demand for products initially stimulated by competitors' advertising; and

6. capitalizing on traffic generated by communitywide promotions or shopping-center promotions and, concurrently, contributing to the total shoppers' traffic during such promotions.

RESERVATIONS ABOUT ADVERTISING

Some persons have reservations about retail advertising. Attitudes range from apathy through misunderstanding and suspicion to vigorous objections and even downright hostility. Most of those on the outside challenge retailers as to whether the goals we have just enumerated *should* be sought through advertising. This questions is part of what advertisers must take into account in designing advertising, since any promotion that arouses the ire, rather than cultivates the goodwill, of significant customer groups, community spokespersons, or power-wielding officials is, per se, "bad" advertising. For now, however, we shall assume that we are dealing with advertising that is clearly legal, inherently ethical, and does not raise the hackles of advertising critics.

The questions asked about advertising by a retail management team usually center on whether spending for advertising will accomplish the objectives described above, not on whether advertising *should seek to* accomplish them. What the retail executive faced with determining the size of the advertising appropriation for a given store for a given period wants to know is, "Is the appropriation justified? Will the advertising work?"

As we have already observed, one can always find an exception "to prove the rule"—a small merchant who seems to succeed even though claiming to do no advertising. However, such a retailer is usually found to be heavily emphasizing other means of sales stimulation, perhaps at a greater cost than the cost of regular mass-media advertising, or to be enjoying the temporary shelter of a protected market growing out of an unusual competitive situation. And the shopkeeper who explains that a host of happy customers do all the "advertising" for the store, gratis, "by word of mouth," never comes up with a convincing answer when asked how much *more* the store might prosper if the conventional forms of advertising were used.

There is also another exception to the general run of advertisers—the store that overadvertises, seeking to achieve a greater sales volume than is possible (or than it can profitably handle) in a given phase of the business cycle or a given marketing environment. Though such a store might increase its apparent profits (at least temporarily) by reducing its promotional investment somewhat, the problem is often more a question of the irrational *timing* of advertising than advertising extravagance.

Some merchants point out, correctly, that advertising is only *one* element in the total marketing mix that causes people to buy a certain product or shop at a given store. They consider, quite rightly, that other elements—the nature of the product and its package, the personal selling ability involved in the final sale, the store image and its reputation among satisfied (or dissatisfied) customers—have a major impact on sales and can, without question, reinforce or greatly diminish some or all of the benefits of advertising.

The fact that cheerful, well-trained, and highly motivated salespersons—along with effective window displays, a wise choice of merchandise, and an impeccable reputation for adjusting complaints and rendering service after a sale—contribute to a rising sales and profit curve does not detract from the importance of advertising. A retailer should isolate, if possible, the contribution to sales of *each* element in the marketing mix. Even if advertising has relatively little beneficial influence on sales, this "little" can have a major effect on a store's profit margin.

WASTE IN ADVERTISING

Most hard-headed business executives' suspicions about the effectiveness of advertising can be traced to the kind of thinking that prompted the nineteenth-century "merchant prince," John Wanamaker, to declare, "I know that half of all the advertising I do is wasted, but I've never been able to determine which half." The primary reason some merchants budget for advertising so parsimoniously is that *their* advertising has not worked very well. They "don't believe in advertising" because they have rarely seen much in the way of

results from it themselves. Too much of their own past advertising was wasted; too little was profit-producing.

Why does this happen? Let's stop here, briefly, to examine a few of the major causes of ineffectiveness in advertising. Retail advertising will surely be wasted

1. if shoddy, uninteresting merchandise of little or no real value to the ultimate user, or a service or idea lacking true merit, is advertised;

2. if advertising is sporadic, unplanned, and not linked to a budgeting system that insures consistency; and

3. if advertising is expected to do the total marketing job all by itself, without adequate follow-through at the store—without displays, a large-enough stock of merchandise, or an enthusiastic, well-informed sales force.

As John O. Whitney pointed out in the *Harvard Business Review,*

> Far too often, [advertising] budgets are set by conventional "rules of thumb" instead of through analysis of the current competitive and environmental conditions. Often, too much is spent.... Conversely, some retailers spend far too little....
>
> ...another area of waste is the limitation of advertising's role to the sales function. Advertising can be a powerful tool in...employee relations ...as a "window" to examine the store from the customer's viewpoint...[and] for reviewing and making policy....
>
> The primary reason why waste is not eliminated is that [advertising] is usually discussed only in the context of its effect on sales, and more particularly its short-term effect. The measurements used are weekly sales

volume, item count ... and customer count. These short-term indicators are valid as such but limited in usefulness. They neglect the idea that because advertising communicates certain things about a business, its effect on sales cannot be evaluated separately from that which it is communicating.[1]

In addition, Laurence Jacobs of the University of Hawaii notes,

> There is a threshold level of impact for advertising, and if a store cannot afford to advertise at a sufficiently high level the manager would probably be better off putting his money into some other form of promotion. Too little advertising is clearly more wasteful than too much.[2]

THE PSYCHOLOGY OF BUDGETING

Retailing is, as we have established, a business of people. Advertising is equally a business of people. So also are the internal planning, management, and budgeting of advertising. Budgeting is in essence a method by which top management allocates operating resources and establishes priorities (in dollar terms) for different facets of a firm's marketing plan. Since people are emotional as well as rational, some emotion may enter into the budgeting process.

Budgeting may be viewed as "a psychological process involving the interactions of people with their motives, attitudes and emotions," according to Charles C. Gibbons, administrative consultant for the Upjohn company. He points out that everyone has a tendency to want to see his own activities accorded respect, and a large budget indi-

cates that a function is considered important. Gibbons suggests that "[t]here is no way to eliminate the emotional component of budgeting, but problems will be minimized if managers are allowed to participate in setting their budgets, if they are consulted when changes are made, and if they have every opportunity to explain unfavorable variances [such as overspending their allotted funds or failing to achieve the sales goals the expenditure of those funds was expected to attain]."[3]

A psychological climate inimical to rational decisions about advertising budgeting may develop when a company has all the business it can handle—or at least all the business it can handle efficiently at the moment. In such a situation, the management may well "see an opportunity to move money from the advertising expense column into the profit column."[4] But advertising has a cumulative effect. Done when business is good, it lays the groundwork for future business. Advertising done only when the store needs business may be advertising that is too little and too late.

Some advertisers also tend to throttle back on the ad budget during a business recession. They look on advertising "as a business expense rather than an investment," and slash it when there is an economic slump.[5] Historical studies of groups of firms with consistently high ad budgets and others that cut their ad funds in times of prosperity or recession show, however, that

> [t]he firms which are willing to invest the most dollars for advertising are more able to ward off the effects of recession and to rebound from

them. . . . [A]lso . . . firms with liberal advertising budgets and policies tend to grow faster than those with more restricted policies. Finally, . . . though advertising expenditures and sales do not show a perfect correlation, . . . the most liberal advertisers usually experience the fastest growth in sales.[6]

A compatible series of studies of ad expenditures by companies in basic industries, including the recessions of 1949, 1954, 1958, 1961, and 1970, all confirmed this point: the cut budget was associated each time with moderately lower sales during years of poor business and with dramatically poorer sales during years immediately following recessions. More significantly yet, the budget-cutting companies during the 1968 to 1973 period also experienced significantly poorer net income (profits), thus taking into account the cost of sustained advertising by those that did not cut ad budgets so severely. By 1973, the companies that continued advertising at levels the same or higher than before the slump reported a 76 percent gain in net income over the last prerecession year (1968), while those that did cut their ads in the two worst years of the recession reported only a 30 percent improvement in net income.[7]

2 Methods of Budgeting for Advertising

While there are fifteen or twenty loosely-defined "methods" of arriving at an advertising budget (even including "what's the competition doing?" and "how much money have we available to spend?"), we shall deal here only with two commonly used systems, the *percentage-of-sales* and the *objective-and-task* methods.

THE PERCENTAGE-OF-SALES METHOD

This method has been the most popular method of budgeting for advertising for many decades, among both retailers and other types of advertisers, but its preeminence has been challenged in recent years. Essentially, the percentage-of-sales method is a passive budgeting approach. It denies the whole idea of advertising as a *dynamic management tool* whereby the *goals* of a business can be achieved. It relates advertising directly—indeed, mathematically—to the dollar volume of business done by the firm in the *past*, the dollar volume of business estimated for the *coming period*, or the dollar volume of business done by *other stores*.

How does a retailer using this method of budgeting determine what percentage of his sales revenues to devote to advertising? One way is to examine the *average* advertising-to-sales ratios reported by trade associations, trade magazines, and government agencies and use a figure equal to or near the average for the store's trade line. Another way to determine the percentage figure is to find out what the store invested in advertising last year (or, more rationally, what its average advertising investment was over the past three or five years), express this amount as a percentage of sales, and adopt that figure.

Uses of the Percentage-of-Sales System Many experts find so little merit in this method of allocating advertising dollars that they point to its utter simplicity as its chief advantage. Anyone who has mastered grade-school arithmetic can handle it. Nevertheless, comparing the ratio of advertising expenditures to sales for different trade lines can be useful in judging the best allotments of ad funds among departments of a large store. In addition, facts about the emphasis placed on advertising by other specialty stores can help establish guidelines for managers of smaller stores.

The percentage-of-sales system is useful for large chains with widely scattered stores. For the corporation as a whole, a tightly controlled advertising budget that is a constant percentage of sales makes sense, though the funds allotted to individual stores may vary greatly. A certain large variety-store chain operates with an overall ad budget equal to 1.5 percent of sales; its individual stores' budgets range from around .5 percent to well above 2 percent. A women's specialty chain based in the Midwest functions profitably with an advertising-to-sales ratio of 2 percent in its home area, 4 percent in outlying markets, and a little under 3 percent for the corporation as a whole. A nursery and garden-products retailer moves masses of merchandise profitably at advertising costs equal to 3 percent of sales in its home city, 4.5 percent overall, and as much as 13 percent when it is breaking into a new metropolitan area with many better-known competitors.

Average percentages may well serve as a *floor,* below which no progressive, forward-looking business would want to set its budget, or as a base-point for a new business with little knowledge of its market and only *estimated* sales figures to work with.

Sources of Advertising Percentages Lists of ratios of advertising to sales can be found in an annual tabulation, "Percentage of Sales Invested in Advertising," derived from an analysis of corporate tax returns by the IRS and last printed in the October 20, 1975, issue of *Advertising Age.* Ratios for retail businesses can also be found in *Expenses in Retail Business,* a booklet published at intervals by the Marketing Services Division of the National Cash Register Company, Dayton, Ohio 45409. Trade associations and trade magazines also supply figures for particular trade lines.

However, "average" figures for the percentage of sales invested in retail advertising should not be taken too seriously. Even estimates from the most respectable and impartial sources, reported in the *same* magazine (also known for its impartiality and integrity), were, for the same recent year, almost three-quarters of a percentage point apart: *1.51* percent versus *2.21* percent. Translated into cash terms for particular stores, this can mean a difference of thousands of dollars in the ad budget.

The differences among trade lines are incomparably greater. Figures range from as low as about .5 percent for many to as high as about 5 percent for others—*ten times* as much, on the average, for lines traditionally committed to heavy advertising as opposed to those typically using proportionally less advertising. Among individual stores whose reports are combined to create averages, the differences are wider still. Some report no advertising at all, or miniscule figures like .01 percent, while others in the same table report expenditures of 10, 12, or even 15 percent of sales.

Examples of *low-budget* trade lines, with advertising expenditures ranging from .8 to 1.5 percent of sales, include auto dealers, bakeries, building materials dealers, farm supply stores, food stores, service stations, taverns, and children's and infants'-wear shops. Others with ratios of advertising to sales well below the overall average are beauty shops, book stores, confectioneries, custom tailors, hardware stores, insurance agents, liquor stores, and paint and wallpaper stores.

Relatively *high-budget* retail advertisers include department stores, with ratios ranging from 2.4 to 3.8 percent, movie theaters, and sporting goods stores. Other "high" spenders are camera shops, *large* dry cleaners, *large* floor coverings stores, florists, furniture stores, hotels and motels, jewelry stores, laundries, photo studios, real estate agents, shoe stores, specialty stores, and toy dealers.[8]

There are enough contradictions among different reporting sources, and enough fuzzy definitions of the kinds of store included in each category, to shake the perfectionist's confidence in the whole idea of basing his budget on that of the elusive "average" store. For example, the NCR booklet mentioned above is based mostly on surveys by national retail trade associations composed largely of small, independent merchants—which in turn are based on very small samples drawn from those who choose to respond to questionnaires. The IRS figures published by *Advertising Age* derive from *corporation* income

tax returns and exclude the hundreds of thousands of stores organized as sole proprietorships or partnerships.

Limitations of the Percentage-of-Sales Method

1. It puts the cart before the horse. It bases *advertising on sales,* ignoring the fact that *sales derive* (in part, at least) *from advertising.*

2. It *looks back* rather than forward. It assumes that the percentage appropriate *a year or two ago* is appropriate for a *future* budgeting period.

3. If an "average" industry ratio of advertising to sales is used, it may be all wrong for a particular store. An average is simply the product one obtains by adding a long list of widely disparate figures, then dividing the sum by the number of figures on the list. Many profitable stores may have a substantially higher or an appreciably lower ratio. Industry averages also include (and tend to be *reduced by*) stores which do *no* advertising, some of which may be about to fail for lack of customers or in the process of being bought out by more aggressive competitors.

4. An undue fascination with averages or with past ratios may cause a small independent store to give up one of its main advantages over the larger chain-store competitors and the big discount houses: *flexibility* in adjusting to rapid changes in local market conditions.

5. The percentage-of-sales method fails to recognize rising advertising costs; using the same ratio of advertising to sales as in a prior year may actually result in a store's doing *less* advertising than was really intended.

6. If the ad budget is based on a sales

forecast that is too optimistic, the store may end up *overspending* early in the year and face a drought of funds for important promotions during the peak end-of-year season.

The writers of some of the country's best texts on advertising have issued some pretty sobering warnings about the shortcomings of the percentage-of-sales advertising budgeting habit. They say, for example,

> [It] leads to unreasoned imitation . . . influences stores to match blindly the expenditures of other stores . . . induces a shortsighted one-sidedness. [Its] use . . . is strongly discouraged.[9]

> [It] is illogical because it assumes that advertising is a result of sales rather than a cause. . . . It makes no allowance for the possibility that sales may decline because of too little advertising. . . . There is a large variation in the productivity of advertising at different levels of operation; so it is entirely possible that the return on extra advertising expenditure[s] may diminish, rather than increase, after a certain level of sales has been reached. . . . A company that uses [a] percentage of past sales may underspend when the potential is great and overspend when the potential is low.[10]

> The [percentage-of-sales method and others] are not necessarily opportunity oriented. . . . Conditions are constantly changing. By basing expenditures upon past experiences (either past sales or a percentage of sales that was established under past conditions), the retailer may not take full advantage of future changes and opportunities.[11]

> . . . if the budget is specified as a certain percentage of projected sales, and this ratio . . . is simply an arbitrary figure used uncritically year after year, the presumed cause-and-effect relationship between advertising and market response is reversed.

> Advertising, like any other element of the marketing mix, can be viewed as an independent variable— a factor the company can control for the purpose of accomplishing something. The "something"—sales or other desired market reaction—is the dependent variable—the hoped-for result of the marketing stimulus. But when advertising expenditure is rigidly or arbitrarily fixed as a ratio to projected sales, it is *determined* by sales, rather than being treated as something that helps determine *them*.

> . . . most companies tend to guard against the possibility of an advertising/sales ratio hardening into an inflexible budget determinant that replaces analysis and judgment, and threatens to make the company a prisoner of habit.[12]

THE PREFERRED METHOD: OBJECTIVE-AND-TASK BUDGETING

If a retailer does not use the percentage-of-sales method (or some other method with even less to recommend it), how *can* a store's advertising budget be established?

A consensus of informed opinion and the trend of the times point to the objective-and-task-method—sometimes referred to simply as the *objective method* or the *task method*. This system has received nearly unanimous approval from opinion leaders and the most successful practitioners of both advertising and retailing. It is being increasingly accepted throughout American industry, where *management by objectives* permeates the executive outlook.

No more lucid and concise statement of this budgeting method can be found than that of Delbert J. Duncan of the University of California, Charles S. Phillips of Bates College in Maine, and Stanley C. Hollander of Michigan State University, authors of an all-time classic volume on retail management:

> In deciding how much money to spend for advertising during a given period [the retailer] should (1) analyze his situation carefully, (2) define his objectives, (3) decide upon the methods he will follow in attaining these objectives, and (4) set aside the money required—provided he can afford to do so.[13]

How to Use Objective-and-Task Budgeting In this advertising budgeting method, the advertising appropriation is built up in successive steps. The process starts with *identifying the "target" customers* in a market, the *position of the store* in the retail complex, and *the role of advertising* in the store's total marketing concept. These topics were dealt with in depth in Part 1.

Out of these steps emerges a set of *objectives*. There may be just two or three, or the list may run to dozens. Some objectives originally proposed may be weeded out: the impractical ones, those least likely to contribute to the growth of sales or profits, and the ones the store is not quite ready to tackle. Those objectives finally assigned to advertising define the advertising *tasks* for the budgeting period. Other objectives may be assigned to public relations or sales; still others may be sought by physically remodeling the store or altering merchandise and service policies.

The tasks assigned to advertising will almost always include the day-to-

day *catalog*, or *item-price*, promotion of proven traffic-builders and profit-makers. Not all advertising tasks are exotic, innovative, or "creative."

The next step for the retailer is to estimate, roughly, the probable costs of the advertising needed to accomplish the firm's objectives. Space, time, and production costs and the cost of incidentals are tabulated and totaled. Their sum, if the store can afford it, is the advertising budget. If the proposed budget is too high, the list of advertising tasks for the period must be trimmed down, perhaps by postponing the pursuit of one or two objectives or trying to accomplish them in some other way. It is better to focus on fewer tasks and do them really well than to make across-the-board cuts and try to do too much with too little. Table 5–3 shows some typical advertising objectives for a small store and a hypothetical trial budget.

What would happen if, after the trial budget was drawn up, the store found that its tax rates for the coming year had increased, the cost of remodeling for the boutique was exceeding estimates, merchandise appealing to older residents would not soon be fully stocked, and new surveys by the local newspaper and AM radio stations indicated that new apartment residents were being reached quickly through those media as they moved in? To conserve cash to meet its higher tax and remodeling expenses, the store might reexamine its advertising objectives. Perhaps the last two are less important than they originally seemed and could be postponed; perhaps, too, the reserve fund could be trimmed a little. The store's appropriation then might be as shown in Table 5–4.

Table 5–3

Advertising Objectives and Trial Budget for a Small Store

Objectives	Estimated Cost
1. Hold normal share of regular trade (via weekly promotional ads in town's principal newspaper)	$5,000
2. Reinforce seasonal promotions and clearances (via bulk-rate radio spots on two AM stations)	1,800
3. Promote new youth boutique to be opened midyear (via ads in college and high school newspapers; six-months' budget)	400
4. Attract residents of new apartment complex in nearby suburb (via series of "welcome" letters)	125
5. Increase traffic of elderly and retired persons (via sponsorship of health-care programs on FM radio)	1,300
Trial Budget Total for Specific Objectives	**8,625**
Reserve for Unforeseen Uses	875
Total Trial Budget	**$9,500**

Evaluating the "Pros and Cons" Puts Objective-Task Budgeting on Top Among the manifold advantages of this progressive budgeting method are its

1. flexibility (both in concept and application).

2. forward-looking, rather than backward-glancing, orientation.

3. propensity to force management to think carefully about what its advertising is expected to do. This results not only in a more potent advertising effort, but often in better overall planning for the business as a whole.

4. correct concept of advertising as a tool for generating sales and profits.

5. tendency to force management to solve, in advance and rationally, the twin problems of media choice and copy themes. Since this method of budgeting starts with determining specific tasks for advertising to accomplish, these basic decisions have been made on functional grounds long before a detailed campaign has been developed.

6. focus on making profits through pleasing people. This is the most significant advantage for this is, after all, what retailing is all about.

Table 5–4

Final Advertising Objectives and Budget for a Small Store

Objectives	Estimated Cost
1. Hold normal share of regular trade	$5,000
2. Reinforce seasonal promotions and clearances	1,800
3. Promote new youth boutique	400
Final Promotional Budget for Specific Objectives	**7,200**
Reserve	800
Total Final Budget	**$8,000**

Although the advantages of objective-and-task budgeting far outweigh its limitations, the following objections are sometimes raised:

1. It requires more effort and more judgment on the part of management than mechanical budgeting methods.
2. It can lead to overspending if the goals set for advertising are wildly overoptimistic or if the firm tries to accomplish too many objectives when prudence would dictate seeking a few at a time.
3. It is difficult to predict precisely the results (in terms of sales) of any given investment in promotion.

However, with respect to this last point, research is finding ways to narrow the limits of error, and retail management is becoming increasingly capable of applying and interpreting such research. Better record-keeping due to EDP is also shortening the amount of time needed to reach valid conclusions about advertising effectiveness.

Authorities such as those quoted earlier in the chapter who reject the once-popular percentage-of-sales method are nearly unanimous in endorsing the objective method as the preferred alternative. Others also endorse this view. John Crawford, dean of the School of Journalism at the University of Oregon and formerly vice president of a leading advertising agency, calls the objective method "the one method receiving the most attention by forward-looking advertising people." [14] David Hurwood and James Brown of the Conference Board note that

> [A] growing number of companies are giving emphasis to an approach in which advertising needs are carefully analyzed in a broad context; i.e., marketing objectives are spelled out, the role of advertising in the marketing program is defined, and funds are appropriated in accordance with the best knowledge or estimate (based on experience and/or research) of the amount of money needed for advertising to do its assigned job. [15]

And according to John Burke, vice president of Compton Advertising,

> The task method, although it requires the most marketing sophistication and the most budget preparation time, is recommended to national and retail advertisers alike. [16]

3 How Much Is "Too Much" Advertising?

Whatever budgeting method is used, a retailer eventually comes up against this key question: How must *at the very most* can this store profitably invest in advertising? The objective-and-task method leads directly to this question, since its basic premise is that a firm should invest every penny in promotion that will pay for itself and increase profits—no more and no less!

Advertising can, *up to a point,* return rich rewards. Table 5–5 shows the effect on *profits of succeeding increments* of advertising, *assuming all other factors remain constant.* Increased advertising is the *only* variable in this hypothetical situation. The store is operating at a *loss* when only $20,000 is invested in advertising; its total expenses (including, of course, the cost of the merchandise purchased for resale)

Table 5-5

The Return on Advertising Investment: A Hypothetical Case

		(1)	(2)	(3)	(4)	(5)	(6)	(7)
Sales Volume		$690,000	$940,000	$1,050,000	$1,120,000	$1,150,000	$1,150,000	$1,150,000
Less Cost of Merchandise (65 percent of sales)		448,500	611,000	682,500	728,000	747,500	747,500	747,500
Gross Profit Margin (35 percent of sales)		**241,500**	**329,000**	**367,500**	**392,000**	**402,500**	**402,500**	**402,500**
Expenses								
Fixed expenses	$	150,000	150,000	150,000	150,000	150,000	150,000	150,000
	%	21.74	15.96	14.29	13.40	13.04	13.04	13.04
Variable expenses								
Advertising	$	20,000	30,000	40,000	50,000	60,000	70,000	80,000
	%	2.89	3.19	3.81	4.46	5.22	6.08	6.96
Other	$	82,800	112,800	126,000	134,400	138,000	138,000	138,000
	%	12.00	12.00	12.00	12.00	12.00	12.00	12.00
Total variable expenses	$	102,800	142,800	166,000	184,400	198,000	208,000	218,000
	%	14.89	15.19	15.81	16.46	17.22	18.09	18.95
Total expenses	$	**252,800**	**292,800**	**316,000**	**334,400**	**348,000**	**358,000**	**368,000**
	%	**36.63**	**31.15**	**30.10**	**29.86**	**30.26**	**31.13**	**32.00**
Net Profit		**(−11,300)**	**36,200**	**51,500**	**57,600**	**54,500**	**44,500**	**34,500**
	%	—	3.85	4.90	5.14	4.74	3.87	3.00

Note: All expenses and profits are reported in dollars and as a percentage of sales.

Source: Adapted from Charles M. Edwards, Jr., and Russell A. Brown, *Retail Advertising and Sales Promotion* (Englewood Cliffs, N.J.: Prentice-Hall, Inc., 1959), p. 100.

are more than its total revenues from sales. Something must be done, and management decides to increase the advertising budget by 50 percent—to $30,000. The added promotion creates a spectacular increase in the store's gross profit margin. (For the purposes of this example, we shall assume that variable expenses other than advertising increase proportionally with sales; that is, they remain 12 percent of sales no matter what the sales figures are. In actuality, variable expenses rarely increase as rapidly as sales, so in a real-life situation the increase in the gross margin is likely to be even greater than it is here.)

If an added $10,000 in advertising changes an $11,300 loss into a $36,200 profit, should the store increase the advertising budget still more? Management thinks so and raises the advertising investment to $40,000, a 33 percent increase. Again, the results are happy, but they are not as dramatic as before. The sales volume increases somewhat more modestly, as does the gross margin. The store's profit again increases; it is now 4.90 percent of sales instead of 3.85 percent, and the store has $15,300 more in its bank account than it had at the end of the preceding budgetary period. When still more money is put into advertising, the sales volume, gross margin, and net profits increase again, but only slightly, while the store's advertising *costs* rise to 4.46 percent of sales.

Management is so pleased with the results of its advertising that it adds still another $10,000 to the ad budget, bringing it up to $60,000, or three times what it was at the beginning. Now, however, though the store's sales do rise, they do not rise sufficiently to compensate for the increase in advertising costs, other variable expenses, and the cost of mer-

chandise. The store's profit actually *drops* by $3,100, even though its sales have increased by $30,000. Advertising has reached its *point of diminishing returns.* Maximum profits were obtained with $50,000 of advertising. This was enough to coax practically every potential customer in the store's market area to come in and buy merchandise. The added $10,000 did not pay its way! If management was unaware of this leveling-off process, or if it wanted to gamble and try the effect of spending still another $10,000 for ads, it would discover that there would be *no* further increase in sales and the whole of the added $10,000 in advertising was an *expense* that had to be deducted from profits. Still further spending for advertising would start the store back toward the point of *negative profits.*

One reason increased advertising so often pays off in higher profits, up to a point, is this: fixed expenses remain the same regardless of the number of customers or how much they buy. Therefore, fixed expenses become a *declining proportion of total income* as sales increase, compensating in whole or in part for the increasing proportion of sales revenues allotted to promotion. In addition, as has been pointed out, variable expenses actually do not increase as rapidly as sales, still further increasing the opportunity for profit as ads bring in more sales. Even the cost of merchandise purchased for resale may decline as a percentage of sales.

MARGINAL ANALYSIS

To determine the most profitable advertising expenditure for *any* business, one must analyze the *marginal* (or *hard-to-get, extra*) *sales* that can be, should be, or have been generated as a direct or indirect result of *marginal* (*extra* or *better*) *advertising*. One can then determine, through research or trial and error or a combination of both (plus judgment) just how far it pays to go.

Marginal analysis is explained in scholarly but lucid terms by David Hurwood and James Brown of the Conference Board:

> ... to maximize profitability, money should be spent on advertising ..., once the break-even point is passed, until the last dollar spent brings in one additional dollar of *revenue;* or, in the terminology of economics, until the marginal cost ... of advertising equals the marginal revenue ... it produces. [A smaller] advertising budget ... is not optimal, because ... an additional dollar spent on advertising will yield more than an additional dollar of revenue. [A larger] advertising budget ... is not optimal, because the last dollar spent on advertising will result in less than an extra dollar of revenue. ...[17]

Hurwood and Brown observe that retailers are foremost among the types of firms that have been generally able to apply marginal analysis to advertising decisions.[18]

A simple example of marginal analysis is presented in Table 5–6. The analysis is based on three simplifying assumptions:

1. advertising is the only element of the marketing mix in which a change is being considered;
2. sales revenue is revenue net of all nonadvertising costs (i.e., the amount left for the store after the cost of merchandise, fixed expenses, and variable expenses other than advertising have been deducted); and
3. advertising must be purchased in units of $50 (because of the price of minimum-sized ads in local newspapers and the minimum charge for a broadcast or billboard ad in the store's community).

Table 5–6 shows the records kept by a small, hypothetical retail store during a period in which it took pains to trace the results of its advertising to determine the most profitable level of advertising. Starting with no ads at all, the store added $50 to its advertising budget each week for an extended period to test the effect on sales. Means were devised to separate new sales stimulated by the increased advertising (column 4) from the total sales (column 3). The last two columns of the table give the store's total profit and the added profit each week attributable to the extra (marginal) advertising.

How much should the store allot for advertising in the future, assuming that there is no change in its overall marketing situation? An inspection of the table, in particular column 5 (total profit), provides the answer: $300. Spending this amount for advertising produces the greatest total profit for the store: $310. The marginal profit produced by the final $50 of ads is $10. If further advertising could be purchased for less than $50, the store could profitably increase its ad budget until its *marginal* profit fell to zero (or one cent short of zero!). In no case would it increase its ad budget beyond $350, since this would cause its total profit to drop to $300. Instead of a marginal *profit,* it would have a marginal *loss.*

What happens toward the lower end of the scale of advertising investment is also important. There is an advertising effectiveness *threshold.* When ads are too few and too small, they have *no* effect on sales whatsoever, and *all* the money spent on them is wasted. It takes a certain minimum amount of advertising to get any action at all. For the store in Table 5–6, spending $50 a week on ads is useless. Even when the advertising budget is raised to $100, nothing results but a bigger loss. An ad investment of $150 produces neither a profit nor a loss; the store merely breaks even. It takes an ad budget of at least $200 per week to bring in enough extra business to pay for the ads *and* add to the store's profits.

At the other extreme, continued overspending for advertising can wipe out all the store's profits. With an ad budget of $350 or more, total profits begin to shrink. Spending $650 for advertising produces a marginal deficit of $250 that wipes out all the profits ac-

crued as a result of the former, more moderate levels of advertising, leaving the store in the same profitless condition it was in originally.

In real life, the point of diminishing profitability given increasing increments of advertising is usually not reached as quickly as it might appear from theoretical models and tables. The reason is a *lag* in the effect of advertising and the *carryover effect* of much advertising. Every ad run by a store may (and usually does) open up a stream of business that continues over a period of time, not just a single burst of business that can easily and unmistakably be attributed to the ad. Each day, each week, and each month, *some* business comes in as a result of ads in previous periods. This tends to sustain a store in a profitable

Table 5–6

Marginal Analysis: Alternative Advertising Levels and Associated Sales and Profits

(1) Total Advertising Investment	(2) Marginal Advertising Expense	(3) Total Store Sales	(4) Marginal Sales (due to extra ads)	(5) Total Profit (3 − 1)	(6) Marginal Profit Produced by Final Increment of Advertising (4 − 2)
0	—	0	—	0	—
$ 50	$ 50	0	0	− $ 50	− $ 50
100	50	$ 25	$ 25	− 75	− 25
150	50	150	125	0	75
200	50	400	250	200	200
250	50	550	150	300	100
300	50	610	60	310	10
350	50	650	40	300	− 10
400	50	650	0	250	− 50
.	.	.	.	.	.
.	.	.	.	.	.
.	.	.	.	.	.
650	250	650	0	0	− 250

Source: Adapted from Edward Hurwood and James Brown, *Some Guidelines for Advertising Budgeting* (New York: The Conference Board, 1972), p. 16.

condition even after advertising reaches its point of diminishing returns. Even though the store in Table 5–6 realized no profits with ad budgets from $50 to $150, it is quite possible that *after* a long period of advertising at the optimal level it could then cut back its ad budget to those levels and continue to prosper for a while. Sales might continue at a high level due to the momentum of the earlier ad campaign, the lagged effect of good-sized ads for products with a long buying season, and the acquisition of new steady customers from those attracted by previous ads. Eventually, of course, the store would revert to its original unprofitable condition, just as a top will eventually quit spinning or a toboggan sliding down a hill onto a level plain will sooner or later come to a standstill.

Now let's see graphically, using Figure 5–1 and Table 5–7, how the most profitable advertising level for a small store is determined. During one week in the late spring, its annual peak season, South Side Hardware Store is trying to increase its market penetration for one product line: power lawn mowers. It is assumed that 70 new mowers might possibly be sold in the community as a whole during the week. Prospective buyers may be classified into seven groups, A through G, in order of their likelihood to buy a mower and to buy it from South Side Hardware. Ten possible purchasers are in each group. The prospect groups are as follows:

A Close relatives of the owners of South Side Hardware living anywhere in the larger community; immediate neighbors of the store and fellow businesspersons in the same shopping strip; long-time charge customers; enthusiasts for the brand of mower featured by South Side Hardware (which has an exclusive franchise); persons whose old mowers have just broken down who have tall grass needing immediate attention.

B Residents of the South Side and its adjacent suburbs who have bank credit cards recognized by the store (and so advertised by it); their old mowers are becoming balky and hard-starting and do a poor job of cutting grass.

C Residents of the entire city and its surrounding suburbs who often travel to the South Side for shopping and other business and personal errands, who are affluent and not concerned with price or credit, and who are conscious of the brand of mower sold by South Side Hardware because of reading its ads; their present mowers are serviceable but too small for easy cutting of their predominantly larger lawns.

D Residents of North, East, and West sides of the community who usually shop near home and who have each just received a "windfall" (a raise, a bonus, or a larger-than-expected dividend on an investment); they have faulty mowers showing signs of decay, and each is ashamed because neighbors have newer, better machines.

E Residents of North, East, and West sides who are very loyal to stores in their own neighborhoods; they have old but smooth-running mowers and would someday like larger machines with improvements such as those exclusively on the brand of mower sold at South Side Hardware.

F Residents of the entire larger community who have recently experienced financial reverses such as reductions in salary, prolonged layoffs, and unexpectedly large medical bills due to family illnesses; they possess mowers in good working order.

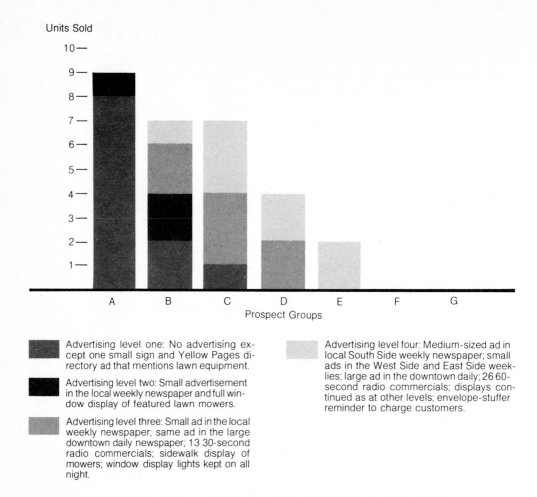

Figure 5–1 How the Most Profitable Advertising Level for a Small Store Is Determined

Table 5–7

Profit Margins at Various Advertising Levels by South Side Hardware Store

	Advertising Expenditure Level			
	1	**2**	**3**	**4**
Total Number of Units Sold	11	14	21	29
Total Gross Margin @ $40 Each	$440	$560	$840	$1160
Less **Cost of Advertising**		40	205	610
Net Margin after Advertising Cost	440	520	635	550
Less **Sales at Level 1 without Advertising Cost**		440	440	440
Net Increase in Gross Profit due to Advertising		80	195	110

At advertising expenditure level one, with no special expenses being entailed for ads to promote lawn mowers, our store does well with group A and makes a few more or less accidental sales to groups B and C. The store's profit on those 11 sales is $440. At level two, inexpensive local-area advertising brings in three additional buyers, one from group A (thus virtually exhausting the potential for sales to that group) and two from group B. Net profit, after advertising costs, increases by $80.

The proprietor of the store, seeking still more sales, now expands the store's effective trading area for mowers through more widespread advertising. At level three, the store deepens its penetration of its prime (neighborhood) market by increasing sales to group B, and it pulls some marginal sales from the city as a whole as it sells mowers to more people from group C and even draws buyers from group D. These additional sales more than pay for the advertising costs, so that the total profit now rises to $635.

Since advertising worked so well at level three, the store believes it might do even better with still larger, harder-hitting ads reaching the entire community, so it goes "all out" in advertising the mowers. However, it becomes increasingly difficult to motivate people who live so far away and have so little incentive to come to this store for this particular make of mower, and the *law of diminishing returns* defeats the merchant's well-intentioned plan. The additional sales drawn by the advertising at level four are not enough to compensate for the costs of the advertising. Net additional profit falls to less than it was at the previous level. The store finds that it does not pay to spend money on more ads that do not reach enough really good prospects. The same kind of thing happens in all kinds of stores every week and every day. The proper level of advertising is in reality determined by customers and their needs.

How much *should* South Side Hardware allot to its advertising? Some figure, as yet unknown, that is more than $40 (level two) and less than $610 (level four). It is probably somewhere near $205 (level three). Further experimentation and research by the store will determine the correct amount.

JUDGING "HIGH" VERSUS "LOW" ADVERTISING ALLOTMENTS

Regardless of a given merchant's method of determining the promotional budget (the objective-and-task method, the percentage-of-sales method, or some other variation), and irrespective of the amount of research done or the EDP data available, a substantial amount of *judgment* must ultimately be brought to bear on *any* advertising appropriation decision. One can list certain factors that logically support either a "high" or a "low" ad expenditure: *high* or *low*, that is, relative to (1) last year's ad costs, (2) the ad budget of another store in the same chain or group, (3) the ad expenditures of the trade line or industry's "average" store, or (4) the ad budget of a similar store in the same town.

After setting up a trial budget, it is wise to evaluate it in terms of this list, putting a *plus* after each item that supports a large ad budget, a *minus* after each item that argues for a low budget, and a *zero* if a particular factor is irrelevant.

Some factors that should be considered are discussed briefly below.

The Position of Advertising and Its Goals in the Store's Basic Promotional Policy If a store maintains a highly skilled sales force, if its in-store and window displays are of superior quality, and if it features exceptionally liberal policies regarding returns, alterations, service, and warranties, it is likely to be a *high-expense operation.* It probably has less money available for advertising than a store with opposite characteristics, but it also has less *need* for ads. Its costly sales force, displays, and customer services will buy some of the same things advertising might be expected to produce: impulse sales, tie-in sales, repeat sales, long-range customer loyalty, and effective word-of-mouth "advertising" by satisfied customers. Such a store may safely operate with a subnormal ad budget, since it has elected to depend more heavily on alternate means of stimulating sales.

The Amount, Quality, and Effectiveness of Manufacturers' Advertising If most of a retailer's merchandise is heavily promoted in the makers' national advertising, a lot of people in the store's trading area will be presold. The advertising battle will be fought, to a substantial degree, by the manufacturers; the dealer need only establish his or her particular store as the place for those people to buy their products—and to buy them *now,* at stated prices, and on given terms. This is particularly true of retailers dealing exclusively or largely in the products of a franchisor—car dealerships, gas stations, and many fast-food restaurants. Many manufacturers reinforce their national advertising with dealer aids to stimulate point-of-purchase sales and with cooperative ad allowances to beef up retailers' ads. Stores so favored may well find a modest local ad budget sufficient. On the other hand, stores dealing chiefly in nonbrand or less-advertised merchandise will have to carry far more of the ad burden themselves (though they may enjoy a higher markup on what they sell).

The Length of Time the Store Has Been in the Area A new store in a community must "overadvertise" initially. It must lure traffic with advertising until it has become established and developed a core of repeat customers. An old rule of thumb among retailers says that to get a new store going one must invest the equivalent of one year's normal profits in *extra* advertising. In effect, the store must run for a year with no profit, or for two years at half the normal profit, or for three years at one-third the normal profit, so that it can "overadvertise" for the introductory period. A new department in an existing store, a new merchandise line, or a new service must also be heavily advertised at first.

The Location of the Store Location can have a great bearing on the need for advertising. A store in a high-traffic site adjacent to municipal parking in a busy downtown area or in a lively suburban mall that conducts frequent traffic-building promotions and is "anchored" by several heavy advertisers will be able to get along with less advertising than normal. Its windows and its sign will do much of the job. Conversely, a merchant on an out-of-the-way street will need to do considerable advertising to compensate for this disadvantage.

The Nature of the Market If many people in an area are highly mobile— vacationers or college students, perhaps —a store there is *always* a "new" store to a large proportion of prospective customers. It must, therefore, put a heavier emphasis on advertising than similar stores in areas with large settled populations. If a neighborhood has gone downhill and a store's best customers have moved to suburban or "exurban" areas, its advertising must have enough long-range pulling power to keep them coming back to the store. This is especially true if the less affluent families now living in the neighborhood, who may be reached less expensively, cannot afford to buy enough merchandise at a normal markup to make the store prosper.

The Physical Nature of the Trading Area Major rivers or lakes, mountain ranges, and nearby state lines can cause a trading area to have an unnatural shape, unlike the typical and more easily cultivated "roundish" trading zone. New traffic arteries, the creation of new shopping centers, and the renovation of downtown areas in nearby towns can also force a store to advertise more heavily and alter definitions of what makes a good location.

The Media Available and Their Rates The *fewer* and *better* the newspapers, broadcasting stations, and other media available, the less costly it is for merchants to deliver their advertising messages squarely on target. An overabundance of media, none of which is dominant, makes it more costly to obtain

effective market coverage. Like fish in an overstocked pond, media in such a situation tend to be small and weak. Their audiences frequently overlap, and their rates per page or per minute are invariably high in relation to the amount of sales they generate.

The Competition: A Critical Factor An ad budget that served a store well in the past may have to be doubled if a new store opens up across the street.

The Effect of Business Cycles on the Trading Area Historically, it costs more per dollar of sales to promote merchandise during hard times than in periods of prosperity. Advertising must work harder when sales and dollars are difficult to come by.

The Perishability of the Store's Merchandise How fast a retailer's stock loses value also affects its need for advertising. The produce department of a supermarket whose refrigeration system goes dead during a July hot spell has a lot in common with the high-fashion apparel shop facing a sudden switch in customers' moods that leaves "dated" items clogging its shelves as a season draws to its end. In both cases, some quick and hefty advertising expenditures may save the day. Neither soggy cantaloupes nor passing fads in clothing can be held over, and extra advertising to sell them before they become distress merchandise may be the lesser of two evils from a profit standpoint.

The Size of the Store and the Variety of Merchandise Carried A big and growing store with diverse departments may need to reach out with its ads to people with varying lifestyles, tastes, and buying habits in order to keep all departments equally busy and profitable. A smaller store that is diversifying the goods and services it offers for sales may also need to cultivate different target audiences. Investing extra ad dollars to reach customers in neighboring communities or to motivate selected market segments may be a wise idea. On the other hand, a neighborhood specialty store offering a single line of merchandise may make attractive profits with substantially less advertising that reaches a sharply defined, homogeneous group of nearby customers. Consider the floral shop in a major hotel or the restaurant selling before- and after-shift snacks to workers at a factory across the street. Both have virtually a captive market.

WHAT IS AN ADVERTISING EXPENSE AND WHAT IS NOT

One final problem faces many advertisers: finding a workable definition of the word *advertising* itself!

Very large department and specialty stores, according to the National Retail Merchants Association, usually have a *sales promotion budget* that is different from but includes their *advertising budget*. Sales promotion expenditures may equal as much as $3^1/_2$ percent of large department stores' sales and over 4 percent of large specialty stores' volume. Their advertising costs are likely to cluster around $2^3/_4$ percent. The difference represents the cost of activities that stimulate sales and build goodwill. Although these activities may be related to

advertising, their cost is *not* considered an advertising expense.

Small stores typically lump all sales-stimulating activities into one budget or charge the nonadvertising portion to a general catchall account. This is one of the reasons comparing advertising costs among stores is difficult.

Many people confuse sales promotion, public relations, and advertising expenses. There will never be complete agreement on which is which, but a few guidelines can be helpful.

Legitimate advertising expenses include the payroll of the store's advertising staff (if any); the cost of space, time, and production materials for media ads; professional fees paid to outside consultants, survey specialists, and advertising agencies; printing and postage for direct-mail ads; the cost of supplies and materials used in the production of advertising; the cost of outside services such as the production of TV or radio commercials; and the cost of travel by the advertising staff.

Some items to question if a retail ad budget seems inflated are charitable donations (even those in the form of advertising, such as "Compliments of Store XYZ" listings in garden club programs or high school yearbooks); store tours for the public or civic groups; scholarships for local school students; the cost of entertaining guests of the store; employee house organs; product (as opposed to advertising) research; sponsorship of recreational activities such as bowling and baseball; gifts of merchandise; "Help Wanted" ads in the classified section of local newspapers; and signs on store-owned vehicles.

Cooperative advertising, joint advertising by a manufacturer and retailer (and sometimes a middleman or wholesaler as well) in a local market over the store's signature, often leads to faulty accounting and budgeting procedures. The total amount invested in this kind of advertising through the store's account with the local newspaper or broadcasting station is shown on the store's books. The medium bills the store, which pays the bill but receives a rebate of a portion of the cost (usually 50 percent) from the manufacturer.

Only the *net* cost to the store properly belongs in the retailer's own ad budget. For accounting purposes, the merchant's books may show its total "advertising disbursements," a deduction for "advertising rebates from vendors," and a balance reflecting the true "net advertising expenses." A retailer that includes the vendors' portion of co-op ad funds as part of its own ad budget is only kidding itself—and watering down its real advertising investment.

Questions for Discussion

1. Assume that you are the assistant manager of a medium-sized store, destined soon to take over the active management from the person who founded the business many years ago. Your boss has counseled you that when you assume control you need not waste much time or effort on advertising but should "just give the ad manager a budget and see to it that he sticks within that figure." For what reasons should you *not* follow that advice, but, on the contrary, plan to be actively involved in many of the basic decisions affecting advertising?

2. In what ways is advertising like insurance?

3. Why is it often possible to *increase* a retailer's advertising expenses, both in dollars *and* as a percentage of sales, and increase the total net profit? Explain, using figures or a diagram.

4. Why are some retail advertising dollars wasted? What would you do, if you were the advertising manager of a store, to avoid this kind of waste?

5. Why is percentage-of-sales budgeting considered "passive" and "backward-looking"? Why may this system be of some use to retail managers even if it is not adopted as the primary means of determining the advertising appropriation?

6. Although objective-and-task budgeting is looked upon by many experts as the best system, it does have certain limitations. What are those limitations? Do you believe that its limitations (or the advantages of any other budgeting system) outweigh its advantages? Why?

7. If a store's average cost of merchandise purchased for resale was 60 percent of the selling price, how much could it afford to pay for an *extra ad* that was sure to bring in at least an extra $100 in sales?

8. If the average furniture store invests 3.1 percent of its sales revenue in advertising and you are starting a new furniture store in a low-traffic location in a town with many other such stores, will you have to have an ad budget that is a much higher percentage of your projected sales? What factors *might* allow you to suc-

ceed with an advertising appropriation equal to or only slightly higher than 3.1 percent of your sales?

Suggested Projects

1. Interview 20 people (friends, neighbors, classmates, or relatives), and ask them (1) if they believe retailers' advertising in your community costs consumers money by adding to the prices they must pay for merchandise, (2) whether they think stores could sell goods at lower prices if there were no local ads, and (3) if they ever find advertising by stores personally useful because it saves them time, energy, or money—for example, when sales or "specials" are advertised. Then interview the managers of 10 local stores and ask them whether, in the long run, they consider their advertising an expense or an investment. Find out if they believe they know how much more profit their stores make with advertising than they might expect without it. Tabulate the replies, and do a reasonably brief report on the consensus of consumers and merchants about the usefulness and value of retail ads.

2. Go to a library where you can secure back copies of *Advertising Age* and find the latest "Percentage of Sales Invested in Advertising" report. Or obtain a copy of "Expenses in Retail Business" from the National Cash Register Company. Using data from either of these publications, construct a table or graph showing ad costs as a percentage of sales for various lines of retailing. Put the lines whose ad costs are the highest percentage of sales at the top and

those whose ad costs are a smaller percentage of sales at the bottom. Why, do you think, are there such wide differences in the ratio of advertising to sales among different trade lines?

3. Collect all the local newspaper ads of one store in your area for one calendar month; clip them from the paper and keep them in a file. Then study them. Can you determine one or more *objectives* the store evidently intended to accomplish with its ads? Go to the newspapers where the ads appeared and secure local or retail rate cards; then measure the size of the store's ads. Tabulate its frequency of advertising and its total volume of ads for the month. From this, you can calculate the store's probable rate for its newspaper ads and estimate its total advertising expenditure for the month. Draw up a statement of the store's probable advertising goals for the month, and see how important its management thought the accomplishment of those objectives was, in terms of money appropriated for newspaper ads. For this exercise, you should select a store that does a substantial amount of regular advertising.

Notes

1. John O. Whitney, "Better Results from Retail Advertising," *Harvard Business Review* (May–June 1970), pp. 112–113.

2. Laurence W. Jacobs, *Advertising and Promotion for Retailing* (Glenview, Ill.: Scott, Foresman, 1972), p. 60.

3. Charles E. Gibbons, "The Psychology of Budgeting," *Business Horizons* (June 1972), pp. 47–50.

4. John M. Trytten, "Why Advertise When You're All Booked Up?" *Sales Management* (February 19, 1973), p. 38.

5. Charles W. Hubbard, "Cut Your Advertising Budget Lately?" *Business Ideas and Facts* (Summer 1969), p. 3.

6. Ibid., p. 9.

7. *How Advertising in Recession Periods Affects Sales* (New York: The American Business Press, Inc., 1974). In addition to this booklet, historical evidence that the continuation of heavy advertising during periods of recession produces beneficial results both during and following the business slump may be found in the Hubbard article; Neil H. Borden, *The Economic Effects of Advertising* (Chicago: Richard D. Irwin, 1942), p. 716; Arno Johnson, "Selling Ourselves Out of a Slump," *Broadcasting* (February 24, 1958), p. 82; "How Does Advertising Affect Sales and Growth in Recession and Boom?" *Printer's Ink* (August 29, 1958), pp. 25–26; *How Advertising in Recession Periods Affects Sales* (New York: The American Business Press, Inc., 1974); and "Cutting Ads Costs Future Sales," *Advertising Age* (June 23, 1975), p. 34.

8. The figures reported here are approximations derived from surveys by various trade associations and reports of government agencies.

9. Charles M. Edwards, Jr., and Russell A. Brown, *Retail Advertising and Sales Promotion,* 3rd ed. (Englewood Cliffs, N.J.: Prentice-Hall, 1959), p. 91.

10. S. Watson Dunn and Arnold M. Barban, *Advertising: Its Role in Modern Marketing* (New York: Holt, Rinehart and Winston, 1974), pp. 254–255.

11. Laurence W. Jacobs, *Advertising and Promotion for Retailing,* p. 67.

12. David L. Hurwood and James K. Brown, *Some Guidelines for Advertising Budgeting* (New York: The Conference Board, 1972), pp. 7–8.

13. Delbert J. Duncan, Charles S. Phillips, and Stanley C. Hollander, *Modern Retailing Management,* 8th ed. (Homewood, Ill.: Irwin, 1972), p. 441.

14. John W. Crawford, *Advertising,* 2nd ed. (Boston: Allyn & Bacon, 1965), p. 355.

15. Hurwood and Brown, *Some Guidelines for Advertising Budgeting,* p. i.

16. John D. Burke, *Advertising in the Marketplace* (New York: McGraw-Hill, 1973), p. 201.

17. Hurwood and Brown, *Some Guidelines for Advertising Budgeting,* p. 15.

18. Ibid., p. 18.

Preview

Unplanned, hit-or-miss advertising spells failure. All stores need a goal-oriented advertising plan. Primary and secondary goals should be defined, and short- and long-term strategies constructed. Selecting specific target markets is essential for a realistic advertising plan.

A good advertising plan often starts with setting aside a reserve fund to provide flexibility. A store may also decide at the outset whether to emphasize immediate-sell ads or institutional ads. Funds may be set aside for group advertising with other stores in the same shopping center or retail district to build traffic.

Once this has been done, the advertising funds for promotional advertising must be divided among the store's several departments and/or merchandise lines, taking into account (1) the sales of each department or line; (2) the profits it generates; (3) the opportunity it provides for building store traffic; and (4) its growth potential.

Making the best advertising allotment involves (1) determining the total promotional funds available; (2) finding out the percentage of annual sales for each month in past years; (3) dividing the total available funds among the coming year's months on the basis of these percentages; (4) making necessary adjustments for months when extremely high or low sales are expected and allowing for holidays, weather, paydays, special events, and changes in the competition; and (5) considering special situations calling for "contracyclical" advertising.

A good advertiser always is alert to special situations that may force late changes in advertising plans.

Learning Goals

Chapter 6 will teach the student to establish a sound advertising plan tied to a store's overall promotional goals. It should help in understanding the aims of promotional and institutional advertising, and the reasons for a reserve fund and an allotment to build areawide traffic.

The reader should learn how to give each department or merchandise line or a store a proper share of the available funds so as to insure the highest profits and growth rate for the store as a whole. The student should master the simple but vital techniques for determining variations in potential sales during the planning period and for distributing advertising funds over time.

The student should also learn the use of planning calendars and become aware of the need for flexibility when changes in the advertising plan are occasioned by unusual or unforeseen circumstances.

6

Planning
the Advertising
Program

1 The Importance of Planning

An investment in advertising generates the greatest return if an intelligent advertising plan is developed in advance. This may seem an obvious conclusion. Who would make a trip without a road map or build a house without a blueprint? Yet retailers who would not dream of doing either of these things may tell you that they are "too busy" to think ahead about promotion. With luck, a store may get by with this kind of management, but the retailers who profit most from their ads are almost invariably those who have put the most effort into planning.

In stores where the advertising appropriation was "built up" in the first place by objective-and-task budgeting, a basic plan will have already been established. Goals will have been defined, means of accomplishing them will have been approved, and the funds needed for the program will have been earmarked for it by top management. The

ad manager's job, then, will be to refine the general plan still further, breaking down the advertising tasks into more detailed assignments, and putting the machinery in motion to get them accomplished.

If some other budgeting method such as the percentage-of-sales method was initially used to determine the advertising appropriation, the advertising department's planning at this stage will have to be more complex and time-consuming. Advertising goals will have to be defined at this point (since they were not defined before), means of attaining them suggested, and conferences held with other executives to secure management approval of the programs developed.

In either case, an *advertising plan* (simple or comprehensive, sketchy or complex, depending on the size of the operation and the diversity of its goals) should be evolved to guide the actions of advertising personnel and others involved in the advertising process throughout the budgeting period.

When advertising is planned in advance, there is adequate time for the preparation of ads, for checking for errors, and, if necessary, for the preliminary testing of merchandise appeals before a full-scale mass-media campaign is begun. Planning enables a store to keep its advertising investment in proportion to the sales that can reasonably be expected for each department and merchandise category each season, each month, and each week. It makes possible the effective coordination of advertising with buying and the preparation of displays, staffing, public relations, and other store functions without which ads seldom produce maximum results. It enables retailers to anticipate and prepare a response to new trends and events that will affect sales. It increases their chances of being able to repeat past successes and cancel out past failures. It enables a store to meet competitors' challenges more intelligently, to tie in its advertising more effectively with manufacturers' advertising, and to obtain more promotional allowances and cooperative ads from wholesalers and manufacturers.

For the smaller merchant, who must serve as his own advertising manager in addition to performing a myriad of other duties, advance planning is even more urgent than it is for the large store. By postponing planning until a week or a few days before an ad is needed, the small retailer is flirting with luck. Unpredictable interruptions that have first claim on the owner's time are the rule, not the exception, in small retailing operations. Sales representatives make unannounced calls, customers get angry about billing errors, clerks fall ill and fail to show up for work, stock fails to arrive as ordered, furnaces quit on cold days, and family duties beckon at awkward moments. A general advertising plan for the months ahead and a more specific plan for the coming weeks allow others to fill in for the absent owner-manager. His or her secretary or senior salesperson or account executives from various media can carry on. A general advertising theme has already been determined, approximate budgets have been set, tentative feature items have been selected, media contracts have been signed, and outside copy, art, and continuity services have been arranged for.

The small-store proprietor can perfect promotional plans for a coming busy season during the preceding slack season. The merchant can work on advertising for *next* month (not *this* month), unburdened by pressure. With tasks paced this way, well in advance of critical dates, the plan-oriented retailer is assured that the store's promotional blueprint will not collapse even if a week-long convention beckons or the proprietor must stay in bed with the flu or rush out to Kansas for Aunt Agatha's funeral.

Generally speaking, the larger the retail organization the farther in advance individual ads are prepared, within the framework of a long-range overall plan. A dynamic women's wear chain in the Midwest with a very professional approach to its advertising prepares newspaper ads a full month in advance, and its television commercials have a three-month lead time. The average supermarket chain's newspaper ads are planned five weeks in advance, and the layout is completed 10 or 11 days before publication. Big mass merchandisers who are increasingly using magazine-type color roto inserts in newspapers allow a three-month lead time for their preparation and distribution.

2 Advertising Goals and Strategies

Styles in marketing strategy change from time to time, just as styles in wearing apparel, home furnishings, and hairdos change. *Creativity* was considered the major determinant of advertising success during much of the 1960s. The emphasis was on finding the one creative innovation that would make a company's ads stand out from its competitors' ads and produce better results. Also important was the *image* a product or a store projected through its ads.

The recession in the 1970s made *price* an important factor in ads, as it had been during the depression thirties. *Positioning* also became a chic word among marketing people for a while. Advertising was used to establish the "position" of a given product or store vis-à-vis its competitors in the minds of consumers. Years ago, *media selection* received a great deal of attention on the *national* advertising front, especially as television came into its own. People argued for or against the proposition that the medium *was* the message. A preoccupation with media—that is, with the *channels* through which advertising messages are delivered to the consumer —became noticeable among *retail* advertisers in the early seventies. For the first time they began to experiment seriously with a broader media mix. At about the same time, the mass of new data that emerged from the 1970 census and subsequent measurements of changing demographic characteristics reinforced interest in *market segmentation*.

Much as one might wish to simplify the work of retail management by isolating one element as the key to advertising success, the fact remains that despite the shifts in emphasis on various aspects of the marketing mix, a number of factors must be taken into consideration in developing an effective advertising plan.

PRIMARY AND SECONDARY GOALS

Pinning down concrete objectives and goals is the first step in retail advertising success. The ad manager may be fortunate enough to have such goals preestablished as a result of objective-and-task budgeting, or there may be only a general mandate to get all the business possible. In either case much detail work remains to be done, and many intermediate decisions must be secured from colleagues and superiors in the store's management hierarchy.

The primary objectives of any retailer's advertising, sales promotion, and personal selling must forever be *to keep its present customers coming back and to develop new customers*. Keeping a store's existing customer base is essential to short-run survival, and developing new customers is equally crucial to long-term success.

Once these two broad strategic goals have been recognized, a vast number of tactical choices emerge. To keep old customers and induce new ones to come to the store, a retailer must set up intermediate objectives that lead ultimately to the accomplishment of these major aims. Often the same action will attract both present and prospective customers. But sometimes these two groups require totally different advertising approaches. This may mean some painful decisions as to priorities and some hard thinking about which courses of action will have the highest payoff if the store cannot afford to include all of them in its current ad plan.

Advertising may be called on to perform any or all of the following specific tasks:

- increase the variety and volume of merchandise and services sold to present customers;
- step up traffic in dull periods;
- clear left-over merchandise at the end of a selling season;
- develop weak departments into strong ones, and create ad awareness of new departments (or services that may not have been offered in the past);
- turn special opportunities like manufacturers' cooperative advertising offers or townwide promotional events into sources of sales for the store;
- attract new customers from among newcomers to the community, those dissatisfied with other stores, and those interested in new products, new fashions, and bargains;
- penetrate or create new markets for the store's goods and services;
- hold on to present customers when competitors make overtures to them and win over other stores' customers;
- build the store's reputation;
- introduce a new product;
- increase the sales of a product by suggesting new uses for it;
- build goodwill by providing a public service;

- directly support the store's personal selling program;
- reach customers who seldom or never come in person to the store;
- acquire a list of prospects for salespersons to call on;
- increase shopper traffic (and hence sales) in the district or shopping center as a whole;
- increase consumer awareness of the assortment, quality, fahion, or low price of merchandise with a particular appeal for specific market segments;
- encourage more people to become charge-account customers of the store or use bank credit cards;
- make people more aware of conveniences offered by the store, including free or inexpensive parking, delivery service, and evening, weekend, or holiday shopping hours;
- build consumer confidence by explaining how to select, use, and care for certain types of merchandise;
- identify the store with specific nationally advertised brands;
- produce telephone and mail orders;
- contribute to the store's overall public-relations effort;
- explain store policies, including "negative" ones that will have a less adverse effect on the public if they are fully understood; and
- reach the public quickly with messages of an emergency nature.

Some of these advertising goals are overlapping; a few may seem a bit contradictory. The priority given to accomplishing each of them will depend on the store, its advertising budget and resources, and its marketing environment.

Not even the largest and most diversified store will attempt to accomplish all these goals simultaneously.

WHAT ADVERTISING CANNOT DO

Just as important as knowing what advertising *can* do is knowing what it *cannot* do. Why waste time and money trying to do the impossible? Advertising cannot make a store better than it is or create a market when conditions are unfavorable. It cannot turn lemons into oranges, develop public confidence in a store overnight, or overcome a poor reputation in a short period of time. In brief, it cannot substitute for good merchandise, good service, a good operation, and other basics of retailing.[1]

SELECTING TARGET MARKETS

To whom may advertising messages be most profitably directed? A few years ago this question would have seemed superfluous, if not silly. Stores advertised to everybody. Now *to whom* a store advertises has become more crucial even than *why* and *what* it advertises.

The mass market, if it ever existed, has disintegrated, and the emphasis has shifted to *targeted marketing, segmented advertising, and selected audiences*. Ads no longer seek to elicit a response from "all those people out there" but focus with laserlike intensity on narrowly defined target groups. They are aimed directly at those people who are most likely to respond to a particular appeal and to become customers of the store.

At the very beginning of this book,

we observed that retailing is essentially a *people-pleasing business.* Any given retail store must determine *which* people it is most likely to please with its merchandise, its services, its distinctive, intangible atmosphere and image. *Those are the people it must seek out with its advertising, not just people in general.* The large, departmentalized store with many kinds of goods and services often divides its internal advertising staff into specialized units, each dealing with a different target group: patrons of the main store, the basement store, the suburban branch stores, the men's store, the ladies' fashion departments, the home furnishings department, the cluster of boutique shops, and so on. Each unit operates a separate advertising program. The smaller specialty shop has an easier task—zeroing in on one type of customer or a few very special groups.

Effective advertising must be *planned from the beginning* to touch the real buying motivations of such diverse groups as city-dwellers, suburbanites, small-town and rural inhabitants, home-owners, apartment-dwellers, mobile-home residents, farmers, whites, blacks, local ethnic groups, the affluent, the middle-class, and lower-income groups. It must be designed to appeal to the young, the middle-aged, the elderly; to the college-educated, those with a high-school education, and those who have less education; to professional and managerial workers; to white-collar workers, blue-collar workers, and unskilled laborers.

It must speak to men and women equally well, taking into account any sex-related differences in shopping patterns and buying motives.

3 Funds Set Aside for All-Store Purposes

THE RESERVE FUND

Like the prudent family with money tucked away for a rainy day or the wise general who never commits all the unit's soldiers to battle at the very beginning, the smart advertiser sets aside a portion of the ad budget as a reserve. It is rarely possible to foresee *all* the opportunities for profitable advertising that may arise in the course of a year or some other budgeting period. The alert merchant feels the pulse of the market as the months roll by and keeps constantly in touch with new developments in the store's segment of the industry. This advertising tool of reserve funds allows the retailer to act quickly and decisively in carving out profits when unforeseen opportunities come along.

The reserve fund provides flexibility. It need not be spent at any particular time, and a portion of it may not be spent at all. In the event of an unforeseen recession or a slowdown in the growth of the local economy, it can be "frozen" while the rest of the store's advertising program continues as planned.

The reserve fund typically constitutes from 5 to 10 percent of the total ad appropriation. The more stable the market and the more secure the position of the store, the smaller it need be. Conversely, the greater the uncertainties and the more unknown factors the store faces at the beginning of the advertising planning period, the larger the reserve fund should be. New stores, new branches, stores in fast-changing, dynamic communities, and stores facing new competition must keep more promotional ammunition in reserve to deal knockout blows or intensify defensive advertising at the right moment. Those dealing in relatively staple merchandise, such as food and gasoline, need much smaller reserves than those in highly volatile segments of retail trade, such as fashion merchandisers and dealers in luxury goods acutely sensitive to fluctuations in disposable income and buyers' moods.

THE INSTITUTIONAL
ADVERTISING PROGRAM

How much emphasis should be placed on selling the *store* (including its services), and how much on the *merchandise* it sells? Of course, the ultimate goal is to sell the merchandise and those services that turn a profit in their own right. But so often now the tangible goods sold in vastly different types of stores are identical or nearly identical. Somber carriage-trade shops with thick-piled carpeting and frockcoated sales attendants standing imperiously behind polished hardwood counters actually stock and sell items from the same production line as gaudy discount houses that pile these identical products in wire-mesh bins!

What, then, makes people buy from one store rather than another?

First, the packet of *services* provided by the store is important. This may include everything from the courteous, low-key counselling service of trained professional salespersons to alterations, delivery, gift-wrapping, credit, return privileges, repairs, and maintenance.

Institutional ads tell the story of these merchandise-related services.

Second, intangible store attributes, not necessarily directly related to any specific merchandise, create an *atmosphere* or *image* that will draw a certain clientele. These attributes derive from the store's physical appearance, both outside and in; the demeanor and attitude of its personnel; its decor and furnishings; the people with whom one rubs shoulders at the sales counter; refinements and amenities like restrooms, in-store restaurants, and parking arrangements; the carpeting (or absence thereof); and the window and interior displays. All this is in part *reflected* in the store's advertising (both institutional and promotional), but it is also *created* by the ads, whether they are deliberately institutional or well-designed promotional ads reflecting the intangible attributes of the store.

Although there is a resurgence of promotional ads during each period of business recession, the long-range trend is toward more institutional advertising. Even discount houses and other self-service stores are backing away from exclusive reliance on price-centered, "hard-sell" ads. That type of advertising was ominously characteristic of many stores that have fallen by the wayside. Some advertising experts have even been moved to predict that, among *national* advertisers, corporate (i.e., institutional) ads will soon outnumber product ads. Whether the same situation will prevail in *retail* advertising is open to question, however.

The rise of the *consumerism movement* in the late sixties and its growth in the seventies have weakened the appeal of emotional, suggestive, exaggerated, and "gimmicky" ads. Simultaneously, rational, explanatory, and educational ads—whether totally separated from ads for particular products (purely institutional ads), as is Figure 6–1, or straightforward ads for specific merchandise (promotional ads), as is Figure 6–2—have increased in popularity. The intensification of public interest, especially among the young, in problems of the environment and ecology has also stimulated institutional advertising and reinforced the effect of promotional ads with institutional touches. Stores now say more about their relationship to the local environment and use institutional advertising to take stands on hotly debated public issues.

THE CASE FOR THE "HARD SELL"

On the other hand, despite the general trend described above, few retailers are likely to entirely eliminate item-price ads in favor of soft-sell or purely institutional appeals. Determining the best balance between the two kinds of advertising in a particular marketing environment is a fundamental, and difficult, top management decision. The case for the highly promotional ad was made crystal clear by one retailer, the owner of a floor covering company in Parsippany, New Jersey:

> [T]he so-called creative ads, soft-selling ads, ads with lots and lots of white space, just don't do as good a job of selling carpets and rugs as hard-hitting, hard-selling every-day ordinary retail carpet ads, and selling carpets and rugs is the name of the game.
>
> [The] hard sell is . . . the basis for good business in this industry as in

almost all others. And it has helped us grow to New Jersey's largest specialty chain, with 17 stores . . . plus . . . 21 floor-covering departments in discount stores.

> Our fundamental philosophy when it comes to advertising is that it must produce results . . . it must sell our product. . . . We find [that] people look for price first once they get to the point where they're seriously shopping carpet ads . . . our ads are designed to get them in their pocketbooks, and to get them into the stores where the sales are made. And our ads SELL HARD to do this. . . . [The] hard sell, especially in advertising, does what it's supposed to do . . . it sells hard for us.[2]

WHEN AND WHY TO USE INSTITUTIONAL ADVERTISING— AND HOW MUCH TO USE

Much institutional advertising can be run at any time of the year. Some of it is even used as a *rate holder,* to fulfill contractual obligations to the media during slack selling periods. Other institutional ads, because of their nature, must be keyed to specific dates like the store's anniversary, national holidays, election days, the beginning of a season, or Christmas, or to local community events. Generally speaking, however, the institutional portion of the advertising appropriation is seldom allotted to specific seasons or months but goes into an overall "kitty" somewhat like the reserve fund.

About 5 to 10 percent of a store's total ad budget has traditionally been assigned to institutional tasks, but this percentage is rising. Depending on store policy, it can range from as little as 1

Learn, before you bite.

Over the years at Publix we've learned just about all there is to know about apples.

Just like we've tried to become experts on all the fruits and vegetables you buy.

Because we want you to have the best. Any apples that come to Publix that don't come up to our standards are refused.

We want you to know your apples. We figure, the more you do, the more you'll want to buy them from people who know theirs.

Apples are amazing.

There's practically no end to the ways you can enjoy them. Eat them out of your hand, slice or dice them in salads, boil them, bake them, fry them, sauce them, candy them, or squeeze and drink them.

They're healthful too. They contain pectin, fruit acid, natural fruit sugar, vitamins and minerals.

Apples keep down cholesterol, pep up the system, aid digestion and are one of the world's great natural toothbrushes.

And since an apple can satisfy hunger with only 90 calories, it's a favorite of diet watchers.

How to pick apples.

Look for freshness and good color. Color depends on variety. Red Delicious, Winesap and Jonathan should be a rich shade of red. McIntosh, two tone red and green. Cortland, red with a green "cheek". Golden Delicious, a soft yellow with gold flecks.

Skin should be relatively smooth and bruise free. Apples should be firm to the touch. (Don't squeeze though, they'll bruise.)

Read, before you cook.

For applesauce, use only enough water to keep from scorching. No water for pies or betties.

Use sugar sparingly. Too much can spoil the natural flavor and make apples mushy.

When you slice or dice for salads, dip the bits in lemon juice or in cold water and add a pinch of salt for each apple. They'll stay white longer.

Clip and file this handy guide. It'll help you pick the best variety for every use.

Red Delicious, best for eating fresh and in salads. Winesap and Jonathan, excellent for fresh eating, and cooking too. McIntosh, delicious for eating out of hand, salads and applesauce. Cortland, excellent for pies, salads and baking. Golden Delicious, tops for just about any use.

Publix Apple Orchard

publix

percent to half or more of the total ad funds.

The specialty shop appealing to a sophisticated clientele drawn predominantly from better-educated and more discerning segments of the population, and many a "youth-oriented" retailer, may devote far more of the ad budget to institutional promotion than the average store. Retailers moving rapidly into consumer-service operations need to capitalize fully on this commitment to changing times, and institutional ads often do that best.

COOPERATING WITH OTHER STORES TO BUILD AREA TRAFFIC

In addition to maintaining a reserve fund and allotting funds for institutional advertising, most retailers set aside still another portion of promotional money for purposes not directly and immediately related to selling specific merchandise. This is the amount that each store in a retail district contributes to promoting traffic in the district, or that the store in a shopping center contributes (voluntarily or as required by provisions in its lease) to generate traffic in the center. A merchants' association of some sort usually manages the combined funds, drawing crowds with a series of seasonal events, special promotions, and even entertainment designed to familiarize the public with the district or center.

This amounts to a form of *horizontal cooperative advertising* among the merchants involved. A formula is set up to allocate the cost of the overall program among the various stores, and each store's management takes its expected contribution into account when it develops its ad budget. A calendar of district or center promotions should be published in advance, so that individual stores can tie in their own ads to them to take advantage of the traffic produced.

SUMMARY: SET-ASIDE FUNDS NOT AVAILABLE FOR MERCHANDISE ADS

Three allocations must be considered, and deducted from the total ad budget, before detailed planning for merchandise ads can begin:

Figure 6–1 A Purely Institutional Ad

This is not really an ad for an orchard but an ad for a supermarket chain. What appears to be the "signature" is actually a clever way of saying the message is from the fresh produce department of Publix Supermarkets. The purpose is to create an image of quality and friendliness for the company by informing the reader—and potential customer—about apples. It tells how to buy them for particular uses, takes the mystery out of the names of different varieties of apples, and even suggests how to prepare them in the kitchen, either for applesauce or salad. It is one of a series, each dealing with one chosen kind of food item, and originally it appeared in bright, attractive "apple red" color.

But did it actually *sell* anything? Probably not, at least on the day it appeared. It was justified, though, because of its long-range impact. The objective was to change food shoppers' *attitudes* toward Publix, to gain a more favorable image than the many other food stores competing in this hotly contested segment of retailing. The profit to Publix accumulates over a long period of time and is hard to measure in specific dollars-and-cents results from any one ad. Publix is reputed to consistently maintain the most eye-appealing, best image-creating advertising with the highest-quality artwork of any food group in the U.S.

Source: Ad reproduced from International Newspaper Advertising Executives, *Sales & Idea Book* (August 1973), p. 41.

Figure 6–2 A Typical Item-Price, Immediate-Sell Promotional Ad

This ad exemplifies the price-oriented, multiproduct promotional ad that is intended to produce immediate sales of specific items within hours after it appears. Nearly 40 items appear on this originally massive two-page spread that had eight super-features blazoned out in price figures that were nearly three inches high! The ad contains no institutional elements as such, but the advertised low prices do contribute to the image of this store as a thrifty shopper's best place to buy. Compare and contrast this with Figure 6–1. Both are ads for supermarkets, and of course both are designed to make profits for the advertisers. Figure 6–1 aims at long-range profits, but this one intends to make cash registers ring right now. Both types of ads have their places in a well-balanced retail advertising plan, whether for food stores or any other type of merchandiser.

Source: Picture from International Newspaper Advertising Executives, *Sales & Idea Book* (Spring 1970), p. 52.

	Possible Low Figure	Possible High Figure
1. The Reserve Fund	5%	10%
2. The Institutional Ad Fund	1	50
3. The Assessment for or Contribution to a Joint Ad Fund (if any)	2	15
	8%	75%

Thus, depending on many variables, the total set-aside funds may range from a mere pittance to a large portion of the store's advertising appropriation. For most stores, it will fall well between these two extremes; possibly 15 to 20 percent would be a good overall average for retailers today.

4 Allocating Advertising Pressure Among Departments

The yearly, semiannual, seasonal, or monthly advertising plan of any large store is a thick document detailing the sums laid out for the promotional ads of its many merchandise divisions and departments. Each receives advertising support roughly in proportion to the contribution it is expected to make to total sales and/or profits. Since this varies through the year as the demand for different kinds of goods fluctuates, a given department's share of ad funds will vary accordingly. More money will be spent to advertise yard and garden supplies in May than in January; formal gowns will be more heavily advertised in December than in August.

The smaller store with a dozen departments, or perhaps just two or three, should take a careful look at each in allotting its advertising funds, too. Its ad plan may be less formal, its budget less rigid, and its marketing strategy less complex, but there should be a plan! Even the one-line specialty merchant should give some thought to the allocation of advertising funds to different merchandise and price lines. In a sense, each represents a different "department" for advertising planning purposes, even though all are sold within a 20-foot space by the proprietor, a family member, or one clerk.

BREAKDOWNS BY SALES, BY PROFITS, BY TRAFFIC, OR BY GROWTH POTENTIAL

The first and most obvious step in drawing up departmental budgets is to determine what proportion of total store sales is generated by each department (or is likely to be generated in the budgeting period). Expected sales can be projected from known past sales figures. A departmental breakdown of sales for a typical retail store with three departments might look like the table below.

Department	Sales Volume		Advertising	
	Dollars	Percentage of total	Percentage of total	Dollars
A	120,000	60	60	6,000
B	60.000	30	30	3,000
C	20,000	10	10	1,000
Total	**200,000**	**100**	**100**	**10,000**

In the absence of any other information, about all a retailer can do is allocate advertising funds in exact proportion to its projected sales volume. For many a small store, this is enough. And for all stores, it is a first step toward a sound advertising plan.

But what about modifications of this simple and obvious breakdown, so that each ad dollar will make the greatest long-range contribution to the profits of the store as a whole?

An effective cost accounting system may reveal differences in *profit* percentages among the store's various departments, merchandise lines, or price lines. These differences may be due to variations among them in the average gross margin on sales or to unequal departmental operating costs expressed as a percentage of sales. In large home supply centers, for example, a cost and profit analysis has shown a 33 percent average gross profit on furniture and only a 25 percent profit on major appliances. To the store, then, a dollar of furniture sales is really worth more than a dollar of appliance sales. If furniture is sold by department B and appliances by department A, the advertising breakdown might look something like the table below.

The store will now spend $600 less on advertising for the less profitable department, A, and $600 more on advertising for the more profitable department, B. It will favor the higher profit department, B, since *any* increase in B's sales stimulated by advertising will be more profitable than a similar increase in department A's sales would be.

Another consideration, easily tracked down by an analysis of *transaction counts* among the departments, is their rank in terms of *drawing traffic*. A department with a low sales volume (and even one that makes a low contribution to gross profits) may turn out to be one in which a high proportion of the store's total customer transactions occur. Its *unit volume* and customer count may greatly outpace either its gross sales or its gross profits, in relation to other departments.

Such a department may be directly or indirectly responsible for big and profitable sales accomplished by (and credited to) other departments. A film processing service in a camera shop, a cosmetics counter in a dress shop, a meat department in a supermarket, a tobacco counter in a drug store, or a small-appliance repair service in an electrical-goods store may draw traffic and be more important to the store's overall profits than is at first apparent.

Department	Gross Margin		Advertising	
	Dollars	Percentage of total	Percentage of total	Dollars
A	$120,000 × .25 = $30,000	54	54	5,400
B	$60,000 × .33 = $20,000	36	36	3,600
C	(No change. C generates 10 percent of the store's sales and profits and is allotted 10 percent of its ad funds.)			

Department	Sales (percentage of total)	Gross Profit (percentage of total)	Traffic (percentage of total)	Advertising (percentage of total)	Advertising (dollars)
A	60	54	40	50	5,000
B	30	36	20	35	3,500
C	10	10	40	15	1,500

Suppose, for example, the manager reexamines the store's "small" department and finds that although it generates a mere 10 percent of the store's sales it accounts for far more than 10 percent of the customer traffic. By bringing in so many customers, it feeds business to departments A and B, where effective displays and personal selling ability result in both immediate impulse sales and leads for future sales.

To reward department C for its contribution to building store traffic and compensate for the fact that some of the sales of the other two departments are actually the result of traffic drawn by C, the ad budget may be further revised to look somewhat like the table above.

As a result of this adjustment, department C will get 50 percent more advertising than its sales volume or contribution to profits might seem to justify, in order to stimulate still further the traffic it generates (upon which the two "big" departments depend for some of their sales and profits). With some careful in-store research, it may be possible to pinpoint the exact volume of department A and B sales being made to persons who *first* make purchases in department C. An analysis of traffic patterns within the store at intervals may also provide a concrete basis for this sort of adjustment. By tracing the path of shoppers from the time they enter until they leave, the store can determine what proportion first visit department C and later enter the other departments to make purchases or inquiries that may result in later sales.

A marine-products dealer on the shore of Lake Michigan had focused most of his promotion, for years and years, on outboard motors, his big source of sales and profits. A professional advertising counsellor then stepped in to help and noted that he had never featured ads for life preservers, cushions, canoe paddles, bilge pumps, waterproof batteries, anchor ropes, corrosion-proof boat hardware, or spar varnish for wooden decks. He carried all this merchandise but found it rather slow-moving, somewhat of a burden in terms of inventory turnover, yet a seeming necessity as a service to those who spent big money buying new motors every few years.

The counsellor suggested that these nickel-and-dime items were what drew boating enthusiasts into a store repeatedly throughout the boating season (and even off-season). He coaxed the merchant to include and even to emphasize them in his ad program.

With this new plan in effect, business in all departments increased dramatically. Traffic and transactions skyrocketed and, most importantly, *outboard motors sold as never before.* People who came into the store frequently throughout the season to buy fittings, accessories, and minor items for their boats saw those bright-and-shiny new motors on display, picked up current manufacturers' catalogs to take home and drool over, and were often persuaded by the store's salesmen to take out demonstration models to see how they liked the new motors on their own boats.

Much of this *spillover business* from the sluggish marine-supply department had been missed in previous years as customers and could-be customers searched elsewhere in the community for those seemingly insignificant "little" things every boat owner needs so often. The prior exclusive emphasis on outboard motors in the store's ads had given it the image of a great place to visit every four or five years when one could afford a new motor. Its new image was that of the weekend skipper's headquarters for *all* his or her needs. And it paid off in a spectacular increase in overall profits, as well as more profits than ever on motors.

In like manner, a druggist might sell an expensive perfume to a woman who came to the store for a lipstick refill, or a clothier a $150 suit to a man who responded to an ad for his favorite kind of undershorts. Spillover sales are particularly likely in stores with effective displays and alert sales staffs.

The *growth potential* of a department or a merchandise line must also be considered. This means analyzing market trends, eyeing the competition, and using judgment rather than simple arithmetic. Let's take a look now at another hypothetical store, this time a large hardware outlet with three departments: A, which handles general hardware, B, a lawn-and-garden supply center, and C, a small basement sporting-goods shop with

room to expand. Building permits in the store's community are running three-to-one for apartments and townhouses as opposed to private single-family homes, and two of its major industries have just announced that they are adopting a four-day work week.

It looks like there will be a shrinking market potential for lawn and garden supplies used by homeowners and an expansion of the leisure-time market, for two reasons: (a) apartment-dwellers have less need to spend evenings and weekends working on lawns and gardens, and (b) people with three-day weekends must find something to do with all that time. The town has four garden-and-lawn supply centers, but the only sporting-goods shop in the area has just announced a "going-out-of-business sale" after a long period of inept management (including, no doubt, a weak advertising program). People are traveling many miles to the neighboring town for sporting goods or ordering them by mail and telephone.

The hardware dealer's cues are plain: Sporting goods have a great future! The storekeeper makes some estimates and assigns a five-year growth factor to the three departments as a goal, which advertising will help to achieve. The ad budget then looks like the table at the top of the next page.

A shrewd merchant will also take a look at special situations affecting the departmental advertising budget breakdown. These could include, for example, the availability of cooperative advertising funds from manufacturers. A department that deals mostly in merchandise whose vendors are generous with promotional funds may generate heavy traffic and return handsome profits even though the retailer's own allotment of

Department	Present Percentage Contribution to Sales	Planned Growth Over Next 5 Years	Percentage of Total Advertising Allocated to Department
A	60	10% per year = 50%	50
B	30	5% per year = 25%	25
C	10	20% per year = 100%	25

advertising funds to that department is relatively modest. Some other department, dealing chiefly in products whose manufacturers provide little or no co-operative ad money, may need a larger proportional share of the store's ad funds. Still another department may face new head-on competition this year, which it did not have to contend with before, while other departments may have a near monopoly on the goods they sell. Obviously, the challenged department will need extra promotional funds for defensive purposes. An entirely new department or a greatly expanded one will also need extra advertising initially to draw consumers.

USING EDP DATA AS A BASIS
FOR MAKING STRATEGIC
ADVERTISING DECISIONS

A computer programmed to maintain a constant tab on inventory movement by department, by merchandise category, and even by specific items can also provide reports on gross margins and handling costs by the same breakdown. Further, it can relate them to the space occupied by a department or product line, to sales of goods from a particular vendor, or to goods bearing a certain brand name. This enables management to determine the relative profitability of each department, product line, item, or brand. If the store's advertising strategy is to concentrate on the

most profitable departments, merchandise categories, or items, the EDP system can be very useful indeed.

Some retailers will question this strategy, however, because the most *profitable* items may not be the most *popular* ones, and if the concentration is on ads for them, the productivity of the store's advertising dollars may actually be reduced. Ads are most effective when they are used to accelerate the turnover of products that are already good sellers because of their inherent appeal to the customer, their newness, their timeliness, or their price.

A computer system can also be used effectively if management decides to concentrate on advertising popular departments, merchandise categories, or items. It can be (and usually is) programmed to report the velocity at which merchandise moves. The EDP reports thus provide a virtually automatic guide to what should be advertised.

Programming a computer system to generate *both* kinds of information can be the most productive advertising strategy of all. The store can then identify and feature in its ads items that are fast-moving and inexpensive to handle and that produce a high gross margin—items that are *sure winners*. At the same time, as we have noted, computer technology enables the store to target its ads precisely to the most likely customers and to evaluate specific sales results of those ads.

5 Timing Ads for Best Results: The Key to Scientific Ad Planning

Big-time national advertisers, whose multimillion-dollar promotional funds are allotted through the glamorous Madison Avenue agencies, can well be jealous of retailers—especially smaller, local retailers—in one respect.

Why?

Because those large-scale manufacturers cultivating nationwide markets perceive the superior opportunity enjoyed by local stores to fine tune the *timing* of advertising messages.

Part of the potential sales-stimulating power of a national advertiser's most extravagant television campaign or its most exquisite magazine spread is unavoidably wasted. It is wasted because it does not always arrive at the point of impact (the customer's mind) at precisely the time when the customer is most receptive. Schedules and messages are necessarily tailored to the mythical nationwide mass market. Inadequate recognition is given to strictly local climates, customs, and economic and social factors, and even less to the peculiarities of individual dealers in a given community. The very long lead-time associated with nationwide advertising makes it impossible to foresee the exact marketing environment at the magic moment when the ads are supposed to do their job.

Retailers, on the other hand, *can* adjust the flow of advertising pressure to coincide with buyers' moods and to swing with local variations in national or regional habits. Many, if not most, of the very large retail chains that in the past have controlled advertising quite tightly from national or regional headquarters have tended recently to delegate more authority downward to group or store managers (so that they can adjust the scheduling or alter the content of ads). But it is the smaller, local, and usually most "independent" merchant operating in one community or in a few areas (usually contiguous) who is in the best position with regard to the timing of promotions. Hence, smaller stores' ads can and often do outpull those of the gigantic national advertisers on a dollar-per-dollar basis.

Stores can easily accumulate local records of fluctuations in sales from year to year, month to month, and week to week—broken down by departments and merchandise categories. These can be a valid guide for future planning, enabling the merchant to use advertising precisely at the moment when it will elicit the best response. Retailers know in advance about local quirks in climate, regularly staged events, promotional programs of merchant groups and even major competitors, payroll days, vacation periods and seasonal layoffs in local industries, and harvest dates of crops. All these things cause seasonal, monthly, and weekly ebbs and flows in the volume of sales, and each affects different merchandise categories differently. The records of any store's past performance will reflect the combined effect of such variables.

THE DISTRIBUTION OF ADVERTISING BY MONTHS

The *calendar month* is by far the most popular planning period for allotting advertising funds within a budget year. Large stores sometimes use intermediate periods, such as first and second half of the year or a quarterly (seasonal) breakdown. A few use a 13-month "year" ("months" being 28-day periods with equal numbers of peak weekend shopping days). For our purposes we shall think of a year as having the normal 12 months.

There are five simple steps in breaking down any store's total advertising appropriation into 12 monthly segments that reflect 12 different levels of selling opportunity.

1. Determination of the Total Annual Advertising Appropriation (discussed in Chapter 5) Deduct the reserve fund and the all-store institutional advertising appropriation. The remainder is the yearly promotional ad budget:

Total Advance Appropriation	$10,000
Less Reserve	−1,000
Less Cost of Institutional Ads	−1,000
Year's Promotional Advertising Budget	$ 8,000

The larger, departmentalized store will have to consider two or more sales curves and will further divide the promotional budget into allotments for specific departments that enjoy different "peaks and valleys" in selling opportunities throughout the year:

Total Advance Appropriation	$50,000
Less Reserve and Funds for Institutional Ads	−8,000
Promotional Advertising Budget	$42,000
Departmental Allotments:	
Department A	$12,000
Department B	20,000
Department C	10,000
	$42,000

2. Ascertainment of the Proportion of Annual Sales Realized Each Month in the Past Last year's sales records are

the obvious source for this data, but it is often better to take an *average* of the figures for the preceding three- or five-year period. One simply divides the monthly figures by the year's gross sales to obtain the *percentage* of sales that occurred each month. For example, suppose we have the following data:

Gross Sales for the Past 12 Months	$250,000
Gross Sales in March	25,000
Gross Sales in July	15,000

Since

$$\frac{\$25,000}{\$250,000} = .10$$

March sales were 10.0 percent of annual sales. And since

$$\frac{\$15,000}{\$250,000} = .06$$

July sales were 6.0 percent of annual sales.

In the case of a new store, national and/or regional figures can be obtained from the Newspaper Advertising Bureau (through the nearest member paper), from the National Retail Merchants Association or other trade associations, from government bureaus, from trade journals, and from manufacturer's representatives. However, these figures will not be as accurate a guide as the store's own records and should be discarded after a year or two of normal operations.

One way to decide how heavily to promote each line each month is to use the *Neustadt Red Book,* available from National Retail Merchants Association. It reports the actual newspaper advertising volume of 90 commodities in major markets for the past year, and the average for five past years. In effect, a retailer can base plans on the consensus of the nation's major retail advertisers as to when advertising should be done. Using past advertising rather than past sales as a basis for future advertising eliminates the "lag time" between the appearance of advertising and the consummation of sales as a factor in the timing of ads. This lag is more important in some merchandise categories and not so important in others.

An expanding chain retailer moving into territories distant from its home base must be especially cognizant of *regional variations* in buying patterns (based on differences in climate, industries, and social customs). To illustrate, study Figure 6–3, which contains extracts from the 1971 edition of the Newspaper Advertising Bureau's *Timetable of Retail Opportunity* (based on sales figures for 1961–1965 reported by the Federal Reserve Board). Imagine that you are a chain store ad manager helping your company expand from its New England base to the Pacific coast. Sales in your Massachusetts units (Federal Reserve District #1) reflect the patterns shown on the upper half of the figure. You are tempted to allot advertising funds for the coat department in a new Los Angeles store accordingly.

What a disaster this could be for the new store! The sales potential for women's and misses' coats is more *than* twice as great in June in Southern California (Federal Reserve District #12) as it is in New England: 4.6 percent of annual sales versus a mere 1.9 percent. Assuming the same sales volume, the Los Angeles store should have two times the June ad budget for coats as the Massachusetts stores. Furthermore, you have never had a sharp sales peak in December, which accounts for 12.1 percent of annual coat

sales in New England, and were considering spending at least as much of the new store's budget for coats in October as in December. Then you examined a table such as the one shown in the figure and learned that in Southern California people do not buy coats heavily early in the season but all in a rush in December. There, the sales potential is *more than half again* as great in December as it is in New England (19.7 percent of annual sales, compared to only 12.1 percent in the chain's home territory). And in October, California stores have *scarcely two-thirds* the sales opportunity of those in Massachusetts. Had you overspent that badly in October in Los Angeles, a third of the money might have been wasted, and had you starved the new store's December ad budget for coats, a third of the sales opportunities might have been missed.

In addition to variations in spending patterns that arise on a regional basis, other fluctuations exist. Locally, patterns will vary month by month for different types of stores (see Figure 6–4). Within the departments of a large store (Figure 6–5), and even among closely related merchandise lines sold in the same specialty shop (Figure 6–6), selling opportunities will be unique for each month. Such variations necessitate separate plans for timing the release of ads for each product category.

3. Division of Next Year's Advertising on the Basis of the Proportion of Last Year's Total Sales That Actually Occurred Each Month For the month when 10 percent of the total sales occur, the advertising should aproximate 10 percent of the year's total advertising effort. In another month when only 6 percent of the total sales generally occur, not much more than 6 percent of the promotional funds should be spent—lest they be largely wasted at a time when people just don't want to buy.

Figure 6–7 demonstrates the right and wrong way to use ad funds. It suggests that it may be wise to "underadvertise" slightly (in proportion to the expected sales volume) in peak sales periods and, conversely, "overadvertise" to a moderate degree during periods when weaker sales are expected. (See Step 5, below.)

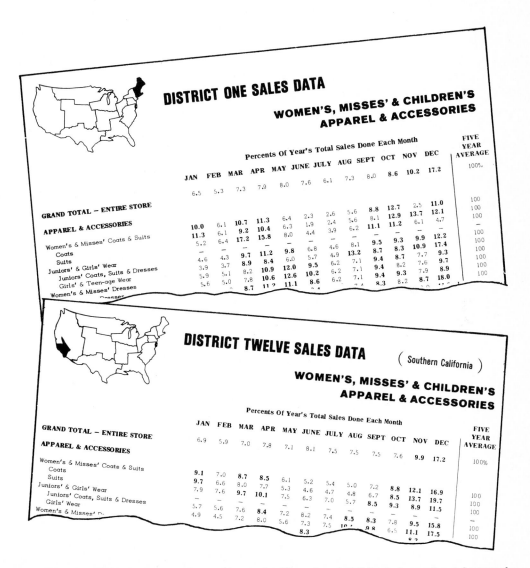

Figure 6–3 Regional Variations in Sales of Women's, Misses', and Children's Apparel and Accessories

4. Adjustment of Monthly Allot-ments for "Floating" Holidays and Var-iations in the Number of Weekend Peak Shopping Days   In basing an advertis-ing plan on records of past years' sales, a retailer should recognize that direct month-by-month comparisons from one year to the next contain a hidden flaw: The calendar is not exactly the same for any two years running. An adjustment is in order to allow for holidays that fall either on a different date, on a different day of the week, or within a different month.

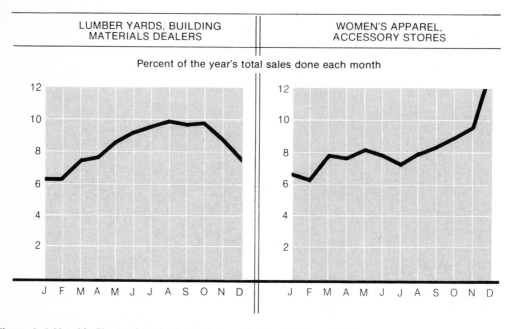

Figure 6–4 Monthly Fluctuations in Sales Volume for Two Types of Stores
These graphs are based on national totals compiled by the U.S. Department of Commerce. Note the sharp differences in sales volume done by these two types of stores. Sales for lumber yards and building materials dealers begin to climb steadily as the warm weather sets in and reach a peak during the late summer and early fall months. This is contrary to the typical industry sales pattern with its December peak, which is illustrated by the graph for women's apparel and accessory stores. Here, sales climb from a February "low" to the December "high." The smaller peaks throughout the year reflect closely the greater sales brought by holidays and the start of new seasons. While the sales curves of many other types of stores may reflect similar overall patterns, specific peaks within the year will be different for most.
Advertisers must pay close attention to the sales pattern for their specific stores in order to allot advertising funds most effectively. In using such data as this, they also must realize that each region, state, city, or neighborhood would offer a somewhat different pattern of buying behavior index. A store must have the latest available figures peculiar to its own market and its own experience. Therefore, adver-tisers will need to refine such data to reflect more accurately their store's own market by referring to com-parable data tabulated separately for each of the nation's 12 Federal Reserve Districts. (Figure 6–3 shows examples of this data, which is available from Federal Reserve banks.) The national data can be brought up to within about three months of the current date at any time by referring to the monthly Department of Commerce publication, *Survey of Current Business*.
Source: U.S. Department of Commerce, 1972.

Most retailers realize significantly more sales on Fridays and Saturdays than on other days. Depending on local laws and customs, many stores also find Sundays an important shopping day while others do not. It is important to determine the number of weekend "peak sales" days in any given month "last year" and compare this figure with the number of weekend days in the same month this year or next year. When a 31-day month begins on either a Thursday or a Friday, it guarantees *five* full Friday-Saturday shopping "peaks"; when such a month begins on a Wednesday or a Saturday, it contains $4^{1/2}$ such weekend shopping bonanzas. But when a 31-day month begins on a Sunday, a Monday, or a Tuesday, it will contain only *four* Friday-Saturday combinations. In planning advertising support for any month, based on a prior year's sales, a retailer must take into consideration whether the month has more or fewer weekends this year than in the base year or years. Thirty-day months involve a different pattern, of course, and February is a special case; it always has the same number of choice shopping days during ordinary years, but in leap years it may have $4^{1/2}$ weekends.

Holidays can have either an exhilarating or a depressing effect on buying. A winter holiday may release thousands of people from the routine of going to work, and stores open for business may have an exceptional opportunity for peak sales. A summer holiday may stimulate a mass exodus from the community as families go to the lakes, the mountains, or the seaside—while the stores back home are as empty as tombs.

Any given holiday can have an opposite impact on different lines of merchandise, too. The immediate preholiday period in the summer may be a great time to sell automotive goods and services, sporting goods, beachwear, and luggage. But it will be a poor time to promote food sales because everyone will want the refrigerator as empty as possible before going out of town.

Holidays falling adjacent to a weekend create three-day "mini-vacation" opportunities and have a more pronounced impact on sales than holidays

Figure 6–5 Monthly Fluctuations in Sales Volume for the Nine Typical Departments of a Hardware Store
    This page appears in the annual *Advertising Promotion Planner* (1974 edition), published by the National Retail Hardware Association. It demonstrates the kind of help offered by the many national and regional retail trade associations to their members. (Such data is often sold to nonmember stores, but at a premium price.)
    Note how different product lines reach their sales peaks and valleys at different periods of the year: Lawn and garden supplies, paint, and sporting goods dominate sales increases in the spring, while housewares and gifts go wild in December. Meanwhile, hardware itself and building materials offer steady volume, sales being virtually the same during every one of the 12 months. Read the comments the hardware association makes in regard to advertising timing for each of the nine lines. Because of the differences in the sales curves of the lines, a single advertising timing plan for the whole store could well lead to wasteful overadvertising on specific products at certain periods or to tragically wasted selling opportunities during other months.
    The association directs special attention toward the growth area for hardware people: building materials. By being aware of the potential for sales here, a store may wish to expand into this line of merchandise and divert advertising funds from some less profitable line.
    Source: By courtesy of the National Retail Hardware Association.

THE IMPORTANCE OF TIMING IN ADVERTISING

What you advertise can be just as important as the ad itself. Here are graphs showing how sales in various departments are affected by the seasons. Plan ads that capitalize on these national sales trends.

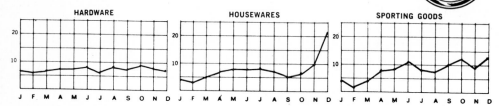

Note that the sales of hardware items remain fairly constant throughout the year while housewares sales rise drastically in November and December. The sales of sporting goods are also highly influenced by normal seasonal sales patterns.

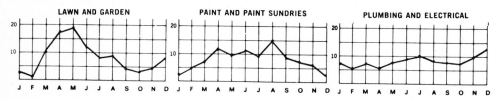

Unless lawn and garden lines are advertised in the March thru June period, the advertising is largely wasted. Paint and paint sundries sales also follow a spring and summer sales curve that should be noted. Electrical and plumbing sales are quite stable.

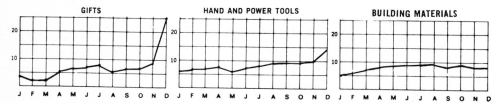

Seasonal influences on sales of giftwares depend largely on how much emphasis you place on the gift department. Unless an attractive gift department is maintained throughout the year, giftware sales are primarily made in November and December. Hand and power tools are now attractively packaged and can also be sold as gifts throughout the year.

GROWING IMPORTANCE OF BUILDING MATERIALS

Building materials of all types, from concrete to lumber, are rapidly becoming a stock item in more and more hardware stores and home centers. Hardwaremen who have added building materials lines report that they tend to increase store traffic, sales and profits. Hardware customers are beginning to expect larger hardware stores to carry some building materials lines.

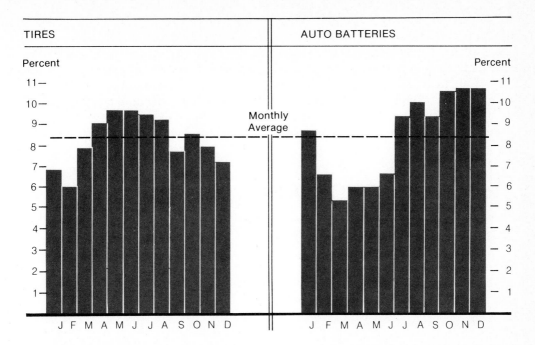

Figure 6–6 Monthly Difference in Sales Volume Between Two Closely Related Merchandise Lines
These two graphs show the very different sales curves of two closely related products—tires and batteries—sold by a store specializing in automotive goods. People buy tires primarily during the spring and summer, perhaps because of the summer travel season when they put more miles on their cars and want to be assured that the family vacation trip is not spoiled by tire trouble. Midwinter, especially February is a slow season for tires. In contrast, motorists need new batteries all the way from late summer through midwinter, and the first cold spells that konk out the old battery are most likely the buying motive that causes the all-year peaks in November and December. Early spring is a bad time to try to push batteries: If the old one survived the winter, it will probably crank the car pretty well for a few more months as the weather warms up! The advertising of these two lines should be adjusted according to the months when the merchant can reasonably expect to sell the products.
Source: By courtesy of the Newspaper Advertising Bureau, Inc.

that come at midweek. Sometimes a Thursday or a Tuesday holiday results in the closing down of places of employment on the intervening Friday or Monday also, producing a four-day "weekend" with a correspondingly heavier impact, either pro or con, on sales.

"Floating" holidays, the most important of which is Easter, actually shift from one month to another in different years. The date on which Easter falls

especially affects fashion-related apparel purchases and can make either March or April the spring's best selling month. The trend toward casual living and the decline of traditional religion as a motivating force in our society are, however, weakening its effect on buying patterns. The calendar date of Thanksgiving and the day of the week on which Christmas falls affect the number of effective shopping days for the great pre-

Christmas gift-buying spree. When Christmas and some other major holidays fall on a weekend, local custom often dictates that employers give their workers an extra day off to compensate for the missed "time off." But will that day be the preceding Friday or the following Monday? This could have a sig-nificant influence on retail sales from one year to the next.

Table 6–1 lists many of the more important holidays for three successive years (1974–1976). Note how the day of the week or the date of the month on which they fall can change. A table like this helps a store schedule its advertising

make this timing test...

Today, merchants are keenly aware the *timing* is essential to sound, profitable advertising. Making the simple check suggested here, they are often surprised and shocked at how far out of line their advertising is.

If you want well-timed advertising to sell more merchandise at lower unit cost you want a sales and advertising pattern which month by month looks —

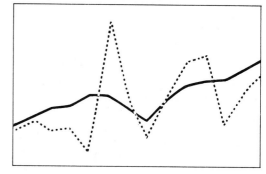

LIKE THIS   NOT THIS

Figure 6–7 Make This Timing Test

This test enables a store's management to tell at a glance if the timing of its advertising is roughly parallel with its sales opportunities or whether it is out of time and thus less likely to produce maximum sales results. In the "Like This" chart at the left, sales and advertising are distributed in about the same proportion. When sales fluctuations are plotted in terms of each month's percentage of the year's gross sales, the graph (the solid line) is seen to closely parallel the graph of the percentage of the year's total advertising budget allotted to each month (the dotted line).

When the store fails to plan its advertising distribution to the 12 months in proportion to projected sales, the actual sales will turn out to be very similar, from month to month, to former years, but the advertising will be erratic. It will shrivel up at times of the year when sales are good, and it will expand beyond reason at other times, when people simply do not want to buy that much from this particular kind of store (whatever its merchandise lines may be). As shown in the "Not This" chart, the dotted line representing the month-by-month variation in the proportion of the total advertising budget allotted to each month bears no resemblance whatsoever to the sales curve. Much money will be wasted when advertising is done on this hit-or-miss basis.

Source: *Advertising Planbook* (New York: Newspaper Advertising Bureau, 1974), p. 2.

to harmonize with the current year's calender (not last year's).

5. *Consideration of the Contra-cyclical Theory of Advertising Timing* The basic premise up to now has been that advertising should *accelerate natural demand* when people are in a mood to buy. From this premise we have derived a procedure for allotting portions of an annual advertising appropriation to each of the 12 months in a year roughly in proportion to the contribution of each month to the past year's (or the average of several past years') business. This presumes that advertising cannot greatly change people's buying habits, that it cannot alter established shopping preferences to any great extent. It must reinforce customer's natural inclinations,

Table 6–1

Important Dates: 1974, 1975, 1976

Event	1974	1975	1976
New Year's Day	Tuesday, Jan. 1	Wednesday, Jan. 1	Thursday, Jan. 1
Lincoln's Birthday	Tuesday, Feb. 12	Wednesday, Feb. 12	Thursday, Feb. 12
Valentine's Day	Thursday, Feb. 14	Friday, Feb. 14	Saturday, Feb. 14
Washington's Birthday *	Monday, Feb. 18	Monday, Feb. 17	Monday, Feb. 16
Ash Wednesday	Wednesday, Feb. 17	Wednesday, Feb. 12	Wednesday, Mar. 3
St. Patrick's Day	Sunday, Mar. 17	Monday, Mar. 17	Wednesday, Mar. 17
Palm Sunday	Sunday, Apr. 7	Sunday, Mar. 23	Sunday, Apr. 11
Good Friday	Friday, Apr. 12	Friday, Mar. 28	Friday, Apr. 16
Jewish Passover	Sunday, Apr. 7, thru Apr. 13	Thursday, Mar. 27, thru Apr. 3	Thursday, Apr. 15, thru Apr. 22
Easter Sunday	Sunday, Apr. 14	Sunday, Mar. 30	Sunday, Apr. 18
Mother's Day	Sunday, May 12	Sunday, May 11	Sunday, May 9
Victoria Day (Canada)	Monday, May 20	Monday, May 19	Monday, May 24
Memorial Day *	Monday, May 27	Monday, May 26	Monday, May 31
Father's Day	Sunday, June 16	Sunday, June 15	Sunday, June 20
Dominion Day (Canada)	Monday, July 1	Tuesday, July 1	Thursday, July 1
Independence Day	Thursday, July 4	Friday, July 4	Sunday, July 4 (200th anniversary of signing of Declaration of Independence)
Labor Day	Monday, Sept. 2	Monday, Sept. 1	Monday, Sept. 6
Jewish New Year	Tuesday, Sept. 17	Saturday, Sept. 6	Saturday, Sept. 25
Columbus Day *	Monday, Oct. 14	Monday, Oct. 13	Monday, Oct. 11
Thanksgiving Day (Canada)	Monday, Oct. 14	Monday, Oct. 13	Monday, Oct. 11
Veteran's Day *	Monday, Oct. 28	Monday, Oct. 27	Monday, Oct. 25
Halloween	Thursday, Oct. 31	Friday, Oct. 31	Sunday, Oct. 31
Election Day	Tuesday, Nov. 5	Tuesday, Nov. 4	Tuesday, Nov. 2
Thanksgiving Day	Thursday, Nov. 28	Thursday, Nov. 27	Thursday, Nov. 25
Christmas	Wednesday, Dec. 25	Thursday, Dec. 25	Saturday, Dec. 25

* These holidays, in some states and localities, are still observed to some extent on their original, or "traditional," dates also.

Source: *Advertising Planbook* (New York: Newspaper Advertising Bureau, Inc., 1974), p. 42.

not combat them—strike while the iron is hot.

There is a contrary theory of advertising called the *contracyclical theory.* Instead of reinforcing the cycle of consumer demand, stores can advertise when people *do not* want to buy. They can use advertising to build up sales when they would otherwise be low, and they can cut back on advertising during "hot" selling periods when everybody seems willing to buy without prodding. For example, a store may schedule 10 percent of its advertising for a month when it normally does only 5 percent of its annual business and allot a mere 6 percent of its annual ad budget to a month that accounted for 12 percent of its total sales in the preceding year. Hopefully advertising will jack up sales in the poor month, and natural demand will keep people buying during the month in which the store did so well in the past.

To some retailers, this approach seems to make sense. But does it? Contracyclical advertising is based on the premise that advertising is such a powerful force that it can drastically change people's normal buying patterns.

In some cases this is true. But many decades of experience and years of research say that under typical circumstances it is *not* true in the overwhelming majority of cases. Advertising is *not* a strong enough force to coax very many people to buy air conditioners in December in northern Minnesota when the temperature stands at 25 degrees below zero. It is *not* sufficiently powerful to induce people to buy expensive Christmas gifts for their loved ones in June, to be delivered six months later.

However, well-conceived advertis-ing used consistently over a long period *can* alter *some* customers' shopping habits *gradually.* In particular, it can, in time, extend a *buying season* at both ends. It has, for example, extended the pre-Christmas shopping period back into early November and even early October. It has extended the buying season for major yard-and-garden purchases (like power lawn mowers) back into the very early spring and even the late winter. It has convinced people to take advantage of "end-of-season" savings on air conditioners in September, thus extending the buying season for these appliances by several profitable weeks. Operators of ski resorts have extended their active season by having snow brought in on trucks or manufactured on the slopes by machines and by advertising this fact.

All businesses could operate more profitably if their sales volume could be made more nearly constant. Increased profits often accrue when some business is actually lost during peak selling periods, provided the same or a greater overall volume is generated by improving sales during low-volume periods. This is true for several reasons: During peak periods, it becomes necessary to hire part-time help that adds payroll costs and may lose sales through inefficiency or ineptness. Extra warehouse space has to be rented to carry inventory overload just before peak, whereas the store's stockroom could handle the inventory if sales were constant all year long. Also, ads are less effective and less conspicuous when all stores are advertising heavily.

In practice, then, many retail advertising experts advise stores to include a little dose of contracyclical advertising in their program to build up sales in weak selling months. Shaving a little from the ad appropriation for the busiest selling months and adding a little to the budget for poor months usually pays off over time. For example, if a store made 20 percent of its annual sales in December, 8 percent in November, and only 6 percent in October, it might redistribute its peak pre-Christmas sales by heavier advertising in late October and throughout November: by allotting 15 percent of its budget to December, 10 percent to November, and 9 percent to October.

Contracyclical advertising also accomplishes two other useful objectives. It stimulates sales in periods of the year when people might otherwise forget about a retailer and makes it less likely that they will deal with a competitor during the next busy season. And it gets people thinking about purchases of big-ticket items like houses, autos, major appliances, and furniture, so that by the time the peak selling season for those goods arrives they have already mulled over the buying decision. People like to have time to consider such important purchases, to shop around, and to discuss them with other members of their family. Though contracyclical advertising may not stimulate an actual "pre-season" purchase, it will give the retailer a running start by planting the seed of the purchase idea well in advance.

This advertising distribution contrary to the normal buying cycle is the *one* sensible way for a business to advertise *if* it is already operating at its full profitable capacity during its top selling period and cannot economically handle any more business at that time. A summer resort may be fully booked for July and August, with or without promotion. The only rational advertising approach, then, is to advertise for June and September business. If a restaurant is crowded beyond belief five days a week with business people, its advertising should aim at getting more weekend business from families. If an auto dealer's service department is strained to handle all the jobs it gets during the peak season for new-car sales, it need do no advertising at all during that period, and a big share of the dealer's ad budget can be allotted to the off-season for new cars, to get people with older models to come in for service.

DETERMINING THE BEST WEEKLY AND DAILY ADVERTISING APPROPRIATION

If a store's ad budget for a given month is $1,000, it does not necessarily follow that $250 should be invested each week. When the month is one of those with five top-sales weekend periods, the store may wish to allot $200 of advertising to each weekend period. Or it may want to "borrow" $100 or more from the budget for the following month if the present month ends on a Thursday and that day's ads will stimulate sales during the first couple of days of the next month. Holidays must also be taken into account. Does the second week contain a holiday that has a depressing influence on sales (by creating, say, a long summer weekend that drives half the people out to the country)? If so, it may be best to cut back that week's ad budget to $100 or so and use the money the preceding or following week when selling opportunities are greater. On the other hand, if a week contains the sort of holiday that stimulates sales, or one to which special promotions are traditionally pegged (like St. Patrick's Day or Valentine's Day), an ad investment of $300 or $350 may be justified for that week, even if it means a smaller amount for the other weeks in the month.

Local paydays are a vital factor in fine-tuning a month's ad allotment to maximize sales, especially of discretionary items and big-ticket purchases. People will spend more freely when their pockets are full. If paydays for the major industries in the area fall on the 15th and 30th of the month, for example, more advertising will be in order the second and fourth weeks of the month. Smaller retailers should take into consideration the actions of major stores that draw heavy traffic into a downtown district, a neighborhood shopping area, or a shopping mall. By pacing their advertising to match that of the larger stores, they can get their share of the traffic drawn to the vicinity.

Weather, insofar as it can be predicted, should be considered in developing a monthly (or weekly) ad budget. The National Weather Service issues 30-day and 5-day forecasts, which can be obtained from local newspaper or broadcasting stations. Commercial meteorologists sell both short- and long-range forecasts and count retailers among their clients. Beachwear sales collapse on a cool, wet summer day, and sales of snow blowers and snow tires perk up when a sudden blizzard hits the community. Beer, soft drinks, and sunburn lotions move best when it turns hot and dry, while air conditioners reach their peak in sales if the heat wave includes high humidity. Top sales opportunities for hay fever remedies are related to weather cycles that cause weeds to pollinate, and other medicinal products (even menthol cigarettes) move quickly

at times when more people catch colds. Bad weather favors stores near home and those in covered malls; good weather induces people to make long-range shopping trips and to go to open-air plazas.

News and feature content of the media influence people's response to adjacent advertising. When the sporting goods dealer knows that officials will announce the census of deer herds or the forecasts for migration of flock of ducks, he has a great opportunity to maximize results from his hunters' goods ads. So, too, the dress shop proprietor enjoys a special advantage if major ads can break just as a round-up feature on the coming season's styles is printed or broadcast. To assist advertisers in this particular, the Newspaper Advertising Bureau surveyed 1,335 daily and 463 Sunday papers to determine when each of 43 categories of advertising-related news and feature material is most often printed. Food, motion picture, and fashion news, as well as many other categories, were covered.[3]

It only makes sense to adjust ad allocations to take advantage of all these factors, increasing them on days and in weeks of greatest sales opportunity and avoiding wasted promotional effort when conditions detrimental to sales are likely to arise.

6 A Checklist of Factors That Can Force a Retailer to Modify a Planned Advertising Program

Even though a year's, a season's, or a month's advertising and promotional scheme has been neatly planned and is being skillfully executed, some problems are bound to crop up. This is the reason for the reserve fund mentioned earlier in this chapter, and it is also the reason for continuous Johnny-on-the-spot work by the advertising staff and merchandising people in the store. An ad plan must be flexible. Quick adjustments are almost the rule, rather than the exception, in today's fast-paced retail industry. Many factors can cause a store to alter its ad plans.

Regional Differences Climate, customs, industries, habits, lifestyles, and values vary from one locality to another, a fact that is of increasing importance as stores open more and more branches, single stores turn into mini-chains, and regional chains sprawl into national chains. Rapid changes in strictly local situations pose real problems where ads are managed from top headquarters.

Weather This variable plays all sorts of tricks, both bad and good. And it does not necessarily repeat itself from year to year even in the very same spot. Some of the statistical data derived from an analysis of a store's prior-year sales may suddenly become useless as a guide for advertising this year because of variations in weather. Some product lines whose sales are erratic and thus difficult to predict because of shifting weather patterns from year to year include swimsuits, snowmobiles, rainwear, heavy outer garments, and car batteries. The effects of weather may create unique and unusual sales opportunities. In the mid-sixties, the Upper Mississippi Valley experienced heavy rainfall and massive floods that left stagnant water that bred billions of mosquitoes, much more than in a normal year. Then came unusual winds that blew the mosquitoes by the hundreds of millions eastward into the Middle Great Lakes region. The Mississippi Valley mosquitoes were several times as large as the mosquitoes native to the Great Lakes area and had a much greater flying range. By being so big and ranging so far, they created a whole new and totally unexpected market for all kinds of mosquito-control chemicals, devices to spread insect fog, and the services of insect-control firms. Those who had what the public needed enjoyed a sales bonanza, until they ran out of stock. Those able to replenish their stock found an explosive response to their advertising announcing the happy news.

Fashions Styles are extremely volatile, as every seller of ladies' wear knows well. The switch from mini- to would-be-midi- to maxi-skirts and back again is an old story. The big news in fashion merchandising, however, is that style changes now dominate *men's* apparel merchandising as well as women's. Pants went from tight-fitting to flared; cuffs came, went, and returned; white shirts lost their traditional status then returned to the fashion scene (with long collar points). The long-range trend has been toward casual clothes and away from traditional and formal clothes, but that is about all one can be sure of. The Nehru suit, the Mao jacket, the thirties look—who could have predicted their advent, and known what to stock and how to advertise?

Changing Customs Failure to correctly estimate how established trends are being altered can lead retailers into costly traps. Evidence is mounting that traditional sales-stimulating holidays are becoming less of an incentive to spend: Christmas is declining in influence, as is Mother's Day and Father's Day, as family ties weaken in our mobile society. Until recently, almost all wedding-related promotion was geared to traditional June weddings. However, only 13.4 percent of weddings now occur in June. Almost as many, 12.1 percent are in August; July, September, November, and December also have an above-average number of weddings. Youth's rejection of "materialism" has reduced the overall appeal of lavish manufactured items and increased that of do-it-yourself materials, tools, and courses. The weakening of formal, organized religions is altering the prospects for sales of baptismal and confirmation gifts.

Economy   Inflation and recession, overtime work and layoffs, welfare payment changes and investment income fluctuations all play a dominant role in expanding or contracting sales opportunities. But they affect different categories of merchandise differently. International, national, and local economic developments are all watched by an astute retailer.

International events, such as currency devaluations, greatly affect the relative selling potential of imported versus domestic goods. Dramatic events abroad can trigger shifts in buyer attitudes and in the salability of various lines of merchandise.

National inflation rates, unemployment rates, wage levels, strikes in basic industries like energy-production, transportation, and raw materials extraction —these and many more factors can have an immediate and unpredictable effect

in every town and hamlet, every store and shop.

Local industry is the lifeblood of retailing in every community. A plant shut down by strikes or materials shortages, an industry lost by a corporate merger, bankruptcy, or removal to a distant site can kill merchants' hopes for growing sales. New industries, higher wages, increased employment, longer vacations, more holidays, a shift from blue-collar to white-collar employment as factories automate—all these things can have a stimulating effect on a retail business if it is properly managed and takes advantage of its opportunities through advertising. Local advertising strategies must always be flexible enough to keep in tune with changes in the local economy.

Consumerism and a Concern for Ecology   Consumer sentiments and the ecological effect of products have become important factors to consider in recent years. They can suddenly focus local public opinion on some particular aspect of retailing—the kinds of merchandise offered for sale or the types of service and warranties provided. They can affect the particular features of a given product that should be promoted and the nature of the advertising message itself.

Government Intervention   Regulation that originates at federal, state, or local levels of government is having an increasing impact on the retail segment of the industry. Every retailer must be aware of the possibility of legal restraints on ways of doing business and must keep as broadly informed as possible about laws that may affect the store. The products sold, the services offered, the message content of the ads, and the media through which ads are delivered can all feel the instant impact of a new ordinance, statute, or regulation or a new interpretation of an existing law by courts or administrative agencies. What was perfectly legal (and presumably ethical) yesterday can become illegal (and presumably dishonest) tomorrow!

Special Events Activities contrived by merchants' associations, chambers of commerce, shopping-center associations, and other local groups may be spur-of-the-moment ideas hatched by community leaders (or would-be leaders). Or they may arise in connection with unforeseen natural phenomena or community happenings. A store's advertising plans should be flexible enough to be integrated with such events.

Social Trends A local society may respond to trends at a faster or slower pace than the nation as a whole. The basic trends traced in Chapter 1 have unequal significance at different points in time, for any given locality. Increasing crime rates stimulate sales of firearms, burglar alarms, special locks, and protective devices of all kinds. A single dramatic event can create a "hot" temporary market for some special item. A highly publicized "moon journey" by Apollo astronauts and the much-touted visit of the comet Kahoutek in 1974 increased sales of small home telescopes (even though they were impractical for observing either of these phenomena).

Changing Technology New gadgetry or innovations in automation can quickly alter shopper's interests. Years

or decades of work may be needed to achieve a technological breakthrough, but it usually bursts on the consumer market all at once. Television changed from a scientist's dream to a reality in nearly every American home in the course of a very few years in the early 1950s. Rotary engines—or steam or electric cars—may precipitate a whole new era for automobile retailers and service stations if, as, and when they find general public acceptance. Microwave ovens may change centuries-old ways of preparing food. New fabrics can alter apparel stores' opportunities and their problems.

Merchants face the double danger of being slow to "get with" a new technological development and thus losing out to more progressive competitors, or, on the other hand, of rushing in too soon (with both their merchandising and their advertising) and suffering losses because the consumer market fails to respond as expected.

Disasters and Emergencies Unpredictable crises can arise in the store's community that negate the effectiveness of a planned advertising campaign and force a quick change to ads explaining what actions the store is taking to cope with the crisis. A retail establishment itself may fall victim to calamities of many sorts—fires, floods, wind damage, accidents, robberies. These can interfere with or disrupt entirely the normal operation of the store. Ads intended to stimulate shopping will then have to be halted as quickly as possible to prevent an undue waste of funds. New ads, informative in nature, will have to be gotten out as quickly as possible to clarify the situation for customers and let them know what the store's management is doing to meet the crisis. Later, ads announcing the retailer's emergency plan for resuming business may be needed. The only asset a destroyed or damaged business has is its intangible franchise in the public mind, and advertising can be used in time of distress to protect that all-valuable piece of "property" while the physical plant is being rebuilt, cleaned up, repaired, restocked, or otherwise made fit to resume business.

Of course, even catastrophes can have a beneficial influence on the sale of certain items. A California earthquake in 1971 boosted sales of blankets, flashlight batteries, power units, dishes, and roll-away beds as 80,000 people were evacuated from their homes. Fears of running out of regular fuel hiked sales of free-standing, wood-burning fireplaces more than 30 percent in the winter of 1973–74.

Availability of Merchandise When goods are not available as was expected when ads were planned, a selling event may have to be cancelled or postponed. Materials and parts shortages, strikes at manufacturing plants, transportation difficulties, and other unwelcome happenings can intervene to thwart some portion of any long-range promotional plan. Other merchandise must then be advertised, or ad schedules readjusted. This situation is especially critical in chain or branch-store operations where the advertising originates at a central office. The local-store ad manager in such circumstances spends a great amount of time coordinating advertising with merchandise stocks and making substitutions or altering insertion dates for ads.

7 Putting It All Down on Paper

An advertising plan, even for the smallest business, will not work if it is simply carried in the proprietor's head. It should go down on paper, right from the start. It may be enough, in some cases, to have a simple notebook with a page or two reserved for a statement of advertising objectives and methods of determining the ad budget, a page for a basic media allotment system, and one page for each month of the budgeting year. The same notebook might provide space for pasting down copies of each ad used during the budget period, together with a notation of its cost, the results obtained, the weather conditions that day, and perhaps copies of competitors' ads. Or it may be very complex. A very large, highly departmentalized store or chain would, of course, have a much more formal ad plan.

Retail and media trade associations provide a great deal of material to help the small and medium-sized merchant organize and record an advertising plan. By using such materials, any store can make its ad planning more professional. And by using standardized planning materials as a guide, the medium-sized but growing store can readily devise its own tailor-made planning aids.

An example of a planning calendar provided by a media association is found in Figure 6–8. Assuming that a good long-range plan for the year's advertising has been established, the successful working out of the plan depends in large part on a good breakdown into monthly plans that are related to more specific details. Usually, the best working guide for a monthly plan is the actual calendar for the month itself. In small stores, virtually all necessary notations for the monthly plan can actually be inserted on that calendar page. In large stores, a system of keys or symbols can relate the calendar to a written list of weekly and daily ad themes, media to be used, headlines of key ads, departmental considerations, and so forth.

Questions for Discussion

1. What are four or five reasons why planned advertising is preferable to unplanned, or "hit-or-miss," advertising? Which of these reasons do you consider most important?

2. What special benefits accrue to the smaller merchant who carefully plans his advertising in advance (other than general benefits equally applicable to stores of all sizes)?

Both retail and media trade associations provide simple monthly planning calendars to aid small stores in planning their ads, such as the one shown in Figure 6–8. Study that figure. In which week of the month did the merchant plan to use more advertising than in any other week? Determine from notations on the calendar why that merchant chose that week for the heaviest advertising within the month. (There are two distinct reasons revealed by the notations in the calendar.) Do you notice any difference between the ads the merchant has scheduled for Sunday papers to stimulate early-week shopping and the Thursday ads to promote end-of-week business? What do you think is the reason for this difference?

3. How does the amount of *institutional* advertising used by typical stores, the period of time over which it is expected to produce benefits for the

Figure 6–8 One Retailer's Approach to Scheduling

A planning calendar like this is usually all that the average smaller merchant needs to set the store's advertising plans down in an orderly fashion, and thus to guide buyers and advertising personnel through a month of well-timed advertising. Down the left margin of this monthly calendar sheet is a simple four-step plan for systematizing the month's ad program, with provision for goals, budget, and departmental breakdown. The daily details of the program can be written in on the face of the calendar itself.

This calendar looks as it would after a typical retailer had filled in the specifics. It is important to the store that the community's businesses are open Monday and Friday nights, and that on Thursday of the first week there comes a holiday on which the store will be open. Very critical points are noted concerning citywide "dollar days" (doubtlessly scheduled by a retailers' promotion committee of the chamber of commerce) during the second weekend, and payroll days for local industries on the second and fourth Fridays. The final special event for the month is the store's own end-of-month sale early in the fifth week.

Key ads are planned to take full advantage of night openings, the holiday, the townwide promotion, and paydays, and to promote the sale most effectively. These ads are written in on the calendar on the days when they will appear, with notations as to their size, the amount of space each department of the store will get, and the general type of ad to be prepared. As the number of departments increases or the media plan becomes more complex, separate calendars can be used for each merchandise division or department and for each advertising medium the store uses on a regular basis.

This calendar is the one provided to retailers by newspapers that belong to the Newspaper Advertising Bureau and is reproduced from the NAB's annual *Advertising Planbook*. Similar calendars are provided by other media and by retail trade associations for use by their member stores.

This sample worksheet represents

1. set a sales goal

Department	Sales Goal	% of Goal
A	$ 7,500	25 %
B	$ 2,400	8 %
C	$ 3,900	13 %
D	$ 4,800	16 %
E	$ 5,100	17 %
F	$ 3,600	12 %
G	$ 2,700	9 %
	$ _____	____ %
	$ _____	____ %
Totals	$ 30,000	100 %

2. decide how much advertising

5	% of sales
$1,500	dollars
$3 / Col. in.	rate
500	linage

3. decide what to promote

Write in percents of month's sales which each department contributes. Allot percents of the month's advertising on an equivalent basis. Calculate the linage for each department.

Department	% of Sales	% of Adv.	Linage
A	25%	25%	125"
B (plus co-op)	8	6	30"
C (expanded)	13	15	75"
D (overstocked)	16	19	95"
E	17	17	85"
F	12	12	60"
G	9	6	30"
	___	___	___
	___	___	___
Total	100%	100%	500"

Sunday	Monday	Tuesday
1 Depts: C=20" F=25" — 45 Col. in. ad — Lead Item...price, Item...price, Item...price, Item...price	**2** Night Opening	**3**
8 Depts: E=25" D=15" — 40 Col. in. ad — Lead Item...price, Item...price, Item...price, Item...price	**9** Night Opening	**10**
15 Depts: A=30" F=25" — 55 Col. in. ad — Lead Item...price, Item...price, Item...price	**16** Night Opening	**17**
22 Depts: G=10" B=10" + co-op =10" — 30 Col. in. ad — Lead Item...price, Item...price, Item...price	**23** Night Opening	**24**
29 End of Mo. Sale ad — Depts: A=25" G=10" E=25" B=10" + 10" Co-op — 80 Col. in. ad — Sale Item...price, Sale Item...price, Sale Item...price	**30** 2-Day "End of Month" Sale — Night Opening	**31**

one retailer's approach to scheduling.

Wednesday	Thursday	Friday	Saturday
"Holiday Sale" ad 4 All Departments 10 col. Inches 【 10 Col. in. ad 】 Lead Item....price Item....price Item....price Item....price Item....price	5 Holiday Store Open	6 Night Opening	7

11	"Dollar Days 12
	Sale" Ad
	Depts: A=35"
	    C=25"
	    D=20"
	【 80 Col. in. ad 】
	Sale Item...price
	Sale Item....price
	Item...price
		Payroll Day 13
		
		City Wide
		
		Night Opening
			14
			
			Dollar Days

18	19 Depts: A=25" D=15" 【 40 Col. in. ad 】 Sale Item...price Item....price Item....price	20 Night Opening	21
25	Depts: C=20" 26 E=25" Sale →D=35" 【 80 Col. in. ad 】 Sale Item....price Item....price Item....price Item....price	Payroll Day 27 Night Opening	28

store, and its content differ from the amount of *promotional* advertising used by the average store, the duration of its impact, and its content?

4. Assume that you are managing a store that has three distinct departments, each of which contributes about one-third the total sales volume. What three factors might make you consider appropriating much more than a third of the total ad budget to one of the departments and substantially less than a third to one of the others?

5. What are the essential steps in determining the monthly allotment of funds for advertising a store or a department? How would you work out ad budgets for February and December for a store with a total annual promotional ad budget of $12,000 (in addition to its funds for institutional ads and its reserve funds) if the store expected to do 4 percent of its annual business in February and 12 percent in December? What would the dollar budget be for each of those months?

6. What adjustments are suggested for a monthly promotional budget to take into account such things as the number of holidays and weekend shopping days, which vary from month to month; the contracyclical theory of advertising; industry paydays; weather; and townwide events? In what circumstances might the contracyclical theory be the dominant factor in the allotment of funds for a given month, day, or week?

7. What are two broad, strategic goals of any store's advertising and promotion? Which one must always be considered the primary goal, and why?

Suggested Projects

1. Examine as many current ads by retailers in your community as you can. Clip ads from the local newspaper, secure copies of direct-mail ads, and jot down the essence of broadcast commercials you hear or see. Then, after reviewing the section of this chapter headed "Primary and Secondary Goals," which lists 25 possible tasks for advertisements or series of advertisements, try to pinpoint the tasks these local ads seem to be designed to accomplish. Which goals seem to be most often sought by your local retailers? What are some probable reasons for these goals?

2. Assume that you are assigned to define, as narrowly as possible, the several different target markets for products sold by retailers in your community. First, set up a tentative list of market segments drawn from your own knowledge of the people who live in your area. Define them by their age, sex, occupation, income, education, place and kind of residence, ethnic affiliation, and lifestyle. Then spend some time in the nearest reference library examining federal, state, or local statistics that may help you to define these market segments further and give you a cue to their size. Having done this, discuss how this kind of knowledge can be used by local department stores, supermarkets, auto dealers, specialty shops, and service businesses in formulating their advertising plans.

3. Collect a dozen or more ads recently run by a local store where you yourself seldom go shopping. Or get newspapers from a neighboring town, and pick out a heavy adver-

tiser whose store is not too well known to you. After you have studied these ads carefully, noting the merchandise and services mentioned and the general format and "tone" of the ads themselves, draw up a description of the store (including its decor and fixtures) and its merchandise and services (including its personnel) *as you visualize them to be* after studying the ads. Then go to the store and compare your description with what you find. How accurate was your description? How good a job did the store's advertising do of building a true image in your mind? How would you suggest that the store revise its advertising thrust in the future (if at all)?

4. Obtain a calendar and spot the holidays for the coming month. (A comprehensive sales promotion calendar, possibly from a local advertising medium, a nearby department store's offices, or a chamber of commerce, would be best.) During the month, make a collection of retail ads that have a holiday motif. In what different ways do local retailers associate their merchandise and services with the holidays? Do you think some merchants missed opportunities to use holiday themes in their advertising?

5. For a period of two or three weeks, keep a record of the daily weather in your community. During the same period, collect all the weather-related retail ads you can find. Then analyze how well these ads related to the actual weather in your community, with special emphasis on any weather-related advertising themes that went awry (because the weather turned out to be unseasonable or contrary to normal expectations for the time of year).

6. Visit or call the payroll department at several of the largest employers in your community, and ask what the factory and office payroll dates are for the coming month. Show on a calendar how this will affect local advertising plans. (Note: The chamber of commerce, the bank, or the newspaper may also have this information readily available.)

Notes

1. Joseph R. Rowen, "F.Y.I., Ideas for Independents—Sales Promotion" (July 1970), p. 22.

2. Alvin C. Schottenfeld, "Two Four-Letter Advertising Words: HARD SELL," *Carpet Industry Review* (1970), pp. 32–37.

3. *How to Select the Best Days to Run Ads* (New York: Newspaper Advertising Bureau, Inc., 1974).

Preview

Retail advertising links with sources outside the retail industry itself in a common purpose: to move goods from manufacturer to merchant to consumer. The national advertising campaigns conducted by manufacturers stimulate a demand for goods and services that can benefit local outlets for those products, especially if their own promotion relates to and reinforces that of the manufacturer.

Advertising agencies can often contribute greatly to the advertising effort of the retail, as well as the national, advertiser. Generally, stores will continue to handle their own printed promotional advertising while turning over broadcast advertising and institutional messages to an agency. Retailers must understand what limitations are on their use of agencies, how to select the right one, and how to make their relationship with that agency a smooth one.

In cooperative advertising, a manufacturer joins directly with a retailer to promote its products that are sold by that store, sharing the cost of the advertising and perhaps even supplying the advertising messages and materials. Co-op advertising offers many advantages to both retailers and manufacturers when used as part of a larger marketing plan that serves the objectives of both and when carried out within the rules set forth by the Federal Trade Commission.

Learning Goals

Chapter 7 should give the reader an understanding of the role of national advertising in the marketing process and of the ways in which agencies work to produce and distribute advertising for their clients, both manufacturers and retailers. Students need to know how to choose an agency and what services it will render. A clear knowledge of the principles and methods of cooperative advertising is essential for any substantial retail advertising program. The reader should learn sources of co-op funds, the sort of obligations and restrictions found in contracts for this type of advertising, and the manner by which retailers can work smoothly with manufacturers. Readers will gain an understanding of the limitations of, and possible pitfalls in the use of, cooperative advertising.

7

Retailers'
Advertising Allies

Our purpose in this chapter is to examine the forces *originating outside the retail industry* that help create retail sales. National advertisers, advertising agencies, cooperative advertising, and other dealer-support measures help to accomplish the same end as the promotion originated and paid for entirely by a store. That end, of course, is to stimulate consumers to buy from retailers.

Merchants have allies; they do not carry the full burden of the advertising job themselves. But they must carefully integrate their own efforts with this aid from outside and make of it a team effort. Understanding manufacturers' advertising implies an appreciation of the role of advertising agencies and a recognition of their increasing role as adjuncts to the merchant's own ad program.

1 National Advertisers

Manufacturers, processors, and producers of goods did abut $14.8 billion worth of advertising and promotion in 1974 and an estimated $15.6 billion in 1975. This was 55 percent of all the advertising in the United States. The remaining 45 percent, costing $12.8 billion, was paid for by local (chiefly retail) advertisers.[1]

HOW NATIONAL ADS
DIFFER FROM RETAIL ADS

There are marked differences between retail advertising and national advertising. For one thing, few national advertisers actually prepare their own ads, purchase time and space in the media, or handle other technical details themselves. This is done for them by advertising agencies. Another difference is that national advertising functions at three levels. There is (1) national consumer advertising, aimed at influencing the ultimate user of a product or service to buy it; (2) trade advertising, designed to coax the retailer to carry the nationally advertised product; and (3) dealer support, to help the retailer sell the particular manufacturer's products.

The message content of national consumer ads is usually very different from that of retail ads, with a focus on the product or the company that makes it. Retail ads may indeed deal with the product, but only as a means to an end: to get the buyer to come to *a particular store.* The national advertiser cares little about *which* store the customer visits as long as it is a store that stocks its product. The national advertiser often mentions no price, simply because it does not know at what price its many dealers may choose to sell an item. When its ads do include a price, they may hedge by calling it a "suggested retail price." Retailers, in contrast, generally tell potential customers precisely what an item costs.

National ads have to be general and all-inclusive, rather than precise and specific. A national advertiser usually makes many different products, so that few, if any, of its dealers can stock large quantities of every item. It cannot be sure which models, styles, sizes, or colors are immediately available to the reader or listener in his own community. Its ads must therefore focus on the total line, on the brand as a whole. A merchant, on the other hand, knowing exactly what is in stock at that moment, can advertise a concrete item.

The advertising message of a national advertiser is more likely to include emotional and imaginative appeals, while that of the retailer tends to contain more rational and factual elements. Institutional advertising may be done by a national advertiser, just as it is done by retailers, but it is less likely to be included in an ad designed to sell products. Ads related to immediate happenings, news, and the weather, are less practicable for the national advertiser for two reasons: (1) its ads may go into dozens, hundreds, or thousands of communities, conditions in all of which cannot be the same at any given moment, and (2) working with an agency and with gigantic national media like network TV or magazines, the national advertiser has little of the flexibility with respect to ad timing enjoyed by local advertisers. The lead-time is so long that it cannot get out ads soon enough to take advantage of fast-breaking circumstances.

Because of its generally much larger ad budget, the availability of the professionals at its agency, the greater time span for the preparation of ads, and the spreading of each ad's preparation costs over many repeated insertions and over many different local market areas, a national advertiser can afford generally higher-quality art, design, talent, and production. However, the disparity between national and retail ads, especially ads for big-volume department stores and the great national and regional chains, is tending to decline.

There are striking differences in the media used for delivery of the message. Newspapers are the dominant media for retailers, accounting for about three-fourths of all local media expenditures. The situation is different in the case of national advertising. No one medium carries so large a share of ads because national advertisers employ a complex mixture of media, as Table 7–1 shows. Many people do not include mailings when they think of mass media. If we exclude this means of advertising, television leads the media pack by a very wide margin with respect to national advertising. The amount invested in TV ads is two-and-a-half times the amount invested in magazine ads and three times the amount invested in daily newspaper ads. Among the very large national advertisers, TV is by all odds *the* major medium and often accounts for from 60 percent to as much as 90 percent of their ad budgets. The cost of a single commercial announcement on national network TV in prime time can reach $60,-000, and the cost of producing a good TV commercial is often $25,000 to

Figure 7–1 A National Ad Appealing to Nostalgia
This famous brand of chicken noodle soup, Campbell's, has been known to several generations of American consumers. The manufacturer does not have to stimulate primary demand for a whole class of products but simply wants to remind shoppers how much they themselves have enjoyed this product all their lives. Thus, the ad is dominated by the picture, which shows the hot, tasty soup on a table with some attractive-looking grapes and bread in the background. The small inset picture at lower left shows the can with its universally known label. The brief wording of the copy deals with the many happy memories this product elicits and ends with the company's much-advertised "M'm! M'm! Good!" theme of recent years.
Source: By courtesy of Campbell's Soup Company and their advertising agency, Batten, Barton, Durstine & Osborn, Inc., New York, New York.

Campbell's Chicken Noodle Soup. You know how good it's going to taste before you even lift the spoon.

Just looking at a steaming bowl of Campbell's Chicken Noodle Soup makes you feel hungry. Hungry for those tender pieces of chicken, those golden egg noodles, the richness and flavor of two chicken stocks. Share Campbell's Chicken Noodle or Chicken Vegetable or Chicken 'n Dumplings Soup today with someone you love. Before you even lift the spoon, you know how good they're going to taste.

M'm! M'm! Good!

Table 7–1

National Advertising Media Expenditures, 1974

Medium	Billions of Dollars	Percentage of Total Media Expenditures
Direct mail	$3.986	33.2%
Television (network plus spot)	3.640	30.3
Magazines (excluding farm & business magazines)	1.504	12.5
Daily newspapers	1.194	9.9
Business papers	.900	7.5
Radio (network plus spot)	.480	4.0
Outdoor signs	.225	1.9
Farm publications	.072	0.6

A large category of national advertisers' expenditures, the "miscellaneous" category, includes money used for ads in various lesser media, the manufacturers' share of cooperative advertising costs, point-of-purchase expenditures for displays and other retailer aids, internal overhead costs of advertising departments, weekly newspapers, and the like. These expenditures amounted to $2.759 billion in 1974.

Source: Robert J. Coen, "Advertising Volume 1973–1974," *Advertising Age* (September 15, 1975), p. 51.

$30,000. These sorts of costs effectively rule out this medium for the small advertiser.

Magazines are the most-favored secondary medium, and medium-sized and smaller national advertisers sometimes use them as the primary medium. They are a selective medium in that their readers tend to be better educated, have better jobs, and enjoy more discretionary buying power than nonreaders. Furthermore, there are hundreds of special-interest publications reaching specific segments of the market. Some big magazines divide their circulation along geographical lines, selling regional editions that can serve even retail chains or very large department stores in major cities.

Newspapers and radio are used primarily as *spot media* by national advertisers, to reinforce their messages in selected markets where sales opportunities are best. This compensates for the sometimes too-broad audience of television and magazines, which put as much emphasis on reaching communities where the advertiser has no dealers, or

Figure 7–2 A Retail Ad Featuring National-Brand Products

This retail advertisement seeks to sell Campbell's chicken noodle soup, as does the ad in Figure 7–1, but it also aims to sell any or all of the 38 other products. The same distinctive and well-known soup can is shown as appears in the soupmaker's national ad. The copy is ultra-brief, only sufficient to identify the product, and then the price is emphasized. Price, of course, was not mentioned in the national ad, because different groceries will have different prices from city to city and even from week to week. Working together, making an impression on the same shoppers at about the same time, both ads help sell this brand of soup. The more national advertising behind any branded product, the easier it is for retailers to sell it, with a minimum of their own advertising.

only a very few, as they do on reaching other areas where the dealer network is excellent. Spot advertising also permits adjustments for seasonal variations in sales opportunities. Newspapers or radio stations can be selected to deliver an ad just when the time is ripe, in the case of weather-related products.

THE TREND AWAY FROM SINGLE-ITEM NATIONAL ADS

In recent years there has been a trend in national advertising toward an emphasis on branded product *lines,* rather than specific items, and on image-building ads to promote goodwill. Retailers have been shouldering more and more of the task of describing specific products. Some observers forecast a quickening of this trend in the future and predict that eventually very little specific product information will be disseminated through national advertising.

It is essential to the complete success of any national advertising program that local dealers relate their own promotion and sales efforts to the manufacturer's advertising. Much of the space used in trade journals by national advertisers deals with "merchandising" the ad campaign "to the trade." Unless a retailer is aware of the national advertising in advance, relates some of the store's advertising to the same theme and the same merchandise, uses the window and point-of-purchase displays provided, and trains the sales force to sell the advertised line, neither the merchant nor the manufacturer will profit. Merchants receive notice of projected national advertising campaigns affecting the merchandise they buy for resale not only from ads such as the one shown in Figure 7–3, which are found in trade publications, but in literature mailed to them and from the vendors' salespersons.

MAJOR RETAIL CHAINS AS NATIONAL ADVERTISERS

A significant phenomenon in recent years has been the entrance of large retail chains into the national advertising arena. A pioneer in this field was the Great Atlantic and Pacific Tea Company, which began long ago to promote its "8 O'Clock Coffee" and a few other

Figure 7–3 A Trade Ad to Merchandise the Manufacturer's National Advertising to Retail Dealers
    Much of the *trade advertising* of makers of nationally branded merchandise is devoted to telling the retailer what the manufacturer is doing with national advertising to make the public aware of the product. This enhances the value of that merchandise to the dealer, because local consumers are, in part, *presold* by this national advertising. In this trade advertisement, which appeared in a retailers' trade newspaper, the maker of Burlington pantyhose announces in huge letters on one page of a spread, "This spring, Burlington's fancy lightly turns to a heavy advertising schedule." On the other page, shown here, it tells about the heavy seasonal schedule of advertising on network and spot television and network radio and in selected national magazines appealing to the target market (women). A total of 400 million impressions on the nationwide market are promised. This ad appeared in *Women's Wear Daily* on January 7, 1972, sufficiently far in advance of the spring selling season to influence women's apparel store buyers to stock the pantyhose for that season's selling. The final words of the copy urge merchants to see the Burlington salesperson and stock up, so that they will capitalize on the demand created by the manufacturer's advertising.

What do we mean by heavy? We mean more than **400 million advertising impressions** this spring. Your customers will see ads and commercials for Burlington pantyhose— Brief-top, Cantrece II, Opaques, and all the Burlington best-sellers—in all these places:

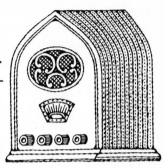

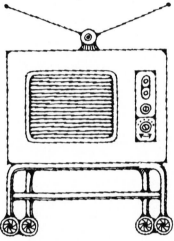

Network TV. The Carol Burnett Show, Sonny & Cher, and other top-rated shows. **Network radio.** On the news, the rock music programs, and special personality programs. **National magazines.** Ads in Cosmopolitan, Glamour, Harper's Bazaar. **Spot TV.** Campaigns in special markets, with free store credits for you.

And a big campaign for our **Annual Sale.** On network TV, spot TV, network radio, and in Cosmopolitan. **Are you ready?** See your Burlington salesman, and make sure you're stocked up. With Burlington's spring campaign about to begin, the customers can't be far behind!

house brands with magazine ads. By 1974, Sears, Roebuck had become the nation's third-largest national advertiser (with over half its national ad investment credited to its mail-order catalog). According to *Advertising Age* estimates, Sears' total 1974 national advertising investment was $220 million. J. C. Penney ranked 32nd among national advertisers with an investment of $69 million. A & P, Woolworth, and Ward had also ranked among the top 100 national advertisers briefly in the early seventies.

In terms of mass media usage, the big chains' national ads are primarily a television venture. In 1974, Sears put $66.4 million of its $106.0 million total media budget into TV, and Penney allotted $20.1 million to television out of a total media budget of $29.3 million. Both also used much radio, and Sears ran a substantial magazine schedule.[2]

Much of the national advertising by big retailers concentrates on promoting the retailers' brands. These ads simply take the place of the national advertising for the manufacturers' brands sold by their competitors. Some retailers use national ads for corporate image-building, to acquaint people with their stores and company policies. It becomes sensible to launch national advertising, quite obviously, only when a chain achieves near-national coverage with its stores. As more chains spread beyond their home territory, more national advertising by retailers can be expected.

Now for the first time ever, retail companies are advertising on two levels: at the national level, as the large chains push their own brand-line products and images through nationwide media (mostly television), and at the local level,

as they continue providing direct support to individual stores (or clusters of stores in the same metropolitan area). Their local ads employ all media but continue to be based on a heavy newspaper schedule. Close coordination throughout a retail organization is needed to get the most from a combination of national and local advertising. Both the timing and themes of the ads at each level must be synchronized. There must also be follow-through at store level. The merchandise advertised must be available on the sales floor, and related displays set up. The sales staff should be advised of the advertising.

For the first time, too, we are launched into an era when virtually all very large retailers employ advertising agencies. At the national or regional level, agencies handle retailers' ads just as they have long done manufacturers' advertising. But they are also entering the retail picture by doing local ads for medium-sized and small stores. Agencies employed by retailers are upgrading the overall quality of retail advertising and helping stores develop a more judicious media mix.

In Chapter 2 we explained that some "chains" actually consist of networks of independently owned stores affiliated with wholesalers, manufacturers, or simply with one another. These types of chains engage in advertising at the national or regional level, as do both national and regional specialty chains. They may employ ad agencies. Manufacturers that are moving into the retail field, setting up chains of stores as outlets for their products, are also advertising on two levels, adding retail promotion for their stores to their long-established national advertising programs.

2 The Advertising Agency: Its Role in National and Retail Advertising

Nobody knows for sure how many advertising agencies there are in the United States. In its "agency list," published every five years, the 1972 Census of Business reported 5,912 in the 83 metropolitan areas that census officials consider to have important agency business. *Advertising Age,* in its annual report for 1974, listed data on 699 that responded to the magazine's request for information.

The agencies doing the largest volume of business in the United States in 1974 were Young and Rubicam International; J. Walter Thompson Company; Batten, Barton, Durstine and Osborn; Leo Burnett Company; Grey Advertising; Doyle Dane Bernbach; and Ted Bates and Company. Each was reported to have billed more than a quarter of a billion dollars that year. (*Billed* is the expression used in the advertising business to rate and compare the gross volume of business handled by an agency. It refers to the amount of advertising placed by an agency in all media for all its clients, plus charges for special services and materials.) There were 72 agencies with billings of over $25 million each, and they billed a total of $10.4 billion.

Some widespread misconceptions held about agencies are that all of them are big and glamorous, all charge fees beyond the budgets of smaller retailers, and most of them are in New York City. This is not the case. Small local agencies, which are of special interest to retailers, can spring up almost anywhere. They differ greatly in size, complexity, and the quality of work produced for their many and varied clients.

The 699 agencies in the *Advertising Age* report billed a combined $13.6 billion in 1974. Since only 72 agencies billed $10.4 billion of this total, this leaves $3.2 billion to be shared among the 627 small and medium-sized agencies—or an average of about $5.1 million for each. Any agency's gross income (the portion of the billings it keeps for itself) tends to approximate 15 percent of its billings, so the typical smaller agency earned about $765,000, out of which it had to pay expenses and make a profit. Examined that way, the agency business is not exclusively a glamorous world of giants but rather a mixture of a few big ones and many small ones. The latter serve smaller clients, each one of which is very important to its agency and gets the same kind of attention the largest corporations enjoy at their own much larger agencies.[3] Agencies are scattered widely around the country and are thus available to assist stores virtually everywhere. While it is true that 1,038 agencies, including most of the giants of the industry that handle large corporations' national advertising, are concentrated on or near famed Madison Avenue in New York, nearly 5,000 others are distributed among 82 other metropolitan areas in every part of the country. Sixteen cities have 100 or more agencies, and 80 cities have 10 or more, reports the Bureau of the Census in its 1972 tally.

Students of retail advertising should understand how agencies work for two reasons:

1. so they can appreciate the channels through which most national advertising, with its huge impact on the sales potential of many items, comes into their communities, and

2. so they can evaluate the performance of particular agencies that may provide advertising services for stores, where such students, either now or in the future, may be employed.

THE FUNCTIONS AND STRUCTURE
OF AN AD AGENCY

There are six basic services an ad agency can perform for retailers:

1. study the client's store and the products it sells in order to determine the advantages and disadvantages inherent in the store, in its merchandise, and in its relation to competitors;

2. analyze the present and potential market of the store and the store's competitive position;

3. use its media expertise to determine the best channels for the store's advertising so its ads may reach the greatest number of desired customers at the least cost;

4. formulate a definite advertising plan and present this plan to the client for approval;

5. execute the plan: write, design, and illustrate advertisements; produce TV and radio commercials; contract for space or time; and perform all the other tasks involved in the ad campaign;

6. help coordinate advertising with the store's other sales efforts to ensure that it has the greatest effect.[4]

Figure 7–4 is an internal organizational chart of a hypothetical agency. The names of the units and officials suggest their functions, and the lines of authority trace the relations of each unit with the others. Even in a moderately sizable agency, some of the work is contracted to outsiders, especially production work and some marketing services. The time and space buyers, of course, work closely with the various media. The ad managers of the various client companies, in this case assumed to number eight in all, make contact with the agency through one of the several account executives.

Most agencies operate on a "committee" system, with periodic meetings in which the account executive for a given client holds planning and coordinating sessions with heads of the various operating departments. Some large agencies use the "account group" system, in which the account executive for a particular client uses the services of a group of specialists drawn from each of the functional units on a permanent basis. Some observers believe that the agency organization shown in Figure 7–4 will change drastically in the future as specialty shops carry more of the workload.

The Account Executive   This key official explains the agency to the client and interprets that client's needs and wishes to colleagues in the agency. The account executive is deeply involved in the planning function (including budgeting); assembles facts, suggestions, and concrete proposals from other personnel of the agency and presents them to the

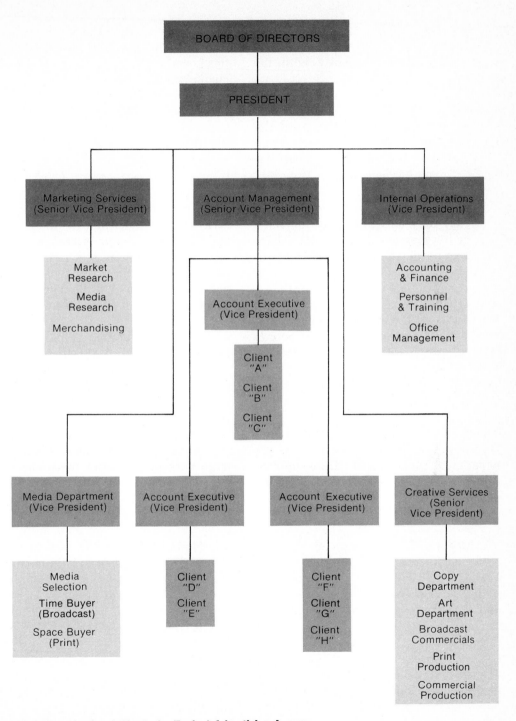

Figure 7–4 Organizational Chart of a Typical Advertising Agency

client for approval; and rides herd on other agency workers as the program unfolds, checking frequently with the client.

Copywriters   The people who write the ads, or *copy*, constitute one of the largest departments in an agency. Many of them are specialists in particular kinds of copy (perhaps retail). They prepare the actual contents of all ads, working under a *copy chief*. Print and broadcast copy may be handled by the same unit or by separate departments. There is close coordination with art and production people.

Artists   People with talent and training in art lay out printed advertisements (and perhaps also the *story boards* used to rough out television commercials). They arrange the various elements of an ad so that it will attract the attention of the right audience and communicate whatever the planners expect it to communicate. Finished artwork and photography is either created within the art department or obtained from outside studios. The art department may also design visuals for television commercials.

Media   The primary job of the many media people in an agency is to evaluate and select the media through which advertising will be done. *Time* and *space buyers* arrange contracts with the media selected, unless this task is farmed out to independent media-buying firms. The media department works with a mass of statistical data about the audiences, "gross rating points," coverage, and technical specifications pertaining to all the media any of the agency's clients

might wish to consider. It keeps on top of choice time slots or page "availabilities" and does the bargaining when media rates are "negotiable."

Research   The research unit is a key unit of a modern agency, usually found within the marketing department. Agency planners and clients are always thirsty for more facts on which to base decisions in today's complex market. Large agencies may actually have their own survey teams and do their coding and tabulating of data internally; smaller ones will engage the services of professional research firms. All will maintain voluminous files and libraries as secondary sources of data. (See Chapter 4.)

Production   Often separated into *print* and *broadcast* divisions, the production departments work up the product of the several creative units into the proper technical form to be distributed to the various media. A few big agencies actually do the technical work themselves, but all small agencies and most large ones contract out these chores to separate companies specializing in typography, photoengraving, printing, or the production of commercials.

Merchandising   For their national clients, large agencies usually have merchandising specialists to plan retail promotions and point-of-purchase materials and to explain and promote ads to the clients' own sales forces and dealers.

Accounting   The great mass of clerical work done in the accounting department insures that the media are paid for all ads they have carried for each client and that the agency's commission on such payments is correctly deducted; that suppliers of special materials and services are paid and that the proper client account is charged; and that the client is billed for agency services on schedule.

HOW AGENCIES EARN A LIVING

Originally, agencies served literally as *agents of the media* and attempted to sell to advertisers as much space as possible at the highest rate they could get. In 1876, the N. W. Ayer and Son agency introduced the notion that an agency worked essentially for the *advertiser* and should try to get the lowest possible rates from the media, even though it derived its compensation from the media in the form of a commission. In 1893 this arrangement was formally accepted by the nation's principal publishers' association, which also made it a matter of policy not to allow commissions to be paid directly to advertisers. Commissions have continued to be the primary source of agency income ever since. The rate of commission has long been standardized at 15 percent (with 2 percent discount for payment by the 10th of the month following the appearance of ads).

Ad media may charge a higher rate for national advertising (all of which is presumed to be handled by agencies) than they charge for local advertising (most of which they receive directly from the advertiser). They get about the same amount of actual cash either way. So in reality it is the national advertisers who compensate agencies for their services, not the media.

Surveys by the American Association of Advertising Agencies (AAAA) reveal that about three-fourths of the income of the big agencies is from commissions, while only a little more than half of the total income of the medium-sized and small ones is from this source. The other two sources of agency income are (1) *add-on service charges* for purchases made from outside sources for the client (usually pegged at 17.65 percent of net, which turns out to be the same as the 15 percent commission on media costs), and (2) *fees for the agency's own services* if the account is not using enough commissionable media to compensate the agency for its work. These fees are negotiable, of course, and are specified in an exchange of letters when a client agrees to appoint an agency to handle its ads. Most agencies require a *retainer* from small clients, usually a flat sum per month.

RECENT CHANGES IN THE STRUCTURE AND FUNCTIONS OF THE AGENCY BUSINESS

In recent years, many independent limited-service agencies, dubbed *ad boutiques,* have sprung up. These special-service shops differ from the traditional full-service agencies described in the preceding section in that each specializes in just one facet of advertising service, such as buying media space or time or creating ad messages. They now occupy a recognized niche as specialists, along with the long-established research firms and production houses that have traditionally been used by advertisers and by full-service agencies.

In addition, responsibility for the planning and management of advertising has gradually been shifting away from the agencies as the executives of client companies have become more aware of the vital role of promotion and have acquired greater competence in this area. Moreover, companies nowadays tend to employ the best advertising managers they can find, further reducing their need for outside help. This trend dovetails with the trend toward the proliferation of advertising boutiques, because, as a firm strengthens its ability to plan and manage its own advertising, it automatically develops the capability of going into the marketplace itself to engage specialists for the advertising tasks it cannot or does not choose to perform. These tasks may include research, media evaluation and selection, copywriting, art, the production of broadcast commercials, or even such prosaic chores as typesetting. Besides obtaining help with these technical aspects of advertising, some firms elect to retain outside consultants or consulting firms to help with the long-range planning and evaluation of their advertising program (another task with which traditional full-service agencies were typically concerned).

House agencies have been maintained by some national advertisers, both large and medium-sized, for many years, and this practice is increasing. In some cases, house agencies are treated and identified simply as the company advertising department; in others, they have a separate name from the parent company and resemble regular, independent agencies. They may even take on a few noncompeting clients to help pay their expenses. These expanding internal ad departments, or *captive agencies,* purchase outside services on an *a la carte* basis, like diners who choose the items they want from a large menu instead of ordering the full-course din-

ner the chef has designed. They tailor advertising operations to the company's specific needs at the moment and seldom make long-range commitments. This is in marked contrast to the traditional client-agency relationship, wherein the advertiser and its full-service agency were expected to work together over a long period of time. While the vast majority of large national advertisers still use full-service agencies, the number of defectors is growing. Moreover, a pattern is emerging with special implications for retailers. It has always been normal for *stores* to have their own ad departments and to buy outside services as needed; now that this system is spreading among other kinds of advertisers, *agency people* are becoming more aware of it.

The traditional full-service agencies have reacted to these trends by setting up separate departments that provide particular advertising services on a piecemeal basis. Instead of expecting all their clients to turn over all their advertising problems and functions to them, many agencies today welcome the part-time client. They offer the do-it-yourself advertiser whatever specialized services it needs at the moment, for a fee, rather than a commission. Thus the temporary client, who literally "goes shopping" for its ad services, can choose to deal with either special-service firms or various departments of one or more full-service agencies. This development has eroded another long-standing tradition—that no agency should have two or more clients in the same line of business.

Another, related trend is the movement away from the commission system. More advertising services are being purchased on a fee or "cost-plus" basis. Instead of paying a uniform 15 percent commission as in the past, clients are increasingly forcing agencies to compete on a price basis, as well as on the basis of service.

Recent years have also seen a weakening of consumer loyalty to national brands, especially among the young, and a correspondingly wider acceptance of retailers' private brands. As some agencies' business from brand-name manufacturers declines, they will inevitably become more interested in finding retail clients with house brands to promote. Since the agencies already have expertise in brand-line advertising (often the very thing retailers themselves lack), the result could be a very profitable partnership.

3 The Agency and the Retailer

The trends we have just described play directly into the hands of merchants who seek a workable compromise between two dangerous alternatives:

1. to continue planning, creating, delivering, and evaluating all their advertising and promotion internally in the face of an increasing need for professionalism in meeting the challenges of segmented markets, new media mixes, a higher type of creativity in ad design and production, and more effective evaluation, or

2. to break completely with their own tradition and turn all their advertising over to outsiders who, despite their technical expertise, may lack a true understanding of retailers' problems.

Conditions are now better than ever for a middle-of-the-road solution to this dilemma. Store managements can instruct their promotion executives to tailor their operations to fit changed and changing needs, retaining the bulk of their established day-to-day promotional advertising programs "in house" but enriching their overall promotional efforts by a selective use of outside specialists. Agencies are increasingly seeking retail clients, learning to work with them and at their rapid pace, and setting up special retail units geared to retail (not national) advertising needs.

Some big retail firms are already advertising at the national level, as we have observed. Many more retail giants that operate on a regional basis are rapidly adopting a two-layer system of advertising: using regional ads that saturate a wide area as a backdrop for hundreds of stores, plus strictly local ads to back up each individual unit. Their regional advertising is virtually the same as national advertising, and agencies are invariably engaged to handle it. Even the biggest ad agencies are now recognizing this trend and have established special subsidiaries or departments to deal with the particular needs of retail clients.

The big news of the early seventies has been the increasing use of agencies for local advertising by so many regional and even purely local stores. The huge retailers doing national or regional advertising through agencies are tending to assign some of their local ads to agencies also—either to the same agencies that handle their top-level ads or to different (usually smaller) agencies. And local retail organizations are forming affiliations with branch offices of major agencies or with smaller, locally oriented agencies that handle their ads for individual stores.

The local retailers seldom, if ever, are interested in contracting for the whole spectrum of agency services. They may be interested in media buying only, in research, in creative work for institutional ads, or just in television and radio advertising. The store ad manager generally retains overall control of the ad program and supervises it, and the day-to-day promotional ads (primarily newspaper and direct-mail ads) are still handled internally.

To sum up, the current relationship between retailers and ad agencies can be described as follows:

1. The "marriage" is still in the honeymoon stage, except in the case of a very few large retailers that have long been involved in national advertising.

2. The development of house-brand merchandise and the spreading out of retail operations over wide and diverse geographical areas have accelerated the retailers' use of agencies.

3. Increasing emphasis on institutional advertising in all media and increased use of the broadcast media have tended to precipitate retailers' decisions to affiliate with an agency. Merchants' own ad departments are seldom equipped to make their own TV commercials or to buy TV time.

4. Rarely does any store, large or small, turn to an agency for its full range of services. The vast bulk of retail advertising of a promotional nature (for specific items at stated prices) remains in the hands of the retailers' internal advertising staffs (and most of it is done through newspapers or direct mail ads). Hence, most retailer-agency arrangements are for handling specific and limited portions of the stores' ads.

5. Most retailer-agency relationships involve fees, not the traditional 15-percent commission. However, commissions earned by an agency on retail clients' ads, if any, are typically deducted from its fee.

6. Big retailers employ different agencies for specific tasks. Therefore, some agencies have more than one retail client.

FACTORS LIMITING THE USE OF AGENCIES BY RETAIL CLIENTS

There is no evidence from current trends that retailing as an industry is about to transfer the advertising function from its own internal personnel to outside agencies. The latter appear destined to serve as valued auxiliaries, but not as substitutes for the stores' own ad staffs. The limitations on the usefulness of agencies for retailers stem from a number of factors.

The Size of the Ad Budget Except for the very largest retail chains and the greatest of the local department and specialty stores, retailers do not have ad budgets (or do not choose to turn over to agencies a portion of their ad budgets) large enough to seriously interest most of the agencies. The small or even the medium-sized store does not generate enough billings from commissionable media to become an attractive client for the agency.

If a retailer has a budget of $100,000 and turns it all over to an agency working on the traditional commission system, the agency grosses only $15,000 a year from the account. It is, at best, a marginally profitable account, especially since the time consumed in servicing the retailer may well exceed that devoted to a manufacturer with a much larger budget. Retailers need many, many ads and frequent changes in copy to match seasonal, monthly, and weekly sales patterns. In contrast, many national advertisers of consumer or industrial goods need relatively few copy changes throughout the year.

Agency people say that a retail budget of less than about $25,000 rules out the use of even the smallest and hungriest of agencies. And all work done for small stores will, of course, be on a fee basis because the media billings will be too small for the agency to break even on commissions. Essentially, this means that a retailer pays a great deal more per dollar of advertising than a national advertiser.

Local vs. National Media Rate Problems Local media, especially newspapers, which are the mainstay of retail advertisers, often insist that when a store places its ads through an agency, the *national* advertising rate must apply. The steeply discounted local rates were developed years ago to reward the local retailer for its consistent, high-volume business without benefit of an agency claiming a 15-percent commission.

Many merchants question whether they can really afford sharply increased rates in order to enjoy the luxury of retaining an agency on a full-service basis. They usually settle for partial agency service and continue to place their own ads directly with the media, typically obtaining discounts of as much as 30 to 40 percent off the national rates they would pay if agencies placed ads for them.

The Time Factor Retail advertising operates at a pace unknown to most agency people. National advertisers, whom agencies are geared to serve, work on an extremely long lead-time. Campaigns are prepared months in advance, and there is little or no opportunity or necessity for quick copy changes or sudden shifts in ad strategy. In stores, sudden, unexpected changes in advertising needs are the rule rather than the exception (as we saw in Chapter 6). An agency simply cannot react as rapidly as an in-house ad department whose members meet buyers, merchandise managers, and department managers many times daily on a face-to-face basis.

Expertise in the Wrong Media For 20 years or more, the focus of national consumer-goods advertising has been on television (with a secondary emphasis on magazines, which are seldom a factor in local retailing). Agencies (especially the larger ones) are staffed primarily to serve the large national advertisers, and consequently their creative staffs and media-evaluation services have been, and in most cases continue to be, TV-oriented. A whole generation of agency people has been wedded to TV as the prime medium; few of the most talented personnel have been assigned to, or chosen to work in, print.

Because, in sharp contrast, retail stores' advertising has been, is now, and by most predictions will long continue to be essentially newspaper-based, the question arises as to whether an agency is really staffed, equipped, motivated, or competent to do any better job for the retailer than its internal ad staff. The store can be led to overemphasize the rightful role of broadcast advertising as a supplementary medium and try to use it as a primary medium, with disastrous results. Or the quality of work done for a retailer's newspaper ads can be below the standards agencies are famous for in other media—with equally dismal results for the advertiser. These criticisms, of course, do not apply to those few agencies—many of them smaller ones—that have retained a better balance among the media, do have top-flight newspaper-oriented copywriters and layout artists on hand, and are wise in the ways of evaluating and buying space in print media.

Questions About the Need for Change   The primary reason for calling in an outside expert to reinforce a store's internal resources in any area is to get better service than the store can provide itself, at a competitive cost. There has been a marked upgrading of the quality of retail stores' own advertising personnel and facilities and of that supplied by local media to their retail clients.

Whereas 25 years ago it was rare to find a truly professional advertising person employed by any but the very largest retail companies, newspapers or radio stations, this is no longer true. Many observers feel that only when a store begins television advertising, for which its own personnel may be untrained, and the local stations do not offer full or free production services to advertisers, need it go outside for help.

AD AGENCIES AND
THE SMALL RETAILER

For the smaller merchant, the basic questions are whether to employ an advertising agency at all and what sort of firm to hire if the decision is made to go the agency route. Let's see what advice we can obtain. Joseph R. Rowen of the National Retail Merchants Association offers this answer to the question, "Should you use an advertising agency?"

Perhaps. Many leading department stores with large staffs of creative people have turned to agencies to handle their broadcast advertising, while retaining production of print advertising on their own premises. The manager of a smaller store who is shoulder deep each day with the many responsibilities of store merchandising or operations may find it advantageous to assign the mechanics of advertising preparation to an ad agency (or a free-lance ad man).

The smaller advertiser, if he uses a large proportion of radio or TV time, may well consider an agency for a degree of expertise not ordinarily found in print-oriented advertising people. The smaller retailer could find it more economical to pay an agency for the time of skilled artists, copywriters and other specialists than to maintain people on his own payroll. Certainly, he should consider the quality of his advertising, for although advertising may seem less tangible than merchandising, advertising dollars are very real and valuable and quality is no less important than the quantities of time and space purchased. . . .

Where payment of the agency increases the cost of a retailer's advertising space or time, it is possible—and often likely—that the better quality of advertising produced will more than justify the agency's services. Moreover, real agency pros who understand retailing can provide long-range planning and objectivity.[5]

On the subject of what sort of agency to choose, Rowen has this to say:

Some local agencies . . . can assist the retailer with marketing data, merchandising recommendations, promotion ideas, and advice for strengthening the store's position in its market. Certainly, the most valuable ad agency is the one that has expertise in media selection, and a good knowledge of retailing. The retailer, on the other hand, must be prepared to work closely with the agency's representative and keep him well informed. The agency must know the store's over-all objectives and seasonal merchandising plans long in advance if it is to develop an efficient media schedule and advertising that reflects purpose, continuity, customer-appeal, and creativity while telling the store's important stories with good timing and impact.[6]

A Small Business Administration book on advertising offers these comments:

> Selecting an advertising agency is like hiring a new employee. An advertising agency is people—people offering their talent, experience, and time. . . .
>
> First, you must decide what sort of agency you want. . . .
>
> . . . If you are a retailer or in some other local business, you would certainly look for an agency with experience in newspaper, radio and direct-mail advertising. Few agencies are so specialized as to be entirely industrial or retail. Most of them are general agencies with diversified accounts. They plan and prepare advertising for all media. . . .
>
> As a small advertiser, you may feel that your agency should be small, too. That is not necessarily so.
>
> Many small agencies are well equipped to give good service. Often your advertising would get the personal attention of the principals. But do not be influenced by the fear that you might get lost in a large agency. In many cases, an agency that appears large is really

a collection of small agencies under the same roof and operating under the same name. . . .[7]

Small retailers often wonder how to develop a smooth working relationship with an ad agency. The same SBA publication gives this advice:

> Do not ask an agency for a speculative plan for your advertising. . . . you should not expect [the agency people] to prepare an adequate plan until they are more familiar with your business. The experience of the staff and what it has done for other advertisers are better ways of sizing up an agency. . . .
>
> . . . Before you tell an agency that it is your final choice, be sure that you and the agency agree about how your advertising will be handled. Formal contracts are not common, but letters of understanding should be exchanged. . . . Know what you will be charged for and how you will be billed.[8]

4 Linking Arms with the Manufacturer Through Cooperative Advertising

Broadly speaking, *cooperative advertising* can be any advertising whose cost is shared by two or more businesses, each of which will benefit by increased sales, prestige, and consumer awareness.

COMMON TYPES OF CO-OP ADVERTISING

Joint advertising is sometimes undertaken by two or more national advertisers selling complementary goods or services, such as a manufacturer of outboard motors and a manufacturer of boat hulls or a resort hotel and an airline that flies to the resort area. This is *national* co-op advertising that is *horizontal* in nature.

Retail horizontal cooperative advertising is becoming increasingly common and is taking many forms. All the independent jewelers, pharmacists, realtors, or insurance agencies in a given community may join in sponsoring institutional ad campaigns to professionalize their public image. The stores in a given shopping center or downtown shopping area may advertise jointly to generate traffic, especially for specific promotional events. Associations often sponsor and coordinate such advertising. Auto dealers that sell the same make of cars within a given metropolitan area habitually channel much of their advertising jointly through an agency.

Vertical cooperative advertising typically involves a manufacturer and its dealers. This is by far the most widely used and most important kind of cooperative advertising. It reaches the consumer in the form of retail advertising, bearing the name of the retailer as a "signature," but including the name and often the distinctive emblem or logotype of the manufacturer or its brand.

A third party may also be involved—the producer of the raw materials used in making the product. Wool growers' associations, orange growers' groups, or makers of synthetic fibers may contribute to an ad program, provided the source of the materials is mentioned in the advertising. Wholesalers or distributors may also join in advertising products, adding their own funds to what the manufacturer puts in.

Cooperative advertising is *both horizontal and vertical* when a manufacturer (possibly backed by a raw-materials producer and a wholesaler or distributor) joins with *two or more* of its dealers in the same community to advertise a product. The advertisements present the manufacturer's story of its product or product line and identify all the outlets where it may be purchased. In print ads, this means that anywhere from two or three dealers (in a small town or suburban area) up to 15 or 20 (in a major metropolitan area) have their names, addresses, and probably their telephone numbers listed in the ad.

In broadcast ads, several dealers' names may be flashed on the screen for a few seconds at the end of a commercial, or (particularly in radio ads) the dealers may take turns being identified

Figure 7–5 Horizontal Cooperative Advertising Combined with Vertical
Here three dealers have joined to sponsor an ad for the same product offered at the same price. They are not competitors; one is located in Milwaukee, and each of the others is in one of the city's suburbs. The dealers might choose to jointly sponsor an ad to enable each of them to make a greater impact in a major metropolitan newspaper. Rarely could a small dealer afford an ad this size in a large newspaper if the entire cost had to be paid out of the store's own budget. From the manufacturer the dealers may get only the professional artwork, distinctive headline, and well-written descriptive copy. In all probability, however, the maker of the Sylvania TV sets also paid a share of the cost of the space for this ad. Typically it is 50 percent, and if that was the case here, it reduces each dealer's cost to a mere one-sixth of the cost of the total space. Note that this ad is entirely product-centered in content and is totally devoid of institutional messages for any of the dealers, except for listing their names and addresses.

at the end of the product commercial each time it is aired.

The combination of horizontal and vertical cooperative advertising can be very inexpensive for the retailer, and it is sometimes the only way a very small store can be represented in a very large ad medium such as a big metropolitan daily or television. In the case of a $2,000 ad, for example, the manufacturer's share of the costs might come to $1,200 (60 percent) and the retailers' joint share to $800 (40 percent). With 10 dealers participating, each dealer's share would be just $80.

Promotional allowances are a sort of cross between cooperative advertising and a *trade discount,* an *inducement to carry merchandise,* a *rebate,* or a *bribe.* Theoretically, they started out as a form of true cooperative advertising in which the retailer was granted maximum freedom to use the manufacturer's money to promote the sales of its product in any way the merchant preferred. No restrictions or qualifications attach to dealer allowances, usually stated in terms of a number of "cents off" per case (for food and drug products) or as a simple percentage of gross wholesale purchases.

In practice, this type of allowance usually degenerates into a back-door method of gaining a better price. Dealers allege that by giving products prominence on store shelves or in displays, they have "promoted" them adequately. However, some manufacturers insist that each store that accepts an allowance must show proof of having mentioned the product in at least one ad of a specified minimum size, within a season or a year. The rest of the allowance, over the cost of that ad, the store can use as it sees fit—either for legitimate promotion and advertising or simply to augment its gross margin.

TRUE COOPERATIVE ADVERTISING

For our purposes, we shall focus primarily on vertical cooperative advertising involving at minimum a manufacturer and a dealer and at most a manufacturer whose contribution is augmented either by a wholesaler or a producer of materials and two or more retail dealers. Our working definition of co-op advertising, then, might be "advertising mutually sponsored by a manufacturer and retailer which is placed locally by the retailer and sells a branded product to local consumers." [9]

HOW MUCH IS COOPERATIVE ADVERTISING USED?

No one has precise figures on how much co-op advertising is used; they are impossible to tabulate accurately. But educated guesses by industry leaders indicate that the vendors' share (including allotments from manufacturers reinforced by producers' and distributors' contributions) totals about $2.5 billion per year and that another huge sum, perhaps as high as $1 billion, is appropriated for the purpose but *not used by retailers.* At least 75 percent of co-op ad money is used for local newspaper ads, though broadcasters are now making strenuous efforts to get a larger share of it. Co-op funds represent roughly one-fourth of all retail advertising media dollars, according to some reliable authorities; if stores' matching shares are included in the tally, co-op funds may be involved in half of all retail-store advertising.

The use of cooperative advertising varies by trade lines among manufacturers and by type and size of stores among merchants. The Newspaper Advertising Bureau estimated in 1975 that the following percentages of ad budgets are co-op: television, radio, and appliance dealers, 80 percent; food stores, 75 percent; drug stores, 70 percent; shoe stores and department and specialty stores, 50 percent; clothing merchants, 35 percent; jewelers and furniture and household goods stores, 30 percent; and discount stores, 20 percent.

THE GROWTH OF CO-OP ADVERTISING

Co-op advertising is one of the most hotly debated topics among national marketers, retailers, and government regulators. Someone is always predicting its imminent demise or its rapid growth. The operational mechanics change periodically, within a company or a group of companies in the same industry. The emphasis shifts among retailers. And the whole scheme is supersensitive to amendments issued at intervals to Federal Trade Commission guidelines and specific court decisions in cases involving the use or misuse of co-op funds.

Despite the fact that some companies are withdrawing from co-op arrangements and there are some segments of industry where less money is available now than was once the case, the overall balance favors growth. Increasing government supervision has forced users of co-op advertising to study the rules more carefully, but the net effect has often been to help eliminate abuses.

The fragmented national market of today makes co-op advertising seem more sensible to many makers of merchandise than further increases in national advertising. Cultivating market segments in specific localities through joint ad programs with retailers who are knowledgeable about the area may make manufacturers' ad dollars go further after all. Professionalism in the field of co-op advertising is being fostered by the emergence of a new title in the marketing world, that of the *cooperative advertising coordinator* in national brand-name corporations, in the larger retail stores or chains, and on the staffs of the principal local media. Nationwide associations and private companies dedicated to serving the co-op field have developed, making this type of advertising easier to use and more likely to succeed. The repeal of fair trade laws in 1975 was expected to stimulate increasing use of co-op advertising both by discounters newly freed from manufacturers' price regulation and by independents seeking more aids in competing with the discounters and other mass merchandisers.

Some of the mystery about the growing proportion of advertising defined as "local" disappears when one understands the growth and potential of co-op advertising. Quite bluntly, it means a shifting of national-brand manufacturers' dollars out of *national* advertising channels into *retail* channels.

REASONS FOR CO-OP ADVERTISING'S POPULARITY WITH RETAILERS

The basic advantages of co-op advertising for a merchant may be summed up thus:

1. The store sells more merchandise, at little or no increase in its own advertising costs, through more frequent, larger, and more effective ads than could otherwise be afforded.

2. The total exposure of the store to media audiences increases as a result of these ads.

3. The merchant usually obtains a lower per-unit ad rate from the media (especially from the much-used newspaper medium) by doing a larger total volume of advertising. This permits the store to either increase the total annual advertising expenditure at no cost to itself (as it should) or to maintain the same total level of exposure at a smaller net cost.

4. The retailer realizes the most value from wholesale purchases only when co-op allowances are fully utilized, since the manufacturer's share of the costs is built into the wholesale prices it charges its dealers. In effect, the retailer has already paid for the co-op funds (and must pass the costs on to retail customers). The store can recover the costs only by *using* the allowances.

5. For small merchants lacking internal ad staffs—who are often served by small media, equally unable to offer top-grade creative services—a true bonanza comes with the co-op ads: manufacturers' art and copy, professionally done by their big-time ad agency's creative experts (see Figure 7–6). This can enhance the image of the smaller store, gain greater attention, assure higher readership or listener attention, and produce a greater response than the less professional efforts of store-keepers and local ad salespersons.

6. A local retailer who employs co-op ads is probably plugging into a total marketing plan devised and paid for by the vendor, including national ads that reinforce the same themes and slogans as the local co-op ads. Furthermore, the co-op ads are backed up by store and window displays, and perhaps also by envelope stuffers and other sales-stimulating literature and devices. All this integrates the store, even the smallest one around the corner or on a sleepy Main Street, with a massive and professional marketing effort, virtually certain to expand the sales volume of the fortunate merchant.

7. Because most co-op plans include a requirement that matching funds be reimbursed only when specific ads are used during a particular season, the merchant is protected against one of the greatest sources

Figure 7–6 Cooperative Advertising Material Supplied to the Dealer
Small retailers lacking their own internal advertising departments are forever beset with problems in obtaining suitable art, copy, and professional commercials for print or broadcast ads. With "co-op," the manufacturer solves these problems for them. Pictured is a newspaper ad in the form provided by one major appliance and home-entertainment manufacturer to its dealers. The dealer has only to indicate the price of the appliances, replacing the zeros that come as shown here, and insert the store's logotype or signature at the bottom. Perhaps the phone number, address, parking and credit facilities, and store hours would also be added. A "mat" is supplied for dealers working with "hot type" newspapers, or a "repro" for those whose local papers use "cold type" ad composition. When entering into the co-op agreement, the dealer orders whichever form is needed.
Source: Material supplied by courtesy of Major Appliances Business Group, General Electric Corporation.

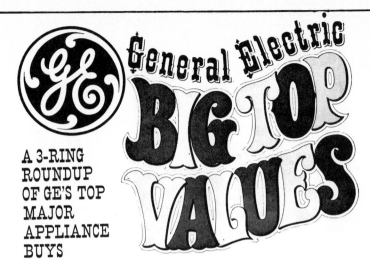

General Electric BIG TOP VALUES

A 3-RING ROUNDUP OF GE'S TOP MAJOR APPLIANCE BUYS

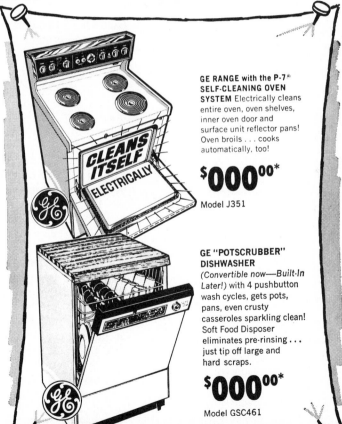

CLEANS ITSELF ELECTRICALLY

GE RANGE with the P-7® SELF-CLEANING OVEN SYSTEM Electrically cleans entire oven, oven shelves, inner oven door and surface unit reflector pans! Oven broils . . . cooks automatically, too!

$**000**⁰⁰*

Model J351

GE "POTSCRUBBER" DISHWASHER (*Convertible now—Built-In Later!*) with 4 pushbutton wash cycles, gets pots, pans, even crusty casseroles sparkling clean! Soft Food Disposer eliminates pre-rinsing . . . just tip off large and hard scraps.

$**000**⁰⁰*

Model GSC461

of advertising failure: promoting the product at the wrong time. The co-op contract is based on the manufacturer's research, timed to match its national ads, and can be a much more accurate indicator of the right time to advertise than a storekeeper's hunches or whims.

8. Traffic drawn to the store in response to co-op ads can be converted into storewide sales of many items not included in the mass media advertising. Hence, the co-op ads help create an opportunity to sell many other items, increasing the merchant's overall profit.

9. Since many manufacturers, in addition to their share of basic space costs, pay 100 percent of the cost of *color* in newspaper ads, the retailer gets a huge bonus. Adding color to black-and-white ads has been proven to increase readership 80 percent, retention 100 percent, and sales from 50 to 168 percent. But color is usually too expensive for the small store to use unless the cooperative vendor will pick up the tab (which it often does). Furthermore, the expensive color-separation plates or negatives needed to do a good job are sent free by the manufacturer, solving the store's color production problem as well.

10. When a local store is connected with a famous national brand in the minds of customers, some of the prestige and fame of the nationally branded merchandise rubs off on the retailer. This makes co-op ads, in effect, valuable institutional promotion for the lesser-known or small store.

In short, everyone concerned benefits from co-op advertising that is properly employed.

LIMITATIONS AND SOME DRAWBACKS OF CO-OP ADVERTISING

All is not peaches and cream in every co-op advertising venture. Improperly used, or overused, the co-op system can do harm as well as good to the local merchant. The following points should be kept in mind by a retailer considering a co-op arrangement.

1. Co-op ads should be used *only* when they truly fit in with the store's overall, profit-oriented advertising and budgeting plan. If a store can sell more units of some other item, perhaps at a higher profit than the co-op item, it should use the money it would have to contribute to the co-op ad costs to promote those other items and let the co-op proposal go by.

2. The *overuse* of cooperative advertising can decrease, rather than increase, a store's total annual profit in at least two common situations. One occurs when virtually the whole of the store's ad budget is used to match manufacturers' co-op funds, leaving little or no money to pay for image-building institutional ads that set the store apart from its competitors. Co-op ads for two or more stores that may be direct, head-on competitors look precisely the same. Spending too much for co-op ads may also create problems for a store that lives largely off the traffic generated by fast-moving staple items with a low unit price for which little or no co-op ad funds are provided. The big-ticket items (for which there is more likely to be co-op advertising) may be sold, in large part, as a result of the traffic. If there are insufficient funds for advertising the fast-moving traffic-builders, the big items themselves may move more

slowly, even when they are featured in co-op ads.

3. Retail ad budgets can be skewed out of line, and advertising may for that reason fail to produce highest profits, when the availability of co-op money is allowed to dominate decisions about the allotment of store ad funds to given seasons, months, and weeks or to particular departments, merchandise lines, or product categories. If store ad money is used solely to match co-op offers, the merchant may muff opportunities to exploit seasonal buying trends peculiar to the community. Or the retailer may neglect profit-making or traffic-building departments or lines. (Review the discussion of a true case in Chapter 6, pp. 149–150.)

4. Administrative chores associated with co-op contracts can be misunderstood or neglected (especially in the small, one-family type of store). This may result in time-consuming correspondence, late payment, or even eventual nonpayment of the vendor's share if the red tape never does get unwound.

5. Either through misunderstanding or deliberate design, retailers and advertising media can be enticed into unethical and illegal practices such as "double billing." Double billing is used to deceive the manufacturer into paying more than its agreed share. Some co-op contracts explicitly state that the manufacturer will reimburse the retailer at the medium's *national* ad rate (the same rate it would pay for an ad handled through its agency) or at the local *open* rate (which a small retailer might have been paying before it "earned" a lower rate because of the increased volume credited to its ac-

count by virtue of co-op ads). But in most cases the contract specifies that the manufacturer will pay only its half (or 75 percent or some other agreed-upon fraction) of the net, actual retail advertising costs, including any year-end rebate the store may have "earned." Violating this agreement with the cooperative manufacturer, willfully or unintentionally, can lead to a withdrawal of co-op privileges (at the least) and can make the store, the medium, and the factory subject to citation by federal authorities for violation of the Clayton Act, the Robinson-Patman Act, or the Federal Trade Commission Act.

6. The proper use of co-op ads is as a bridge, linking the planned, long-range, market-oriented promotion plan of a manufacturer with the equally well-planned, long-range, market-focused promotion of a retailer. If the two coincide, cooperative advertising is in order. If they do not coincide, the store must have the courage to stick to its own plans.

FTC REGULATIONS

FTC regulations concerning co-op advertising are specific and far-reaching. Regional FTC offices are under orders to "police" the advertising practices of local retailers in all parts of the country, and co-op advertising is one great area of concern.

To be fully informed about both its rights and its obligations, the retail participant in cooperative advertising or vendors' promotional allowances should obtain a copy of the FTC guidelines (with latest amendments) that govern this process.[10] Among the most important FTC requirements is the rule that vendors must offer "proportionally equal" co-op opportunities to *all competing stores* handling their merchandise (but not necessarily throughout the whole country) if they offer it to any store. They cannot legally favor the big stores over the small ones, chains over independents, or prestigious shops over lesser-known merchants in the same "natural" trading area. Moreover, the vendor is held responsible for promptly and completely informing all its dealers about its co-op programs, and the retailer who accepts is even forbidden to do so if that retailer knows that a certain "deal" is a special one that has not been offered to competitors. A landmark decision by the United States Supreme Court in 1968 (the famed "Fred Meyer case") established that there can be absolutely no discrimination against retailers who buy through wholesalers, and in favor of direct buyers, in giving out "proportionally equal" promotional assistance. New FTC guidelines issued in 1969 promulgated this doctrine and further refined its application by including a requirement that the original seller (the factory) retain responsibility to "take affirmative steps to verify" that the intermediaries are in fact carrying out the maker's written instructions to offer and handle the program for stores who buy from them on exactly the same basis as the manufacturer's plan for those who buy direct.

Geographical, media, or other trick limitations are forbidden unless they provide for exceptions so that even the littlest store can participate in a reasonable manner. And everyone involved—vendor, media, and merchant—is held

responsible if double billing is resorted to as a means of "conning" a manufacturer into paying its proportion of a fictitious advertising rate higher than the actual rate a retailer paid for advertising (including the store's year-end quantity discount, if any). The general thrust of recent amendments and new policy statements has been to increase the protection of smaller dealers against past practices that tended to benefit the larger stores and to spell out more plainly the prohibition of billing practices that defrauded the manufacturer. Recently the Federal Communications Commission, which regulates broadcasting, launched its own stepped-up enforcement measures against radio stations that resort to double billing, with penalties as severe as cancelling a station's license to broadcast. The Department of Agriculture has struck out against those in the meat industry who participate in the same illegal practices.

HOW A STORE GETS ITS SHARE OF AD FUNDS, AND HOW THE SYSTEM WORKS

In large department or specialty stores and chains, the merchandise manager is as involved in, and concerned for, cooperative advertising as the advertising manager and his or her immediate associates. The store's buyers naturally try to get advertising support for every line they take on. When the price of products, their customer appeal, their quality, the terms of delivery, and other factors are about equal, a buyer will normally give the nod to the one whose maker offers co-op advertising. Advertising help from vendors is one of the things buyers "buy," in addition to tangible merchandise. The closest coordination between buyers, merchandise managers, publicity directors, and advertising managers is essential. They must continually exchange information.

Where to find co-op deals is the first and most obvious problem for any merchant who wants to obtain all the co-op advertising possible or who feels that the store's resources (suppliers) have not adequately notified all their retail customers about available opportunities for this kind of aid. While FTC *Guide 8* insists that it is the "seller's duty to inform" every "competing" dealer about the availability of co-op plans, the "seller" (manufacturer or wholesaler) is free to "make the required notification by any means he chooses." The FTC suggests this notification can be made through "wholesalers, distributors or other third parties," by means of "appropriate announcements on product containers or inside thereof with conspicuous notice of such enclosures on the outside," by publishing notice "in a publication of general distribution in the trade," or by "advising customers [dealers] from accurate and reasonably complete mailing lists." [11] Quite obviously, any or all of these notification methods can fail. It behooves the managers, buyers, and advertising staffs in the stores to be constantly alert and even aggressive in seeking out vendor funds on their own initiative. If enough retailers persistently ask for advertising help, and perhaps drop hints that other suppliers do offer co-op funds, a company may offer some, even if its former policy did not include this kind of backing.

A few dollars invested in sending a form letter to every one of the store's resources, asking for co-op funds, may work wonders. Salespersons sometimes forget to mention co-op funds, or neglect to mention them except to favorite customers. Letters to the home office will quickly resolve the issue of whether anything was missed by the smaller merchant. Retailer's trade associations maintain lists of companies supplying co-op programs within any trade line, which are sometimes published in bulletins or association magazines. The National Retail Hardware Association not only provides lists of co-op programs but actually administers many of those programs for its member stores.

Local media, especially in larger cities, compile lists of cooperative advertising opportunities for their clients. The Newspaper Advertising Co-op Network functions nationwide to provide member newspapers with the information needed by local advertisers in their towns. The Newspaper Advertising Bureau, regional and state press associations, the Radio Advertising Bureau, and the Television Bureau of Advertising all help their members to alert local clients to co-op opportunities.

Directories of co-op advertising sources are available and may pay off richly, especially for the merchant who carries many diverse merchandise lines from a large number of resources. The *Tripac Co-op Ad Guide Book,* published by Tripac, P.O. Box 627, Middlesboro, Ky. 40965, is inexpensive and easy to use. It should more than pay its way for even the smallest store that suspects it is missing out on some co-op ad funds. The *Standard Directory of Advertisers* (the classified edition) is another goldmine of information. Though more expensive than the Tripac guide, it is updated more often. It is available from the National

Register Publishing Company, 5201 Old Orchard Rd., Skokie, Ill. 60076.

Finally, a store should watch other stores' ads. It is easy to spot a co-op ad, with a little practice. If someone else in an area—or a nearby larger city—appears to be getting help in advertising a product or line the store carries, it too can hop on the bandwagon.

CO-OP ADVERTISING CONTRACTS

Entering into an agreement for co-op advertising involves signing a contract with the vendor. There is no such thing as a "standard" co-op contract; each company makes up its own. All the contracts tend to cover the same basic points, but they *can* be modified to suit a retailer's special needs (provided no violation of FTC guidelines is involved). A typical contract is reproduced in full in Figure 7–7.

The four basic parts of most co-op contracts pertain to (1) allowances, (2) performance, (3) specific requirements, and (4) billing for reimbursement.

Allowances must provide for proportionally equal payments to all stores, large and small, as required by the FTC. They may be *fixed* or *accumulative*. A fixed allowance may be a set dollar figure, such as $500, to be employed for the grand opening promotion of a new store, throughout a designated season of the year (like the pre-Christmas season), or for a holiday promotion (perhaps at

Easter). Or, the amount may be tied to the size of the ad and the circulation of the medium. The manufacturer might pay a blanket 50 percent of the cost of 500 column-inches of newspaper advertising (or 50 30-second commercials) during each six-month period. Some fixed-allowance agreements permit a store to run a given amount of advertising (such as 200 column-inches) totally at the manufacturer's expense, with or without purchases of its products in any stated volume. Or the agreement may be a simple "open-ended" contract saying that the manufacturer will pay half the cost of any and all advertising the merchant uses for the product involved. (See Table 7–2.)

Allowances based on purchases take the form of *earnings* accumulated by the store. Their size is proportional to its volume of business with the manufacturer or its level of purchasing of specified branded products. They may be a specific percentage of *dollar* purchases, say 4 percent. In that case, a $1,000 order produces a credit of $40 in the store's co-op account, or a purchase of $5,000 entitles the retailer to $200 of the manufacturer's money to match its own when it advertises the products. But in some industries, notably the food and automobile industries, the credit accumulates as a specified dollar amount per *unit*: 50¢ per bag or case, or $50 per car. Sometimes the percentage allowed for ads is 5 percent throughout the year but is raised to 10 percent for a brief

Figure 7–7 Example of a Cooperative Advertising Contract
     This is a typical cooperative advertising contract that is actually used for the dealers of products made by a manufacturer of home entertainment electronics components. (The name, address, and so forth are fictitious.) It contains most of the provisions common to cooperative ad contracts for all lines of merchandise.

CLEAR VOICE . . . A Division of United and Consolidated Electronics, Inc.

1616 E. West St.
Plain City, N.J. 07999
Telephone: (201) 349-3485

CO-OPERATIVE ADVERTISING ALLOWANCE FOR HIGH FIDELITY PRODUCTS

1. Clear Voice will allow 5% of an authorized dealer's gross purchases of high fidelity products (dollar value based on distributor cost) to be used for co-operative advertising of Clear Voice High Fidelity Products.

2. Co-op advertising funds are cumulative over six month periods, i.e., the 5% is computed back six months from the dealer's purchases "to date." The 5% accumulated co-op fund will be applied to 50% of the cost of the dealer's advertising of Clear Voice High Fidelity Products. Co-operative advertising funds not used expire in their entirety.

3. The fund may be used for payment of media space and radio time costs (PRODUCTION COSTS ARE NOT APPLICABLE TO CO-OP FUND), or for the purchase of special promotional material that will be made available by Clear Voice from time to time. Co-op funds are applicable only to nationally recognized local media listed by Standard Rate and Data Service, Inc. Co-operative funds will be paid at the best rates available to the local advertising dealer.

4. Co-op advertising will be available only to those franchised stocking dealers who have an adequate stock and prominent in-store display of Clear Voice High Fidelity products. Only high fidelity products will be eligible for co-op funds.

5. All printed media and radio advertising must include the standard Clear Voice trademark prominently displayed and no competitive product to the Clear Voice product being advertised is to appear in the same ad. Example: "X" loudspeaker and Clear Voice loudspeakers is not permissible; Permissible: "X" loudspeakers and Clear Voice tuners, amplifiers, etc.; or Clear Voice loudspeakers and "X" tuners, amplifiers, etc.

6. Clear Voice will provide newspaper ad material of "Stereo High Fidelity Products" to dealers. When material other than that supplied by Clear Voice is used, copy and layout or commercials must be cleared by Clear Voice.

7. Credit for co-operative advertising will be based on the actual date coinciding with the date of the media invoice.

8. To receive credit for printed media, Clear Voice requires a full-page "tear sheet" of the advertisement and receipted copy of the paid media invoice attached with the dealer's invoice claiming 50% credit of the total cost of that portion of space devoted to Clear Voice products and then forwarded to the Advertising Manager, Consumer Products Division, Clear Voice, Plain City.

9. To receive credit for radio advertising, copies of commercials, station affidavit of performance and receipted copy of paid station invoices, attached with the distributor's invoice claiming 50% credit of the total cost of that portion of time segments devoted to Clear Voice products must be forwarded to the Advertising Manager, Consumer Products Division, Clear Voice, Plain City.

10. Such claim for credit will be checked against your purchases to determine if it has been earned. You will be advised by letter from the Consumer Products Division Advertising Department, as to the exact amount credited to your account. Again, this amount will be 5% of your previous six-months' purchases, as detailed in paragraph one. This amount will be credited 50% of the invoice sent us. We will be glad to answer all questions concerning this program if you will write:

ADVERTISING MANAGER
CONSUMER PRODUCTS DIVISION
CLEAR VOICE
1616 E. West St.
Plain City, N.J. 07999

Table 7-2
Cooperative Advertising Allowances to Retailers: A Survey

Product Category	Number of Contracts Included in Survey	Proportion of Advertising Costs Paid by Manufacturer						Proportion of Purchases Used as Basis for Accumulation of Co-op Advertising Credits (up to proportion indicated)									Fixed Amount Per Unit
		Below 50%	50%	60 to 70%	75%	80%	100%	1% or less	2%	3%	4%	5%	6% to 9%	10%	Over 10%	No Limit	
Appliances	61	0	23	1	22	0	15	1	7	8	8	17	0	0	0	1	4
Hardware, garden, and farm supplies	47	0	34	2	0	5	6	1	6	6	2	1	0	4	2	13	2
Automotive (cars and supplies)	58	2	37	1	1	0	17	6	5	0	0	7	1	0	0	7	18
Heating, electric, lighting and plumbing supplies	11	0	9	0	2	0	0	1	1	1	0	2	0	0	0	2	1
Floor coverings, furniture, and household goods	67	0	40	13	2	0	12	2	7	12	6	17	3	7	1	5	1
Office equipment and supplies	9	0	3	0	0	0	6	0	0	2	0	3	0	1	1	0	1
Builder's hardware, paint, and building materials	54	0	40	4	1	0	9	6	4	9	1	5	4	3	2	10	1
Luggage and leather goods	9	0	7	0	0	0	2	0	2	1	0	6	0	0	0	0	0
Photographic equipment and accessories	7	0	1	0	0	0	6	0	0	0	3	1	2	2	0	0	0
Watches	14	0	11	2	1	0	0	0	0	0	3	7	0	5	2	0	1
Apparel	21	1	18	0	0	2	0	0	8	4	4	4	0	1	0	0	0
Miscellaneous	23	2	13	0	1	0	7	3	1	1	4	3	0	7	4	3	1
All trade categories	381	5	236	23	30	7	80	20	41	44	27	73	10	30	12	41	31

Note: In this analysis of a representative group of manufacturers' contracts in several important product lines, when the same company offered different types of contracts for several lines, each contract was included. Contracts were *not* selected on the basis of a true probability sample; hence the table does not necessarily represent the relative preponderance of the various types of contracts. It does reflect the general practice in the different product groups current in 1973 and 1974. The figures for the proportion of purchases used as basis for accumulation do not equal the total number of contracts analyzed, due to options in some plans and an absence of information in others.

period to stimulate local advertising that coincides with top sales opportunities and the manufacturer's heaviest national advertising campaign.

An allowance is normally paid in cash or by a credit to the store's account, but it can also be paid in merchandise: one extra case free for every 10 cases ordered, provided the retailer runs an ad of given size for the product.

Performance requirements are clearly stated in the co-op ad contracts, and the retailer must understand them in order not to invalidate the agreement and lose the co-op funds the manufacturer offers. The most important thing to know is the *split,* the proportion of the advertising to be paid for by each of the two parties that have agreed to "cooperate." Although the 381 contracts surveyed in Table 7–2 were not systematically chosen to reflect a true cross-section of all manufacturers who offer co-op support to their dealers, the sample is sufficiently representative to permit a few broad conclusions to be drawn about the proportion paid by each party. (1) Since 62 percent of the contracts (236 out of 381) provide that the manufacturer will pay half the co-op advertising costs, one may declare that the "50–50 deal" is typical. (2) Because 5 percent leads all other figures by nearly two to one as the percentage of purchases used as a basis for accumulating co-op credits, this is the figure most likely to be encountered. (3) Only in the automotive field is a per-unit basis for the accumulation of credits significant. (4) The percentage of manufacturers who will pay *all* the advertising costs is highest in the camera, office supplies, miscellaneous, and automotive categories. (5) Those who place no limit on the

proportion of a retailer's sales that can be used as the basis of co-op advertising credits are most likely to be found in the hardware field and related lines. (6) The appliance category is dominated by manufacturers who pay *more* than 50 percent of the ad costs.

The terms of the split make a big difference, particularly if the proffered co-op campaign is of marginal value to the store. If the manufacturer, who has perhaps received contributions from raw materials suppliers, pays 75 or 80 percent of the costs, the retailer is almost sure to get a good value, even if the advertising is partly a gamble. But when the store must supply 50 or 60 percent or more of the money, the co-op offer should be accepted only if (1) it is squarely on target with the store's pre-planned, profit-oriented merchandising plan and (2) the store's share of the money would have been spent on that merchandise regardless of the co-op rebate.

Restrictions on media may influence whether or not a given store wants a plan. Virtually all co-op programs specify the use of a paid-circulation daily newspaper acceptable to the manufacturer for ads. Some prohibit the use of weeklies or of controlled-circulation (free or partly free) papers or shopping guides. FTC rules now make it easier for lesser media to be acceptable if a store cannot effectively use the medium preferred by the manufacturer. Radio or television ads are optional in many co-op programs. Some manufacturers will approve outdoor or direct-mail ads, too.

Most co-op programs for seasonal items restrict the period during which the ads may appear. A grass-seed company would hardly appreciate spending money for ads run in November in the northern states (even if the retailer were so foolish as to waste its own share of the money at that season). The approved season may be rigidly stated in the contract, or the store may be gently nudged to use the ads at the right time by a clause stating that the manufacturer will pay 80 percent of the cost of ads appearing, say, during May and June and 40 percent of the cost of ads used at any other time of the year. This type of clause is more than a gentle hint that it is to the advantage of the store to use the co-op advertising when the manufacturer prefers it!

Some manufacturers require only a minimum of advertising; one ad or a few small ads may be all that is required for a store to receive a large "promotional allowance." However, this practice, like double billing, is being phased out under FTC scrutiny.

Some manufacturers are very rigid in their insistence that the entire contents (excepting a very small and precisely defined unit for the store's own identification) of all co-op ads they sponsor *must* be supplied by their own agencies or ad departments. Such ads are totally hard-sell item-price ads, lacking any institutional overtones, and are the rule when the dealer is a franchised outlet. Other manufacturers allow considerable flexibility under certain conditions: if groups of dealers jointly engage a local ad agency to assist with preparing professional-quality local advertising for the group as a whole (vertical-horizontal co-op advertising); if an ad medium works up the ads; or if a store has a good internal ad staff and a well-established reputation and prestigious image. It

often takes special personal contact with high officials of the cooperating firm to secure advance clearance for such deviations from its established policies.

Essentially, the two main factors that influence the performance required of the store are *the manufacturer's basic marketing program* for its products and *current trends in its industry.* These change from time to time, and so do "typical" co-op advertising performance provisions.

Specific requirements (the "fine print" in contracts) vary greatly from industry to industry and from manufacturer to manufacturer, and are constantly being influenced by reinterpretations of federal law by the FTC and the courts. Contracts may become increasingly complex in the future, as all concerned (manufacturer, wholesaler, retailer, and the media) seek to clarify their positions and have everything down in black and white lest some legal complications arise to plague them as the FTC pushes more deeply into the active regulation and policing of cooperative advertising at all levels.

Billing for reimbursement can be complex, and procedures differ from one company to another. As far as the media are concerned, the store is the sole advertiser and must pay the whole bill. In most cases, the retailer's contract with the medium establishes the rate, and because co-op ads count toward any rebate or earned rate to which the store may be entitled, both store and medium are responsible for informing the manufacturer of such rebate -possibilities or earned rates. Ad allowances cannot be used as credits against merchandise invoices due the manufacturer; the advertising arrangement is an entirely separate transaction.

Within a stated period after appearance of the advertising, usually thirty to sixty days, the merchant must bill either the manufacturer or its representative— such as the Advertising Checking Bureau, a service agency that processes co-op ad claims for nearly 400 manufacturers, or a retail trade association. Each claim must be supported with a full page tearsheet from each newspaper in which the ad ran or, for a co-op commercial, with an affidavit of broadcast plus a notarized copy of the actual script. To each claim, the store must attach an invoice showing the amount of space and time used and the rate previously agreed upon—most commonly the retailers' net rate, taking into account the discount and, possibly, rebates, but sometimes a *fixed line* rate set by the manufacturer, the lowest local contract rate, the medium's national rate, or whatever. This invoice shows the total cost, less the store's share, and the balance due from the manufacturer. Color surcharges for print ads are usually handled separately, but they count against the dealer's earned co-op ad allowance.

Some agreements require the store to include copies of the merchandise invoices on which the co-op allowance is based in order to prove that sufficient credits have been built up to cover the manufacturer's share of the advertising cost. They must be dated within the current year, because unused balances are rarely carried over from one year to the next. Many vendors require a receipted bill from the medium (usually unnecessary when dealing through ACB), which helps the manufacturer detect fraud. When a medium and a retailer conspire to provide an alleged "paid bill" for a larger sum than was actually paid for the advertising, both are subject to prosecution by the FTC for double billing, and, in the case of broadcasting stations, the Federal Communications Commission can revoke the station's license.

The administration and planning of co-op advertising can be simplified and made more accurate and effective by the use of various forms. Large stores develop their own; small ones can get them from retail trade associations in some cases, and from the local media.

BUDGETING FOR CO-OP ADVERTISING

There is a lot of fuzzy thinking associated with budgeting funds for the store's share of co-op ads, especially among smaller merchants. Some kid themselves into treating the vendor's money as if it were part of their own ad budget, instead of a welcome "bonus" to augment it. The Newspaper Advertising Bureau, in its 1974 *Advertising Planbook*, suggests that when a retailer has set up a monthly ad budget for each department or merchandise group (like that discussed in Chapter 6) and co-op deals come along, co-op support for each line of merchandise should be calculated as demonstrated in Table 7–3.

Questions for Discussion

1. What are some of the main differences between *national* and *retail* advertising? On which "levels" do

Table 7–3

Adjusting a Monthly Departmental/Merchandise-Line Budget for Cooperative Advertising

Merchandise Eligible for Co-op	Projected Co-op Contribution (% of purchases)	Amount of Month's Adv. Already Budgeted for This Project	Terms of Co-op (vendor to retailer)	Advertising Budget Adjusted for Vendor Co-op
Product A	5% × $2,000 = $100	$50	⅔–⅓	$150
Product B	4% × $5,000 = $200	60	50/50	120
				(unused co-op = $140)*

* The projected co-op contribution should supplement the amount of month's advertising allocated for a particular line of merchandise rather than determine that amount, because a revision of the budgeted amount just to match the co-op terms may adversely affect the amount of advertising linage necessary to effectively promote that department or other departments and thus the traffic, sales and profits of the entire store.

Source: *Advertising Planbook* (New York: Newspaper Advertising Bureau, 1974), p. 8.

national advertisers operate, what use do they make of advertising agencies, and which media do they most prefer for ad messages?

2. Why should people working in retail advertising know something about advertising agencies?

3. What are at least five functions an agency performs for its clients? Draw a rough diagram to show how an agency is organized to accomplish those functions. Who in an agency has the most direct contact with and the most personal relationship with its client companies, and what are that person's main duties?

4. How do agencies "earn their living"? What changes are taking place in the methods by which agencies are paid for their work? Will these changes encourage or discourage the use of agencies by retail stores?

5. Of what should a retailer be careful if it is going to employ an agency to handle all or some of its advertising? If you were a retail manager,

what qualities would you look for in selecting an agency for your store?

6. What are the advantages of cooperative advertising that make it popular with most merchants?

7. What are some of the possible pitfalls merchants must be aware of in using cooperative advertising?

8. How does a retailer go about finding which manufacturers whose merchandise the store sells offer cooperative advertising support? Which means do you think would prove most fruitful for a small store searching for advertising dollars it might be missing?

9. What four basic points does any cooperative advertising contract cover?

10. If a store has purchased $10,000 worth of merchandise at wholesale from manufacturer A, which allows an accumulation of advertising funds equal to 5 percent of purchases, how much cooperative advertising credit has it built up? If

this manufacturer pays 75 percent of the cost of co-op ads, how much of the store's own money must it put in to secure all the co-op money to which it is entitled? If it uses all the money for newspaper ads and the newspaper charges $5 per column-inch for display advertising, how many column-inches of advertising can the store run and get the 75 percent rebate?

Suggested Projects

1. Secure several popular consumer magazines and a number of copies of a relatively large daily newspaper. From them, select a dozen or more national consumer advertisements. Select a like number of retail ads from the newspaper or from a local magazine that carries retail ads. Compare and contrast the national and retail ads. Consider the amount of specific facts given about the products, prices, purchasing terms, service, and the breadth of the product line; the timeliness and the relation to current events and seasonal weather patterns of the ads and their consistency with local economic conditions; their use of rational as opposed to emotional appeals; the quality of the artwork; and any other factors you see fit. Does a clear pattern emerge that distinguishes the national ad from the local retail ad? What are the chief distinguishing characteristics of each type of ad, as you perceive them after this exercise?

2. Go to an advertising agency in or near your community. Ascertain if it has retail clients, and if it does arrange to interview the account executive who is responsible for them. Learn all you can about how the agency works with the store management, and ask to see examples of materials the agency has prepared for its retail clients' campaigns. Thereafter, make a point of seeing and hearing ads for local or area stores that you know come from this agency, and compare them with ads for other local retailers that are not handled by an agency. See if you can spot points of superiority in the ads created by the agency.

3. In local newspapers and broadcast media, try to spot advertising that is probably run on a *cooperative* basis, with manufacturers and stores both involved. Horizontal co-op ads, where two or more dealers' signatures or ID's are used, may be easiest to spot. Study a number of these ads, and compare them with other local retail advertising. Consider the main focus of the ads, their overall appearance or sound, their use of artwork, and the quality of the copywriting. Also compare the amount of "store copy," or institutional material pertaining to the retailer.

4. Interview the cooperative advertising coordinator or the retail advertising or sales manager of a local print or broadcast medium. Ask how the newspaper or broadcasting station helps its retail advertisers find cooperative advertising opportunities, how the medium helps prepare the material to be published or broadcast, and how it assists the advertiser by making it easy to conform to the manufacturer's rules and secure prompt reimbursement for the vendor's share of the cost. Do you find the local media generally helpful in this respect and aware of the importance of co-op advertising to their clients and to themselves?

Notes

1. Data from "Advertising in '75 Expected to Be 6% Above Last Year," *Advertising Age* (September 15, 1975), p. 3.

2. "The top 100 national advertisers of 1974," *Advertising Age* (June 30, 1975), p. 56.

3. James V. O'Gara, "U.S. agency billings hit record $13.6 billion," *Advertising Age* (February 24, 1975), front cover and p. 16.

4. Adapted from "Agency Service Standards," a code developed by the American Association of Advertising Agencies, New York, N.Y.

5. Joseph R. Rowen, "F.Y.I: Ideas for Independents—Sales Promotion," *Stores* (January 1974), p. 18.

6. Ibid.

7. Harvey R. Cook, *Selecting Advertising Media* (Washington D.C.: U.S. Small Business Administration, 1969), pp. 91–97.

8. Ibid.

9. C. M. Bresnehen, Howard Nicks, and Charles E. Treat, *The Cooperative Advertising Concept and Use* (Oklahoma, City, Okla.: pub. by Bresnehen, 1971), p. 3.

10. Federal Trade Commission, *Guides for Advertising Allowances and Other Merchandising Payments and Services* (Washington, D.C.: Federal Trade Commission, promulgated May 29, 1969; amended August 4, 1972). All information in this and the next paragraph is derived from pages 6, 12–16, and 19 of this booklet.

11. Ibid., pp. 8–10.

PART **3**

Characteristics of Advertising Media: How to Choose and How to Use

In Part 1 we examined the sweeping changes in society as a whole that are making retailing and advertising so dynamic and so challenging, and how stores are responding to these changes. Part 2 dealt with the management of retail advertising, the decisions participated in by top executives of retail firms, and the many interlocking relationships between advertising people and their colleagues on a store's staff who also have a direct interest in advertising.

Part 3 deals essentially with the tasks allotted to the advertising professionals who put any store's advertising program into effect, although basic, long-range media selection decisions in a large organization also involve the highest echelons of management.

Advertising starts with *ideas* the advertiser wants customers or potential customers to accept and act upon: "My store is good; my merchandise will benefit you, you need it, and you can afford it; come in this very day!" To put these ideas across, the merchant must "translate" them into advertising copy, graphic designs, and illustrations, or into commercials involving music, words, motion, color, and so on.

Then a *medium* carries the advertisement to the reader, listener, or viewer—the intended customer. The delivery may be interrupted or the message distorted along the way. The newspaper's truck may get wrecked and fail to deliver the paper, or a thunderstorm may blow up static that blocks radio reception. When the message reaches the eyes or ears of the intended receiver (the customer), that person may misunderstand it and draw a different meaning from its words than was intended, may react negatively to the music or the color that was chosen, or may see the illustration in a different way than the advertiser saw it when it was designed. Then, too, the medium may deliver the message to the wrong kind of people, people who do not need or cannot afford the product, who cannot be convinced that the store is a good one, or who have their attention fixed on some other matter at the moment the message arrives.

We shall first school ourselves in general guidelines for choosing media, recognizing that no store, small or large, can always afford all the advertising *coverage* (or the *quality* of coverage) it really wants, with the *impact* and *frequency* it wants. Which media excel in each of these desired characteristics, and which have limitations of which retailers should be aware?

A cliché among advertising professionals says that "the medium *is* the message." Surely a gross oversimplification of a complex subject, this maxim does, nonetheless, help us recognize that media decisions do depend in large measure on the nature of the message (i.e., the content and purpose of the ad)—and, of course, on the audience the advertiser seeks to reach. Most retail media reach partially overlapping but nevertheless different audiences. And they deliver advertising messages through different senses, while the audience is in different environments, doing different things, thinking different thoughts, in different stages of receptiveness.

In this part, we shall investigate the various ways in which different local media are used to carry out advertising plans. No medium is perfect, either at finding the right audience or at delivering the message in ideal form at the one best moment in time to maximize results. The best the advertiser can do is to narrow down the areas of imperfection in both the medium and the message, as both relate to the intended audience. We shall investigate each retail medium in turn, and later, in Part 4, we shall consider the basic ideas out of which the advertising messages for transmission by the media must grow.

Preview

Few stores, not even the largest, can afford heavy and frequent exposure in all the means of reaching the consuming public—the local advertising media. Hard choices must be made to concentrate the advertising messages in the most suitable media. Historically, newspapers have been the most effective medium for retailers, and they continue to play a primary role in reaching retail customers; however, today the "multimedia" concept prevails, and most stores use one or more other media as well.

A good choice of media calls for a fine balance between these attributes:

1. coverage, or the quality and size of audience reached;
2. impact, or the force with which the messages are delivered and the extent to which they are recalled by the consumer after they have been read, heard, or viewed; and
3. frequency, or the amount of continuity and repetition, both of which are essential to sustaining awareness of the message at a level sufficient to trigger purchases.

In comparing the advantages and limitations of competing media, after accounting for the three factors listed above, the astute retail advertiser considers the rates for time and space, the services rendered by each medium, the availability of desired time or space, the problem of "clutter" (caused by too many distracting ads), intervention by the government and other extraneous forces that mitigate against a completely free choice, and the nature of the message.

Learning Goals

This chapter is intended to lead the reader to a clear understanding of the basic strategy for choosing media, employing a few of the best for the primary advertising program and perhaps (but not necessarily) adding others for special purposes. It provides guidelines for making rational choices and outlines some of the dominant characteristics of the leading local media. The reader should also gain an appreciation of outside influences that may affect the value of a medium and learn how to draw up a media plan as part of an overall advertising plan.

8

Media Planning Strategies

The specific characteristics of the many different media available to today's retailer, including the advantages and limitations of each, will be discussed in depth in the following chapters. The focus here is on the fundamental principles of efficient media planning that guide management in choosing among its many options. Essentially, we are seeking to provide an overview of the media situation from the merchant's point of view, before we get to the particular claims and counterclaims of aggressively competing media, all trying to woo and win the retail advertising dollar.

Each advertising medium—daily newspapers, AM radio stations, weekly newspapers, television, FM radio stations, mailings, shopping guides, billboards, and the rest—has merit. But few stores, not even the largest, can use effective amounts of all media at the same time. Choices have to be made, often hard choices. Some good media have to

be omitted or underused at one time, added or increasingly used at another. The *mass of available funds* must be conserved for use in the few media selected for *primary tasks*.

Except for a very small handful of the very largest retailers, the dissipation of funds over too broad a selection of media can be disastrous, even though the use of each medium can seemingly be justified in each instance. Such a practice can result in weakness everywhere and strength nowhere, and it leads to advertising in driblets rather than in torrents, at the crucial time to reach the primary target audience.

1 Relative Use of Local Media

One way to begin to understand the complex media choices open to local advertisers is to examine the apparent relative popularity of the several largest local media, which is implied by the amount of money invested in each of them by advertisers nationwide. Table 8-1 shows the historical trend in local advertising expenditures since 1940.

To trace the development of each local medium in which expenditures were measured over the 34-year period that ended in 1974, go along the top line to any year you choose, then go down the column to see how much local advertisers used each medium at that point in time. Comparisons may be made in *dollars* or in *percentages*—either of *measured media* costs or of *all* local advertising costs.

To follow the progress through the years of any one medium, go down the left side of the table to the appropriate line, then move across the page to the right and see how the dollar and percentage figures change for each ten-year base period. Essentially, this table records the evolution of local advertising from virtually a one-medium proposition (daily newspapers) in the 1930s to mixed-media status in the 1970s.

Radio gained ground at a fantastic rate in the forties. Its growth then leveled off for nearly two decades, until it made a spectacular comeback in the late sixties and early seventies. Television became significant as a local medium in the early fifties, and began to gain rapidly in popularity in the early seventies. Outdoor advertising actually declined in the early sixties, but has, surprisingly, revived in more recent years. Note, however, that daily newspapers continue to overwhelmingly dominate local advertising; expenditures for newspaper ads account for about $5.5 billion more than the ads in any other medium. In fact, the dailies' dollar volume exceeds the combined volume of the three measured media by $4.1 billion, and the increase from 1970 to 1974 alone ("new" money flow-

Table 8–1

Historical Trends in "Local" Advertising Expenditures, 1940–1974

	1940			1950			1960		
	Expenditures (in millions)	Percentage of Measured Media Costs	Percentage of Total Local Adv. Costs	Expenditures (in millions)	Percentage of Measured Media Costs	Percentage of Total Local Adv. Costs	Expenditures (in millions)	Percentage of Measured Media Costs	Percentage of Total Local Adv. Costs
Daily newspapers [a] (weeklies included in "Miscellaneous" category)	$654	90.2%	71.6%	$1,552	80.6%	63.2%	$2,903	78.9%	62.4%
Radio [b]	60	8.3	6.5	273	14.2	11.2	428	11.6	9.2
Television [c]				55	2.8	2.3	280	7.6	6.0
Outdoor media	11	1.5	1.2	46	2.4	1.9	66	1.8	1.4
All measured media	725	100.0	78.8	1,926	100.0	78.9	3,677	100.0	78.9
Miscellaneous advertising costs [d] (including expenses to unmeasured media, adv. staffs, etc.)	195		21.2	514		21.1	978		21.1
Total local advertising costs [e]	920		100.0	2,440		100.0	4,655		100.0
Percentage of total advertising costs attributable to local advertising costs [f]	44.6%			43.8%			38.9%		

Note: Figures include both media costs for space or time and production costs.

a. The cost of local advertising in daily newspapers first topped $1 billion in 1947, $2 billion in 1953, $3 billion in 1963, $5 billion in 1971, and $6 billion in1973. The papers' proportional share of ad dollars has slowly declined for many years but has become almost stable in the 1970s.

b. Radio ad costs first exceeded $1 billion in 1972, but radio advertising expenditures reached their peak as a percentage of total local advertising costs in 1945.

c. Television ad costs reached $1 billion only in 1973, but their growth rate had surpassed that of other local media expenditures since the mid-sixties.

d. Miscellaneous local advertising expenditures (including those for minor media) first reached $1 billion in 1962 and passed $2 billion in 1972.

Table 8–1 (cont.)

Historical Trends in "Local" Advertising Expenditures, 1940–1974

	1970			1974			197...		
	Expenditures (in millions)	Percentage of Measured Media Costs	Percentage of Total Local Adv. Costs	Expenditures (in millions)	Percentage of Measured Media Costs	Percentage of Total Local Adv. Costs	Expenditures (in millions)	Percentage of Measured Media Costs	Percentage of Total Local Adv. Costs
Daily newspapers [a] (weeklies included in "Miscellaneous" category)	$4,813	74.3%	58.7%	$ 6,807	71.7%	56.6%	$	%	%
Radio [b]	881	13.6	10.7	1,355	14.3	11.3			
Television [c]	704	10.9	8.6	1,211	12.8	10.1			
Outdoor media	80	1.2	1.0	120	1.3	1.0			
All measured media	6,478	100.0	79.0	9,493	100.0	78.9		100.0	
Miscellaneous advertising costs [d] (including expenses to unmeasured media, adv. staffs, etc.)	1,722		21.0	2,527		21.0			
Total local advertising costs [e]	8,200		100.0	12,020		100.0			100.0
Percentage of total advertising costs attributable to local advertising costs [f]	41.4%			44.9%			%		

e. Total local advertising expenditures first exceeded $1 billion in 1943, topped $5 billion by 1962, and passed the $10 billion mark in 1972.

f. This line traces the decline of local advertising expenditures as a proportion of all U.S. advertising expenditures from 1940 until the mid-sixties, after which spending for local ads increased much more rapidly than spending for national advertising. In 1972, 1973, and 1974, expenditures for local advertising reached their highest percentage of total advertising costs since before World War II.

Source: Compiled from figures prepared by McCann-Erickson, Inc., for *Advertising Age* (August 27, 1974, and September 15, 1975).

ing into the medium) was nearly $2 billion, far exceeding the total spent for any other local medium. Buried away within the miscellaneous category is perhaps another half billion or so dollars of newspaper advertising carried by weekly newspapers, not credited to the newspaper medium in this data.

The last three columns at the right have been left blank for the student to do the research and insert the final revised figures for 1975 or a later year. Local figures can be extracted from *Advertising Age* data (check the August or September issues), but the student must calculate the subtotals and percentages. (See Suggested Project 1 at the end of this chapter.)

One big chunk of money shown in Table 8–1—that in the "Miscellaneous costs" row—frustrates those seeking a clear view of advertisers' use of the various means of delivering messages to audiences. Spending for ads in the measured media totals up to just a little less than four-fifths of the gross amount of money invested in advertising by local advertisers. What about the rest—the one dollar in five labeled miscellaneous expenditure? This category includes salaries, office costs, travel costs, and so on for stores' advertising staffs, and other advertising department overhead expenses. But it also includes some rather big chunks of money that go into "unmeasured" media.

Two media in particular, data for which are not reported separately, deserve special mention: weekly newspapers and direct-mail ads. Both loom large in the media planning of a vast number of retailers. Together, they absorb nearly a billion dollars of local advertisers'

money each year. Using available sources, one can arrive only at something between a rough estimate and an educated guess about the importance of these media in the overall picture. However, even a crude calculation of the probable importance of the two missing media permits us to see a somewhat different (and more realistic) distribution of the local advertisers' media dollar. Table 8–2 shows what the 1974 distribution *might* have been, had reasonable estimates for the two large "unmeasured" media been included.

And there are other "unmeasured" media like the *Yellow Pages,* free-circulation shoppers' guides, retail magazine ads, car cards in mass transit vehicles, and motion picture "trailers," each of them potentially useful for some retailers in special situations.

Tables 8–1 and 8–2 both measure the cost of *local* advertising, which is not precisely the same thing as *retail* advertising. There is evidence that strictly "retail" advertising by stores selling tangible merchandise represents a little over 60 percent of the broader classification "local" advertising. The remainder is chiefly the advertising of transportation companies, communications agencies, public utilities, financial institutions, insurance agencies, real estate firms, and consumer service businesses. These kinds of businesses are well within the intended scope of this book, and everyone interested in retail advertising in this age of services should accept them as so closely related to the retail scene that they are, in a broad sense, part of it. For our purposes we shall, therefore, use the term local advertising as equivalent to retail advertising.

Table 8–2

1974 Local Advertising Expenditures, by Media, Revised to Include Author's Estimates of Spending for Advertising in Weekly Newspapers and by Direct-Mail
(Compare to 1974 data in Table 8–1.)

	Expenditures (in millions)	Percentage of Media Costs	Percentage of Total Advertising Costs
Newspapers			
Dailies [a]	$6,807		
Weeklies [b]	550		
Total	$ 7,357	70.2%	61.2%
Radio [c]	1,355	12.9	11.3
Television [d]	1,211	11.5	10.1
Outdoor [e]	120	1.1	1.0
Direct-mail [f]	450	4.3	3.7
All local media	**10,493**	**100.0%**	**87.3%**
Miscellaneous advertising costs [g]	1,527		12.7
Total local advertising costs [h]	**$12,020**		**100.0%**

Note: Percentage figures do not add to 100 because of rounding.

a. From Table 8–1, line 1.
b. Estimated.
c. From Table 8–1, line 2.
d. From Table 8–1, line 3.
e. From Table 8–1, line 4.
f. Estimated.
g. From Table 8–1, line 6, after deducting estimates of spending for direct-mail ads and advertising in weekly papers.
h. From Table 8–1, line 7.

2 Media Planning

Some words of wisdom on media selection were written by a senior vice president of the famed Doyle Dane Bernbach advertising agency, Montgomery McKinney:

"There is no such thing as a bad medium—only the bad use of a good medium."

At first glance that could well be considered one of advertising's most obvious and least valuable truisms, but in my experience it sometimes has proved to be both a provocative and productive thesis. . . .

Frequently, the discussion which followed [the introduction of that thought at a media-planning conference] centered on what could be called secondary media and brought forth examples of how true creativity could make these media highly effective and efficient. . . . Most seasoned advertising people could add innumerable examples of secondary—or "weak"—or "bad" media—being used freshly and daringly with deservedly successful results.

It's a safe bet too that every advertising man [or woman] could cite dozens of horrible examples of the bad use of good media—campaigns which ignored well-known demographic, market and purchase data—or schedules which ignored the fundamentals of reach, frequency, continuity and cumulative effect.

All too often there is a common cause of these serious, expensive and wasteful mistakes. The nice phrase to describe this common cause is "lack of objectivity." The not-so-nice words are stupid prejudice, unprofessional bias, autocratic ignorance....

In recalling the origin and uses of the "no-bad-medium" thesis, I remember another usable truism which, in a way, parallels it. I now generously pass it along to anyone who dares or cares to use it: Each time you decide to spend a dollar in one medium you simultaneously decide *not* to spend that dollar in a dozen other good media. [Maybe two dozen.] [1]

One of the most prolific and articulate writers on media planning in recent years has been Herbert Maneloveg, formerly vice president of the Batton, Barton, Durstine and Osborn and the McCann-Erickson agencies. He details six key factors:

1. *The communication requirement.* This is normally the most important element ... selling ... remains the most important ingredient of advertising.... The selection of media is always tied to the message.... Accordingly, before a media planner starts building his proposal, it becomes essential that he knows what the copywriter is trying to say and in what media form it can best be said ... [T]he communication idea is the key element.

2. *Emphasis on the prime prospect.* Here is where the media man must do his best work—analyzing media vehicles in order to maximize concentration on prime prospects.... Here he becomes a market expert rather than just a media man [and] must secure a fund of knowledge about who buys the product or service being advertised....

3. *Geographic sales analysis.* Here he [the media planner] must decide where to place his weight ... and in what proportion.... Here is where demography [the target audience], geography and [the] budget mesh.... As advertisers, we must logically go where the people are....

4. *Efficiency/effectiveness balance.* When exploring various media alternatives we must take into account unit costs and attendant efficiencies. In the past we have measured cost ... in relation to *homes* delivered. But today, in an age of market segmentation and product proliferation, as we concentrate on specific audiences, we now view media vehicles in relation to the cost of delivering our prime *customers.* Our criterion is the cost-per-thousand *prospects* delivered....

5. *The pressure of competition.* ... Before a media plan is developed we examine the delivery of our own previous efforts [compared to] that of [the] competition.... Coverage and frequency patterns *vis-a-vis* competition form a framework for many of our media decisions.

6. *All this must be measured in relation to the dollars allocated to advertising: the budget.* It must be remembered that advertising budgets are determined within the framework of the over-all marketing expenditure.... Advertising is but one facet. [2]

3 The Triangle of Media Characteristics

The essential factors to be evaluated in selecting retail advertising media may be thought of as a *triangle of desired qualities.* The three sides of the triangle are (1) *coverage* (or *reach*), (2) *impact,* and (3) *frequency* (plus *continuity*). (See Figure 8–1.)

In long-range media planning, say, for a full year, this triangle should approximate an *equilateral triangle,* with all three sides in balance. If one media characteristic is pursued too avidly at the expense of either of the others, the overall media plan may be ineffective. Although special circumstances and specific short-range goals may sometimes make one media attribute more important temporarily, then the advertiser should still strive for some sort of balance in making media decisions.

Advertisers using the percentage-of-sales budgeting method (discussed in Chapter 5) must constantly adjust their plans to fit their budgets. Those using objective-and-task budgeting will have dealt in broad terms with media choices at an earlier stage of the planning process. They will also have determined tentative ad appropriations needed to achieve their goals, in advance.

COVERAGE AND REACH

Coverage is defined by Webster as "the portion of a group or community reached by an advertising medium." Merchants naturally seek media that effectively *cover* their normal trading areas (plus areas just a little beyond, to attract new customers—but not too far beyond, to avoid waste). In practice, the coverage of a medium is invariably much greater than the number of households or

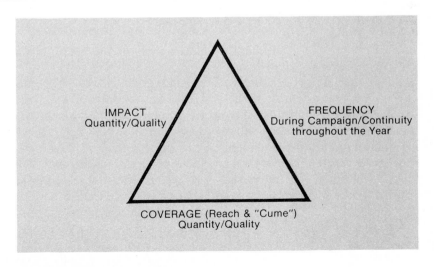

Figure 8–1 Triangle of Media Characteristics

persons definitely exposed to a given advertisement or commercial. It is the ideal, theoretical maximum number that *might* be reached. A newspaper's *circulation* (which can be measured easily and precisely) may indicate that it "covers" 90 percent of the homes in the retail trading area of a community. But, on any given day, some of the families who take the paper may be out of town and they may give it only a cursory glance when they return. Or they may be too busy to read more than the front page. Furthermore, certain members of the family may read the paper thoroughly one day and skip through just a few pages the next day. The coverage of a radio or television station depends on the geographical area within which it is technically possible to receive its signal. Its "circulation" is the average number of homes where one or more persons listen to or view programs in a given time period, such as a day or a week. An outdoor sign will be passed by a known volume of traffic, but who knows how many of the passersby actually see it? A medium's *reach* is always some *fraction* of is coverage.

Cumulative Reach and Audience Duplication A medium's actual reach accumulates over time. Its cumulative reach, or *cume,* as it is called by advertising people, is always more than its one-time reach, but never as much as its theoretical total coverage. Some people buy a paper at a newsstand now and then, but not regularly; some members of a household read the Sunday paper and certain weekday editions consistently but pay little attention to the paper on other days. One family regularly views TV on Mondays and Thursdays but seldom watches on other evenings.

Radio (primarily a personal and individual medium) attracts relatively few listeners at any given moment, but it gets the attention of a great many people over the course of a whole day as various audiences come and go. The cume of any medium over a period of time increases the net audience ultimately reached (and is obviously directly related to the frequency side of the triangle of media qualities, which we shall discuss shortly).

A medium's *unduplicated* audience must be considered in comparing two or more media. If a retailer is now advertising in the morning paper, how many other households will it reach by putting ads in the evening paper? If it is now airing commercials on one TV channel, how many new viewers will it reach by buying time on a second (or third) station? To the extent that there is an overlapping, or duplication, of media audiences, the *reach* of advertising is not improved by using more media, but there is an increase in the *frequency* with which consumers are exposed to the ad messages. This, of course, increases the likelihood that they will be remembered. Thus audience duplication affects all three sides of the media triangle.

Effective Reach: The Quality Factor Thus far we have examined only gross coverage and total reach—the *quantity* aspect of advertising. To some merchants, this facet of coverage may be all that matters. Stores that sell products with a basic, universal appeal and those that offer a wide variety of merchandise in all price ranges may, quite literally, seek to reach *nearly everyone* in a given market area. Most food stores, gas stations, pharmacies, variety stores, and perhaps the very largest general merchandisers draw their trade from every social and economic class, every age group, both sexes, and all the geographical subzones within a trading area. For them, the quantity dimension of coverage and reach is paramount, and they care little what the audience profile of a medium may be. Sheer gross numbers, and numbers alone, govern their media choices.

Another factor makes the quantity aspect of coverage important. The number of active "prospects" for a given item on a certain day in a particular community is limited to a very few individuals. Thus it follows that the more people a store reaches with its ads, the more likely it is to influence at least *some* of the minority who are both able and in the mood to buy.

But even merchants whose products have a wide market know that although they can sell something to almost everybody, certain kinds of customers tend to buy in larger quantities, to visit a store more often, and to choose products on which the store makes greater profit than do other types of customers. Furthermore, many general merchandisers have recently split up their selling areas into highly specialized shops appealing to clear-cut and often quite narrow market segments.

The specialty shop, because of its nature and function, can profit only from reaching certain types of shoppers with its ads. Specialized merchants, in particular the smaller ones, obtain their primary trade from specific groups, specific *target markets*: particular income groups, age groups, occupational groups, people who adhere to special lifestyles, those living in clearly defined types of homes, members of ethnic minorities, or people having some other identifying characteristics. These merchants (and there are vast numbers of them) seek media that influence special market segments, and this brings us to the *quality* dimension of coverage and to the only *effective reach* for such retailers.

A farm-supply dealer cares less than nothing about the city-dwellers reached by a medium. A ladies' apparel shop urging women to buy clothing for themselves wants to reach women. It is not interested in reaching men, except during gift-giving seasons when it advertises items men can buy for women. For the men's store featuring protective workshoes, the only portion of a medium's coverage that matters is that of blue-collar workingmen. A women's shoe store emphasizing expensive, high-fashion footwear wants only to reach upper-middle-class women with both the incentive and the means to match each of their outfits with just the right shoes.

Of course, all these special groups may be found within the audiences of the great mass media. Unfortunately, they often provide too much coverage for the store searching out a target market. Since all this coverage must be paid for, the cost *per effective prospect* may be too high. Merchants dealing in limited merchandise lines often find that they spend less and get better results by using carefully selected *lesser* media— lesser in terms of their total coverage, but able to reach most, if not all, of the desired target group. Thus the best medium for an ad campaign aimed at teenagers may be high school newspapers, a quality-coverage medium for that particular group. Ads aimed at blacks may be most effective if they are carried by a black-oriented radio station.

Advertising to farmers may produce the largest response if it is placed in a farm journal. A promotional program aimed at Catholics may fare best in a diocesan magazine and parish bulletins. Like everyone else, high school students, blacks, farmers, and Catholics read regular newspapers and watch television. But the cost of reaching just these groups through these media may be prohibitive. For small stores the crucial consideration may be the geographical selectivity of a medium. There is little profit in reaching too large a trading area at an unacceptably high cost per ad. To insure quality coverage, a retailer's target markets should match, as closely as possible, the target audiences of the media it uses.

The Cost-per-Thousand Formula   A simple method of measuring the relative efficiency of two or more media, the *cost-per-thousand* formula, or CPM, was developed years ago by national advertisers. It is considered less valid for retailers and is used less now than in the past for two reasons: (1) the number of media choices has increased, and (2) the increasing diversification of target markets calls for a more sophisticated delineation of audience segments, not just gross audience figures. However, the CPM idea can be refined and adapted to satisfy some of the needs of present-day retailers wishing to improve their media-selection techniques.

The CPM system is really quite simple: Take the total *cost* of a given ad or series of ads in a specified medium and divide this by the *number of households* (or persons) presumably reached by the medium, moving the decimal point in the circulation (or coverage) figure three digits to the left. This gives you the amount of money it takes to reach 1,000 homes (or persons) with that particular ad or series of ads.

For example, if a newspaper has a circulation of 16,800 and its rate for a one-page ad is $336, the CPM is found as follows:

$$\frac{\text{Cost in dollars}}{\text{Circulation in thousands}} = \frac{\$336}{16.8} = \$20$$

If a radio station accumulates an audience of 7,000 homes in a 24-hour period and offers a saturation "package" of 20 one-minute commercials for $100, the CPM is figured thus:

$$\frac{\$100}{7} = \$14.29$$

The CPM system is most useful for comparing the efficiency of two similar media, such as two newspapers of roughly equal circulation or two broadcasting stations with about the same size audience. It tends to fall down when cross-media comparisons are undertaken —for example, comparisons between radio and direct-mail ads or between newspaper and TV ads. In such a context, the crucial question is "cost-per-thousand *what?*" Only if one could determine how many 30-second radio commercials were equal in *selling power for a store* to a given number of letters or circulars mailed to a select list of consumers would a comparison of the CPM of radio and mail advertising be meaningful. Only if we knew what size newspaper ad would equal the selling power of a television commercial of a given length would the CPM of those media be a reliable tool for comparing them.

A variation of this formula may be useful, nonetheless, when a retailer wishes to make a broad comparison of the relative value of the audience quality of two or more media, provided the media being compared can supply valid demographic and geographic breakdowns of their respective audiences or circulations. If, going back to the first example cited above, a store wants to advertise merchandise appealing to *homeowners,* and it can be ascertained that 80 percent of a newspaper's circulation does go to privately owned residences, then the effective CPM can be found as follows:

$$16,800 \times .80 = 13,440 \text{ (the circulation } relevant \text{ to the ad campaign)}$$

$$\frac{\$336}{13.44} = \$25.00 \text{ (the cost per 1,000 homeowners reached)}$$

In the second example, if the advertising were for sporting goods or automotive products sold almost entirely to *men,* and the radio comercials could be scheduled entirely during commuters' "drive time" when surveys show that 75 percent of the listeners are men, the real, useful CPM would be

$$7,000 \times .75 = 5,250 \text{ (the audience } relevant \text{ to this campaign)}$$

$$\frac{\$100}{5.25} = \$19.05 \text{ (the cost per 1,000 men reached)}$$

The CPM for *small media* is invariably much higher than the CPM of large media, which explains the preference of national advertisers and large chain stores for big media. Single-location stores, or small chains serving a compact trading area, may find that smaller media have lower effective CPM's when the portion of the coverage that matters, instead of the gross coverage, is used in the CPM formula. A large medium may have a raw, unadjusted CPM of $5 per 1,000; but this figure can jump to $25 or $50 if the coverage is adjusted to include only those members of the audience who live in the smaller stores' natural trading areas.

To sum up, in considering the coverage of a medium retailers must pay attention not just to gross numbers, but to the usefulness of the medium in reaching the kind of consumers a given campaign or a specific ad is aimed at. A media plan that overemphasizes coverage of the greatest possible numbers of potential customers may fall flat because there is not enough money left for ads with adequate impact or for advertising with sufficient frequency.

IMPACT

When we talk about the *impact* of an ad, we mean its ability to attract and hold an audience long enough to arouse interest, transmit information, create feelings, do a selling job, or convince people to inquire about products. Seldom will all readers, listeners, or viewers notice every ad in any medium; and of those who do notice an ad, only some will attend to the whole message. Fewer yet will remember it the next day, the next week, or whenever they go shopping. The impact of an ad determines how deep an *impression* it makes on readers, listeners, or viewers.

Impact depends in part on the medium used and in part on the ad message

—how cleverly it is conceived, designed, written, and produced. We shall see what makes an effective advertising message in Part 4. Here we are concerned only with impact as a factor in the media-selection decision. As in the case of coverage, there are two factors to be considered: *quantity* and *quality.*

The Quantity Factor   The impact of an ad always depends to some extent on its size. How large or long an ad need be depends on the nature of the ad message and the technique chosen for getting the core idea across. Sometimes, advertisers will depend primarily on the sheer size of an illustration, an emblem, a slogan, or a headline to make an impression on consumers. Thus they will select media like huge outdoor signs or two-page spreads in standard-sized newspapers to carry the ad message. The same kind of massive impact could not be achieved in a tabloid-sized paper or on a nineteen- or twenty-one-inch television screen,

If the ad message must be long in order to satisfy the consumer's need for adequate facts or to demonstrate the advantages of a complex and unfamiliar product or idea, broadcast media have a basic drawback: a rigid limitation on the length of any commercial. Even full 60-second commercials can contain about 150 words at the very most (if they are "all talk" and done by a very fast announcer). When a 200- or 300-word message is needed to insure adequate impact, one of the printed media is essential. The same media choice is virtually unavoidable when, as so often is the case in retail advertising, it is necessary to mention a large number of different items in the same ad. Nevertheless, in a great many cases, the greatest impact can be obtained by the simultaneous use of sound, sight, motion, and color. Television and only television offers this combination of sensory stimuli.

Often, advertising planners face a hard choice between having great audience coverage and reach and making a superior impact on a smaller group of customers. Little is gained by buying so much coverage that little money is left to support the impact factor. Presumably, a full-page newspaper ad has more impact potential than a quarter-page ad; at least, its impact *can* be superior if it is properly designed and worded. Suppose newspaper A reaches 100,000 potential customers, but space costs so much that the advertiser is forced to use only quarter-page or smaller ads. Newspaper B reaches 25,000 subscribers in the same trading area, but its advertising rates are so much lower that the store can afford several full-page ads. Quite possibly, the impact consideration will tip the balance in favor of the paper with the smaller circulation. Or suppose broadcasting station X can solidly document its audience of 25,000 prime prospects for the store, while station Y claims a scant 5,000. However, time is so costly on the larger station that messages must be compressed into 20-second spots, leaving no time for sound effects, music, dialogue, or the mention of more than one item of merchandise. The store may wisely elect to go with the station reaching 5,000 consumers, because its lower costs permit the use of 30- and 60-second announcements containing the full message, properly dressed up with attention-getting techniques.

The Question of Quality   The second determinant of impact is the *quality* of an ad. Before making a media-selection decision, an advertiser should find out what facilities each medium offers its clients. If its creative and production facilities are few and rudimentary, the advertiser who buys space or time gets only space or time for its money. If the medium has skilled creative and production personnel, top-grade materials, and good internal equipment that it makes available to its advertisers, the cost of space or time includes services that can significantly improve the impact of advertising and increase its profitability.

Some newspapers maintain staff artists to assist in designing and illustrating ads, and copywriters to add sparkle and zest to the words. Many papers subscribe to several syndicated art services and can offer their advertisers a wide choice of illustrative material to magnify the impact of their ads; others provide a bare minimum of such material, and no assurance of exclusivity. Some radio stations maintain sound libraries containing thousands of tapes and records for sound effects, background music, or opening and closing musical signatures. On many stations, popular newscasters and disc jockeys will do commercials. Their prestige and familiarity to listeners also improves the impact of local advertisers' commercials. Stations that offer these extra values may be preferred, even over competitors with higher audience ratings. Unfortunately, substantial numbers of television stations are still geared primarily to serve national or regional advertisers, rather than local retailers; their facilities for the production of local commercials are minimal, at best. Merchants may well prefer to deal with stations that can do the whole production job, and get more professional ads at little or no extra expense.

When the amount and quality of assistance to advertisers provided by two or more local media is about equal, differences in their *technical capabilities* may make one medium preferable. If the color of an illustration is of paramount importance, an advertiser will not choose a newspaper that can print only in black and white or whose color ads are normally of poor quality. Nor will it choose a newspaper noted for sloppy proofreading and ads full of typographical errors if alternative media are available. By the same token, if a broadcasting station's signal is frequently interrupted or distorted, advertisers may go elsewhere.

In essence, advertisers should be striving to get the most value possible from the content and form of their ads. Some broad classes of media have inherent advantages or limitations with respect to particular types of ad messages. And some specific, individual media offer superior facilities for creating high-impact ads. Often, it is better to sell successfully to 20 percent of an audience of 10,000 (2,000 persons) with high-impact ads than to try to sell to an audience of 50,000 with low-impact ads and succeed in motivating only 2 percent of them (1,000 persons) to buy.

Both the coverage and impact sides of the media triangle are related to the third side—*frequency*—and still more compromises may have to be made before an ideal media plan is devised.

FREQUENCY, CONTINUITY, AND REPETITION OF THE MESSAGE

The *frequency* of advertising is measured by the number of times an advertisement (or a series of similar, related ads directed at the same audience and promoting the same product, merchandise line, service, or idea) is delivered through the same medium (or group of media) in a stated period. That period may be a three-day weekend, a week, or a selling season such as the back-to-school or Christmas season. Closely related to the frequency of advertising is its *continuity* over a much longer period of time, such as a calendar year. Advertising continuity is measured by how often, over a relatively long period, a store and its merchandise are brought to the attention of the public. Regular advertising in some medium or some combination of media is an essential, if not *the* essential, prerequisite to advertising success. Many inexperienced advertisers miss this point; they "shoot the works" on occasional and intermittent massive coverage and heavy impact, then run short of funds to maintain the momentum of their ad program.

Consumer awareness fades rapidly without repeated nudges. Some experts have likened advertising to the geological process by which water dripping on a mass of stone wears it away—provided the dripping continues for tens of thousands of years. Others have sized up the situation by noting that "advertising pulls; it doesn't jerk!" Recently, the concept of an *advertising-awareness threshold* has come into vogue to explain this innate psychological phenomenon. An isolated ad, repeated at infrequent, irregular intervals, may actually produce *no results whatsoever*. It may never "sink in." All a retailer's ad money can be wasted by an infrequent, inconsistent ad program that never crosses the threshold of consumer awareness.

The same advertisement or advertising campaign, of course, should not be continued forever. The fifth time one person sees or hears an ad is the first time some other member of the potential audience notices it; the tenth time some people are exposed to it is the second time others see it and the first time still another group pays it any attention. People are not always equally receptive to an ad. Some are prodded into making an instant purchase; others barely begin to be aware of the store and the merchandise it offers. Ultimately, a point of diminishing returns is approached. Nearly everyone who is exposed to the medium used for the store's ads has become aware of them, all those who are capable of being convinced to shop at the store have become patrons, and all those who are going to buy an advertised product have done so. At that point the store may alter the impact of its ad program by retargeting a portion of its ads to appeal more emphatically to a different market segment within the audience of the same medium or media, or a wholly different product or merchandise line may be selected for promotion. Thus the whole process begins anew. Alternatively, an advertiser may shift all or a portion of its media budget to another medium, one that reaches different people, changing its tactics with respect to coverage.

Media differ greatly in terms of their ability to provide a sufficient *frequency* of advertising impressions during a given short-run ad campaign, and to a lesser degree they also differ in their ability to provide long-run continuity. Moreover, some media reward the frequent advertiser by offering a rapidly declining rate per unit of advertising as the frequency of insertions increases. The advantages of various media should be examined with these considerations in mind. One or two media may be selected because they offer a satisfactory degree of coverage and impact and also lend themselves well to adequate repetitions of the ad message. Other media may be included in a media plan because of their massive coverage or their mighty impact, even if frequent insertions are impossible. Still others may be chosen mostly because ads can be inserted with great frequency.

Picking High-Frequency Media Among newspapers, a daily plainly permits frequent advertising that a weekly cannot match. And those dailies with Saturday, Sunday, and holiday editions offer better frequency opportunities than those which are published only five days a week. In some communities, morning and evening papers offer combination rates when the same ad is carried in both papers. For very little more money, the advertiser can make two impressions on the same day on those who read both papers, while simultaneously widening its total coverage. The broadcast media, by their very nature, allow an advertiser to make multiple impressions during the same day or half-day, or even within the same hour. But not all broadcasting stations are equal in this respect. Some radio stations are licensed to operate only during daylight hours, and others must cut down their power (and consequently their reach) after sundown. Few TV stations remain on the air during the early morning hours, but some radio stations operate 24 hours a day. Stations affiliated with networks have fewer time slots open when audiences are at a peak than unaffiliated stations, all of whose programming is under local control.

Ads sent through the mail can be timed to arrive each business day but not on Sundays or postal holidays; however, the postal service cannot always be depended on to deliver mail on a specific day. Outdoor advertising can make a great number of impressions on people who often circulate through the areas where the signs are posted, but very few on those who get out little or live in isolated areas. The number of impressions daily is also less for outdoor signs that lack artificial illumination during the winter months.

The type of advertising contracts offered to regular advertisers by daily newspapers, radio stations, and outdoor advertising plants favors frequency, as the rates normally decline sharply when weekly or daily space or time is purchased for a whole year, even though the individual ads may not be large. On the other hand, such contracts are less common in television, magazine, and weekly newspaper advertising. Printers will often reduce their rates if they are asked to provide periodic mailing pieces, when they know the advertiser will order a similar format at predictable and frequent intervals.

The Media Mix and the Frequency Factor Small and medium-sized retailers typically assign the task of maintaining a continuity of impressions throughout the year to one primary medium, and schedule high-frequency advertising in one or more other media only during peak promotional seasons. If, for example, a store's budget will not permit television advertising all year with reasonable frequency, the store may still be able to get on the screen several times a day during the four or five most important selling seasons of the year. It can schedule a saturation campaign for selected weeks or weekends that mean the most in terms of potential results. Meanwhile, a less costly medium can be used for steady advertising year-round.

Successful Advertising Pulls—It Doesn't Jerk As one management manual puts it, "Continuity, or advertising consistency, is probably the biggest single factor in advertising success. Advertising is not a stop-and-go proposition. Advertising success is built on regular advertising—preferably daily advertising, or at least weekly advertising." [3]

James T. Mace, a retail advertising executive of the Seattle *Times,* tells this dramatic story:

> The following [ad] schedule [was] for a grand buy-out sale held by a Seattle camera shop:
> Thursday, 6 July . . . 25 "teaser" ads, one column by two inches and two columns by three inches [very small ads].
> Friday, 7 July . . . 25 teaser ads, same size.
> Saturday, 8 July . . . 10 teaser ads.
> Sunday, 9 July . . . 25 "page finder" ads [directing the readers to the store's main ad in the same edition], one column by two inches and two columns by three inches, plus two full pages, one in color.
> This [ad series] was a real winner. By 10 A.M. on the morning of the sale, the store had to call the police to control the crowds. There were 2,000 persons lined up when the doors opened.

The Seattle store ran *85 small ads in four days,* plus two big ads. The 85 small ads doubtless had an effective reach equal to virtually the whole of the newspaper's circulation, gathered a larger cume each day, and focused attention on the massive ads that trigged an immedi-

ate response from 2,000 people and brought untold thousands more to the store during the remainder of the sale.

There is no better way for professional advertising people to remind themselves of the importance of repetition than to adopt this charming little verse (whose author is unknown) as their guide.

> One step won't take you very far; you've got to keep on walking. One word won't tell 'em who you are; you've got to keep on talking. An inch won't make you very tall; you've got to keep on growing. One little ad won't do it all; you've got to keep them going. The constant cooing lover carries off the blushing maid; and the constant advertiser is the one who gets the trade!

4 Special Problems in Choosing Media

In choosing the most suitable media for a particular store with its own peculiar advertising objectives, a merchant may take into account many factors in addition to the three major considerations we have just discussed. Where the choice is close, these special considerations tip the balance one way or another.

Rates and services provided to local advertisers by media—two topics that are relevant to media selection—will not be discussed here because they are covered in great depth in later chapters.

LIMITS ON MEDIA OPTIONS

A merchant does not always have a *free choice* of media. Forces beyond the merchant's control—and equally beyond the control of local media managers —sometimes restrict the *availability* of media space or time useful to the retailer. Most broadcasting stations (especially television stations, but to a lesser degree radio stations too) have commitments to the networks with which they are affiliated. These, in effect, limit the available *prime-time* periods they can sell to local advertisers. Long-standing orders from national "spot" advertisers also tend to limit the options of local retailers shopping for broadcast time.

Outdoor advertising plants have a limited number of signs in any given community, and they too have orders far in advance from national advertisers. This will often allow the local retailers only a choice among the "leavings."

Newspapers are not equipped to print all *colors* every day. Presses can handle only a certain number of colors on any given day, and a merchant may have to select a day other than the day he prefers to insert a particular color ad or use the same color already ordered by some other advertiser. Supplies of newsprint are not necessarily infinite, and at times some newspapers have had to ration their advertising space because of lack of paper, as in 1973 when paper mills were not geared to meet a growing demand and railroad strikes had slowed down the flow of what paper there was.

Intervention by various government agencies affects the kind and amount of advertising local media can offer retail accounts and affects media options. Progressive increases in third-class postal rates in recent years have limited the amount of direct-mail advertising possible with a given budget. In many cases the net result has been a bonanza for newspapers, for big retailers will now

ship them preprinted circulars to be inserted in the papers as supplements instead of sending them out by mail as before.

When the Federal Trade Commission issued new guidelines for cooperative advertising, protecting the small store against long-established policies that had favored larger retailers, one important result was to broaden the media options of small merchants. This redounded to the benefit of free-circulation shopping guides in some communities, which had not previously been taken seriously by major manufacturers.

FTC investigation of sliding-scale retail advertising rates, whereby a store earns increasingly attractive discounts as its volume of ads increases, has inhibited extension of such discounts by some media. Believing that their rates unduly favor large advertisers, the FTC may intervene to equalize per-unit rates for both large and small advertisers. Should this happen, it will make some media seem more attractive and others less desirable—depending on the size of a given advertiser's budget.

When federal authorities, acting on the findings of the surgeon general about the effects of cigarette smoking, ordered cigarette manufacturers to cease advertising on TV, more TV time became available for other advertisers (including retailers whose business had never before been sought by TV salespersons). Every time the Federal Communications Commission licenses additional radio and TV stations in any given listening or viewing area, it cuts down the effective audience of all existing broadcasting stations in that area. Conversely, this tends to make available increasingly attractive "buys" for highly specialized stores seeking narrowly segmented audiences at a minimum cost.

The U.S. Highway Beautification Act, administered by the Federal Bureau of Roads, has had a major impact on the outdoor advertising industry. In states that have chosen to participate in the act's provisions (and there were strong financial incentives to do so), the number, location, and nature of highway signs have been altered drastically. This legislation (unintentionally, no doubt) has stimulated changes that tend to favor the big and the rich advertiser and penalize the small local retailer or service business dependent on outdoor advertising to direct customers to its door and attract the attention of tourists.

Some media are subject to *interruption or suspension* without notice; others are perhaps more dependable. Large metropolitan newspapers have suffered occasional strikes that forced them to suspend publication for prolonged periods. AM radio is subject to unpredictable interference from static electricity, particularly during thunderstorms. Both TV and radio time may be preempted when important presidential announcements are made, high-ranking officials have key speeches to make, or catastrophic news events require total coverage. Billboards can blow down in high winds, and the U.S. mail is sometimes so swamped with advertising literature that it is physically impossible to deliver all of it prior to the special holiday to which it is keyed.

CLUTTER

Closely related to the question of the availability of advertising space and time is the matter of *clutter*, which some academicians have dubbed *information overkill*. There is evidence that the reader, listener, or viewer who is bombarded with an excessive number of ads within a short span of time becomes confused, irritated, and even repelled. The person to whom these many ads are all directed may mix up their meaning or even credit an advertiser's message to the competitor. The din may simply cause the confused reader, listener, or viewer to tune out all the ads.

The problem of clutter is considered most acute in the broadcast media. A trend toward shorter commercials, and more of them, has accentuated this effect. In one three-week period in the second quarter of 1967, the total number of 30-second spot commercials on television was 7,057. Only three years later, in the same period the number had exploded to 333,936! [4]

Clutter occurs in all media, not just TV and radio—and paradoxically, the more successful an ad medium is, the more cluttered it becomes. Newspapers, the retailer's prime medium, are far from immune. They tend especially to become overloaded on "grocery day," when supermarkets insert most of their big ads, and on other days when merchants flood them with ads to take advantage of peak shopping periods. On such days, many daily papers contain hundreds of ads, big and small, interspersed with relatively little news matter.

The media do try to alleviate the problem as best they can. Broadcasters usually schedule ads to give "protection" to each advertiser—for example, by not airing one store's commercial within 15 minutes of a direct competitor's. FM radio stations in many communities take pride in being the least cluttered of local media; they make it a point to schedule but few commercials within each program segment. Newspapers try to avoid direct confrontations between similar advertisers on the same two-page spread. However, this practice is often modified (with the concurrence of the advertisers) when the ads are for specialty merchandise like apparel, automobiles, and sporting goods, which the reader always looks for on certain pages. Outdoor media have long made it a policy to avoid placing more than two signs together.

Advertising clutter may not always have a negative effect. There is little solid scientific research substantiating strong consumer displeasure with ads that are seen or heard adjacent to other ads. In a 1963 study, *The Impact of Blank Space in the Daily Newspaper,* conducted in Des Moines, Iowa, the Newspaper Advertising Bureau, Inc., compared "recognition scores" for ads on pages containing three ads, versus scores for ads on pages from which one of the three ads had been removed. The average score was 36 percent with three ads; and 29 percent with two. The ads on the more cluttered pages actually attracted more notice! More recent studies based on magazine ads also indicated that ads on pages with other ads get more (not fewer) readers than ads standing alone on a page.[5]

Although the general feeling among merchants is that clutter is undesirable, it is often the lesser of two evils. Where a retailer has a choice between putting an exclusive ad in a weak medium with a small audience or putting an ad in a strong medium where it will be only one message among many, the consensus favors the latter course.

A third alternative may be a medium that has elected to rid itself of clutter, at a price—by raising its advertising charges to a point where few can afford to pay them. A small number of well-heeled firms may prefer exposure in such a medium to sharing the limelight with other advertisers.

THE ROLE OF THE MESSAGE

The nature of the *message* itself is a key determinant of media choice among advertising professionals and, all too seldom, among retailers. This is one more good reason why things work out better when objective-and-task budgeting precedes media selection. A merchant should first decide what to say to whom, and then explore the best way (or ways) to say it. Only then should the advertiser consider which medium to use. The nature of the message and its intended audience should, at least, narrow the range of media options; at best, it should make the most appropriate medium obvious.

A clear-cut exposition of the role of the message in media selection was presented by Andrew Vladimir, president of the Vladimir & Evans ad agency:

> ... in planning a media mix, there are other important factors to be considered than simply which medium or combination of media offers the greatest reach and frequency or the lowest cost per thousand. In fact ... these should be the last factors to be considered. ... At our agency we believe that the function of media is simply to transmit the creative message, and until we determine what that message is, we can't write any [media] plan at all.

. . . The media I select to transmit my message is a function of what kind of a message it's going to be, because different media are appropriate for different messages.

When we discuss what media mix is right for any retail store, I think we first have to discuss what we are advertising and what we have to communicate. For example, are we selling items or image, or both?

. . . Too often advertising budgets are drawn up and then arbitrary amounts for each medi[um] are assigned. People say to me all the time, "We've allocated 15% of our budget to television or 75% to print or 10% to radio . . . do you think that's enough?" I never know whether it's enough or not because I think that's the wrong way to approach the whole subject.

One way to approach the whole problem is to consider whether the item you're advertising is a planned purchase or not. If it's a planned purchase, the consumer has probably decided he wants or needs one of these things and the function of advertising is to let him know that you have what he wants. . . . Newspapers, by their very nature, are informational. And any advertising message where the real thrust is needed information works better in newspapers because a consumer can study it and re-read it and even tear it out and carry it around in her purse if she wants to. Moreover, if it's a planned purchase, we know the consumer is looking for a place to buy that item, [and] she "shops" the newspaper looking for it.

But what about something that is not a planned purchase, [which] the consumer has to be motivated to buy? Or a seasonal promotion . . . your store is holding that as a consumer I don't care about or wasn't planning to go to? Or an image-building campaign to at-

tract younger customers to your store? There the excitement of the electronic media—the color, sounds, music and total impact—can really contribute something. And again, where demonstration is an important factor in making the sale, television is invaluable.

Ideally, of course, you should use more than one medium to sell anything. There's a synergistic effect that's been demonstrated time and again that shows that the use of any two media together has an effect more powerful than the sum of the same media used by themselves.[6]

MULTIMEDIA PLANNING

The *synergistic* results of two or more media used as a team are worth thinking about. Advertisers should try to utilize all the effective media they can afford. It may even be justifiable, in some cases, to add extra money to the budget to permit the use of additional media.

The record is full of case histories of increases in sales and profits when the right media mix was used. Usually, ads are concentrated in a *primary medium* and supplemented with ads in *secondary media.*

In Junction City, Kansas, a fellow named Gerald Robinson, owner of the Gambles store, tried multimedia planning. When he expanded his store in 1969, he went into a newspaper-plus-radio mix. The newspaper delivered intensive coverage of the local community, while the radio station provided added *reach* in neighboring counties where folks read other papers. Robinson promoted his merchandise simultaneously in both media, using the same copy, which was "targeted" to specific audiences such as housewives and teenagers. (It was modified, of course, to suit the technical characteristics of the two media.) When the results were in, Robinson's sales had risen by 120 percent over sales for the same month the previous year.[7]

In Ann Arbor, Michigan, a medium-sized city, Dick Berger took over ownership and management of the century-old Wagner's Menswear Shop just in time to face the challenge of the 1969–70 recession. His innovative management policy included a broad media mix. He outlined his advertising policy this way:

> We're big in advertising. We don't look to our competition to lead the way. We decide where we want to go and gear our advertising accordingly.
>
> Occasionally I advertise in the *New York Times*. That makes Ann Arbor sit up and take notice. Newspaper ads emphasize the now look . . . the cosmopolitan buyer . . . if you've seen it in Paris or London, Wagner has it. . . .
>
> [Our] advertising firsts among menswear stores in Ann Arbor: . . . off-beat ads . . . [an] eight full page supplement in the *Ann Arbor News* . . . color TV on Detroit's UHF . . . and Detroit's WQRS-FM [radio] . . . and billboards. We're first in the amount of color newspaper ads we run.
>
> [Our] ad budget breakdown [is]: 60 percent newspaper (25 percent of this is in color); 20 percent radio and TV; 10 percent mailings; and 10 percent window display.[8]

The results of this store's multimedia advertising plan are impressive:

> While some retailers were tightening their belts we were ringing up fantastic sales. Last year our total volume was 33 percent ahead of the year before.[9]

Putting additional advertising dollars into a different medium often produces sales gains greater than those attainable by putting those same added dollars into further ads in the primary medium.

Retailers can use newspaper ads to direct readers' attention to forthcoming circulars or catalogs to be sent through the mail and to build interest in sponsored radio and TV programs. They can use radio announcements to call attention to key ads in newspapers. They can arrange to project the same visual symbols and graphic devices via TV, billboards, newspapers, window displays, and mailing pieces, and use the same musical jingles and sound effects on radio as they do in their television commercials. It all pays off.

DIFFERING MARKETS

Localizing the media situation and understanding patterns of media usage in any given store's trading area are essential to a successful retail media plan. Communities differ, and what is suitable nationwide may not apply in a particular place. Nationwide media usage patterns are merely guides; local inquiries and investigations must be made to translate these guides into a meaningful plan for a given city or area. This is one of the reasons why local advertising at its best can be more efficient and more productive than national advertising. And it is why local independent stores can, if they go about things the right way, get more profit from their advertising investment than large national or regional chains that may not be aware of special local situations.

In Minneapolis, one radio station (WCCO) captures a larger share of the listening audience than any one station in most other major metropolitan area markets. It actually has a greater audience than any one television station in its market (a most unusual situation, since nationwide there are 10 times as many radio stations as there are TV stations). In Providence, Rhode Island, and Peoria, Illinois, newspaper coverage is near 100 percent—higher than in any other U.S. cities.

The Los Angeles market is different from the rest of the country in many ways. Network TV stations get a smaller share of the audience than elsewhere because there are so many independent stations. Radio is strong because of the amazing total of 44 stations, the high proportion of cars with radios, and the great amount of time Angelinos spend in cars. Major downtown dailies, mighty as they are, share the newspaper audience with no less than 17 lesser dailies and 300 free-circulation shopping guides (60 published in conjunction with daily newspapers).

ADAPTING TO CHANGE

Technology is constantly altering the balance among the various media. Color TV became widespread during the 1960s. When TV itself first emerged in the late forties, it was thought of as a sort of elaborate improvement on radio. No one at first knew just how to harness its great advertising potential. Now wired television, an outgrowth of Community Antenna Television (CATV), is growing in popularity. It may eventually alter drastically the relative potency of all other media. Some prophets foresee a total home communications system through which the consumer will be able to respond immediately to advertising and place orders electronically.

Newspapers are going through their own technological revolution. Not long ago, most small newspapers did a poor job of printing, and rarely if ever could they handle color. In recent years, smaller papers have pioneered the shift from the letterpress process to offset lithography, and they are now wholly competitive with the largest metropolitan dailies with respect to the quality of their printing and their ability to reproduce top-grade color ads. Big papers are fast switching to the cold-type process for producing display advertising, even though the material is later printed on letterpress equipment, to gain some of the advantages the weekly and community papers gained by adopting the new processes.

Changes in the media picture derive from social upheavals and altered lifestyles. Increased leisure time leads to more time spent away from home, weakening the pull of newspapers and television and increasing audiences for radio and outdoor advertising. Increases in the number of women who work full- or part-time reduce the daytime audiences of the broadcast media. Increased education tends to increase the hunger for knowledge throughout life and builds the readership of newspapers and magazines.

Media planners must be flexible and keep an open mind about innovations yet to come. No set pattern will be appropriate forever; no rules of thumb will endure to eternity. The wise merchant will repeatedly test media plans, keep records, and analyze the results of various forms of advertising. We will investigate how this can be done, by large and small stores, in Part 4.

5 Writing Down the Media Plan

The media plan should be put down on paper in an orderly way, and a calendar indicating the tentative allotment of funds to each medium each season, month, week, and day should be drawn up. This can be integrated with the overall ad plan for the store, and in the case of larger stores, allotments can be broken down by department or merchandise line. Dollars of budgeted funds can be translated into units of printed advertising space (usually column-inches, but sometimes pages or "agate lines") and into "spot announcements" of stated lengths or sponsored programs for broadcast commercials.

A simple media plan for one month for a small store is shown in Table 8–3. The buyers, the department managers, and the person responsible for advertising will work out a weekly and daily ad

Table 8–3

A Media Plan for *The Style Shoppe*, May 1977

Media Advertising	
Total allotment for media advertising	$1,200
In downtown *Daily Gazette*	
(for 225 column-inches of space @ $4 per column-inch)	900
In suburban *Weekly Journal*	
(for 50 column-inches of space @ $1.50 per column-inch)	75
On radio station *KSEL*	
(for 20 30-second spot announcements @ $10 per spot)	200
Total media funds committed	**$1,175**
Amount under or over budget	−$25
Special Promotion	
Cost of special promotion (231 institutional letters to brides and graduates)	
Cost of printing on store letterheads	$20
Postage (@ 13¢ a letter)	30
Total cost of promotion	**$50**
Funds available from media budget surplus	25
Funds available from institutional advertising/reserve fund	25
Total funds available for special promotion	**$50**

Departmental allotments for May

	Better Dresses	Sportswear	Shoes	Accessories	Total
Daily paper (column-inches)	50	100	50	25	**225**
Weekly paper (column-inches)	30	20			**50**
Radio (30-second spots)			12	8	**20**
Letters	231				**231**

schedule for each department based on the monthly plan. They will decide whether to use a series of small ads or one or two big ones for each department and whether to use *omnibus ads* featuring items from two or more departments or have separate ads for each merchandise line. They will also decide whether radio announcements will be concentrated in peak sales periods or scattered throughout the month.

Questions for Discussion

1. What things must be considered in choosing among various advertising media? What are six or seven specific points authorities urge the advertiser to investigate? Which are most important in the community with which you are most familiar? Why?

2. How would you draw a "triangle of media characteristics"? How would you label each of its three sides? What is meant by each of the three basic characteristics sought after in media? Why must all of them be given some attention in devising a successful media plan for stores?

3. Which desirable media characteristics (desirable from the standpoint of local advertisers) are *especially associated* with each of the following: television, outdoor advertising, radio, direct-mail advertising, and newspapers?

4. Why does an advertiser not always have a completely free choice among advertising media?

5. What is the CPM formula? Why does it often have little application for local retail advertisers seeking to compare media? How can the CPM concept, nevertheless, be converted

into a useful aid for such advertisers in evaluating media?

Suggested Projects

1. Table 8–1 shows the approximate proportion of local advertising that went into each of the major retail media early in the 1970s. Go to the nearest business library to secure recent copies of *Advertising Age* containing similar data, and bring the table up to date. What are the most recent trends in local media use? Why? How do you think media preferences among local advertisers will change in the next five years? Why?

2. Make a roster of all available local advertising media in your or your school's community. Include daily and weekly newspapers, AM and FM radio stations, VHF and UHF television channels, outdoor advertising plants, shopping guides, local-area magazines, and any other media you can find. (Check the *Yellow Pages*.) Does your community offer all, or nearly all, the media choices discussed in the text? Is this an advantage or a disadvantage for local advertisers? Can larger media in neighboring cities be used satisfactorily by local stores? Why?

3. Study the *clutter* in your local media. Count the total number of local display ads in the local newspaper for several days, and strike an average; also, counting only pages that contain two or more ads, determine the average number of smaller ads exposed to the reader's view on each two-page spread. Listen to a local radio station for a full hour, and note the number of commercials you hear. (Choose a desirable time period such

as the early morning, the noon hour, or the late afternoon, when many commercials are usually scheduled.) Do the same, for a local TV station during a period when the program being shown is a local one rather than a network show dominated by national advertising. Collect a week's supply of direct-mail advertising from your family's mailbox. Which local medium do you think is most "cluttered" with competing ads? Do you think this problem is a serious one for advertisers in your community right now?

4. Find five recent examples of print or broadcast ads that could *not* have been delivered as effectively by *any other medium* than the one used. In other words, identify five ads whose message is such that *one medium* in particular is more appropriate than any other. In doing this, think of how you would have handled the same message, had you been required to use a different medium. Do you think most local advertising could be transmitted to the public just as well by two or more available local media? Why?

Notes

1. Montgomery McKinney, "The Good, the Bad and the Best Use of Media," *Broadcasting* (November 1, 1971), p. 12.

2. Herbert Maneloveg, "How Media Men Buy Media—Six Factors for a Good Plan," *Advertising Age* (November 21, 1973), pp. 62–64.

3. *Advertise . . . to promote your business* (Dayton, Ohio: National Cash Register Co., 1958), p. 4.

4. *Broadcast Advertisers Reports* (New York: Broadcast Advertisers Reports, Inc., 1967 and 1970).

5. *The Impact of Blank Space in the Daily Newspaper* (Newspaper Advertising Bureau, Inc., 1963).

6. Andrew Vladimir, "No Magic Formula for Media Mix," *Stores* (June 1973), pp. 28–29.

7. Budd Gore, "Newspaper and Radio Combined," *Stores* (January 1970), p. 30.

8. "Wagner's Is Ann Arbor Catalyst," *Daily News Record* (March 18, 1970), pp. 20–21.

9. Ibid.

Preview

There are nearly 9,000 newspapers in the United States. These include evening dailies, morning dailies, Sunday papers, weeklies, and special-interest papers. Together they form the dominant medium for retail advertising.

There are various reasons why retailers prefer newspaper ads. Local papers tend to reach just the right people for local stores. Newspapers permit flexibility with regard to the format, timing, size, and cost of ads. They can be custom-designed to reflect each store's personality and needs. The preparation and production of newspaper advertising is easy and inexpensive. The public tends to accept and to believe newspaper advertising, and newspaper ads stimulate immediate sales.

The limitations of newspapers include possible wasted circulation, duplication, weak coverage of specific groups such as the young and the poor, inferior reproduction, competition for the reader's attention, and a lack of technical uniformity among papers.

Display ads, classified ads, and supplements are popular forms of newspaper advertising. Space is usually sold on a contract basis by prior agreement, with great savings to regular or large advertisers. Most newspapers offer ads in color at a premium rate. Much research has been done to help advertisers get the most value from ads in this medium.

Learning Goals

The student should become familiar, in this chapter, with the wide differences among newspapers and learn which types best fit certain stores' needs. The reader should see why so many retailers favor this medium but also what its limitations are. It is necessary to learn the meaning of frequency contracts, bulk-space contracts, and earned-rate contracts and to know which kind best suits a given advertising plan.

9

Newspapers—
The Primary
Retail Medium

Daily newspapers contained an estimated $6.9 billion in local advertising in 1975. Weeklies are estimated to have contained about half a billion dollars more, bringing the total to at least $7.4 billion. This was nearly three-fourths of all local advertising media expenditures. Investments in newspaper ads include expenditures by individuals for ads in the classified columns and those by service-related, rather than strictly retail, firms. The purely retail portion of newspaper advertising is estimated to cost about $5 billion. Department stores are the largest newspaper advertisers, followed by discount houses; food markets; furniture, household goods, and appliance stores; and apparel shops.

1 Domination of Retail Advertising by Newspapers

Overall, newspapers have received nearly the same proportion of retailers' ad budgets in recent years, despite the spread of the multimedia approach to media planning. Over the last quarter century, which has been, essentially, the *multimedia era* in local advertising, the yearly local ad volume of daily newspapers alone (excluding weeklies) increased by more than $5 billion; of television, by $1.2 billion; of radio, by $1.1 billion; and of outdoor media, by $69 million.[1] In 1974, daily newspapers contained $4.1 billion more local advertising than the other three media *combined*.

The extent to which newspaper advertising dominates ad budgets varies for different kinds of stores. The leading advertising trade paper estimated the 1973 advertising budgets of the 25 largest general merchandise firms, with media breakdowns for most of them. The total dollars these retailers placed in daily newspaper advertising reached $633 million and the next most favored medium, local television, received $126 million—a ratio of 5 to 1 in favor of the dailies. Among the 25 largest food retailers, the magazine reported $368 million in 1973 daily newspaper advertising and $58 million in TV— a ratio of 6 to 1 in favor of dailies. Among the 10 largest general merchandise retailers, some of them national chains and some of them department store groups, 83 percent of the dollars were invested in daily newspaper ads, 12 percent in television commercials, and the remainder in miscellaneous media, chiefly radio.[2] Department stores (especially the big ones), discounters, women's apparel shops, and such smaller segments of the retail field as office supply outlets traditionally allot well above 75 percent of their budget for newspaper ads. Sporting goods, photographic supplies, menswear, luggage, housewares, and drug outlets spend approximately three-fourths of their ad dollars (the average for retailers) on newspaper ads. Tire dealers, furniture stores, hardware outlets, and restaurants tend to place slightly less emphasis on the medium. Auto dealers, hotels, banks, and food markets have traditionally used significantly less of their ad budget for newspaper ads than the typical retailer (though newspapers are still their number one medium).

2 The Diversity of Newspapers

Each of the 1,768 dailies in this country (with a gross circulation of 62 million) and the 7,612 weekly papers (with a combined circulation of 36 million) has its own personality, reflecting the particular community it serves. The *evening dailies,* 1,449 of them, have the largest circulation, nearly 36 million. They are the prime medium for most retailers in most communities, save only the very small towns that can support only a weekly paper, and a few very large metropolitan cities. They offer a high degree of geographical coverage, which tends to decrease as the interest area of the next daily paper is approached. The coverage of a city and its suburbs will be in quantity, with quality coverage in exurbia and the hinterland. The evening dailies' average circulation is only 25,000, reflecting the large number of such papers in smaller cities and suburban communities.

The *morning dailies,* of which there are 340, have a circulation of over 26 million (an average, per paper, of three times the circulation of the evening papers). They tend to offer a substantially different kind of coverage to retail advertisers. Most of them are based in larger cities. They circulate to a great many families who also read an evening paper, and they tend to appeal most to those who, by virtue of more education, higher-status jobs, and more wealth, seek more and quicker coverage of both local and worldwide news through news and feature stories. Their much larger circulation tends to take in a vastly greater geographical area than that of the average evening paper. Although some have levels of circulation competitive with those of the evening papers in their own city, most morning papers reach a smaller (but richer) segment of the population there, and then penetrate into dozens, scores, or hundreds of other communities which do not have morning papers of their own. In these outlying areas, their circulation is even more "class-oriented," taking in largely business leaders, professional people, and government officials. In effect, a morning paper is "the" morning paper not merely for its own city but for many other areas as well.

Retailers appealing to *lower*-income groups or to *all* economic classes, especially those with stores chiefly in the central city and close-in suburbs, almost always make the evening paper their primary medium. Those with many branches farther out or in other smaller communities in the region and those appealing to higher-income customers (who also tend to be more mobile shoppers) may consider the morning paper a better deal. Big department stores, chains with stores scattered over a wide area, and class-oriented specialty merchants can ill afford to miss advertising in either kind of paper, if they are located in a city that offers both. The content of ads and the treatment of copy is often designed especially for each paper, to appeal to their different audiences and to take into account the different time of day the two kinds of dailies make their impact.

Sunday papers number 641 and have a combined circulation of about 52 million. They are always published (in the United States) as the seventh edition of a daily paper; on the average, they have a larger circulation than their weekday counterparts. Their circulation, like that of the morning papers, tends to be scattered over a wide area, thus giving regular advertisers coverage of a larger geographic area once a week. Sunday papers carry a great deal of retail advertising, especially from fashion-oriented department stores and from discounters that have Sunday shopping hours. They are read in a more leisurely fashion, typically have far more pages than daily issues, and usually contain a number of special-interest news and feature sections where ads can be placed to reach special target audiences—stamp collectors, antique lovers, avid book readers, and the like.

Weekly papers used to be especially widespread in rural areas, but now half their circulation is concentrated in suburban communities where most of their subscribers also read at least one daily. Many are distributed at no charge to the readers. Emphasizing highly localized news and advertising content, weeklies are the fastest-growing segment of the newspaper industry. Like the smaller community-centered dailies, they offer the retailers of their districts a compact coverage pattern (an average circulation of 4,715 per newspaper) at relatively low cost per unit of space (but a comparatively high cost per thousand homes reached).[3] A study released in 1975 found that over half of suburban adults read these local papers (most of which are weeklies), with women leading men both in readership of the papers as a whole and in use of the ads that appear in them as a guide to shopping. Sixty percent of the suburbanites who read such papers read three-fourths or more of each issue they see, compared to 47 percent who read that much or more of the large metropolitan dailies. Readers of these papers include a higher proportion than the United States population as a whole of homeowners (especially owners of more expensive homes), of multi-car owners, of new-car owners, of families with high incomes, and of persons with professional and executive occupations. Readers look at service advertising, classified ads, and food store ads more frequently than they do in metropolitan dailies.[4]

Most weeklies use the offset lithography printing process, which permits high-quality retail ads with fine-screen reproduction of photographs and other forms of art and with excellent color printing. Many weeklies are linked together in small "chains" under joint ownership and offer advertisers a choice of circulation zones via one or several different papers serving contiguous communities. Some papers are delivered free of charge to the homes in a given area, making the coverage "100 percent"; others send out a free-circulation shopping guide containing ads, but not news, to nonsubscribers.

Special-interest newspapers, such as school newspapers, farmers' papers, businesspersons' publications, foreign-language papers, and papers oriented to black readers are also available. Obviously, for target campaigns aimed at those market segments, they are highly suitable.

3 Advantages of Newspapers for Advertising

There are six basic reasons why newspapers are the most popular medium for local advertisers: (1) their effective reach; (2) their flexibility; (3) custom-design of ads; (4) easy and inexpensive preparation of ads; (5) acceptance of newspaper ads by the public; and (6) stimulation of immediate sales.

EFFECTIVE REACH

The sheer number of newspapers available guarantees retailers an efficient means of delivering their messages to those they want to reach, without paying money to reach people who are not potential customers. Newspapers (like stores) are local. Even in large metropolitan dailies, much of the news is local. In smaller papers, local events, interests, and problems receive by far the most attention. This produces two benefits: (1) compact, efficient coverage of stores' real trading areas and (2) a connection between local retail and service outlets and the news in readers' minds.

Newspapers reach huge numbers of people every day and every week. Nationwide studies show that from 73 to 77 percent of all U.S. adults read at least one paper each weekday, and a fifth of them read two. Over the span of five weekdays, adult readership of at least one paper zooms to 92 percent, with the average reader seeing four papers during that time. In the demographic and geographic population segments most important to a majority of local advertisers, daily readership hovers around the 80 percent mark, and readership over a five-day span tops 95 percent.[5] Only about a dozen U.S. cities have more than two daily papers, and the number of cities with as many as two dailies is about 100. Elsewhere, in the smaller towns, one single daily newspaper delivers saturation of a prime local market.

Newspapers have a known audience. Their coverage is precisely measured by the Audit Bureau of Circulations or some other authoritative certification service, so there is no guesswork about how many homes are being reached. Furthermore, on the average more than two adults actually read each copy of a paper—a huge bonus in effective reach above the basic circulation paid for.

Newspaper ads also reach those most ready and able to buy. Of the readers of ads for specific merchandise, persons who are actively considering purchase of that merchandise are twice as numerous as those who are not in the market for those products. People sort out newspaper ads that relate to intended purchases and focus on those which are most likely to cause them to buy—which is precisely what most retailers want from their ads.[6]

Countless studies through the years confirm that newspaper circulation is skewed toward consumers with discretionary income to spend. Readership is highest among families with incomes above $15,000. It is also highest among those with college educations and professional and managerial workers—groups that tend to have more purchasing power than average.[7]

Prime-time space is available to every newspaper advertiser. All ads reach every subscriber in every edition, so there is no shopping for "availabilities" when audiences are large (and premium rates exclude all but the largest advertisers). In peak selling periods, when retailers need ads the most, newspapers can add pages and sections to accommodate them. Unlike the broadcast media, they are not locked into a 24-hour day and a 60-minute hour.

FLEXIBILITY

The vast variety of sizes and forms of newspaper ads and the many choices of rate structures make newspapers a medium that can suit the special needs of any merchant. Display ads, classified ads, display classified (a combination form), inserts, supplements, run-of-paper color, and preprinted color pages are some of the options available. Each, on occasion, may be the answer to a store's problem.

Quick changes can be made in newspaper ads in response to sudden changes in marketing opportunities or conditions. A store can also gear its ads to current events, as newspapers are by nature topical and up-to-date.

CUSTOM—DESIGN OF ADS

The content and format of newspaper ads can be varied in an infinite number of ways. No two need be alike. The copy can be long or short, with or without a headline; the layout, typography, border, and white space can be tailored to fit a store's image; illustrations can be faithfully reproduced from any art medium, and they can be few or many, large or small, black or white, or any combination of colors. Stores can also make up their own ad supplements for the paper to deliver. Coupons can be used, and ads can ask for (and get) phone or mail responses.

Stores can give *exposure to as many items as they choose* in each ad. The one-item ad can do a fantastic job on today's special-promotion "leader" item. A big store can put 200 products in its day's ads, presenting a virtual catalog of its huge stock. Typical food stores name 62 items (12 of them features) in their 2½ pages of weekly newspaper ads, and a fifth of such stores mention more than 100 items weekly.[8] Advertising such a wide range of products at one time is possible only in newspapers or circulars. Institutional, image-building, and idea-oriented elements can also be readily included in print ads.

Newspaper ads have a *visual im-pact.* Printed words that can be read and reread at will can be linked with pictures that hold still and can be examined, shown to others, and studied over again. A store can simply picture its merchandise, or it can show the products being used. Printed pictures can reflect the satisfaction to be derived from a purchase, or reveal the construction features or materials that make it a good value. Art can be put to work to establish a mood and stimulate emotion. Typography and design can also transmit their own kind of graphic message.

Color is now available in nearly all U.S. newspapers. Many surveys over the years have proven that the added cost of color is less than the value of the added sales it produces (see Chapter 14). The full cost of color is often absorbed by cooperating manufacturers, too. Color makes merchandise seem more exciting. It magnifies the readership of ads and the readers' response to them. It also has a psychological effect, stimulating emotions and creating moods.

In a newspaper ad, the essential facts are a *matter of record* and can be easily referred to again. The advertiser's name, address, phone number, hours of business, and credit arrangements are set down in black and white; so are specific prices and models of merchandise.

Classified ads are very popular with certain types of retailers, like auto and boat dealers, and with good reason. Millions of people search out classified ads daily to find jobs, locate homes, hire help, rent rooms, recover lost articles, dispose of unused items, hunt for bargains, and find services they need. Classifieds attract $2.1 billion from advertisers annually, and in 70 percent of families that read newspapers, one or more family members look at classified ads at least once each week.[9] Some 85 percent of daily papers accept display-classified ads, the form most used by retailers. More than six out of ten general merchandise items bought through classified ads in newspapers are purchased from stores or dealers rather than from individuals. This reflects the increased recognition of the value of classified ads, the visual impact of display classifieds, and the willingness of consumers to accept dealer as well as consumer ads in this part of newspapers.

EASY AND INEXPENSIVE PREPARATION OF ADS

Writing and designing newspaper ads calls for less technical skill than the creation of ads for other local media. Ordinary business people can do much of the work themselves—easily, quickly, and effectively. With newspapers, ad preparation costs are minimal, and the amount of media help is maximal. The majority of the dailies with circulations above 30,000 maintain copy and layout departments, as do many smaller papers. Newspapers provide planning and budgeting guides, promotional calendars, timetables of selling opportunities for various merchandise lines, market research, and massive supplies of syndicated professional artwork for advertising illustrations on which all advertisers can draw. Many have cooperative advertising coordinators to assist stores in getting aid from manufacturers, and increasing numbers of papers sponsor periodic seminars at which merchants can learn to improve their advertising.

Because preparation costs are so low for newspaper ads, retailers can use all or most of their funds to buy space. There is also less need to hire an expensive agency or build up a big in-store ad staff.

Newspapers carried well over $1.2 billion in national ads in 1975, and are likely to run more such advertising in the future. Much of it is for automobiles and related products, foods and beverages, transportation, tobacco, and household equipment and appliances. Stores can capitalize on this national advertising with tie-in ads in the same paper. Often, their suppliers will furnish art, copy, and print materials to make this easy and inexpensive. Newspaper staffs habitually alert retailers to products for which national advertising is scheduled.

ACCEPTANCE OF NEWSPAPER ADS BY THE PUBLIC

People like newspapers and their ads. Readers pay out over $3 billion annually for their papers, and they do look clear through them: Page opening averages 84 percent and is quite constant throughout the paper. (Even women's pages are opened by 80 percent of men and sports pages by 70 percent of women.) [10]

Consumers' preference for newspaper ads, when measured by impartial research with no "axe to grind," simply verifies and confirms parallel research sponsored by the newspaper industry itself. Recent studies all arrive at the same conclusion: that shoppers say newspaper ads are most helpful, believable, and sought-after. A syndicated report by Alan R. Nelson Research based on replies from 3,235 men in a National

Family Opinion consumer panel in 1974, measured *attentiveness to advertising* in several media. It revealed that 80 percent were receptive to newspaper advertising because it is "better if you want to comparison shop," and 75 percent were attentive to newspaper ads because "you can look for sale items." By contrast, top score for magazines was 72 percent—because "you have more time to respond"—and for television, 47 percent—because " 'catchy' phrases and slogans often stick in your mind." [11] In a 1971 survey by the Mass Retailing Institute, 92 percent of the discount store shoppers questioned said that they recalled seeing or hearing store advertising. Of these respondents, 85 percent said it was the stores' newspaper ads they recalled, while television and radio advertisements were far behind with a recall of only 15 percent. [12] Another survey conducted by the institute in 1973 reported that 69 percent of the shoppers questioned said they read printed advertising when comparison-shopping for price, quality, or both. [13] When the Sindlinger and Company research firm interviewed 2,234 consumers in 1974, asking upon which medium they most relied when looking for the best buys before shopping, 78 percent said that they relied on newspapers, while only 4 percent relied on television. Fifty-eight percent of the same respondents rated newspapers as the "medium [that] presents the most useful and believable advertising," as opposed to 16 percent who rated TV in this way. [14] The Super Market Institute in its 1975 annual report declared that its research affiliate found that 71 percent of people surveyed considered food ads in newspapers "generally helpful" and that 41 percent of

them "almost always" clipped coupons from their newspaper. [15]

Newspaper ads are read in favorable circumstances. They are not considered interruptions that must be borne or irritants. People look forward to reading a newspaper, including the ads. Readers can control their exposure to newspaper ads—scanning, skipping, or dwelling on them at will. The slow reader can take much time to comprehend the ad, and the fast reader can grasp the essence of a message in a flash.

Newspaper ads benefit from the aura of authenticity associated with the printed word—and with the factual, specific, hard news that surrounds them. In broadcast media, particularly TV, fantasy tends to dominate the programming and is often reflected in commercials.

STIMULATION OF IMMEDIATE SALES

Quick action at the cash register is more likely with newspaper ads than with other kinds of retail promotion. When a West Coast specialty chain runs an ad for sleeper blankets at $3.99 and sells 12,000 in two days, it isn't even news; things like this happen every day, everywhere. Top executives dub newspapers "the action medium," and for good cause. They can advertise today and sell tomorrow.

4 The Other Side of the Coin: Newspapers' Drawbacks

For relatively large merchants with big enough ad budgets to obtain adequate impact and frequency in two or more media, it is no longer a defensible proposition that newspapers are the *only* effective local medium. Though many stores do continue to grow and prosper without using other media, they are becoming the exception rather than the rule. The specific advantages of other media cited in Chapters 10 and 11 constitute, in effect, the case against making newspapers a store's *sole* ad medium.

The following limitations of newspapers must be kept in mind.

1. *Waste circulation,* which a retailer has to pay for but does not benefit from, is sometimes a problem. Some metropolitan papers "zone" their circulation on certain days to give retailers coverage of target areas at a lower cost. Excess coverage is not always a matter of geography, however. Newspapers may also reach some socioeconomic groups that are not potential customers of a particular retailer.

2. *Duplication of coverage* occurs when two or more newspapers—a morning and an evening paper in the same town or a downtown daily and a suburban weekly—reach many of the same people. Some retailers may prefer to make two impressions on the same people (doubling the impact factor in advertising). Others

may choose to broaden their coverage by cutting out advertising in the "second" paper, to release dollars for media that reach entirely new audiences. This problem of duplication, however, is decreasing as the number of two-newspaper towns dwindles, leaving one daily dominant in the great majority of communities.

3. *Competition for attention* may be too stiff for the small-budget newspaper advertisers, whose ads are forever surrounded by larger competitors' bigger and better-produced messages. Thus they may turn to a smaller paper or to other media not so heavily saturated with advertising. Essentially, this is the clutter problem discussed in Chapter 8.

4. *Poor reproduction quality* may be found in a paper that has failed to keep up with improvements in graphic processes. Many ads may look substandard, destroying much of the quality of their impact.

5. *Decreasing circulation* often hits poorly managed papers in spite of population growth in the areas they serve. They may not attract the young or the newly arrived residents of an area, whom retailers need to reach through ads.

6. *Inferior personnel* on newspaper

Figure 9–1 Zoned Editions Appeal to Retailers
Small-city newspapers, suburban weeklies, and community-centered newspapers everywhere tend to develop circulation patterns that closely approximate the natural trading area of individual stores. Large metropolitan papers spread over huge areas—central city plus the vast suburban fringe—and tend to price themselves out of the market for one-store retailers' advertising. To make advertising more economical for merchants whose pattern of store locations does not justify use of the vast total circulation available, large papers may divide up their circulation into zones and offer zoned editions (often just on certain days of the week) targeted on a specified segment of their metropolitan areas.

This map shows how one midwest metropolitan paper has divided its coverage area into four zones, available individually or in any combination the advertiser prefers. Rates are substantially less than for the total metro-area coverage, enabling smaller retail stores to utilize such papers to reach their own more local markets without waste.

News Metro Zones were determined by geographic boundaries and the shopping patterns of people in the various areas.

Each News Metro Zone boasts its own staff of reporters. Each zone edition features editorial content of interest to readers in that particular area.

1. Metro Detroit—City of Detroit plus the cities of Highland Park and Hamtramck.

2. Metro West—Wayne County south and west of the city of Detroit, including such cities as Dearborn, Livonia, Dearborn Heights, Grosse Ile, Taylor, Lincoln Park and Redford Township.

3. Metro North—Oakland County which includes such cities as Birmingham, Pontiac, Southfield, Royal Oak, Lathrup Village, Bloomfield Hills, Bingham Farms, Beverly Hills and West Bloomfield.

4. Metro East—Macomb County, including the cities of Warren, St. Clair Shores, Sterling Heights, Roseville and East Detroit. Also including the Grosse Pointes in Wayne County.

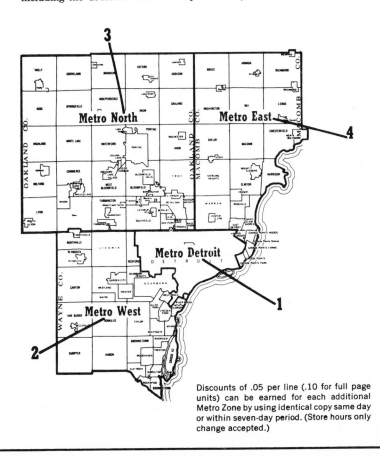

Discounts of .05 per line (.10 for full page units) can be earned for each additional Metro Zone by using identical copy same day or within seven-day period. (Store hours only change accepted.)

staffs may be unable or unwilling to actively assist retailers (in particular the small ones) with their advertising. This forces merchants to other, more helpful, media.

7. *The rapidly increasing advertising rates* of newspapers are due primarily to high inflation in the cost of newsprint since 1970. This rise in rates has not been matched by growth in circulation, and this has resulted in a more rapid gain in *cost per thousand* homes or persons reached than has been the case with competing media. To counteract this trend, however, most newspapers have deliberately trimmed circulation outside the normal trading areas of their communities rather than in areas where retailers find their prime markets. Therefore, it remains an unanswered question whether the *effective* CPM has increased any more than that of other media.

8. *Lack of uniformity in technical specifications* for ads among newspapers means that chain stores advertising in different papers in different towns must take into account different page sizes, column widths and lengths, different printing and typesetting methods, and different capabilities for printing in color in preparing ads. This increases ad preparation time and the cost of advertising. By 1975 there were 214 different page formats in use among the 1,569 dailies belonging to the American Newspaper Publisher's Association. In that year, the American Association of Advertising Agencies and the Printing Platemakers Association issued joint specifications for standardizing ad materials supplied to newspapers. In response, the newspapers' association developed and publicized throughout the industry its own new advertising dimension standards, compatible with those of the agencies and platemakers, with a goal of reducing the 214 different formats to only six: three standard formats for newspapers using eight or nine columns on their pages, and three for newspapers using a six-column page (tabloids excluded). This will simplify newspaper advertising preparation and reduce its cost, as the newspapers conform to these standards.

From time to time, speakers for major retail firms and for agencies that have retail clients have voiced the opinion that the era of newspapers' dominance in retail advertising is drawing to a close. Predictions have been made that broadcast advertising will displace printed ads as merchants' most-favored medium. The great majority of industry leaders, however, express the view that other media (especially television, in the case of very large stores) will be increasingly used in a more balanced media mix, but a majority of retail advertising dollars will continue indefinitely to be invested in newspaper space.

5 How to Use Newspapers Most Effectively

KINDS OF NEWSPAPER ADVERTISING

Display Advertisements These are the kinds of ads most commonly used by retailers. They are usually in black and white, but are sometimes in color. They almost always include one or more illustrations of featured items, and they carry the main load of continuous item-price promotional advertising for the great majority of stores.

Classified Ads. These are a prime medium for realtors and car dealers. They are also widely used by retailers of recreation vehicles, boats, and other leisure-related items; furniture outlets; appliance stores; farm-supply businesses; and those who offer services of all kinds. Increasingly, other retailers are turning to classifieds to reinforce other advertising, including that for "sale" goods and new merchandise at the low end of price lines. A few papers accept certain kinds of illustrations in these ads, and most of them permit large-type commercial ads called *display classifieds* for those who want extra impact.

Supplements Newspaper supplements are a fast-growing form of retail advertising. Many supplements are pre-printed by large chains or big department stores and inserted into the newspaper; others are part of the newspapers' own weekly feature supplement. Both kinds of supplements are usually printed on premium-quality paper in bright colors. There are also preprinted *Hi-Fi* or *Spectacolor* pages that appear within the regular section of a paper. Their brilliant artwork is very costly and is shipped in advance to the newspaper by the advertiser, usually a large chain or cooperating manufacturer, with some space left open for local imprinting.

NEWSPAPER RATE STRUCTURES:
HOW TO BUY SPACE

Display Rates Rates for display ads are figured by the *agate line* by large met-ropolitan dailies. An agate line occupies $\frac{1}{14}$th of a column-inch. An ad approximately four inches square would be two columns wide by four inches deep. It would occupy eight column-inches, and 8 times 14, or 112, *lines*. A paper with a *line rate* of 50 cents would charge $56.00 for this much space. In smaller cities retail display rates are normally figured in *column-inches,* which are much simpler to visualize. A full two-column ad in a newspaper having 21-inch columns, is called a "2 × 21" (or a "2 × full") and occupies 42 column-inches. If the rate per inch is $5 (as it might well be for a paper with a circulation of roughly 100,000), the ad will cost $5 × 42, or $210. A smaller paper, perhaps a daily or a weekly with 10,000 subscribers, might charge $1.50 per inch and run the same ad for $63 (42 × $1.50).

Volume Discounts Discounts for volume advertising are allowed by newspapers (and other media), just as other business firms charge less *per unit* as the size of the order increases. A newspaper gives stores a special deal when they buy space by the thousands of inches or order ads by the dozens. Special rates for newspaper space are designed especially for retailers; rarely does a paper offer similar breaks to its national advertisers. This is a primary reason why long-range preplanned advertising is so much less costly for retailers than advertising concocted on the spur of the moment and run at the newspaper's open rate.

Frequency discounts are always the lowest rates on any newspaper's retail rate card. They usually call for a minimum of one ad, of a specified *minimum size, per week* for a 52-week period (modified to 26 or 13 weeks for seasonal

644 Household Goods

BED — Queen size and chest, walnut, $75; triple dresser, walnut, $50; desk and chair, $25; sectional, 3 pieces, $75; double springs and mattress, $25. Ph. 485-0697.

BED — $35, bunk $85, twin $85, dresser $35, chest $35, TV $55, refrigerator $75, stpve $50. Ph. 393-3957.

BEDROOM SUITE — Bed, chest of drawers, double dresser with mirror, innerspring mattress, and box springs, all for $298. Terms you wouldn't believe possible. Berk's (Old School House) Furniture Co. Ph. 482-6241. Open Mon. and Fri. 'til 9, other days 'til 5:30.

BEDROOM AND DINING — Room clearance sale. Moving this department to another area of the store with less space so take advantage of the savings now. Bell Furniture Sales, N. U.S. 27. Ph. 487-0121.

BISHOP'S FURNITURE — Shop Bishop's scratch and dent department for super savings on odd lot items. Sofas, lounge chairs, dining tables, chinas, chairs, beds, recliners, starting at $48.88 mattresses, etc. Save up to ½. 5814 S. Pennsylvania.

BOX SPRINGS — And mattress, full size, like new. $70. Ph. before 6 p.m., 337-0245.

BRIDGE TABLE — And 4 upholstered chairs, coral, $50. Ph. 351-8240.

BUNKS — $45; antique sewing rockers, $35; Sleigh dresser and bed $95; recliners $25; rockers $8, Hide-a-way bed $50; sofa $25; headboards $2 up; dishes, pots, pans. Bell Furniture Trade-in Sale. Ph. 487-0173 and 487-0121.

CARPET — Beige, wool, high-lo, pile, 12x20, 12x10, 12x9, excellent, $225. Ph. 646-6006.

CARPETING IS A BIG PART — Of our business. We represent over 10 major mills. Compare! Also draperies and wallpaper to correlate. Bell Furniture Sales, N. U.S. 27. Ph. 487-1021.

COUCH —$ 75, bed $35, bunk $85, twin $85, chest $35, dresser $35, TV $55, refrigerator $75, stove $50. Ph. 393-3957.

GET AQUAINTED! — Holmes Road 2nd Hand Store and Antiques, 2323 W. Holmes Rd., open 7 days, 10-6. Ph. 882-3022.

GOOD SELECTION — Used and repossessed furniture. Sofa, chairs and miscellaneous items at Tony Coats Trade-in Floor. Ph. 332-0805.

HOUSEHOLD GOODS — Formal dining set, made to seat 12, cane back chairs, velvet seats, pads included. Ph. 485-5332 after 5.

MOVING — Furniture, files, beds, vacuums, 5' round table, dehumidifiers, lots, lots more. Fri., Sat., Sun., 10-6, 6129 Coachouse Dr., off N. Hagadorn.

NEED CARPET? — At discount prices. Credit no problem, we finance our own. Ph. Credit manager, 694-1138, Carrousel Carpets.

REMODELING — Must sell. 2 colonial love seats, like new, $135 each; purple traditional chair and foot stool, 36" Kenmore gas stove, 5 pair gold drapes. Ph. 663-4198, 6270 Steele Hwy., Eaton Rapids.

USED KERBY — Upright vacuum cleaner, very good condition, attachments available. New $295, must sacrifice $54.95. Call 372-4497.

100 USED VACUUM CLEANERS — Tanks, canisters and uprights. 1-year warranty. $7.88 and up. Dennis Distributing Co., 316 N. Cedar, Lansing, Mich. Ph. 482-2677.

3 CHAIRS — Tables/chairs, canopy bed, miscellaneous. Ph. 372-6820 after 5.

646 Appliances

APPLIANCE — Headquaters at Dave's furniture, 75 good used appliances in stock all guaranteed and delivered. Most reasonable prices in town, ADC orders accepted, 1814 S. Washington. Ph. 371-2843.

COOLERATOR — Humidifiers. Early bird buys now. Shop and save at Whalen's Distributing Co., 2709 W. Michigan. Ph. 487-6074.

businesses, at a slightly higher cost). There is no limit on the number of ads, and all ads, large or small, are charged for at the contract rate. These rates favor department stores, supermarkets, and drug stores, which obviously have a relatively flat sales curve, with few variations from month to month and week to week. For other retailers, too, it often saves so much on the total cost of advertising that a moderate degree of *over-advertising* during slack periods is acceptable. Ads run solely to fulfill contracts during a store's off-season are called *rate holders,* and they are usually institutional ads prepared well in advance. Reductions of as much as 40 to 50 percent from standard, or open, rates are typical for big users of regular space with *frequency contracts.*

Two typical *rate cards* are shown in Figure 9–3.

Bulk contracts appeal to stores that concentrate ads in peak sales seasons and throttle back to little or no advertising during slow periods. In these con-

tracts rate discounts are based on the *total* volume of space used during the year (or, possibly, a six- or three-month season). They sometimes do require a stated minimum of ads per month, making them, in effect combination *bulk-and-frequency contracts,* with the emphasis on the former. Bulk rates are invariably higher, for the same total volume of space, than frequency rates. However, for store that are very large in-season advertisers and very small advertisers the rest of the year, it is cheaper, on the whole, to go the bulk route.

A newspaper with a $5.00 open rate, might, as shown above, offer a $4.25 per-inch rate for 52 weekly 10-inch ads, and also a 500-inch annual bulk rate of perhaps $4.50. The 52 10-inch ads required as a minimum under the frequency contract would total 520 inches during the year and cost $2,210. With a bulk contract, 520 inches would cost $2,340, or $119 more. However, if the store wanted to use 300 inches in De-

Figure 9–2 Types of Newspaper Ads Used by Retailers
On the right is a single, one-item promotional ad for a small-town shoe store. It exemplifies the great majority of retail newspaper ads, called *display* ads. The headline, illustration, text (or *body copy*), price, distinctive store signature (or *logotype*), white space, and decorative border are the essential elements of most display ads, which may vary in size and shape at the advertiser's option. *Classified* ads are the mainstay of some types of local businesses and can be used to great advantage in special circumstances by all of them. The illustration on the left shows both the regular classifieds (sometimes called "liners"), which are in small print, and a *classified-display* ad, a hybrid variety combining some of the advantages of both display and classified ads. Many newspapers restrict the amount of pictorial matter, special type, and other attention-getting facets of classified displays, but all place them in the appropriate classification along with similar ads to facilitate quick discovery by the reader.

Preprinted ads, a relatively recent development in newspaper advertising, are not shown here. One version of preprint ads, the *insert* (or advertising supplement), is the fastest-growing kind of newspaper retail ad. It closely resembles direct-mail circulars, being entirely prepared by the advertiser and delivered to the newspaper in bulk to be inserted into the paper. The other kind, *roll-fed* preprints, are very spectacular, in full, rich natural colors on high-grade magazine-type paper, often supplied by manufacturers with a strip down the side or center for local imprinting by the store. These ads, which are too costly for any but the very largest of retailers, bring maximum impact to the newspaper medium. An example of a roll-fed preprint can be found on the last page of the color insert in this text.

cember, 120 in November, and 100 in May, the bulk system would be best since a frequency contract would force it to also use 10-inch ads every week during nine months when it did not want any ads at all—at an additional cost of $1,527.50!

Short rates are applied when an advertiser defaults on an ad contract and does not use the minimum amount of space agreed upon at the beginning of the contract period. A short-rate bill takes into account the difference between the amount of space the advertiser contracted for in order to get a reduced rate and the amount of space it actually used.

Suppose a store had agreed to use 20 inches of space weekly, all year long, in a small local paper, which had promised to bill him at $1.00 per column-inch instead of at its open rate of $1.80. What would happen if, despite the contract, the store either skipped a week or two now and then or cut the size of its ads to 10, 8, or 6 inches? Whether the store also ran a few huge ads before Easter and Christmas would be immaterial, since the agreement was for a *minimum* size and a *minimum* frequency. When the contract expired (or perhaps before!) the paper would, quite rightly, examine its rate structure and determine what rate the store actually "earned" with its irregular advertising. If it had run no ads smaller than 10 column-inches and had not skipped any weeks, it might be charged the paper's regular 10-inch weekly frequency rate, perhaps $1.10. But since it missed some weeks entirely and used very small ads at other times, it really should be charged a bulk rate for whatever total volume it used. This might bring its costs up to $1.30 per inch. Hence, if the store had used 400 inches (which it paid for at the contract rate of $1.00, in monthly bills), the *short rate* to be paid at the end of the contract period would be the *difference* between that amount ($400.00) and the corrected amount billed at $1.30 per inch ($520.00), or $120.

Some papers give a *rebate* if things work out in the opposite way, with stores running far more ads (or bigger ones) than they had anticipated when a contract was signed. The stores may get a break if the paper will adjust the rate *downward* at the end of the contract period. Usually, a newspaper will notice an unexpectedly large volume from a store long before a contract expires and will suggest terminating the contract and arranging a new one, establishing lower rates based on a greater frequency or volume of ads. Rebates are an especially sensitive subject when some of a store's ads have been cooperative ads, for which a manufacturer has agreed to pay a portion of the costs. The cooperative ad contract usually specifies that the vendor must get its share of any rebate, along with the retailer, and FTC guides specify that this *must* be accomplished even

Figure 9–3 Newspaper Rate Cards for Local Advertising
All media publish rate cards to inform advertisers and the media departments of their agencies of the cost of a given advertising proposal, the restrictions and limitations involved, the technical specifications, and the opportunities offered for special rates when a contract is agreed upon. These examples are typical, but there is no one "standard" form for newspapers or any other medium. Local rate cards, especially for newspapers, are very different from national (or general) rate cards; they invariably suggest great savings in cost for volume and frequency of advertising.

On the left is a page from a 20-page *retail rate* booklet. Like other very large newspapers, the *Cleveland Press* rates include the usual frequency and bulk schedules, offering substantial reductions from the "open" rate; on other pages would be found various special classification rates. Note that these rates are quoted both in *lines* (first column) and *inches* (second column). In large cities, some advertisers think in terms of the (agate) line rate, which is one fourteenth as much as the inch rate. Everywhere, smaller retail advertisers use the cost per inch, which means a *column-inch,* or a space one column wide by one inch deep.

The card on the right is a *classified rate card,* with one page of a 12-page booklet shown. This page shows the classified contract rates for the San Jose, California, *Mercury & News.* The lines referred to in a classified rate schedule are not the same as those used in connection with display advertising. They are the actual lines of classified ad type used in any given newspaper (seldom, if ever, 1/14th of an inch in depth as are the agate lines shown in the *Cleveland Press* rate card). Contracts for classifieds, like this one, tend to call for shorter contract periods but greater frequency—in this case an ad of a specified minimum size *every day* during the contract period.

THE CLEVELAND PRESS
Retail Display Rates

Effective May 15, 1974

	Line Rate	Inch Rate
OPEN RATE	$1.33	$18.62
TIE-INS with General ads or Press promotions-7 lines or more	1.08	15.12

FREQUENCY CONTRACTS

1 inch-13 times within 1 year	1.02	14.28
3 inches-26 times within 1 year	1.00½	14.07
5 inches-52 consecutive weeks	.99	13.86

BULK SPACE CONTRACTS

50 inches-within 1 year	1.05	14.70
100 inches-within 1 year	1.01½	14.21
500 inches-within 1 year	1.01	14.14
1000 inches-within 1 year	1.00½	14.07

SUBURBAN (Business with one outlet qualify) (East of 40th St., West of Cuyahoga River)

OPEN RATE	1.14	15.96

CONTRACTS

1 inch-13 times or 50 inches within 1 year	1.01	14.14

Friday Showtime Magazine, and Saturday Home Magazine back page premium-$100

LOCAL COLOR ADVERTISING

Spot Color - - - - - - - - - - - - - - 90 inch minimum
Multi Color - - - - - - - - - - - - - -180 inch minimum

	ROP	TABLOID
One Color and Black-Contract rate plus	$ 480	$300
Two Colors and Black-Contract rate plus	$ 900	$500
Three Colors and Black-Contract rate plus	$1000	$600

Tabloid Double-Truck-Full page R.O.P. color rates apply.

Above rates apply to process colors only.

(Special colors or Day Glo Color Rates on request.)

CONTRACT RATES

Classified contract rates are determined by the number of lines in each ad AND the number of consecutive days the ad is published without change of copy.

INDIVIDUAL CLASSIFIED ADS OF	1 Day	2 Days	3 Days	4 to 6 Days	7 or More
2-6 Lines	1.16 Per Line	.78 Per Line	.70 Per Line	.57 Per Line	.52 Per Line
7-13 Lines	.99 Per Line	.69 Per Line	.62 Per Line	.54 Per Line	.50 Per Line
14-41 Lines	.89 Per Line	.60 Per Line	.56 Per Line	.52 Per Line	.48 Per Line
42-139 Lines	.86 Per Line	.58 Per Line	.54 Per Line	.50 Per Line	.47 Per Line
140-499 Lines	.84 Per Line	.56 Per Line	.52 Per Line	.48 Per Line	.45 Per Line
500 Lines or More	.83 Per Line	.54 Per Line	.50 Per Line	.45 Per Line	.43 Per Line

Requires signing an advertising agreement for three (3) consecutive months or longer. A minimum of at least two (2) lines of classified advertising to be inserted each day regardless of the frequency or volume of classified advertising published. Cancellation of agreement prior to minimum period of three months will require rebilling at open rate. The agreement is not transferable and does not include any joint advertising arrangement.

FUNERAL NOTICES
(CARD OF THANKS and IN MEMORIAM)

SUNDAY or DAILY COMBINATION
68¢ Per Line

MORNING or EVENING ONLY
51¢ Per Line

though it obviously involves a great deal of extra clerical work long after the co-op ads may have run.

An *earned-rate* contract specifies a modest monthly minimum of advertising coupled with a sliding-scale *monthly bulk rate* based on the total volume each month. With such an arrangement, a given store might be obligated to use at least 40 column-inches each month at a basic rate of $2 per inch; but if in, say, May, June, September, and December, its ads far exceeded 40 inches, it might enjoy a reduction to $1.90 or $1.80. This system reduces misunderstanding and disagreement between merchant and medium and has become increasingly popular in recent years.

Ad Placement Most retail ad contracts are for "ROP" (run-of-paper) ads, which may be placed anywhere in the paper, as the newspaper chooses. Large papers offer a guaranteed *position* for an additional premium rate, and some have special rates for different categories of local advertisers. Commonly, the frequency rate is lower yet if the store commits itself to a *stated day* for all its ads.

Color Color is normally charged for at a *flat rate,* since the newspaper's costs for adding color to an ad are virtually the same whether the ad is large or small. *Any* use of color, even for a single letter or a tiny part of a simple picture, requires about the same amount of extra labor and specialized equipment as using a large amount of the same color. So color ads carry a surcharge, over and above the regular space rates. Typical *color premiums* may start at $75 to $100 in small papers and go as high as many hundreds of dollars *per color* in big ones. In effect, color rates

favor large advertisers; most papers will not accept color ads of less than 1,000 lines (72 column-inches), thus preventing the very smallest retailers from even considering them.

The *availability* of color is not assured everywhere, but it is nearly always obtainable. One color (plus black) is offered by about 1,500 dailies, which have over 90 percent of the circulation of U.S. dailies, and by most of the larger weeklies. Extra charges for color average 19 percent for full-page ads and 36 percent for 1,000-line ads. However, these averages are based on the top national space rates (which are usually equivalent to the high local open rates) of all newspapers. For retailers, the *added* cost is much higher, simply because their basic black-and-white rate is so much lower. Furthermore, color premiums are *relatively* higher among smaller papers than among large ones. For retailers in smaller markets with limited space budgets, the expense of adding one color may *double* the total cost of a given ad.

Three or more colors can be printed by over 1,300 daily papers having better than 85 percent of the gross circulation in the country. This costs an average of 34 percent more than the open rate for full-page ads and 70 percent more than for smaller ads—plus very costly preparation charges (which are sometimes, happily, absorbed by cooperating manufacturers). In papers with a circulation of less than 25,000, the three-color premium averages 92 percent for 1,000-line units. Color cannot always be used every day of the week, due to mechanical limitations on certain popular days, and closing dates for color ads average two to seven days earlier than those for black and white ads. Merchants often have to schedule such ads far in advance, especially if they want three colors, and they may even have to accept a one- or two-day optional insertion date.

Classifieds Classifieds are usually charged for by the *line* (but not by the agate line mentioned earlier). The classified type chosen by the newspaper for its small, solidly set *liner ads* becomes the unit of measure for all classifieds, including big ones with white space and larger type sizes for headlines and signatures. The rate may be 80 cents *per line,* hence $8 for a ten-line ad *or* for an ad containing larger type or white space that occupies an equivalent amount of space. Ads with larger type or extra space, called *display-classified ads,* are usually preferred by retailers. Contracts are available for classified ads, usually based on the frequency system but with rate breaks at 3, 6, 30, and 90 consecutive daily insertions.

Preprinted Ads Rates for preprinted ads (either supplements or rolls of Hi-Fi or Spectacolor) and for space in the newspaper's own special supplements, vary considerably. Nearly all papers accept advertisers' supplements and *wallpaper* (preprinted rolls). The smaller papers generally do not have weekly feature supplements, but many schedule supplements for particular seasonal events.

GETTING THE MOST MILEAGE FROM THE NEWSPAPER ADVERTISING DOLLAR

Newspapers are a versatile medium capable of producing tremendous results when used properly. Both the content and form and the timing of newspaper ads should be tuned to the kind of audience the newspaper delivers and the special segment of that relatively undiversified audience the ad seeks to reach.

The geographical dimensions of daily newspaper coverage are pinned down by Audit Bureau of Circulation (ABC) reports. There is no guesswork involved; the reports are authenticated periodically by impartial outside auditors. ABC reports show both absolute circulation figures and the percentages of occupied households reached in each paper's *city zone* (central city and immediate suburbs) and *retail trading zone.* They show how the paper is delivered, how subscriptions were obtained, and how many copies go to outlying communities. Most newspapers that are not members of ABC have other data to pinpoint their geographical coverage.

Retail advertisers can learn a great deal from the great mass of research assembled by the Newspaper Advertising Bureau in recent years on how best to use ads in newspapers. NAB member newspapers may have much of this data on file locally.

NAB studies show, for example, that newspaper readership varies little from day to day through the week. They show that greater per-dollar results are likely from a series of small ads than from one big ad. Greater exposure can also be obtained by scattering insertions throughout a week. Readership does increase with increases in ad size, but not in *proportion* to increases in size (and costs).

Research has also demonstrated that there is practically *no* difference in readership between ads on right- and left-hand pages, and that only *minor* differences occur as ads are placed farther toward the back of a moderate-sized newspaper. Numerous studies certify that in very "thick" editions, readership beyond the first 16 pages varies according to special-interest groups rather than according to page numbers. Even though they are "buried" far back in the paper, sports pages, financial pages, society pages, and food and fashion pages attract large numbers of readers.

Questions for Discussion

1. For what reasons may a small store whose trading area is compact and nearby, and which sells merchandise with a general appeal to all social and economic classes, prefer an *evening* newspaper (rather than a morning one) for the bulk of its ads? In contrast, why may a very large store that sells relatively expensive big-ticket durable goods put much, if not most, of its advertising in a *morning* newspaper?

2. What trends in society as a whole, and in the rapidly changing retail industry, explain the rapid growth of community weekly newspapers (especially in suburban areas)? What role would such papers play in your advertising strategy if you had a small store on the fringe of a large city? How would you use them (if at all) if you were the advertising manager of a large downtown store with many branches?

3. Which of the reasons for retailers' strong continuing preference for newspapers as their primary ad medium impress you, personally, as being the most valid and most important? Which drawbacks of newspapers as an ad medium do you think are most serious?

4. Why do merchants usually sign frequency contracts with newspapers, instead of bulk-rate contracts? What kinds of retail outlets and service businesses might prefer the bulk-rate system?

Suggested Projects

1. Procure several copies of each of these kinds of newspapers: a large metropolitan daily, a smaller daily newspaper, and a community weekly newspaper. Analyze the news contents of each, and discuss how they differ in terms of coverage of worldwide and national news, regional and state news, and local news, and in the type of informative or entertaining feature articles they contain. Then analyze their sources of advertising revenue. How important is na-

Figure 9–4 Special Advertising/Feature Supplements

Newspapers, large and small, issue special feature supplements targeted on particular market segments, such as brides, college students, homeowners, apartment-dwellers, newcomers, and many others. These are much used by retailers, who place special ads in them to seek out the particular segment of the newspaper's gross circulation they most want to cultivate. These supplements are much like magazines, containing a great deal of information, feature articles, and pictures to back up the ads. They are often taken out of the paper by the subscriber and kept for prolonged periods—such as football supplements that sports fans like to keep on hand throughout the fall season or gardening supplements that become the garden hobbiest's reference book all summer long—thus insuring prolonged exposure for the ads.

Shown here is the first page of a supplement on outdoor living in which retailers of sports and leisure-time products placed many advertisements.

Join us... in the GREAT OUTDOORS

Outdoor Living Supplement
to
OXFORD LEADER - ORION REVIEW

tional advertising, retail display advertising, and classified advertising to each of them? Finally, examine the apparent use of each type of newspaper by these different kinds of retailers: conventional department stores, national chains, discount houses, supermarkets, auto dealers, high-fashion apparel shops, other specialty shops, and realtors. When you have finished, summarize the distinguishing characteristics of each type of paper.

2. Clip from local newspapers a number of ads that demonstrate the great versatility of this medium in terms of the forms of advertising it offers. Include local retail display ads in black and white, local retail display ads in one color (plus black), local retail display ads using two or more colors (plus black), regular liner classified ads by retail or service firms, display classifieds by a retail or service business, and preprinted ad supplements inserted into the papers by retailers. If possible (they are rare), find roll-fed preprinted ads with retailers' signatures (ads using Spectacolor or wallpaper Hi-Fi).

3. Secure a local retail rate card from the nearest daily newspaper. Study the various kinds of rates it offers, then decide which contract rate you would prefer if you were the ad manager of (a) a food store desiring to use 160 column-inches (2240 lines) of advertising per week, year round; (b) a department store needing 20,000 inches (280,000 lines) of advertising a year, a low of 1,000 inches (14,000 lines) in February and a high of 3,000 inches (42,000 lines) in December; (c) a specialty shop desiring 2,000 inches (28,000 lines) of advertising from May to June and 3,000 inches (42,000 lines) from No-

vember to December; and (d) a seasonal business needing 1,000 inches (14,000 lines) of advertising monthly from May through September only.

Notes

1. Media expenditure figures were calculated from McCann-Erickson research reported in *Advertising Age* (August 27, 1974; September 15, 1975). (See Table 8–1 in Chapter 8.)

2. "Top 25 in retailing in 1973, with ad totals" and "Supermarketing's top 25 in 1973," *Advertising Age* (September 30, 1974), pp. 30–32.

3. These figures were compiled from daily newspaper statistics found in *Editor and Publisher International Yearbook* (New York: *Editor and Publisher* magazine, 1975), p. 7, and from weekly newspaper statistics found in *Directory of Weekly Newspapers* (Washington, D.C.: National Newspaper Association, 1975), p. 6.

4. *A First Measurement of the Suburban Newspaper Household and Reader,* by H. D. Ostberg Associates, Inc., sponsored by Suburban Research Center (New York, N.Y., 1975), pp. 11, 12, 16, 28, 29, 36, 37, 56, and 57.

5. *1973 Daily Newspaper Readership Demographic Tables,* based on survey by W. R. Simmons (New York: Newspaper Advertising Bureau, Inc., 1973); *Quantitative and Qualitative Aspects of Daily Newspaper Reading: A National Study,* survey by Audits & Surveys, Inc. (New York: Newspaper Advertising Bureau, Inc., 1973).

6. *The Daily Newspaper and Its Reading Public,* survey by Audits & Surveys, Inc., sponsored by the Newsprint Information Committee (New York: Newspaper Advertising Bureau, Inc., 1961).

7. Ibid.

8. *New Views of a $100 Billion Indus-*

try (New York: Newspaper Advertising Bureau, Inc., 1973), p. 24.

9. *Classified Advertising: Readership and Use Among Purchasers of General Merchandise and Recreation and Leisure Items,* data from National Family Opinion, Inc. (New York: Newspaper Advertising Bureau, Inc., January 1975), p. 5.

10. Bureau of Advertising and American Newspaper Publishers Association Research Center, "News and Editorial Content and Readership of the Daily Newspaper," *News Research Bulletin* (April 26, 1973).

11. *Media Insight* (New York: Alan R. Nelson Research, Inc., 1974).

12. *Consumer Buying Patterns in Self-Service General Merchandise Stores* (New York: Mass Retailing Institute, in cooperation with E. I. du Pont de Nemours and Company, 1971), p. 6.

13. *Where Shoppers Buy General Merchandise in Competitive Areas and What Prompts Their Decisions* (New York: Mass Retailing Institute, in cooperation with E. I. du Pont de Nemours and Company, 1973).

14. *Special Media Study Number One* (Swarthmore, Pa.: Sindlinger and Company, Inc., October 25, 1974).

15. *The Super Market Industry Speaks —1975* (Chicago: Super Market Institute, Inc., 1975), p. 12.

Preview

The two broadcast media account for about a fourth of local advertising. Though traditionally used to supplement newspaper advertising, radio and television are sometimes assigned a primary role.

About 7,000 stations make radio universally available. Its strong points include great selectivity of audiences by station, program, and time of day; a personal, human appeal; great flexibility; individuality; mobility; timeliness; and immediacy. The absence of pictures, inadequate audience measurements, the perishability of messages, its intrusive nature, too much clutter, the brevity of commercials, and the inexpansibility of time are its drawbacks. Radio time is usually purchased in series of spot announcements of from 10 to 60 seconds, but program segments can also be used (especially on FM stations). Advertisers should carefully select stations that attract the type of audience they wish to reach and schedule their broadcasts when these audience segments are listening.

Television has about 500 stations that make it effectively available in all larger communities. Its penetration of U.S. homes is nearly universal (with color sets in almost two out of three TV homes), and viewing time averages over six hours daily. Retail TV use tends to be concentrated among larger stores. Its greatest advantages over other media are its superior impact capacity and its ability to closely approximate a personal selling message. Its key limitations are the high cost of both time and production; coverage of too wide an area (especially for smaller stores); and the limited availability of the most desirable time periods, due to the dominance of the medium by large national advertisers rather than local businesses. Buying time on TV involves much the same consideration as buying time on radio, but selectivity by program segment and time period is the key, rather than the choice of a station. Many retailers lack experience in TV advertising and miss great opportunities because they do not hire outside specialists or add TV-trained personnel to their staffs.

Learning Goals

Readers should study Chapter 10 carefully to learn the differences between print and broadcast advertising and the special attributes of radio and of television. Students should learn how to buy time for both broadcast media. The suggestions provided by the Radio Advertising Bureau and the Television Bureau of Advertising with regard to the best ways to use time on the air should be mastered and used to evaluate the potential of these media for retail advertising generally and for particular stores.

10

Radio and Television—
Media That Generate
Extra Sales and Profits

The two electronic media account for about a quarter of local advertisers' investment in measured media. Overall, the split in billings between radio and TV is quite even. However, most retail television advertising is by a relatively small number of very large chains and big local general merchandise stores, auto dealers' groups, franchised restaurants, and financial institutions. Radio is almost universally included in the advertising programs of both large and small stores and service businesses.

Normally, broadcast media are used in a secondary role, to reinforce advertising in newspapers, among retail stores of all sizes and in all tradelines. The stores may find, by research and experimentation, that once newspapers are saturated with their ads to or slightly beyond the *optimum point of profit per dollar of advertising cost,* additional ad funds can be more effectively used in an-

other medium. Rather than overadvertise in the primary medium, they may prefer to put additional "growth dollars" into a second medium.

In some cases small or medium-sized stores that cannot hope to achieve much relative impact through newspaper ads (due to consistently heavy advertising by several much larger competitors) may profitably make TV or radio their *primary medium,* using the bulk of their limited funds for time on one or two good stations carefully chosen to reach *particular* prospects. Habitual listeners will think of these stores as "big advertisers" and, even though these people are not a majority of the community's population, the stores will benefit from the fact that *these selected listeners* feel they are the "big stores" for their particular lines of merchandise. The stores will get greater advertising impact and frequency among a limited segment of their market.

Stores may use a significant, though minor, portion of their ad funds for broadcast advertising (especially on radio) to appeal to target audiences best reached by that medium: Use of black-oriented, foreign-language, youth-cult–oriented, farmer-oriented, or sports-dominated stations may be the best way to cultivate a following among special-interest consumer groups.

1 Radio: What It Offers and How to Use It

Before the advent of television, radio was essentially a national ad medium, used mainly by big manufacturers who sponsored network broadcasts. Then during the 1950s radio advertising faltered, but during the sixties it staged a comeback by *going retail* in a big way. In 1974 local advertisers invested $1.4 billion in radio, or 14 percent of local media dollars. The very largest retailers tend to allot a major share of their broadcast advertising dollars to television, but smaller stores actually assign a larger role to radio, which may often get from 15 percent to 30 percent of their ad budgets. The heaviest local users of radio are auto dealers, department stores, banks, clothing stores, and supermarkets. In medium-sized and large cities, theaters and restaurants are also big radio advertisers.[1]

As radio went retail, it also became less of a mass medium. Stations developed target audiences and by so doing became a favorite ad vehicle for tens of thousands of alert retailers from Main Street to Manhattan whose merchandise has a special appeal for particular population segments. Radio advertising not only pays for itself, but actually increases the good results obtained from ads in other media. Newspapers and radio make a very effective media mix, provided their quite different capabilities are properly employed. Radio can reinforce consumers' recall of TV commercials at low cost.

The Federal Communications Commission reported 7,123 commercial radio stations on the air as of April 30, 1975: 4,440 regular AM stations (ranging from small daytime-only broadcasters in rural county seats to big, clear-channel giants with massive audiences throughout entire regions), and 2,683 of the newer FM kind (short-range, static-free, usually 24-hour broadcasters, and typically inexpensive "buys"). The FCC is now permitting more radio stations to be established in outer-fringe suburbs and rural communities in order to provide service for those fast-growing areas. FM stations originally tended to be "highbrow" and picked up loyal but small audiences among more sophisticated listeners; some still do have these kinds of audiences. But the majority of homes now have at least one FM receiver, and from 80 to over 95 percent of the homes in large metropolitan areas have them. Congress has even considered making FM capability mandatory for all radios (except the very lowest-priced models) sold. About a third of radio listening is now to FM stations, many of which *simulcast* the programs of affiliated AM stations. However, simulcasting is being discouraged by the FCC, which recently ruled that combination AM/FM stations in the larger cities must offer separate programs throughout much of the broadcast day. The purpose of that ruling was to insure that the public has access to the maximum number of information channels and the greatest choice of programs. Small AM stations are often ruled off the air during hours of darkness to avoid interference. This used to leave many small towns without any night radio (until FM arrived). Each station, of whatever kind, develops a personality all its own; and on this peg hangs both the size and kind of its audience and its usefulness to advertisers.

By 1975, close to 99 percent of U.S. homes had radios and 95 percent of all cars were so equipped.[2] Research indicates that during the average quarter-hour from 6 A.M. to midnight, 18 percent of all adults are listening to radio. In the course of a full day, however, 82 percent are in the radio audience at some time. Weekly cumulative audiences include 96 percent of those over 18, virtually all teenages 13 to 17, and 96 percent of all persons over 12.

Studies indicate that men listen to radio slightly more than women, and the young substantially more than the old or middle-aged. Audiences are considerably larger on weekdays than on the weekend, particularly among those over 18.[3]

ADVANTAGES OF RADIO
AS AN AD MEDIUM

The continued great popularity of radio among retailers derives from a number of fundamental advantages:

Audience Selectivity This is modern radio's strongest suit, and it fits in perfectly with today's emphasis on target-audience advertising and the fragmented markets stores must reach. Because there are so many radio stations on the air, none of them can attempt to be all things to all people. Each deliberately adopts a specific program format to collect as listeners certain types of consumers. Different audience segments attend to the programming during the day, so targeted advertising is possible both by *time of day* and by *type of program*. The store can reach a maximum of the people it does want to hear its message, while spending a minimum amount broadcasting in vain to those it does not seek to motivate. Smaller radio stations (especially FMs) may also have a geographic coverage that approximates the trading area of a store quite nicely.

Personal Appeal   The personal, intimate appeal of the human voice makes a radio station seem like a friend to many people in this "nation of strangers." Listeners become emotionally attached to the voices of favorite announcers, disc jockeys, performers, and newscasters—and those who make commercial announcements. Type on the printed page cannot equal in impact this close personal involvement with radio "personalities." Sometimes, merchants favored with suitable voices produce their own commercials, or they have persons on their sales staff make commercials, creating a sense of familiarity with the store's personnel among consumers.

Flexibility   Among mass media, radio offers the most alternatives for advertisers. Radio advertisers can sponsor programs (hopefully, directly related to their businesses), air spot announcements in given time periods, or purchase *run-of-schedule* saturation spots throughout a day, week, season, or year. They can use 60-, 30-, 20-, or 10-second commercials, as many or as few as their budgets allow and their sales opportunities dictate. They can have music, sound effects, or dramatizations that conjure up vivid mental images of products, services, or stores.

Mobility   Radio is a mobile medium that matches the mobile society of our age. Radios are found in every room of the home and in nearly every car. More than half of all adults and three-fourths of teenagers own battery-powered radios, and two out of every five receivers sold are portables.[4] They accompany couples, groups, and "loners" on hikes through the forest and to mountaintops, and on the beach. They are tucked in the pockets of sports fans who cannot resist listening in when their favorite team has a big game. Radio audiences hold steady even during midsummer months when people travel and spend most of their leisure time outdoors, in contrast with the summer slump experienced by other major retail media.[5] In addition, it is often the one best way to reach visitors in the community: tourists, conventioneers, and businesspersons.

Timeliness   Radio commercials can be arranged in hours, sometimes even in minutes, when market conditions suddenly shift. A scheduled announcement can be changed shortly before airtime, and in some cases a special one can be squeezed in at short notice when an emergency arises. The response to radio is fast, too. Not infrequently, a sale is made because someone heard an announcement on the car radio while en route to a shopping center. Radio draws its largest audience in the morning, just before the hours when most people go shopping; by contrast, TV's big audience is in the evening, as is the newspapers' largest circulation.

Economy Radio is not expensive as modern media go. Inflation in the cost per thousand for audiences reached by spot radio was favorable when compared to similar increases in costs of other media during the early 1970s, and projections for the remainder of the decade indicate that radio costs will not rise as rapidly as those of its chief competitors.[6] Virtually any store can afford to advertise on some station (not necessarily on a 50,000-watt big-city station, but on one of the many smaller stations in each big metropolitan area and in small towns). A moderate slice of any retailer's ad budget will buy sufficient coverage, impact, and frequency to make radio worthwhile.

Universality Radio is the most nearly universal of all media. More people and more households have more radio receivers than they have TV sets, newspapers, or magazine subscriptions. All social classes and all economic and educational groups have radios and listen to them, so that over a week's time virtually the whole of the U.S. population is part of the radio audience.

High Frequency Radio is a high-frequency medium, by means of which it is possible to reach listeners very often in a given time period for the same money as it costs to place a very few ads in a newspaper or on television for that same amount of time.

Sole Daily Medium in Small Markets In smaller towns without local daily papers, radio offers the only mass medium opportunity for reaching consumers on a daily basis.

Lack of Distractions When a store's radio announcement comes on the air, there are no other distracting advertisements presented at the same time, as in newspapers, to compete for consumers' attention.

DISADVANTAGES OF RADIO AS AN AD MEDIUM

Despite its many very real advantages, radio does have severe limitations that make it unsuitable as a primary ad medium for most retailers.

An Absence of Pictures This is a fundamental disadvantage of radio that is not shared by any other medium. Far more products are purchased because of what they *look* like than because of what they *sound* like. Psychologists remind us that we live in an "eye-oriented" society, and that visual stimuli greatly outweigh auditory stimuli as a source of information. Radio must depend on *word imagery* to compensate for this drawback; and unless first-quality, top-flight commercials are available from professional sources, it is usually hard to create the necessary picture in the listener's mind. Retailers themselves, or station personnel, can rarely do the job well enough on their own. Radio works best either for institutional ads, or if it is used to sell specific items, when it is linked with visual media in a multimedia mix.

A Paucity of Firm Audience Measurements Small stations can afford audience surveys by recognized research firms all too seldom; and even the data provided by larger stations gets out of date as stations compete with one another for listeners by changing their format, adding features, and adopting other strategies. All audience data is tentative at best, since nothing really matters but how many of the kind of people a store wants to reach are actually listening at the time its commercial goes on the air. This is virtually impossible to predict with accuracy, making each commercial announcement, to some extent, a gamble.

Perishability of the Message The transient nature of radio announcements and their consequent brief retention time worries many radio advertisers. Radio commercials are much more easily forgotten than either television commercials (with sight plus sound and dramatic action) or printed advertisements. Even if a listener is attending to a message details may be forgotten. People cannot save a radio ad to show their wives or husbands, study the particular details that interest them, refer to the ad when they are ready to go shopping, or take it to the store with them.

The Intrusive Nature of Radio Advertising Because the consumer is merely a passive listener to radio commercials, radio is a poor medium for tapping the existing, conscious demand for specific merchandise. Consumers can scan printed media, go seeking ads for what they want. They do not sit by the radio hoping ads for particular products will come on the air.

Clutter Too many commercials at peak listening hours reduce the value of all of the commercials. People learn to tune them out and resume active listening when the music or the news resumes.

The Brevity of Messages A store cannot successfully use radio to tell the world about its big stock of merchandise during a peak selling season or a big storewide promotion. Only two or three items can be adequately described in each radio spot; literally hundreds can be, and often are, promoted simultaneously in print. All that one can expect of a radio ad is that it will make one or two important points and make them stick via repetition.

Limited Time Availabilities Time (unlike pages of printed matter) is not expansible. Not every store can obtain a desirable time slot for its commercials. Popular programs attract more commercials than the station can fit in. An advertiser cannot always secure desired time on the air to reach the size and type of audience preferred. It may have to wait months or years to earn enough seniority among the station's clients to get the first choice of a time slot.

Too Many Stations Proliferation of stations fragments available audiences, reducing the share held by any one station at the moment a particular commercial is aired. The more stations there are, the fewer people there are to listen to each one of them. Yet the number of stations keeps increasing, especially with an ever-growing number of FM stations being licensed. When 10, 15 or 20 stations are heard well in an area, how much coverage of a market can a retailer expect to get with any one commercial announcement?

Technical Problems Radio advertising is often harder to plan than advertising for media that a store has long used for the major share of its ad program. It takes special talent, training, and equipment to do *good* commercials. Except for large businesses that can afford to hire a radio specialist, in-store production may be too difficult. The average smaller retailer is thus heavily dependent on what the station can do (which is, of course, the same as what it can do for the competition), unless there is a budget and adequate time to turn production over to a professional studio, which may perhaps be many miles away.

Excess Reach Radio stations may have *too much reach* for small stores in a large community. That is, too much of their coverage may be of areas beyond the effective trading area of the store. Conversely, a large store in the smaller community may find that local radio stations *fail to carry far enough* (especially when power is reduced after dark, as it often is) to cover their entire trading area. Because people choose stations essentially for their entertainment content, and not because of an inherent interest in the community in which the stations are located, geographical profiles of their audiences do not necessarily match natural retail trading areas.

BUYING RADIO TIME

The costs of radio advertising are, as we have noted, moderate, and hardly a retail store exists that "can't afford" radio. Most buy *spot announcements* rather than sponsor programs, which is more expensive. Spots may be 60, 30, 20, or 10 seconds long, and rates for them decline sharply with volume. *Price breaks* usually start with weekly *package plans* and become quite substantial for volume within 13-, 26-, 39- or 52-week periods. Unlike newspapers, radio stations do not heavily emphasize the frequency contract, and their rate cards generally favor bulk buys. Since audiences vary with the time of day, rates are coarsely graded to match audience levels, with "Class A" time the best, "Class B" time the next best, and so on. Small-station rates can be as low as $1 per spot, and even in middle-sized towns retailers can get on radio for $5 to $10 a spot. Big cities have many stations (and the major metropolitan areas have *dozens*), and except for a few of the very biggest, most of them offer specialized audiences at a reasonable cost.

Each station establishes its own time classes. Research indicates that weekday audiences are greatest from 6 to 10 A.M. (when some 24 percent of all persons over 12 listen). Weekend audiences peak at slightly over 22 percent from 10 A.M. to 3 P.M. Saturdays and Sundays.[7] Men are much more avid listeners to out-of-home radios (primarily those in cars), not only during morning and evening *drive time,* but throughout the day.[8] Summertime audiences are slightly smaller than winter ones during morning hours, and slightly larger at midday, except among teenagers. The number of teenage listeners from 10 A.M. to 3 P.M. more than triples in the summer months, and the number of evening listeners increases sharply among adults.[9] But all these patterns can vary in a particular community or for a given station, and local surveys should be consulted whenever they are available.

The following advice from the Radio Advertising Bureau has been reprinted, with permission, from its 1974 *Radio Planner* for retailers.

CHECKLIST FOR BUYING RADIO

1. Don't rely completely on your own taste. Your customers may prefer other station formats that do not appeal to you. Temper your taste with considerations 2 through 7 below.

2. Study audience surveys available from local stations to see which stations are strong with which customers.

3. Listen to all the stations in your market and add your judgment to the ratings and station research which you've reviewed.

4. Give stations as much advance notice as you can on your schedules. This will enable them to give you their best availabilities.

5. Finalize your weekly or monthly buy in writing: a signed contract, written instructions on how many spots are to run which days and which copy is to be used for each spot. This is particularly important when you have more than one item schedule running at the same time.

6. Let station[s] know if you need verification for co-op and what you need when you finalize the buy: exact times spots run, notarized scripts, station affidavits, invoices, airchecks ... whatever. This is much easier for a station to do in advance than after the schedule has run.

7. Listen to your spots on the air and encourage your staff (merchandise managers, buyers, salespeople) to listen, too, by notifying them [of the] approximate time spots will be on. This is one way to involve store people with their radio advertising. This procedure will also enable you to make suggestions to station personalities on what you like about their delivery of your spots.

8. Keep track of results [of] radio campaigns as you go along on the weekly planning sheets and try to figure out the elements that made the campaigns successful.

9. Plan your next campaign to take advantage of past experience with stations' pulling power, time slots, item selection and impact of schedule.

HOW TO USE RADIO ADS

Radio's prime value, according to many of its most enthusiastic retail users, is not just its substantial ability (over time) to gather a massive total audience, but its high-quality coverage. It delivers the particular audience a certain store most wants to reach, with its selectivity by *station,* by *time of day,* and by *type of program.* One can predict a big male audience during commuters' drive time, a housewife audience in midmorning, and an adolescent audience after school; one can also predict the listeners to sportscasts, homemakers' programs, newscasts, and hit music. Some advertisers effectively guarantee themselves a desired type of listener by sponsoring programs such as sports or news broadcasts. Most use run-of-schedule (ROS) commercials, but stations try to put most of them in the logical places in their daily program log to catch the best prospects for each advertiser (with due consideration for preceding and following program segments).

Since its beginning, radio has been a great medium for *institutional* advertis-

Share of Cumulative Audience in 5 Basic Age Groups

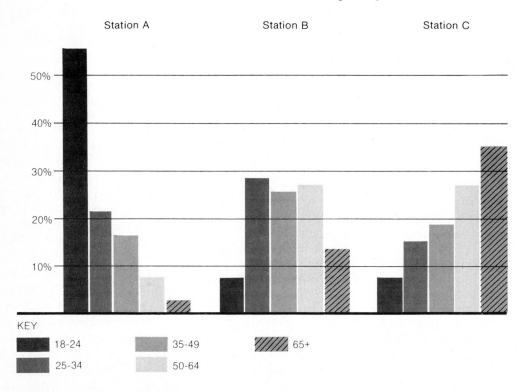

Figure 10–1 Importance of Selecting the Right Station
This chart highlights the opportunities a store enjoys to select the best station for its particular advertising needs; it also underscores the danger of choosing the wrong one. If a store or product appeals to younger age groups, Station A could do a terrific job of delivering the message, which would surely fall flat on Station C. Those seeking to motivate senior citizens would have a real opportunity for efficient advertising on Station C, while Station B delivers the middle-aged market exceptionally well. Specific time periods on any of the stations might also reveal even greater discrepancies in age-group segmentation of audiences. This chart is extracted from *The Radio Retail Revolution,* a publication of WCBS Newsradio (Retail Sales Department), and is typical of many useful aids the broadcast industry makes available to its clients to help enhance the effectiveness of broadcast advertising for retailers.
Source: ARB San Francisco Survey, Cumulative Daytime Audiences, April/May 1972.

ing, and it still is. Many stores that put most (or all) of their promotional ads in print media will devote most (or all) of their broadcast time to building goodwill and an image. However, radio can be an effective medium for properly conceived and well-executed item-price advertising too. Increasing co-op advertising (which *has* to focus on products, not stores) has reinforced the trend toward more item-price ads on radio. Retail media-mix strategies usually assign radio the task of reinforcing promotional ads, and make it a primary medium for institutional ads. Stores with a large budget or stores that use an exceptionally low-cost station may spread their radio commercials throughout the year but increase their frequency during peak sales periods. When the radio budget is very meager, this medium should be employed only for major promotional events (giving up *annual* continuity in favor of *seasonal* frequency).

Radio's speed and flexibility should be exploited. After the first rush of shoppers on the opening morning of a big sale, a store can tell other shoppers via radio which items are still in good supply. It can push rubber boots while storm clouds are still in the sky or tell listeners about a truckload of fresh produce that has just now rolled up to the unloading dock!

Jack Byrne, when president of Jack Byrne Advertising in New York, gave this advice, which succinctly summarizes how retailers can best use radio:

> Newspaper circulations are slipping, circular costs are rising and television is expensive as hell. So what is a retailer to do? He can turn to radio. . . .
> Radio should be used as a retail image maker. Retailers generally accept

print efforts blindly, as people accept taxes, parents or warts. And people do shop newspapers for bargains. . . .

> There is, however, radio. And radio can push price and image simultaneously or alternately, hour by hour. Radio has a lot of nice things about it, if retailers use it right. . . . Give radio a proper test. Give it the break you give newspapers. Give it money . . . time . . . freedom to breathe and speak . . . facts . . . variety. Give it identity. . . .[10]

2 Television: A Powerhouse of Impact for Big Retailers

The 511 commercial VHF stations, most of which are affiliated with one of the three major networks, provide television coverage for almost the whole of the populated United States. Broadcasting from about 400 cities, they have an effective range of 60 miles each. The 190 newer UHF stations, most of them independent and locally oriented, reach out about half that distance. These commercial television stations vie for viewers' attention with 242 educational stations and 3,240 cable systems; the latter extend the viewing area of regular TV broadcasting, but more than 600 of them also originate programming in their own studios as one option for their subscribers.

Some 97 percent of all U.S. homes have TV sets. Some 41 percent of TV homes have two or more receivers, and 68 percent have at least one color set. The studies indicate that the average viewing time per TV-equipped home is $6^{1}/_{4}$ hours daily. It is over 8 hours in households of five or more persons (implying much viewing by children) and about 7 hours where the woman of the house is from 18 to 54 years old. It is 5 hours in one- and two-person households, somewhat below 4 hours in households where the woman has a job outside the home, and a bit above 5 hours where the head of the household has one or more years of college education. There is a significant variation in viewing hours associated with income. The heaviest viewers are in the $10,000–$15,000 income range. But the less affluent and the more affluent spend considerably less time in front of the "set." [11]

TV reaches 77 percent of American men in an average day, and 94 percent in a week. Women are somewhat heavier viewers: 83 percent see TV in a day, and 95 percent see it in a week. Teenagers (especially boys) view television less than adults, but children are the heaviest viewers, both daily and weekly. There is considerably more evening viewing in the winter than in the summer, but daytime and late night audiences decline only slightly, if at all, in the summer. [12]

Prime-time (evening) network TV at its peak gathers in the world's greatest advertising audience—at a cost of perhaps $15 to $20 million for a winter season's sponsored weekly program hour, or $50,000 for a single commercial, 30 seconds long. Obviously, this is big business, and it should be no surprise that a relatively few large national advertisers dominate the medium. More than three-fourths of all TV advertising is from national, not local, sources. But the local portion has been rising by leaps and bounds, especially during the early seventies, and in 1974 it reached $1.2 billion. Television continues to close in on radio as the second-place local me-

dium, but it still carries barely one-sixth the combined volume of the daily and weekly newspapers.

During the 1960s a number of big retailers, chiefly department stores and a few national chains, began getting into the local TV scene, often on a frankly experimental basis. Stores like Woodward & Lothrop in Washington, Carson Pirie in Chicago, and Neiman-Marcus in Dallas tried it for a while, then backed out, then tried again. Others such as Marshall Field in Chicago stayed aloof, and some, like Macy's in New York and the May Company on the West Coast and in Cleveland, tested the medium very sparingly.

In the 1970s, the situation changed considerably. Two big things happened. Sears, having done some testing and research, led the retail pack into local (as well as national) television advertising. In many markets where Sears had an adequate number of stores, it outadvertised all other general merchandise retailers on TV. To compete, a number of less gigantic merchandisers allotted very significant portions of their much smaller ad budgets to television. At the same time, federal authorities ruled $100 million of cigarette advertising off the air, leaving wide gaps in TV's national and local schedules. This suddenly available time was often sold to retailers, sometimes, reportedly, at special rates. Many of them thus learned to use TV at discount prices, at least until other national advertisers were rounded up to take the place of the tobacco companies.

It is safe to say now that TV has arrived as a serious competitor for big stores' ad dollars. Table 10–1 details the sources of a $17-million, 34-percent gain

Table 10–1

Nonnetwork Television Investments by Leading Retail Companies, 1972–1973

Company	Rank	1972	1973	Percentage Change
Sears Roebuck & Co.	1	$18,842,100	$19,779,900	+ 5
Marcor, Inc. (Montgomery Ward)	2	7,203,200	12,228,100	+ 70
J. C. Penney Co., Inc.	3	5,107,900	5,587,200	+ 9
S. S. Kresge Co. (K-Mart)	4	2,468,200	4,931,900	+100
Arlen Realty & Development Corp. (Korvette & other stores)	5	3,178,800	4,260,600	+ 34
Federated Department Stores, Inc.	6	2,965,300	3,215,700	+ 8
Vornado, Inc.	7	560,900	2,536,700	+352
Allied Stores Corp.	8	2,268,000	2,456,900	+ 8
W. T. Grant Co.	9	1,202,400	2,360,500	+ 96
Zayre Corp.	10	590,300	2,127,000	+260
May Department Stores Co.	11	974,900	2,096,600	+115
Interstate Department Stores, Inc.	12	2,546,800	1,834,500	− 28
R. H. Macy & Co., Inc.	13	1,151,200	1,755,800	+ 53
F. W. Woolworth Co. (Woolco)	14	1,316,300	1,687,500	+ 28
Associated Dry Goods Corp.	15	594,700	1,235,300	+103
Total Top 15		**$50,971,000**	**$68,094,200**	**+ 34**

Source: Dollar figures are from *Broadcast Advertisers' Reports* (New York: Broadcast Advertisers' Reports, Inc., 1973 and 1974); supplied by courtesy of the Television Bureau of Advertising.

in local TV advertising by 15 of the biggest retail firms in the 75 large markets (that is, cities) where expenditures are measured by Broadcast Advertisers' Reports, Inc. Table 10–2 portrays the change in spending for TV advertising in single major markets by 10 major department stores in the same period. (A number of very large department stores that were among the top 10 in sales volume for the same year did not appear among the top TV users.)

In 1974, total estimated television expenditures by local advertisers in the 75 markets measured by BAR reached $912 million, a gain of more than 20 percent over their 1973 investment of $756 million. Table 10–3 sorts out these TV costs by the 20 leading categories of businesses. Throughout the whole country, local advertisers increased TV expenditures from 1973 to 1974 by 8.6 percent (based on a comparison of the data reported in Table 8–1 and data from a similar report from the same source for 1973). This was greater than the increases reported for newspapers and for radio, but less, on a percentage basis, than the gains experienced by outdoor advertising. However, it must be borne in mind when examining these impressive *percentage* increases in local TV advertising, that television started from a relatively low base in terms of dollars, and that other media are also experiencing large gains and holding their relative places among the local media in a rather stable relationship.

Table 10–2

Department Stores' Television Investments: Data for the Top 10 Users, Based on Dollars Invested in a Single Market, 1972–1973

Store/Market	Rank	1972	1973	Percentage Change
Macy's/New York	1	$ 423,300	$ 908,400	+115
Jordan Marsh/Boston	2	894,800	761,400	− 15
Rich's/Atlanta	3	550,400	671,500	+ 22
Sanger Harris/Dallas	4	503,400	582,300	+ 16
Foley's/Houston	5	483,800	581,800	+ 20
Abraham & Straus/New York	6	305,500	503,200	+ 65
May Co./Los Angeles	7	196,900	500,100	+154
Rike's/Dayton	8	448,300	468,500	+ 5
Schottenstein's/Columbus, O.	9	265,800	450,600	+ 70
Goldbatt's/Chicago	10	243,600	433,000	+ 78
Total		**$4,315,800**	**$5,860,800**	**+ 36**

Note: National chains (Sears', Ward's, Grant's, and Penney's) were not included in this listing.

Source: Dollar figures from *Broadcast Advertisers' Reports* (New York: Broadcasting Advertisers' Reports, Inc., 1973 and 1974); supplied by courtesy of the Television Bureau of Advertising.

ADVANTAGES OF TELEVISION AS A LOCAL MEDIUM

An examination of the strong points and the limitations of television at the retail level shows quite clearly why it may soon catch up with radio in terms of the total dollar investment by local advertisers, and also why it is used mostly by a relatively small group of very large chains and major department or specialty stores, rather than by small merchants.

TV offers the following essential advantages.

Superior Impact TV is truly unique among the mass media with respect to impact. The combination of sight, sound, motion, and color—delivered right in the consumer's own home—cannot be approached in effectiveness. Psychologists agree that when appeals are made si-multaneously through two human senses (the eyes and the ears), the message penetrates into the mind and is retained in the memory more clearly than when separate stimuli are applied first to one sense, then to another (as, for example, when a newspaper ad is followed or preceded by a radio commercial).

Each of the two stimuli (visual and auditory) reinforces the other, and the whole thing becomes a dramatic event of great force, especially when motion and color are added. A portrayal of the advertised product actually in use by real human beings lifts the top-quality, professionally produced television commercial into a class by itself.

Personal Appeal The personal, intimate, human nature of the well-done TV ad does all that the voice appeal of the radio commercial can do, plus very much more. Often, television and

Table 10–3

Leading Users of Local TV Advertising in 75 Top TV Markets

	Millions of Dollars Invested		Percentage Change
	1973	1974	
Restaurants and drive-ins	$ 82.6	$112.5	+36
Department and discount department stores	88.3	104.3	+18
Banks, savings and loan associations	83.4	95.0	+14
Food stores and supermarkets	66.0	80.1	+21
Movies	37.1	67.4	+82
Auto dealers	66.5	51.6	−22
Furniture stores	41.4	46.2	+11
Amusements and entertainment	20.0	26.3	+32
Appliance and repair stores	17.8	22.5	+27
Clothing stores	19.6	22.1	+13
Builders and real estate agents	18.9	19.1	+ 1
Leisure time activities & miscellaneous services	12.8	14.0	+ 9
Carpet and floor covering stores	11.9	13.3	+12
Loan and mortgage companies	13.8	13.0	− 6
Home improvement contractors	9.0	11.7	+30
Gas, electric, and water companies	15.2	11.7	−23
Local schools and colleges	8.7	10.9	+25
Newspapers	6.8	9.0	+33
Variety stores	8.1	9.0	+11
Drugstores	8.1	9.0	+11
Total	**$635.9**	**$748.5**	**+18**

Note: The data shown here for 75 top TV markets is not projectable for all TV cities.

Source: Broadcast Advertisers' Reports, Inc., data published in *TV Basics* (New York: Television Bureau of Advertising, 1975).

motion-picture actors already well-known to large audiences appear in the commercials, reinforcing the commercials' believability and creating a greater feeling of empathy in the audience.

TV is the *closest approach possible to personal selling*, right in the customer's home. A good newspaper ad, properly illustrated, in effect extends the store's showcases and displays into the home, along with printed copy explaining the products. A radio commercial is equivalent to a good salesperson's verbal exposition of product benefits and reasons to buy. But a television commercial can do the whole selling job: It can show merchandise in its most favorable light, and it can let a good salesperson project his or her whole personality into a sales appeal.

Timing TV generally reaches audiences when they are in a relaxed mood, with their attention fixed on the screen. When the commercial comes, it is on "center stage." There are no distractions —no other ads or news clamoring for attention, no other things people are busy doing while they are watching. The commercial has a captive audience, even if it is only for a brief 30 seconds. It catches the viewers' attention *whether or not* they are consciously seeking shopping information.

Mass Audiences   The top-rated TV stations deliver mass audiences during prime time. Though all the mass media ultimately reach nearly all the people, cumulatively, over a week's time, few deliver as large an audience at a given moment as television. Hence the effective reach of a given TV ad can exceed that of ads in most, if not all, competing media. There are less than one-eighth as many TV stations as radio stations (including noncommercial stations for both media) and about half as many TV stations as daily newspapers. Granted that nearly everyone attends to all the major mass media, it obviously follows that more individuals can be reached through a single telecast ad because TV, at its best, deals with masses of people rather than fragmented smaller groups. More people spend more time watching TV than reading or listening to any other medium, too.

Selectivity   A medium's *flexibility* in reaching certain audiences is a plus factor for some types of stores and ad messages, but not for others. TV audiences are well measured by recognized research agencies and the demographic characteristics of those viewing specific programs are reported reasonably soon. Some programs, notably sportscasts, local homemakers' hours, and children's shows, reach obvious target groups. This permits a degree of demographic selectivity in placing adjacent commercials. VHF stations (the majority) cover a very large area (described as an *ADI* or *area*

of dominant influence), a desirable feature from the viewpoint of chains having outlets throughout that area. The coverage of shorter-range UHF TV outlets (which are growing in number) is likely to roughly approximate a medium-sized city's actual prime trading zone, improving the geographical selectivity factor for one-location retailers or local chains.

Improving Acceptance and Believability   There is an inherent element of credibility in personal delivery of an advertising message—a technique that reaches its apex in television. There is also a general consensus among advertising experts that the believability and prestige of any medium tends to rub off onto the advertisements it contains, as the public transfers its acceptance of its news or entertainment content, to some degree, to the ads also. A series of nine attitude studies conducted by The Roper Organization for the Television Information Office from 1959 to 1974 traced the acceptance of TV by the public and its credibility among consumers as a source of information. Those choosing TV as their favored source of world news rose from 51 percent of the respondents to 65 percent during the 15-year period, while those naming newspapers dropped from 57 percent to 47 percent and those citing radio slipped from 34 percent to 21 percent. The surveys showed an increasing number of people favorable to television when asked which medium they would be most inclined to believe in case of conflicting reports. TV drew 29 percent of such responses in the first survey and 51 percent 15 years later, but newspapers' adherents dropped from 32 to 20 percent and radio's from 12 to 8 percent during the same period. The proportion of respondents who said they disliked practically all commercials or who declared they found most of them very annoying changed but little through those years, from 39 percent in 1959 to 40 percent in 1974. On the other hand, those who considered most commercials all right, or who even said they actually enjoyed them, rose more significantly: from 51 percent to 58 percent.[13]

WHY SOME STORES,
ESPECIALLY THE "SMALLS,"
THINK TWICE ABOUT TV

TV and its retail users must face up to and solve some essential problems before stores in general can be expected to launch into any substantial further use of this medium. We shall now take a brief look at these problems.

Costs   The primary stumbling block for retailers interested in TV advertising is its cost. Both TV time and TV production are expensive. A well-recognized expert on retail television has advised, quite frankly, that "if you can cut $3,000 a week out of your newspaper campaign, you can be on TV with a modest but very effective program [depending on your market."[14] This implies a $156,000 annual budget for television as the minimum a retailer should consider.

The cost of TV time can range from $30 to $40 for 30 seconds, in a small community, to $1,000 and up, in a big city. Few stations have separate rates for retailers, and those in larger cities generally charge local stores as much as big national advertisers. Even so, *package deals* for multiple buys abound, especially for daytime, when TV audiences

are relatively small, in smaller markets. As in the case of radio messages, *frequency* is a necessary ingredient in advertising success, but with costs so high, only the large merchants can afford enough repetition. Even the big stores usually concentrate their television advertising in key periods and make little or no use of the medium between top sales seasons. It can take half or more of a smaller store's ad budget to make a big enough splash on TV to reach the "threshold" level of advertising effectiveness. Buying "cheap" time, during periods when few are viewing, is hardly a solution; it defeats the whole purpose of TV advertising, which is to reach a big audience. Calculations by media experts at advertising agencies indicate that the cost of spot TV advertising as related to the size of audiences reached (the cost per thousand, or CPM) did not increase as rapidly during the first half of the seventies as did the costs of other media, but they were already very high when the decade began. However, projections to 1980 of probable CPM, especially in the popular *fringe time* (early evening hours), indicate that TV costs will increase at a faster rate than those of competing media.[15]

The cost of production is not a serious factor in either radio or newspaper advertising, but it looms large when a retailer considers TV. TV commercials are no do-it-yourself proposition for any but the greatest of retailers. Hiring an advertising agency or a TV production house to produce commercials is a must if the very benefits TV has to offer— great impact and high consumer motivation—are to be realized. Cheap commercials, sometimes made locally, usually turn out to be motionless, perhaps even colorless—to be, in effect, radio commercials plus still pictures of merchandise or the store. They lack the drama that makes TV a great medium for those who can afford it. Such ads may look quite shoddy when they appear on the screen seconds after a national advertiser's professional ad that cost $25,000 to $50,000 to produce, used nationally famous actors, and had all the zip and dazzle of a Hollywood production. A fair commercial may be obtained by a retailer from a production firm for $500; a good one, for perhaps $2,000; a really superior one, for $5,000 or more. Adding figures like these to the cost of TV time and calculating the frequency necessary to keep the ball rolling make it very obvious why few medium-sized stores and hardly any small ones use TV (except via the co-op route, with manufacturers' commercials rebroadcast locally and the retailer's portion a brief video flash at the end or a few seconds of audio recognition tacked on).

Decreasing Length and Increasing Numbers of Messages Even more than in radio, the brevity of the TV message is a problem, even though more information can be given in a stated time period because both sound and sight are available. High costs have made the 30-second commercial standard, even for big chains and national advertisers, and even 10-second commercials are becoming increasingly common as TV advertisers try to maintain adequate frequency with an acceptable budget. In 1974, no categories of local advertisers reported by Broadcast Advertisers' Reports in 75 major markets used 60-second units for as much as a quarter of their TV commercials, and among most categories only a

negligible number were that long. Conversely, among many important types of local businesses, from a fifth to a quarter of their commercials were only 10 seconds in length (see Table 10–6 on page 294). The president of a prominent ad agency has predicted that by 1985 the 10-second commercial will be the basic length, and the "30" will be as rare as the "60" is today. Furthermore, he has noted that because of this trend to shorter commercials and greater numbers of them coupled with increased costs, it took twice as much money to make the same impressions on an audience in 1975 as it did in 1965, and he foresees that by 1985 this cost will double again to four times the 1965 level.[16]

Few products can be advertised with sufficient persuasion, few stores identified adequately, in these flashing bits of time crowded one after the other. Nor do people remember the messages well. Sometimes they remember the wrong product, the wrong sponsor, or the wrong store—it all comes and goes so fast. The clutter problem is worst of all in TV advertising, further discouraging the retail advertiser who can use only a small unit of time and whose commercial is likely to be conspicuously inferior in quality to adjacent national commercials. Data from on-air commercial-testing services suggest that during the period when average commercial lengths have decreased and more of them have been broadcast, the proportion of program viewers who stay at the set to see the commercial has declined only slightly—from 71 in a hundred in 1966 to 69 in 1973. But more worrisome for TV advertisers is that the average recall of the contents of commercial messages by those who did view them appears to have slipped greatly, resulting in an over-all loss of effectiveness of about 10 percent. The same sources indicate that it has become increasingly critical for a television advertiser to have a commercial shown *first* in the series of the typical dozen or more nonprogram items broadcast at each "break." The first such item drew an average of over 71 percent of the program's audience throughout the 1965 to 1971 period, but those "buried" in the middle (preceded and followed by three or more other commercials or promotional announcements) held the attention of only about 61 percent of those who were viewing the program.[17] A more recent study based on 1,000 viewers in two cities found that the average half-hour program had 15 commercials, and that only 12 percent of TV viewers could recall the last commercial they saw (compared to 18 percent who could recall it in a comparable survey ten years earlier).[18]

Excess Coverage The broadcast range of the standard VHF TV station (about 60 miles) results in an area of dominant influence roughly 120 miles across. An ADI of such magnitude is of interest to national advertisers and sometimes to big chains whose stores are spotted in a number of communities throughout that coverage area. But because TV time rates are based on the area and population reached, these big ADIs represent waste coverage for which small or medium-sized, one-location stores must still pay. For these stores, media that reach their natural trading zones are most cost-efficient.

A Shortage of Prime-Time Spots Retailers can usually get all the TV time they want when few people are viewing (daytime or late night periods). But during prime-time evening hours, they are in direct, head-on competition with the big-budget national advertisers (including, of course, those few giant nationwide retail chains that have recently allotted millions of dollars annually to TV). Most stations with high audience ratings belong to one of the three national networks, and much of their prime time is committed to network programming and commercials. The remaining prime time is sold, months in advance, to national spot advertisers or to large local retailers whose agencies or time-buying services go shopping for desirable availabilities. Except in a few smaller towns and on a few nonnetwork stations that draw unimpressive shares of evening audiences, two or three major general merchandisers that are seriously committed to TV and have big ad budgets could absorb *all* the available open slots in the evening television broadcasts of a community. This, of course, leaves virtually nothing for medium-sized or smaller retailers when they need to buy—often on short notice because of their more flexible promotional plans—television time.

Inadequate or Inappropriate Audience Selectivity for Many Retailers TV audiences, as a whole, tend to be too undifferentiated for specialty merchants. Of the great mass of total viewers reached, far more are likely to be non-prospects than prospects. Furthermore, numerous surveys by different audience-measurement services have all agreed on one point: that the heaviest viewers of television have lower incomes and less education and are older than the lighter viewers. For merchants, this means that the best prospects for most kinds of merchandise are less exposed to TV commercials than the poorer prospects. Repeated commercials (high frequency) are necessary to reach those who are likely to buy the most merchandise, and especially the higher quality merchandise; meanwhile viewer impressions are continually piled up among the poorer prospects.

Possible Irritation of an Important Minority of Viewers Retailers must face the question of viewers' actual annoyance with television advertising, of the potential for a sort of *reverse image-building*. Even though a slim majority of people seem to accept TV commercials in stride, the minority who dislike them is of significant size among all socioeconomic groups and is largest among those with the most education and the highest incomes. The latest study conducted for television interests by The Roper Organization found that two-fifths of respondents either disliked practically all commercials or found most of them very annoying (only a little more than one-third made such a response in a similar survey 10 years earlier). The same survey reported that while the median number of viewing hours stood at an all-time high of over three hours daily, it remained substantially below three hours among the college-educated and the higher income groups. Furthermore, of those respondents who viewed TV less than three hours per day, half said they found the commercials either seldom helpful or never helpful. This was in marked contrast to the 38 and 39 percent of the heavier-viewing groups (generally composed of the less educated and

less affluent) who voiced dissatisfaction with commercials.[19] When Alan R. Nelson Research polled 3,200 men through National Family Opinion polls the same year, it found nearly three out of four were unreceptive to TV advertising because the stations show the same commercials so many times that even the good ones become annoying.[20] The Mass Retailing Institute had shoppers interviewed in their homes and asked them if they liked to see retail store advertising for specific merchandise on TV; half said they did, but almost as many, 47 percent, replied no.[21] With so many people, often the best potential customers, so cool toward television advertising, many retailers use extreme caution to avoid irritating viewers.

Reaction Time Changes in ad messages to match shifts in marketing conditions can sometimes be handled by local TV stations, but such "flash bulletins" usually lack the punch of top-quality TV commercials on which more preparation time has been spent. Television cannot compare with radio when it comes to this type of flexibility, and it may not even be competitive with the daily paper. TV ads do, however, generate immediate sales. In this respect they are on a par with other means of delivering the ad message.

Technical Problems Finally, television advertising is much harder to plan for and produce than other forms of retail advertising. Few retailers have the experience, the personnel, or the TV know-how to create good ads. By contrast, they feel at home with newspapers, radio, and direct-mail advertising. Adding TV to the media mix virtually forces a retailer to employ an outside advertising agency.

Buying TV time is very different from buying radio time. There are far fewer stations to choose from, which simplifies the decision as to which station to use, but there is far less demographic segmentation of audiences. While this is helpful to large, diversified general merchandisers, food outlets, and other businesses appealing to a mass market, it creates a problem for the specialty merchant or the retailer seeking to publicize a specific department or store service. For such firms, a knowledge of audience demographics at specific times of the day, and of those drawn by a particular program, is essential. Considerable research is being done continually on TV audiences, but most of it is national, and breakdowns for local markets are not as adequate. Both the A. C. Nielsen Company and the American Research Bureau, however, do check out the demographics of TV audiences in about 200 markets, so local advertisers there can determine in advance what to expect from given time slots and types of programs.

Though evening prime-time TV is viewed, according to Nielsen reports, by up to 60 percent of all U.S. households, its expense and the limited time available for smaller, local merchants make most of them turn to daytime or fringe-time advertising, where lower costs make more adequate frequency possible. Then, gross audiences fall to somewhere in the vicinity of 25 percent of all TV households, and there are wide variations at different hours in the kinds of people viewing. Finding out which ad schedule reaches the most of the right kind of audience for any given store, department, or product is the problem, and it is a big one. Tables 10–4 and 10–5 demonstrate the wide fluctuations in a national sample of TV households, in types of viewers at different times of day and for different types of programs. Table 10–6 details how some categories of local advertisers actually buy their TV time. For each category, the table shows the peak months for TV campaigns and the proportion of the advertisers' total TV ad budget allotted to each, the percentages of commercials scheduled during each part of the day, and the distribution of the commercials according to their length (mostly 30-second units). Note the small proportion of advertising that is scheduled during prime time.

Except in smaller cities, few retailers endeavor to deal with the TV stations themselves; most of those who seriously enter the TV field employ advertising agencies or time-buying services to "go shopping" for time that reaches the right numbers and kinds of people. (See Chapter 7.)

Large stores with big budgets can afford enough commercials to include many that sell key traffic-building items. But even they devote most of their TV time to image-building and institutional reinforcement of major special events.

Table 10-4
TV Program Household Ratings and Percentage Audience Composition

Program Type	Average Number of Homes (in millions)	Average Household Rating	Total Viewers per 1000 Viewing Households	Percent of Total Viewers					
					Women			Men	
				Total	18–34	35–54	Total	18–34	35–54
Evening									
General Drama	12.49	18.2	1946	46	17	13	29	10	9
Suspense & Mystery	12.81	18.7	1879	44	16	14	36	13	13
Situation Comedy	15.72	22.9	2057	43	14	14	30	9	11
Western Drama	13.21	19.3	2058	41	12	12	30	10	10
Feature Drama	13.93	20.3	1953	41	18	14	35	15	12
All 7:30–11 P.M.	13.29	19.4	1939	42	16	13	34	12	12
Early Fringe									
Informational 6–7:30 P.M.	9.36	13.7	1701	48	11	14	38	9	12
Daytime									
Daytime Drama	5.69	8.3	1244	76	27	24	13	4	3
Quiz & Audience Participation	4.77	7.0	1344	61	17	20	21	6	5
All 10 A.M.–4:30 P.M.	5.12	7.5	1307	67	21	21	17	5	4

Source: *Nielsen Television Index* (November 1974).

Table 10–5
TV Program Viewers Ratings

	Persons Ratings Percent of Persons Viewing in Each Age/Sex Category							
		Women			Men		Teens	Children
Program Type	Total	18–34	35–54	Total	18–34	35–54	12–17	2–11
Evening								
General Drama	15.2	15.0	13.6	10.6	9.5	10.3	10.2	10.5
Suspense & Mystery	14.6	14.4	14.2	13.2	11.6	13.7	8.8	7.2
Situation Comedy	19.2	16.6	19.2	15.0	11.7	15.6	14.0	14.3
Western Drama	15.3	12.4	13.7	12.6	10.1	11.7	9.9	14.8
Feature Films	15.4	17.6	15.6	14.6	15.3	15.2	13.0	8.7
Informational 6–7:30 P.M.	10.5	6.3	9.4	9.2	5.3	8.4	3.5	**3.8**
All 7:30–11 P.M.	14.9	14.8	14.5	13.3	12.1	13.7	10.8	**9.9**
Daytime								
Daytime Drama	7.4	6.9	7.1	1.4	1.2	1.0	1.3	1.3
Quiz & Audience Participation	5.4	3.9	5.3	2.0	1.5	1.4	1.5	2.1
All 10 A.M.–4:30 P.M.	6.1	5.2	5.9	1.8	1.4	1.2	1.5	1.9
Total U.S. Base (persons in millions)	73.04	27.52	23.71	65.28	25.92	22.11	24.80	35.82

Source: *Nielsen Television Index* (November 1974).

Table 10–6

How Some Advertisers Use Local Television

Categories of Advertisers	Peak Months for TV Advertising, with Percentage of Annual TV Ad Budget Allotted to Each	Percentage of Television Commercials						
		By Day Parts in Which Broadcast				By Length of Commercials (in seconds)		
		Daytime	Early Evening (Fringe)	Night (Prime)	Late Night	10	30	60
Automobile dealers	June 9.8, May 9.4, July 9.3	25	22	20	33	16	72	12
Carpet & floor covering stores	Oct. 11.0, Mar. 9.3, Nov. 9.2	53	16	14	17	13	74	13
Clothing stores	Dec. 15.8, Nov. 10.5, June 8.8	36	21	17	26	18	75	7
Department & discount stores	Dec. 14.2, Nov. 11.9, Oct. 9.7	46	21	15	18	21	77	2
Food stores & supermarkets	Apr. & May 9.2, Oct. & Nov. 9.1	46	20	19	15	13	80	7
Hardware stores	Nov. 11.1, Apr. 10.8, May 10.7	43	25	10	22	9	87	4

Source: *How Advertisers Use Local TV* (New York: Television Bureau of Advertising, 1975).

Smaller TV advertisers generally leave item-selling to newspapers, radio, and direct-mail, and allot TV a primary role in their institutional, image-building program. The exception is where manufacturers' cooperative advertising is used on TV; this, of course, must focus on the specific merchandise the manufacturer wants promoted. Many small stores can afford virtually no TV unless a cooperative arrangement with suppliers helps pay the bill.

The Television Bureau of Advertising (TvB) itself, which sponsors periodic workshops for retail advertisers, tends to emphasize the medium's image-building potential rather than push item-selling as the wave of the future for local TV. A nine-market study of shoppers' habits by Group W (Westinghouse) stations indicates that television is especially useful for reaching those who are not already customers of a store and for influencing younger age groups.

The Television Bureau of Advertising, in its booklet *Merchants of Change*, draws conclusions from hundreds of successful case histories of retail TV use. These tips are adapted from that booklet:

1. When something you're doing in television works, don't abandon it if it's "old"; update it [for] today's marketplace.

2. You may not need strict "image" commercials, because [everything a store does] . . . on TV [including item-selling] creates image.

3. Periodically, redefine your customers and how best to reach them.

4. Don't expect your agency to solve your problems by itself.

5. The amount you spend may not be as important as how you spend it.

6. To run many different commercials often, you may have to cut their production costs.

7. To buy the best time periods for the right merchandise, plan ahead.

8. You can reach selective audiences of value to your store with special programs and packages.

9. Use television to create positive reactions, not just to overcome the negatives of your competitors.

10. Don't be afraid to "do it your own way." You may be setting a precedent for your good future.

3 Summary: The Broadcast Media in Retail Advertising

This cogent summation of the present and probable future role of retail broadcast advertising, with the synergistic impact it can bring to the media mix, comes from Ed Libov, president of an agency noted for its many retail clients and its expertise in preparing radio and TV advertising for them:

Don't kiss off TV because you're too small or too specialized. In many cases TV or radio will pay off for retailers where newspaper advertising doesn't. Don't give up newspapers either. A definite synergism develops between broadcast and print that either alone couldn't develop. The most cost effective pattern seems to be to lead off with the new products and new promotions via broadcast, then follow through with them in print. TV and radio advertising for retailers isn't the wave of the future. It's here now. It's here to stay. And it's working.[22]

The best source of specific help with either radio or television advertising for any store is the local station's sales staff. If the store plans a heavy use of either or both broadcast media, an ad agency may also have to be consulted. The two national trade associations of the broadcasting industry, the Radio Advertising Bureau and the Television Bureau of Advertising, also have much useful information for retailers available through their member stations. The great national retail trade associations are still another source of data and advice. With such help the retail advertiser can learn to use the broadcast media properly and effectively to fit the store's individual needs.

Questions for Discussion

1. Assume that you are counseling a store about its advertising media plans. The community has a good newspaper, which, in the past, has produced effective results for the store. What special circumstances might lead you to recommend that (a) the store adopt a multimedia mix, allotting a substantial, though minor, portion of its advertising funds to radio and/or TV, or (b) the store relegate the newspaper to a secondary position and elevate broadcast advertising to the status of a primary medium?

2. What are the fundamental advantages of radio and television as retail ad media? Which do you think is the most important advantage of radio? Which is the most important advantage of television? What are the chief limitations of each?

3. Assume that a store wishes to make a strong thrust into broadcast advertising and must choose between either radio or television as its principal medium. (a) How will it evaluate these two media if it is a large department store or major national or regional chain? (b) How will it evaluate them if it is a small, one-location, independent store?

4. Assume that you are buying radio time for a series of commercials advertising a high-fashion ladies' apparel shop. What specific things would you investigate in evaluating several local radio stations? What sort of "personality" would you want a station to have? What sort of programs should it present, and what time of day would you want your announcements to be heard? Answer these same questions, assuming that your store is a hardware store; a sporting goods outlet.

Suggested Projects

1. Visit each radio and television station in your community (or a nearby larger city, if there are no local stations), and secure rate cards for retail commercials. Also ask each station for any audience-rating reports they have available and for maps showing coverage areas. Inquire about the production facilities they have for local retailers' commercials. Also ask what participation programs they have for target audiences, what remote pick-up equipment there is for broadcasts originating at a store, and what other special services are available. Determine which stations, on balance, offer the most,

and which the least for (a) large local stores, (b) local units of chain
stores, and (c) smaller, independent
local shops.

2. Determine what, as far as you can
judge, the future of television as a
retail medium is likely to be in the
next five to ten years. First, review
the text and tables in this book pertaining to TV; then do some of the
outside reading suggested in the bibliography. Finally, go to the library
to obtain new data from government
reports, advertising media, and retail trade papers. Use your reading
and research to explain your conclusions about TV.

3. Call on the advertising managers of
stores in your area that are using
television extensively in their current advertising program, and ascertain what they are doing about the
production of TV commercials. Poll
them on whether they rely mainly on
local stations, agencies, TV production houses, manufacturers, or other
sources for help. Then find out how
they *buy time:* direct from stations,
through a full-service ad agency, or
through the services of a time-buying
firm. Find out what reasons underlie
their policies with respect to production and the buying of time. Do
you think all of them are getting as
much as possible out of their investment in TV? Why or why not?

Notes

1. *Sources of Local Revenue* (New
York: Radio Advertising Bureau, 1972).

2. *Radio Facts* (New York: Radio Advertising Bureau Research Department,
1975), pp. 3–4.

3. *Radio's All Dimension Audience
Research.* Study by Statistical Research,
Inc. (New York: Radio Advertising Bureau,
Inc., November 1974), Tables I, II, and IV.

4. *Radio Facts,* p. 5.

5. *Radio Weekly Cumulative Audiences by Season* (New York: American Research Bureau, 1973).

6. "Five-Year Trend in Media Costs,
Circulation, Audience Per Dollar," *Advertising Age* (August 11, 1975), p. 42, and
"Media Cost Projections 1974–1980," *Advertising Age* (February 24, 1975), p. 169.

7. *Radio's All Dimension Audience
Reach,* Table V.

8. American Research Bureau audience surveys (Beltsville, Md.: ARB, 1973).

9. Pulse audience surveys (New York:
The Pulse, Inc., 1973).

10. Jack Byrne, "Radio Advertising: It's
Tailor Made for the Retail Trade," *Broadcasting* (June 12, 1972), p. 15.

11. *Nielsen Television Index,* NTI/NAC
Audience Demographics Report and Market
Section Audience Report (November 1974).

12. Ibid.

13. *Trends in Public Attitudes Toward
Television and Other Mass Media 1959–
1974.* Report by The Roper Organization,
Inc. (New York: Television Information Office, 1975), pp. 3, 4, and 21.

14. Ed Libov, "Ten Points for Fine Tuning," *Stores* (November 1974), p. 28. © 1974
NRMA.

15. "Five-Year Trend in Media Costs,
Circulation, Audience Per Dollar," p. 42, and
"Media Cost Projections 1974–1980," p. 8.

16. "Less for More for Television Advertisers?" *Broadcasting* (November 4, 1974),
p. 28.

17. Erwin Ephron, "How (and how not)
to solve tv clutter" (with accompanying
tables from Gallup and Robinson, and

Burke), *Advertising Age* (April 21, 1975), pp. 57–58.

18. Burke Marketing Research, Inc., *TV Commercial Recall: A Coincidental Telephone Survey* (New York: Newspaper Advertising Bureau, Inc., March 1975), pp. 13 and 21.

19. *Trends in Public Attitudes Toward Television and Other Mass Media 1959–1974*, pp. 6, 21, and 22.

20. *Media Insight* (New York: Alan R. Nelson Research, Inc., 1974).

21. *Where Shoppers Buy General Merchandise in Competitive Areas and What Prompts Their Decisions* (New York: Mass Retailing Institute, in cooperation with E. I. du Pont de Nemours Company, 1973).

22. Ed Libov, "Ten Points for Fine Tuning," p. 28. © 1974 NRMA.

Preview

Special-purpose mass media can, and often do, effectively support the primary advertising campaigns of stores in the three major media. In particular cases, these less-used vehicles can become the primary factor in a promotional campaign. They include (1) outdoor advertising (and similar transit advertising, where available), (2) shopping guides, (3) magazines, (4) cable television, and (5) miscellaneous other media, such as directories, movie trailers, and specialties.

Direct-mail advertising is flexible and selective and can be highly personalized. It is unique in that it is entirely under the control of the store itself. Direct advertising can be adapted to item-selling or to institutional purposes, it produces results that are easily traced, and in some cases it can be the sole practicable means of advertising. This medium takes many forms, including letters, postcards, leaflets, folders, booklets, circulars, and catalogs. Success depends above all on a good mailing list and requires a knowledge of postal laws and printing processes.

Window and in-store displays can greatly magnify the power of the other advertising and sell a great deal of merchandise in their own right. They work best when they are well planned, have an adequate budget, and are closely coordinated with other facets of a promotional program. Sales promotions, special events, public relations, and personal selling are also part of a complete promotional operation.

Learning Goals

Chapter 11 will introduce the student to supplementary advertising media. The reader should learn the essential advantages and limitations of these useful but lesser retail media, and be aware of situations in which they can assume great importance. The need to integrate promotion by these means with advertising through the primary media and with other phases of store promotion must be understood. The reader should focus much attention on the direct advertising handled by the store itself, becoming knowledgeable about mailing lists, postal regulations, printing, and so on. An appreciation of the role of sales promotions and special events should be acquired, along with a knowledge of some examples of their effective use by small and large stores. The student should also become aware of the role of public relations in retailing and its relation to advertising. He or she should acquire a healthy respect for effective retail salespersons and know why, without good on-the-floor selling, even the best advertising programs are likely to fail.

11

Other Media and Means of Advertising and Promotion

The bulk of a typical retailer's promotional dollar will be spent for advertising in, and most of the work of its advertising staff or agency will be focused on, the three great mass media we have just discussed in depth. But that is not all it takes to generate sales, bring in and hold customers, and make a profit. In special situations, certain forms of mass media, less used on the whole, may be of great value to, or even turn out to be the primary medium for, a particular store. And a program of direct advertising, usually through the mail, plays a significant role for nearly all retailers. Some even rate it as their number one means of communicating with customers.

In addition to all the measures designed to communicate with consumers outside the store, a whole complex of activities on the store's own premises must take place to complete the selling job. Window and interior displays can

be considered *advertising,* or they can be defined as another part of the broader function of *sales promotion.* Then, too, *sales promotions* (in the limited, more specific sense of the word) are vital to any store, and they are themselves "the thing advertised," more often than not. *Special events* are a part of these promotions, and they may be employed either to sell specific product lines or to build the store's image, just like advertising itself. *Public relations* overlaps in function and in technique the institutional portion of advertising; and *personal selling* is the one priceless ingredient, for most stores, without which many other sales-stimulating activities would be wasted.

All these functions must be closely coordinated, for they are interdependent. In very large stores, the vice president in charge of sales promotion supervises both the display and special-events departments as well as the advertising department. In medium-sized stores, displays are often a duty of the same people who prepare the advertising, and they work as a team with the merchandise manager and/or buyers on special promotions. Small merchants usually perform all these tasks alone, automatically coordinating them.

1 Special-Purpose Media

OUTDOOR ADVERTISING

The oldest form of mass advertising, outdoor advertising, is a "measured" medium that accounted for $120 million in local advertising expenditures in 1974. This was only 1.3 percent of the total local media investment, but the medium has been growing rapidly during the sev-

enties. The Institute of Outdoor Advertising estimates the purely retail portion of the outdoor ad investment at $150 million, made chiefly by national general merchandise chains, department stores, supermarkets, car dealers, restaurants, clothing merchants, and malls and retail associations. Outdoor signs can play a useful role in reinforcing ads in other media, and they sometimes get the nod as the prime means of delivering an ad message because of their inherent virtues. Co-op aid for this type of advertising is offered by many manufacturers.

The following advantages are offered by outdoor advertising.

Outdoor Signs as a Mass Medium They cumulatively reach virtually the whole population of a community and have a very high frequency of exposure that builds up very rapidly. The vast numbers reached and the high incidence of repetition make their *cost per 1,000 per exposure* very *low.* No other medium reaches so many people, so many times, for the same money.

Reinforcement of Other Advertising Outdoor signs are essentially a "reminder" medium, highly recommended by many impartial experts to reinforce other media with their massiveness, color, and visual continuity (i.e., they repeat visual cues that relate to the advertisement of the same product or store through the other media).

Strategic Locations Billboards are often seen on the way to a shopping district or adjacent to parking areas, making a final impression on consumers before they actually choose stores or make purchases. They often do their work, literally, just minutes before the cash register rings. Directional signs can lead customers to stores not favored with high-traffic locations.

Attraction of Transient Business Restaurants, hotels, motels, resorts, recreational facilities such as theaters, golf courses, and marinas, and sporting goods merchants may choose signs as a primary medium for reaching visitors, travelers, tourists, and resort-goers. They are often the sole means of intercepting transient traffic, and they are most effective in the summer rather than in the winter, when fewer people are moving around and driving on the roads, and when darkness falls earlier. It is because of signs' effectiveness in attracting customers that associations representing many lines of business vigorously protest government attempts to restrict the normal deployment of this medium.

Creation of Interest and Emotion Human interest and emotional appeals are outdoor advertising's strong suits, making it primarily useful in institutional campaigns, although they can sell specific items. An auto dealer produced fantastic results by featuring massive, bigger-than-life-sized photos of his salesmen on a huge billboard near a busy intersection. The whole town came to feel that it "knew" those salesmen, as individuals.

Outdoor ads can rarely do the whole promotional job, however, because of their limitations.

Brief Exposure Time Because fast-moving vehicular traffic gets only a very brief exposure to outdoor media, the ad message must be short: eight words, at the most (a few more, perhaps, where pedestrian traffic predominates). In contrast, 25 words can be included in the shortest of broadcast commercials (10-second spots) and 12 to 15 in a small, three-line newspaper classified ad.

Long Lead–Time and Infrequent Copy Changes It takes months, usually, to arrange "showings" and to prepare the "paper." New advertising can go up only once in 30 days on standard billboards, or every 60 days on smaller "junior" posters. Others, "painted bulletins," call for new copy only once or twice a year. This makes them an inflexible medium for item-selling.

Lack of Selectivity Audience selectivity of billboards is the lowest of any mass medium, and audience research data is very sketchy, except for total traffic-counts provided by the Traffic Audit Bureau. Their geographic selectivity is obviously perfect, however; advertisers do know precisely where their boards are, though they do not know just who sees them or how often they see them.

Public Hostility Toward Outdoor Advertising Billboards sometimes create adverse public reactions among some consumer groups. As a result, federal legislation has been passed that has caused most states to enact laws rigidly limiting where signs may be posted. Often, where the desired traffic is heaviest, they must be at least 660 feet (⅛ mile!) from the road. Giant boards beyond that distance may soon be ruled out also. About 800,000 boards were scheduled to be torn down because of these laws by 1976, a great many of them *nonstandard* signs (that is, not part of the recognized, professional outdoor industry). However, the fuel crisis caused authorities to defer the removal of directional signs pointing to travelers' accommodations, since lost motorists might waste a considerable amount of gas. Furthermore, a series of state court decisions has halted the spread of local antibillboard ordinances on constitutional grounds.

Standard "24-sheet" posters measure 12 by 25 feet. Local outdoor advertising companies (called *plants*) sell them in units called *showings*. The number of billboards in a showing will vary depending on the size of the town and its traffic patterns, but a *100 showing* means that a theoretical 100 percent of the adult population will see the ad message at least once in the month's time each ad is normally exposed. One can buy a 50 or a 150 showing, or other showings that cost more or less and reach more or fewer people with greater or reduced frequency. Recent surveys report that a 100 showing reaches a cumulative audience of 89 percent of the adults in a market in four weeks and that the average person sees the ad message 31 times; a 50 showing reaches 87 percent of the adults in an area, but they see the messsage only 16 times. In a big city like Chicago, there are 360 panels in a 100 showing (about half of which are usually lighted at night), and the cost is $48,000 monthly; in a smaller market, such as San Diego, there are 86 boards and the cost is $11,000 for 30 days.[1]

TRANSIT ADVERTISING

Car cards inside mass-transportation vehicles and posters on station platforms are much like outdoor advertising. They are effective, of course, only where mass transit is highly developed, as in the large cities of the Northeast. But since people see the message for a longer time as they ride, the copy can be a bit more complete. If urban revitalization efforts succeed and proposals to limit the use of autos in downtown areas materialize, as many think they will, this medium may come to be a very effective one for local stores.

SHOPPING GUIDES

The "shopper," blending the virtues and faults of both direct-mail and weekly newspapers, is found in many isolated rural towns and in urban areas too. It thrives especially where other media are notoriously weak. Resembling a newspaper in format, but containing no news, it is mailed by its publisher to a pre-selected list of "occupants" or delivered by carriers in a specified zone in an effort to achieve 100 percent coverage of a trading area. Its prime selling point is this "full" coverage, though there is no proof that everyone to whom it is sent actually accepts, opens, and looks at it.

In most cases, shopping guides are dominated by highly promotional, bargain-centered, price-oriented merchandising, which does indeed appeal to some market segments. The use of such guides is often rejected by quality stores seeking to retain a high image among better classes of shoppers. In addition, "full" coverage sometimes proves difficult to achieve where postal delivery routes do not jibe with natural trading areas. Either some families who do trade in a town are skipped or persons who live too far from a shopping area to be likely customers receive the guide. The cost, including the postage cost, of this wasted advertising is necessarily passed on to the retailer in the form of higher rates. Duplication of coverage is frequent, too, where papers go both to homes and business places.

In typical towns, about the same proportion of people read the regular paper and the free one, according to George Brandsberg, author of the only full-length book devoted exclusively to free papers. After examining the evidence, he declared:

[The data] pretty well explode any sweeping generalization that the public does not read shopping guides. At the same time, these figures do a good job of deflating shopping guide people's claims that everyone who gets a shopper reads it. . . .

. . . The dramatic all-or-nothing differences some people believe exist between paid newspaper and shopping guide readership were not found in . . . the studies discussed. . . . Most people read at least some of the shopper and at least some of the local newspaper. [2]

Demographic breakdowns of data indicate a lower occupational status for most shopper readers and a higher status for subscribers to regular papers.

A research study conducted in the St. Louis area in late 1972 by the Newspaper Advertising Bureau

. . . confirmed past findings that the readership of dailies tends to increase along with family incomes; 81% of those having incomes of $15,000 or more read a daily "yesterday." In contrast, the past week's readership of the laregly free group [of] papers was highest in the bottom income bracket, while readership of the independent [mostly paid-circulation] weeklies peaked in the midddle-income group. [3]

The NAB study showed that only 52 percent of those with family incomes above $15,000 read the largely free papers, while 65 percent of those in the below-$10,000 bracket read them—a

Figure 11–1 Understanding the Language of Outdoor Advertising
Like other media used by local advertisers, outdoor has a language of its own that advertisers will find mysterious at first. This figure explains what "24-sheet" and other posters are all about. It also tells what is meant by the term "showings."
Source: Extracted from *This Is Outdoor Advertising,* a highly informative booklet published by the Institute of Outdoor Advertising.

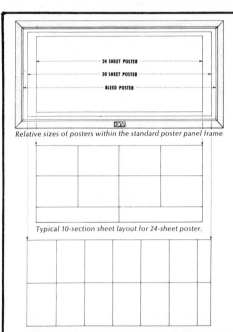

Relative sizes of posters within the standard poster panel frame.

Typical 10-section sheet layout for 24-sheet poster.

Typical 14-section sheet layout for 30-sheet poster.

COLUMBIA, S.C.
Traffic Flow Map

Streets shown in bold are the main arteries of travel in this typical market. Generally, 80-90% of traffic is carried on 10-20% of the streets.

POSTERS

The terms "24-sheet" and "30-sheet" do not mean that the posters are made up of that many individual pieces of paper, although they were many years ago. Today presses are larger, and posters are usually printed in 10 to 14 sections. They are mounted on the Outdoor panels, centered within the uniform copy area and surrounded by white blanking paper.

The 24-sheet poster measures 8'8" x 19'6". The 30-sheet poster measures 9'7" by 21'7", and affords the advertiser 25% more display area. A recent development is the "bleed" poster, which extends the artwork right to the frame of the panel by printing on the blanking paper as well as the poster. Size of the bleed poster averages 40% larger than the 24-sheet poster. There is no additional space charge for the larger sizes.

OUTDOOR SHOWINGS

The number of a showing does not refer to the number of posters, but simply indicates a relative measure of coverage provided. The basic unit, a #100 showing, includes the number of posters required to provide a daily effective circulation approximately equal to the population of the market. Obviously, the number of posters in a #100 showing in a large city will be much greater than in a small town. In either case, the degree of coverage of the market will be about the same. A #50 showing generally will include approximately half as many posters as will a #100. A #200 generally will include about twice as many as a #100, offering twice the intensity of market coverage.

skew toward low-income readership not shared either by dailies or paid-circulation weeklies.[4]

The value and quality of shopping guides varies drastically from place to place, making it impossible to evaluate them in general terms. They are, however, here to stay in many communities, where they fill a real gap in media availabilities. Recently they have become more professional than in the past, with improved printing facilities and state and national trade associations of their own, and they are becoming increasingly acceptable for co-op ads among manufacturers who formerly frowned on free-circulation media. Some newspaper publishers put out their own "shoppers," reprinting newspaper ads for distribution to nonsubscribers. Still another variation of the shopper idea is to send a complete newspaper (with small amounts of news) free to everyone in a community. The *Detroit Shopping News,* one of the oldest and largest-circulation (792,000) shopping guides in the country, switched from all ads to including three pages of news and features in 1974, when it found that many copies were not being picked up from doorsteps.

MAGAZINES AS RETAIL MEDIA

For more than a century, magazines have been a powerful *national* medium, largely middle- and upper-class oriented; they remain so today and are second only to TV on the national scene. But they are also now employed by retailers, in five different ways:

1. Major national chains put some of their own national ads in them,
pushing house brands and their corporate image.

2. Large magazines like *Time* and *Esquire* have arranged to split up their huge circulations via *zoned* editions for advertising purposes. *TV Guide,* the largest-circulation magazine, offers 74 such localized editions. This system permits advertising to be directed to one region, state, or metropolitan area at but a fraction of the cost of nationwide coverage (but the CPM is substantially higher than the cost of full-run national editions). This zoning makes magazine ads feasible for chains, big department stores, larger specialty shops, and voluntary, wholesaler-based store groups. Manufacturers also split the costs on a co-op basis in some cases, buying big ads with long lists of dealers at the bottom or on the facing page.

3. Since the sixties, magazine network firms, the largest of which is New York-based Media Networks, Inc., have arranged joint advertising in *groups* of magazines by collecting local advertisers' ads. They insert these ads in all copies of the selected magazines that go into the *specific geographical areas,* some as small as a county, chosen by each advertiser. The total circulation of perhaps half a dozen of these magazines mounts up to a considerable figure and is heavily concentrated among families in upper income and educational groups—a very attractive market segment for many local advertisers.

4. The numbers and circulations of purely local magazines are increasing in both large and medium-sized cities. The largest of these magazines is *New York,* one of the oldest is *Philadelphia,* and others bear

names like *The Chicagoan, Palm Springs Life,* and *Texas Monthly.* Their circulations are usually small compared to those of other local media, but they consistently reach "quality" audiences like those of national magazines. Over four-fifths of their revenue is from local advertisers.

5. For many years, certain prestigious apparel shops, jewelry stores, gift stores, and the like have carried purely retail ads in *The New Yorker* and several top-flight women's fashion magazines. These ads permit retailers to capitalize on magazines' unparalleled ability to faithfully reproduce superior artwork and to reach an affluent and sophisticated market segment, thus building local and national prestige as well as bringing in extra business through mail orders.

The primary drawback of magazine ads for all but the very largest stores (which can spread their costs over insertions in many zoned editions and more than one magazine) is the very high production cost—for art, typesetting, printing plates, and so forth—plus the relatively hefty space charges. Ad production costs far exceed those most retailers are accustomed to, and employment of an ad agency to handle the ads is virtually a must. Another limitation of magazine advertising is the long lead-time involved. Far-in-advance "closing dates" mean that it does not have the flexibility so vital to much promotional advertising. Monthly or twice-monthly publication also makes some magazines a poor choice from the standpoint of ad frequency.

As a result of these limitations, retailers' advertising investment in maga-

zines remains minimal. The Publishers' Information Bureau in New York reported that only $68 million was invested in them by both retailers and direct-mail marketers in 1973. Thereafter the apparent volume shrank because the advertising of big chains like Sears and Penney was counted as national, not retail, advertising. (In the national area, too, large chains' ad investment in magazines has been declining in favor of TV.)

CABLE TELEVISION

Although wired television is primarily used to bring the signals from up to a dozen regular TV stations into areas where geography limits reception too severely, this may soon change. In the United States, there are 10 million homes hooked into 3,240 CATV systems. These constitute about 15 percent of TV households. In several dozen medium-sized markets, CATV penetrates 50 percent or more of the homes. Many observers believe that most local CATV operators will soon sell local retailers advertising on channels reserved for local programming, or possibly during station breaks on other channels (a suggestion bitterly resisted by regular TV broadcasters). More than 600 systems already transmit local programs, and half of them carry local ads, including, in some places, commercials for Woolco and Sears stores.

This highly selective and decidedly local medium has great advertising potential, especially in smaller markets without local TV stations of their own. However, CATV faces many problems yet to be solved, not the least of which

Jacobson's Michigan, and Toledo, Ohio

Jumpsuit by JOHN ANTHONY...soft and sumptuous.
Of course it's **Nyesta** nylon jersey. Platinum or mocha, 4 to 14 sizes. $175.

Also at Jacobson's in Florida: St. Armands Circle, Sarasota, Winter Park and Longvood

*Registered Trademark of Rosenan Industries, Inc.

are wrangles with municipal authorities over franchises. The boom in CATV has not been as great as was predicted a few years ago, and many now believe it will be well into the 1980s before as many as 60 percent of U.S. homes are hooked up. It may ultimately prove to be the forerunner of the "homecom," the all-purpose home information device futurists forecast for late in this century.

MISCELLANEOUS SPECIAL–PURPOSE MEDIA

Directories, especially the *Yellow Pages* put out by the telephone companies, help new residents find particular types of stores and retailers of various national brands. They are especially useful for advertising services and the kinds of things people need in a hurry when emergencies arise: household repairs, sickroom equipment, rentable formal wear, tools, cars, and professional counsel. Audits & Surveys studies indicate that 77 percent of all adults use the *Yellow Pages,* turning to them an average of 40 times in a year.

Theater-screen ads (movie trailers), *Beetleboards* on Volkswagens cruising through college towns, ad messages on teenagers' sweatshirts, *Evatone* plastic records sent through the mail or bound into magazines, *skywriting* by aviators and on balloons, *searchlights* (some of which can project images on low-lying clouds), and old-fashioned *sandwich signs* carried on busy streets by pedestrians hired for the purpose are all advertising media that may, in special cases, pay their way well. A great deal of experimentation is under way involving in-store or mall advertising, both audio and visual. Most of this capitalizes on the large numbers who go to a food store or a shopping center frequently. Consumers may see closed-circuit TV or giant ads projected on walls and hear radio-like commercials between selections of piped-in music.

Specialties like calendars, books of matches, pens and pencils, key chains, ash trays, and little gifts of all sorts

Figure 11–2 Fashionable Specialty Shops Build Prestige with Magazine Ads

Jacobson's, a specialty chain with stores in Michigan, Ohio, and Florida, ran this ad in the November, 1975, issue of *Vogue.* The picture was taken by a New York specialty photographer, using a professional model, and the copy was written by the chain's own advertising staff in Jackson, Michigan. This ad was hardly expected to substitute for the store's many local ads appealing directly to people in the communities where it has outlets. But it was intended to reach patrons of high-fashion shops in all parts of the country, in order to build a following for the store. The company's resort shops in Florida benefit directly, because their patrons have permanent homes throughout the country, and any one of the firm's stores can benefit when people move, as they so often do, from one area to another and find Jacobson's a familiar name as a result of these magazine ads. Further, the shopper who has seen such ads in a recognized fashion magazine will feel happier about buying at this store, even if the specific item advertised is beyond her means.

Prestigious specialty stores and some major department stores find that magazine ads like this reinforce their local advertising with a most desirable image-building punch. Exquisite artwork can be faithfully reproduced in slick-paper magazines, showing detail that cannot be duplicated on coarse newspaper stock. Such ads appear in company with authoritative fashion news commentaries by leading experts and with ads from other well-known fashion merchandisers, both retailers and big-name designers and manufacturers. The manufacturers often reimburse half the space cost on a cooperative basis.

bearing the name of the advertiser serve as a reminder of the store and create goodwill when they (1) are unusual items that will really be valued and used and (2) relate in some way to the advertiser's business—as, for example, does a thermometer given out by a heating and air-conditioning dealer, a tire-pressure gauge distributed by an auto-supply business, or a ruler or level provided by a building-supply house.

2 The Direct Advertising Approach (By Mail or Otherwise)

Before postal service costs increased so drastically and service deteriorated so sadly, a major form of advertising—considered by many a "medium" in its own right—was called *direct-by-mail advertising*. More and more, the term is being shortened (and thus broadened) to *direct advertising*, though of course much of it is still delivered either through the U.S. mails or through one of the commercial delivery systems that have sprung up in recent years. Not the least of these systems is the ordinary, traditional newspaper carrier, who either includes the "mailer" as a supplement to the paper or, in addition, undertakes to drop off a copy at each house along the way, regardless of whether the occupant is a newspaper subscriber. Western Union's *Mailgram* service provides a quick, impressive delivery of brief messages to special lists of prospects.

This is surely not a "measured" medium, and national data, such as that in the tables in prior chapters, lump all its messages together as "national," not local, advertising. Studies by the NRMA

and others indicate that it probably accounts for about 5 percent of the average retailer's ad budget, though for some stores it will run to as much as 75 percent. It is the one form of advertising almost every store uses to some degree. Most stores handle their own direct advertising, though specialty houses may exist in larger towns that do a better, quicker, more professional job (and even, perhaps, their own printing).

ADVANTAGES OF THE
DIRECT APPROACH

Selectivity and Flexibility Direct advertising can be the most selective and flexible way to deliver messages. It can consist of a postcard or letter to one prospective customer or blanket mailings to hundreds of thousands, even millions, of prospects chosen by computer or by a geographical analysis of a market as most likely to respond. Its form, cost, timing, and frequency can be tailored to suit any marketing objective and any budget. It can take the form of a simple handbill stuck under doors or windshield wipers, or a 1,500-page, brilliantly colored catalog; it can be sent daily or once a year; and it can be directed only to that slice of a market known to be most likely to buy. Computerized mailing lists can be used based on the demographic characteristics of each zip code area.

Personalized Messages Personalized messages can easily be used in this kind of promotion. A letter (perhaps accompanying other sales literature in the same envelope) can be addressed specifically to Mr. or Mrs. John C. Smith and signed with a pen by Mary Jones, the store manager, or by Bill Johnson, their favorite salesperson. This one cannot do with any "mass" medium, although computer-driven typewriters can insert "personalized" references into mass-produced letters.

Total Control over the Ad Effort Retailers can tailor direct ads to suit themselves, unencumbered by the rules and regulation of the mass media. The ad is all the store's own work and can be unlike anything a competitor has ever done. (Competitors will not even know about it; it will be just between the store and its customer or prospective customer.)

A Direct or Long-Range Effect Direct ads can stimulate a *direct, immediate response,* or they can have a *long carryover effect*—as when they warm people up during a preseason period to make big-ticket purchases when the time is ripe. Actual samples of merchandise can be enclosed for prospects to see, feel, smell, and in some cases even taste. The advertising can lead directly to a sale if the prospect returns an enclosed order card, calls a specified telephone number, or makes a trip to the store. Or the aim can be to generate leads for in-home selling.

Measurable Results Sales results are more easily ascertained than when any other medium is used. Simple arithmetic is all that is needed to tabulate the exact sales results per dollar of cost. Direct advertising can also be used to test various copy appeals, different headlines and pictures, and the effect of timing advertising in a certain way. The results may even help the store learn something that is also applicable to its other advertising.

No Competing Ads No competing ads face readers at the "moment of decision" when they view direct advertising. It has their undivided attention, if it gets any attention at all.

Economy Nothing is less expensive than including advertising with the monthly bills sent to a store's own charge customers. No extra postage is incurred as long as the advertiser does not exceed the weight limit for that type of mail, and often there are no additional printing costs, since suppliers offer billions of envelope stuffers to dealers each year, either free or at the cost of the store's imprint.

Practicality for Small Areas For some small neighborhood stores, direct advertising is the *only practicable way* of advertising because their trading area is only a tiny fragment of the area covered by the local mass media. It is also the only practical system for certain highly specialized categories of merchandisers, those appealing to limited segments of a market scattered over a large area, for whom media advertising is far too costly in terms of the number of *real prospects* reached.

DISADVANTAGES OF DIRECT ADVERTISING

Despite its advantages, direct (by mail) advertising can lead rapidly to disaster, especially if it is adopted on a large scale as the primary or major back-up medium for reaching consumers, unless its drawbacks are recognized and compensated for. Merchants considering direct advertising should be aware of the following disadvantages, which should be weighed against its advantages.

A High CPM   The cost per 1,000 of direct advertising is higher than that of ads in the mass media, even for the simplest, plainest sort of mailing—many times higher. The cost of postage, especially for the third class mail so often used by commercial mailers, is rising year by year. A knowledge of current postal regulations and the various mailing options is vital in keeping down costs. Ignorance of the rules can delay the receipt of advertising beyond the date of a promotional event or result in mailing pieces that will be rejected by the post office. Retailers should confer with local postal authorities before going into any sort of mail campaign and learn how to set up their mailing lists in zip code order. They should find out whether a permit is desirable and what physical form mailings should take in order to comply with the rules and increase the probability of quick delivery at a minimum cost. Postage accounts for *half* the total cost of direct-mail advertising, and misunderstanding or inefficient use of the mails can kill off all possible hope of a profit. If possible, a retailer should select a printer who knows postal rules and offers a complete addressing and mailing service.

The rising cost of purchasing mailing lists from list houses also drives up the CPM of direct advertising for some retailers, and even those who develop their own lists must pay the hidden costs of their maintenance and use. The discrepancy between the CPM of advertising in mass media and direct advertising will widen, not narrow, in the future.

Isolation of the Message   Top quality copywriting and art are essential in direct advertising in order to attract and hold the reader's attention. The ad message is not part of an entertainment or news package he or she has chosen to tune in or purchase. Its credibility is not backed up by the prestige of a mass medium, and it will be judged solely on its own merits.

Few small retailers are equipped to produce really good direct advertising on their own, and the copy, art, and makeup techniques they use for newspaper ads are not always suitable for mailings. Generally, either a specialist in direct-mail must be added to the staff, or the store must use the services of a firm specializing in direct-mail advertising.

Dependence on the Quality of the Mailing List   Success in direct advertising depends very much on just one factor: the quality of the mailing list. Retailers do have one advantage over other advertisers in this regard—their files of charge-account customers. Stores with computerized billing, in particular, can operate a very efficient direct advertising campaign, classifying and sending mailings to customers according to their location, past buying habits, volume of purchases, and credit standings. Reaching noncustomers is harder. Stores that want to blanket a trading area with advertising can use "occupant" mailings with a third class permit. This type of advertising is cheap to send and to address, but it is also more likely to be thrown away unopened as "junk mail" than advertising addressed to specific individuals. Nevertheless, direct advertising is a good medium for some stores, such as supermarkets that issue periodic circulars.

Mailing lists can, of course, be bought from mailing list houses, borrowed from noncompeting stores, or developed by store personnel from such sources as directories, club or union membership files, newspaper clippings, and records of building permits and marriage licenses. Any list, whether bought, borrowed, or drawn up by store personnel, should be tested before funds are committed to a large-scale direct-mail campaign. Lists deteriorate rapidly in our mobile society, where nearly a fifth of the people move every year, and if one is not productive, it should be revised or scrapped before more money is wasted.

Indifferent Recipients Much direct advertising is delivered, but never opened or looked at. An increasing spate of computerized mass mailings by nationwide direct marketers makes it harder and harder for any one ad to stand out and get attention. A 1972 survey by the U.S. Postal Service found that the only kinds of mail ads significant numbers of people "particularly liked" were sales notices (popular with 43 percent of those questioned), other store ads and catalogs (both liked by 25 percent of the respondents), direct marketers' offers of merchandise (liked by 11 percent), and cents-off coupons (liked by 10 percent). However, some people also disliked them. Some 7 percent disliked sales notices, 5 percent disliked other retail ads, and 9 percent disliked offers of merchandise. Insurance offers and land offers and deals were much disliked and produced *no* favorable responses. A 1973 survey by the A.C.

Nielsen Co. for the Direct Mail Advertising Association produced rather more favorable results. Some 67 percent of the respondents said that they actually made purchases from mail catalogs, and 57 percent said that they responded to other direct-selling offers. More than three-quarters reported that they actually opened both kinds of advertising.

In general, there is evidence that the higher the socioeconomic status of a family, the more mailing lists it will be on and the greater the mass of unsolicited mail it must sort out each day. Hence, those with the most money to spend are more likely to be irritated by, and perhaps to ignore, what they perceive as unwarranted pestering by too many advertisers. As a rule, genuinely personalized mail from well-known, prestigious local stores can expect better treatment than third class missives addressed to a "boxholder" or an "occupant." Direct advertising tends to be least valuable for stores whose customers are members of upper income groups, stores located in very large cities, stores that do a great deal of other promotion, cash-sales-only stores, and stores in communities with many transients. For choice target audiences, it pays to use first class mail (or even airmail or special delivery), with individually stamped and personally addressed envelopes. This also provides some protection against the embarrassment and waste that occurs when "cheap" third class mail arrives days after a sale is over.

Robert Stone, *Advertising Age* columnist and a leading authority on direct marketing, offers these "don'ts" for retailers tempted to rush too quickly into full-scale direct marketing, to fend off the inroads of the specialists in that field:

> Don't expect retail newspaper advertising techniques to work successfully for mail-order or phone-in sales. Don't expect success in selling big-ticket items by mail, unless you can offer installment credit. Don't expect much success with *saturation mailing.* (Credit card customers are the best prospects.) Don't think all credit card customers offer the same potential. (There are tremendous differences in [their] sales potential, depending on the *recency* of [their] last purchase, the *frequency* of purchase within selling seasons and *monetary* value (dollar amount) of each previous purchase....)
>
> Don't expect "everyday necessities" to sell readily by mail order. They don't. Don't expect your retail advertising people to be mail order experts. They are retail advertising experts. (The best way to test and build mail order is by using the expertise of direct response experts.) [5]

3 Window and Interior Displays— An Indispensable Adjunct to Advertising

A customer may have been exposed to every form of mass-media advertising known, both national and local, and be most favorably impressed with all of it. The advertising may have done its job well, so that the consumer is at least impelled to look at merchandise but hopefully already inclined to buy it. At this critical stage in the process of turning prospects into purchasers, effective merchandise display can make a world of difference. Inviting windows, an interior atmosphere that stimulates a buying mood, and tastefully designed merchandise exhibits form the all-important connecting link between mass advertising and face-to-face personal selling (or, indeed, may become a substitute for it, in the case of self-service stores). Only at this point in time and place can actual sales transactions occur. Laxity in performing the display function can negate much of the potential benefit from a store's advertising; superiority in display can magnify the profits from a good ad program or compensate for the weaker results of a mediocre advertising effort.

MERCHANDISE DISPLAY AS ADVERTISING

Window and interior display are potent advertising media in their own right. Stores in high-traffic locations pay a high rent; this is one of the ways they *"buy" an audience* for their window displays. How tragic it is if a merchant fails to capitalize on the built-in audience of passersby he or she has already paid for by not having sales-stimulating window displays!

Window displays may feature the *same items* as current media ads, an excellent technique for reminding customers of what they saw or heard yesterday or the day before. The main themes of recent ads can also be echoed and reemphasized in window arrangements for a dramatic final impact. In addition, windows should show an array of items related to, or purchasable instead of, the items featured in the ads. And too, merchandise lines unmentioned in the ads may be given exposure via window displays.

The fundamental challenge for today's windows, which must often appeal to busy, time-conscious shoppers disinclined to merely "window shop," is to stop as much pedestrian traffic as possible and to convert more of those who do shop into actual purchasers. The weakest displays often stop less than 10 percent of the traffic; the best, more than 90 percent. What a difference!

Lucrative, profit-building *suggestion selling* can well commence right in a store's window. Convenience items, seasonal necessities, and the red-hot traffic-building specials featured in the ads bring people to the store. Once they are there, the master merchant will suggest purchases of accessories, related items, newly arrived merchandise, gift articles, and other merchandise, as well as "trading up" to better-quality goods. Few ads are paid for entirely by profits derived directly from the sale of the merchandise mentioned; the real added profits from advertising come when other items and higher-priced units are sold as an indirect result of the traffic it generates. It is important to remember that less than 15 percent of the stock of any store can ever receive direct exposure in media ads.

The modern display director might be more appropriately described as a *director of visual merchandising presentations*. Increasingly, he or she is responsible for the *total store environment*. In some stores, the person in charge of displays is a full-time executive with a big staff; in others, one individual does the job alone, working either part-time or full-time as a store employee or operating as an independent contractor. Display directors must maintain close and continuous relations not only with the advertising manager, but with the merchandising manager, the fashion coordinator, and even the financial and store operations executives. Display people normally work at night and on weekends to set up displays. Much of their time during regular store hours is spent preparing the displays in their workshops and assembling clean, fresh-looking merchandise from buyers and department managers. Every well-managed store provides a reasonable budget for the purchase of materials and equipment. A regular, planned schedule of changes is necessary; nothing kills interest or downgrades a store's image faster than a Thanksgiving theme the first week of December or an Independence Day window on July 6th.

THE EYES OF THE STORE: ITS WINDOWS

Window displays should embody the same principles of good design as other good ads: balance, unity, emphasis, contrast, eye motion. Good merchandise, set off by color backgrounds that create a mood and surrounded by functionally related accessories and compatible items, speaks for itself. No-window stores may use *shadowbox miniatures* of traditional storefront windows for a few very choice items. Those with all-glass fronts or mall stores opening directly onto a pedestrian thoroughfare can use interior displays in the front-facing departments to draw in all-store traffic and at the same time to stimulate those departments' sales. Such "look-in" stores are especially attractive to younger shoppers.

Like other advertising, displays

should focus on popular, timely merchandise. Like mass media ads, they may have an institutional flavor and reflect the store's image or highlight a special event. Color is important and costs the store no extra money. Lighting is critical, especially during the winter and evening shopping hours. At night, a time switch can be set to keep the windows alive when passing traffic is substantial and to save energy by cutting off the lights when passersby are few. A coordinated theme, perhaps the same theme used currently in media ads, can unify a whole series of windows. An Alabama menswear store used the theme "Best of the Show—Fashion with a Pedigree" for its eight windows, in each of which a well-dressed mannequin held a fine show dog on a leash. Another shop piqued the curiosity of passersby with a window covered with black paper, containing cut-out "peek holes." A Cincinnati chain coordinates its window displays with dramatic newspaper ads and sets off featured items with contemporary artwork.

INTERIOR DISPLAY:
THE FINAL PRESELLING STEP

Interior, or point-of-purchase, displays are the final step in nonpersonal selling. In self-service food, drug, and discount stores, they are *the* final inducement to buy. Mass-merchandisers of packaged convenience goods solve most of their interior display problem by a judicious selection of the many materials offered by manufacturers and processors. In apparel shops, department stores, and many other types of retail establishments, manufacturer-produced displays are selectively employed, but materials purchased, designed, and erected by the store itself are more the rule. *Traveling displays* for windows or interiors of the best a vendor has to offer are often animated and equipped with built-in "voices" and other sophisticated features.

Interior displays should sell merchandise. They should attract the eye and turn shoppers into "stoppers"—people who stop and examine goods. One department-store group attributes half its sales volume to special displays; and an NRMA survey of independents shows that, on the average, 25 percent of their sales volume derives from in-store displays.[6]

Good interior displays involve a blend of several basic ingredients: (1) Good *fixtures* show merchandise advantageously, in a proper arrangement, and have few distracting elements. (2) The right *colors* help create a buying mood, either blending or contrasting with the color of walls, ceilings, and floors and the merchandise shown. (3) *Signs* tell a story or do the talking for a display, giving significant details about the size, color, or style of items, about prices and product features, or about the location of goods. Good signs inform, they look professional, they are neat and clean, they are kept timely, and they are focused (like all good ads) on consumer benefits. (4) *Lights* make it possible for customers to see merchandise clearly and quickly, add drama to a display, and set a mood or create an atmosphere through spots and color filters.[7]

Interior display is gaining more and more recognition as a stimulus to *impulse buying,* not just in high-fashion apparel and home furnishings stores, but in more prosaic hardware, home supplies, and discount outlets. A study of nearly 7,000 discount-store shoppers revealed that 30 percent made unplanned purchases an average of 1.6 times per shopping trip. When asked why they bought an impulse item, half of those questioned said it was because they "saw it displayed."[8]

The Newspaper Advertising Bureau, whose member papers, like other local media, are as anxious as retailers themselves to insure that adequate display backs up media ads and produces sales, offers this cogent summary of how stores should "show their stuff":

- Keep window display simple and uncluttered. Business is stimulated by displaying fewer items to their maximum advantage.

- Give windows a central theme by determining (1) your particular prospects, (2) the merchandise you want most to move, (3) possible tie-ins with local or other newsworthy events and (4) the kind of image you want your store to have.

- Be sure that your windows tell the public about your policies and services. A simple sign can draw layaway, charge, budget accounts.

- The lighting in the windows must be adequate and kept on late enough to take advantage of after-hours traffic.

- Avoid clashing colors and distracting backgrounds. Show the merchandise as it is ... make the most of it.

- Make sure that window merchandise is clean and free of finger marks and smudges.

- It is generally agreed that the judicious use of prices adds to the effectiveness of a display.

- When you've finished, walk outside and see how your windows look to your prospects.[9]

"ATMOSPHERICS," THE SILENT LANGUAGE OF CUSTOMER COMMUNICATION

The increasing importance of store services as part of the "product" people seek has been discussed in preceding chapters. But just as goods themselves have already become so much alike that the emphasis has shifted to service as a means to distinguish one store from another, soon the services themselves may reach parity. What, then, can a store point to that distinguishes it from its competitors? Some merchants are turning sharply toward *store atmosphere* as their main appeal. The way a store "feels" to its customers is increasingly becoming the only distinguishing feature the store can offer.

This turn of events in the search for the "something different" leads top management to rapid upgrading of the display function and to broadening its scope into *atmospherics*. This has been defined as the business of *consciously designing a store's environment to produce emotional effects on the shopper that enhance his or her purchase probability*.[10] The new visual merchandise director (who is replacing the old display manager) will deliberately plan every facet of the buying environment—from the exterior store structure to window displays and the interior layout; decor; furnishings and fixtures; floors, walls, and ceilings; and, of course, the merchandise displays. Atmospherics planning will integrate all the factors that impinge on the customer's sensory organs and focus them on one crucial point: the ultimate buying decision. This process involves, above all, the *visual* approach, paying primary attention to everything customers see, but it may also include impressions made through the other senses.

Thus used, atmospherics reinforces and assists advertising by silently communicating with the store's chosen customers. It can be used to signal a store's intention to serve specific and predetermined social classes and lifestyle groups, attracting desired market segments and even repelling the others. It can be used as a message-creating medium, the differentiating advantage that serves to get attention that helps one store stand out among the many. Atmospherics can even be used as an effect-creating medium to arouse emotional reactions favorable to buying and triggering sensations that help convert shoppers' buying *intentions* into the *actual purchase* of merchandise. Atmospherics thus encompasses a broader function than display in its traditional meaning.

Many stores are presently using atmospherics, with great effect. A shoe shop that recreates the atmosphere of a Victorian English club draws a clientele willing and able to buy the fine, expensive shoes it sells. A huge furniture mart, anxious to differentiate itself from nearby barnlike showroom warehouses, divides its interior space into an endless succession of intimate, integrated room settings where customers can visualize a piece of furniture in an environment like that of their own homes. Another store's bargain basement, appealing to different social classes and other buying motives, attracts throngs of busy buyers through crowded aisles and counters

chaotically strewn with piles of goods. This, too, is a *calculated* atmosphere, consciously contrived by perceptive store management to suggest one prime buying motive: bargain prices.[11]

All this greatly affects the store's advertising. Atmosphere often dictates how well the product advertising will actually work in terms of completed sales once the prospects go to the store in response to the ads. The feeling generated within the store must be consonant with the image projected by the advertising. The atmosphere of the store can make the ads seem to ring true so that first-time customers induced to try out the store as a result of its ads will become loyal repeat customers, or it can disappoint them and lead them to discount the ads from then on. In the future, as both products and services lose their importance, the store atmosphere itself may become the main thing advertised. This all adds up to the certainty that advertising people of the future will have an even greater stake in what display and atmospherics-planning people are doing and how well they do it, and vice versa.

4 Making the Whole Team Pull Together: Promotions, Special Events, Public Relations, and Selling Ability

"A store," Herbert Wittkin, president of Stern Brothers, pointed out in the late 1960s, "has a multi-faceted personality which cannot be easily conveyed to the public ... through ... advertising alone." Successful retailers, he noted, do not "overlook the field of special events activities and the chance to insert editorial news into the newspaper." [12] This is just as true today, if not more so.

We shall use the term *sales promotion* in this section to refer to a specific promotional activity or event—either ongoing and recurring or a one-shot deal—and not to the general field of promotion, of which advertising is a part.

When a Columbus, Ohio, department store sends 19 buyers and executives to Europe to prepare for its annual three-week-long import fair—and flies in noted artisans and designers from two continents to lend authenticity, glamour, and drama to the event—this is all part of a sales promotion.

When a Texaco service station in Cheboygan, Michigan, sends out a man to clean windshields in nearby motel parking lots, leaving a modest card informing the visiting motorists whom they have to thank for the courtesy, this, too, is a form of sales promotion. So is the car litter-bag, the generous packet of candy for the kids, and the calendar a motorist gets if he or she chooses to gas up at the service station before leaving town.

Both these retailers are using sales promotion techniques wisely and well. Both may gain some immediate sales thereby; but, more importantly, both are building an image upon which future sales may depend.

In-store events, out-of-store events, free merchandise giveaways, contests, offers to sell a second item for a ridiculously low price to those who buy a featured product, secondary articles or accessories offered at bargain prices along with the major purchase, and trading stamps redeemable in attractive merchandise are among the leading forms of promotion today. *Incentive promotions,* which offer the customer a special price inducement for immediate buying, have rapidly increased in popularity during the 1970s. In big stores, about a quarter of all promotional events are storewide, and three-fourths are departmental. In small stores, even promotions in support of a single merchandise line usually generate all-store traffic and involve the whole staff to some degree.

SOME EXAMPLES OF PROMOTIONS IN SMALL AND LARGE STORES

What sort of promotional events are in vogue these days among large and small stores?

Fashion Shows The fashion show is doubtless the oldest, most widely used, and most thoroughly exploited special-event promotion throughout the apparel industry. It can be staged within the selling department or elsewhere in the store; it can even go "on the road" to exhibition halls, clubhouses, schools, or conventioneers' hotels. The big news in recent years is the success of men's fashion shows, not just the feminine variety. In Frederick, Maryland, Mel King of King's Men's Wear stages a youth-oriented music festival and fashion show twice yearly. In 1970, he drew 1,200 youngsters to the local armory where each paid $2 to get in. The ticket stub was good for a 5 percent discount on anything in the store purchased within 30 days—an offer 25 percent of the audience took up.

Supermarket Promotions Supermarkets have their own bevy of sales promotion stunts, most of them very different from the kind of activities that help clothing merchants, but equally effective. Trading stamps are still very big business, and so are the fast-growing cents-off coupon offers and free samples. Items in a series (artworks, books, chinaware, and other products) are offered one at a time at low prices to keep folks returning to their food mart week after week. Manufacturer-sponsored food demonstrations, with portable ovens and grills providing hot mini-lunches for shoppers to munch on while trooping down the aisles, have appeal. Games and contests with prizes for the winners also attract a following in these stores and in other kinds of highly promotional stores in other trade lines—especially when customers are low down on the socioeconomic scale.

"How-to-Use-the-Product" Demonstrations "How-to" demonstrations are popular in many trade lines and among department stores as well as smaller specialty shops. Often they are arranged in cooperation with manufacturers. Sewing classes are provided by fabric houses and sewing machine stores, cooking lessons are given by food marts and appliance dealers, the use of wigs and cosmetics is demonstrated by ladies' specialty shops and beauty salons, and golfing, tennis, or skiing classes are sponsored by sporting goods stores. A prosaic paint merchant acquires a more glamorous image by sponsoring a demonstration of the use of color in interior decoration by a member of a paint manufacturer's staff, or a dealer in garden supplies wins customers by running lawn-care classes.

Closed-Door Sales A "CLOSED" sign and windows blanked out with sheets of brown paper at a suburban appliance shop startle passersby twice a year. Meanwhile, through the back door come regular customers, each showing entrance tickets to a guard. The tickets have been sent by mail, with a letter of invitation to the semiannual "customers only" closed-door sale. They entitle the holder to buy goods at a discount and without a down payment. They go only to preferred credit risks, but each person who receives one is also given another ticket, which he or she is authorized to give to a friend or neighbor who is also a good risk! This approach flatters; it works. It builds sales to old friends and brings in scads of new ones, too.

Accent on Atmospherics A youth-oriented chain in college towns insists that all its sales personnel dress in "ultracontemporary" styles (including beads and bare feet). It has no chairs because it expects customers either to dance in the center of the floor or sit cross-legged around the edge for informal chats with store personnel. A stereo plays the latest in rock music, and the store's mascot (a tame *fox*) is trained to be friendly to customers' animal pets, which they are urged to bring along.

Free Samples New parents receive a soft pair of "baby's first shoes," gratis, from a neighborhood children's shoe store. A car wash gives customers free service on their birthdays. A night club serves dinner and a beverage "on the house" when a person turns 21. A gas station affixes neat, embossed owners' license plate numbers on its customers' gasoline credit cards. Purchasers of new movie cameras are invited to a camera shop's miniature theater in the basement to view their first reel while the store manager watches and offers pointers for better pictures next time. All these give-aways of goods and services are sales promotions. Many of them involve advertising materials; others do not.

Free Transportation   Half a century ago, Chicagoans received free transportation by horse-drawn carriages from a commuter train terminal to Marshall Field's State Street store. The basic idea is still a good one, though the means of transportation have changed. Downtown stores in Kalamazoo operate a free bus service to and from nearby Western Michigan University for the convenience of student shoppers. A new supermarket in the heart of a once riot-torn urban district has two busses to carry carless patrons safely to and from market, provided they live within a mile of the store and spend $5 or more.

Personal Appearances   Sports heroes can build a store image, bring fame, and magnify profits for merchants with appropriate tie-in promotions. In Dallas, when Ken's Man's Shop moved to downtown from a suburban base, it cleared a whole floor for the stage and featured Dallas Cowboy football players as models and hosts for its grand opening. The Cowboys had already worked with Ken, appearing at the store and making TV commercials. Ken also sponsors such events as interviews with *Playboy Magazine's* Playmate of the Month and a series of radio talks offering advice on men's wear, which he himself narrates.

Consumer Panels   College fashion advisory boards, high school panels, and ladies' clubs sponsored by a store are well-known devices for obtaining feedback about the store and involving customer groups in its promotional activities. A St. Louis retailer even has a "Huddle Club" of boys who go to athletic events as guests of the store and who also earn money as part-time junior salesmen on the floor. Institutional advertising often includes pictures of members of such groups, with which customers can identify.

Special Events   The special events most commonly promoted are store anniversaries. Some, like 25th, 50th, or 75th anniversaries, can be the whole theme for a year. A Chicago firm celebrating its "50th" used antique cars, historic fashion shows portraying style changes over the five decades, and special period garb for store personnel. Christmas is the biggest of all promotional events, and good planning can make the most of Mother's Day, Valentine's Day, Easter, Father's Day, and other holidays as well. A real Christmas party for selected regular customers, the familiar "Men's Night" when salespersons help husbands pick out gifts, even the cheering bottle the proprietor draws from a desk drawer to express the spirit of the season with a customer, are well-known facets of sales promotion.

Increasingly, socially responsible retailers will be combining promotions with altruistic community services, many of which offer no direct or immediate return but help to build their communities and contribute to their success in the long run. In Reading, Pennsylvania, Boscov's department store backed a series of promotions aimed at increasing understanding of various segments of the local population. One event, a two-day "Festival de Puerto Rico," brought over 60,000 people to the store. Local Puerto Ricans worked for weeks building pavilions, cooking specialty foods, and sewing traditional costumes. The store, meanwhile, arranged for folk dancers, singers, sports figures, poets, artisans, writers, actors, movie stars, and government officials to attend the festival. Other promotions in the same series included a senior citizens event and a "Black Heritage Festival."

PLANNING PROMOTIONS FOR
INDIVIDUAL STORES AND
RETAIL COMMUNITIES

Good promotions are planned well in advance and involve all departments of the store. They should stimulate enthusiasm among store personnel, and the best of them are those that are repeatable (with variations) from year to year and that thus build up impetus as time goes on. Careful evaluation of each special event after it is over is a must. Usually, the associated advertising (institutional or promotional) is a key factor in success or failure. Promotions should increase the loyalty of present customers and leave them feeling closer to the store. At the same time, they should coax noncustomers into the store's orbit and turn them into regular customers.

Shopping centers and associations of downtown merchants sponsor all sorts of joint promotions—cultural events, celebrity appearances, parades, carnivals, and the like. They coordinate their clearance sales, sometimes using the traditional sidewalk sale or dollar day theme, but increasingly adding more imaginative wrinkles. Midnight Madness sales find the stores open and doing a great business until midnight, or in many cases all night long. Special price inducements keep the crowds happy, such as when a gong rings every hour to signal extra discounts for selected merchandise. Meanwhile coffee and snacks are free as shoppers wait to see how deep the price on some item will be cut the next time the "mad" merchants ring the bell. Some stores feel that a prestigious image will suffer by identification with such group activities, and they may be right. But few merchants will deny that building area traffic improves business.

A promotion legitimately pegged to a key local industry, an ethnic heritage, or a significant local historical event has great potential. Stoughton, Wisconsin, for example, celebrates Norwegian Independence Day, sometimes with members of the Norwegian royal family in attendance. Holland, Michigan, holds an annual Tulip Festival that attracts visitors from all over to see such sights as the state's governor clomping down the street in wooden shoes. Fremont, Ohio, recalls its spirited defense against the British and Hessians during the War of 1812, led by a Major Croghan, whose trusty cannon, "Old Betsy," still stands before the city hall, during its annual "Croghan Days." The nation's Bicentennial in 1976 became a theme for commercial and civic festivities all over the country starting in 1975.

In addition to promotion based on historical themes, there are nostalgic events that bring back memories of "the good old days," the sixties, the fifties, the forties, and that attract shoppers of all ages. Ideas for promotions that build store traffic, enhance a retailer's prestige, and build sales come from all sorts of sources. Retailers' trade associations will often provide ideas, plans, and case histories of successful promotions accomplished elsewhere. Figure 11–3 shows the down-to-earth, practical suggestions for succesful store promotions provided by the National Retail Hardware Association. Local media and the national media advertising bureaus provide other sources of promotional ideas, such as the suggestions from the Television and Radio Advertising Bureaus for seasonal events shown in Table 11–1.

PUBLIC RELATIONS AND THE RETAILER

As businesses grow and become more impersonal, public relations departments are set up to explain their operations and policies to the various publics they must deal with: customers, townspeople, vendors, financiers, legislators, government administrators, civic leaders, employees, stockholders, even competitors. Lines of communication with these groups are developed and maintained in various ways (in some cases, through institutional ads in mass media). Speeches before community groups, store tours for visitors and students,

and publications (internal and external house organs) are among the public relations expert's tools.

The owner-managers of small stores are their own PR departments. They are traditionally members of numerous civic groups and willing workers for community projects. Public relations has become an increasingly important collateral duty for managers of branch stores or chains. In medium-sized stores, some of the PR duties are usually delegated to the advertising staff and to different executives, such as the assistant to the general manager. Only the very largest stores maintain full-time staffs solely for this function.

Pure publicity, in the form of *news releases* to the various media, is one aspect of public relations, but hardly the most significant. If a store hires 200 extra employees to handle the Christmas rush, sends a couple of buyers overseas, or adds an exclusive franchise to its stock, it is hardly front-page news; such facts should be publicized through paid institutional ads, if at all. But a $3 million addition that will revitalize a downtown or the promotion or death of a major executive is legitimate news, and the store's PR staff can be of real service to the news media by assembling the facts, making them quickly available, and providing appropriate pictures. If disaster

Figure 11–3 Tips on Store Promotions for the Smaller Merchant
Large department stores and big chains have built-in promotion units in their headquarters to guide store personnel in planning and executing promotions, which are always closely related to the media advertising. Smaller merchants get the same kind of service from their wholesalers and suppliers, and especially from their trade associations. Here the National Retail Hardware Association outlines four good seasonal promotional events: a preseason sale, lawn and garden specials, home security specials, and the Christmas sale. This material shows how to relate the overall promotion program to the advertising and explains what in-store "backup" is necessary in each case. The NRHA also offers ten constructive pointers for getting the personnel and store ready to fully capitalize on each event's advertising plan.

BUILDING STORE TRAFFIC WITH **PROMOTIONS**

In meeting competition, hardware stores must become more adept at creating store traffic with store-wide and departmental promotions.

As crowds continue to flock to discount houses, department stores and other giant retail outlets month after month, at least part of the pulling power can be attributed to continuous promotions. Here are some promotion ideas that have been used successfully both by hardware retailers and by other competing retailers. We suggest you read these ideas carefully and adapt them to your own trading area. Slight adaptions and variations can make them very effective promotions for your store. We suggest you read HARDWARE RETAILING and other trade magazines each month to keep such promotion ideas continually flowing to those who help you plan your promotional activities throughout the year.

IDEA

To attract the do-it-yourselfer and sell more service type merchandise.

AD

Run an ad featuring paint up, clean up items (see sample ad). Feature ads in as many departments as possible. For example, tools, vacuum sweepers, paint, unfinished furniture, building materials, etc., a few genuine specials help build store traffic.

BACKUP

Spot "Paint up, Clean Up Sale" signs throughout the store. Identify all specials in each department with attractive signs. Have a few demonstrations of some of the products wherever possible—especially floor covering products.

PRE-SEASON SALE

IDEA

Setting the pace by getting the season off to a flying start. Encourage the early bird shoppers with "hot" sale items.

AD

Show "extra good" value specials to establish your image as a real price breaker. Then round out your ad with associated items priced at good values.

BACKUP

Always keep your salespeople informed in advance of the promotions. Arrange displays that tell the story. Have good bold pricing on the "hot" sale items with associated items well priced and in some immediate area. Sometimes mass displays are in order. Display your ad at the door, counters and merchandised areas.

LAWN AND GARDEN SPECIALS

IDEA

To attract gardeners and homeowners to your store at the rose planting season.

AD

Offer rose bushes at genuine bargain rates. In some areas of the country bare root rose bushes can be obtained in truck load lots and sold at 39¢ each. State clearly what type of rose bushes are being offered. Advise that they are available on a first-come, first-served basis.

BACKUP

Build a mass display of the rose bushes in the lawn and garden section. Build attractive displays of all other related lines.

HOME SECURITY SPECIALS

IDEA

To let customers know how many items you sell that will make their home and family safer and more secure.

AD

Feature a wide assortment of interior and exterior locks of all types. Be sure to show unusual lock items such as window locks, sliding door locks, etc. Devote a section of the ad to fire extinguishers, stair treads, and other safety devices.

BACKUP

Build an attractive display of security devices in a prominent spot in the store. Try to get your local newspaper to run an article or a news release on the importance of home security. Prepare a typewritten list of "Things to do to make your home more secure" and offer it to all customers. Almost all home security suggestions will involve the purchase or use of items sold in hardware stores.

CHRISTMAS SALE (AND LAY-AWAY TIME)

FREE SNAPSHOTS OF THE KIDDIES

IDEA

To attract young mothers and grandparents and make them aware of the merchandise and services offered by your store.

AD

Offer a free color snapshot of the kiddies with the Easter Bunny at Easter time or Santa at Christmas time. Arrange for someone to wear a bunny or Santa suit and for another person to take the photographs. A color Polaroid camera and an adequate stock of film is all the equipment needed. Arrange for adequate seating while the parents or grandparents are waiting for the snapshots to be made.

BACKUP

Offer attractive specials in various departments throughout the store. Spot these specials so they are clearly visible to the parents or the grandparents while waiting for the snapshots. Alert all sales people to suggest these specials to every customer.

GETTING THE STORE AND PERSONNEL READY

FOR PROMOTIONS AND OTHER ADVERTISING EFFORTS . . . Here are tips and suggestions on how to get the most out of all advertising and promotional activities.

1. **Display The Advertised Products Attractively**
   Before running any ad or promotion be sure the merchandise to be advertised and promoted is in stock in sufficient quantity to handle demand and attractively displayed within the store.

2. **Price And Tag All Advertised Merchandise**
   The ad serves to get the customer into the store, but the merchandise and the price tags on it must help close the sale after the ad does its job.

3. **Plan Your Ad And Promotion Well In Advance**
   No ad or promotion is successful unless it is well planned. Give the ad a lot of thought. Make sure it is timed correctly.

4. **Let Your Employees Know What Is Being Advertised And Promoted**
   Always post the ad conspicuously near the time clock or wherever all employees can see it. Be sure they are alerted to what is being advertised and are aware of the product's location on the sales floor.

5. **Get Your Employees Ready**
   There is more to being ready for a sale than just knowing where the merchandise is located and what is being advertised. Successful hardwaremen hold store meetings to create a team spirit to successfully back major advertising and promotional efforts.

6. **Plan Your Cutoff Date For The Ad Or Promotion**
   Some ads and promotions lose their effectiveness by running too long. Limited departmental promotions usually lose their effectiveness after three days. Major promotions usually become ineffective after a seven to ten day run.

7. **Back Up The Ad or Promotion With Signs And In-Store Decoration**
   Create a gala buying mood by using manufacturer advertising and promotional materials or originating material of your own.

8. **Strategically Locate Your Advertised And Promoted Items**
   Don't make the mistake of putting all advertised and promoted specials in one central or forward location. Spot the advertised products throughout all departments to draw traffic to those departments.

9. **Mark Merchandise Back To Normal Price At The End Of The Sale Or Promotion**
   This is important! Unless merchandise is marked back to its original price at the close of a sale or promotion, the sale becomes meaningless in the eyes of the customer and the store loses money by selling merchandise at reduced prices over too long a period.

10. **Appraise The Results**
    Make an analysis of each promotional effort at its conclusion. If the idea was good, try it again. If it was bad, forget it and try something else next time. If it had some merit, try to revise it to make it work better with minor or major revisions.

Table 11–1
Promotional Ideas to Boost Retail Sales

Occasion	Suggested Promotion
New Year's	Free case of champagne with purchase of _____.
January	13th-month sale (items priced in combinations of 13).
Valentine's Day	Recipes from the heart—submitted to supermarket. Winners read on the air (and shown) . . . prize of "your weight in groceries," etc.
February	Snowflake sale . . . for every inch of snow on the ground, a discount is given on items (or for every degree the temperature falls below freezing, below zero, etc.).
March	Hawaiian luau . . . to "hasten warm weather"—pineapple milk shakes at drive-ins, supermarkets decorated like tropical isles.
Easter	Men's store with "bunny-costumed" sales girls . . . who record commercials themselves and tell audience to ask for them by name at the store.
	Easter bunny gives candy to children—clothing stores, candy shops, etc.
	Guess the number of jelly beans in _____.
	Hidden Easter eggs with magic discounts inside.
	Bunny hop . . . dance featuring local radio (TV) personality . . . in connection with clothing store.
Memorial Day	Safe driving contest (best essay) . . . tied in with car dealer.
Flag Day	Flag cleaned free of charge by dry cleaners with $_____ cleaning job.
4th of July	Sale on red, white, and blue items (cars, etc.)
Summer	Heat wave: discount on fans, air conditioners, etc., for every degree the temperature climbs above _____.
	Picture-taking contest in local area within _____ distance of camera shop.
	A sale held outdoors in circus tent which moves around the city. Clowns, free cotton candy, etc.
	Outdoor cooking contest . . . supermarket or barbecue appliances.
	Swimming pool in parking lot at department store: kids can swim while parents shop. Parents register at store for drawing at summer's end (pool given away).
	Ice cream shop: build your own sundae from smorgasbord of ingredients provided (flat price).
	Moonlight sales for hottest day of year . . . store open all night with prices decreasing along with the temperature!
Fall	Square dance . . . apple cider/pumpkin pie (supermarket).
	Car dealer: free bushel of apples with demonstration ride.
	Football tickets free with purchase of car on certain days.
Columbus Day	Free pizza and other Italian foods (Italian food festival).
	Appliance dealer gives free Italian cookbook with purchase of kitchen range.
Halloween	Hidden pumpkins (with names of prizes, discounts) at stores.
	Witching hour . . . prices de-escalating every hour after midnight.
Thanksgiving	Free turkey with _____ purchase. Or, guess the weight of turkey on display. Or, free dinner given away.

Source: Adapted from materials supplied by Radio Advertising Bureau and Television Bureau of Advertising

strikes an area, in the form of a fire or tornado, the public will want to know what local stores (as well as other local businesses) are doing to cope with the situation. This too is a task for the PR staff.

A public relations person must have a wide variety of skills. Good copywriting ability is necessary for such PR functions as writing letters for executives to sign, getting out press releases containing store news, writing and editing employee bulletins and stockholders' reports, preparing store-sponsored magazines, or perhaps even writing the copy for some of the public-service institutional ads. People who can write in a way that sounds right in spoken speech, can compose good continuity for radio commercials or "ghost write" speeches to be delivered by store executives at important civic events. Outside of writing ability, skills needed for the many different facets of public relations work include a liking for people and an ability to speak well before groups; the necessary polish, manners and social grace to greet and escort important visitors; an understanding of government and the knack of making friends among legislators; and a feel for handling store tours by such diverse groups as school children and convention visitors.

PERSONAL SELLING IN THE STORE

A few years ago the author, while teaching a course in retail promotion at a large university, sent an advanced retailing student out into the town to conduct a little survey. Its purpose was to test the response of salespersons on the floor to a "customer" who had seen the stores' current advertising and wanted more information, presumably with a view to buying one of the products mentioned. The student read and memorized pertinent facts about various products advertised in the local paper the eve-ning before. She then posed as a "customer" interested in the advertised items and sought additional facts about them from salespersons.

Eighteen "contacts" were made in nine different stores (in two or three different departments in some of the departmentalized stores). The results were as follows:

Twelve salespersons (two-thirds of those contacted) were totally ignorant of the advertising their store had carried in the previous evening's paper. Of these, ten asked the "customer" to look through the store and try to find the advertised item; all were able to give some product facts once the "customer" had identified the advertised item.

Two were not only unable to identify the advertised item, but once the "customer" found it they were also unable to offer any additional facts to enhance its value, justify its price, or serve as a reason for buying it. Of the ten salespersons who did offer product information, seven behaved gracefully but not enthusiastically when the "customer" backed off from buying and gave an excuse for leaving the store. Two tried suggestion selling and sought to interest the "customer" in an alternate item. One showed severe temper and behaved discourteously in the face of the impending customer "walk-out."

Only six salespersons (one-third of those questioned) were aware of their store's advertising and immediately showed the advertised item to the "customer," giving additional product information. Only two gave thoroughly professional sales presentations on behalf of the advertised product.

What a tragic waste of advertising dollars, of the hard work of the advertising staffs, managers, and media people! It is absolutely essential that a store's merchandise people, buyers, and department managers be involved—deeply so —with every advertising campaign and each advertisement, from its inception. It is also essential that they keep their front-line salespersons (including part-timers who often miss scheduled sales meetings) aware of forthcoming advertising. Proofs of newspaper ads and copies of radio and TV scripts *must* be placed on employee bulletin boards before the public sees or hears them, and special selling features of the advertised products must be reviewed.

A store's management has no other task more crucial to success than recruiting, testing, selecting, training, motivating, inspiring, holding, and retraining its sales force. Good salespeople know their merchandise and they know human nature. They alone can answer customers' questions or parry their objections to a product. They can overcome sales resistance and close a sale expeditiously. With increasing numbers of retailers' ads urging response by telephone, a good salesperson well-trained in the special techniques of telephone selling can often convert an inquiry into a completed sale right then and there, or can use slack periods of time to initiate calls to special customers and ring up added volume.

When customers are matched with merchandise properly chosen to insure satisfaction, the store gets repeat business and word-of-mouth advertising. And when they are encouraged by salespersons, with proper consideration for their true needs and ability to buy, to either trade up to better quality merchandise and/or to buy additional (usually related) items, the store is on its

way to big-time success, because its per-customer and per-transaction sales volume is *greatly increased* without a material increase in any of its expenses. Only when this kind of effective selling is done can advertising make its maximum contribution to profits.

Questions for Discussion

1. Why is it that, despite its many virtues, outdoor advertising cannot do the whole advertising job for most retailers? In what kinds of businesses does outdoor advertising often play a leading role?

2. What kinds of retail stores are most likely to profit from direct-mail advertising, and why? If you were called in as a consultant to one of those stores, to set up a direct-mail program, what dangers and possible limitations of this kind of advertising would you discuss with its management (assuming that it has had little experience in this area)?

3. Why should advertising people be interested in and involved in window and interior displays? How does a good advertising professional work with the people responsible for store displays?

4. If you were assigned the task of preparing a year-long series of sales promotions for a large store, where could you turn for ideas? Which sources do you think would be most useful? What promotions mentioned in the text would be suitable for a particular store with which you are familiar, either as an employee or a regular customer?

5. If you were public relations director of a retail firm, in what ways would

your work be different from that of the advertising manager? In what ways would all or most of your long-range objectives be similar to the advertising manager's?

6. What is the relationship between advertising and personal selling? Why is each important to the other?

Suggested Projects

1. Drive or walk around the main thoroughfares and principal business streets of your community for an hour, with a pocket notebook and a companion to assist you. Note down the number, names, and types of local consumer-oriented businesses whose highway signs and outdoor posters you see. (Do not include signs on the premises of the businesses themselves.) Analyze your results in terms of the categories of retail stores and service businesses whose signs you saw. Which kinds of firms used the most and the biggest signs? How many were standard "24-sheet posters" (about 25' by 12' in size)? How many directional signs were there?

2. If there is a shopping guide or a free-circulation paper in your community, secure two or three copies and compare the kind of advertising it carries with the kind comparable issues of the paid-circulation paper carry. Which kinds of businesses run the most and the largest ads in the free publication? Which run the most and the largest ads in the newspaper? What do you think is the reason for the difference?

3. Visit your post office and get the latest pamphlets, bulletins, and booklets pertaining to third class mail and postal permits. Ask for information on the total number of patrons served by your post office, by post office boxes, city carriers, and on rural mail routes. Study this material, and calculate the cost of sending a minimum-weight mailing piece by third class to every resident and business in your community. Compare this with the cost of sending the same piece by first class mail. What would be the advantages of sending such a mailing first class? If you had only 150 names on your mailing list and planned to make two mailings a year, would it pay to take out a mailing permit?

4. List ten retail sales promotions you have recently learned about in your community, through advertising or because you were in the store during the promotion. Which ones interested you the most? What kinds of promotions do you think the people of your community respond to the most? Verify your conclusions by polling 25 friends, classmates, or neighbors.

Notes

1. Data supplied by Institute of Outdoor Advertising, 1974.

2. George Brandsberg, *The Free Papers* (Ames, Iowa: Wordsmith Books, 1969), pp. 70, 71, 76–78.

3. *A Comparative Study of Dailies & Community Weeklies in the St. Louis Metropolitan Area* (New York: Newspaper Advertising Bureau, 1973), pp. 11, 22.

4. Ibid.

5. Robert Stone, "Energy Crisis Do's and Don'ts for Retailers, Manufacturers," *Advertising Age* (March 4, 1974), pp. 34–36.

6. The material in this section is based

on Gabriel Valenti, *Interior Display: A Way to Increase Sales,* SMA #111 (Washington, D.C.: U.S. Small Business Administration, 1971).

7. Ibid.

8. Ralph Head & Affiliates, Ltd., *Why Shoppers Make Unplanned Purchases in Mass Merchandise Stores* (New York: Point-of-Purchase Advertising Institute, 1971).

9. "Show Your Stuff," *Selling News* (New York: Newspaper Advertising Bureau, Inc., 1973).

10. Adapted from Philip Kotler, "Atmospherics as a Marketing Tool," *Journal of Retailing* (Winter 1973–1974), p. 50.

11. Ibid., pp. 48–64.

12. Herbert Wittkin, "An Image Is a Many-Faceted Thing," *Readings in Modern Retailing* (New York: National Retail Merchants Assn., 1969), pp. 221–222.

PART **4**

Creating and Producing Retail Advertisements

Thus far, we have examined modern consumers, the retail industry that caters to their wants, and the management planning involved in setting up a goal-oriented advertising program. In Part 3 the focus was on the media through which a store's message is delivered to consumers.

The message itself will be the center of attention in this, Part 4. Its creation is a job for the active practitioner of advertising, the man or woman who works for a retail company, an advertising agency, or the media through which the message will flow. Advertising plans are implemented through specific advertisements designed to achieve specific goals and delivered through chosen media.

A successful advertising message is one that is well thought out, well written, well designed, and suited to the medium it flows through. We shall examine, first, the thinking process that must precede the writing of any successful ad. We shall then investigate how the thoughts of a store about its merchandise and itself can be expressed in ways that will influence the reader, listener, or viewer to respond favorably. We shall see what makes good advertising good—in any medium. Once we have done this, we will be equipped to explore the tools used in the day-to-day preparation of advertisements.

Here we turn to the creative and technical side of retail advertising to see what kinds of messages attract and hold the attention of consumers and motivate them to buy, and to examine certain limitations placed on advertising message-content from the outside. Finally, we consider the follow-up work done by advertising people and their colleagues in the store to insure the greatest possible success for today's ads and tomorrow's.

The first three parts dealt mostly with material based on hard facts, supported by frequent statistical references and experts' opinions, as well as the established practices of major retailers. As our attention turns to advertising creativity, there are far fewer hard facts and solid data for guidance. The coming chapters are concerned with choosing the words, pictures, and sounds that will influence the human mind—a task that is mysterious, ever-changing, complex, and but little explored in any thoroughly scientific way. Because so much that has to be said can never be proven conclusively, there is no *always-right* way that can be easily contrasted with an *always-wrong* way to do the job. Simple trial-and-error is the most practical method of validation. Judgment rather than authority becomes the keynote, and the reader is urged to feel free to let his or her own ideas take wing. Hopefully many readers will be students in courses where at this point actual exercises in copywriting, layout and art, and broadcast continuity writing are introduced. Others, engaged in self-education, may now be employed in retailing or advertising; they will apply the principles and suggestions in their everyday labors. No two creators of advertising do their work in exactly the same manner, nor should they try to. Each is free to find his or her own way, to test out what is best in a particular case, and to accept the guidance of text or teacher only to the gentlest and most general degree. The reader should not submerge personal creative impulses or instinctive judgment solely to conform to some implied norm. Rather, these chapters should be the source of guidelines (especially for the beginner), with the student retaining comfortable latitude to create freely in his or her own style ads to promote a product, a store, or an idea in classroom exercises or daily business.

Preview

Purchasing advertising space or time merely provides an opportunity for advertising success; the content (and execution) of an ad determines whether it brings a profit to the store. The results produced by two ads of the same size carried by the same medium at the same time can be very different indeed, and the advertiser who goes to great lengths to select the best items, store policies, and ideas to advertise, and to choose the best words, pictures, and sounds to tell their story will be richly rewarded.

Retailers should select items for their ads that are (1) wanted by the consumer, (2) timely and newsworthy, (3) stocked in depth, (4) typical of the store, (5) the best possible values the store has to offer (though not necessarily the lowest-priced items), (6) coordinated with other items in the same ad, especially as to price line, and (7) heavily promoted by the manufacturer.

Institutional ads should build a store's image by telling the story of store personnel, giving instructions or information, commenting on important issues of the day, recognizing an anniversary or local event, featuring store services, emphasizing a well-known brand, or rendering a public service.

Before creating an ad, a copywriter (or an artist) must thoroughly study the product or service to be advertised and consumers' motives for buying it. Determining the customers' level of awareness of their need for the product is also necessary. Only then can the creative strategy, theme, and copy platform be developed.

Learning Goals

Chapter 12 should give the readers an understanding of the importance of good copy in making ads work and of the way to choose the best items and ideas to advertise. It should demonstrate the essential preliminaries to successful copywriting: an in-depth study of the product or service and the means by which consumers can be motivated to buy it. This chapter should also teach the students how good advertising ideas can be developed, and the "five steps" involved in creating productive print or broadcast advertisements.

12

Creative Thinking That Produces Creative Ads

Is it worth it?

Is it worth the *effort* to improve the quality of retail ads? Thousands of them are simple announcements of fact or repetitions of familiar slogans. Tens of thousands are mere price lists, containing only the names of items and their cost (with perhaps a word or two of prosaic description). Yet they work. They sell merchandise and services and remind people of a business that, as a result, they patronize.

However, not all stores need to settle for this kind of ad *every time,* and many stores refuse to do so at *any* time. Let's see what could happen to store profits if *even a few ads* were truly creative, the result of an investment of thought, time, and energy.

Let us assume that half a store's business comes the "easy way," without advertising, and half is the result of its ads. Let us also suppose that the advertising people are too busy to give really

professional attention to more than one ad in five. Finally, let us make the conservative assumption that increased effort in the preparation of ads will make them a mere 25 percent more effective than run-of-the-mill "uncreative" ads. The store's goal, then, is to make *one ad in five* work just *one-quarter harder.*

The country's 50 leading retailers averaged net profits of 2.02 cents per dollar of sales in 1973.[1] If improved ads increased only 10 percent of their sales by one-fourth, there would be a 2½ percent increase in their sales, overall ($10\% \times 25\% = 2.5\%$). Since across-the-board gross profit margins in retailing are around 30 percent of sales, the heightened advertising quality would add a seemingly small three-fourths of 1 percent to their net profits (assuming the small amount of increased business did not increase other variable expenses, as discussed in Chapter 3). But since the average store realized a net profit of only

2 percent to begin with, a three-quarter percent gain in sales bring an increase of 37½ percent in profits. If a store's profits were $100,000 last year, improving the *quality* of ads could raise them to $137,-500 this year.

Solid evidence that the extra effort given to the creative ad is well placed comes from studies of what kinds of ads are most noticed by consumers. For many years Daniel Starch and Staff, a copy research firm, has issued syndicated reports that measure three levels of printed advertising readership: (1) *noted*—the percentage of those who have read a publication who remember having seen the ad; (2) *associated*—the percentage of readers of the publication who saw any part of the ad and can recall the name of the product or the advertiser; and (3) *read most*—the percentage of readers who read half or more of the written material in the ad. Readership of component parts of the ad are also mea-sured, including the headline(s), subheadline(s), illustration(s), logotype (the advertiser's signature), and the copy block(s) containing the main text. Obviously, for an ad to do a complete selling job, the copy or text must be read. This firm's findings demonstrate the wide variations in readership between poor ads and good ones.

For a large group of black-and-white newspaper ads tested over a period of years, the Starch reports revealed that the *lowest-scoring* third were "noted" by an average of 22 percent of the people surveyed who saw the paper; the *highest-scoring* third (for the same kinds of products) "noted" 53 percent—a difference of 141 percent. What store would not like its ads to attract and be remembered by 141 percent more people? [2] Another test dealt with two versions of the same ad, of the same size, in the same medium, and using the same illustrations. Only the overall design arrangement, the size and background of the pictures, and the words of the headline and text copy differed. At bottom are the readership scores in percentages of total publication readers.[3] While the better ad was noticed by more than twice the number who saw and recalled the poorer ad, the difference in readership of the crucial part of the ad, the copy block containing the text, was *1,000* percent (1 percent versus 10 percent).

Hundreds of similar sophisticated research studies have demonstrated that one ad of specified size in a given medium can "outpull" another by a factor of five, ten, or fifteen—even though each ad costs the same. A well-planned, well-designed, and skillfully executed ad that is appropriate for a medium and its audience will always outpull a poorly conceived, ill-constructed, and indifferently executed ad that is inappropriate for a medium, its audience, or both.

1 Choosing What to Advertise

The "pull" of any given retail ad depends largely on its *content. And* whether an ad is worth an all-out creative effort by advertising technicians depends on whether the content offers real promise for success. Buyers, merchandise managers, manufacturers who will pay part of the cost, and the availability of merchandise are often the factors that determine what items are to be promoted. In institutional ads, the firm's top management often decides what will be said.

It is traditionally the prerogative of the merchandisers to determine *what* to advertise—and the domain of the advertising staff only to decide *how* to advertise it. Nevertheless, many opportunities arise for advertising people to have a share in choosing the items to be included in promotional ads and the facets of a store's services and "personality" to be featured in image-building ads. Often the budget is not large enough to advertise all the items the merchandise people want to promote, and the ad people can help to choose those most likely to make an ad successful. In well-managed stores, merchandisers and advertisers work as a team, share a basic viewpoint, and agree on what makes a good ad. The manager of a smaller shop typically works jointly with one or two senior salespersons and representatives of the ad media in deciding on ad content.

The following checklist will help advertising managers, agency account executives with retail clients, and media representatives counseling advertisers to choose items to be included (and especially those to be *featured*) in promotional, item-selling ads.

WHAT TO PUT IN ITEM–PRICE PROMOTIONAL ADS

1. *Popular Items*   Stores should advertise items that are wanted by the public, products that seem to be selling

	Noted ad	Associated ad with name	Read most of words	Read headline	Read copy block (text)
Ad A	57	46	8	15	10
Ad B	25	23	1	8	1

well. They should never waste advertising money trying to push buyers' mistakes on unwilling customers. If last week's ad "pulled well," perhaps certain items mentioned in it should be included again. There is no law against keeping a good thing going! Change just for the sake of change seldom makes sense. Retailers make the most profit on ads that feature items people really want, for their own intrinsic value, and for which they are willing to pay the full, normal retail price.

2. *Timely Items* Stores should advertise items that are timely—ones that are wanted *now*. Their sales records for the same week last year will give them clues as to seasonal wants. In many trade lines (especially costly durables), ads for specific items should *precede* the actual buying season. They should get the buyer thinking about a store before the height of the season when the media are inundated with ads. The woman buying a new fall dress may be thinking about it in August; the family that needs a power lawn mower knows it in March.

3. *Items Stocked in Depth* Stores should advertise items stocked in depth. Then they will have enough of desired sizes, colors, and models to please all the customers who come to buy, even those who come late in the day. A retailer should not risk having to turn away people whom an ad brought to the store!

4. *Items That Are Typical of the Store* Retailers need to advertise items that are typical of the store. Actually, every promotional ad is also an *institutional ad*. It tells people what kind of store they will be dealing with. It creates an impression of being or not being their kind of store. Advertising items out of character with a store's image may drive away present customers and fail to attract new ones. People on a tight budget will stay far away from a store whose advertising makes it sound like Tiffany's or Saks Fifth Avenue, while those looking for the ultimate in service will be repelled by the image of a warehouselike trading mart.

5. *Items That Are Good Values* Stores profit most if they feature items that are good values (regardless of their price). A high-quality item at a fair price is a better bargain than a shoddy item at a low price, and most people have sense enough to know this. Good values become an increasing draw as merchants deal with more-educated consumers.

6. *Items in the Same Price Line* A store should coordinate the price lines of all items advertised. If it offers $200 suits, it should not advertise $10 hats in the same ad. If it features a $160 lawn mower, it should not push a 98¢ garden hose at the same time. The best price line to feature is the one that suits most customers' budgets. A large store for which all price lines are equally important may run separate ads for each line.

7. *Newsworthy Items* Stores should concentrate on newsworthy items where possible—a new model of a popular product or an old model with an attractive new price; an item directly related to a particular local event such as the opening or closing of school, a storm or a dry spell, a visit to an area by a celeb-

rity, a sports victory, or industrial or political news.

8. *Items Being Promoted by Manu- facturers or Other Stores* Stores can often benefit from including or featuring in their advertising items being heavily promoted in manufacturers' national advertising. Literature sent to dealers will provide schedules of factory ads to which retailers can tie parts of their own programs. Co-op programs are usually geared to coincide with manufacturers' own ad programs. Small merchants and those in isolated towns may be able to follow a big store's lead by watching its ads closely. Often the cue to promote a given item is its appearance in others' ads. A big store or a chain's ad for a given product may have appeared at a specific time as a result of some expensive consumer research, and small stores can cash in on this research by following suit a couple of days later. By stirring up a *primary demand* for a product, a large store's ads indirectly help smaller stores sell comparable products.

One thing retailers should *not* do is go wild on price-cutting "clearance" items. The major fault of many retail ads is that they use *nothing but* low prices to attract customers. Clearance sales are a normal part of any retail operation, provided they are what they purport to be: season-end clearances of items that should be sold quickly to avoid the expense of storage. Phony "clearance" sales announced once or twice each month merely destroy a store's credibility. Ads for clearance sales should be the exception, not the rule, in promotional campaigns.

THOUGHT–STARTERS FOR INSTITUTIONAL ADS (AND INSTITUTIONAL ELEMENTS WITHIN PROMOTIONAL ADS)

The first step in an institutional ad campaign may well be an analysis of the store's *image,* as seen by its customers and noncustomers. This image is derived from *people's ideas* about the store's prices, its variety of merchandise, its employees, its appearance, its clientele, and its advertising. Whether these ideas are correct or not is not relevant. One can determine a store's image by asking customers and noncustomers what they think of it or by doing some other simple attitude research.

Having determined a store's *present* image, a retailer can decide what aspects of that image need changing (if any), what aspects should be reinforced (among present customers), and what aspects should be introduced (to noncustomers). Some of the public's ideas about a store may be woefully erroneous. They are the cue for a series of ads setting things straight by publicizing the facts.

Things that are really wrong with the store from the viewpoint of customers and/or noncustomers should be changed or modified. Ads alone cannot work miracles, change poor merchandise or service, make an unattractive store appealing, light a fire under a listless store manager, or alter a deserved bad reputation. *Improvements* in any of these areas may, however, constitute material for ads designed to wash away the old image and create a new one.

A sustained, long-range campaign of institutional advertising with specific objectives will ultimately add up to more volume and greater profits, even though this kind of promotion rarely brings instant results at the cash register. Institutional ads for stores and service businesses can center on one or more of the following themes.

Store Personnel Often *the* advantage the small, local, independent store has over the retail giants with their sometimes faceless masses of ill-mannered and indifferent "sales clerks" is its personnel. Quotations from satisfied customers who have been assisted by courteous sales or service personnel, credentials that substantiate the desire and ability of a store's personnel to serve its customers well, have powerful appeal for today's shoppers. Reports of attendance at factory training seminars, sales courses, and meetings, perhaps written in a news-story format, can create an image of personnel constantly improving their ability to sell and service a store's merchandise.

Pictures and biographies in print, their own voices in radio commercials, and appearances on TV can literally "introduce" store employees to customers. Stressing these friendly *merchandise counselors*, with their special ability to assist people in buying and using merchandise, can bring many customers to a store.

Instruction and Information Helpful facts on how to use and enjoy a store's products are in tune with the age of consumerism. Impartial, authentic aid in choosing among various options, and in preserving and taking care of the purchases they make, will please and impress customers. Stores catering to buyers of fabrics, foods, cars, sporting goods, medical products and drugs, yard and garden items, home furnishing, appliances, and the like will find eager readers for institutional ads offering unbiased, practical information in simple language.

Comments on Local, State, and National Issues Vast numbers of citizens, especially the high-spending and fast-growing young adult segment of the population, react coldly to what they preceive as selfish, impersonal business "interests." The store management that speaks out openly on vital issues may be happily surprised to find how responsive customers are to frankness. The viewpoints of the store and its customers may not coincide on every issue, but willingness to express an opinion will impress them; it is hypocrisy that irritates modern youth, not honest opinions courageously aired.

Merchants of today and tomorrow may be richly rewarded for taking the lead in urban renewal and community beautification programs, in preserving the ecology, in curbing pollution, in promoting fair play among the races, and in protecting consumers. Often, advertising on such issues can be scheduled to coincide with specific local events or campaigns that are government-related or privately sponsored—becoming, in effect, part of the day's news. It can also be timed to coincide with traditional holidays, perhaps replacing banal platitudes and bland generalities featured in past institutional ads.

Anniversaries The traditional *anniversary sale* may still have a place in a retailer's promotional calendar, but there is evidence that it is a worn-out, trite approach. Modern stores can take a great stride forward by converting anniversaries into occasions for telling true and interesting stories about their origins and their evolution, tracing their own growth in relation to the development and improvement of the local business district and the community as a whole. (This sort of institutional promotion, backed up with appropriate in-store displays and special events, need not, of course, *exclude* simultaneous merchandising events.) Anniversary salutes need not be confined to the store's own birthday, nor to milestones in the lives of store executives, either. The founding of the city or the establishment of a primary local industry, a nearby college, a civic orchestra, a local theater, or some other local institution provides valid opportunities for special institutional messages.

Cultural and Sports Events   Art shows, dramatic productions, concerts, lectures, tournaments, and conventions can often be topics for institutional ads appealing to specific segments of the local population. Some of these ads may be a pure community service or a way of building general goodwill. Others may be related to actual merchandise—clothing for sports and athletic events, records or tapes of musical shows, or furnishings and home decorations on display at a home show. Retailers can use institutional ads both to generate goodwill *and* to build store traffic that sells merchandise, by wisely relating them to local events.

Store Services   Services are increasingly the determining factor influencing the consumer to buy from store

A rather than store B. No store can ever fully capitalize on the cost of the extras it offers unless *everyone knows about them:* what they are and how they work. Retailers should play up such customer conveniences as credit facilities, parking, in-store food service, alterations, professional decorating or fashion consultants, exchange privileges, postsale servicing, delivery services, gift wrapping, and mailing services. A store that offers such services should say so, often; if it does *not,* it may even be wise to run occasional ads explaining *why* it does not. When customer comfort is enhanced by better lighting, more luxurious customer lounges, new escalators, and the like, ads should tell people about it.

Name Brands   Making customers aware that a store sells famous brand names (especially those for which it is the exclusive distributor) is profitable, especially when it must compete head-on with chains offering house brands. Ads featuring branded merchandise can give a store a share of the recognition accorded well-known manufacturers. The retailer can use their emblems and trademarks and spell out the reasons their brands were chosen above others.

Special Communications   Advertising should be used whenever the store has a special message for the public, such as an explanation for changes in store policies regarding the hours or days it is open for business, the extension or contraction of delivery services, credit, the return of merchandise, or billing procedures. A store may be changing its name or its location. Sometimes unusual problems are caused by weather, strikes, transportation delays, or new laws and regulations. Even in these potentially negative situations, a forthright explanation of what is going on is often preferable to an ostrichlike atitude that permits customer ill will to fester silently. Radio is an ideal medium for emergency announcements; direct-mail permits a store to contact its regular customers in regard to a matter without giving details to noncustomers; and newspapers are an economical way to publish a long and thoughtful message to the general public.

Store Visits by Celebrities or Experts in a Field These events are usually part of a store's planned promotional program, and must of course be heavily publicized to be effective. They increase traffic and they enhance a store's prestige. The visitor may be a noted dress designer giving a fashion show, a famed golfer demonstrating his or her swing, or an author autographing books.

Trade-at-Home Ads Merchants in smaller communities with competition from big retail complexes burgeoning in larger towns nearby often use a portion of their advertising to build traffic and keep shoppers "at home." They may run individual or jointly sponsored ads expounding on the convenience of shopping locally and the variety of goods and savings available.

Public-Service Ads These should be kept to a minimum and should be well chosen. Retailers' ad budgets are not unlimited, and there are many uses

for their ad dollars. When a community activity has real worth and does in fact make an area a better place to live and shop in, merchants should not hesitate to give it their active support. However, ads should really *say* something, have some real meat for the reader, some attractive art and a message worth remembering.

Store Expansion and Improvements Closely related to ads for merchandise are those institutional ads occasioned by the opening of a new branch or department, the remodeling or expansion of a store, the installation of new fixtures or equipment, and the acquisition of a local distributorship for a noted merchandise line. Institutional ads should really sing and shout about these events, as well as about the sprucing up of a business district or shopping center as a whole, either through a government project or through private initiative.

2 Integrating the Advertising Campaign

All retail ads should be in harmony with the broad goals of the store and the tasks assigned to its advertising. (Review the discussion in Chapter 6, especially pages 138–141.) Most of them are also preplanned in series to fit into unified themes over a year, a season, or the duration of a promotional event. Themes, slogans, and graphic symbols connect each successive ad, in each medium, to a campaign as a whole, to build up layer upon layer of awareness and impact. A whole year's campaign can be related to observance of a store's 100th anniversary, one of several months' duration to the opening of a new store, and a shorter campaign to seasonal merchandise promotions. Some campaigns are designed to support and build up a given department or merchandise division, such as fashion apparel or home furnishings, and others are called *umbrella* campaigns because they cover the whole store. Increasingly, campaigns are focused on demographic and lifestyle characteristics of specific customer targets, such as working women, sports enthusiasts, apartment-dwellers, campers and backpackers, students, and senior citizens.

All ads related to a campaign should reflect a common image, carry a common slogan, emphasize a unified theme, display the same graphic symbol; these integrating devices are then carried *across media* to tie the whole campaign together. Colors and type styles are coordinated among all printed ads, and where feasible, the same, or at least compatible, illustrations are used. Musical identity is enhanced by coordinating radio, television, and in-store audio devices. Slogans like "Downtown, we know what you have in mind" or "Caring about you is our first concern" are less used than in the past because they tend to wear out and become meaningless after long repetition. Themes of shorter duration carry more specific connotations, such as "Summer Fun Time," "Man's World," "The Jingle Bells Store," or "The Now Shop." Campaign symbols can be a stylized flower, a cartoon character, or a clever variation on the store's established logotype. A distinctive color may also be used, carrying across media from mail, newspaper, and billboard ads to the in-store displays.

3 Thinking Through the Advertising Proposition

Traditionally, retailers have sorted out, classified, and labeled their individual ads according to the *function* they are expected to perform for the store: They run promotional ads, including regular price-line merchandise selling, special promotional ads to push big planned selling events, and clearance ads to turn end-of-season inventories into cash. They also run institutional ads, either to build prestige (image) or to tell about the store's services. These classifications of advertising relate well to three discernable types of stores: the highly promotional store (using mostly special promotion ads, often disguised as clearance ads); the nonpromotional store (emphasizing institutional and regular price-line ads when it advertises, but doing much less advertising as a whole); and the semipromotional store, blending all kinds of advertising in a balanced mix.

Today, these simplistic distinctions are becoming blurred, but they remain useful concepts for the creator of advertising—with due modification to conform to an ever-fragmenting market and the continuing diversification of retailing and service businesses. We must indeed be aware of the overall promotional plan, and of the characteristics of each medium we are to use, before we get down to the particulars of writing, designing, and otherwise creating an ad.

But especially must we know the product (a tangible item or line of merchandise, a service or group of services, or the store itself, which more and more is the "product" retail ads are called on to "sell") and, finally and most importantly, the people, the consumers we seek to motivate.

Let's start with the product, defined in limited or broad terms.

STUDYING THE PRODUCT TO BE ADVERTISED

Just as a salesperson cannot effectively sell merchandise in a face-to-face situation unless and until he or she knows a great deal about it, so too an advertising person cannot begin to create an effective ad until he or she has studied the product, service, or store thoroughly.

Where do advertising people get information about the products they are to advertise? Figure 12–1 shows an *advertising requisition form* used by the Wieboldt Company, a large Chicago-based department store group. Note how much information about the product the store's buyer, who normally initiates the request for any specific promotional ad in a big store, supplies. (The buyers for this store are required to submit the form two weeks before the publication date of the ad.) Three things on this form are especially crucial: the *actual merchandise sample* to be supplied to the illustrator and copywriter who will work on the ad; the buyer's definition of the *major customer benefit* of the product; and the six *selling points* to be specified, in order of importance.

Obtaining this data is a good beginning. When time and the importance of the ad justify it, a whole lot more should be done. For example:

1. *Use the product yourself.* Wear it (if practicable). Drive it, if it's a car, a motorboat, or a motorcycle. Take it home and show it to your wife or husband. Try it in your own home, your own yard or garden. If it's a service—dry cleaning, gift-wrapping, or the Auto Club's emergency road service—try it. If it's food, smell it, taste it, and eat it; if it makes music, listen to it. Many small merchants have an advantage over big stores because they do all this. Their advertising rings true, just as their personal selling does, because of their superior knowledge of their limited merchandise lines.

2. If you can't use it, *find out what users say about it.* Talk to people who bought the product, after they've had it a while. Salespersons on the floor often hear effective "testimonials" from satisfied repeat customers, which can be passed on to advertising people as cues to selling points. Keep in touch with the front-line troops of retailing, the floor salespeople. They also know which specific points in their own oral "sales pitches" persuade a customer to buy.

3. The very large store may even have a *testing laboratory* whose reports on products are available to advertising staffers. Read those reports carefully and visit the lab when you can.

4. Finally, *learn what the manufacturer says about the product.* It has probably made tests; its advertising agency has developed a selling

strategy for national ads pegged to product virtues that satisfy consumer needs. Examine these national ads and the tags, labels, package information, and owner's manual that come on or with the product, and find out what the manufacturer's catalog and sales representative have to say about it.

Absorb all the facts you can about the product—how it is made and what it is made of, how well it is made, how it works, how it compares with competitive products, how it is identified, what its price is and why. And keep thinking always about how its attributes can be *useful to those who buy it.* What does it *do* for them? And for what specific kinds of people will it do the most? Will some product features appeal to one kind of user, and other features to different segments of the market? One woman may buy a refrigerator primarily because it comes in a wide choice of colors and she can match it to her kitchen decor; another may be interested chiefly in its capacity. One man may buy shoes because he likes their style, another because he thinks them well made. What specific feature would make *you,* your wife or husband, the fellow next door, or the lady across the street want the product?

STUDYING CUSTOMERS AND
THEIR BUYING MOTIVES

By far the most important part of the preliminaries to the actual writing, designing, recording, or staging of an advertisement is the work you do to relate the product, service, or store's key benefits to the people who will be the *target* of your ad. Draw on everything you know about the store's customers and those you seek to make customers. What motives, in addition to the obvious practical applications of the product, might some or all of them have for buying it? Many creative experts recommend the *problem-solving* approach: find out what problems the prime prospects have, then determine precisely how the product, service, or store can help solve those problems. From this line of thinking come ads that are essentially *solutions to consumers' problems,* and there is no better way to go about it.

Solving customers' problems requires knowledge of their psychographics, demographics, lifestyles, logic, and emotions. Not all their problems are obvious: People are not necessarily conscious of all their problems themselves, and different groups and individuals have different kinds of problems. The person buying a bicycle to ride to work in order to save on gasoline and avoid parking problems, and incidentally to improve health, faces different problems from the one who buys a bike for a son or daughter. Because of limited time at home, the employed women's problems associated with cooking and housecleaning stem from entirely different circumstances than those of the full-time housewife. Advertising appeals must be quite different to motivate each kind of consumer.

A recent study by the Newspaper Advertising Bureau described psychographic analyses of customer target groups as follows:

An effective aid in identifying the best sales prospects and in devising advertising appeals . . .

ADVERTISING REQUISITION

Due in Advertising Department 14 WORKING DAYS in advance of the week ad is to run

Department _____ Paper _____ Date of ad _____ Space _____

Name of Sale or Promotion _____

ART INFORMATION

Actual merchandise sample supplied ☐   Old art or engraving _____

Glossy photo supplied ☐   When run _____

Specification sheet supplied ☐   Paper _____

Fill in information below. Use separate sheet for each item

ITEM HEADLINE: _____

_____

MAJOR CUSTOMER BENEFIT: _____

_____

SELLING POINTS (List in order of importance):

1. _____

2. _____

3. _____

4. _____

5. _____

6. _____

Be sure you have listed sizes and colors by customer preference

REGULAR   IF REDUCED   CHECK IF
PRICE: _____   STATE SALE PRICE: _____   SPECIAL PURCHASE ☐

If item above comes in additional sizes and or styles, list below with additional prices:

_____   _____   _____

_____   _____   _____

_____   _____   _____

SPECIAL REQUIREMENTS

USE PROCESSOR'S LOGO ☐   USE BRAND NAME LABEL ☐   PHONE ORDER ☐   MAIL ORDER ☐

INCLUDE COUPON ☐   SPECIFY IF NOT AT ALL STORES _____

COPIES TO: Advertising, Merchandise Manager, Buyer, Section Manager

F 101 (4-66)

Figure 12–1 Advertising Requisition Form

Extremely useful in devising copy and art appeals because they provide insights into individual differences and prejudices.

Most useful for defining product prospects when markets are specialized and limited. For universally used products, [they are] most useful in defining prospects for individual brands.[4]

The study turned up certain broad personality groups likely to react to different advertising appeals: among females, the conformists, the drudges, the free spenders, and the striving suburbanites; among males, the achievers, the discontented, and the traditionalists.[5]

Which kinds of customers are the primary prospects for a product, and which of its features will appeal to them the most?

The reasons people buy are not necessarily obvious. Consumers may purchase a given product from a particular store for any one reason or any combination of reasons—for example,

1. *Price.* The price of the product may be lower than the price of the same or a comparable product in other stores in the same trading area.

2. *The brand name.* It may bear a favorite trademark or label, whose popularity has been established by national advertising, habitual use, or the reputation of the maker.

3. *Convenience.* The store may carry a wide array of similar products, conveniently displayed, and have an adequate stock of related items.

4. *Seasonal needs.* Vacation periods, school years, holidays, and climatic factors affect traditional and customary wants.

5. *Sequential buying.* A customer may be acquiring a set of something, adding to a collection, or looking for accessories to items already owned.

6. *Celebrations and anniversaries.* Many people buy things for others, to mark birthdays and other anniversaries, successes in school or on the job, or simply to express love.

7. *Ethnic customs.* Racial, religious, and ethnic traditions motivate purchases of some foods, apparel items, home furnishings, and religious articles.

8. *Subconscious identity.* Some products reinforce a desired self-image by connoting virility, sweetness, youth, wealth, education, or social status.

9. *Psychological compensation.* Buying can be stimulated by domestic quarrels, feelings of loneliness, a sense of unfulfillment, or by periods of distress or loss. The act of "going shopping" or of accumulating possessions provides a form of relief.

10. Fads, a momentary attraction to a product, a desire to imitate others, and pressure from peers or family members can also move people to buy.

Very important to the planning of an effective ad is an estimate of the state of mind of the intended customers at the moment the ad has an impact on them. In part, this will vary with the medium used. In part, it will be created by forces not under your control or subject to much manipulation through advertising (but which you must take into consideration): the state of the local economy, unemployment, inflation, the weather. You must also determine whether a product or service is primarily aimed at a replacement market (because it is better than something the typical customer has now) or whether it is something that is essentially new and untried, from the consumer's point of view.

Most essential is an estimate, based on research if it is possible and on judgment if it is not, of which of *three levels of customer interest* you can assume, prior to the reception of your ad.

Conscious Need Are some customers aware of a need for the product? If people are actively seeking information on a product or service they know they want to buy, and buy now or very soon, they will respond well even to prosaic catalog-type listings of simple facts. But even if this kind of ad is all that is needed, it should be well done. Emphasize the product's one, two, or three best selling points and give enough information to answer consumers' questions, as interestingly as you can. Most retail ads go no further, and they do not need to.

Subconscious Need Do customers have a need for the product that is just below the conscious level? Will advertising make them recognize this need and fire them with enthusiasm to buy? To do this ads must often blend the bare facts about a product with art or copy that has an emotional appeal—that is imaginative, creative, sprinkled with subtle implications, or that tells a story or amuses. The focus in such ads is generally on customer benefits more than on the item or service proper, on getting the reader, listener, or viewer personally involved. The advertiser touches

psychological wellsprings of feeling by appealing to such basic human needs as the desire for acceptance, for comfort, for fun, for safety, for admiration, and for love. Indirectly, an ad implies that the product is a good one, but the main emphasis is on how good its buyers will feel after they have purchased it.

This kind of appeal, designed primarily to persuade consumers with a subconscious need for a product to buy it, is called *stimulating primary demand*. This is normally the job of national, not retail, advertising. Nevertheless, the memory of a retailer's well-done ad may inspire people to buy a product at a particular store once repeated national advertising and the example of more innovative consumers has transformed their subconscious need into a conscious one. The store whose advertising works jointly with the manufacturer's ads to arouse need awareness among the people of its own marketing area will get more than its share of new business as people buy new or improved items they once ignored or thought they did not need.

No Need or Interest Some consumers may have no need for or interest in a product, at least at the moment. Immediate response from ads aimed at them may seem disappointing, and many merchants consider efforts to motivate them a pure waste. While it would surely be folly to concentrate a major share of a store's advertising appeals exclusively on this market segment, some effort to draw the attention of these people can be a wise investment. A young man with little interest in fine jewelry, perfumes, or women's accessories may fall in love and want to buy gifts for his girl. A single woman living in a small furnished apartment downtown may have little interest in home furnishings, but if she marries and sets up a home, her needs have drastically altered. The person with a desk job near home cares little about luggage or travel service; then the company shuffles job assignments and this person is required to do much traveling.

By proclaiming its variety of merchandise, its helpful sales staff, and its unsurpassed concern for customer satisfaction with service back-up and warranty performance, a store may realize a future return on its advertising that well rewards present efforts. In short, such consumers as these, with little or no existing motivation to buy, are the ones to be reached by the store's institutional ads or the institutional elements included in product ads.

Through no fault of the persons who prepare the ads, or of the stores that run them, an ad may be fighting an uphill battle against public dissatisfaction with a whole segment of a retail or service industry. Conversely, it may benefit from a relatively favorable public attitude toward the type of products or services being advertised. In 1973 the Conference Board surveyed 10,000 people to find out which industries and products they were satisfied or dissatisfied with. At that time, *positive* attitudes were most prevalent toward black-and-white television sets, eggs, and milk, while *negative* feelings ran strongest against movies, repairs on autos, appliances, and homes, and prescription drugs. Table 12–1 shows further details.

Another factor to take into account before preparing advertising is the *de-gree of knowledge* that the intended audience already posseses about both the product and the store. This determines in large measure the amount of detail that needs to be included in the ad, both for product descriptions and for "store copy" (the institutional elements of the ads). You can skip lightly over description of a well-known product or go into complex details for a new or substantially improved item. You can rely on a store's well-known logotype and signature or include much institutional information in the message to make noncustomers or new residents aware of the store's attractive features. Defining the target audience in terms of its degree of familiarity with product and store can be very difficult because no two people will ever be equally familiar with either one. Few single ads can be appealing to all persons in the audience. Consequently a store doing a great deal of advertising may find it profitable to prepare special ads directed at certain groups: (a) consumers presumed to know a great deal about both the product and the store (such as regular customers urged to buy staple merchandise); (b) those presumed to know much about the store but little about the item (such as regular customers being urged to buy a new, improved, or fashion-related article); (c) people presumed to have substantial knowledge of the product but who are unfamiliar with the store (such as newcomers to the community or customers of competing stores that one tries to woo away from them); and (d) those presumed to know little about either the product or the store. Figure 12–2 suggests one way of looking at those to whom ads are directed, in terms of their awareness of and attitude

Table 12–1

How 10,000 Consumers Appraise the Value Received for Money Spent on Goods and Services

Product or Service	Percent Distribution of Responses *	
	Good Buys	Poor Buys
Foods		
Beef	16	44
Poultry	30	21
Eggs	42	12
Fish	26	22
Milk	40	13
Fresh vegetables	24	29
Convenience foods	13	38
Restaurant meals	15	28
Apparel		
Men's suits	14	24
Women's dresses	10	40
Children's clothing	9	43
Shoes	11	39
Home Furnishings		
Upholstered furniture	11	30
Wood furniture	13	27
Major appliances	25	15
Small appliances	27	13
Carpets	20	13
Home Maintenance and Utilities		
Appliance repairs	5	57
Repairs on home	4	57
Telephone	25	26
Electricity	28	21
Moving expenses	4	40
Transportation		
New cars (domestic)	13	36
New cars (foreign)	22	23
Used cars	11	36
Auto repairs	6	59
Auto insurance	13	40
Local transportation	14	40
Air fares (domestic)	17	16
Air fares (foreign)	21	15
Medical and Personal Care		
Doctors' fees	13	40
Dentists' fees	12	43
Prescription drugs	9	48
Other drugs	8	35
Health insurance	14	40
Life insurance	19	17
Beauty shop services	14	28
Finance		
Credit charges	8	49
Bank service charges	19	26
Recreation		
Television (black and white)	40	8
Television (color)	29	18
Movies	6	64
Magazines	18	25
Children's toys and games	13	36

* Responses of "average buy," which were tabulated in the original survey, are not included here.

Source: National Family Opinion, Inc., 1973 survey (New York: The Conference Board).

toward the store and the product advertised, their ability to buy and need for the product, and their shopping or buying actions. The store's institutional and reminder ads can help at the first two stages, starting from the top of the model. The ads can do little about the next two stages, except perhaps to stir up consciousness of a hidden need. The ads can be a decisive factor in getting those who can afford and do want the product to visit the store and be predisposed to making a purchase—the final stages.

DETERMINING THE CREATIVE STRATEGY FOR AN AD

Assume that you have examined the thing you are to advertise from every angle, to find out what it really offers the consumer—whether it is a product, a service, or an intangible attribute of the store as a whole. Assume, too, that you have examined the needs and wants of various target groups that can be satisfied by the item, service, or store. Along the way you have matched product attributes with customer needs and desires, to find the *one most important product benefit* that will stimulate action both by those with a felt need for the product and those with a subconscious need for it that you can, with skill, fan

into an open awareness and buying action.

What is the one best way to present the product, to tell its story, to move the consumer to act?

Many advertising people rely on a system propounded long ago by a man named James Webb Young. Young said, in a nutshell, that you should learn all you can about the product and the customer, then *go to sleep on it.* Shelve thinking about the problem and let your subconscious go to work. Tomorrow, or the next day, inspiration will strike.

Some call this the *"aha"* system. You suddenly, in a flash, perhaps while driving, shaving, curling your hair, riding a bus, eating a meal, or riding an elevator, "see the light." A basic advertising theme keyed to a primary product benefit comes to mind. The details you can work out later.

But things do not always work out this way. There is not always time to wait for ideas to percolate up from the subconscious. Most ads have to be ground out the hard way, by thinking the problem through. One way to make things easier and to increase the chances that an ad or commercial will really work is to reduce the audience (in your mind) to one person. Out of the hundreds, thousands, or millions in the target audience pick out one real human

Figure 12–2 A Model of the Different Audiences of a Retail Ad, According to Their Proximity to the Buying Decision

* Possible secondary benefits to the store resulting from the influence of its advertising on these groups: (1) those who become customers in the future; (2) those who influence others favorably, recommending that they buy from the store.

** Persons who buy may include (1) repeat purchasers of the same product at the same store; (2) regular customers of the store who are new purchasers of the product; (3) enthusiasts for the product or its brand who search out the dealer; (4) new customers who have switched from competing stores; (5) new customers recently moved into the community; (6) new young customers just entering the market as shoppers.

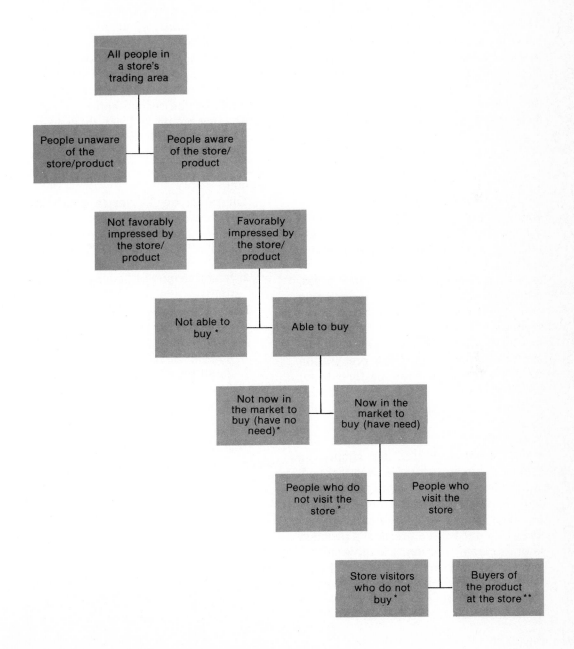

being—a friend, a neighbor, someone you met in the store, on the street, or at lunch—who, in your judgment, is fairly typical of the group you seek to motivate.

Some authorities recommend that the first rough draft of any ad be in the form of a personal letter to that one person, telling him or her, in plain language you would both feel comfortable with, what is so great about the product, the service, the store. This draft can then be converted into suitable copy for a print or broadcast ad. Another approach is to wait until you are alone in your office or at home, then tell the product's story out loud while a tape recorder takes it all in. Use everyday language and explain why your typical customer would benefit from buying what you are advertising. This latter method is particularly applicable to broadcast commercials. In some cases, the tape may need just a little doctoring by technical specialists to become the ad itself.

Those who have ever done any personal selling (an excellent preparation for advertising) can draw on their training (if any) in that field and on their experiences. Years ago, a man named John Kennedy (not the U.S. president, but an early-20th-century advertising professional) defined advertising simply as *salesmanship in print*. He was right. A successful ad is a sales call that works. Modern sales staffs are trained to look on their work as "problem-solving." They find out what a prospect's problem is and offer a solution. Effective advertising does the same thing. It shows people how their needs and desires can be satisfied by merchandise or services.

Ultimately, the preliminary work on an ad will be refined into a *copy platform* or an *ad strategy* based on the product's *one* best selling point, its *one* primary benefit for the kind of customer you want to motivate. That one product *feature* will be emphasized in the main headline and probably also in the illustration of a print ad, or in the opening words, first sound effect, initial "mood music," or beginning dramatic scene of a broadcast commercial. Further on, you may mention the second and third most potent sales points and use them to reinforce the urge to buy.

All that has been said here is applicable to the creation of ads for any medium.

On radio, on TV, or in print, the basic goals are the same:

1. to attract attention (favorable attention);

2. to arouse interest (in a benefit to the user);

3. to create a desire (for the product, to obtain that benefit);

4. to establish conviction (that the product, service, or store really will do all the ad promises, and perhaps more); and

5. to stir people to action (to buy the product now, not "someday").

Just how all this can be done, using words, pictures, type, sound, color, motion, and all the tools of the advertising trade in each of the retail media, is the subject of the next three chapters.

Questions for Discussion

1. Why is it so well worth the effort to produce first-class retail ads, even

though the majority of them seem to sell merchandise quite well *without* much creative effort? How can busy, overworked retail advertising people improve a store's profits by making a few of its ads of the best possible quality?

2. List at least eight guidelines for selecting the best items to advertise. Which do you think are most important? What sort of things should be emphasized in institutional ads?

3. Where does an advertising writer get information about a product to be advertised? Which are the best ways of getting facts, in your opinion?

4. What three levels of need may exist among readers, listeners, or viewers with respect to an advertised product? Which group offers, on the whole, the greatest potential for retail advertisers? Which group offers the greatest potential for greater results, when ads are more thoughtfully planned and better prepared?

Suggested Projects

1. Take an item of merchandise you recently purchased and reflect on what you have learned about it since you bought it and put it to use. You may still have a label, an instruction booklet, a package, or some other material that, in effect, tells what the manufacturer has to say about the product; and you may recall what the salesperson told you when you bought it, or even what the ad that first stimulated your interest in the product said. Now list all the good and bad features of the product and rank them in order of importance. Pick out what you think is the one best thing about it, the feature you would emphasize were you yourself to prepare an ad for the item. What are its second and third best selling points? Now, consider how someone else might rank the product's selling features, someone whose age, occupation, interests, or lifestyle is different from yours. Is the main selling point the same?

2. Collect at least one example of each of the themes for institutional ads suggested in the text from local papers. Which do you think is the best ad? In what other ways do you think the same or a similar theme could be handled?

3. Go window shopping in the nearest mall or retail district for about an hour. Examine the merchandise displayed in or outside the stores, and **decide which item** you yourself would most enjoy buying, right now, for your own use, assuming you have plenty of money to spend. Now sit down and write a letter to a friend—to a real person who has needs, tastes, and interests similar to your own and who you feel would enjoy owning the article you selected as much as you would. Start by describing the enthusiasm you have for the product, to arouse your friend's attention and interest. Then stir up your friend's desire to have the item, and convince him or her that it will perform well and be a pleasure to own. Conclude by urging your friend to go see the article in the store where you saw it displayed and to consider buying it. (Note: You may wish to go back to the store before writing the letter to examine the article more closely and ask the salespersons more about it.) Your letter is your first step to becoming an effective advertising copywriter.

Notes

1. "The Fifty Largest Retailing Companies," *Fortune* (July 1974), pp. 121–122; average of 46 figures in net income as percent of sales column.

2. Daniel Starch and Staff research (1964–1966). Reported by Newspaper Advertising Bureau (1971).

3. Johanna Rock, "Which Ad Attracted More Readers?" *Advertising Age* (September 3, 1973), p. 28.

4. *Psychographics: A Study of Personality, Life-Style and Consumption Patterns* (New York: Newspaper Advertising Bureau, 1974).

5. Ibid.

Preview

An effective retail newspaper ad depends for its punch on both its copy (the wording) and its design and graphic elements. This chapter will focus on the copy, which must (1) get attention, (2) arouse interest in the product and create a desire for it, (3) distinguish the offer from all others, (4) generate confidence and belief in the product, and (5) stir consumers to buy it now.

Copywriters inform and persuade via a factual (rational) approach, based essentially on the product itself, or an imaginative (emotional) appeal, based on the benefits or results of using the product. The best ads often combine both approaches, but one is usually dominant.

Headlines may contain news, product benefits, promises, or advice, or words that select an audience segment. They may arouse curiosity, make a suggestion, give a command, or simply name the product for sale.

The text, or body copy, can also do many things, among them, (1) state reasons for doing something (buying the product, patronizing the store), (2) make promises, (3) give testimonials, (4) publicize the results of performance tests, (5) tell a story, (6) report a real or imaginary dialogue, (7) solve a predicament, or (8) amuse.

Writing for ads should be clear and direct. Words should be short, sentences simple, punctuation frequent, and paragraphs brief. Copywriters must use the idiom of their audience, language it can readily understand. Special care is called for in writing sale or clearance copy (which is often neglected) and copy for classified ads (in which graphics cannot serve as a crutch). Before any copy is published, it should be checked for technical mistakes and substantive errors or omissions.

Learning Goals

Chapter 13 should point the way to organizing the contents of any printed advertisement in a logical sequence that leads the reader through various psychological stages, from attention and interest to belief and an urge to act. Students should be able to recognize the two types of copywriting and learn to express product benefits either way, or through a blend of the two. The extreme importance of headlines should be understood, and the several different kinds of headlines most used in retail advertising thoroughly examined. Readers should learn how to select a method of presenting body copy suitable to the needs of any given ad, and they should begin developing writing styles suited to their talents and the type of advertising they hope to do.

13

How to Write
Newspaper Copy

The retail store's internal advertising department is equipped, staffed, organized, and geared primarily to produce advertising for local newspapers. In larger stores, the advertising department includes *copywriters,* who write the copy (i.e., the words) for ads; *artists,* who create or procure the pictures, design the ads, and draw layouts to show how the ads will look and to guide compositors and printers in producing them; and *production* people to arrange for the actual manufacture of necessary materials. Very large stores will also have a research unit, a special-events unit, a planning unit, a broadcast coordinator to tie print and broadcast ads together, and liaison people to work with the display and merchandising staffs.

In the small store, all this will be done by one person, perhaps in a few hours each week, with help from various outside sources: the local newspaper's advertising staff, an agency that handles some (but rarely all) of the print ads, a special-service house that supplies art, or local freelance specialists. How well the job gets done determines, to a large degree, whether the store's ads will fall flat (like the 85 percent of modern advertising said to go unread), be among the 10 percent that are merely noticed, or ring bells as part of the slim 5 percent or so that really registers.[1]

Each member of a store's advertising staff has a role to play in increasing the impact of its ads. We will first discuss copywriters, who are at the heart of the whole business of retail advertising. Their challenging job is the creation and production of newspaper ads.

1 Ad Structure, Ad Strategy, and Copy Approaches

The word *copy* as used in the advertising business is a hangover from the early days of printing when hand-written advertising messages were given to a printer to "copy" in type for the printing press. The word has come now to have a broader meaning, to apply to the entire content of an advertisement; but we use it here in the limited sense of the words used in an ad.

THE STRUCTURE OF A RETAIL AD

Basically, the structure of all good ads stems from their fundamental *functions*: getting attention, arousing interest, creating desires, establishing a *unique selling proposition* to distinguish the offer from all others, creating conviction that the claims are true, and moving the reader to positive action. The following checklist is a good starting point for planning any ad. Not all the points apply to every ad, but all of them pack power when they fit the selling strategy.

Get attention—Make the headline work.
  —Be brief if you can.

- Mention the prospect and his or her interests.
- Promise benefits.
- Use news if it relates to the product or its uses.
- Provoke curiosity in a pertinent way.
- Mention the product. Tell how it saves money or time or labor or is easy to use.

Arouse interest and create desire

- Enlarge on the promise in the headline in the words that immediately follow. Clearly state the benefits to be obtained.
- Tell the story in the first paragraph.
- Emphasize one basic idea.
- Present the product's main selling points.
- Show that it is easy, economical, and agreeable to use.
- Imply that it will enhance the masculinity, femininity, popularity, or pres-

359

tige of the owner/user (if that is true).

- Use negative inferences. Point out the ills avoided by purchasing the product.

Distinguish the offer

- Contrast it favorably to other products.
- Point out its superior features.
- Refer to its exclusive features.
- Emphasize exceptional claims you can support.

Create conviction

- Present the main idea three times.
- Use bona fide testimonials, research results, and authorities' approvals.
- Give assurances and proof of the product's effectiveness.
- Guarantee it if you can.
- Be definite about its value.

Try for action

- Give the reader good reasons and excuses for buying.
- Make choosing easy by stressing just one model.
- Tell how, when, and where to get the product.
- Give prices and terms of sale. Make it easy to buy or order items.
- Consider a coupon or a direct offer for response by mail or phone.
- Sell *now* as the time to buy.

The basic copy for any ad has the following parts:

- the main headline
- a subhead (optional, often depending on the size of the ad)
- a lead-in paragraph (usually set in larger type than the text)
- the body copy, or the text of the ad (the "small print")
- the store's signature and necessary related information

AD STRATEGY AND THE COPY PLATFORM

A copywriter must first develop a *copy strategy* that takes into account the store's goals, the advertising tasks, current campaigns, the nature of the product or service to be promoted, and the audience to whom the ad is to be directed. It may be as simple, as direct, as narrow, and as specific as the motivation of construction workers to come to the shoe department to buy a new line of steel-reinforced workshoes. Or it may be as broad, as inclusive, and as complex as wooing and winning younger customers who are not yet aware that the store has been remodeled and redecorated to be in tune with the times, and that it has increased the stock of casual, youth-oriented merchandise in its apparel and home furnishings departments.

Once a copy strategy has been determined, a *copy platform* is constructed: a guide for organizing the material in the ad in such a way that it will achieve its objective. A *basic promise* will be declared or implied in the headline, the subhead, and the opening words of the text (and reinforced, hopefully, by related artwork). A fundamental decision as to the specific type of *audience* the ad seeks to reach will be reflected either openly in the words of the headlines and the ad or implicitly in its design and illustrations. The basic promise of the ad will be expressed in language and pictures that members of the selected target audience will relate to when the plan for the ad is actually *executed*. Finally, specific features or attributes of the product, the product line, or the store (when that, itself, is the "product") will be listed and convincingly amplified, to prove that the promise can be made good. The most important features (to the customer) are mentioned first; the less important ones are added further on to reinforce the product's appeal.

TWO COPY APPROACHES

The copywriter's approach will be based on one or the other of two basic types of appeals: a *factual* (rational and direct) appeal or an *emotional* (imaginative and indirect) appeal. Many of the best ads blend the two, but one usually predominates.

The *factual* school of copywriting developed in the late 19th century as a retailers' reaction against the bombast and rank emotionalism then prevalent in advertising. Most regular promotional ads simply describe merchandise in a factual, but hopefully interesting, way and illustrate it realistically. Such advertising does, after all, sell merchandise—hundreds of billions of dollars worth of it every year. It provides, in effect, a "catalog description" of products, and millions of people seek it out for its informational value, every day of the year.

Such copy appeals mostly to the mind; hence the term *rational* copy. It reasons with the customer and focuses on inherent qualities of the merchandise: durability, style, beauty, comfort, safety, economy, compactness, a moderate price. It deals directly with the product, whatever it may be, and is therefore called *direct* copy. Readers are presumed to know that a product with such desirable characteristics will, indeed, benefit them personally if they buy and use it. They are expected to make the connection between *product features* and *customer benefits* in their own minds. Pants that hold their crease offer the wearers benefits that they can easily visualize. Carburetors that will not flood with rapid changes in humidity make cars pleasanter to drive. Garments carefully sewn with strong thread are obviously less likely to come apart. Factual ads expect customers to understand these things without having them spelled out.

People who are conscious of a need for a product and who have already visualized in their minds how they would benefit from it are the primary target of factual copy. People in such a frame of mind tend to seek out information on the products they are interested in. Consider the following copy:

> BOYS' SLACKS AND JEANS
> IN RUGGED NO-IRON BLENDS
> A Good Buy at $5
> We bought these for four good reasons: They're long-wearing, easy to take care of, they look great, and they're just $5. Choose from a big group, including casual slacks in fancy patterns, blue jeans, faded denims, and solid-color twills—cuffed and uncuffed models.

It gives people the facts—useful facts if they are in the market for slacks.

The same product can be advertised using factual or emotional copy. Take two versions of an ad for trash cans, for example:

**beauty
more than surface deep,
beauty in function.
At Lazarus, naturally.**

LAZARUS

the naturals
(clear wood)

It's the clean appeal of pure wood color and grain, finished with a clear rich, patina. It's beauty with purpose. The "naturals" look is solidly functional. For example, economize space as you turn an idle wall into a panorama of nestled artistic units as in the arrangement we've shown. Your room gains a refreshed light, airy, openness as you display books, artifacts and stereo components. Small rooms seem spacious. Large rooms gain unity. Brisk cubic tables or tables with a crisp flash of chrome accent the look. Available by custom order. Allow six to eight weeks for delivery, (it's worth the wait). Shown: top three middle units, each $155; bottom three units, each $175; end top units, each $110; end bottom units, each $135. Chromed: end table, $117; dining table, $269. These and more "naturals" furniture in Furniture D606, Downtown Fourth Floor; and Home Store East.

For more Lazarus shopping news, see pages 6, 7 and 34

DURABLE, GALVANIZED
TRASH CANS $12.95

Big, 45-gal. heavy-gauge steel cans. Tight-fitting covers, rustproof, hard to bend or dent. Guaranteed leakproof for 2 yrs. Made to our own specifications. $12.95 ea., $24.00 a pair; cart to fit 2 cans, $8.00. We deliver locally.

This is a perfectly adequate factual ad. However, a clever copywriter might sell more cans by being more precise about the benefits of owning the cans:

MAKE YOURS THE TIDIEST
HOME ON THE BLOCK
with Jones's special Trash Cans—
just $12.95

No more messy leaks on your garage floor. Heavy-gauge steel and tight-fitting lid discourages dogs and rodents. Guaranteed rustproof for 2 yrs; saves you money in the long run. Huge 45-gal. capacity allows for large families and "overload" weeks without smelly overflow. Hard for the roughest collection man to dent or bend. Ordered to our own specifications, especially for big suburban homes. Only $12.95. Why not buy 2 for $24.00? Handy tote-cart fits 2 cans, saves back-breaking labor, only $8.00. Delivered free in county.

Unlike the ad with product-centered, purely *factual* copy, this version focuses on *indirect* product values. It suggests specific benefits of using the trash cans. It stimulates the imagination of the readers, making them see their own cleaner garages, the frustrated dogs and rats, the reduction in work for the family that owns this product.

Emotional copy, in its purest form, focuses almost exclusively on how the owner or user will enjoy the product, to the near-exclusion of information on its tangible attributes. It stimulates people to see themselves using the product, and its subordinates direct exposition of the tangible merits of the item to a description of user benefits. Only *indirectly* does it imply that the product must be a good one (since otherwise it would not do all that it does).

If it is overdone, and if it makes exaggerated claims for a product, this type of advertising can drive people away—especially the more sophisticated consumers whom retailers can expect today. It can also get a store in trouble with the law if the claims made are proven false. However, statements made in ads need not always be literally true. Emotional copy takes "poetic license"; it employs figures of speech, similes, analogies. It is part fiction, and frankly so. A wedding gown is described as the "Dress Made of a Thousand Dreams," a garden tractor is called a "Weekend Happiness Machine," a toy department

Figure 13–1 Examples of Factual Retail Copy

In this ad from the Lazarus department store, the picture dominates; the headline, not too prominent, is the simple, provocative declaration, "the naturals." The subheadline and the copy block in the lower corner of the ad are packed with informative words—facts about the advertised product that repeatedly suggest its usefulness to the owner. The word *beauty* is used several times, and the copy is properly "you"-centered, referring to *"your* room" and suggesting that *"you* turn an idle wall into ... artistic units." The copy constantly mentions customer benefits, yet it is direct, rational, and factual in its approach. Toward the end come specific details like price, availability, delivery time, and the products' location within this large store.

Source: By courtesy of Lazarus of Columbus, Ohio.

is billed as "Santa's Workshop." This is fantasy, of course—but it sells merchandise, often much better than *factual* copy.

It is easy, and true, to proclaim that a store has "Summer Dresses in Cool Colors." But how much better the same idea comes through when you say "Come see our Frosty Lime Fizzes—Dashed with a Twist of Lemon!"

Famous-Barr of St. Louis sold nighties with this ad:

ROMANTICALLY INCLINED NIGHT SHIRTS

Borrow the tender look of frills and ruffles from days gone by for sweet dreams now. Famous updates the night time shirting role by shortening, shaping and pairing these pretties with wisps of matching bikinis. What a lovely finale to the drama of the day! [Thus far, the ad is virtually pure emotional copy; but as it proceeds, it slips deftly into factual information on the product.] Billowly pleated sleeves on Formfit Rogers' nylon Romeo shirt in blush pink or blue; small, medium, large $13.... Call 421–4500 or mail order. Famous-Barr Lingerie—all stores.

This is good retail advertising, and it *combines* the two schools of copywriting (factual and emotional) as do so many of the great ads of today.

Here is another example of an emotional, indirect, imaginative appeal:

CALLING ALL LAZY PEOPLE

No more getting out of the car in bad weather to open your garage door. No more fussing with seat belts. No more turning on your lights in your garage at night. No more heavy lifting for the woman in your life. For a limited time only we are offering a Nutone Door Operator for $182.

Institutional ads, like those often used to open a major selling season, can repeat the same old clichés—"Winter's Wonderland Opens Friday at Zilch's Toy Department"; "Discover a Holiday Shopper's Paradise at our Downtown Store." But consider this choice example of institutional, season-opening copy from a full-page ad in a Pittsburgh paper containing chiefly white space and a pale green picture of a forlorn pine tree:

THE BALLAD OF PENELOPE
Out in evergreenery,
In cedar and scotch pinery
Stands, pining, poor Penelope
December snows enveloping
Her lonely dreams of finery
She longs for light and candy canes
And ornaments and icicles
And presents laid in panoply
From turtlenecks to tricycles

Figure 13–2 Examples of Emotional Retail Copy

Created by a noted retail-oriented ad agency for Osmun's, a group of menswear stores, this ad deals with a special-price promotion. Perhaps 99 percent of ads for price-off promotions turn out to be dull—purely factual in nature. But this one uses a refreshingly different, imaginative approach that compares the price reduction with an eagle swooping low. Because the name brand of these suits is Eagle, this is a most appropriate way to combine emotional imagery with a factual attribute of the advertised product. Note that the copy block, located at the top of the ad, continues the imagery of birds, with words like "swoop" and "peacock."

Source: By courtesy of Osmun's of Pontiac, Michigan, and its agency, Jaffe, Stone and August, of Southfield, Michigan.

In one fell swoop a whole flock of famous-name Eagle suits go down at a $55.10 saving. Each one a magnificent specimen in imported worsteds and wools with scalloped flap pockets and smart two-button styling.

They're available in a wide selection of new shades. In regular sizes 37-46, short sizes 38-44 and long sizes 40-48. Alterations are free.

So come over to Osmun's. In your new Eagle suit, you'll be proud as a peacock.

Today and tomorrow, the eagles fly low.

Eagle suits, regularly $155 really low at $99.90.

Osmun's
Fashion for men and young men.

OPEN SUNDAY, NOON TO 5 P.M. IN THE TEL-TWELVE MALL.
Open evenings 'til 9 in the Tel-Twelve Mall (Telegraph and 12 Mile in Southfield), Tech Plaza Center (12 Mile and Van Dyke in Warren) and Tel-Huron Center (Telegraph and Huron in Pontiac). Our downtown Pontiac store is open daily 'til 5:30 P.M. You can charge what you want with your Osmun's Charge, Bank Americard or Master Chargecard.

Sprucelike, she lingers silently
Long gone is Cousin Juniper,
Who went to the distillery,
And Uncle Jack in Omaha—
A pole for some Utility;
They left, bereft, Penelope
And Father's gone; a table leg,
And Brother? Off to tournaments
(a hocky stick in Winnipeg)
Now only Christmas ornaments
Can comfort poor Penelope
Will joy reclaim Penelope?
Will fate reverse its hellish bent?
Will she become your Christmas tree?
Will Horne's supply embellishment
To furbish her with finery?
Why, absolutely! Otherwise,
The ad would not be half this size
                           Joseph Horne Co.

This is great copywriting, with a very effective emotional appeal and a uniqueness that makes it stand out above other ads.

Imaginative copy means simply that copywriters don't sell cars; they sell transportation, economy, safety, glamour, or style. They don't sell a house; they sell a home, comfort, prestige, and security. They rarely sell clothes; instead they sell "a look." They seldom sell shoes; but they sell feet that feel warm in winter and free in summer. They don't sell books; they sell pleasant hours spent reading, facts at one's fingertips, a well-stocked mind. They don't sell electric drills; they sell holes that are perfectly round. They don't sell perfume; they sell romantic nights.

In composing copy, the copywriter should carefully consider which of the approaches—factual or emotional—will best suit the ad's purpose. Wise, effective use of either approach will be a very important factor in the ad's success.

2 Headlines

No single part of a retail ad is more important than the headline, and where there is no picture, the headline must do even more. Its primary function is to *gain attention for the ad*. If it is any good at all, however, it states or implies a product *benefit*. Often, too, it identifies the kind of audience the ad is aimed at. Every good headline should contain a verb, or an implied verb; and active verbs far outperform passive ones. A good headline *gets the reader involved*. And the more specific it is, the better. The headline, "Everyone Is Enjoying Smith's New Restaurant" will not sell. "Come, Enjoy Smith's Air-Cooled Luxury" will do much better.

The main headline for any ad may grow out of the copy, as it does in the newsrooms, where editors, not reporters, write headlines based on the fact-crammed first paragraph of a story. A head may also be suggested by an illustration, and its length or size dictated in large part by the overall design of the whole ad. For these reasons, planning a good ad involves a preliminary conference between copywriter and artist when a separate art unit exists. The two work together on the strategy and copy platform and also coordinate headlines and other copy elements with pictures and layout. Sometimes the headline is decided upon first, before anything else in either copy or art; sometimes not.

Some experts say that from 40 to 70 percent of the effectiveness of an ad depends on the headline. If it does not get the reader's attention, the rest of the ad will never be read. If it attracts the wrong kind of readers, those who do not need or cannot afford the product rather than those who do need it and can afford it, the ad will just not work. It should, normally, tell people what the ad is all about, not pose riddles or create mysteries; people are too busy to fool around with trick headlines or to wade through three paragraphs to find out what a product or service will do for them.

The ideal length of a headline is often defined by "experts" as x number of words, and no more. Like Abraham Lincoln's long legs, however, if heads serve the purpose for which they were made, they are just the right length. A headline should say enough to attract the attention of the intended readers and make them want to read the rest of the ad. In some cases one word may be enough, or five. There have been very successful ads with heads of 15 or even 20 words.

A headline for a half-page ad by a large and growing Midwest apparel chain, obviously slanted at a particular target market, used 22 words:

Doll on your Snood and Your Carmen Mirandas and your Kicky MISS SKEF-FINGTON Dress & Beat your Daddy Eight to the Bar.

One of the most famous heads in all advertising history had 18 words:

At sixty miles an hour the loudest noise in this new Rolls Royce comes from the electric clock.

Other classic heads (also, incidentally, advertising foreign-built cars) have been very short indeed:

Think Small

Nobody's Perfect (coupled with a picture of a car with a flat tire)

(Both of these were Volkswagen ads, of course.)

Copywriters have many options as to the kinds of headlines they can use. The most common types are described briefly below.

NEWS HEADLINES

"Shrinks Gain Prominence in the Field of Fashion." "Suddenly, the Knit Pullon Has Real Pazzazz!" These heads are particularly appropriate in the newspaper, which people read to keep up to date on world and local events.

SELECTIVE HEADLINES

"Haggar Mustang Wide Tracks— The Slacks for the Untamed Young Man." "If you know a graduate, we know a perfect personal care gift." In this era of fragmented markets and targeted ads, the headlines directed at particular groups have become more important than ever.

BENEFIT HEADLINES

"Lowest-Priced Dependable Mower on the Market." "Mann's Iron Pants Are Tougher Than Kids." Research indicates that heads that merely "boast" about a product are only two-thirds as effective as those that stress customer benefits.

17 PEOPLE IN MILWAUKEE ARE REALLY GOING TO GET A BARGAIN!

Now that you're reexamining your clothing dollar, shouldn't you also reexamine your clothing store?

PROMISE HEADLINES

"In by 9, Out by 12 at Phillips Cleaners." "Summer Dreams Come True in Miss Elaine's Sleeping Beauties." The copy that follows this type of head *must* ring true; it must *offer proof* that the promise will be fulfilled.

"HOW TO . . ." OR ADVICE HEADLINES

"How to Get More Interest on Your Savings." "Why Doctors Advise Daily Exercise to Keep Fit." These heads too contain a kind of promise, and the ad must provide a real reward in the form of useful information and guidance in making a purchase for the reader who takes the trouble to read the fine print. Such ads are very much in tune with the current stress on intelligent shopping.

CURIOSITY—QUESTION—CHALLENGE HEADLINES

"Why Don't You Ask?" "Plain Keds Are Dead!" These heads are tools of the seasoned professional and are *not* rec-

ommended for beginners. They usually violate the basic rule that a headline should reveal what an ad is about. Skillfully written, this type of head can pique the imagination, making readers curious enough to read on to find out what the message is. If they are disappointed when they read on, however, watch out! You have made an enemy for the store. And if the head does not make people want to read the message, the ad will flop.

Rhetorical questions, a variation of this type of head, are safer: "Haven't You Done Without a Toro Long Enough?" "Why Not Come in TODAY and Let Our Motor Analyzer Check Your Car's Engine?" If the typical reader's reaction is an automatic yes, fine; but if this kind of head is clumsily handled, it, too, can backfire.

IMPERATIVE OR "COMMAND" HEADLINES

"Come Sew Up Spring at Macy's." "Enjoy Our New Color TV TONIGHT." These heads get readers involved be-

Figure 13–3 Retail Headlines
An example of a *label* headline, which is the easiest and quickest type to write, is shown at top left. These headlines serve a purpose, merely to identify the advertised product or idea, and when coupled with a related picture and associated with a well-known store's name, they can do well. Special selection of an "old-fashioned" typeface helps create an image that relates this headline well to the product.

At the opposite extreme among retail headlines are the *curiosity* or *challenge* and *question* headlines that seek to stimulate interest and tempt the reader to go into the ad and find out what it is all about. Those shown at bottom left are typical. The first one, by itself, fails to explain what product is involved, and the casual reader could miss the point entirely. In fact, this one was in an all-type ad, without pictures to help explain. But the signature was that of an automobile dealer familiar to Milwaukeeans, and that served to imply what the product was. Those sufficiently motivated to read the text of the ad found out there were 17 slightly used "company cars" available at much-reduced prices. The second such headline made it clear it was talking about a clothing store, as did a small illustration at the bottom of the ad. This was a provocative headline approach for an institutional ad; it ran the risk of being rejected by the busy reader because of its great length. But the advertiser probably sought to motivate only a few, to challenge those with inherent interest to read the meat of the message.

cause they urge them to act; they preview the final element in any good ad, the "call to action" at the bottom of the text. Tactfully and subtly written, they can be very good indeed, and far less experience and skill are required to make them work than to handle the more risky "challenge" heads successfully. Generally, the commands should focus on the customer ("Do yourself a favor . . .") and not on the store ("Buy from us . . . You can't go wrong.")

LABEL HEADLINES

"Vibrant Velours." "The Norell Classic Lipstick." These are the weakest heads of all, though as subheads for sections of a large omnibus ad they are sometimes justified. Unfortunately, a high proportion of retail advertisements still contain nothing more creative in the way of headlines. Coupled with an adequate picture, and when used for items for which there is already a demand, they still sell merchandise. But how much *more* might be sold by a more imaginative approach, one can only guess.

Some headlines make a play on words. When deftly handled, they are very good; but when they strike out, they really strike out. Some heads contain humor, also very difficult for beginners to handle. Others relate cleverly to the advertised merchandise— for example:

"For Power-Hungry Men" (An ad for power tools that has a touch of humor, a double meaning, and a selected audience.)

"Barney's Presents New York's First Exterior Decorators" (An ad for famous clothing store that "decorates" the "exterior" of the men who are outfitted there.)

"Ralph Nader, Come See Us!" (An institutional ad telling the public about a furniture store that insists on telling the strict truth in all its ads; has liberal warranty, repair, exchange, and refund policies; and never engages in hanky-panky about alleged "cut" prices. Tied to a name often in the news, it is a form of "challenge" head that arouses curiosity.)

"One Thing We'll Say About Our Bank Robber: He Sure Picked a Good Bank!" (An ad for a bank in a small midwestern town that had been robbed the day before. It capitalizes on the recent news and uses tongue-in-cheek humor.]

Subheads   Set in smaller type than the main head, subheadlines may appear directly under it or be scattered throughout a large ad to relieve the typographical monotony, identify different types of merchandise, or underscore secondary product benefits not mentioned in the main headline.

3 Body Copy

The advertising battle is half won if a good headline stops readers and arouses their interest. But an ad must also *capitalize* on the attention it gains. Dull, unconvincing, irrelevant, difficult, or tasteless body copy can throw away the sales opportunity a good headline (or an attention-getting picture) has created. Incomplete, unenthusiastic, prosaic, or timid copy *may* be read; it may even give its readers some useful information—but it will not sell merchandise. Good copy must follow through on what the headline promises, cite chapter and verse (blending both rational and emotional appeals) to convince readers that they will, indeed, benefit in a particular way by buying the product. The text should also describe other benefits, if the ad is large enough, to increase the readers' conviction that they need the item, and conclude with a compelling reason to buy now (not tomorrow or next week).

How does a copywriter do this?

There are number of different ways to develop the theme of the ad stated in the main headline.

The *"lead-in" paragraph* (in a large ad) connects the headline with the text, makes the transfer from big type to little type, and either amplifies the benefit-centered main headline or describes a secondary product benefit. Good copywriters shift back and forth smoothly between painting word pictures that make readers feel the satisfaction, fun, safety, or esteem the product will bring them (the emotional approach) and describing the actual product features—its design, construction, materials, and so on—that make it so satisfying to own and use (the rational approach).

Various types of copy are associated with each approach.

WRITING FACTUAL COPY

Rational, factual, direct appeals generally contain a great deal of product information, nearly always including (but not necessarily emphasizing) price, and they can be presented in an attrac-tive manner that goes far beyond the stark catalog listing technique. Among the ways most often used by retail advertisers to present factual copy are those named, briefly explained, and demonstrated in the following paragraphs.

Descriptive or Explanatory This copy is used in the bulk of retail promotional ads. Product benefits predominate in this simple, straightforward, lay-it-on-the-line method. But a little effort can make the ad interesting, well written, and appealing, with an occasional word or phrase borrowed from the imaginative branch of copywriting.

ZIPPER TOOL CASE. Excellent for glove compartment. Case is genuine cowhide with suede lining. Precision tools made in Germany. 13.50.

[Following headline, "Pucker Pow!"] Our favorite shirtmakers turn tailored classics into sexy stretchies. Which cleave like crazy, do sensational things for even the skimpiest curves. Most are of stretch nylon or acetate, all puckered up in bubble or lacy finishes. Choose turtlenecks, polos, zip-fronts, mockturtles, tie-backs, florals, geometrics, stripes, solids. You wear them in or over skirts, pants, hotpants, for day or evening. By Alice Stuart, Lady Manhattan, Weber, La Matthews, Fanfare and others. Sizes S, M, L. $10 to $17. Declare yourself for pucker pow now! First, Third, all nine stores.

Reason Why This logical copy tells the readers exactly why they should buy a product or shop at a store, and perhaps how an item is best used, and why.

[Following headline, "A Whole Flock of Reasons Why!"] ★ Zayre's

Shopper's City is best for back-to-school shoppers. Zayre Shopper's City *has* what you want! You get super selection because we're a complete discount department store...over 40 departments and all under one roof, with convenient, free parking outside. You'll find every back-to-school need in our A to Z(ayre) selection. ★ Zayre Shopper's City *guarantees* it! At Zayre Shopper's City you'll find hundreds of top-quality, famous-name brands, plus fine imports. Compare our quality and you'll truly appreciate Zayre Shopper's City. *And* you must be satisfied with every purchase or we'll cheerfully refund your money. ★ You *save more* at Zayre Shopper's City! Why? Because your local Zayre Shopper's City stores are **part of a** 200-store buying group. This vast group of purchasing power means better buys for us, and for you. Come take advantage of Zayre-power!

Promise If the headline or the first part of an ad makes a promise, the body copy must back it up by giving the facts that enable the retailer to make that promise.

[Preceded by headline, "Accentuette Makes Fitting a Bathing Suit As Easy As Fitting a Bra and Panty."] How? It's easy! You buy tops and bottoms separately. So you can mix-up the sizes and styles to suit you perfectly. Plus, wait till you see our sensational prints ...all California's best. Push-up bra, 16.00. Fuller cup style, 15.00. Then add the hipster. It converts to a bikini. Sizes S, M, L, 10.50. And a mini coverup, S, M, L, 27.00.

Testimonial (*implied or actual*) This kind of copy can be very convincing, especially if the person quoted is a local personality.

[Following headline, "Why women like going to Don Jacobs Buick."] It's a great place for a single woman to come because the mechanics are honest and they're friendly. You can bring your car in here and you know that they're going to service it and not play a bunch of games on you. I just keep going back because they're friendly people. This is my fourth and our family's sixteenth or seventeenth Buick from Don Jacobs.—Bonnie Buege, Waukesha.

Performance Tests and Construction Methods and Materials This kind of copy is more common in national ads than in retail ones, but any retailer can easily convert manufacturers' ads for local use. Large retailers with house brands made to their specifications and those with product-testing facilities can emphasize such copy. So can other stores, by quoting manufacturers', trade associations', or government agencies' test reports on brand-name items.

[Beneath the headline, "Our Heritage Is Quality."] Tests determine quality: tests of science, tests of use. Long before sportsmen put their Rolex timepieces to tests of use, we at Rolex tortuously check the accuracy and reliability of each Rolex Chronometer for **15 days and 15 nights** at an official Swiss **institute** for Chronometer tests.

WRITING EMOTIONAL COPY

Imaginative, emotional, indirect appeals are most likely to focus on the users' satisfactions derived from the product and to give only the minimum of actual information about it. Warm, personal terms predominate in these methods of copywriting. The following examples, together with the name and a brief description of each, suggest the sharp contrast of such appeals with the factual methods just discussed.

Telling Stories This kind of copy can include references to classic literature and to history; it can be in the form of a fable or fantasy, or it can come from the mouths of fictitious characters or real people.

[With a headline, "A Bedtime Story."] Once upon a time, there were a King & Queen who wished for a throne that would turn-into-a-bed. They proclaimed throughout the land how long they had searched for the perfect throne on which they could both sit and sleep, both reign and dream. Near-by, in Robisonland lived a sofa named Simmons (on sale!). A royal hide-a-bed indeed! I, Simmons, was plaid and stain-resistant with separate reversible cushions and strong steel frame. They bought me and I became the prize of the palace. And King, Queen and hand-some, versatile Simmons lived happily, happily, happily, ever after.

Dialogue This sort of copy, phrased as if two people were talking, seems more human and believable than other kinds of copy. To be effective, however, it must be cleverly done, ring true, and sound the way real people really talk.

[The first in a group of eight women pictured in a department store's ad for its new sewing center speaks.] All I've got to say is that a sewing center just isn't a sewing center unless it has the basic knits . . . all the knits . . . in stock at all times. Knits are it! [Then the store, talking through its ad

copy, responds . . .] How right you are. Knits play a very important role in our Sewing Center. That's why you'll find knits by Wm. Heller for all seasons in stock at all times. Finessa polyester/wool. Ponteroma virgin wool. Carmelle acrylic doubleknits. Savoy polyester crepe knits. All the knits! [Then an-other woman tells of her needs . . .] With three young school children to dress, you can bet I've already started on their back-to-school wardrobes! Can I find the fabrics I need . . . even at this early date? [The store reassures . . .] Clever little early bird! You'll be happy to hear we've already stocked our Ernest Einiger fall wools and woolens. Plus, from Concord Fabrics, polyester/cotton kettlecloth, cotton Chatel prints, acrylic polyester knits . . . and more . . . all perfect for back-to-school dresses, skirts and jackets!

Predicament When copy solves a problem or resolves a predicament, the copywriter has touched the very essence of effectively motivating consumers. Clever writers can employ this technique for either institutional or item-selling ads. Both products and services can solve problems for those who use them.

[Following headline, "Do You Have a Fitting Problem?"] Well, no one's per-fect. But if your physique is something less ideal than that of a Greek god, come to Hughes & Hatcher. We've got a magic nondiet formula for shaping you up, whatever shape you're in. It's called tailoring . . . and all it requires is for you to stand still for a moment. It begins with highly trained fitters who know exactly what to do to make you look slimmer if you're stout, taller if you're short, smoother if you're bumpy, and evened-up if you're lopsided.

Humor If it is really funny, humorous copy can be terrific. But it is not for the amateur or the beginner. Before you submit funny copy, make sure someone else thinks it is funny.

ONE OF OUR BANK GUARDS TAKES MONEY FROM HIS WIFE'S PURSE—We're people, too.

Cox's department store in Pennsylvania, which found remodeling a pretty messy proposition, demonstrated very well that ads do not all have to be serious.

The plumbers are plastered. The plasterers are hammered. The carpenters are all lit up. The electricians are spackled. The painters are swinging from the pipes. And when you come to see what they've done to Cox's, you'll probably do what Bob Cox did when he saw the bill: You'll pop your cork.

You can well imagine how the public must have enjoyed this full-page newspaper ad, dominated by a near life-sized picture of a bottle of champagne in a bucket of ice.

CHOOSING WORDS AND A WRITING STYLE

How you write advertising depends on the audience your ad seeks to motivate. Write in their language, not yours. Nothing is gained if your ads are essentially a demonstration of your massive vocabulary or of the trade jargon (which the customer will probably not understand) you have picked up.

A story is told about a plumber who poured a gallon of hydrochloric acid down a customer's stopped-up drain. Shortly after, the customer reported that the basement was full of water; and, upon investigation, the bewildered plumber noted that the drain pipe was no longer there. He wrote to the chemical company that had supplied the hydrochloric acid and asked for an explanation. The reply, from a college-educated chemical engineer, was as follows:

In reply to yours of the 15th instant, this is to advise that hydrochloric acid, while often effective as a decongestant agent in certain cases of waste-disposal systems stoppages, is, nonetheless, potentially inimical to the permanence of metallic substances.

The plumber (and his wife) read the letter over several times, shaking their heads in wonderment, then wrote a second time to the chemical works, pleading, "But *what happened* to the pipe?"

The second reply from the company was written by the office boy, a bright fellow, but one who had dropped out of school after the ninth grade. He was forced to reply because his boss, the engineer, was on vacation. His letter was short and to the point:

That stuff eats the hell out of pipes.

Needless to say, the plumber got the message.

Write *for* your audience, remembering always that the purpose of copy is to *communicate*, quickly, accurately, and painlessly. Use short, familiar words and uncomplicated sentences. And be specific. General words will not call up mental images of the product or the benefits it provides. Say "cherry red," "daffodil yellow," or "midnight blue," not "variety of colors in stock." Say "walnut" not "wood"; "cotton," not "washable fabric"; "fits in your pocket," not "small." Write "Come in, you skinnies and you talls, you shorts and you plumps," not "suits to fit all sizes, heights, and weights."

Construct active sentences that involve the reader, not bland passive statements, and try to include words with double meanings that keep people thinking about the subject: "Reflect on our door mirror savings" is better than "Save on door mirrors." "See the light; save on four styles of lamps" is better than "Prices reduced on four styles of lamps." You can make reading advertising fun, rather than a bore, with phrases like "See-worthy nauticals" (swimsuits); "The McGregor anti-freeze" (winter jackets); "Italian dressing" (pant suits imported from Italy); and "Your pet turtleneck" (sweaters).

Small words move big items. They read fast and make their point every time. And one very short three-letter word should be used often: YOU.

Advertising writing can be clear, clean-cut, and expressive in many different idioms, each designed to suit a particular audience. Compare and contrast the vocabulary, the style, and the image-creation of these two bits of copy —each so obviously directed at different target readers:

MACY'S FOR TEAWARE

Our cup runneth over with more tea-and-coffee sets than ever Santa took a shine to. From tea services with sterling character to silver plate with polished manners, stainless steel, the prettiest of pewters. From tea-for-two temptations to splend'rous silver services lavished with fluting, trays with chasing, ingratiating styles from the opulent to the optimum in sleek contemporary taste. . . .

THE DON'T–BLOW–ALL–YOUR–BREAD–ON–CLOTHES SALE

There's a way to get the up-tight look at hand-me-down prices. There's a way of wearing an Australian Lamb's Wool sweater without looking like a mother kangaroo. There's the cable-front, $12.99. And the plain V-neck, $11.99. There's a way of wearing a shirt, and having a half inch show at the collar and a half inch show at the sleeve without it being custom made. . . . There's a way of wearing rugged pants without looking like you just came off the farm. . . . There's a way of wearing a nylon football jacket without having your name plastered across the back, to show who owns it. . . . AT DANBY'S

Both are very good ads. Both are appropriately worded for their intended audiences. Both use words that create mental images.

"Puffery," bombast, bragging, and exaggeration may have moved merchandise in Grandad's day. People today, however, are turned off by overdone claims; they automatically assume that they are false. The consumerist movement and government policing of misleading advertising have had plenty of publicity and have helped to educate shoppers. In advertising, *an overproven understatement is vastly more compelling that an underproven overstatement.* Candor, realism, simplicity, modesty are keywords now. And research has verified that a *two-sided approach* (admitting what is bad about a product as well as proclaiming what is good about it) finds the greatest favor among the better-educated, most affluent segments of the population who control the most disposable income.

GETTING PEOPLE TO BUY

All retail ads should end with words that urge the reader to buy, just as personal sales calls must lead up to "asking for the order." The final words of the copy, often a separate paragraph, may remind the readers that a sale ends Saturday (and they had better hurry to the store since prices will go back up on Monday). They may point out that the stock of merchandise is limited and that inflation is pushing up list prices all the time. Or they may remind readers that they can enjoy that new color TV set *tonight,* use that new power mower on their lawn *this* Saturday, wear that lovely new dress at *this week's* party, or start saving gas on *tomorrow's* driving with an engine tune-up today.

At the end of the ad is the *store copy,* commonly part of the store's *signature.* This copy details how easy it is to shop at the store doing the advertising, what credit cards are accepted, when the store is open, if telephone and mail orders are accepted, if delivery service is available, what parking facilities the store has, whether the merchandise is available in branch stores, and so on.

Though these things may seem trivial, they increase the probability of a quick and definite response to the ad, because such things are important to the customer. They *remove barriers* to buying action and get the reader thinking positively at the end of the ad, where it counts so much. An ad should always include a store's address and telephone numbers, even if they are well known. Almost every shopping area has a significant number of newcomers and transients who are not familiar with local stores. Very large stores should also specify in what part of the store the advertised items are found—"Men's Store, State Street Side" or "Basement Lingerie only." Mail orders can be stimulated by including in the ad a coupon that serves as an order form.

Attending to all these bottom-of-the-ad details is part of the copywriter's job for each ad prepared. Because they are so often placed with or near the signature logotype and because they appear in every ad, there is a dangerous tendency simply to repeat the previous form of this information by the clip-and-paste method or by marking the copy sheet "pick up sig[nature]." When hurried copywriters do this, they may well see printed in the paper such errors as "Open till 9 tonight" on days when the stores closes at 6, or "Air conditioned for your summer shopping comfort" after the fall weather has brought freezing temperatures.

4 Special Problems in Copywriting

The foregoing section dealt with the broad problems of writing copy for all kinds of ads. Certain special problems arise, however, and certain specific types of ads require a particular kind of treatment. We shall take a look at some of the most common of these special situations here.

OMNIBUS AND MULTI–ITEM ADS

A large and diversified store will almost always do much of its advertising through *omnibus* ads, in which two or more departments are represented. Other ads, both for department stores and larger specialty shops, may promote products sold in one department, merchandise division, or "shop," but there will be a great number of items mentioned. In both cases, the store's institutional copy pertains to the store or department as a whole, and a central theme, under an "umbrella" headline, attracts the attention of the desired readers and sets the tone for each item that follows.

The copywriter then works on each item as if it were the only item in the ad, but wherever possible relates it to the overall theme. Copy can strengthen the ad as a whole when it cross-references items that can be used together, mentioning how the one serves to enhance the benefit the customer gets by buying the other (as in the case of co-ordinated wardrobes in apparel advertising). The overall tone, word choice, and style of writing should be the same for all items in order to maintain the unity of the ad and preserve the image of the store. Particular attention must be paid to this matter when the copywriter converts a manufacturer's national ad copy or suggested retail copy to the store's use; it must be made to sound, always, like the store is talking, and not the manufacturer. The copywriter working against a tight schedule should first concentrate effort on the one feature item that sets the pace; the more abbreviated copy for the rest will tend to fall into place.

FASHION COPY

Since the illustration is relatively more important in fashion ads than in any other kind, the copy must begin where the dramatic art leaves off. This does not mean that the copywriter's job is easy. Fashion copy is by far the hardest to write; not everyone can do it. The fashion copywriter must thoroughly know the subject, understand the latest trends in styles, and be acutely aware of the mood of the moment. Moreover, the fashion copywriter must also know, personally, how it *feels* to wear or use the product. Because fashion is capricious, ephemeral, and illusive, a comprehensive knowledge of fashion cycles and of the consumers' whims and enthusiasms is even more important than writing ability. While selling a mood and the feel of fashion is paramount, there is more to writing these ads. People also want facts, and the writer must mix fanciful details with practical information.

High fashion, typical of exclusive specialty shops, aims to sell a fashion concept to people who *set* the pace, and the individual ad is designed to motivate them to accept a style rather than to buy a specific item the store has in stock. Volume fashion, on the other hand, is the domain of department stores and chains, and for them the mission of the ad is to sell merchandise to people who must *keep* the pace. High fashion copy can be quite formal, somewhat informal, or a blend, and price is always subordinated. Volume fashion copy cannot neglect mood, emotion, and glamour, yet it must include more specific product facts. Price becomes important, but it must be handled subtly or it can repel (or even insult) the reader. Brevity is at a premium, for large masses of type should not detract from the more important pictures. Each word counts: The copywriter must work the miracle of saying a lot by saying scarcely anything.

The language of all fashion copy

begins with active verbs that tell what the item does for the consumer, not what it is; adjectives are minimized. Headlines are brief, sometimes even mere labels, and the message must be newsy, authentic (perhaps subtly mentioning famous designers), and, above all, very personal and human. Once confined to ads for women's apparel and accessories, fashion copy has spread to menswear, home furnishings, and other lines of merchandise.

COMPARISON COPY

A recent trend in advertising is the return to favor of copy based on direct comparisons between products, their manufacturers, and stores. Once thought to be unethical, many recent ads of this sort have been tactfully written and are accepted by the public as an effort to provide more meaningful information on which buying choices can be based. This kind of copy calls for the most thorough study of the products to be compared, and written documentary evidence should be available to sustain any comparative claims included in the copy. The copywriter must be a diplomat, so as not to offend a friendly competitor by the way the message is phrased. Price comparisons are impressive but dangerous unless there is conclusive proof that prices of your store and the competitor actually are as stated. We will discuss this further in Chapter 16.

COPY FOR COOPERATIVE ADS

Within certain latitudes, manufacturers encourage localizing the copy in the ads they help pay for. Retail copywriters, revising manufacturers' copy in such cases, must be aware of the limits to which each vendor will permit ads to be altered. The copy can then be revised up to that limit to make it as much like the store's other copy as possible. In that portion where alterations are allowed by the agreement with the manufacturer, the copywriter should overlook no opportunity to introduce the same kind of vocabulary, tone, and feeling that characterize ads completely created by the store itself. Both vendor and merchant will benefit most when the copy rings true to the store's established image and style.

THE PLACE OF PRICE IN RETAIL COPY

The most commonly asked question among retailers attending advertising clinics conducted by the author in several states over a long period of time has been, "Should the price be mentioned in *every* ad?" For the typical promotional ad run by the average store, the answer is simple: *yes.* A good rule is to *always mention* price but to *seldom emphasize* it. Often independent merchants facing discount house and chain store competition believe that ads without price are safer, since they can never beat the competition on price. Actually, research studies have shown that when no price is mentioned, readers tend to think the price is still higher than it actually is. Moreover, the advertising of a higher price, in and of itself, is seen as evidence of greater quality and value.

Well-written copy always seeks to build consumers' belief in the value of the product advertised, to make it seem worth the price. Beyond this, the institutional portion of the small merchant's ads should emphasize the services this kind of merchant offers, for these are very often superior to those of the competition and thus compensate for somewhat higher prices. Major stores, both locally owned and chain outlets, rarely, *if ever*, run product ads without the price. But only the highly promotional stores put the price in huge print and make it, and it alone, the feature of the ad.

Highly prestigious shops often shun figures and use words, with prices fully spelled out: "This lovely brooch can be hers for only four thousand dollars." Such stores rarely print the price in type any larger than the smallest used for the text copy itself. Few stores use the dollar sign ($) to indicate price; the public assumes prices are in dollars and this is adequate: 22.50, not $22.50. Many stores omit the zeros when the price is in even dollars, but in that case the dollar symbol is called for to make sure readers understand: $35, rather than $35.00 or 35.00. Prices should not be buried within the text copy, as the public expects to see them at the end, in the case of nonpromotional or semipromotional stores' ads, or, often, at the beginning, as the feature of the copy itself, in ads run by highly promotional stores.

Prices, and other details of finished copywriting such as abbreviations, capitalization, and punctuation, are usually a part of established store policy, and their use differs from store to store as management dictates. The copywriter is responsible for implementing such policies consistently from ad to ad.

WRITING COPY FOR SALES

The chief feature of the ad for sales and clearances is always the *price* of the product, for the chief interest of the ad's readers is presumed to be *economy*. This does not preclude mentioning secondary selling points in the copy. Reducing the price of merchandise will not make people buy it unless they believe it is worth *at least* the sale price. In writing copy for sales and clearances, it is crucial to *justify* the sale, to make it believable. The reason for reducing prices may be a manufacturer's introductory or season-end special, an overlarge postseason inventory, a serious financial problem facing the store, a special purchase of odd lots of merchandise, a need to clear out last year's models so fresh merchandise can be displayed. Whatever it is, it should be spelled out in the ad.

The use of *comparative prices* in sale ads has created considerable controversy in recent years, and federal and state requirements regarding proof of the alleged "regular" price have become increasingly stringent. Ad policy-makers must also consider whether the savings offered will be sufficient to motivate people to buy. Merchandise managers, not a store's advertising staff, determine price reductions. But the latter can and should voice their opinions when decisions are made and do all they can to make this type of advertising both legally correct and believable.

A 1972 survey by a fashion chain operating in six midwestern, eastern, and southern states turned up some unnerving statistics about the credibility of sale ads and the kind of price reductions needed to motivate people to buy. More than 72 percent of those shoppers questioned were skeptical to some degree about sale advertising. Barely 28 percent answered yes to the question "Do you believe sale advertising?" About 48 percent said they believed

A winter clearance to bring out the beast in you.

After you go ape over our prices, you may get cowed by our selection.

You won't know, for example, whether to pounce on those famous-name Ronald Bascombe 100% **double knit sport coats**, regularly $75.00, **now $59.90.**

Or to swing over to the **half price sweaters.**

Or to feather your nest with a smashing new **famous-name Eagle suit,** regularly $155, **now $99.90.**

Or to attack that formidable array of famous-name 100% polyester **double knit dress slacks,** regularly $29.95, **now $23.96.**

So come over to Osmun's and stalk our selection.

You may walk out with some pretty wild stuff.

Osmun's
Fashion for men and young men.

most, but not all, sale ads; almost a quarter said that they believed either very little or no sale advertising. Nevertheless, people did seem to respond to sale ads. Some 47 percent of those surveyed "frequently" went to a store because of a sale ad. About 45 percent would go to a store because of a sale ad only when they had already been looking for whatever was on sale. But only 8 percent "rarely or never" attended an advertised sale.

Ninety percent of the respondents said that stores should list both the regular and sale prices of items, and 82 percent thought prices should be reduced by 25 percent or more before advertising a sale. More than a third of the respondents felt that prices should be reduced by 50 percent. Barely 7 percent of the respondents felt that 10 percent was a sufficient price reduction.[2]

Copywriters, then, may have to really work at sale ads to get a favorable reaction from consumers. The general rule that being *specific* is more convincing than being *general* applies to sale copy too. "Save $20" is better than "25% off" if an $80 item has been reduced to $60. Dollar figures should be used whenever possible instead of percentage reductions. Readers can visualize instantly what it means to save $20; they have to do some arithmetic for "25% off" to have any meaning.

WRITING CLASSIFIED ADS

The basic rules of good copywriting apply even more strongly to classified ads, since illustrations do not normally accompany the copy. The words must do the whole selling job. And where *liners,* or straight classified listings "set solid" in small type, are used, there is not even a headline to catch the reader's eye. However, the *target audience* has already been shown where to find the ad by the newspaper itself, which uses *column heads* to attract the notice of buyers in the market for a particular type of item.

Like the display ads, classified ads should start by revealing a product *benefit.* Since there is no headline, this is accomplished in the *first few words* of the copy itself (which are often printed by the newspaper in capital letters or boldface type). Classified copywriters must bear in mind that there is a very marked difference in *reader attitude* that calls for a different type of copy approach than the approaches used in writing display ads. Research has shown that eight out of ten of those who purchase merchandise as a result of classified advertising had definitely planned to buy the kind of item they purchased before they saw the ads at all. Only two out of ten are *impulse* shoppers who just happened to come across the ad and at that point became

Figure 13-4 Sale Ads Can Be Interesting!
In welcome contrast to the typical retail sale ad with its dull listing of comparative prices and its screaming, overdone headline is this clearance ad for the Osmun's stores. The ad departs from tradition and goes humorous. It is in the imaginative copy school, of course, and carries the simile of the "animal" from the headline through the massive picture to the last words of the text. Nonetheless, there is such factual material in the copy as specific prices, materials, and brand names.
Source: By courtesy of Osmun's and its agency, Jaffe, Stone and August.

interested.[3] Thus, for most readers, the copy need not stir up a desire to buy (it is already there, in the readers' minds), but it must highlight very specific benefits of the one particular item the ad seeks to sell, to distinguish it from all the many hundreds of others advertised on the same page. Creating *primary demand* is the problem in only 20 percent of the cases; *competitive selling* is the mission in all the rest.

An ad that says "CAR FOR SALE" is terribly weak when the whole page is full of cars for sale. To distinguish one ad from a mass of ads, be specific. Instead of "CAR," say "PONTIAC '76 WITH AIR."

Why say "UNUSUAL DINING TABLE" when you can say "DINE ON ANTIQUE WALNUT, 5 legs"?

Many common errors in writing classified ads derive largely from misguided efforts to "save" on their cost. The classified ad, even more than any other kind of ad, seeks an immediate, specific response and a quick sale, often to the *one* person in the whole community the product or service appeals to at one moment in time. It must tell the complete story about the product, give all the details necessary to produce a telephone response or a quick trip to the store. Sellers should give all the data necessary to distinguish their offer from others on the page, even if the cost per insertion is greater.

One does not save money by running a brief ad that fails to produce a response for six days at $4 a day ($24), when one insertion of a good ad, costing $12, could have sold the item. In one instance, a real-estate man ran a 16-word ad for a house and got six responses. Then he rewrote the ad, using lively, interesting wording and giving readers enough information so that they could visualize the house as a home where their families would be happy. This time, he used 49 words, not 16, but he drew 48 responses. He spent three times as much, but he got eight times the response. Which ad was really "cheaper"?

A second major error caused by trying to save money with brief ads is using a mass of abbreviations—trade jargon which the writer understands but which the average reader finds puzzling. No word should be abbreviated in a classified unless the abbreviated form is understood by the public at large. Using "Ave." for "Avenue" is surely all right; so is using "A.M." for "morning." Used-car dealers may understand that "full power" means power brakes and power steering, but most car buyers may not; the letters "r.r." in a real estate ad will not convey to the average home-seeker that the house for sale has a recreation room.

But unnecessary words that do nothing to help sell the product can be dropped in classified copy. The word "the," for example, is seldom necessary. Another space-waster is "and." Classified copy can be *telegraphic* in style, as long as it includes the specific descriptive words needed to make the reader able to visualize the product and want to buy it.

MOW TO MAKE DO:
THE SMALL STORE AND
THE PART-TIME COPYWRITER

Small-shop proprietors and managers who double as their own advertising "departments" have insufficient time to do a proper job all by themselves. Yet their stores must advertise, and effective copywriting is near the heart of advertising success. What can they do?

If the store's advertising budget is too small to enable it to turn to an ad agency, the local newspaper may offer help with copy. When rough copy with good ideas is turned over to the newspaper's ad department, experts there may rewrite it, smooth it up, and add just the right touch to make it sparkle. In many communities, a freelance copywriter can be found to write, for a small fee, the one or two ads a small store places each week. Such outside help will need to make periodic visits to the store to see the advertised merchandise and to thresh out basic copy strategy with the manager.

The merchant who decides to go it alone can keep a file of clippings from both consumer magazines and retail trade journals and convert some of the best of the manufacturers' copy into local ad copy. A prime source of ideas, expressions, clever words, and appropriate ways of expressing sales ideas is the copy used by other stores in *distant* communities (but *never* those who are direct local competitors). A merchant can subscribe to a newspaper published in another city that may be two or three states away and save from it ads for stores in the same trade line. There are endless opportunities in borrowing from ads that no one in the community has ever seen. Often this source will provide copy ideas for the very same products for which ads need to be prepared. (The legalities of borrowing from others' ads will be covered in Chapter 16.) In addition, the small-store proprietor can subscribe to syndicated services that

provide both art and copy. (These will be identified in Chapter 14.)

All copywriters, part-time or otherwise, can benefit from having at their fingertips a good dictionary, *Roget's Thesaurus* (for expanding vocabulary by looking up synonyms), a standard book on English usage such as *Fowler's English Usage,* and perhaps some specialized publications like *Bartlett's Quotations* and Eric Partridge's *Dictionary of Clichés.* A special volume intended as a working tool for local copywriters is Edmund J. Gross' *Copy Stimulators,* which contains 2,000 headlines classified by 56 merchandise categories and 1,000 advertising words arranged in alphabetical order.[4]

5 Wrapping It All Up

PREPARING COPY FOR THE PRINTER

Different newspapers have different suggestions for preparing copy for their typesetters and printers, but the form demonstrated in Figure 13–5 is a good, standard, generally accepted one. All copy should be typewritten and double-spaced, with wide margins. Beginners often become confused trying to make typewritten copy "fit" a specific area of an ad's layout; they write short lines to try to show what the printed type will ultimately look like. This is unnecessary and confusing. Use a standard line length for all copy, and let the "mark-up" people in the store's production unit or the newspaper's composing room indicate

Advertiser: Lund's Furniture Store

Newspaper: Daily News - Record

Insertion Date: September 25

Size: 3 columns x 10 inches

Headline: Enjoy luxury in limited dining space

Text: (A)

               Here's all you could ever hope to ask for in apartment-sized

               versatility, in the life style of your choice. Table and 4 chairs

                                                              $329.95

               (B)

               Superb all-wood styling. Each piece is constructed of selected

               hardwood veneers and solids. Genuine pecan veneers are featured

               on the 40" round table tops, which extend to 58" with included

               18" leaves. Fashion-upholstered chair seats complement luxurious

               woven plastic cane backs. Authentic detailing and exquisite

               turning complete the unmistakable look of quality. Craftsmanship

               you'll be proud of forever. Deep, lustrous finishes.

Signature: (Lund's Furniture - standing logo)

Figure 13–5 Form of Retail Copy

the correct length for the type to be set. Watch out when you write a headline on the same sheet of paper as the body copy; be sure to indicate that it is a head. Instructions for special handling of heads should be given in the margin and circled.

CHECKING YOUR WORK BEFORE THE AD GOES TO PRODUCTION

Figure 13–6 offers an example of checklists for advertising copy widely used by larger stores. Developed and sponsored jointly by newspapers and retail associations to help copywriters check each ad for all the necessary selling points, they come in a series for dozens of different merchandise lines and products.

Common copywriting errors that can still be caught and corrected after copy is written but before it goes off to be set in type include (1) *"wordy" copy* that does not really say anything specific; (2) *formal words* and writing that seems stilted, cold, or impersonal, more like a high-school English theme than the way people really talk and think; (3) *too-long sentences* and paragraphs that will form an uninviting grey mass on the newspaper page unless they are broken up by heads or white space; (4) *too much copy in capital letters,* which are harder to read than small letters, when boldface or italic type could be used for emphasis instead; (5) *poor spelling and grammar;* and (6) *small but crucial oversights,* like forgetting the "each" or "per dozen" beside the prices in a promotional ad or not giving the full store copy with the signature at the end.

REVIEWING THE FUNDAMENTALS

After you have finished writing copy for an ad, take a break (if you can); then, before sending it out to be printed, review your own work in the light of the following selected bits of wisdom from several leading experts in the field. If there is no time for this before the ad is published, look at it when the paper comes out, and using these guides, prepare to do better on the next ad.

The ground rules for effective copywriting have been condensed by John W. Crawford, dean of the University of Oregon School of Journalism, author, and former creative vice president of a major advertising agency, into this brief admonition:

> [There are] four specific things to say:
> 1. This product benefits you,
> 2. because it has these features,
> 3. which work to your advantage in this way,
> 4. and see how easily you can get it.[5]

Paul S. Hirt, a practical newspaperman, promotion manager of the *Chicago Sun Times,* and the author of a widely used copy-service newsletter, offers this advice:

> As a retail copywriter, your job is to make love to the prospect. Making copy love follows the same rules as person-to-person courtship: letting the object of your affection know you are interested in what matters to him or her; addressing that interest in compelling terms; and enhancing the desirability of whatever you offer.[6]

Judy Young Ocko, a retail ad consultant, author, and, for years, a copy specialist at Macy's in New York, gives

Upholstered Furniture

- ❖ Brand name—well-known trademark or descriptive trade name.

- ❖ Specific style, type, design, shape, period, motif, purpose, matching or decorative application to rooms.

- ❖ Number of pieces and type of each.

- ❖ Finishes or tones of wood or metal parts, frame, decorative trim, hand-rubbed, antique, etc.

- ❖ Materials of upholstered parts:
  fabric, weave, stitching, leather, synthetic, blend, gauge or thickness, finish, texture, grade, type & number of coils, foam rubber or other stuffing, tufting, tufting buttons, quilting, trim.

- ❖ Colors, tones and patterns of upholstered parts & trims, matching or decorative possiblities with color schemes.

- ❖ Sizes:
  over-all widths, lengths, heights, depths and thicknesses.

- ❖ Features:
  long-wear, comfort design, resiliency, color-fast; unique construction? Sectional pieces? Curved or contoured pieces? Reversible cushions? Stain-resistant? Reinforced? Weight? Zip-off covers available?

- ❖ Cleanability:
  washable, foam clean, dry clean, wipe clean.

- ❖ Prices; delivery.

- ❖ Payment plan.

- ❖ Name and location of store or department. At branches, too?

- ❖ Hours store is open.

- ❖ Phone number.

- ❖ Phone and mail orders accepted?

this description of copywriters and their job:

> A copywriter is not just a person with a knack for words, although we must know our way around words. A copywriter is not just a long-haired creative artist, although the more creative we are, the better we are.
>
> Instead, a copywriter is actually a salesman behind a typewriter. We use our typewriters to sell, sell, sell. Whether we are promoting an idea or an item, whether we're writing hard-hitting prose that screams SALE or salutes the Red Cross in chaste language, we are always selling our store. . . .
>
> Test your own copy by asking two questions: (1) Does my ad include customer benefits? . . . (2) Does my ad give a reason for buying at my store? Giving the customer benefits and the reasons for buying at your store will bring people in, provided you have been honest, and the merchandise is both right and priced right.[7]

The copywriter can improve his or her performance by asking these questions about every ad and checking all copy against these summaries of the fundamentals of effective retail advertising copy:

- Does the ad start with a bang, focused on *a single main selling idea?* One primary advantage must make itself heard above the din and clamor of "me too" ads.
- Does it speak from *the customer's point of view,* in the customer's own language? "You"-centered copy in plain talk—honest, believable, and specific—will work. "We"-centered copy will fail.
- Is the copy *brief but clear?* Ads must communicate rapidly, often relying on the art to help make the main point and to stir up emotion. Favor lively verbs and visual words that dramatize key points. Copy must fill in all the necessary specific details without becoming wordy. Use no word that is not needed; use every word that is needed to make the proposition clear even to the least-interested reader.
- Can the reader *get involved?* Customers will tune out ads that do not make them feel a part of it all. Create empathy.
- Does the copy *ring true?* Friendly, enthusiastic, honest, and candid copy, written in a personal, natural, and conversational tone, will sell. Overstatement, brag, and bombast will turn off the readers.

Figure 13–6 A Checklist for Copywriters
This is one of a series of checklists for all types of products available to the copywriter at a minimum cost and sponsored by the Sales Promotion Division of the National Retail Merchants Association, the Newspaper Advertising Executives Association, and the Bureau of Advertising of the American Newspaper Publishers Association. As the original instructions point out: "Before placing your ad in the newspaper, check your descriptive copy against this suggested checklist to make sure every important feature is included. This will insure more reader-interest and buying action and also will reduce costly correction time after the first proof. Readers want ALL information about your merchandise when attracted to your newspaper ad. In addition to the above technical check, be sure to tell how your merchandise and its various features will benefit the reader. The prospective purchaser is interested principally in the benefits he or she is going to derive from a purchase."
Source: Reprinted by permission of the International Newspaper Advertising Executives, Danville, Illinois. Copyright 1962 by INAE.

- Does the ad encourage *buying action*? Conclude with a powerful nudge to *do something—right now.*

Advertising copy is so closely linked with the art, layout, and mechanical production process that anyone concerned with copywriting must be almost equally involved with, and interested in, those facets of advertising. In smaller stores, in fact, advertising personnel seldom enjoy a complete specialization of duties, and often one person must handle all these functions in the course of a normal day's work. Therefore, our overview of copywriting fundamentals cannot stop here but must continue in Chapter 14. There, among other things, the matter of fitting copy into the layout and estimating how long it can or must be to fill its assigned space is dealt with in section 3, *Understanding Type.* Copyfitting deeply involves every copywriter, and that section should be studied intensively as an extension of the copywriter's duties that were outlined in this chapter.

Questions for Discussion

1. What are the main purposes of the headline in a retail newspaper ad? Which of them do you think is usually most important? Why?

2. Which of the several different kinds of text, or body copy, appeals would be most appropriate for (a) an ad for a local dry cleaning establishment, (b) an ad for slacks and sports shirts from a men's clothing store, (c) an ad for wedding dresses by a high-fashion ladies' apparel store, (d) an ad for season-end reductions on lawn and garden equipment from a hardware store, and (e) an ad for living-room furniture by a better-quality furniture store?

3. Why is it important to include something more than a list of items, their former prices, and their current reduced prices in a clearance sale ad? What are some of the things a merchant may say in such an ad to increase its believability?

4. Why is a headline not as necessary in a classified ad as in a display ad? What should the first few words of a classified ad say?

5. To be complete, an ad should encourage potential customers to buy the product *now.* What are six things you can say near the end of an ad to stir the reader to buy promptly? Which would work best if the reader was (a) an elderly man or woman, (b) a college student, (c) a young housewife, (d) a prosperous executive, (e) a very busy person with long working hours every weekday?

6. After an ad has been completed, what points should the copywriter check before the ad goes to production? What do you think that you yourself would be most likely to overlook or need to improve or correct?

Suggested Projects

1. Go through a consumer magazine and pick out six or eight ads that employ an emotional, imaginative, or indirect approach. Then take a local newspaper, and see how many ads you can find from local retail and service businesses that employ similar imaginative approaches. (Don't select ads that appear to be

cooperative ads with manufacturer-supplied copy.) Then select some of the mass of local ads that have factual, rational, or direct copy and rewrite them to make them more like the imaginative kind of ads you found in the magazine, while still giving readers all the necessary facts about the product or store.

2. Examine the retail ads in a local paper and count how often each of the several types of headlines explained in the text are used. Which kinds are hardest (or impossible) to find, even by going through several issues of the paper? Find several headlines that simply identify the products for sale (label heads) and rewrite them to make them more interesting.

3. Get the classified section of a large daily newspaper, and select a page containing chiefly liner ads, not display classifieds. Go through that entire page and count the number of meaningless, unnecessary, "nonselling" words you find. Also count the number of abbreviations whose meaning is not clear to you. Then rewrite several of the worst ads, substituting informative and pointed words for useless words and mysterious abbreviations. (In some cases, you may want to telephone the advertisers and ask what the abbreviations you did not understand meant.)

4. Rip a page at random from any consumer-goods mail-order catalog. Choose any item on that page and try to rewrite it as a mass media ad (a newspaper ad, for example). Assume that you will have space only for half the number of words used in the catalog ad. The catalog copy will probably be almost totally factual and direct; try to convert some of it to imaginative and indirect appeals as you rewrite the headline and the body copy. If you wish, choose a particular target audience for your ad.

Notes

1. Robert E. Karp, "An Approach to Creative Advertising for the 70s," *Arizona Review* (January 1972), p. 5.

2. Survey by Sheldon M. Berman Public Relations-Advertising, Inc., Columbus, O., for Limited Stores, Inc., July 9, 1972.

3. *Classified Advertising: Readership and Use Among Purchasers of General Merchandise and Recreation and Leisure Items*, data from National Family Opinion Poll, Inc. (New York: Newspaper Advertising Bureau, Inc., January 1975), p. 22.

4. This book is available from Halls of Ivy Press, 13050 Raymer St., North Hollywood, Calif. 91605.

5. John W. Crawford, *Advertising*, 2nd ed. (Boston: Allyn & Bacon, 1965), p. 196.

6. Paul S. Hirt, *Designing Retail Ads for Profit* (New York: International Newspaper Promotion Association, 1968), p. 117.

7. Judy Young Ocko, *Retail Advertising Copy: The How, the What, the Why* (New York: National Retail Merchants Association, 1971), pp. 1, 3–4.

Preview

Most retail ads use pictures to (1) show how a product looks, (2) tell how it is used by people, (3) demonstrate the pleasant results of owning it, (4) make a point humorously, (5) relate the ad to current news and events, or (6) attract attention and arouse curiosity.

Original art used in ads usually consists of drawings or paintings. Larger stores have staff artists to make these pictures; smaller stores obtain art from specialized service firms, freelance artists, manufacturers, newspaper service departments, or syndicated services. Photographic art has the advantages of realism, the visual impact associated with news, the ability to focus on the selected *feature* of an ad, and speed.

A layout organizes the elements of an ad into a pleasing design and serves as a blueprint for production technicians. Design involves (1) balance, (2) gaze motion, (3) emphasis, (4) contrast, and (5) unity.

Type selection is an art essential to effective design. Roman and sans serif typefaces are the most common. Type conveys subtle emotional overtones by its physical form, size, weight, width, and posture. Layout artists fit copy into the space available, using systems that measure the area that a particular typeface and size will occupy.

Color in retail ads attracts attention and carries emotional messages. Specific colors affect readers in different ways and reinforce the impact of words and pictures. Quick, simple, and inexpensive production of ads by *cold type* composition and *offset lithographic* printing is offered by most newspapers. A few still use *letterpress* printing, but most of them can also set ads in cold type.

Learning Goals

Chapter 14 discusses the purposes, kinds, and sources of illustrative material suitable for retailers' uses. Students should gain from reading it, and especially from a careful study of the many examples presented in the figures, an understanding of the basic fundamentals of good advertising design and of the steps to making an effective layout. They should become aware of the many variations of type and the importance of choosing the right kind for each ad. They should learn to estimate how copy can be fitted into a given area of a layout. They should also come to see how color influences the effect of an ad and in what ways color can be used. Everyone connected with the preparation of advertising needs a basic understanding of the technical processes involved, the opportunities they present, and the limitations they impose.

14

Graphics for Newspaper Advertisements

The graphic portion of a newspaper ad includes the illustrations, the fundamental design or layout, the type used for the headline and body copy, and the colors used in the printing process. The graphic elements of an ad facilitate the quick and easy comprehension of the printed word, offer additional information, and provide an emotional element that speaks without words.

To properly synchronize the copy and the graphics, there must be close teamwork between copywriters and artists; their efforts must be tightly coordinated from the very conception of each advertising idea, whether it be for a whole campaign or an individual ad. It is primarily by means of visual symbols that each store develops a distinctive style that distinguishes its ads from those of other stores, and it is also by this means that it secures cross-media unity among all its advertising messages.

1 Illustrations

WHY ILLUSTRATIONS ARE USED

Illustrations can have many different purposes, and the more precisely the artist can define the purpose of a given picture, the better the job he or she can do. Nearly all retail ads use illustrations of some kind, and in some cases they tell the story so well that the copy becomes of minor importance. Illustrations can have any one (or combination) of the following functions.

To Show What the Product Looks Like This is all that illustrations do in the great majority of immediate-sell, item-price ads. They act as extensions of the store's display counters. Usually, pictures that simply show the product are factual descriptions of each item, as in an illustrated catalog. They are most effective when readers are already aware of their need for the product. When the product is the store itself, as in institutional ads, the interior, the exterior, a featured department, or even a person who is "the store" to its customers may be pictured.

To Show the Product Being Used by Someone Hopefully the subject in such illustrations is one with whom the intended readers can "identify," someone they will accept as being much like themselves or like the person for whom they are contemplating purchasing a gift. This type of illustration can also serve two further purposes. It can stir to consciousness a need or a desire for the product that was not felt before, and it can reinforce a headline designed to attract a particular target market or make

the wording that does this unnecessary in the head. A picture of a baby is sure to attract the attention of mothers, a man ploughing is certain to catch the eye of farmers, and a smiling, well-dressed person will make the reader think of being invited out to a gala party.

To Demonstrate the Happy Results of Owning or Using the Product or Shopping at the Store This may be done either realistically or symbolically. Usually, this type of picture is associated with emotional, imaginative copy. It is especially helpful if the advertiser wants to reach persons who have no felt need for the product. It attracts the interest of hard-to-motivate "prospects" by making them want to experience the same joy and satisfaction as the pictured users. It makes them begin to get interested in the product or service, hopefully enough so that they read the rest of the ad to

Figure 14–1 Illustrating Ads

The artwork that is chosen to illustrate an ad can fulfill many purposes. The ad at top left employs cartoon characters that lend a light, humorous touch while visually picturing the happy results of shopping at Lazarus stores. The smiling faces show that it is the norm to get the proper size dress, to have a package delivered on the correct day, or to have an easy time parking your car.

The next ad is an example of the use of graphic symbol that can transmit to the consumer an idea, image, or intangible attribute, rather than concrete information. Here the symbol is the familiar mortar and pistil, a symbol that has long been associated with the profession of pharmacy. This symbol, the predominate feature of the ad, conveys an image of dignity and professionalism and thus overrides any tendency on the part of the consumer to think that poor, untrustworthy service would be found at this "cut rate" drug store.

The ad for ladies' footwear uses artwork to establish associations for the product that add to the perceived value of the advertised product. Shown in the ad are the footlights of the stage, and the headline proclaims "bright footlights." The idea is subtly conveyed: The wearer of these shoes will be "on stage," the center of attraction, the focus of admiring eyes. With a well-chosen picture, the product has become associated with glamour, romance, and mystery.

The final ad pictured here uses illustration to demonstrate materials from which the product is made. Four samples are shown from the collection of 300 distinct materials that this store has in stock. Such a choice of art conveys well the idea that these are not ready-made shirts, but shirts that the customer can choose and create to suit his own tastes and needs.

Other examples of the use of art to illustrate ads can be found throughout this book. The ad for Campbell's chicken noodle soup in Figure 7–1 on page 179 is an excellent example of artwork effectively used to show what a product looks like. The art in the Jacobson's ad in Figure 11–2 on page 308 serves two purposes: to show the product used by someone, and to establish a psychological relationship by picturing someone whom the reader (the woman who wishes to be a high-fashion leader) would want to be like.

Source: Photo at left by courtesy of Lazarus of Columbus, Ohio.

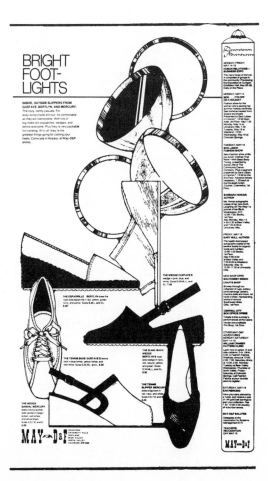

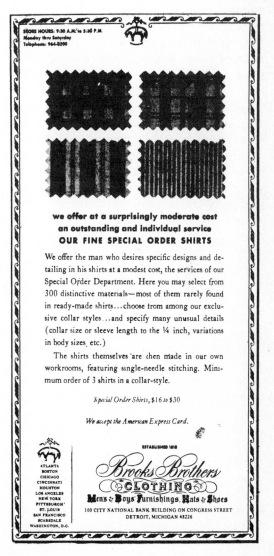

find out more about it and perhaps decide that they do "need" it after all.

Such a picture can take either a positive or a negative approach, or two pictures can be used, one negative, the other positive. They can show a predicament and its solution or any variant of the "before-and-after" approach. The *unhappy* results of *not* using the product or shopping at the store can be the focus, sometimes in a humorous fashion.

Where a creative art service is available or can be purchased from outside sources, and where there is adequate time to prepare an ad, this technique often produces superior results. Smaller retailers or account representatives of smaller newspapers sometimes try to get this type of impact by converting "stock" pictures from syndicated *art service catalogs* (which are always replete with drawings or photos of laughing men, smiling women, sleeping children—contented, relaxed, joyful faces). Deftly used, such pictures can contribute to the effectiveness of an ad.

To Imply Psychological Relationships Associated with the Product or Its Users This type of art, a near-cousin of the type described above, emphasizes the background and environment of the product's users or portrays people with whom readers would want to be associated or like whom they would choose to be. It must invariably be reinforced by imaginative, emotional copy. Often employed in the past by national advertisers, this type of illustration may eventually become more popular among retailers as more of the burden of promoting products and services falls on them.

To Symbolically Represent an Abstract Quality of the Product or the Store Symbolic art can reflect various attributes of a store or a product—stylishness, reliability, durability, convenience, femininity, masculinity, gaiety, seriousness. It is most often used in institutional ads, to reinforce an element of the store's image—its age, size, dependability, cheerfulness, or other abstract quality. The creation of this type of artwork is not an assignment for the beginner or amateur, but a real challenge for advertising professionals.

To Demonstrate Materials, Construction Features, or Manufacturing Methods Various cutaway techniques or greatly magnified pictures of product details that may never be seen by the user in normal circumstances are common in manufacturer's ads but rare in local ads. Big retailers who control their own production facilities, lay down specifications for their house brands, or have product-testing facilities can sometimes use this type of art. It often goes well with factual copy and is a graphic way of presenting tangible evidence that a product can perform as promised. Generally, manufacturers' ads of this type can be adapted by retailers for their own purposes, perhaps in "How to . . ." ads or *informational* ads about the care, maintenance, and use of purchases.

To Make People Laugh Cartoons and photos used in ads often have a humorous theme, since people tend to respond well to and remember an ad they enjoy.

To Relate the Product or Store to Current Events Illustrations can connect the use of a product or a characteristic of a store with a national or local current event. Or there may be "news" about the store or the product itself. Ads can show photographs of new merchandise being unloaded from a truck, a manager or a buyer at the airport going off to market, the crowd attracted by a special event, or the progress of construction work on a new store.

To Attract Attention, Arouse Curiosity, or "Decorate" the Ad Illustrations that serve only this function are seldom worth spending money on; they should be considered only as a last resort. Often a good, honest headline and effective copy will do the job just as well. Every picture (like every headline) should relate in some way to a user benefit or a desirable characteristic of the product, service, or store, either directly or by implication.

An inappropriate picture, in no way related to the ad message, can actually detract from the ad's impact. It may even arouse readers' ire when they discover its irrelevancy to the copy. Pictures of scantily clad females designed solely to attract the attention of male readers can be particularly offensive.

ARTWORK

What Kinds of Illustration to Use All kinds of art may be used in advertising illustrations. And almost any art form can be used in newspaper ads, provided expensive "full process" color printing is available for run-of-paper ads, as it always is for Sunday magazine sections of large papers and for preprinted, made-to-order inserts for local papers.

Ads may use *drawings,* including (a) pen-and-ink line drawings, possibly with dotted "benday"-process overtones —simple sketches, maps, diagrams, and cartoons; (b) wash drawings, possibly combined with line work and sometimes rendered by a soft-tone "aquatint" process; (c) charcoal drawings; (d) crayon and pastel chalk drawings; (e) pencil drawings; (f) scratchboard drawings; and (g) "litho-pencil" drawings. They may use *paintings* done in (a) watercolor, (b) oils, (c) tempera, (d) casein-opaque pigments, (e) fluorescent watercolor pigments, or (g) lampblack (*Hi-Lite* or *Kromolite*), or done by the (h) dry-brush method.

Woodcuts, an art form that goes back to the days of Gutenberg, are making a comeback, often in the form of linoleum-block cuts like those used in grade-school art classes. This type of art often appeals to the young and to "individualistic" customers, who respond well to ads that look *unlike* mass merchandisers' professional ads. Woodcuts often combine well with hand-lettered printing or script done by the proprietor of the store or a customer who likes to dabble in art.

Because newspapers are printed rapidly on coarse, porous paper, and because most retailers cannot afford to use color printing for the vast majority of their ads, the art media that translate into bold, clear-cut black-on-white pictures are by far the most popular for retail advertising. Fine lines may not come out well; delicate shading can get lost and appears muddy or murky. Even when color is used, newspapers (unlike magazines or better grades of direct-mail) do not lend themselves to subtle

Figure 14–2 Using Syndicated Art Services

Shown at left is artwork for Washington's Birthday promotions that is available from a syndicated newspaper retail art service, and, at right, is that same artwork as it could be used by a dealer in power lawn-care equipment when creating an ad. The picture of the lawn mower is derived from the manufacturer's catalog, and thus it will be precisely the model advertised in the ad. Some syndicated art services also provide generalized pictures of many products sold at retail, which resemble but do not necessarily exactly represent the actual item mentioned. The copy in the ad must make this point plain to the reader, or it can mislead or disappoint. Among retailers too small to maintain internal art staffs to create ads especially for themselves, this type of advertising art is the mainstay.

Source: Copyrighted material, reproduced by permission of Multi-Ad Services, Peoria, Illinois.

gradations and delicate hues and shades. Thus line-and-wash drawings (which are often combined) or charcoal or pencil sketches are the best bets for most newspaper ads. A great deal of high-fashion art produced in retailers' ad departments, by freelancers, or in local studios is of this type. A shaded effect, various gradations of tone and "weight," can easily be achieved using most of these processes by benday overlays of fine-spaced dots.

Sources of Artwork for Smaller Stores' Ads The large store with its own artists or the one that employs an advertising agency has no problem procuring artwork. The smaller merchant must depend on outside sources.

Specialized art service firms, which provide "stock" pictures to pep up small retailers' ads, abound. They provide catalogs of artwork created by top professional artists in their own employ or by the art departments of large stores who are willing to sell material for syndication after it has appeared in their own ads. One can secure weekly, monthly, or quarterly catalogs, containing thousands of illustrations, for each line of merchandise. Suggestions for effective copy and overall ad designs are usually included. Some art service firms will make sketches and drawings to order. They come in the form necessary for reproduction in the retailer's local paper—as metal printing plates, as *mats,* (an abbreviation for *matrixes,* papier-mâché molds used to produce pictures in papers using the letterpress printing method), or as *slicks* or *reproduction proofs* if the paper uses offset lithography or has converted its advertising production to the cold-type process.

Among the largest and longest-es-tablished of these retail art service firms, with clients throughout the country, are Ralph Heineman, Inc., Chicago; Metro Associated Services, New York; SCW, Los Angeles and New York; and Multi-Ad Services, Inc., Peoria, Illinois. Others can be contacted by consulting the *Yellow Pages* of local telephone directories, the headquarters of national or state retail trade associations, the art service director or retail advertising manager of any sizable newspaper, or the advertising manager or promotion director at any major independent department or specialty store. Many are local in scope, highly specialized as to trade lines served, and deal with copy for all media, not just newspaper ads.

Part-time professional help is often available locally from freelance artists, "moonlighting" employees of local ad agencies, and college teachers of advertising or art.

Manufacturers almost all offer free advertising materials to their dealers for local use. Factory salespersons, wholesalers, or home-office dealer-relations departments can be a source of thoroughly professional illustrations and copy ready to print in the local paper.

Local media retail service departments are also a prime source of art for many small stores. Artists and copywriters on larger papers may take over much of the practical burden of advertising production, design, and copywriting—if they are allowed enough lead-time to do a good job. All newspapers subscribe to syndicated illustration services and have tens of thousands (if not hundreds of thousands) of "stock cuts" on file to pep up and glamorize merchants' ads. For an example, see Figure 14–2.

PHOTOGRAPHY

For the small- to medium-sized store, original creative art is too expensive. But photographs are universally available and can be just as creative. Retailers can work with local professional photographers or use the photographic facilities and personnel of their newspaper. The ad department of small papers can "borrow" photo services from the news department. Medium-sized and large papers will have full-time photographers assigned to their ad departments (as will medium-sized and large retail stores). The technical problems in reproducing photographs clearly in newspapers are being rapidly solved as most newspapers, save only the very largest, have moved into offset lithography (itself essentially a photo-based process) for their printing.

With photographs, recognizable local scenes and people—the actual personnel and merchandise of the store in their real background—can be depicted quickly, inexpensively, and convincingly. The impact of photography can be unbeatable, when it is properly used. In essence, it is photo art that gives smaller merchants, working with smaller newspapers, flexibility and control over their advertising art. This permits them to use the illustrations in their ads for exclusive, creative, high-impact purposes. They can stop trying to imitate the big stores whose budgets they just do not possess and build true, individual images for themselves instead of depending on warmed-over, borrowed, or bought art from distant sources.

Advantages of Photo Ads Photos are superior to line art and other types of illustrations in these respects:

1. They are more *realistic* and more *believable*.

2. They bring to ads the *attention-getting power* and *visual impact* of the modern illustrated news or feature article. This makes the ads as interesting, well read, and sought after as the news itself. Research shows that subscribers think of a newspaper as a whole. They do not separate the news and ad portions in their minds to the extent that newspaper people and advertisers thought they did in the past. Photo-based ads raise the level of reader involvement to the same high plane attained by a good, well-illustrated news or feature article.

3. Photos can zero in on the *feature* of a given ad. They can illustrate *the* specific message that ad is intended to deliver.

4. Photos can be obtained quickly.

Limitations of Photo Ads There are, of course, some pitfalls to watch out for in using photos:

1. *Poor quality* (either low-grade reproductions or photos that miss the point of the ad).

2. *Delays caused by the need to get an OK on local photographs to be used in cooperative ads.* Most manufacturers will approve (with enthusiasm) when ads featuring their products are localized and improved by photos; but the red tape involved in getting that approval can be time-consuming.

3. *Extra expenses and delays* if the paper still uses letterpress printing and "hot type."

4. *Poor models.* Not being professional

actors or models, local persons used for ad pictures often behave most unnaturally before the camera's lens, with disastrous or ludicrous results. One solution is to use the candid camera approach whenever possible, and to take several shots of each scene, so that the most natural expressions and poses can be selected later.

How to Use Photos to Sell Merchandise Just how does one go about using photos to stimulate immediate sales of specific products? Photo art in item-price ads might well be discussed in terms of the *functions* the picture is expected to perform within the framework of the ad as a whole:

To illustrate the item(s). One or very few featured items in a major ad can be shown in a static situation, with a neutral background that focuses all attention on the merchandise. This is the weakest and least productive way to use photos, but it may be justified if the store must substitute photos for other artwork that is not readily available.

To highlight a specific feature of the product. This focuses on the "unique selling proposition" of the ad, the primary benefit it offers the customer. It usually means close-up shots with excellent lighting and may involve taking the product apart or removing a hood or cover to expose the special portion to be emphasized. In the lab, before the ad goes to the compositor, the artist can draw a circle to further direct the reader's eye.

To show the item in the store. Ideally, this means posing the product in the hands of a pleasant and knowledgeable-looking salesperson in the act of demonstrating or explaining it to a customer. The background is the store interior itself, and perhaps other (related) merchandise. Those who see the photo are then, in effect, on the customer's side of the counter, or on the sales floor. They can easily put themselves in the picture, in their mind's eye.

To depict the product in the user's own environment. A photo of a product can have much more impact if the advertiser goes to the trouble of taking the item out of the store and shooting it being used. Show a snow blower actually throwing clouds of white stuff off somebody's driveway, a silver bowl gracing someone's handsome sideboard, or a motorboat making a graceful wake through the water. The sales results are more than likely to justify the extra time and effort.

To show an actual or simulated customer using the product. This type of photo can produce the most powerful ad of all. Easily portable items can be shown in the customer's environment as suggested above, but bulky objects may have to be photographed in the store.

A shot of an improvised "actor" (i.e., a simulated "customer") can be adequate. In fact, that is all thousands of effective national ads in big media do. But *local* retailers have a priceless opportunity to "marry" the picture with the most powerful sales appeal of all: *testimonial* letters or quotations from satisfied, real-life customers! Their faces are familiar to many; their names mean something in the stores' trading areas. An auto dealer that shows well-known local people actually behind the steering wheel or an applicance store that shoots local residents cooking on its ranges will have an ad that is a real winner.

Even if the product itself is not

shown, a picture of one or more happy customers, clearly identified as local people, can be very effective. Intangible "products" like insurance cannot be pictured, but the results of buying them can.

Success with this type of picture depends, quite obviously, on the photographer's skill in catching expressions.

To show "before-and-after" situations. A pair of pictures, one taken before and the other after the use or application of the advertised product or service, can be very persuasive. This type of picture calls for some long-range planning, but it may well be worth it. Show a house or room before and after painting, remodeling, or refurnishing; or a yard before and after landscaping or mowing and trimming. Show the customer too, and get a testimonial for the product.

To show related items featured in special promotional events. When a store has a major item-selling promotion based on special merchandise and/or an exceptionally large stock of on-sale products, use an overview of the interior of the store, stockroom, or warehouse. Show dramatically the huge selection and variety of choice available. Or take pictures of smaller groups of related items, such as coordinated wearing apparel that makes a complete outfit. Photograph an actual window or in-store display, or use an attractive local model. The copy in such an ad can refer to the whole group of products or each item separately.

Using Local Photography in Institutional Ads When the ad's mission is to sell the store itself (rather than just its merchandise), photography is a "nat-

ural." There are virtually unlimited ways to use photographs to improve institutional ads. For example, the following types of pictures might be considered:

Photos that illustrate store services. Gift-wrapping, delivery, parking, installation, servicing, repairs, fitting, alterations, and many other things modern stores do for customers in the new services society must be promoted aggressively. One of the best ways to do this is to have ads in the form of news stories and feature articles—illustrated in the same way the news is illustrated. A straightforward report on what the store is doing for its customers can be illustrated graphically through photographs.

Pictures that show store personnel. Humanizing the atmosphere of the retail store is a prime objective of institutional advertising, especially in suburban areas and growing communities with mobile populations where it is no longer true that "everyone knows everyone else." Even simple mug shots of store and department managers, merchandise deliverers, salespersons, stock clerks, and cashiers can be very effective. Portraits of store personnel should be accompanied by brief biographies, emphasizing their special qualifications for the job they are doing—their years of experience, the technical schools and seminars they have attended, their safe driving records if they are delivery persons, or the trade shows they attend if they are managers.

Even more effective are informal pictures taken in or beside the store itself, depicting each employee "in character," doing the things customers will actually see them doing—photographs of a cashier beside a register, a smiling credit manager at a desk, a delivery per-

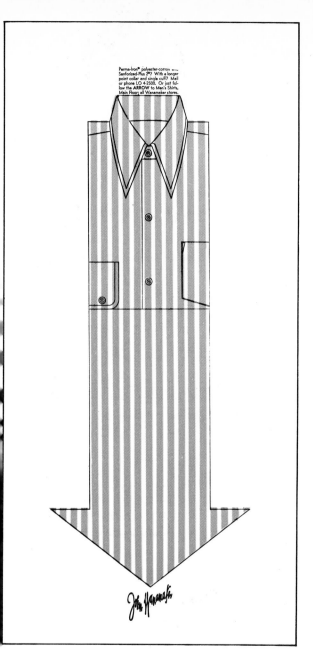

Figure 14-7 Use of Color in Retail Advertising

The ads on these four pages illustrate how color can be used effectively in retail ads. (See the text discussion on pages 424-425.)

This dignified shirt ad from John Wanamaker, a Philadelphia store, uses bright green stripes to de-

pict the product in an idealized, not realistic, style. Gathered into an arrow, the stripes help direct the reader's attention to the small store signature at the bottom of the page.

In a series of ads for an insurance company that had changed both its name and location, yellow type

Mom's the word at Westland Mall.

It's Mother's Day. Today and every day at Westland Mall. 89 magnificent stores sparkle with gift ideas. Fun gifts. Luxurious gifts. Practical gifts. Choose the perfect gift for every mother at Westland Mall. It's where mother loves to do her own shopping.

A development of Monumental Properties, Inc.

On the Palmetto at W. 48th Street, Hialeah. Take the Northwest 103rd Street Exit from the Palmetto.

Color Phil Patton's
face red!
He's really embarrassed. . .

Phil was afraid that General Motors would go out on strike, so he bought every Pontiac, Buick, and Cadillac he could get on his lot!

As everyone knows now - GM's labor problem was peacefully settled - without a strike. He's

Overstocked

that word's an understatement!

Phil must move 100 new Pontiacs, Buicks, and Cadillacs.

Almost all models in stock! Many are air-conditioned, radios, belted tires, fancy upholstery, automatic shifts, power brakes.

Don't pay any attention to the sticker price. . .

We're really dealing...

If anyone in Northwestern Ohio's underselling us - We'll buy you a 10 lb. Christmas turkey!

Patton PONTIAC - BUICK CADILLAC

Phone 599-1421 or 599-0025   1417 N. Scott Street
Napoleon

Open 9 to 9   Monday thru Friday Sat. 'till 6   Yes, we lease.

---

on a black background provides great visibility, thus helping the company keep old customers and also win new customers.

A shopping mall ran this creative, exquisitely simple ad for Mother's Day to build image and create traffic. The red comes from a lipstick; thus the ad

has subtly included an actual product in an actual color that can be purchased for a present.

Good advertising ideas do not come only from big-city experts, as this ad from a small-town car dealer shows. Tying his ad in with the front-page news of a threatened GM strike, the dealer used red

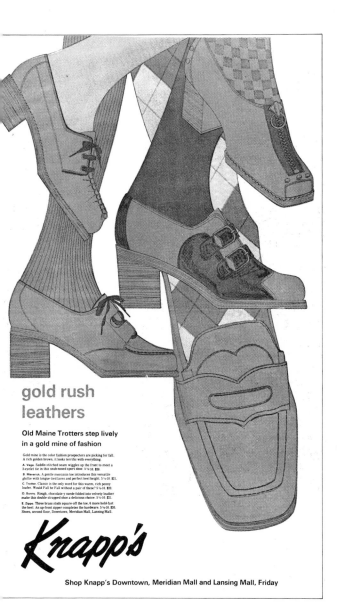

gold rush leathers

Old Maine Trotters step lively in a gold mine of fashion

Gold mine is the color fashion prospectors are picking for fall. A rich golden brown, it looks terrific with everything.

A. Vega. Saddle-stitched seam wiggles up the front to meet a 3-eyelet tie in this snub-nosed sport shoe. 5½-10. $20.

B. Maverick. A gentle moccasin toe introduces this versatile ghillie with tongue-tied laces and perfect heel height. 5½-10. $21.

C. Trotter. Classic is the only word for this warm, rich penny loafer. Would Fall be Fall without a pair of these? 5½-10. $20.

D. Sunny. Rough, chocolate-y suede folded into velvety leather make this double-strapped shoe a delicious choice. 5½-10. $21.

E. Zippo. Three brass studs square-off the toe, 6 more hold-fast the heel. An up-front zipper completes the hardware. 5½-10. $20. Shoes, second floor, Downtown, Meridian Mall, Lansing Mall.

Knapp's

Shop Knapp's Downtown, Meridian Mall and Lansing Mall, Friday

to signal his embarrassment at the situation he found himself in. The dealer must have gotten a lot of kidding from this ad, but also a lot of attention.

The Knapp's shoe ad is an excellent example of one color made to look like many through the artistic use of screens, black ink, and white background.

The color both shows the actual colors of the product and associates the ad with autumn.

In the ad from O'Coin's, color is employed to motivate the consumer's deep-seated desire to avoid the sizzling summer heat (effectively evoked by the red) by having an air conditioner to provide cool-

ness and comfort (two feelings elicited by blue).

Next, a chain supermarket uses full-process color to make the advertised meats appear totally real and delicious, thus stimulating in the consumer a desire to have them on their table. The packer of the meats probably assisted the advertiser by providing color plates.

The final ad uses full color to show the wide range of carpets and colors that this retailer has in stock. This is an example of a Hi-Fi preprint supplied by a cooperating manufacturer. The strip for local imprinting runs down the center.

son boarding a truck, or a salesperson beaming with enthusiasm behind a sales counter filled with attractive merchandise. Such live action shots make an ad come to life in a way no other newspaper technique can.

This type of campaign has especially intriguing cross-media possibilities, since the newspaper ads can be reinforced by radio commercials projecting the actual voices of the store personnel pictured in the ads. On-location shots of television scenes can be included in the store's commercials to further promote the same theme.

Views of the store itself. Pictures of the exterior are OK, especially if the store is new or remodeled; they do establish identity and familiarity. However, even a bright, shiny new building shown in a purely static environment makes a dead, lifeless ad, more interesting to the contractor than the customer. Include normal pedestrian and vehicular traffic to make the scene seem natural —even if the shot has to be "contrived" by assembling store personnel, their families, and their vehicles early some sunny morning! If the picture is taken during normal shopping hours, it may be a success only if the camera can be positioned high enough to get a good shot of the store front as well as of the shoppers and their cars.

Interior views are often much better, and these can more easily be combined with both merchandise and personnel to guarantee realism. Never show a cold, inanimate room full of merchandise alone; include store staff and customers (not gaping at the lens, but in natural poses). Zoom in on *the* feature being promoted: the lounge, the lunch counter, the fitting room, new fixtures,

a new boutique, a youth center, a repair service workshop, a new basement display area, or whatever.

During major promotions, pure news-type pictures of vast throngs rushing in as the doors open, or happily dashing from bargain to delicious bargain, can pack a powerful punch.

Pictures that tell a story of customer education or in-store instruction. Increasingly, retailers are offering information, demonstrations, and classes on how to use the products they sell. Fabric shops hold sewing classes, garages offer maintenance clinics for drivers, food marts provide cooking instructions, furniture merchants and paint dealers give home-decorating seminars. Each of these is a glorious opportunity for follow-up photographic promotion, treated in the same way as any other newsworthy local event: with action photos showing *things happening to people.* The pictures taken at the first clinic or workshop can also be used to attract participants the next time one is held.

Pictures that capitalize on visits to the store by experts or celebrities. When manufacturers send an expert to demonstrate their products, offer advice, and instruct customers, the corporations' public relations departments will invariably supply good, clear mug shots in advance (sometimes hoping the editor of the local paper will run them, for free, as "news"). Use them in the ads, of course. But also get a camera to the event itself and photograph the visitor surrounded by store personnel and interested customers. If the event is scheduled to run for several more days, shots like this can bring in still more crowds in the final days. In any event, they are great material for follow-up institutional promotion.

Sometimes a celebrity, such as a famous sports figure, visits a store. Handled the same way, photos of the event also make for great institutional ads both during and after the visit.

Some Final Tips on the Use of Photography in Local Ads When the first proofs of photographs are sent in so that the best picture out of a group of shots can be selected, consider what can be done to improve each photo by appropriate cropping and touching-up. Often a great deal can be done at this stage either to improve a marginally effective picture or to add sparkle and zest to an already good one.

If customers are shown in such a way that they can be identified by friends and neighbors in the community, they should be asked to sign a simple release form before the photo is used. Legal trouble can arise if this is not done. Any commercial photographer has such release forms, and any lawyer can easily devise one.

Strive to use photo art in a *series* of ads, not just as a one-shot deal. This establishes *continuity of image*. Photos taken in sequence at one time can be used in separate ads later on. This saves time and energy and results in a much lower cost *per picture*. Sometimes shots can be used repeatedly over a period of weeks or months, with the size, the borders, or the cropping varied to keep them looking fresh and new. Results snowball, as continuous advertising with photographs has a cumulative effect.

Pictures can also be used in special institutional elements within ads that are essentially item-selling ads. Food merchants can run columns of advice to shoppers on beating rising prices, gas stations and garages can offer advice on saving gas and wear and tear on cars, and home furnishing stores can provide advice to homeowners—all in insert columns headed by pictures of the store owner or manager or a special "expert" consultant. In place of the standard mug shot, a series of candid photos can show the same person with various different expressions. Stores should keep orderly files of all pictures taken, indexed so that they can get at them easily in the future. There may be many opportunities in the months and years to come to reuse some of the better pictures and to exploit shots that were not used the first time around.

2 The Design and Layout of Ads

The design of an advertisement is shown through a *layout,* which enables the artist, the copywriter, the advertising director, the media representative, and the store buyer or merchandise manager to visualize, in advance, what the finished ad will look like and to suggest changes. The layout also serves as a blueprint for the newspaper's production staff, telling it where to put the various graphic and typographic elements of the ad.

Magazine ads and big newspaper ads prepared by agencies for national or local advertisers often go through several layout stages, from a rough sketch or *thumbnail* (smaller than actual size) *layout* on through to a *finished layout* that looks, often, even better than the printed ad. In most retail operations, there is no time and no need for all this. A rough layout is all that is necessary, but it should not be so rough that it is sloppy, incomplete, or ambiguous.

Most newspapers provide clients with layout sheets with ticks along the edges indicating the width (in columns) and the depth (in inches and sometimes also in agate lines) of their pages. Page size and column width have in the past always varied from newspaper to newspaper (by 1975 there were more than 200 different page formats in use among standard-sized dailies), making the layout of ads a confusing job for stores that advertised in more than one newspaper. A chain store typically has had to make up ads to fit the *smallest* page size among newspapers in all towns where it has stores, letting a little space go to waste in other places. However, in 1975 a joint committee representing retail and national advertisers' associations, advertising agencies, and the newspaper industry drew up recommendations to standardize ad makeup sizes for all newspapers. As quickly as mechanical changes can be put into effect, all newspapers using eight- or nine-column pages will be classed as A, B, or C papers and will have the column widths designated in the upper part of Figure 14–4. Those using six-column pages will be D, E, or F papers, and their column widths will be as shown in the lower half of the chart. In the layout of an ad, the layout artist will only need to know to which of the six groups the local newspaper belongs; this chart can then be used to determine the total width of an ad of any given number of columns in width. For ads more than one column wide, the width includes not only the space in each column but also the width of the spaces *between* columns. For example, the F-classified papers, which will have columns two inches wide, will have $8^3/4$ *inches* of width in their four-column ads, not *8 inches.* The additional $^3/4$ inch represents the spaces between columns within the ad.

The basic elements out of which an ad design is created are (1) headlines; (2) pictures; (3) body copy, or text type (*copy blocks*); (4) the store signature or *logotype,* its stylized nameplate along with "standing," or constantly repeated, store copy; and (5) that mysterious and often neglected element, white space. Some would add (6) typographical devices, borders, column rules, "boxes," and the like, which other design experts discourage and consider a source of distracting clutter.

Headlines are hand-lettered directly onto rough layouts, so that the approximate size, blackness or lightness, and letter forms desired in the finished product can be shown. Both the store signature and illustrations may be pasted down in the desired spot on the layout, or simply indicated by a rough sketch and a notation that they will be supplied later (or "picked up" in the case of the signature or standard logotype).

FUNDAMENTALS OF GOOD
ADVERTISING DESIGN

The essential purposes of design are, first, to organize the basic elements of an ad in a logical fashion to *facilitate communication,* the elementary purpose of all advertising; second, to make it easy to *notice the ad in the first place* (in the case of a small ad, which must fight for attention as one of many at-

Advertiser: Maurice

Newspaper: Journal

Insertion Date: November 6

Size: 3 columns x 9½ inches

Headline: Special November Coat Buys !

Text: (A)

Warm, beautiful Coat Buys ! When the chilly winds blow, be
ready for them in one of our great, new Winter Coats at Very
Special Savings. Warm Woll Meltons, Tweeds, Plaids, Plush
Woolens in Junior and Misses' sizes. Sketched ... big, bold,
wool plaid hooded wrap coat. A Beautiful color blend of red,
blue, green, black

78.00

(B)

AT MAURICE''S DOWNTOWN AND MERIDIAN MALL

Signature: (Maurice - standing logo, reverse)

Figure 14–3 The Layout: From Rough Layout to Printed Advertisement

Often in fast-paced retail advertising, a very rough layout of the ad (as shown in the first picture of this sequence), which serves as a blueprint to the newspaper's production staff, will suffice. The size and shape of the ad are shown, a rough outline of the advertising picture is placed in the correct place within the layout, and that picture is identified with a number (the "mat" or "repro" number that enables the person who does the mechanical work to positively identify the piece of art to be used from the newspaper's, the retailer's, or perhaps the manufacturer's catalog of available art). The location of the main headline and the store signature are indicated, along with

rough lines indicating where to place the text copy.

A finished layout as demonstrated in the second picture will serve the same purpose of communicating the concept to printers, but in addition it can be shown to people in the store (the advertiser, merchandise manager, buyer, etc.) to enable them to visualize what the ad will ultimately look like. A proof of the picture has been pasted down on the layout, and the main headline has been hand-lettered in its correct place in a form that resembles the type style that will be used. The actual store logotype, cut out of one of the store's previous ads, is set in proper relationship to other elements in the ad. The text lines are indicated neatly, with due concern for the varying line lengths needed to accommodate the "copy block" to the allotted space. In addition, the text lines are keyed "A" and "B" to correspond to the copy sheet (next picture). When there is more than one copy block, this guides the compositor in putting the right words in the right place. The *display* type (the large type used for the main headline and the price) are also hand-lettered on the finished layout.

At the newspaper, the copy sheet must be "marked up" to indicate the type style and size that is to be used and to fit the copy into the allotted space in the ad. Since the typesetter who gets the copy sheet may be setting only the small-print text type, with the display type being produced from the layout itself by another typesetter, the display lines will be circled on the copy sheet to indicate that those words are being handled by someone else.

Note that the finished layout is always done in full size—just as it will ultimately appear in the paper—and on layout paper that is typically provided by newspapers to their advertisers. This paper has tick marks along the top and bottom to indicate the width of the columns (in picas) and depth (in inches). The size of this ad is thus three columns wide and 9½ inches deep.

The last picture in the series is the final proof of the ad, which is now ready to go to press (unless the proofreader finds some flaw that must be corrected). This is the ad as it will be seen printed in the newspaper.

tractions on a page); third, to make it easy to *follow the logical progression of the messages* the several elements have to tell; and, fourth, to *communicate in a general way the "feel" and image of the store,* product, or service being advertised.

Headline-picture-copy-signature is the most common sequence, moving from the top left of an ad toward the bottom right, but it is not necessary in every case. Some great ads are arranged picture-headline-copy-signature, and others signature-picture-headline-copy. If the the nature of the artwork and message and the space purchased will allow it, the ad should be in the form of a vertical rectangle, reflecting as closely as feasible the shape of the newspaper page itself. (This applies to less-than-full-page ads, of course.) The human eye rejects *monotony* and is attracted to *variety.* It even rejects monotony in the dimensions of an ad as a whole, and likes contrast in its dimensions. This means, avoid square ads when possible. The ideal shape is a width-to-depth ratio of 3:5. If the nature of the art, an exceptionally long headline, or some other consideration makes a vertical rectangle unsuitable, then a horizontal rectangle should be used, with dimensions as close as possible to 5:3 (width to depth).

BASIC LAYOUT PRINCIPLES

Balance Formal or *static balance* results from centering all elements of the ad on the vertical center-line or from

ANPA Format Committee Recommended Ad Makeup Sizes for Newspapers

8 (and 9) Columns			
Cols	A	B	C
1	1¾"	1⅝"	1½"
2	3⅝"	3⅜"	3⅛"
3	5½"	5⅛"	4¾"
4	7¼"	6¾"	6¼"
5	9⅛"	8½"	7⅞"
6	11"	10¼"	9½"
7	12¹³⁄₁₆"	11¹⁵⁄₁₆"	11¹⁄₁₆"
8	14¾"	13¾"	13¼"
9	16¾"	15⅛"	14⅞"

6 Columns			
Cols	D	E	F
1	2¼"	2¹⁄₁₆"	2"
2	4¾"	4⅜"	4¼"
3	7¼"	6¾"	6½"
4	9¹¹⁄₁₆"	9¹⁄₁₆"	8¾"
5	12³⁄₁₆"	11⅜"	11"
6	14¾"	13¾"	13¼"

The sizes given in this table are rounded off to the nearest fraction of an inch and are not intended to be exact. For this reason, and to avoid the appearance of precision, this table has not been converted to picas and points.

For the time being, not every newspaper's makeup width can conform exactly to the dimensions shown. Papers that are over 14¾" wide are classified as A or D. Papers that are between 13¾" and 14¾" wide are classified as B or E. Those between 13¼" and 13¾" are classified as C or F. Smaller papers and tabloids are not covered by these standards.

Figure 14–4 Standardization of Ad Makeup Sizes for Newspapers

placing pairs or groups of elements at equal distances on either side of it. This type of stable, rigid, conservative design is often considered to lack "life." However, many chain stores use a *block system,* involving an overall design used by all stores, for their ads. This layout contains "boxes," or blocks, in which each local store inserts prewritten copy and headquarters-created art for the items it has in stock or finds best suited to its market. The balance in such layouts must be essentially formal.

Informal or dynamic balance is achieved when an ad is deliberately set up to have a somewhat lopsided, but not awkward, look. There is a *focal point,* slightly above the geometric center and a little to the left, where the eye tends to come to rest when one first glances at an ad. That point is treated as a fulcrum, like the hinge on a seesaw. The elements of the ad are placed in opposite quarters, with "heavy" elements near to the focal point and "light" ones further away. (Picture a heavy adult sitting near the center hinge of a teeter-totter, in balance with a small child far out on the end of the board on the other side.) This arrangement produces a pleasing sensation of motion and informality, arouses interest, and even offers a challenge.

Gaze Motion, or "Eye-Flow" The elements of an ad can be arranged so that the eye flows naturally and logically from some conspicuous item near the focal point (in the upper-left quarter), rightward and downward through all parts of the ad. This is done, in part, by placing any *pointed* item, such as a shoe tip, an umbrella, the corner of a flaring coat or skirt, or an arrow, so that it faces *inward* and usually *downward,* directing the reader to the next logical part of the ad. If the ad shows a person, he or she should be looking inward so that following the direction of the gaze will take the reader to the next part of the message.

This principle even applies to imaginary persons not actually shown in the ad, and produces the phenomenon of *right-hand* versus *left-hand* pictures of inanimate products. A chair tends to make us see a person sitting in it; hence all chairs should face inward, so that when the reader adds to the scene a person sitting in the chair, he or she will be looking *toward* the center or lower-center of the ad. A television set makes us think of a person looking toward its screen, so it too must face inward, never outward, as the reader will add the mental image of a viewer standing or sitting in the ad opposite it.

Sometimes, a *reflector or mirror system* is used to bounce the reader's gaze back into the ad. Placing linear elements along the sides of the ad keeps the eyes from straying to the next item on the page and redirects a wandering gaze back to the ad. Heavy black borders are sometimes fascinating to merchants who think they can lock readers into an ad in this way. Unfortunately, it is just as likely to inhibit people who scan a page from reading an ad at all.

Emphasis, or Focus Retailers sometimes find it hard to understand that every ad should have a focus, even if two or more items are of equal importance. *One* should still be featured more strongly. It should have a bigger picture, a bolder subcaption. The *total ad* will attract more readers when *one* main element stands out. Nothing kills interest like a monotonous array of product descriptions.

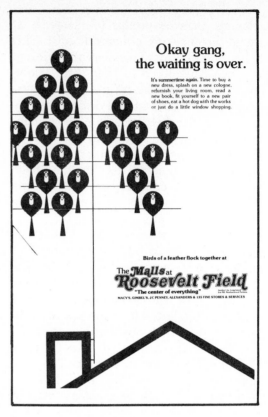

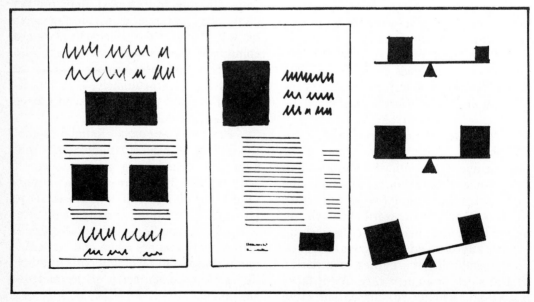

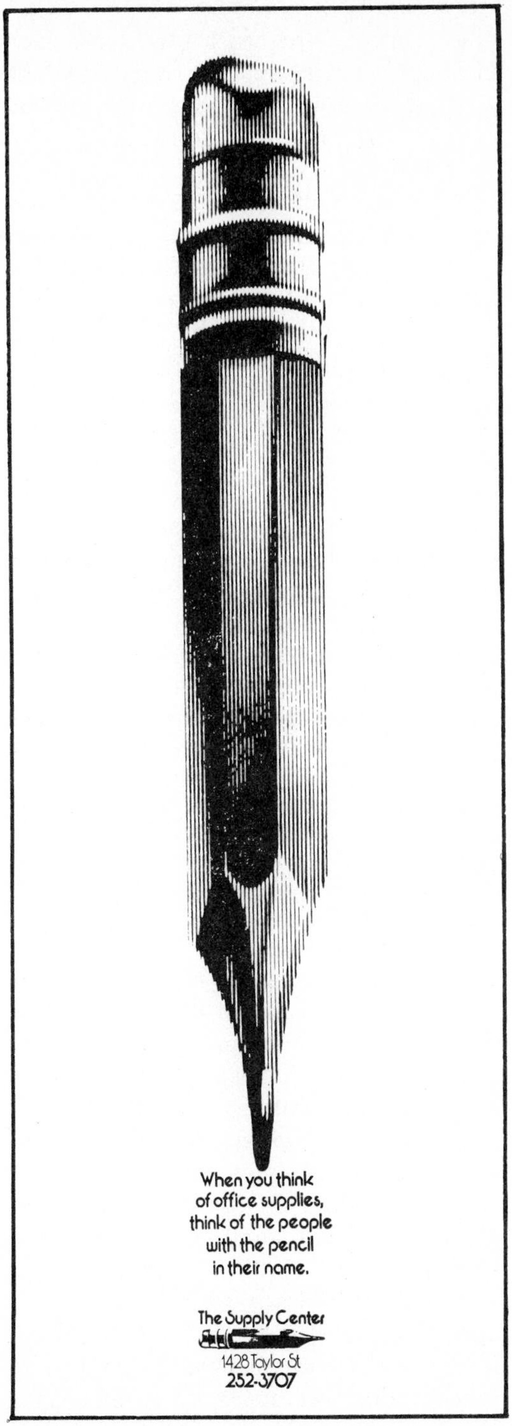

When you think
of office supplies,
think of the people
with the pencil
in their name.

The Supply Center

1428 Taylor St
252-3707

Figure 14–5 Design Fundamentals

Illustrated at bottom left are the two types of balance that can be used in an ad. The first two sketches show *formal* or *static* balance and *informal* or *dynamic* balance, respectively. The idea behind this can be illustrated by the "seesaw principle." Formal balance is achieved by setting two equal weighted graphic elements at equal distance from the focal point, or fulcrum, of the ad. Balance, but of the informal type, is achieved by positioning two masses of unequal weight so that the lighter of the two is nearest the focal point. If the opposite is done, with the heaviest mass nearest the focal point, the ad will be totally unbalanced, as in the bottom sketch. This will disturb the reader and displease the eye.

Informal balance is excellently illustrated by the Roosevelt Field Mall ad. The focal point of this ad is between the two groups of birds. The heavy mass of birds to the left of this point balances well with the type block at lower right, which is positioned farther away from the optical center of the ad. Further balance is achieved in the ad between the copy block at upper right and the chimney of the house at lower left.

Gaze motion is the main design principle used in the ad from The Supply Center, in which a giant pencil first attracts attention and then directs the readers' attention inevitably downward to the brief block of the copy and the advertiser's signature at the bottom.

The Kay Baum ad is a fine example of the use of both *contrast* and *unity*. The store's name at upper right, by being in extremely bold lettering, contrasts well with the copy block at the center of the ad. In addition, the benday background with its moderately heavy screen contrasts with the white lettering and the product picture, but it also serves as the unifying factor that ties the whole ad together and lifts it out of the mass of other ads on the page.

Emphasis has already been illustrated earlier in this book, in Figure 6–2 on page 146. Note how each of the many products advertised there are given varying emphasis. And of the three that are given the greatest prominence, pork chops become the most-noticed item, placed as they are at the very center of the ad.

Source: Ad for The Supply Center reprinted with permission from the International Newspaper Advertising Executives' *Sales and Idea Book* (Winter 1974), p. 21.

Contrast Contrasting elements in an ad are another way of attracting readers' interest. Vary the size of *pictures;* their weight, or tone; or their shape. Vary the size, slant, and boldness or lightness of *subheads and captions.* Vary the boldness and line width of the several blocks, or paragraphs, of *body copy.* Break up all long pieces of copy with subheads, changes in column widths, or different styles of type. Or place a *tint block* beneath some copy elements. (This is a screening device that lays a mass of tiny inked dots over a given area. It is not dark enough to inhibit reading type or seeing the picture, but it gives that area of the ad a *tone* that contrasts with the pure white of the open spaces and the pure black of the larger headlines and bolder pictures.)

Some seek contrast by making the "empty space" in an ad, or some parts of it, solid black, and the printing white. This technique may attract attention when there are few similar ads, but many studies have proven that it is harder to read white type on a black background than it is to read the black type on a white background that we are accustomed to. This makes white type unsuitable for ads that contain a large amount of copy.

Unity An ad must "hang together." It must look like a *unit,* distinct from all the other ads or the editorial matter on a page. This effect is often best obtained by surrounding the elements of the ad with a "sea of white space." This is much more effective, in any event, than either the big, bold borders or the gaudily decorative ones some advertisers still use. Lay out the elements of the ad in the order you have decided on; then

move them all inward a little from each of the four corners. The result will be a pleasing "island" of advertising set off crisply and tastefully from the rest of the page.

A unified effect can also be achieved by a homogeneous background of light gray or some other light tint if color is being used. The tone, shape, and size of illustrations, the copy blocks, the type used in headlines, and other elements can also be uniform. But the need for unity must be carefully weighed against the need for contrast. It is often a considerable challenge to achieve just the right balance between these two equally vital elements of good design. A distinctive border creates a unified effect, but borders in general, and thick, black, and overly ornate ones in particular, are passé. Other unifying methods are preferred. Heavy borders *within an ad* tend to break it up too much; readers either "get lost" or think they are seeing more than one ad.

New Restrictions on Small Ads as Conservation Measures The critical shortage of newsprint that developed by the mid-1970s caused a rapid increase in the cost of newspaper space and led to the adoption of standardized dimensions into which small display ads must fit in order to conform to paper conservation measures taken by newspapers. Where these policies have been instituted, the result has been to reduce the sizes of ads that small shops can afford, to restrict the retailer's choice in the shape or form of ads permitted (in some, not all, papers), and to force small ads into a still more critical battle for attention on ever more crowded pages. When such situations prevail and small-space ads must be designed to fit a pre-scribed format and to appear on crowded pages, close adherence to the funda-mentals discussed in the foregoing pages becomes even more important. One piece of artwork should be dominant; the prin-ciple of gaze motion to direct the eye to the key element near the center of the ad must be skillfully applied; a delicate balance needs to be reached to insure that the ad has a central focus. Also rec-ommended is the use of a large word or two in the headline and a strong identi-fying logotype for the signature. Use adequate white space and consider a well-chosen, truly distinctive border (but not necessarily a reversion to the over-use of heavy borders, which are par-ticularly eye-repelling when many are seen in close proximity).

3 Understanding Type

Type is a key element in presenting any advertising message. It can make or break an ad. But typography is often the least understood and most neglected aspect of the printing process. So, by default, type selection is left up to the production people at the newspaper, who rarely spend much time thinking about the real purpose of an ad and about the delicate, image-building rela-tionship between the product, service, or store and a given type style. The original idea is watered down, the in-tended thrust weakened, in the type-selection process.

This is nobody's fault but the ad-vertisers'. It behooves them, first of all, to be thoroughly familiar with the type-faces, sizes, and variations their produc-tion staffs or those of the newspapers have at their disposal. Larger newspa-pers (and contract typesetting houses) normally have a catalog or sample sheet of *type specimens*. If there is none, one can easily be made up from the ads that have appeared in past issues.

CHARACTERISTICS OF TYPE

Each type style has a *face*, each face belongs to a *family*, and each family is a member of a type *race*.

Roman (or Serif) Type By far the most-used type race is the *roman*, whose major subdivisions are *oldstyle, modern,* and *mixed* type. Almost all *long* units of small body or text type are set in some form of roman. Most persons first learn to read in schoolbooks, newspapers, and magazines using roman body type. So because of their lifelong familiarity with it, if for no other reason, people comprehend printed matter more rapidly when it is in roman. Since legibility and quick comprehension are the prime needs in body copy, it is always a safe choice.

Roman types are characterized by *serifs* (short lines at an angle to the ends of the strokes of letters) and by varia-tions in the thickness of the linear and curved lines that form the shape of each letter. Oldstyle has pointed serifs (which look like little triangular pennants flying from the tops of the ascenders) and only moderate variations in line thickness. Modern roman has straight, clipped-off serifs and very extreme variations in the thickness of the lines that form the let-ters.

Figure 14–6 Races and Families of Type

As the text's discussion of type indicated, there are a great number of specific typefaces available for use in advertisements. Here only a few examples of all those typefaces can be shown, but these serve to illustrate the characteristics of each and to point up differences between them.

A An oldstyle roman face called *Garamond*. The pointed serifs and moderate variations in the line thickness of the letters are typical of this race of type.

B A modern roman face called *Bodoni*. The serifs of roman type are present, but they are straight and squared off. The thickness of the lines varies dramatically within each letter. Modern roman typefaces mix well with modern sans serif types.

C A mixed roman face called *Cheltenham*. The serifs exhibit the angles of oldstyle but are clipped off, as in modern, before they can reach a point. The moderate variations in the line width of the letters are also typical of oldstyle.

D A sans serif typeface of the Gothic version called *Franklin Gothic*. This race of type lacks serifs and can best be described as "blocklike." It has a perfectly plain face, with little variation in the line width of individual letters.

E A modern sans serif typeface called *Spartan*. Again, serifs are absent, but there is greater variation in the line widths of the letters, and the blocklike appearance of the letters has been modified. (For example, compare the dots on the "i's" of **D** and **E.**)

F Another modern sans serif called *Spartan Book*. Here, the letters are extremely rounded, with very thin, uniform lines. Note how much more modern and feminine this looks than typefaces **D** and **E**.

G A square serif typeface called *Beton*. This type race is characterized by thick, square serifs.

H A typeface of the script-cursive race called *Raleigh Cursive*. The space after each letter distinguishes cursive from script, in which all the small letters are connected.

I A text or blackface type called *Cloister Black*. This race of type is used to imply a relationship with something very old or religious or Germanic.

J A special-purpose "open" type. These special-purpose, contemporary, or decorative typefaces do not fit into the classical races of type design. Many are derived from them but are embellished, distorted, and altered for special emphasis. Not all are found in regular typesetting houses, but many can be obtained from advertising art services.

(D) # what can we do to suit you?

(E) **men's shirt sale** save now on terrific selection permanent press dress shirts

(F) ## We're having a sale because we want the business.

(G) # a dress is a coat is a coatdress

(I) ## A Madrigal Dinner=Concert

December 10, 11, 12 & 13, 1974

7:00 p.m.

(H) ## Special Sale!

(J)

Headlines in roman are excellent, too. Ads would look good and sell merchandise well if *nothing but* roman faces were used. Most newspapers and printing plants offer more roman typefaces than faces belonging to any other race.

Sans Serif Type Second in overall popularity (and growing rapidly in acceptance and use, even in smaller sizes) is the *sans serif* type race. It has two branches: the blocklike *gothic* and the trim *modern sans serif*. These typefaces are characterized (as their name indicates) by an absence of serifs and by the uniform thickness of the lines forming the letters. Both the stolid gothic and the modern sans serif faces are frequently used in ad headlines; the latter mix very well with modern roman type in the body text.

Modern sans serif is being increasingly used for selected units of body type, too. It can add variety and contrast, provide emphasis in a large ad, or tell the entire message in a small one. It is a readable, clean-cut typeface with a modern, functional look.

Other Type Designs Other type designs should be used sparingly, for special-purpose headlines or subheads, for store signatures, and as a means of giving continuity and identity to a series of related ads in a campaign. *Square serif* type is much like sans serif, except that thick, bold serifs are added to the ends of the straight, uniform strokes. It mixes well with either sans serif or modern roman, but is a poor choice for the body type for lengthy copy. *Script*, or *cursive* type, which has curved, sweeping strokes resembling handwriting, sets a desired tone when it is used for a word

or two here or there, but it falls flat when it is used too frequently in any one ad. Least legible of all are typefaces belonging to the *text* or *blackface race*, which derive from the ancient hand-lettering used by medieval monks prior to the invention of printing. Their elaborate embellishments retard reading speed and comprehension; in a few cases, however, they can add just the right emotional tone to an otherwise too flippant or too modern design.

Going into specifics about the many type families belonging to each type race would be futile, since there are literally hundreds of them and the production people on any store or newspaper's staff will probably have only a dozen or two to work with. Some type families have classic names like Caslon, Bodoni, Futura, Railroad Gothic, or Memphis; others have names peculiar to the particular company from which a newspaper or typesetting shop buys its fonts.

TYPE STYLES

Most kinds of type come in a variety of styles, especially the much-used roman and sans serif varieties. The usual options are *regular* (straight-up-and-down) type, *italic* (slanted) type, and *bold, medium,* and *light faces*:

regular

italic

bold

medium

light face

Regular-width type, which is easiest to read, is suitable for the typical ad with average line lengths. *Condensed type* permits adjustments for narrow columns or for extra-long words in heads and subheads, while *extended type* is useful in unusually wide ads, when lines are long, or to fill up otherwise awkward white spaces when an ad contains unusually short words.

regular width
condensed width
extended width

All type can be set *solid* (with the lines as close together as possible) or *leaded* (with varying amounts of white space inserted between the lines to enhance the overall appearance of the copy and increase its legibility).

these	these
words	words
are	are
set	leaded
solid	

Adequate leading is especially critical when relatively small type is set in relatively long lines and there are many lines one after the other.

Headlines in large type are often *letterspaced* by drawing the letters out and inserting extra white space between them.

Letterspacing looks like this.

This improves their readability and produces a more appealing visual impact.

No long unit of copy, and no long headlines, should be set in all-capital letters, and some kinds of type, such as text or blackface and script or cursive, can never be set in capitals except for initial letters. Many typographers strongly disapprove of using any italic type in all capitals, too. Left margins should always be set *flush* (in a straight vertical line), but right margins may be set *ragged* (in irregular line lengths).

Sophisticated *photocomposing machines* can play all sorts of tricks with type, introducing unusual slants and angles that may be just right for a particular ad. However, advertisers should beware of using such gimmicks to try to compensate for poor copy or a poorly designed ad. Photocomposition also has other advantages. Screens can be used to make heavy boldface letters in large sizes less overwhelming and type can be photographically enlarged or reduced to sizes in between the traditional point sizes used in letterpress composition. Phototype composing rooms can also produce *reversed* images of given blocks of type (white letters on a black background) quickly and cheaply.

On the other hand, limitations may be placed on the advertiser by the typesetter (or compositor) that will be used. Not all typesetters have all typefaces or styles available, and the advertiser should be aware of this before designing the ad.

Type Measurement Sizes of type are expressed in printer's *points*, each being $\frac{1}{72}$ of an inch. Hence, the body copy or text of an ad will probably be set in sizes ranging from 8-point to 14-point, although subordinate units in small ads, such as detailed specifications of secondary items, may range into sizes as small as 6-point.

This is 6-point type.

This is 8-point type.

This is 11-point type.

This is 14-point type.

This is 18-point type.

Headlines, subheads, and even lead-in paragraphs in larger ads use *display* type sizes, from 18-point up through 72-point (one inch high) and 144-point (two inches high). The actual printed image will not be quite this large because in hard metal or hot type there must be a shoulder on the piece of metal that carries each letter, both above the tallest ascender and below the deepest descender of the letter forms. This space can be eliminated entirely in photocomposition for special headline effects, but doing so endangers readability. Each individual type family, in the same point size, varies as to the actual image size printed.

Linear measurements and area dimensions are figured in *picas;* the pica is $1/6$ of an inch. The *em* of any particular type style is the square of its point size, because the small letter *m* occupies a perfectly square unit of type material. When printers speak loosely of an em without specifying the type size, they refer to the *pica em,* which is $1/6$ of an inch square. Sometimes they call it, even more inexactly, simply "a pica."

GUIDELINES FOR SELECTING TYPE

The basic function of any kind of printing is to facilitate communication. Type itself is only a means to an end, and the advertiser's chief goal should be to *deliver the message,* without necessarily making the reader conscious of the type at all. *Legibility* must always be the first consideration in choosing type. Avoid all capitals and stick to capitals and lower case unless there is a compelling reason to do otherwise. Capital letters are harder to read, less pleasing

to the eye, and more likely to be mistaken for other letters. (To prove this to yourself, hold this page a little farther from your face than you normally would and try to read the following sets of letters:

abcdefghijklmnop

ABCDEFGHIJKLMNOP.

Which letters are easier to distinguish?)

Hold fast to the most-used, best-known faces for all solid masses of type. Use italic sparingly, for emphasis and contrast; it is much harder to read. Seek a reasonable balance between too much variety and too little. Using only type from one family may sound montonous, but varying the posture, weight, width, and size of the type by an appropriate use of italic, boldface, lightface, condensed, and extended type will provide plenty of contrast and variety, plus the *unity* that all good ads should have. Seldom should a small ad contain more than two type families, nor a big one more than three.

Never skip all over the type catalog and include half a dozen different styles of clashing type in the same ad. There are some combinations that do not clash, of course; perhaps a clean-cut sans serif head followed by body copy in a modern roman face; script or cursive for a head, matched with oldstyle roman for the text; a square serif head and a sans serif body type. A mixture of roman styles may also work, but some experts say oldstyle type should not be paired with modern, though either may be associated with the transitional mixed roman.

Despite the fact that simplicity and legibility are the primary considerations in choosing type, properly selected faces can also reinforce the emotional impact or tone of an ad. Oldstyle roman faces can produce a conservative, dignified effect that suits ads for banks, insurance firms, long-established department stores, jewelers, and professional people, as well as many institutional messages. Modern roman is a safe choice for almost any ad. Gothic, the bolder versions of which are more usually encountered, implies sheer physical strength and endurance, useful qualities in ads for hardware, building materials, or construction equipment. Gothic is also traditional for the main headline in clearance-sale ads of highly promotional stores. Some mixed roman families like Cheltenham have similar connotations.

Modern sans serif type, usually lightface or medium weight, is much in vogue for stores that want a new, modern look. It suits fashion advertising, announcements of new stores or remodeled older stores, and ads aimed at the youth market. Square serif type has much the same flavor but has more overtones of physical strength and material toughness. Script and cursive faces are used to approximate stylish handwritten notices or invitations for very dignified special events, such as the grand opening of a prestigious shop, and are often seen in the signatures of better jewelers, ladies' fashion shops, and home furnishings outlets. Text, or blackface, has religious and also Teutonic connotations. It is reminiscent of German script, the sort that might be used in ads for German cars or for skiing at Bavarian resorts. Though too illegible to be used for more than a very few words, it is often seen in ads for funeral homes, professional services, and church-related items and events.

Boldface type often suggests masculinity or ruggedness; lightface styles tend to imply femininity, high fashion, delicacy, quality, or expensiveness. The type chosen for a given ad should suit both the product, service, or store being advertised and the target market. It must also harmonize graphically with the layout and art. One would hardly use thick, bold letters with a delicate line drawing; and, conversely, an ethereal, flowing lightface script would be a poor choice to accompany a bold, massive illustration.

HOW TO FIT ADVERTISING COPY TO SPACE

Most of the worst of locally produced newspaper retail ads suffer from overcrowding. Others contain too little copy, drowning in vast oceans of nonfunctional white space. Advertisers can avoid both these extremes by knowing how to estimate the space needed for a given piece of copy when a particular size of type is used, or, conversely, how much copy to write to fill a predetermined area when a certain size type is to be used.

The Square-Inch System One simple way to estimate, very roughly, how much space copy will occupy is called the *square-inch method*. Take a piece of material already printed in a known typeface, and use a ruler to divide it into a dozen or more one-inch squares. Count the words in each square, then average the results. This will give you the average number of words that will fit in each square inch of space when that type is used. Do this, right now, to this page (if you personally own this book). You will find that the count is 13 words per square inch or thereabouts. And it takes no mathematical genius to go further and determine how much will fit in a space three inches wide and four inches deep or whatever.

The following table shows very roughly the average number of words, set in a typical regular-width typeface, that will fit into a square inch of space both when the lines are set solid and when they are leaded.

	Set Solid	Leaded
8-point type	32	23
10-point type	21	16
12-point type	14	11
14-point type	10	6

This table will *not* be accurate, except by chance, for the particular type you may be using. But it demonstrates how the word content of a given unit of space varies depending on the type size and the amount of leading (if any) used.

When copy contains, say, 400 words, some simple arithmetic will tell you how many square inches you need for an ad (allowing space, of course, for headline, pictures, the store signature, white space, and so on). If a fixed amount of space is available each week or each day, it is equally simple to calculate the maximum amount of copy that can be used.

The Word-Count System The square-inch system, while better than guessing, is a very rough method of fitting copy. Other, more time-consuming methods should be mastered and used,

particularly when an ad is extra-important.

One less rough method is the *word-count system*. It is based on the fact that when any average, normal typeface is used, the average word occupies 3 ems of space if the type size is 10-point or smaller and $2\frac{1}{2}$ ems if the type size is larger. In 8-point type, the average word occupies 24 points; in 18-point type, it occupies 45 points.

Now all you need is the *line length* to calculate the number of words that will fill a line. If a line is 3 inches wide, it contains 216 points (there being 72 printer's points to the inch). Divide this 216 points by 24 and you will get 9 words per line for 8-point type. Or divide by 45 and you will come up with 4.8 words per line for 18-point type. Since words are hypenated when they "break" at the end of a line, using fractional parts of a word is permissible in the smaller type sizes normally used for body copy (especially when one is dealing with large masses of copy that run into many hundreds of words). But for short bits of copy, forget the fractions. Give yourself a margin of safety, and give the compositors a little room to add white space here and there. Of course, when the larger type sizes popular for display purposes (headlines and subheads) are used, it is seldom feasible to break a word at the end of a line. If a line is three inches long and 18-point type is to be used, it is wiser just to let well enough alone and figure on four words to the line. Also, when larger type sizes are used, it can be misleading to work with "average" words. Look and see if the four actual words are long or short, and adjust the space accordingly!

Finally, figure the depth. Eight-point type is usually "leaded" 2 points between lines, so count lines as if they were 10 points deep. Eighteen-point type will probably have 4 or 6 points of leading between lines, so count lines as if they were 22 or 24 points deep. A copy block three inches wide and four inches deep will thus hold 28 lines of 8-point type (four times 72 points per inch, divided by 10 points per line, with the fraction necessarily disregarded). If you can fit 9 words in each line and your space will accommodate 28 lines, you need only multiply to find the total number of words that will fit in the space: 252 words if 8-point type is used.

Another version of the word-count method starts with the assumption that the average word set in an average width of 12-point type will occupy 3 linear picas. For type in sizes smaller than 12-point, one deducts half a pica for each 2 points the type size is reduced, and for larger type, one adds half a pica. Thus, in 10-point type the average word would require $2^{1}/_{2}$ picas of space, and in 14-point it would require $3^{1}/_{2}$ picas.

The Character-Count System A still more accurate but time-consuming method of copyfitting is the *character-count method*. Though it is seldom used in day-to-day newspaper ad work, it may be needed once in a while when a special, top-grade ad is being designed.

The first step is to count the *characters* in the copy, not the *words*. With typewritten copy this step is not very difficult, for it is only necessary to count the characters that are over or under the line length to which the typewriter was set. (This will not work, however, when copy is typed on a machine such as an IBM Executive, whose characters do not all occupy the same amount of space.)

Next, one refers to special tables (provided by the manufacturers of particular type *fonts,* or faces) that give the average number of characters in a pica for the particular size, style, and form of type that is being used. (This count will vary slightly, depending on what typesetting process is used.) Dividing the total characters in the copy by the number of characters per pica will give the exact number of picas needed to accommodate the copy. Finally, divide the figure obtained by the number of picas per line, which will give the number of lines that the copy will occupy when typeset. Fractional lines, of course, are counted as whole lines, because if even a single word or syllable is left over, it takes a whole line in depth to get it all in.

A character-count table, applying to several popular typefaces in frequently used sizes, looks like this:

Typeface	Number of Characters per Linear Pica in Point-size Indicated		
	8-pt.	12-pt.	18-pt.
Bodoni Light and Italic	3.05	2.35	1.65
Bodoni Bold	2.85	2.2	1.5
Century Expanded and Bold	2.8	2.1	1.5
Sans Serif Light and Bold	3.1	2.1	1.45

Note that this table is merely an example, much simplified. Almost all kinds of type are available in more than three sizes. And two fonts of type bearing the same name and in the same point-size will *not* necessarily have the same character-count. Different type manufacturers may introduce slight variations in their design of letters that will make the figures in their tables somewhat different.

Using this simplified demonstration table, one could calculate that copy totaling 300 characters in length would occupy 98.3 linear picas (300 divided by 3.05) if set in 8-point Bodoni Light. Then, assuming a line length of 18 picas (three inches), one divides 98.3 by 18 to determine the number of lines needed. That comes out to 5.46, which must be rounded off to the next largest whole number, 6, because one must count the whole line to calculate depth. Finally, the total area required to accommodate this copy is determined by establishing the depth needed to print six lines of 8-point type. Assuming those lines were to be leaded 2 points, one counts them as if they were 10-point lines (8 plus 2) and multiplies 6 lines by 10 points depth for each line. The answer, 60, is the number of printer's points of depth necessary. Since there are 12 points to the pica, this could be expressed as five picas (60 divided by 12). Hence, the copy block on the layout would measure 18 picas wide by 5 picas deep. If the same copy were to be set in Sans Serif Light, in 18-point type, leaded four points, in lines of the same length, it would have to be 22 picas deep, a great difference.

The distinguishing characteristic of the character-count method is that it takes into account the fact that letters set in printer's type are of varying widths, which differ for different typefaces. For example, the small letters *i* and *l* and the figure 1 are obviously very much narrower than an average character, while the capital letters *M* and *W* are a great deal wider. In preparing copy for magazines or for high-grade mail pieces, when there is plenty of time and extreme accuracy is essential, character-count is the preferred method of copyfitting. In producing retail ads for newspapers, however, there is seldom time for this method to be used, and the compositors will make adjustments to compensate for minor errors in copyfitting that characterize the results of the other two methods that were discussed.

4 The Language of Color

Color ads, used properly, can sell more goods, get more attention, give a store a better image, and bring in extra co-op dollars. They can provide the extra punch that generates extra profits.

COLOR COSTS

The literature of the research profession, the advertising industry, the newspaper industry, and retailing itself abounds with proof that good color ads outpull ads of comparable size in the same media, delivered to the same audiences, on the same day, in black and white. Scores of studies (some involving thousands of respondents, others only a few dozen) have come up with approximately the same results. On the average a full-color ad gets 85 percent more readers than the same ad without color. Despite their higher cost, color ads attract more readers and produce more sales *per dollar spent*.

Consider the following evidence:

In Long Beach, California, tests were conducted over an 11-year period using the *split-run technique*. (Half the readers got the ads in color, and half got them in black and white.) The researchers then followed up on both groups to determine how many of those who saw each type of ad *actually purchased the* products *advertised*. The results were as follows: [1]

Sales Advantage for One-Color Ad over Black-and-White

1958 (6 tests)	Plus 50%
1962 (6 tests)	Plus 79%
1968 (6 tests)	Plus 85%

It is particularly significant that the more recent tests showed an *increasing* advantage for the color ads, because during the 1960s, when the number of color ads was growing, many people suggested that once color advertising in all media became commonplace, the novelty would wear off and individual color ads would tend to lose their advantage. The color ads cost, on the average, only 17 percent more than the same ads in black and white, yet they generated, on the average, 72 percent more sales.

Another series of split-run tests compared the relative efficiency of black-and-white ads as opposed to one-color and three-color (full-color) ads of the same size in the same media. What was tested this time was the readership of the ads, not the sales results. The results are summarized below.[2]

Another recent study, reported by the N. W. Ayer advertising agency, was less favorable. It found only that "color advertising *almost* pays for itself in the additional readership it achieves." (Note, however, that the increase in sales as a result of using color was not measured.) Ayer reported that using one color in 1,000-line (72 column-inch) ads increased readership by 36 percent and costs by 35 percent; using three colors increased readership by 61 percent and costs by 62 percent. Color made more of a difference in small ads than in full-page ads.[3]

A classic test in Battle Creek, Michigan, in the 1950s showed that spending 43 percent more to have full-color ads raised the readership of text copy by 120 percent.[4]

In other tests over the years, (a) 61 percent more women remembered a color ad five days after it had appeared than remembered the same ad in black and white; (b) a commodity producers' association traced the actual sales resulting from its ads at its dealers and

Tests of One-Color Versus Black-and-White	Increase in Readership with Color
Houston (28 tests—national and retail ads)	Plus 53%
Milwaukee (7 tests—packaged goods ads)	Plus 44%
Publications Research Service (28 tests—national ads)	Plus 70%
Average one-color cost premium over B & W	Plus 17%

Tests of Full-Color Versus Black-and-White	Increase in Readership with Color
Houston (5 tests—national and retail ads)	Plus 91%
Milwakuee (5 tests—packaged goods ads)	Plus 78%
Publications Research Service (10 tests—national ads)	Plus 70%
Average full-color cost premium over B & W	Plus 29%

found that color ads brought in from *two to nine times* as many sales as black-and-white ads; (c) a noted grocery chain found that color ads produced 40 percent more direct sales and kept pulling over a longer period of time; and (d) adding one color to sales coupons produced a 28 percent increase in sales for an 11 percent increase in costs, while adding three colors raised sales by 79 percent for only a 24 percent increase in costs.[5]

USING SPECIFIC COLORS TO ATTAIN DESIRED RESULTS

Getting Attention   When getting attention is a retailer's only aim, the process of choosing an ad color is fairly simple. When the Mandel Bros. department store in Chicago ran the first retail ad in color, in 1903, it used red. And an amazing majority of flat-color retail ads are still in red. Psychological studies confirm that red objects tend to appear a little closer to the viewer than they really are. From this, one can infer that a main headline or a featured picture in red will seem larger and attract more attention. And it will. Unfortunately, red is so badly overused in ads that there is nothing distinctive about it any more. But there are other ways to make a main head or a picture stand out, other colors one can use.

Studies indicate that black on yellow is the *most legible* combination for an attention-getting headline, but black on gray, blue on white, blue on gray, and green on white are almost as good. The *least legible* combinations, on the other hand, are red on green, orange on white, blue on black, and black on blue.

In any event, there are many options

in addition to the traditional red on white. (Retailers should not, however, go overboard in using color as an attention-getter. Too many different colors in an ad, or too much of even one color, may repel, rather than attract, readers.)

Adding Realism   If the purpose of using color is to add realism to the product illustration and strengthen the ad's persuasive power, then *full-process color* (the three primary colors, plus black) is the answer, if the paper can provide it and the advertiser can afford it. Often the necessary color-separation proofs, negatives, mats, or plates can be obtained with the help of a cooperating manufacturer. In fact, most process color ads run by medium-sized or even large stores use manufacturer-supplied production materials (with or without a co-op subsidy for space and color costs).

For retailers completely on their own, flat color that matches actual product color closely is not too hard to manage: lush green for lawn-care items, daffodil yellow when a shipment of new spring dresses includes some numbers in that hue, men's suits in chocolate brown, and so on. Colors for women's clothing and home furnishings, in particular, should always match the original as closely as possible, lest customers be disappointed when they get to the store.

Projecting Emotions   Using the symbolic, emotional, and associational aspects of color to increase the impact of ads is a real challenge for retailers, and for other advertisers as well. Color, as well as words, can stimulate emotions and tell people things about products, stores, and services.

Red is the most exciting color. It

speaks of heat and energy, and it is aggressive. *Orange* too can be exciting and exhilarating. Its lighter tones express openness, frankness, gaiety, and youthfulness. Orange also, along with *russet* and *flame yellow*, denotes cheerfulness; like *yellow*, it adds a sense of light. Yellow is considered a neutral color, yet it has many useful psychological connotations. Its paler shades express cheer and warmth. So do such closely related colors as *tan, ivory, cream*, and *apricot*.

Blue is the exact opposite of red in its emotional overtones. It seems cool and has a soothing, constraining effect. Like *plum* and *slate*, two other cool colors, blue can be slightly depressing, but it is also considered the most restful of colors. Its lighter shades create an atmosphere of quiet, freshness, and repose. Like blue, *green* is a cool, restful color whose shades imply quiet, freshness, and repose. Green is also the color of life and growth, and sometimes of envy.

Brown, like red and orange, is a warm color; but it can also imply bitterness. *Gray* is a cold color. *Steel gray* implies weight and solidarity. *Purple* suggests pomp and power; *black*, sobriety and mourning; *gold*, prosperity. *White* suggests purity, peace, faith, joy, and cleanliness.

See the color insert after page 402 for Figure 14–7, which illustrates the use of color in ads.

HOW COLOR CAN HELP ADS
REACH TARGET MARKETS

Different kinds of people react differently to different colors and combinations of colors. Hence, in planning color ads, it is useful to determine the particular *submarket* of readers one wants to reach and choose colors particularly effective with that target group.

Tests show that there is *age group selectivity* for color. In general, infants prefer *yellow* by a wide margin, while the elderly like *blue* best of all. As people grow older, they gradually shift from a preference for yellow toward a preference for blue. Thus young adults are *inclined* toward yellow, and the mature and middle-aged toward blue; but neither shares the very strong preferences of the very young and the very old. Broadly speaking, however, darker tones please older age groups, and lighter tones please and attract younger people. *Red* is attractive throughout the life cycle.

Sex does not seem to have a strong effect on color preferences, but in general men seem to like darker and brighter colors, while women seem to prefer lighter, softer, more subtle tones. There is some evidence that men are more attracted to blue and women to red, and that men have a slight preference for orange while women have a slight preference for yellow. Both sexes tend to be attracted by orange, but both tend to prefer blue, red, and green, in that order. Women seem to respond to any color better than men.

Social class affects some color preferences. People with less formal education, less money, less-prestigious occupations, and a lower status in the community tend to prefer bright, strong primary colors like red, blue, and green. Higher socioeconomic groups tend to respond better to pastel colors, soft shades, and light hues.

Various *personality types* also react differently to different colors. The outgoing, extroverted person responds better to red (a fiery, aggressive, hot color), while the quiet, restrained, introverted customer is more comfortable with cool, restful greens and blues.

COLOR IN THE AD LAYOUT

The rules for using color in an ad layout are fairly simple. In newspapers, color is most effective when used lavishly: for heavy, bold headlines or thick, sturdy line art. Tint blocks of a thin, weak color overprinted with heavy black or a dark color are also effective. It is seldom wise to use color for delicate artwork or lightface type or to attempt overprinting. And for legibility in *bold copy,* the best bet is still black on white.

5 Advertising Production for Newspapers

Advertising people who understand the mechanics of printing copy and illustrations are better able to communicate with those who do this work and to avoid technical problems that can spoil a good ad. And they are aware of the mechanical capabilities and limitations of print media. Printing equipment and procedures differ from newspaper to newspaper, but they are gradually becoming more standardized and uniform. One of the best ways to learn something about the production end of advertising is to visit a local newspaper and take a plant tour. Very large stores' production units contract out some production jobs such as typesetting and engraving and supply complete materials ready for printing to the newspaper.

LETTERPRESS PRINTING

A few newspapers, chiefly large ones, still use *letterpresses,* machines that depend on massive physical pressure to squeeze paper against the raised surface of printing plates made of hard substances, metal or plastic. The first step in this type of printing is to set the copy in type, a process that was once done by hand, but which is now completely automated (except for oversize typefaces). Printing may be done directly from this type. Often, however, such as when the printing plates must be shipped to the place of printing, papier-mâché molds, called matrices or *mats,* will be made from the type blocks. Into these mats is poured molten metal (an alloy of lead, tin, and antimony), which, when hardened, forms a *stereotype,* a plate with raised surfaces that will be used for printing. This stereotyping process is the source of the term *hot-metal composition.*

The printing plates are formed in a cylindrical shape so that they can be attached to a *plate cylinder.* Rubber-composition rollers carry ink to the plates' surface from a *fountain.* An *impression cylinder* then presses the paper *web* against the inked surface to transfer an image.

The coarse-grained paper often used in letterpress printing and the stereotype process may reduce the sharpness of original type or art. Therefore, bold, strong art elements and relatively large, thick typefaces are best to use.

OFFSET LITHOGRAPHY

The biennial survey conducted in 1975 by the National Newspaper Association revealed that 91 percent of weekly papers and 74 percent of dailies were by then being printed by the *offset lithography* method of printing. Of dailies with more than 50,000 circulation, 55 percent had been converted to that system. Forecasts indicate that before 1980 nine out of ten papers will be printed in this way.

In the lithographic process a flat-surface plate does the printing, not a raised-surface plate as in letterpress operations. The image is created on the smooth surface of the plate by rapid and inexpensive photochemical means. The plate containing the image is made of light, flexible metal that easily bends into the semicylindrical form that is fastened to the *plate cylinder* on the rotary press. Then both ink and water are distributed over the surface from two separate fountains. The two substances do not mix, and because of the photochemical treatment, ink collects only on the areas where there is an image to be transferred to the paper. An *offset cylinder,* wrapped in a rubber blanket, picks up the ink in a reversed image on one side, from the original plate, and transmits that image to the other side, to the paper running through the machine, where it is pressed lightly against the *impression cylinder.* The resulting positive image on the paper (a smoother, finer-grained kind than the coarse-surfaced newsprint used in letterpress work) is crisp and sharp. The rubber blanket on the offset cylinder, being flexible, perfectly adapts its printing surface to imperfections and variations in the paper. Thus no detail is lost, as is often the case when the hot-metal stereotyping process is used, and artwork reproduces especially well. Even relatively fine lines in the advertising art or small, fine-grained photographs can be printed.

Advertising copy and pictures to be printed lithographically are "pasted up" on *light tables* using scissors, razor blades, adhesive wax, sticky tape (containing borders and rules), and fine brushes. No time-consuming and expensive engravings are required. And at the same time that the ads are prepared for plate-making, photographs can be divided into fine dots (necessary in connection with either kind of printing) to be reproduced as *halftones* by *screens* used in the camera. Little or no extra time or money is involved in handling artwork of any kind, including photos. The headlines and copy either can be set in regular printer's type or, just as easily, can be hand-lettered or typewritten. Due to the simplicity of the preparation process, some retailers have established their own production departments from which they send *camera-ready* ads, all ready for printing, direct to the newspaper. Small newspapers whose printing is "farmed out" to have the presswork done maintain their own composing units locally—a real convenience to local advertisers.

COMBINING COLD TYPE WITH LETTERPRESS PRINTING

Some larger newspapers continue to print with letterpress but set up ads in what is familiarly termed a *cold-type ad alley* (the composing room). Here, advertising is prepared in much the same manner as for offset lithography. After a complete ad or page is pasted up, a picture is taken of it and a special photoengraving process etches the image into a thin, flexible plate that can be curved to fit the rotary press cylinder. This gives the raised surfaces necessary for letterpress printing without the intermediate hot-metal stereotyping process in which, in the past, image sharpness was lost and ad size often shrunk.

PRODUCING TYPE

Type for letterpresses is manufactured from matrices in *linecasting machines,* out of hot, liquid metal. It is possible to produce type this way for offset printing also. A single copy of the type needed is produced on a *proof press* on clear, high-quality, white paper, and the metal is thrown back into the "melting pot." This copy is then pasted up to be "shot" by the camera and put through the lithography process for actual printing.

Normally, however, "cold type" is produced directly, by one of three methods. In the *strike-on* method, highly sophisticated typewriters, equipped with a variety of typefaces that closely resemble regular printer's type, can simply impress the letters on paper that is all ready to be pasted into the proper position on the ad layout. The right margin will be *ragged,* however, unless the work is done over again in a time-consuming and painstaking second typing to justify the margin. The most commonly used system is photographic typesetting, or *photocomposition.* Phototypesetters op-

erate from taped instructions either from a typewriter keyboard or from a computer that has stored copy fed to it by another machine. These machines are, essentially, complex cameras in which a font of type consists of a strip, roll, or plate like a film negative. Flashes of high-intensity light photograph the image of each letter or character as it moves successively into place in front of the lens. The sensitized paper onto which these images of letters, figures, or symbols have been projected is later developed and then pasted up. A third method, new, costly, and amazingly fast, is *electronic typesetting*. A programmed computer activates a cathode-ray tube that "paints" images on a screen. The resulting lines of text are then recorded on photographic film that is handled the same as the product of phototypesetters. The photographic typesetting machines of either kind can slant, magnify, reduce, or tilt type, and those used for the larger display sizes can insert a screen to give the letters a softer look.

REPRODUCING ADVERTISING ART

In letterpress printing, *line art* (black-and-white art with no intermediate tones) is reproduced by etching the image into hard metal plates with acid. In offset printing, this costly and time-consuming process is unnecessary. Whatever the camera "sees," whether art or type, it prints. Solid black areas are "lightened" by inserting a screen to break them up into masses of fine dots. The screen can be light or heavy, depending on how dark or light an image is desired.

Art service catalogs and other

sources of stock art must supply a matrix, or mat, for each picture if letterpress printing is used. This mat must accompany the advertising layout when it is turned over to the paper. Mats should be treated carefully; that is, the flat margin should not be cut into if scissors are used to cut one mat out of a large sheet, and the mats must be protected from moisture.

In offset printing, mats are not needed. Instead, *reproduction proofs* ("repros"), or *slicks,* are used. These are simply pictures of the art and type, printed on pure white enamel-coated paper so they will photograph sharply. They too must be treated carefully. They should not be scratched, smudged, cut, or defaced in any way.

A retail chain's central ad department will send mats (with proofs to show what the illustrations look like that can be pasted down on layouts) to stores in areas where the papers use the letterpress process and hot-metal composition, and slicks to stores in areas where the local papers use cold-type composition.

REPRODUCING PHOTOGRAPHS
AND OTHER ARTWORK

Before photographs and other kinds of artwork (except simple line drawings) are started through the production process, they should be carefully examined, perhaps with a magnifying glass, and measures taken to improve their quality. They will always *lose,* never *gain,* sharpness when printed. Pictures should be cropped to eliminate undesirable background and help focus attention on the key features. Technicians working with

an airbrush and paint can touch up a picture, lightening light areas further and making the dark portions blacker; slight imperfections can be obliterated. The entire background can be cut away from a figure to make it a silhouette that stands out starkly against blank paper.

Letterpress printing requires that photographs and other artwork, except line drawings, be *screened* before their images are etched in an acid bath onto metal plates for printing. A screening pattern of vertical and horizontal lines is placed between the subject and the lens of a camera; this breaks up the illustration into a mass of tiny dots. The dots are of varying sizes, and the result, when inked and transferred to paper, is a series of infinite gradations in tone that approximate the appearance of the original photo, or that add shades of gray to drawings and painted illustrations. This process is done easily and without a costly additional step, in the case of material intended for offset printing. The screening is accomplished at the same time as the shooting of the ad or the page to be transferred to the plane-surface printing plate. It will not be needed at all if the photographs have been prescreened before being sent to the store or the newspaper.

These *halftones,* as they are called, will produce very sharply defined pictures with crisp, clear details if the screen is very fine, as are the 100- or 120-lines-per-inch screens that are commonly used for offset lithographic printing. The coarser screens, such as 60 or 80 lines per inch, are better suited when the stereotyping process is to be used, but they of course produce illustrations that lack the detail and subtle tonal definitions of the finer-screened ones.

COLOR PRINTING

Flat color means that one or more solid colors are applied to a specified portion of an ad. The layout artist uses a translucent overlay that fits over the basic layout to show the colored areas. The exact colors to be used must be specified to the newspaper (usually by name and a number). Various standard colors are stocked by most papers doing color advertising, and special colors or mixes can generally be obtained by arranging for them in advance.

A separate plate must be made for *each* color used, and a separate press unit set aside for just that task, its fountain filled with the designated ink. There is a limit to the number of colors that can be used in any one edition of a paper, and advance deadlines for submitting material and specifications for applying the color must be observed. When two or more advertisers use the same color in the same issue, the same unit prints all their ads, as it can lay down color on more than one page. Advertising art services often supply *color-separation mats,* or *slicks,* to facilitate color printing and make it less expensive. If these are not available, the newspaper has to "shoot" each color separately, each time blanking out the remainder of the ad. This is both costly and time-consuming.

Process color approximates the appearance of original art by combining the screening process used to make halftones with a photographic color-separation process. In making plates for full-color reproduction, the original art is photographed four times, once for each of the three primary colors (red, blue, and yellow), plus black. Each time, a different filter is placed in front of the camera's lens to filter out all but the desired color. Then a separate screened printing plate is made from each of the color-separation negatives thus produced. When these four plates are printed one over the other in succession, a mass of tiny dots of each color is spread over the printed surface. When perceived by the human eye, these dots of color blend to become any of the infinite number of colors of the rainbow. Few retailers use process color in their ads, largely because of its cost, unless a manufacturer supplies the necessary materials. It is, however, common in magazine and top-grade direct-mail advertising and in the preprinted supplements of big chain stores.

Questions for Discussion

1. What are some of the advantages of using locally produced photographic art to illustrate retail advertising? Do you think this method of illustrating ads is more suited to item-price ads or institutional ads? Why?

2. Why, when a retailer has a choice, is an ad three columns wide by twelve inches deep preferable to an ad four columns wide by eight inches deep?

3. What is the meaning of the terms *balance, gaze motion, contrast,* and *unity* in advertising design?

4. For what kind of merchandise, appealing to which readership segment, might you use each of the following kinds of type: (a) boldface gothic, (b) lightface sans serif, (c) modern roman in a medium weight, (d) script in a light weight, and (e) text or blackface?

5. What colors would be appropriate in each of the following ads: (a) an ad for air conditioners, electric fans, or a summer resort beside a northern lake; (b) an ad for furnaces, space heaters, heavy winter coats, or lined jackets; (c) an ad for new spring dresses, aimed at women in upper socioeconomic classes; and (d) an ad directed at workingmen, telling of a sale on tools to be used in a home workshop? Why?

6. Why will it take longer to prepare ads for the press if they are to be printed in two colors (plus black)? Why are such ads more expensive than black-and-white ads? Why may it be impossible to schedule such an ad for a particular day?

Suggested Projects

1. Pick out of your local newspapers retail ads that show human subjects as well as the items the stores seek to sell. Analyze each ad to see if it has the power to make readers aware of a previously *unfelt* need for the product and to motivate them to buy. If you had unlimited facilities for the production of original, creative artwork at your disposal, what sort of picture would you use to improve one or more of these ads and increase their power to stir readers? Sketch your idea roughly, as you might do if you were explaining to a professional artist what you wanted done.

2. Collect from local newspapers a a number of examples of photography used to illustrate ads. Also collect other ads employing line drawings, wash drawings, and other types of art. Which group of ads pleases you most? Which group seems most professional? Which relates more directly to the stores, their personnel, and the local community?

3. Clip examples of each of the following kinds of headline type from magazines and newspapers: (a) roman old style; (b) modern roman; (c) gothic capitals; (d) modern sans serif; (e) square serif; (f) text or blackface; (g) script or cursive. Also make an exhibit, from the same sources, of (a) italic, (b) boldface, (c) lightface, (d) extended, and (e) condensed type.

4. Clip from magazines and newspapers advertisements that use color (a) to add realism to the merchandise pictured, (b) to create a mood or appeal to the emotion, and (c) to symbolize something.

Notes

1. *Color in Newspaper Advertising: Is It Worth the Money?* (New York: Newspaper Advertising Bureau, Inc., 1970).

2. Ibid.

3. *Media News,* Philadelphia: N. W. Ayer and Son, Inc., Media Department, December 18, 1972, p. 17.

4. John Newman, advertising director of the *Enquirer and News,* Battle Creek, Michigan. Interview by the author on January 26, 1962.

5. Leslie W. McClure and Paul C. Fulton, *Advertising in the Printed Media,* p. 178. © Copyright, The Macmillan Company, 1964.

Preview

While the basic elements of persuasion are the same in all media, the techniques of production for broadcasting are vastly different from those for print. Since radio commercials work best if beamed to a narrow market segment, a clear-cut definition of a target audience is crucial. Forms of radio commercials include (1) straight or "announcer" spots, (2) dialogues, (3) dramatizations or playlets, (4) demonstrations, and (5) humorous commercials. Music and/or sound effects help gain attention, create mood, and reinforce the words. The opening must attract attention and arouse interest. Script must be in the vernacular—the way people really talk—and in short, easily understood sentences and phrases. Exclamations, ejaculations, and action verbs are preferred. There must be repetition of key words such as the store name and any figures, emphasis on primary product benefits, and an interesting ending that suggests action.

Since the best possible production is more important in television than in other media, TV commercials are usually obtained outside the store. The TV ads most used by retailers include (1) announcer commercials, (2) still slides, (3) projections of newspaper copy, (4) live action, and (5) clips of manufacturers' commercials. The visual element should predominate, reinforced by the audio presentation.

Direct-mail and other forms of printed ads call for substantial modification of the copywriting style and graphic techniques that are used for newspaper ads.

Learning Goals

Reading Chapter 15 will not make students experts in creating and producing advertising for all media, but it should give them an appreciation of how to work with those who do produce commercials for a store. It is especially necessary to acquire some guidelines for evaluating scripts, storyboards, layouts, and rough copy before final production begins. Students should know the different options available with each medium, such as the various types of broadcast commercials, opening and ending devices, sound effects, and musical jingles and backgrounds. They should learn how to write simple scripts and be conscious of the difference between writing for print and broadcast media. They should also be conscious of the special opportunities and problems in preparing copy and art for direct advertising, outdoor signs, and other media.

15

Creativity and Production in Broadcast and Other Media

The basic elements of persuasion are the same, no matter by what means an advertising message is delivered. The principles of creative advertising described in Chapter 12 are applied to different *techniques* in broadcast media, but the goals are essentially the same. Always we must attract attention, stir up a desire for the product, persuade people to buy, and move them to action. And always we must take into account the intended consumers' attitude toward and prior knowledge of the product, service, or store; their level of need at the time they receive the ad message; and their fundamental buying motives.

But consumers will be in a different situation as they receive advertising messages in each medium and have a different attitude toward the medium itself. We must fully capitalize on the special advantages of each medium, described in Chapters 10 and 11, as we prepare the ad message, and we must compensate for any limitations. Whether the store's overall ad strategy is to make radio, television, direct advertising, or outdoor signs the primary medium or to give them a supplementary role, the surest way to fail is to think that the methods and means of creating and delivering the message are similar to those that succeed in newspaper advertising. They most certainly are not; the *techniques* involved are vastly different.

Unlike newspaper copy and layouts, most if not all of which is typically prepared within the retail store itself, materials for ads in other media are generally produced by outside technical experts. The store's management and advertising personnel define advertising goals and supply ideas, but they are not usually involved in the technical production of materials. They must, however, evaluate and accept, reject, or ask for alterations in the work presented to them for approval.

1 Radio Commercials

In developing the fundamental concept of a radio commercial, it is even more important than in any other form of advertising (except, perhaps, certain types of direct-mail) to understand the *narrowness* of the target audience. Audiences for radio commercials are preselected by the station format, the adjacent programs, and the time of day the commercials are aired. This is one of the great strengths of the medium. It means, however, that a commercial that tries to be "all things to all people" will not succeed. Ads must be *tailored* to the audience of a given station at a given time.

For this reason, and because radio commercials must be very short (as ads go), the precise *purpose* of the ad must be carefully defined: to reach new customers; to establish a reputation for good values; to enhance an image of a store that is fun to shop in; to create interest in monthly sales; to increase traffic in certain departments; to increase sales of particular merchandise categories; to sell store services; to make people aware of a new branch, a new department, or a new service; to attract older, younger, poorer, or richer customers; to promote a special event; to make an "emegency" announcement; or whatever.

Radio commercials can, of course, be used to sell specific items of merchandise, but not a lot of them at the same time. Experts disagree as to whether one should sell three or only two items in a 60-second commercial, but they all agree that in a 30-second or briefer spot one item only can be promoted. A store should select a *few* items that have a direct, immediate appeal to the selected target audience, and items *bought frequently*, to build store traffic. (It can then sell other merchandise through effective display and personal selling.) Some items sell well on radio, and some do not. New, complex, unfamiliar products, for example, must be advertised in one of the visual media. Radio ads, especially very short (10-, 15-, or 20-second) commercials repeated at frequent intervals may also be used to reinforce ads in other media.

THE IMPORTANCE OF QUALITY COMMERCIALS

Radio commercials are, as we have already pointed out, short. Even the longer ones that run for a full minute can contain only 120 to 150 words or so. They have only a very brief opportunity to have an impact on listeners. For this reason, if for no other, it is foolish to spend a good deal of money for spots or to sponsor a program that will reach a select target group and then attempt to "save" on production costs. Many radio experts advise having a production budget equal to 15 percent of the cost of airtime to ensure that commercials are of adequate quality.

Poor commercials can *irritate,* rather than motivate, listeners because radio advertising is by nature intrusive. It interrupts entertainment or news programs. Hence the sheer quality of the techniques employed to render the message is crucial. In addition to money, it takes *time* to make good commercials. Advanced planning is even more essential for radio ads than for ads in print media. Scriptwriters and production specialists need time to do a good job.

TYPES OF RADIO COMMERCIALS [1]

The Straight Announcement This type of commercial uses a *fact sheet* sup-

plied to the announcer and is read live or taped in advance to allow "proofreading" for miscues and errors. It costs little or nothing to produce and is the most common type of radio ad for small stores using small stations. The following is a typical 60-second announcer spot:

Announcer: THE OPENING KICK-OFF OF THE BUFFALO BILLS' FIRST PRE-SEASON GAME IS MINUTES AWAY. THAT MEANS THE FALL SEASON IS JUST AROUND THE COR-NER. AND AM&A'S MEN'S DE-PARTMENT HAS THE LATEST IN SMARTLY STYLED FALL FASHIONS. WHEN YOU VISIT AM&A'S BE SURE TO SEE THE MAVEST BLAZER SPORT COATS. THESE HANDSOME COATS REFUSE TO WRINKLE BE-CAUSE THEY'RE MADE OF 100% DACRON POLYESTER DOUBLE KNIT. YOU'LL LOOK SHARP ALL DAY LONG IN A MAVEST SINGLE BREASTED SPORT COAT, WITH GOLD BUTTONS, FLAP OR PATCH POCKETS AND EXTRA FANCY LIN-ING FOR THAT SPECIAL TOUCH. THERE'S A VARIETY OF COLORS TO CHOOSE IN AM&A'S MEN'S DE-PARTMENT. THE PRICE? JUST SEV-ENTY DOLLARS.

A straight commercial read by a well-known local radio personality, disc jockey, or newscaster can have a powerful impact. Some merchants also do their own commercials, with great success. In a "remote" (away from the station) broadcast of a special event, the announcer in the station's trailer generally reads the commercials live and intersperses informal comments about what is happening outside.

Dialogues Getting two voices into the act makes an ad a superior attention-getter and adds realism to the commercial. Professional actors can make even a staged conversation seem real, but actual interviews with customers also have a great impact because of their true-to-life sound. Little mistakes in grammar or pronunciation, or a heavy foreign or regional accent, can make an ad all the more effective (and often a bit funny). However, this type of commercial should always be taped ahead of time and edited, never done "live."

The following sale ad demonstrates the dialogue technique as used for a men's specialty-store commercial, and it also shows how cross-media unity of a campaign is achieved:

Roger: THIS IS DAY AND JAY WITH READINGS FROM TUESDAY'S AD IN THE NEW YORK TIMES, NEWS AND POST FOR BARNEY'S WAREHOUSE SALE.

Jack: YOU SEE BARNEY'S NEW INTERNATIONAL HOUSE AND AMERICA HOUSE ARE NOT COMPLETED, YET THOUSANDS OF FASHIONS FOR THEM HAVE ARRIVED.

Roger: AND THE WAREHOUSE IS STOCKED TO THE RAFTERS, JACK.

Jack: WHICH IS WHY BARNEY'S IS HAVING ITS FIRST WAREHOUSE SALE IN HISTORY.

Roger: TODAY'S AD LISTS 44 CONVINCING REASONS WHY YOU SHOULD GO THERE.

Jack: YEAH—LOOK NUMBER 1 SAYS—QUOTE THE SAVINGS GO UP TO 80%.

Roger: LOOK AT NUMBER 3— 291 PAIRS OF PIERRE CARDIN RESORT SLACKS VALUED TO $40 AT $11.89.

Jack: RIGHT AND NUMBER 5 SAYS: 1,408 SHIRTS VALUED TO $7.50 AT 99¢. (LIMIT OF 12)

Roger: I'LL TAKE A DOZEN.

Jack: I DON'T KNOW WHY NOT. NUMBER 6 MAKES SENSE—IT SAYS IT'S OPEN ALL DAY 9 AM TO 9:30 PM.

Roger: HOW ABOUT 9? SAVINGS TO 70% ON SPORT COATS BY GROSHIRE, PETROCELLI, STEIN BLOCH AND LEBOW.

Jack: WE'LL BE READING MORE OF THE 44 REASONS TO GET DOWN TO BARNEY'S WAREHOUSE SALE, 7TH AVENUE & 17TH STREET BETWEEN NOW AND SATURDAY SO STAY TUNED.

Roger: OR GET TODAY'S PAPER AND READ ABOUT IT YOURSELF.

Jack: YEAH ... WHY NOT.

Dramatizations, or Playets The most powerful radio commercials are often of this type, but professional actors (and frequently special sound effects and music) are required to put them over. The typical plot is a problem situation, a "before-and-after" story in which the product or the store is the "hero" that saves the day for the customer. Often, humor is included. People *enjoy* this type of ad immensely when it is well done, and they remember the point.

This miniature drama is a good example of a playlet commercial:

(Musical opening—strains of Wedding March on organ)

Minister: DEARLY BELOVED ...

Bride: WHAT?

Minister: WE ARE GATHERED HERE TO ... EXCUSE ME, THAT'S A WONDERFUL LOOKING SUIT YOU HAVE ON.

Groom: YOU LIKE IT?

Minister: MAKES YOU LOOK LIKE A MILLION DOLLARS!

Groom: UHM, WELL, IT WAS ONLY $75.50.

Minister: WHERE?

Groom: ROOS/ATKINS.

Minister: REALLY? THAT'S ON SALE, I SUPPOSE.

Groom: OH, NO. EVERY DAY THE PRICE IS ON.

Minister: WHERE DID YOU GET THE SHIRT?

Groom: THE SAME PLACE.

Minister: ROOS/ATKINS?

Bride: I DO.

Minister (in background): UHM.

Groom: NOT YET, FELICE.

Minister: HOW MUCH WAS IT?

Bride (in background): OH... OH...

Groom: THE SHIRT?

Minister: YEAH.

Groom: UH, THE SHIRT WAS $9.00.

Minister: AND THE TIE?

Groom: YEAH, THE TIE SETS IT OFF BEAUTIFULLY. THE WHOLE OUTFIT.

Minister: HOW MUCH WERE THOSE SHOES?

Groom: $26.00...LIKE THEM?

Minister: NOT YET.

Bride: DON'T I?

Minister: NOT YET, I JUST DID.

Groom: UHUH, I DO.

Bride: I DO.

Minister: WELL, I'LL LOOK IN THE BOOK. WAIT A SECOND. HERE IT IS...GO AHEAD.

Groom: I DO.

Minister: NOW YOU BOTH DID. SO IT'S DONE.

Bride: ARE WE...?

Minister: I NOW PRONOUNCE YOU MAN AND WIFE. COULD YOU ...COULD YOU EXCUSE US FOR A FEW MINUTES? I'D LIKE TO TALK TO YOUR HUSBAND.

Bride: I WILL.

Minister: I KNEW YOU WOULD.

Bride (muttering in background).

Minister: COULD WE ALL GO DOWN TO ROOS/ATKINS...DO YOU KNOW ANYBODY?

Announcer: SELECTION, IT'S HAPPENING EVERYDAY AT R/A... ROOS/ATKINS.

Demonstrations Despite the lack of pictures, demonstrations can be done on radio—again, with professional help or, at least, the full utilization of the sound effects library that radio stations maintain to assist their local clients (the broadcast equivalent of the "mat book" of stock art newspapers provide). Sounds can conjure up mental images in listeners' minds that can be more dramatic, realistic, and convincing than a visual demonstration. Carefully chosen words and vocal tones, with sound and music, can make listeners paint their own mental picture.

This demonstration commercial (which is also a dialogue and, in addition, contains humor) was used by an Indiana department store. Note how many words are well chosen to create mental images of physical things.

(Sound effects—store sounds and auto bells in background)

Man customer: IS THIS AYRES' NOTIONS DEPARTMENT?

Saleswoman: YES, SIR.

Man: THEY SAY THERE'S A RULER THAT'S LESS THAN HALF THE SIZE OF A PACK OF CIGARETTES. BUT IT CAN MEASURE ONE THOUSAND ONE HUNDRED AND NINETY-NINE INCHES.

Saleswoman: YEAH, THE E&M WALKING RULER.

Man: YEAH? I DON'T BELIEVE IT!

Saleswoman: WELL, HERE IT IS!

Man: HMMM, IS IT HARD TO USE?

Saleswoman: NO, YOU JUST HOLD ON TO THE HANDLE HERE. AND YOU SEE THIS LITTLE WHEEL?

Man: YEAH.

Saleswoman: WELL, YOU JUST ROLL IT ALONG WHATEVER YOU WANT TO MEASURE AND IT REGISTERS THE DISTANCE HERE ON THIS NUMERICAL . . .

Man: WELL, I'LL BE DARNED!

Woman customer: EXCUSE ME, MISS.

Saleswoman: YES?

Woman: IS THIS WHERE THEY HAVE THAT NEW-FANGLED RULER?

Saleswoman: THE E&M WALKING RULER.

Woman: IT'S SMALL.

Saleswoman: IT MEASURES UP TO NINETY-NINE FEET ELEVEN INCHES.

Boy customer: LADY: YOU GOT ANY OF THOSE CRAZY RULERS?

Saleswoman: YES, I'LL BE WITH YOU IN A MINUTE.

Woman: IT MUST BE EXPENSIVE!

Humorous Commercials Humorous

Saleswoman: NO, TWELVE NINETY-FIVE WITH LONG HANDLE, NINE NINETY-FIVE WITHOUT THE HANDLE.

Boy: BUT, LADY, CAN IT MEASURE A CROOKED ELECTRICAL WIRE?

Saleswoman: YES, AND THINGS THAT AN ORDINARY RULER COULDN'T.

Woman: THE CURVES IN MY SEWING PATTERN?

Saleswoman: YEP, AND CEILINGS, SIDEWALKS . . .

Man: AND PRETZELS?

Saleswoman: YEAH, I SUPPOSE IT COULD.

Woman: WHAT A MARVELOUS CHRISTMAS GIFT!

Boy: IT'S A NEW IDEA, ISN'T IT?

Woman: HAVE THEY BEEN AROUND LONG?

Man: YEAH, ABOUT NINETY-NINE FEET!

Announcer: THE WALKING RULER . . . AN EXCITING NEW IDEA IN THE NOTIONS DEPARTMENT AT ALL AYRES STORES.

Humorous Commercials Humorous continuity (copy for radio advertisements) is very popular, not only because it makes a point in a way people will remember, but because it often makes friends for the store. Enjoy the following commercial for men's hats:

Speaker #1 (meek young man): SIR, MR. V.I.P., I'D LIKE TO KNOW HOW YOU FEEL ABOUT HATS.

Speaker #2: WELL SON, I'LL TELL YOU HOW I FEEL. IT TAKES A MAN TO WEAR A HAT . . . THAT'S RIGHT SON, IT TAKES A REAL MAN.

NOW I'VE BEEN WEARING HATS FOR YEARS ... EVERY DAY.

Speaker #1: UH, UH, ...

Speaker #2: YES, YOUNG MAN, YOU CAN TAKE IT FROM ME ... I BUY MY HATS ONLY FROM WEATHERWAX'S IN DOWNTOWN SIOUX FALLS ... YES, MY BOY, NOTHING CAN BEAT WEATHERWAX'S FOR THE STYLES THEY HAVE. WHY, I HAVE ONE TO MATCH EVERY COAT ... I WOULDN'T BE SEEN WITHOUT ONE.

Speaker #1: BUT, UH, UH, I THINK ...

Speaker #2: I THINK EVERY RESPECTABLE MAN OUGHT TO SPEND SOME TIME AT WEATHERWAX'S TRYING ON THEIR HATS ... THEY HAVE THE TOP STYLES, SUCH AS THE FUR FELT HAT AND THE JAUNTY CASUAL WOOL ... MIGHTY FINE HATS MY BOY ... YES SIR, IT TAKES A MAN TO WEAR A HAT.

Speaker #1: UH, UH, SIR? IS IT TRUE? ... THE RUMOR ABOUT YOUR BALD HEAD?

Musical Commercials Music can be used to attract attention in the opening seconds of a commercial and again at the end (the "fade-out"). It can be continued at a lower volume ("voice over") to establish a mood while the announcer (or the actors in a dialogue commercial) delivers the actual message. Singing commercials can be outstanding, but good ones cost money ($500 to $1,000) to produce.

The *bridge* or *sandwich* technique enables many small and medium-sized stores that cannot spend too much on producing individual commercials to include a brief unit or two of top-quality music in every one of them, and still change the main thrust of their continuity very often. An institutional song is created to run for some seconds at the beginning and end of each commercial, and local announcers are given straight copy on merchandise or the store to fill the middle of the spot. The musical part of the commercial is used over and over at no additional cost and eventually pays for itself. As listeners become familiar with the tune, it serves to identify the store in the same way that a logotype (a distinctive visual symbol) does in print.

Even if a store cannot afford to produce its own "musical signature," it can still use a few bars of a suitable musical number out of the station's sound library at the beginning and end of each of its spots. However, the station must obviously put a "hold" on that same piece of music, to keep any other local advertiser from using it.

National honors for effective radio creativity went to Grey Advertising and a Detroit store specializing in selling trousers and tops to "swinging young males" for the following musical spot. The music, a spoof on Hawaiian melodies sung by a vocalist who imitated a popular singer, occupies most of the 60 seconds; there is time for about 40 words of store promotion by the announcer in the middle:

SFX: (Hawaiian music)

Vocalist sings (a la Bette Midler): IF YOU WANT TO MAKE YOUR HOOMAN-ICKI LOOK REAL GOOD AND YOUR AKKA-POUKI NOOY FEELING LIKE IT SHOULD, YOU BETTER BOOGEY WOOGEY HULA DOWN, DOWN TO WHERE THE NEW HAWAIIAN TOPS ARE FOUND

...OH, HO...THE PALM TREES SWAY AND THEY SEEM TO SAY: YOU'LL BE MY WAIKIKI FLIRT IN YOUR WIKI-WACKY SHIRT!

Announcer: IMITATION HAWAIIAN THE NEW LOOK AT THE MIDWEST TROUSER EXCHANGE. THE KIND OF FASHION NOBODY EVER THOUGHT WOULD COME BACK HAS. YES, THE WHOLE PLASTIC THING WITH SHIRTS AND TOPS SO FUNKY YOU'VE JUST GOT TO HAVE SOME!

SFX

Vocalist sings: OHHHHH, THEY'RE MAKING MOTOWN INTO A HULA HONEYMOON! THE MOONEY SHINE AND THE ISLAND BREEZE ROLLS AROUND YOUR SHOULDER AND RIGHT OFF YOUR SLEEVE...YOU'LL BE THE PAIR IN PARADISE...HAWAIIAN BOOGEY IMITATION SHIRTS ARE NICE, OH, HO THE PALM TREES SWAY AND THEY SEEM TO SAY: YOU'LL BE MY WAIKIKI FLIRT IN YOUR WIKI-WACKY SHIRT.

THE OPENING

A number of different techniques have been developed for quickly gaining the attention and arousing the interest of an intended target audience. In the case of *sponsored programs,* the announcer or master of ceremonies who has just concluded a news broadcast, sports report, or a segment of an entertainment program typically directs the listeners' attention smoothly and casually into the sponsor's commercial. That same person, or another member of the cast, may even deliver it. This is an *integrated commercial,* and there is much spillover interest from the program to the advertising. But sponsored programs are less common now than they once were on radio.

Spots that stand alone fighting for attention amidst the clutter can adapt some of the techniques already discussed in connection with newspaper headlines and lead-in copy. A merchant's total campaign is strengthened by cross-media coordination wherein as many as possible of the same words and expressions that appear prominently in print ads are also heard at the beginning of each commercial. This helps listeners to see, in their mind's eye, the recent newspaper ads as they hear the radio versions of the same appeals (and vice versa). The words heard in the first few seconds of broadcast spots are the *headlines of the air.*

The *straight-talk* opening that plunges right into the heart of the message without fanfare can be likened to the simple statement of product features that characterizes print ads with factual copy. Like those ads, it, too, can only hold the attention of those who already have an intense interest in, and a felt desire for, the thing advertised. Since one of the main strengths of broadcast advertising is to reach people who do not have felt needs for the advertised products, the radio continuity writer must usually go further. Often the best opening is a frank statement of a *product benefit* or of *rewards promised* to the buyer of the product or the shopper at the store. As in print ads, subsequent copy must prove the benefit to be true and make good on the promise (or the advertiser will be in deep trouble). Starting with a *news-type announcement* resembling the typical item heard on newscasts is a good way to begin, especially when the station's familiar news announcers make the commercials. Their voices ring true and, when heard on a commercial, are welcomed by listeners. To quickly describe a startling *predicament* or pose a pesky *problem* is another excellent method, provided the listeners soon hear how the advertiser offers a clear-cut way out or a plausible solution. Often, asking a *question* (which the listeners tend to answer to themselves) is a good way to get interest.

Beyond these suggestions common to both print and broadcast ads, radio offers an extra that enables it to grab the interest of and involve the audience: *sound effects* (abbreviated SFX on several of our example scripts). A *contrast* in the level of sound is elementary in designing attention-getting openings. When the commercial starts with either a louder or a softer level of sound than the preceding unit (whether it has been a program, news report, or some other commercial), the battle for attention is half won. The loud ringing of a bell, the clashing of cymbals, the beating of a drum, or some other noise can often do the trick. On the other hand, subdued and soothing music (sometimes the store's own theme song, toned down to a low volume level) or a well-modulated voice speaking softly or even in a whisper can be a perfect opening for certain types of commercials. Such openings are especially appealing to the more sophisticated, refined, and better-educated listeners who tend to be irritated by the loud openings, which are better suited to attract the rough-and-ready types. Soft openings sometimes include a moment when no sound comes out at all, which is akin to the pause for emphasis used by polished public speakers to get an audi-

ence hushed down to complete silence and waiting for what may be said next. Even these volume-contrast openings may be compared, to a degree, with the different appeals of big, black headlines as opposed to smaller, lightface heads and ample white space discussed in connection with print ads.

Special kinds of sounds heard in openings of commercials can include the use of special and unexpected kinds of human voices: children's voices (unusually effective when parents are the target audience); voices pitched exceptionally high or abnormally low; voices capable of rattling off some introductory words at a rapid but understandable pace or of slowing down to a slower-than-usual rate; very authoritative voices that command respect by their very tone and manner; and voices that come through in a thick foreign accent, humorously, or that reflect unmistakable regional dialects. The "voices" of animals are seldom adequately exploited as opening devices for radio scripts, but they possess great possibilities. The spot that kicks off by barking, purring, howling, braying, whinnying, growling, or cooing can be irresistible. Other opening sounds can conjure up instant pictures in listeners' minds, set moods, bring visions of the product, or dramatize the situation about to be described. The creative continuity writer will consider opening with clicking, humming, swishing, thumping, dripping, gurgling, squeeking, thudding, scratching, whacking, whistling, knocking, plunking, whirring, rattling, slamming, or snapping sounds. They can so pique the curiosity of an audience as to virtually guarantee that all ears will be eagerly awaiting to catch the first words that are spoken a few seconds later. Some of these kinds of sounds can make people think of the advertised product in action or motion, or they can set the stage for a problem-solving message by mimicking a bad situation into which the product or store comes forth as the hero to restore contentment and happiness to the lucky listener who acts on the ad's suggestion. Repetition of the initial sound or word (perhaps the name of the product or the store) in a drumbeat or staccato contrasts with the distractions that surround listeners at the moment the broadcast is heard and can help keep the listeners' attention.

The setting up in the opening seconds of a situation that contains humor, offers a provocative dialogue, emphasizes mysterious or challenging sounds and words, or possesses the shock power of the utterly incongruous is a device that professionally prepared continuity can utilize. A store or product can itself do the "talking," words can come forth from the mouths of animals, or a famous personality can be depicted in a fantastically ridiculous circumstance.

The following selected examples, some of which employ the dialogue technique to get two contrasting voices into the act as quickly as possible, demonstrate good ways to open the commercial.

This announcer-presented opening immediately promises a benefit:

Announcer: PAINT IT ON!... THAT'S WHAT WE SAID...IF YOU'RE THINKING OF PUTTING ON A NEW FLOOR... *PAINT IT ON*. IT'S POSSIBLE WITH FLECTO SEAMLESS ...THE NEW PLASTIC FLOORING SYSTEM FEATURED AT COLUMBIA VALLEY LUMBER...

Starting with a blunt question, this opening instantly poses a problem and then humorously soars into a hilarious reference to a historical figure:

1st Man: CAN I SEE SOMEONE? I NEED A LOAN.

2nd Man: WELL, CERTAINLY, WHAT IS YOUR NAME?

1st Man: DO I HAVE TO GIVE MY NAME?

2nd Man: WELL, YES.

1st Man: ARNOLD.

2nd Man: ARNOLD.

1st Man: BENEDICT.

2nd Man: ARNOLD BENEDICT.

1st Man: BENEDICT ARNOLD.

2nd Man: UH...HUM, LET ME FILL OUT A NEW FORM HERE. OCCUPATION, MR. ARNOLD?

1st Man: TRAITOR...PATRIOT...

The initial words of this opening are alliterative (rare in radio continuity), and the unusual sounds alert the listener and create a word picture for him to "see" as an analogy is built up comparing symphony music with "orchestration" of a wardrobe:

Announcer: POLSKY'S PROUDLY PRESENTS A POP CONCERT

SFX: (Orchestra tuning up in background)

Announcer: FOR FATHER'S DAY, POLSKY'S MEN'S FURNISHINGS CONDUCTING

SFX: (Conductor taps baton—symphonic rock music up and under)

Announcer: THERE'S A COMPLETE ORCHESTRATION OF FASHION FOR THE POP IN YOUR LIFE AT POLSKY'S MEN'S FURNISHINGS. GIVE HIM INTERCHANGEABLE HAR-

MONY WITH A DYNAMIC WOVEN PLAID BLAZER AND SOLID DOUBLE-KNIT SLACKS.

Familiar sounds, sharp and attention-getting, open this commercial; they are followed by a fantasy scene in which an animal does most of the talking:

SFX: (2-toned doorbell rings loudly ... sounds of door being unlatched and opened)

Man: (in suspicious, gruff voice) YEAH?

Child's voice (in high-pitched falsetto): HELLO, I'M YOUR BUSY BEAVER AND I'M HERE TO TELL YOU ABOUT MY GIGANTIC OCTOBER DAYS SALE AT ALL MY HOME CENTERS.

Man (laughingly): HEY, ETHEL, LOOK AT THIS. IT'S SOME KID IN A BEAVER SUIT. HA, HA!

Child's voice: BUT, SIR, I'M NOT A KID IN A ... (interrupted)

Man: HEY, KID, ISN'T IT A LITTLE EARLY FOR TRICK OR TREAT?

Child's voice: OH, NO, MY SALE HAS TREATS RIGHT NOW. RIGHT UP TO HALLOWEEN ...

The creative continuity writer will be able to devise just the right opening to attract the listener's attention and hold it throughout the commercial message.

WRITING RADIO CONTINUITY

Writing radio copy is the same as writing newspaper copy in some ways. Again, copywriters should know what they are writing about. They should gather all available information on the merchandise and spend time talking to the merchandiser, the salespeople—even customers—about why they sell or buy what they do. This kind of research is what makes copy believable.

But there are some significant ways in which good radio copy differs from the copy used in newspaper ads. The following rules are useful guidelines for the beginning copy writer:

1. *Write like you talk, not as you write.* Radio is heard, not seen. This means radio copy must be more conversational, more idiomatic than written prose. Sentences need not always be complete; exclamations, ejaculations, and slang expressions are acceptable. So are pauses ... brief periods of silence, for emphasis and for letting a point sink in. Use phrases that are heard in everyday speech rather than literary ones.

2. *Stick to short, punchy, easily understood sentences and phrases.* Make every word count. Avoid alliteration (groups of words beginning with the same sound) and shun adverbs (words ending in -ly). Stay away from long, complex words and sentences, and use contractions and sentence fragments freely. Do not saddle the announcer with the burden of hissing or barking sounds by including in the commercial words like "sensational" and those ending in "-ark" or "-ack." Too many "s's" will surely tie the announcer's tongue. Punctuate liberally to give cues as to pauses and emphasis; even underline a key word once in a while and insert rows of dots or long dashes to help the speaker time the delivery properly. Operate on the general principle that anything that can be either mispronounced by the announcer or mis-

understood by the listener probably will be.

3. *Use short "action" words in common use.* Action words motivate action.

4. *Slant the copy deliberately for the intended audience—the target customers.* Decide whom it is you are selling to and talk to them in their own language.

5. *Emphasize prime customer benefits, while playing down details and bragging.* This is a rule that should be applied more often in writing newspaper copy, and it is even more vital in doing radio ads. Tell customers what the product will do for them, but shun vague superlatives ("brag" words). They only weaken an ad by making it less believable.

6. *Mention key points repeatedly.* Repeat the store's name, the price, and the benefits of owning the product as many times as you can so they will register, to catch those who missed the beginning of the commercial.

7. *Don't run downhill at the end.* Some commercials start out strong, then fizzle, as though the scriptwriter had lost interest in the subject. Build interest and *hold it* to the end.

8. *Try out scripts before airing them.* This is crucial if a commercial is to be broadcast "live." If it is to be taped, it is still helpful to try out the script before the technicians go to the trouble of adding or superimposing the music and sound effects. Don't just read radio copy silently for errors or difficult phrases. Read it aloud to see how it sounds, if it rings true, if some words are hard to pronounce. If it doesn't sound right, rework it. If you can, have someone else read the copy or read it into a tape recorder.

THE FORM OF RADIO SCRIPTS

The form in which the copywriter submits material for radio commercials is important. The examples shown in the book have the script itself written in all capital letters, with the instructions for the readers and the production crew written in capital and lowercase letters. This is the usual form used, but many stations, agencies, or stores prefer to do the reverse, using all capitals for instructions and lowercase for the script. The copywriter should use the style acceptable to the party for whom the copy is written.

The important point here is that there *is* a difference. Much confusion would result if the script itself looked the same as the material that tells the production crew what to do. As a further clarification, scripts for commercials with two voices may be typed with the lines for one reader in black and those for the other in red. This makes a conspicuous contrast that is easy to follow.

SPECIAL WRITING TASKS

Sometimes copywriters are called on to convert a newspaper ad (or circular) into radio continuity. The best approach to this kind of assignment is to focus on the red-hot traffic-building items. If the print ad used pictures to tell much of the story, words will have to be added to fill readers in verbally on significant product details. And both the store's name and the product (with its price) must be repeated more often than in the print ad. The tempo must suit the ear, not the eye.

Special events are a natural for sat-

WVIC AM 730 FM 94.9

2517 east mt. hope avenue
lansing, michigan 48910

CLIENT ___VILLAGE GREEN___

ADDRESS ___MERIDIAN MALL___

DATES RUN ___NOVEMBER 21, 22, 23, 1974___

WRITTEN BY: SMITH   ANNOUNCER: JONES   SALESMAN: BROWN   CART #: 68

15 SECONDS	(ECHO) Hi, I'm speaking to you tonight from inside a pair of Baggies from the Village Green....at the Meridian Mall. Right now I'm down near the cuff. No, your're not going to believe the room in here. These pants must be extra comfortable and super cool. I mean there's so much room to move around in. Now, I'm moving up (GRUNTING SOUNDS). Say, you know the Village Green has got a great selection of Baggies. (GRUNT) There ! I'm near the knee now. Say, I'm amazed by the smooth feel of the fabric. The Village Green has knit Baggies like
30 SECONDS	these and corduroys with or without the cuffs. And they all look super good, and they're very comfortable and stylish. (GRUNT) Still climbing here. Say, you know there's more Baggies at the Village Green II downtown. Now these Baggies are eight bucks, and you can pick up some others for three, four and five dollars. I'm nearing the pocket area, I'll try and get a grip. Now I see some belt loops up there that are extra wide for those big belts. (SOUND OF CLOTH STARTING TO TEAR) I'll try and get a closer look. (GRUNT,
60 SECONDS	CLOTH TEARING MORE LOUDLY) Oh, oh, noooooooo (VOICE FADES, AS THOUGH FALLING A LONG DISTANCE)

uration radio campaigns. Interest in an event can be created by live copy on strong sellers that are exciting in themselves. Commercials taped on the sales floor often make a big hit. "Slice-of-life" testimonials from real or imaginary shoppers discussing values add realism and believability to an ad. Broadcasts direct from the selling floor can also generate excitement and draw people to the store.

PRODUCING RADIO COMMERCIALS

Many stores write their own radio scripts, and the local stations complete the job. Finished tapes are played back (over the telephone, in some cases, to save time and effort) before they go on the air. All stations, no matter how small, employ continuity writers and have sound libraries of both music and special effects.

Other stores are turning to advertising agencies or special commercial production houses for help with radio ads. A local station can often put a retailer in touch with such firms, or they may be listed in the telephone directory of the nearest large city.

The Radio Advertising Bureau provides its member stations with regular bulletins offering fresh ideas for radio ads and has voluminous files of case studies on how to use the medium and write proper commercials. In addition, the bureau has tapes and records of many of the country's best retail commercials. Often, these can provide inspiration for the local store. The National Retail Merchants Association also offers help to member stores (and to nonmembers, at a higher cost).

Manufacturers frequently supply top-quality tapes to advertise their products, with a few seconds blank at the end for the store's "I.D." They will also cooperate with the store by sharing the cost of air time in many cases. This solves the retailer's production problem but does nothing to build an individual store image. Co-op advertising should certainly be used, but only as one element in a more personalized ad program.

2 Television Commercials

Television commercials share certain fundamental features with newspaper and radio ads. You research customers, the product, and the competition, and you create a copy platform or theme pinned on a particular product feature

Figure 15–1 Commercial Forms Supplied by Radio Stations
Forms similar to this one, which is available from Station WVIC in Lansing, Michigan, are supplied by radio stations to their advertisers to assist them in writing up commercial scripts. Note that it serves essentially the same function as the layout sheets provided by newspapers (shown in Figure 14–3 on page 406). The scriptwriter indicates the advertiser's name and address; the schedule for the commercial; the names of the copywriter, announcer, and salesperson; and the number of the tape cartridge onto which the commercial will be transcribed. Tick marks, each representing about 3 seconds of air time, are indicated along the left-hand margin. The copywriter will need to know how rapidly the announcer for the commercial speaks, and then, with typewriter stops set to conform to that speaking rate, the commercial copy can be typed within the box and the announcer can receive a very accurate estimate of the length of the commercial. The copy typed in here is for a 60-second commercial.

or a unique selling proposition. In creating the visual element (which gives this medium its primary appeal), you apply the principles discussed in Chapter 14 for illustrating newspaper ads. In creating the audio portion, you apply many of the rules for radio ads. Music, the mainstay of radio for getting attention and setting a mood, is also used in nearly half of all better-quality TV commercials. But television ads have yet another dramatic element, *motion.* It is the combined impact of *sight, sound,* and *motion* (reinforced by *color,* more often than not) that makes TV ads so effective.

Major chains and a few of the very largest department stores can fully utilize the sophisticated production techniques required to achieve the incomparable impact TV alone can offer. But for other local advertisers, the one overriding problem with respect to TV advertising is money. The effectiveness of advertising in any medium is determined in large measure by the audience reached. And as we saw in Chapter 10, smaller retailers are forever perched on the horns of a frustrating dilemma: media time is "cheap" only when audiences are small; conversely, great masses of people can be reached only by buying extremely costly prime time (if it is available). A store can cut costs by reducing the length of its commercials, but this places great restrictions on what can be accomplished, no matter how creative the ad is. One can do only so much in 10 or 20 seconds.

It takes a great deal of money to buy time when media coverage is impressive and to run commercials with sufficient frequency. Assuming a store has the budget to do this, and further assuming that it can afford commercials at least 30 seconds long so the creative people have a reasonable amount of time to work with, one financial hurdle still remains: *production costs.*

Most smaller retailers have to settle for far less than the maximum impact TV advertising can have, simply because they do not have enough money for really good, original commercials. This presents smaller stores with a problem unique to TV: the difference in quality between their ads and adjacent material. In no other medium is the difference as great between the *worst* and the *weakest* ads and the *best* and the *strongest.* And a store's ad may come immediately after a national manufacturer's commercial into which a small fortune was poured. It may also come during, before, or after a show featuring the world's greatest actors. Many merchants and advertising professionals believe that retail TV's primary problem is finding a way to improve the quality of the commercial.

BEATING THE COST PROBLEM IN CREATING AND PRODUCING TV ADVERTISING

One factor to consider at the outset is the *length* of the individual commercials; obviously, the shorter they are, the lower the production costs and the cost of time. Because two senses are being appealed to simultaneously (sight and sound), a message can be implanted in the viewer's mind more rapidly through TV than through printed media or radio commercials.

Just what can a store expect to do in very short periods of TV time? It is not the *number* of facts crammed into a given commercial that matters; in advertising, what counts is the *impact* of one or a few major points. And in TV, impact can be achieved in a very short time. As one expert points out,

> In :10, we have time for: the Name, and a Claim.
>
> In :20, we have time for: the Name, a Claim, and a Demonstration.
>
> In :30 and :40, we have time for the Name, a Claim, a Demonstration, Supporting Claims.
>
> In :60, we have time for the Name, a Claim, a Demonstration, Supporting Claims, plus Mood or Atmosphere and Dramatization—if we choose.
>
> You have to decide—mood, atmosphere and dramatization are not requisites, but can be effective aids. Supporting claims often help, but too often just muddle up your message.
>
> It's not how long—it's how good! [2]

Another basic consideration related to TV production costs is the objective of the individual commercial (or series). Where does it fit into the overall advertising strategy? The Television Bureau of Advertising suggests that relatively costly commercials be reserved for institutional messages, which are often repeated many times. Smaller stores that need to economize can do so more safely on promotional ads, which have a short useful life, as seasonal items come and go. The bureau offers a useful checklist of characteristics for the item-selling and image-building ads, shown in Figure 15–2.

LOW–BUDGET TV PRODUCTION

Because budgetary considerations are so obviously paramount, TV advertisers must put the cart before the horse. They must investigate production techniques they can afford before choosing copy themes and creative approaches. Some types of commercials (such as full-scale live-action productions that normally cost $10,000 to $20,000) are obviously impossible for smaller retailers to afford. Other types of TV ads are, however, within reason for smaller advertisers.

Commercials Spoken by an Announcer or Other "Presenter" for the Store On television, this type of commercial can be reinforced with still pictures of the product, the store, personnel, or the store logotype. There is evidence that among all users of prime-time TV, some form of the announcer technique is the most common way of doing the job. The presenter can be a local television personality, an athlete, some other well-known personality, or even a member of the store's staff.

Slide Commercials Ordinary 35-mm. color slides of a series of products, the store, or personnel can be used for the visual elements of a TV ad. Sometimes, quick changes of a sequence of slides impart a feeling of motion, too. *Supers* (printed words superimposed on the pictures) or *voice-overs* (oral announcements synchronized with each slide) are used to reinforce the message the picture conveys.

Commercials That Focus on a Newspaper Ad The camera can zoom in on the one, two, or three key items in a store's regular newspaper ad (or direct-mail piece) while an announcer makes oral comments that reinforce the message.

Live-Action Local Commercials Store personnel can be pictured, with the products being promoted, in the local TV station's studio or on *location* at the store itself (by using the station's remote-pick-up van, the kind of vehicle it uses to cover sports events and local news). This is more costly than the types of commercials described above, but the results may justify the expense.

Clips of National Commercials These are often supplied direct to dealers by the manufacturers. Normally, they have a few seconds of open time at the end for the store to identify itself, either orally or visually. Specialty firms syndicate clips of hundreds (if not thousands) of well-known, nationally advertised products for adaptation by local outlets. Since these clips are often full-color live-action or animated ads, this is the *one* route by which small-budget TV advertisers can make use of the high-cost, full-scale dramatic power of TV. The store or its regular print-ad logotype, its address, and its phone number can be shown at the end, or it can be named by a local announcer in the opening and/or closing seconds, using a *voice-over* technique.

1. **Item** advertising requires the selection of items, commercials, and time periods, and all these usually require	1. **Image** advertising usually requires
2. **many people** at the store to be involved. But commercials with items can count on getting manufacturers'	2. **few people** at the store. It is usually paid for by the
3. **co-op dollars** if the store wants them. Different items aim at different	3. **store dollars** because it does not contain manufacturers' items that would entitle the store to co-op dollars. Image usually aims at
4. **target audiences** such as men, women, teens. This means	4. **large audiences** of all family members but, with a limited number of messages, can use
5. **many commercials,** each with its own items, audience, etc. If there are going to be many commercials, they had better be	5. **few commercials.** With few of them, they can afford to be
6. **low cost** in production.	6. **expensive,** which often means
7. **Tapes or slides** are usually the way for many, quick, low-cost commercials. As the TV schedule is tied to the sales of the individual items featured, the store's TV budget and TV schedule can expect to have	7. **film.** Image is year-round and so the television pattern is
8. **up's and down's** day by day, week by week, and season by season. Because items were the original emphasis, results should be measured in terms of	8. **steady** rather than the up's and down's of item-emphasis advertising. With image as the goal, results would be measured in terms of improved
9. **items,** although store image may also be changed. Many items, many commercials, and lots of people...it all adds up to a pace that's	9. **image...**which could also be reflected in sales of items. With fewer commercials, a more steady pattern, the pace is
10. **fast**	10. **slower.**

Figure 15–2 Two Patterns for Retail TV Advertising
Source: Courtesy of Television Bureau of Advertising.

New, innovative methods are being developed to better fit clips to the individual needs of stores. An apparel manufacturer makes available to its dealers "electronic mats" of films shot in Europe showing fashion models in famed historic backgrounds. Retailers can order scenes depicting the specific lines and models they want to promote and can thus get the video free. It costs little to write the script locally just as the store wants it. The audio is the store's very own, as is the ending. An electronics maker urges its dealers to build their own local commercials from modular kits that permit many different combinations of openings, feature-product promotions, and closings. Prefab storyboards come with the kit, and after arranging the segments of the TV spot as they want them, the retailers order tapes for the particular segments they have chosen. Voice-over audio individualizes each commercial locally, or regionally when wholesale distributors participate along with retail outlets. A communications specialist in Chicago, with offices also in New York and Los Angeles, recently rounded up tens of millions of manufacturers' dollars to support a major drive to customize nationally branded products for major chains' TV commercials, even including plugs for the retailers' own house brands. Named "Retail Program," this project involved making as many as 100 different spots for a single sponsor, many of them including specific prices. Both filmed and taped versions were offered.

In some cases, when manufacturers supply clips, they will pick up half the tab for the TV time. The only drawback of such commercials, for the retailer, is that the focus is on the product rather than the store.

Reminder Commercials Stores can air a series of frequent 10-second spots, like very short radio commercials, to remind viewers of points made in other, longer broadcast or print ads. As a relatively inexpensive supplement to more complete ads, they can be effective. Because they are so short, they can make just one basic point, but they should hit that point hard.

OTHER TYPES OF TV COMMERCIALS

Chains or very large department, specialty, or mass-merchandise stores may go whole-hog into TV and set up a production budget adequate for original, creative dramatizations. Though most ads of this type are national ads (be-

Figure 15–3 TV Commercials Converted from Print Ads
    The Television Bureau of Advertising, through its member stations, provides excellent tips on producing low-budget television commercials, for the merchant who wishes to enter this medium at minimum production cost. Among its aids to local advertisers is a comprehensive do-it-yourself kit, employing *print converter screens* to translate the graphics out of a newspaper (or direct-mail or magazine) ad and into the slides that will illustrate a television commercial. The station announcer produces the voice-over audio portion. This figure demonstrates (left) how the converter, shaped like a TV screen, designates the segments of a newspaper ad to be put on slides for TV use. At right, 10 easy steps in this process are detailed, a simple storyboard is shown to demonstrate how the commercial will look, and an explanation is given of how to add variety and motion by making full use of specific camera techniques.

1 Select the print ad you want to convert to a TV commercial.

2 Using the screens of your Print Converter, pick sections of the ad in the screen sizes that highlight them best, and indicate them for your TV commercial.

3 Take the original parts of your ad—artwork, photographs, logos, typography—and from these pick the corresponding pieces you indicated for your commercial.

4 Photostatically or photographically, have all the parts you've chosen made same size—preferably 15 inches by 11 inches—and mount them on cards of light gray stock.

5 Re-touch away any areas you don't want.

6 Since your commercial, like all TV commercials, will be in color, color-wash artwork, add color to logos, typography...

and their backgrounds...and be sure your photographs are color.

7 Arrange the cards in the order you want the viewer to see them...perhaps an order similar to the pattern of the print layout you used.

8 Read the copy of your print ad aloud, and indicate the copy to apply to each section of your TV commercial.

9 Time the number of seconds it takes you to show and tell your commercial and pick a time length for telecasting: 10-, 20-, 30- or 60-seconds.

10 Have an announcer read the copy of your ad as the television camera is aimed at each card...one at a time...in the order and time length you've selected.

To give you an idea of how your ad will appear to the viewer as it's seen on television, here's how your do-it-yourself TV commercial might look. You have created a series of full-page TV ads from a single newspaper ad. And you did it with the simple screens of the Print Converter!

Noble's announces a major event...

where you can save up to $50 on television sets...

like this console model, priced as low as $289...

by Phoenix.

Portables, as low as $99.

Combination stereo-TV sets. Some priced at a small $899 for big enjoyment and savings.

Only at Noble's, today through Saturday! A name known for quality and value.

Should you like to move...step by step...to greater results with the greater range of advertising tools TV offers, you can begin again. Simply. And again with your Print Converter.

Remember that first picture you showed...your opening frame of your commercial? This time, let's add camera action...by indicating it with the Print Converter screens.

Let's come in close, with the smallest screen, and step progressively to larger and larger screens. You are showing how the TV camera can "dolly back" and add motion to each of the still pictures...the many "full-page ads"...of your commercial.

On the next frame of your commercial, let's do the reverse. Let's indicate with the Print Converter screens how the camera can move steadily closer, and in TV this is called a "zoom."

Now let's use a medium size screen, one purposely picked as smaller than the frame of your commercial, and let's move it across the frame. You have indicated a camera "pan"—a steady, same size flow to call attention to individual parts of your TV picture.

By indicating these camera directions, to be followed while your announcer speaks, you have added a dimension of movement—motion—to the sight and sound of TV.

Further skills in television? They're not really hard to acquire. After all, advertising is advertising. It's the medium that offers you ways to change...and you've proven—to yourself—you can do it. With the same principles and creativity that have made you an advertising professional.

To learn more of the language of television (and more of the things you can expect TV to do) ask for "TV Terms," available on request through the Television Bureau of Advertising.

TvB Television Bureau of Advertising, Inc., One Rockefeller Plaza, New York, N.Y. 10020

cause of their cost), large retailers have come to rely more heavily on such commercials. In general, the various types of ads in this category parallel the types of radio commercials discussed in the last section.

Ads with a Story Line (Playlets) The story-line or slice-of-life commercial is the third most popular kind among all TV users in prime time, behind the announcer-type and the demonstration. As in radio continuity, the "story" is usually about how a product or a store solves a problem for consumers. The before-and-after situations have many possible retail applications. These commercials have the most impact, naturally, when they are well done by top actors. A variation is the "suspense" drama, in which interest is built up steadily to set the scene for a punchline at the very end. This kind of scenario has the same virtues as, and runs the same risks as, a newspaper ad that excites curiosity. Unless a truly talented scriptwriter and a fully professional production crew can turn out an utterly superior product, all is lost.

Documentaries   These present facts in a dramatic form and can be a natural for big stores celebrating an anniversary or opening a new branch. Documentaries can trace the travels of a buyer "discovering" merchandise for the store's customers or tell a story about the store's founder in an institutional tone.

Special-Effects Commercials   Close cousins to radio ads using music and sound effects, these kinds of ads often employ quick shots of a variety of still pictures or animated cartoons (at much greater cost). Unusual sounds, lighting effects, and angle photography can make them especially appealing to the "now generation."

Testimonials   These, too, are much like radio testimonials, but the visual element makes the personality of whoever makes the endorsement come across more strongly. The overall effect is also much more realistic.

Humorous or Satirical Commercials Closely related to both playlets and humorous radio ads, these types of commercials have unlimited possibilities if they are tastefully written and produced. But they can also backfire if viewers find them unfunny.

Demonstrations   These are "television exclusives." Merchants can literally put their own salespersons into the consumer's living room to demonstrate the virtues of a product as they would at the store's sales counter (and, indeed, live production may well be shot in the store). Many creative experts recommend that in planning *every* TV commercial this technique should be considered as *one strong possibility*. The demonstration technique is almost as frequently seen in prime-time spots, both for national and local advertisers, as the announcer commercial. Many ads by direct marketers, and a few by forward-looking retailers, use this approach, usually in inexpensive fringe time, with direct, sometimes explosive sales results.

Analogies   Some TV spots try to lead a viewer to a conclusion by implying that the results of one action or event will be similar to the results of another action or event. "Because [some well-known personality] liked this product, you will like it too," or "Since your grandparents traded here, you will surely also like our store today." This kind of logic can be a dangerous way to put across a point unless the analogy really holds up.

Fantasies Commercials that use fantasy have become increasingly popular among big-time national advertisers. Like highly imaginative print ads, they are a job for professionals, and they may involve expensive visual techniques. Though they are not supposed to be "believable," they can backfire if they are too farfetched.

Mood Commercials Often associated with special effects, these commercials rely on musical backgrounds, colors, tones of voice, and the actors' personalities to create feelings or moods. Their applications for purely institutional messages are obvious.

WRITING AND EVALUATING TELEVISION COMMERCIALS

Rarely will a member of a local store's ad staff actually write a TV script. Should the need to do so arise, a few brief pointers should be kept in mind.

First, "think visual" as you write; TV is primarily a visual medium, and a TV commercial is not just a radio commercial with pictures. The copy should fit the pictures, still or moving, and not

vice versa. The essence of the message should come through even if the audio signal goes dead. So, synchronize the script with the picture or scene to be viewed; make the words and the pictures work together, but remember that the picture will make the first and most vivid impression on the audience.

Simplicity is a cardinal virtue in almost all kinds of advertising. Stick to one clear-cut, main selling idea, and use the same kind of colloquial language you would use in writing radio copy. The opening few moments are crucial. This is the time to arouse viewers' interest with news about the product, a conflict situation, a problem that needs solving, a gag, or a startling declaration of some kind. Remember, however, that the opening must relate in some way to the ad message. A far-out opening that gains attention through gimmickry and has nothing to do with the actual content of the ad is likely to leave viewers cold.

Get down to mentioning the product, service, or idea quickly, within the first 15 seconds or so of a commercial. Avoid shifting scenes too often, or viewers will be confused. More than three scene changes in 10 seconds, or more than 10 in a full minute, are too many. Studies indicate that it takes about four seconds for viewers to become oriented to a new scene; on the other hand, they become bored unless there is some motion or action within six seconds. Either way, the advertiser is walking a tightrope.

Retailers are far more likely to be called on to evaluate TV commercials and to approve them than to write or create them, since so much TV advertising is done "out of house." Here are some questions store owners or ad managers can ask themselves: Does the video portion of the ad tell the story so well that you can grasp the essence of the sales message before reading the script? Do the words sound right, like simple, spoken language? Are they timed properly to synchronize with the visuals? Does each scene tie the audio and video elements together firmly so that the viewers hear about what they see and see what they are hearing about?

Like the writing itself, each scene should be simple, not overcrowded or busy. The opening should involve the viewers, to get their attention and interest in a way relevant to the sales message. The ad should have one main sales point that is made, repeated, and hung on a central theme. Like all other good ads, print or broadcast, a TV commercial should sound and look believable, and it should encourage viewers to act immediately to buy the product or visit the store.

TV scripts written for local retailers closely resemble radio scripts but have instructions for the video scenes added. When there is time and money for a full-scale professional TV production, a *storyboard* is used to amplify the script and link it visually with the video elements. A storyboard is simply a series of pictures of each video scene, along with the audio script and technical instructions. (See Figure 15–4). Its function is much like that of the layout for a print ad. It tells the producer, the technicians, the actors, the camera operators, and others what to do. And like a layout, it permits the store's management to see what it is selling, and order changes if it wants them, before huge sums are spent on doing the wrong thing

(or doing the right thing in the wrong way).

THE TECHNICAL SIDE OF TV PRODUCTION

TV commercials can be live, made from slides, on videotape, or on motion-picture film (16 or 35 mm). All full-scale, thoroughly professional ads will be on tape or film. Tape produces a clearer picture and sound, it can be played back immediately after each take, and it requires no processing. However, it is more costly than film and records the picture only. The audio track is run separately and must be "interlocked," or synchronized, later. Film is flexible, versatile, and widely used and is especially good for "on-location" shooting.

Most retailers who seriously go into TV engage an advertising agency to create ads, contract out their production, and buy time. In some communities, local TV stations cultivate the business of local clients and have facilities for producing commercials, for a price. Large stores with ad staffs competent to create their own TV advertising may make their own arrangements with production firms, of which there are many in every sizable city. They then make their own time "buys" from local stations. Large chains do this at national or regional level, too, and send completed commercials to individual stores or stations.

SOME COST–SAVING PRODUCTION TIPS

Smaller local advertisers in the market for quality TV production to upgrade their commercials, can often keep

Asparagus

This is the kind of asparagus found in a package of a Famous Brand Name's frozen asparagus. It's U.S. Government Inspected. Maybe even Grade A.

This is the kind of asparagus found in a package of Pathmark frozen asparagus. They're not only Grade A. You see we're a bit rougher on our vegetables than that.

When we choose a vegetable we take the best part—the heart of the vegetable. And we select them virtually by hand instead of by machine. So nothing but the best ever sneaks in.

Now, with all this, Pathmark frozen foods and frozen juices cost less than the Famous Brand Name frozen foods.

Which could very well be the reason why—in almost every case at Pathmark—the Pathmark brand is out-selling the Famous Brand Names. After all, fame is nice. But you can't eat it.

Figure 15–4 Story Boards of Agency-Prepared Commercials for Chain Stores

This story board was created by Venet Advertising, a New York agency, for Pathmark Supermarkets, a regional food chain on the East Coast. This "demonstration" commercial (others in the same series included "announcer" commercials) shows four pictures plus the retailer's logotype at the end. No specific store is mentioned. To cut down the cost per store to a minimum level, the commercials are broadcast in areas where one TV station covers the trading area of several Pathmark stores. All commercials are thoroughly professional in concept and execution. Most are focused on institutional appeals, but a few go into specific item selling and include prices.

Source: By courtesy of the Television Bureau of Advertising.

costs down by shopping around and getting bids from several production houses, including those some distance away. In many medium-sized cities, producers of TV commercials use amateur actors, adequate to play various character parts, who do not get guild wages for their part-time work; production crews may also be nonunion in such communities, and costs would be correspondingly cheaper.

For certain scenes, cost-conscious producers can use *"stock"* film footage, available at low rates, and can *shoot scenes on location* rather than building costly sets. A script can call for showing just a hand or a pair of feet, not an actor's face, so that anyone (a secretary, say, or a spare camera operator) can "play the role" just as well as a trained actor.

Concentrating creative efforts on material that can be *used over and over* will reduce the cost *per exposure.* The *sandwich,* or *bridge,* technique described for radio commercials works for TV, too. A 10- or 15-second live-action, professionally created opening and/or closing can be linked with simple announcer-type copy in the middle that changes with a retailer's needs at a given time. The sound track for music identifying the store or for jingles can also be converted for use on radio.

SOME EXAMPLES OF RETAIL TV COMMERCIALS

The Television Bureau of Advertising provides a large number of demonstration commercials for retailers. The four presented below vary in length and in approach. They are for different categories of stores and use different production techniques.

A 60-Second Ad for a Furniture Store

(Suggested technique: videotape, film)

VIDEO	AUDIO
Shot of Jane Smith sitting on couch.	Hi, I'm Jane Smith and I'm at Doe's Furniture Store on Broadway. I just bought this heavenly couch for $239.99. It's mine!
Shot of Joe Jones and Sue Bell looking at their bedroom set.	Hello, I'm Joe Jones and this is my girlfriend, Sue Bell. We're at Doe's Furniture Store on Broadway. We'll be getting married in a few weeks, and we just bought this bedroom set, mattress and all, for $343.99.
Shot of Liza Brown jumping up and down on bed, beaming parents to the side.	We're Mr. and Mrs. Tom Brown and this is our daughter Liza. She's 6. We're at Doe's Furniture Store on Broadway. We just bought Liza her first bedroom set for $189.99. You can see how much she's enjoying it.
Shot of John Doe in center of store; camera should pan across store.	I'm John Doe; my friends call me Jack. I own Doe's Furniture Store on Broadway. You've

just met some of my customers, and I'd like you to become one of my customers. As you can see, I have a lot of furniture for sale at low-low prices. Come buy some furniture from me, Jack Doe, at Doe's Furniture Store on Broadway.

Close with exterior shot of store.

A 60-Second Ad for a Women's Wear Shop

(Suggested technique: film, videotape, live)

VIDEO	AUDIO
Large easel with detailed sketch, showing complete outfit . . . spokeswoman standing alongside easel with pointer in hand, spokeswoman must be well dressed.	Here's (*store name*) fashion forecast for today. I'm (*spokeswoman's name*) and I'd like to tell you a little about (*store name*) fashion predictions.
Points to length of skirt. Points to boots. Points to shirt. Points to waist. Points to vest. Full close-up shot of sketch.	As you know, skirts are longer now. Both Paris and American designers have promoted this longer length for fall. To balance out the look, high leg-hugging boots and dark hose should be worn. As you can see, tops are more soft and feminine and waists are again defined and belted by wide gentle leathers. This softer, more feminine look is rounded out by a short, little suede vest. To sum it all up, (*store name*) fashion forecast for right now is soft, and feminine. Of course, the most outstanding new feature is the longer skirt and the new proportion this length demands.
Fade to store logotype.	All the things necessary for this new, long, gentle feminine look are available at (*store name*). This is (*spokeswoman's name*) saying good night for (*store name*).

A 20-Second Spot for a Men's Clothing Store

(Suggested technique: film, videotape, slides)

VIDEO	AUDIO
Girl in pair of bright-colored man-tailored pants with wide bell bottoms—encased in picture frame, so pair of pants on body appears surrounded by picture frame.	Picture pants, pants for play, pants for parties, pants for any place you go. Picture yourself in pants.

Quick changes of pants in frame. (Style, color should be very different in each frame.)

Show girl in pair of pants within frame ...then show full-length girl still in frame.

The pants picture is right-on for right now. Never before have pants been so right for so many. And never before has (store name) had such a wide selection of styles, colors, fabrics, and good looks.

Make the pants picture complete. Put yourself in the pants picture at (store name), the place for pretty pants, play pants, prime pants.

A 10-Second Commercial for a Jewelry Store at Christmastime

(Suggested technique: slides, film, videotape, live)

VIDEO	AUDIO
Close-up of face of man dressed as a Santa's helper with jeweler's eyepiece in his eye, examining watch.	What do you look for in a watch?
Camera zooms back to include "jeweler's" face as he takes eyepiece out and looks at watch, smiling proudly.	Quality, right? But unless you're a skilled jeweler, you must rely on trust.
Super store name and fade to black.	(Store name) has the finest jewelry and craftsmen. We honor your trust.

3 Direct Advertising and Outdoor Signs

DIRECT ADVERTISING

Direct advertising, whether delivered by mail or other means, in general follows the same basic principles of good copywriting and design as newspaper ads, discussed in depth in Chapters 13 and 14. But there are critical differences in certain particulars. A good newspaper ad is not necessarily a good direct ad. First and foremost, a direct ad stands entirely on its own. Its copy and design must arouse interest instantly or it will instantly be thrown away.

But before we get into copy and de-sign tactics, we must back up a bit (as we have in discussing other media) and pinpoint the specific goal of any proposed piece of direct advertising. It may have an institutional, image-building objective; it may aim for immediate sales of one item, either at the store or through telephone or mail responses; it may announce a new store service; it may promote a whole merchandise line, as in a seasonal campaign or manufacturer-aided cooperative venture; or it may be a thick catalog of hundreds of items intended to generate sales in every department of the store during a shopping season. And the recipients may be a store's present charge customers or a purchased list of noncustomers; who they are will make a crucial difference in what the ad must say and how it should say it.

This kind of advertising is the most flexible in form, and both the copy and the graphics can differ widely depending on that factor. *Postcards and letters* call for simple, straightforward announcements or warm, personal words of greeting, with few or no illustrations. *Leaflets and folders* usually rely on art and design to emphasize key copy points and are often manufacturer-prepared, complete with preprinted, professionally written hard-sell copy. *Broadsides,* or *circulars,* typically resemble big newspaper ads. Currently, this form of ad is in fact blending with newspaper spreads; often the same copy is delivered as a newspaper insert to some, while in other areas (the fringe ones in which newspaper circulation thins out) it comes through the mail as a circular. *Booklets* or *catalogs,* by far the most expensive type of direct advertising, are almost always prepared by outside professionals, specialists in catalog printing, and often the high preparation costs are shared by a wholesale house and its many dealers or a group of cooperating retailers. The store merely supplies its imprint for use on the number of copies it orders. Order forms for mail responses are included in many of these kinds of direct ads.

For forms of mailed advertising not designed as *self-mailers* containing an address panel, the *envelope* is a vital consideration. It may contain a conspicuous "preview" of the contents, to entice the recipient to open it. Or it may take an opposite approach: dignified, subdued, displaying the store's normal business address in the corner. (This is more usual for personalized letters, perhaps accompanied by hard-sell leaflets, to charge customers who already feel an affinity for the store.) "See-through" windows in envelopes sometimes stimulate recipients to open them by revealing an intriguing sample of the contents.

Direct selling is growing and eating into total sales available for retail stores. Increasing numbers of merchants, large and small, are entering this field, in self-defense if for no other reason. Many of those that succeed engage direct-mail specialty houses, which have their own staff of artists, copywriters, and designers. Some may even have their own printing facilities. Stores that do their own mailings should choose a printer with prior experience in direct advertising for other clients. A good print shop can make recommendations about printing processes, kinds and grades of paper, typesetting, art elements, the use of color, and other technical matters that will be very helpful. The range of choices for direct-mail pieces is far greater than in preparing newspaper ads. However, the print shop can explain the forms in which copy and layout or art should be prepared for the greatest economy, the quickest service, and the most productive results.

A survey by the National Retail Merchants Association of 71 large retailers that use direct-mail advertising has revealed that the most suitable merchandise for such advertising is cosmetics, hosiery, women's sportswear, gifts, housewares, men's wear, furs, mattresses, lingerie, and ready-to-wear clothing (in that order). Catalogs are used most often for Christmas, back-to-school, and special sales. Leaflets inserted in monthly bills are most suitable for advertising Mother's Day, Father's Day, and graduation items. Cards and letters are preferred for promoting private sales, furs, and bridal goods, and circulars for publicizing anniversaries and storewide sales.[3]

The same survey reported that direct-mail promotions were tied in with other media ads "sometimes" or "usually" by 87 percent of the respondents. The respondents were split 50-50 on preferences for a "hard sell" versus "soft sell" and on the use of artwork or photographs. In general, they felt that both form letters and personal letters should be designed by the store's chief executive or a buyer. Only 34 percent used reduced-price coupons, and of those all said that they helped "substantially" or "moderately." Nearly 9 out of 10 reported that postage-paid return envelopes or cards increased results. The factors having the greatest effect on results were first, the *merchandise itself;* second, the *artwork;* third, the *copy;* fourth, the *tone* of the ad; and, finally, the *price.*[4]

Form Letters   Form letters carelessly prepared and inappropriately worded can tear down a store's precious and long-established image and irritate or even enrage some of its most loyal customers. This often happens when a store's own mailing list or one prepared from its customer list by outsiders (merchandise suppliers, book and magazine firms, travel agencies, and the like) is fed through computers that activate automatic typewriters able to insert local or personalized references into otherwise standardized copy. Salutations like "Dear Sir" make no hit when received by women (but how do you tell a computer that the account in the name of "M. E. Jones" is that of one Mary Elizabeth Jones?). A very touchy point is the salu-

tation for letters directed to women. If the educational and socioeconomic status of the recipient is high, "Ms." is acceptable. But among those of lower educational levels and less sophistication, and often in rural areas, the traditional "Mrs." or "Miss" sets better— provided, of course, one knows which is right. References to "your wife" or "your husband" are well-meant efforts to be warm and friendly, but they surely backfire when sent to single persons, the recently divorced, or the widowed. Mentioning children presumed to be in a family can be disturbing to the childless couple, ludicrous to those whose "children" are now 25 or 30 years old, and devastating to those whose only child recently died. Letters programmed to attract new charge-account customers seem very phony if they go to people who have traded with the store for 20 years, but this often happens if a retailer buys a mailing list and is not thorough when deleting names of those who already have accounts. The computer does not recognize that the W. G. Smith on one list is the same person as the Walter Smith on the other. In short, personal references are best avoided entirely unless a foolproof system has been devised to segregate groups according to accurate and up-to-date information. Separate versions of form letters must then be written to properly suit each of those groups.

Direct-Response Ads   In writing, designing, and illustrating *direct-response* mailers, the selection of items featured is crucial. Not everything can be sold effectively by mail. Ideally, a featured item should be a product not found everywhere else, one that satisfies a specific need, and one that can be offered at an attractive price. Novelties, hobby items, convenience goods, and lower-priced products generally sell well. The basic selling proposition must be made clear *right at the beginning* in the headline, the picture, and the lead paragraph, all of which must focus on *user benefits*. *Believability* and realism are essential. Sometimes a *teaser* headline can instantly interest readers and make them equate the purchase of what the store has to sell with the fulfillment of a particular desire. *News* value is a key to success. Recipients are likely to be intrigued and to read on when they feel a store has gone to the trouble of communicating with them directly to make them aware of *something really new* that will benefit them.

Once interest in a product has been aroused, the direct-response ad must give far more *specific details* than the average mass-media ad. The aim is not just to get people to come to the store, but to actually get them to *buy*. This makes the *call to action* at the end even more important than in other forms of advertising. The ad itself must do what the floor salesperson would ordinarily do. It must "close the sale." This means that complete specifications, all the secondary selling points there is no room for in the mass-media ad, suggestions for multiple uses of the product, answers to the kinds of questions the prospective buyer would ordinarily ask at the store, must be included. The reader should not be left to guess or wonder about anything, even though this means long body copy and some rather fine print.

The ad should also make it easy to buy by giving credit terms and the hours when the telephone will be answered to accept orders. It should, in addition, include a postage-paid reply envelope or card that's easy to fill in.

Catalogs The catalog business is a whole new world. The best—and only the best—values must be *at the front:* on the cover, on the first page spread, perhaps even on the wrapper in which the catalog is mailed. Lesser items with a weaker appeal should go toward the back. Action verbs, benefit-centered descriptions, and testimonials from satisfied users are helpful, and precise, thorough descriptions are a must. The catalog should also have an underlying theme.

Incentive Offers As well as catalog selling and single-item or whole-line leaflets, folders, or circulars, direct marketing thrives on *special incentive offers*. Some popular ones include free samples sent with the mailing, offers of free trials, money-back guarantees, contests and sweepstakes, free gifts of secondary or related items, and discounts for immediate payment with an order.

OUTDOOR COPY AND ART

In outdoor signs, the art is dominant, the copy secondary. Utter simplicity and directness are essential. Art and style should tie in with other advertising to establish continuity. Eight or fewer well-chosen words, perhaps a store slogan or a seasonal campaign theme tied to the massive picture, must do the job. Signs are seldom used for item-selling, except when manufacturers supply "paper" (and pay part of the costs) for special seasonal product promotions. Signs are frequently used for directions ("turn right at the next interchange") or to advertise convenience ("just 3 miles to...").

The Institute of Outdoor Advertising offers these guidelines for stores:

> In outdoor [advertising],... the importance of copy cannot be overstated. The difference in readership and remembrance between a well-designed poster and a poor one can well be 50% or greater.... Two unique characteristics of the medium must be kept in mind: it communicates with people *on the move*, and *at a distance*. Therefore outdoor advertising must be simple, arresting, and legible. It has only a brief period in which to be seen and to register its message. Economy of ideas, elements, words is paramount. All nonessentials must be eliminated.
>
> Good copy starts with a single idea, proceeds with an original expression of that idea, and concludes with the execution in the simplest, most dramatic, most easily visible terms. Each element should do its own job, so that words, picture, and layout contribute without overlapping. Lettering should be clear, simple and bold.[5]

Most outdoor "plants" maintain competent and professional art and copy staffs to assist advertisers.

Other "reminder" forms of advertising usually employ few words and, often, pictorial matter, and those who produce them normally provide copy and graphic services as part of the "package" advertisers buy. A store should integrate all these forms of promotion with its basic image, slogans, and seasonal themes, so they reflect and reinforce its advertising in the major mass media and point-of-sale displays.

Questions for Discussion

1. In writing scripts for radio commercials, why is each of the following important: (a) repetition; (b) the pronounceability of words; (c) music; (d) sound effects; (e) partial sentences, slang expressions, and pauses?

2. From what different sources can the small store with a low advertising budget secure adequate sound effects, music, and other attention-getting devices for its radio advertising at little or no cost? Which sources do you think are best?

3. What are at least five things to consider in creating television commercials at a cost within the means of smaller stores with limited funds for production? What options are available to a small-budget advertiser that wants quality commercials?

4. How would a TV ad campaign aimed at selling particular items differ from a campaign whose objective was to build a store's *image*? Which kind of campaign do you see most often in your area? Which kinds of stores tend to emphasize item-selling on TV, and which stress image-building?

5. How would copy for the following types of direct-mail advertising differ from newspaper-ad copy: (a) cards and letters; (b) leaflets and folders; (c) booklets and catalogs; (d) circulars, or broadsides? In what ways would it be similar to newspaper copy?

Suggested Projects

1. Turn on any commercial radio station and listen to it for at least an

hour, notebook in hand. Identify and make brief notes on the different types of commercials for local retailers that you hear. Which kinds are most popular? Which of the commercials you heard would you judge to be most effective in motivating people to buy? Which, of those you heard, do you think would have had a greater impact on the listener had some other format been employed?

2. Select the type of opening you think best, from among those explained in the text, for ads for each of the following kinds of stores: (a) a ladies' dress shop, (b) a hardware store, (c) a children's clothing department in a general merchandise store, (d) an insurance agency, and (e) a supermarket. Write an opening for each type of store, and indicate any music and sound effects you wish to use.

3. Visit a local radio station and talk with the continuity writer(s). Also ask to hear some of the sound effects from the station's library. Then report on how the music and special effects the station has available could be used to improve some of the worst of the local commercials you have heard recently.

4. Visit the nearest commercial TV station, and talk with the local sales manager and his or her creative staff. Find out what facilities and services the station provides for the production of retail commercials and also what outside facilities it recommends to advertisers who want to upgrade their commercials. Do you think that TV advertising, in your community, is as easy to handle as radio or newspaper advertising, for stores that do not employ advertising agencies?

5. Get a tape recorder, and with friends or classmates, play the announcers' and actors' parts in some of the TV and radio commercials used as examples in the text. Then listen to the performances, and consider what music, sound effects, and simple, inexpensive visual devices you could add to make the continuity more effective.

Notes

1. All examples in this section were provided by the Radio Advertising Bureau, Inc., New York.

2. S. K. Ziegler, ed., *Guides to Successful Broadcast Advertising* (Michigan State University, 1970), p. 14.

3. *Direct Mail Advertising by Retail Stores* (New York: National Retail Merchants Association, 1967).

4. Ibid.

5. *This Is Outdoor Advertising* (New York: Institute of Outdoor Advertising, n.d.).

Preview

For nearly a century the critics of advertiisng have called attention to the problem of deceptive, misleading, and unethical advertising practices. Pressure groups, government action at all levels, and internal self-regulation have produced vast improvements over former standards, though the job is not yet completed.

Stores tempted to engage in deceptive advertising today do well to remember that they may run afoul of federal, state, or local laws; that valuable goodwill and consumer confidence can be lost as a result of conflicts with regulatory agencies; and that increasing consumer sophistication and skepticism makes "bad" ads both unproductive and unprofitable.

Numerous laws now spell out very clearly the difference between acceptable and unacceptable advertising standards. The Federal Trade Commission and other federal agencies stand ready to enforce an increasingly specific and far-reaching body of federal laws and regulatory guides at the national, regional, and even local levels, while more and more states and municipalities are enacting parallel legislation to plug any gaps at the local level. Voluntary regulation is also widespread, effected through trade association codes and the work of local Advertising Review Boards and Better Business Bureaus.

Much of the trouble in retail advertising centers on the substantiation of claims, corrective ads, "bait-and-switch" merchandise offers, "free" offers, credit terms, guarantees, unsafe products, illustrations, mentions of competitors, professional advertising, and definitions of good taste. Many good retailers today go far beyond mere avoidance of such trouble and take a positive stance, launching positive projects to enlighten and educate consumers and sponsoring advertising campaigns emphasizing high standards.

Learning Goals

From Chapter 16 readers should gain an understanding of where to find both official and voluntary regulatory agencies and how to work with them to improve the level of truth in advertising. Students should know the special "problem areas" in retail advertising and be alert to possible misunderstandings and misinterpretations of well-intentioned ads, as well as outright attempts at fraud and deception.

16

Legal and Ethical Restraints on Advertising Creativity

1 The Controversy over Advertising

Advertising has changed considerably since the days of laissez-faire capitalism, when buyers were warned to "beware" and sellers were little bothered by complaints that they had misrepresented products or grossly exaggerated their virtues.

As consumers have become more educated, public opinion, supported in many instances by the mass media, has forced the passage of increasingly restrictive legislation regarding business in general and advertising in particular. Consumers who believe they have been deceived now have many options, from complaints to consumer protection agencies to class-action suits against offending corporations.

Advertising today is criticized mainly on four counts:

1. that it fails to tell the truth about products—that it promises satisfaction from merchandise that turns out to be of poor quality because of inferior materials or a worker's lack of skill, that does not perform as promised, or that is in constant need of repair or servicing;

2. that it coaxes people to buy things they do not really need or cannot afford, including some that may ultimately do the purchaser or the environment more harm than good;

3. that it raises the cost of products; and

4. that it is often boring, inane, or in bad taste.

How do retailers in general feel about these criticisms? As consumers have become more educated, so too have retailers. Attitudes toward advertising have changed in the business community as well as among the public. No reputable merchant today wants anything to do with advertising that is clearly false or deceptive. Nor does any retailer purposely make its ads boring, inane, or insulting to the customer's intelligence.

As for the claim that advertising raises the cost of goods, it has been both proven and disproven by studies. There are lines of merchandise in which advertising undoubtedly raises the retail price of the product. On the other hand, the general consensus among economists is that advertising, by helping to create the mass markets needed to support mass production and distribution, creates economies of scale that actually lower the unit price of goods.

The question of whether advertising should persuade people to buy what they do not need or should not have, for one reason or another, is basically a philosophical one that the average retailer is unlikely to spend too much time thinking about. In the case of definitely harmful products, a government ban on production may resolve the issue. On the whole, the controversy is one in which national manufacturers are more likely to be involved.

Retailers are more likely to come under fire for the way they advertise. They are attacked for using a hard-sell approach when it is not appropriate or for making product claims that, while not actually deceptive, cannot be proven.

Despite continuing controversy, advertising continues to thrive because of the useful role it plays in the free-enterprise system. Its vices, like its virtues, stem largely from the competitive economic system of which it is a part. We cannot even begin to debate here the merits of a capitalist economy, nor can we give much consideration to the arguments of those who would abolish advertising entirely. But we can point out that the call today is for truthful, tasteful, informative advertising that answers consumers' real needs, credits them with some intelligence, and reflects a concern for the total environment of the community.

Not surprisingly, many businesspersons have already changed or begun to change with the times and to develop new attitudes toward advertising. Aside from philosophical considerations, three practical reasons have fostered this trend away from deceptive advertising:

1. *To avoid prosecution by the government.* Government agencies can impose fines on advertisers for deceptive practices, force them to make restitution or pay compensation to "wronged" customers, require them to do "counteradvertising"—to retract in new advertisements false statements made in previous ones—and make them pay for advertising to warn buyers of dangerous or defective merchandise. The Magnuson-Moss Warranty Act became effective in 1975 to control advertisers who offer written warranties on products they sell. This act allows penalties of up to $10,000 per offense to be imposed on advertisers whose ads are judged to be misleading—even if no deliberate intent is proven—plus restitution in cash to customers who have been bilked. In the future, in addition to being fined and required to make restitution, fraudulent advertisers may actually wind up in federal prisons. If passed, the Consumer Fraud Act of 1975, placed before Congress at the behest of the attorney general of the United States, would make criminals of advertisers judged guilty of some of the worst kinds of false advertising (such as "bait-and-switch" tactics and fictitious price comparisons), with penalties of up to five years in prison. Other federal statutes have long authorized criminal prosecution in the food, drug, and cosmetics fields. In 1975 the FTC unanimously upheld the ruling of one of its administrative law judges that a major food chain's ads had misled because some of its stores did not have advertised items in stock. The agency prescribed rigid rules for the retailer to adhere to in future advertising of specially priced products.

2. *To avoid time-consuming, embarrassing, and perhaps image-destroying run-ins with voluntary self-regulatory agencies.* Even though they do not have the legal authority to enforce decisions in disputes with allegedly wronged customers, it does a store no good when one of the voluntary bodies accumulates a largely negative file on them, issues press releases about its findings, or holds open hearings to air grievances. The media associations are continuing to tighten their own advertising codes, and individual media have the legal right to rigidly censor the advertising offered to them. Many have refused ads they have deemed contrary to the public interest, and more will do so as time goes on. The media will refuse questionable ads if for no other reason than to protect the environment of their other ads, those from advertisers with impeccable ethical standards who do not wish to be in "bad company." In terms of public opinion if not of actual legal authority, local Advertising Review Boards, which are affiliated with Better Business Bureaus and advertising clubs, are becoming a force to be reckoned with in many areas of regulation.

3. *To make advertising acceptable and believable to the consumer.* Some 86 percent of the people questioned in a 1972 Harris poll felt that advertising claims were "exaggerated," and only 11 percent agreed that "most advertising claims" were "generally accurate." In the same year, a Better Business Bureau poll of 68,000 people nationwide reported that the second biggest complaint

against U.S. business was "advertising that misleads or claims too much." Newspaper Advertising Bureau research on the attitudes of 500 young men in 15 cities toward automotive ads, found that 54 percent considered almost all or most car advertising "exaggerated or misleading"; another 36 percent felt that "some" car ads were that bad. In early 1972, a Daniel Starch study based on 18,000 personal interviews reported that nearly half the respondents believed "most advertising nowadays attempts to deceive people rather than inform them." In the face of attitudes like these, can a person responsible for the creative content of any type of advertising fail to get the message? Modest, honest, believable ads are not only ethical, but the only kind likely to produce real results.

2 Government Regulation of Advertising

FEDERAL REGULATION

Federal Agencies and Departments The *Federal Trade Commission,* established by Congress in 1914, is the nation's primary regulator of advertising. Originally concerned only with insuring free and fair *competition* among businesses, its scope was extended in 1938 to include protection of the *consumer.* Its most spectacular and most publicized activities have to do chiefly with *national* advertising, but large retailers have also come under its scrutiny—as have increasing numbers of medium-sized stores. All retailers, even the smallest, would be well-advised to adhere to the developing philosophy of ethical advertising growing out of a continuous and increasing succession of FTC guidelines, rulings, and consent agreements.

Many of the new laws designed to protect consumers are enforced through FTC channels. The FTC's administrative law judges exercise quasi-judicial powers, and the agency can turn important cases over to the Justice Department for prosecution in regular federal courts. Regional offices of the FTC are in operation throughout the country to police regional and local business practices, including advertising. The FTC can get court injunctions against deceptive advertising, issue industrywide rules, and levy fines and assess damages in cases of deceptive advertising. It also has authority to set penalties in *class-action* proceedings, in which large numbers of individuals collectively, rather than individually, sue for compensation for some loss or wrong (as may be incurred through deceptive advertising). Furthermore, it is now empowered to deal with *local* situations previously considered by "strict constructionists" of constitutional law to be beyond its jurisdiction. To facilitate enforcement at local levels, the State and Local Enforcement Act, introduced for congressional consideration in 1975, would empower state and municipal courts to assume original jurisdiction in FTC cases. It would also authorize local prosecuting attorneys or individual citizens to petition such courts to issue injunctions and restitution orders or to provide relief when there is evidence that any local business is in violation of FTC rules.

The *Federal Communications Commission* has been known to block renewal of a broadcasting station's license because of improper advertising practices. However, a recent policy decision indicates that most controversies involving false advertising will be handled in the future by the FTC.

The *Postmaster General* can exclude from the mails magazines and newspapers considered to contain pornographic materials either in ads or editorial matter. Postal authorities also enforce rules concerning preprinted inserts, which must bear the newspaper's name and publication date and be charged for at regular advertising rates. Moreover, not more than half of the total distributed may be used as third-class circulars also. The postal authorities wield heavy regulatory clubs over the whole of the direct-mail segment of the advertising industry. A recent Supreme Court ruling has established that individual postal patrons may prevent an advertiser from sending them *anything at all* by notifying the post office they do not want to receive such material.

The *U.S. Bureau of Roads,* together with *state highway authorities,* can greatly restrict outdoor advertising under certain conditions, even to the extent of allotting public monies to tear down specified billboards. The *Alcohol & Tobacco Commission* (an agency dating back to the eighteenth century), the *Securities and Exchange Commission,* the *Civil Aeronautics Board,* the *Interstate Commerce Commission,* the *Federal Power Commission,* and the *Food & Drug Administration* have certain regulatory powers over specified kinds of advertising, too. The *Department of Agriculture,* though lacking direct jurisdiction over retailers, can affect food stores by its control over processors, as in the case of meat packers it has found guilty of con-

spiring with their retail outlets to engage in illegal cooperative advertising practices. And the *Department of Justice* acts on behalf of all other federal agencies, at their request, in actually enforcing compliance with the numerous laws affecting advertising. The Consumer Fraud Act of 1975, if enacted into law, will go a step further and authorize Justice Department prosecutors to initiate enforcement proceedings under FTC regulations *with or without* requests from the FTC itself. The appellate courts and sometimes the Supreme Court, by their decisions, are constantly modifying concepts of what is permissible and what is not. Often it is the courts that must establish clear-cut definitions when statutes and regulations are not clear.

The *Consumer Product Safety Commission,* established in 1972 to deal with the hazardous design and use of products is, of course, indirectly involved with the advertising of such products. One of its first jobs was to tighten standards for flammable fabrics in children's clothing and to regulate their labeling and advertising. A small *consumer protection office* was set up to hear consumer complaints and recommend legislative and other remedies in the early 1970s, and a large-scale *Consumer Protection Agency* for the same purposes was twice approved by the House of Representatives in 1974 and was still being debated in 1975.

CONSTRAINTS ON ADVERTISING IMPOSED BY THE FTC

Substantiation Retail advertisers must have written, documentary proof of any product claims made in their ads (or be able to get it from their suppliers). The philosophy behind this rule was stated in a 1972 FTC case:

> Given the imbalance of knowledge and resources between a business enterprise and each of its customers, economically it is more rational, and imposes far less cost on society, to require [an advertiser] to confirm his affirmative product claims rather than impose a burden upon each individual consumer to test, investigate, or experiment for himself. The [advertiser] has the ability, the know-how, the equipment, the time and the resources to undertake such information by testing or otherwise—the consumer usually does not.[1]

Early in 1974, the FTC began issuing specific *guidelines* for advertising particular categories of merchandise, beginning with furniture. The guideline for furniture ads, which set the tone for guides in other trade lines, prohibits "any representation or circumstance," including a "failure to disclose material facts," that has or could have the effect of misleading or deceiving consumers about an advertised item's utility, construction, composition, durability, design, style, or quality; about the quantity or number of items; about models; or about the origin, manufacture, price, or grade of the product.[2]

The second guideline issued dealt with catalog selling, and those in other categories followed. These guidelines do not have the force of law, but are the principles that govern FTC prosecution of alleged offenders. Claims regarding products more likely to be hazardous to their users' health and safety must be more thoroughly substantiated, as must claims that are difficult for consumers themselves to test and verify. Greater proof must be given of very specific claims than of general claims.

Corrective Ads, or "Counteradvertising" The principle that counteradvertising must be done as "punishment" for false advertising and to correct wrong impressions made on the public by an unsubstantiated ad claim was applied in several cases in 1973. However, the ruling that firms found guilty of misleading advertising must publish or broadcast follow-up advertising disclaiming their prior untrue claims and setting forth the facts has been highly controversial, and FTC spokespersons have indicated it will be applied only in rare and extreme cases in the future.

Constraints on Bait-and-Switch Advertising and Ads for Merchandise That Is Not Available The FTC defines as unacceptable any advertising for merchandise that is not actually available in the store, in reasonable quantities, for sale to those who respond to the ad. It is up to the store to see to it that its original stock is adequate to justify the advertising and to do everything in its power to replenish its stock of the advertised items quickly if it runs out of them. This is often a problem for supermarkets, which sell such a vast number of items, and for chain stores, since certain stores may be undersupplied even though the chain as a whole has a sufficient stock. The FTC has, at different times, filed complaints against all three of the largest food chains for allegedly failing to have advertised specials on hand. Bait-and-switch advertising (when salespersons try to downgrade an advertised item and use excessive persuasion to get customers to "trade up" to a higher-priced model) is also considered cause for action against a store. This is most often a problem for retailers of major appliances and home furnishings, whose salespersons work on commission.

Comparative Pricing   According to FTC guidelines, manufacturers' list prices may be cited as the "reference" price when ads claim a price reduction, provided the retailer "has no reason to believe that they substantially exceed the highest prices at which sales were made in the region" where the store operates. Both the article offered at a cut price and the original reference price must be explicitly identified, and if the store cannot prove that it has recently sold the item at the higher price, it must say so in its ad. When advertising sales during which prices are temporarily reduced, stores must state the period during which the sale will be in progress and give a definite ending date (though it may later be extended).

"Free Offers"   The FTC also regulates promotional gimmicks such as "one-cent sales," giving 50 percent off with the purchase of two items, allowing customers to "buy one—get another free," and "2-for-1" sales. The price of the item that must be purchased in order to get the "free" or one-cent item must not be marked up over its normal selling price during the preceding 30-day period (or the lowest price within that period, if the price has fluctuated). All terms, obligations, and restrictions connected with such offers must be plainly spelled out in the ad. In the case of low-price introductory offers of new products, the store must, after a reasonable period, begin to sell the item at its regular price.

Credit Terms and "Truth in Lending"   A special problem area in advertising has been created by the passage of the federal *Truth-In-Lending Act* (1969). This requires the full disclosure of *all* details of credit terms in an ad if any specific credit term is used. If phrases such as "no down payment," "36 months to pay," or "only $10 per month" are used, advertisers must give all other particulars of their credit terms as well. In describing interest rates, *annual* rates must be clearly disclosed. There are both criminal and civil penalties for violating the Truth-In-Lending Act. The best way to avoid problems is to use general statements such as "credit terms available" or "use our easy credit plan."

Warranties   An act of Congress that became effective in 1975 assigns responsibility for enforcement to the FTC in cases where retailers' (as well as manufacturers') guarantees and warranties are mentioned in ads. Such advertising must clearly specify whether the maker or the store or both stand behind the product, and whether the warranty covers the entire item or is confined to specified component parts. If there is any chance for misunderstanding, the ad must specifically name unwarranted parts, and there must be full revelation of precisely what the warrantor will do (repair, replace, or refund) and exactly what the consumer must do to get performance under the warranty. These requirements are so stringent that spokespersons for the broadcast industry have pointed out that, commercials being as brief as they are, it may be impracticable to try to include a selling message plus all the newly required warranty details, so that any mention of guarantees may have to be eliminated from broadcast ads.

Additional Areas of Regulation The FTC has responded to many complaints from consumerist groups and individuals concerned about TV ads for children and about disclosure of the contents of drugs and the nutritional values of food products. Investigations have been conducted and hearings held in both these areas, with a view to requesting new laws or promulgating new rules and guides to more tightly regulate these kinds of ads. Other areas in which the commission takes an interest include the use of fantasy, humor, and animation; differential rates for national and local advertisers and for small-space and big-space users; price discrepancies between national brands and house brands; implicit claims, literally true but potentially misleading in terms of the total effect of the message on consumers; co-op advertising; and institutional advertising.

In the past, most FTC advertising-control activity centered on *national* advertising. However, beginning in the early seventies, the job of "policing" ads and conducting investigations to uncover infractions of laws and guidelines was delegated to the commission's 12 regional offices, and a definite policy of concentrating attention on local *retail and service businesses,* large and small, was made public. Many actions have been initiated against small local stores as well as against the biggest and most noted of the national chains, discounters, and department stores.

STATE AND LOCAL REGULATION

State Regulation All but a handful of thinly populated states have laws that provide for consumer protection agencies and set rules for retail advertising. The statutes vary from state to state, but in general they blame the *store* for violations and exempt the *medium* from liability. It is rarely a good idea, therefore, to let a questionable ad go through just because the advertising salesperson or manager thinks it's OK. In one case, in Michigan, a sewing-machine shop advertised $38 machines as "bait" for its only really usable machines, which sold for $329. In another, a wig shop advertised that it "gave away free" wigs worth $55, but those who got them were charged a $15 or $20 "handling fee." Both offenders were given just 48 hours to make their advertising comply with the law, and the wiggery was warned that it faced a $1,000 penalty should it drag its feet.

In the East, an appeals court upheld a $1,600 fine and a 30-day jail sentence for a merchant who advertised $219 sewing machines for $63, after witnesses reported that the $63 covered *only the motor and needles,* while the base was extra. A midwestern car dealer found himself in big trouble for advertising and selling a used car with "only 14,000" miles on the odometer after the former owner came to court and said that the odometer (before the dealer turned it back) had read nearly 30,000 miles. In New York, a famous department store was hauled into court for advertising "Super Sweaters of a famous French Designer—Brand New & Just Arrived from Paris," when testimony brought to light the fact that the products had been made in a small town in Pennsylvania. In the same state a merchant was brought up on criminal charges after having advertised a $1 million "distress merchandise" sale because of alleged overbuying of seasonal stock, when it came out that the "sale" items were actually purchased specifically for the sale and had never been sold for anything near their alleged original prices.

California, which has strict consumer protection statutes, has cited merchants for alleging in their ads that retail outlets were warehouses, factory outlets, or wholesale distribution points where wholesale prices were paid by the general public. California also licenses all sorts of service-related retail functions and employs over 800 inspectors to "police" licensees. Texas now provides penalties ranging from injunctions to $50,000 fines for bait-and-switch ads, turning back car odometers, and any false, misleading, or deceptive ads.

Many states have attempted to impose direct taxes on advertising, ostensibly to raise revenue, but these have been bitterly fought by retail and media groups, partly because taxation inevitably leads to regulation.

Local Regulation Cities, counties, and other local municipal units have the power to pass ordinances further regulating advertising. By 1972, 53 cities already had consumer protection agencies, and thereafter the number has increased so rapidly it can be assumed that any large city, and a great many smaller ones as well, have such an agency in operation. Many city ordinances affecting advertising are rougher than the FTC statutes or the best of the state laws and voluntary codes. Chicago's deceptive practices ordinance requires all retailers to list either the sale price or the regular price of each item featured in stores' cents-off advertising coupons. A Cleveland ordinance provides that a store claiming to be a discount house must sell 75 percent of its merchandise at prices at least 10 percent below "list"; that claims of fire, clearance, or "lost-our-lease" sales be documented; that testimonials are prohibited if the endorsers know the claims to be untrue; that an ad must say so if an endorser has been paid for what he says; and that restrictions on sales must be spelled out clearly, and not in fine print. Local ordinances are particularly likely to affect outdoor signs, greatly limiting their effectiveness as an ad medium.

3 Voluntary Self-Regulation

BETTER BUSINESS BUREAUS (BBB)

Better Business Bureaus operate in 139 major cities and usually try to be of assistance in the trading areas around those cities also. The bureaus have been effective campaigners since their founding, more than half a century ago, for truth in advertising through self-regulation. Local chambers of commerce and state and national trade associations usually work with and through the bureaus to set uniform standards and to settle customer disputes.

A bureau publication offers the following guidelines, condensed from the findings in a "landmark" Supreme Court case, for checking the ethics of a store's advertising:

WHEN IS ADVERTISING MISLEADING?

Advertising as a whole must not create a misleading impression, even though every statement separately considered is literally truthful.

Advertising must be written for the probable effect it produces on ordinary and trusting minds.

Advertising must not obscure or conceal material facts, which the consumer has a right to know.

Advertising must not be planned to distract and divert readers' attention from the true nature of the terms and conditions of an offer.

Advertising must be free of fraudulent devices which induce customers to respond or purchase when they would not if a forthright disclosure of the facts had been made.

The BBB, jointly with the American Advertising Federation, had urged businesses of all kinds of adhere to an advertising code long before the passage of the new, stricter federal and state laws and FTC guidelines. Unfortunately, the problem with this and other attempts at voluntary self-regulation has always been their failure to prevent deceptive advertising by the less-ethical minority of firms.

NATIONAL AND LOCAL ADVERTISING REVIEW BOARDS

In 1971, advertisers, with BBB and advertising association backing plus government approval and support, set up the *National Advertising Review Board* to serve as the top echelon of a two-level mechanism to pass judgment on national ads opposed by citizen groups or consumer protection associations. The *National Advertising Division* (NAD) of the Council of Better Business Bureaus processes complaints, dismisses those it finds unjustified, issues corrective directives to advertisers it believes to be at fault, and submits cases in which the advertiser refuses to accept its recommendations to the National Advertising Review Board for further adjudication. The NARB consists of 50 representatives of advertisers, agencies, and the public; a panel of five members studies each case. The board's decisions have no legal force, but it can pass serious cases it considers should result in legal prosecutions on to the FTC or other appropriate federal enforcement agencies or urge the complainant to do so. Moral suasion and publicity (since its findings are made public) are the board's primary weapons, and establishing precedents and standards its most immediate task.

During its first year of operation, the NAD (essentially the staff arm of the NARB) received almost 500 complaints. About a fifth of them appeared justifiable. Most of the advertisers involved accepted the division's findings; the higher-level review board handled only 20 cases in its first two years, and found only 10 complaints justified. Both advertisers and consumer groups seem reasonably well pleased with this score.

Essentially the same system is now operating at the *local* level, dealing largely with *retail advertising problems*, in about 20 cities. The Better Business Bureaus and advertising clubs are pushing to get more local review boards functioning. The first local board was set up in Phoenix, with 20 members. Some cover more than one city. For example, the White Plains, N.Y., board handles cases from throughout the county, and a 60-member board in Los Angeles considers all of Southern California its territory. So far, two state-level boards are operating, in Oregon and Minnesota.

Soon after the local review boards were getting under way in various localities, one such board, the Advertising Review Council of Metropolitan Denver, and its sponsor, the Rocky Mountain Better Business Bureau, were themselves brought into the U.S. district court as defendants. The franchisor of a local slenderizing salon whose advertising had been questioned by the board alleged that the board's activities had violated civil rights and antitrust laws; it asked for a huge sum of money in damages. Individual members of the board as well as the board itself and the bureau were named as defendants. This cast a cloud over the whole self-regulation movement, until ad clubs all over the country raised a legal defense fund for their colleagues in Denver and an insurance company that carried liability insurance for the bureau declared it would pay for the defense costs itself. Activity resumed thereafter, while the advertising fraternity nationwide awaited the outcome of the suit (a long, drawn-out affair still pending as this book goes to press). It will be a landmark decision when finally settled.

OTHER ATTEMPTS AT SELF–REGULATION

Advertising media are increasingly appointing advertising *censors* outside their obviously prejudiced advertising sales departments. According to a recent Supreme Court ruling, broadcasters as well as printed media have the right to reject advertising if they wish to. They cannot be forced to accept ads they do not want, whatever the reason.

Individual media, in many instances, have long enforced more rigid codes of advertising acceptability on their advertisers than the law or industry guidelines require. But such rules are not uniform, and since the advent of chains and increasing numbers of branch stores, there has been much confusion for retail advertisers dealing with several media whose standards vary. Now efforts are in progress to regularize standards. The National Association of Broadcasters has clear-cut, comprehensive codes for both radio and television advertising, available to advertisers in the form of handy 26-page booklets. The International Newspaper Advertising Executives' ethics committee has issued a 57-page model code for its members' guidance in setting up more uniform standards for the press. These codes are generally similar, and both are parallel to standards set by Better Business Bureaus and retailers' associations.

There is evidence that the FTC is willing to give honest attempts at self-regulation a chance. The future behavior of advertisers, and the care their copywriters, scriptwriters, artists, and producers take in complying with accepted standards of ethics in advertising, will ultimately determine whether the grip of the law will tighten, or whether self-regulation will work.

4 Some Special Problem Areas

An analysis of the kinds of cases that have most often been brought to the attention of voluntary and governmental consumer protection units indicates that the kinds of businesses most vulnerable to charges of deceptive advertising and related sales practices are furniture stores, apparel and accessories stores, new and used car and truck dealers, repair shops, jewelry stores, dry cleaning and laundry establishments, television, radio, and phonograph dealers, home swimming pool dealers, sellers of car batteries, retailers of food products and drugs, carpet stores, home repair and remodeling firms, vocational and correspondence schools, insurance firms, companies that specialize in land sales, and marketers of home freezer plans, dance instructions, and medical devices.

Future legislation is likely to require retailers to state, in advertising, the nutritional value of foods and beverages; the cost of operation of home appliances, adjusted for local electric or gas rate structures; the possible damaging effects of the use of food products by persons with special problems; and any potential hazards in the normal use of advertised products. Regulatory agencies can also be expected to keep a close watch on banking practices, on gasoline mileage claims for automobiles, and on all products advertised to children.

ILLUSTRATIONS

Advertising illustrations should portray merchandise accurately. If a manufacturer's illustration shows a Model A and a store has Model Ds in stock, it should not run the picture. A picture can tell a lie as surely as words. If a newspaper or store's general mat-service book offers a picture that is similar, but not identical, to the actual merchandise, this should be made clear in the caption. The advertiser should not in any way imply that the shopper will find a sportcoat, chair, or guitar exactly as pictured.

MENTIONS OF COMPETITORS OR THEIR PRODUCTS

Mentions of competitors is a subject on which attitudes are changing. Formerly, ethical stores shunned any direct mention of a competitor or its goods. Now, consumerists and government authorities tend to encourage ads that honestly and openly make accurate comparisons between products, considering them to be in the public interest. Hesitation about mentioning other stores or brands among older retailers stems from the the era in which most regulation focused on unfair competitive practices rather than on the public's right to know.

The American Association of Advertising Agencies issued guidelines in this area in 1974 that can be applied to retail as well as national ads. The AAAA said, in part, that "the intent and connotation of [an] ad should be to inform and never to discredit or unfairly attack competitors, competing products or services. . . . The advertising should compare related or similar properties or ingredients of the product . . . for [the purpose of] honest comparison . . . and not simply to upgrade [some products] by association."

PROFESSIONAL ADVERTISING

Another area where the attitudes of consumer protection advocates are pressuring regulatory officials to force an about-face is professional advertising. Once considered "above" such a commercial practice as advertising, the professions and subprofessions are now

Figure 16–1 Retail Ads in the Era of Consumerism

A few decades ago, it would have been rare to see ads such as this one, but now they are commonplace. Sears is using its advertising space to warn owners of a product sold in its stores that a manufacturing defect could make it dangerous. Owners of the item are urged to call the Sears repair department to have the product checked before using it.

WARNING!

This Sears MULTI-SPEED Belt Massager with Lighted Switch May be Unsafe...

Only Model 449.29110 (Sears only model with a light), sold from December, 1969 until taken off sale October 4, 1972, is affected.

In order to prevent possible injury to any user, we **are** requesting that you:

1. Unplug unit.
2. Verify that the model is 449.29110—located on a name plate which is on the underside of the motor housing.

THERE IS NO PROBLEM WITH ANY OTHER SEARS BELT MASSAGER.

3. If you have model number 449.29110, call your closest Sears store and a service man will come to your home to inspect and modify the unit.
4. Do not reconnect the plug until the unit has been modified.

THERE IS NO PROBLEM WITH ANY OTHER SEARS BELT MASSAGER.

This notice is being issued as a result of tests which indicate the possibility that some of these massagers may involve a potentially dangerous electric shock hazard if someone should touch the massager while touching a water pipe, radiator, faucet or other ground connection.

Sears, Roebuck and Co.

Sears, Frandor—3131 E. Michigan, Lansing Phone: 351-8000

being encouraged (if not forced) to advertise services and fees. Again, the public's right to *information* underlies the change in attitudes. Civil engineers, lawyers, morticians, optometrists, pharmacists, or realtors who band together in professional associations that prohibit or restrict advertising by their members may actually face prosecution under the antitrust laws. State laws against prescription drug price ads have been overturned by federal judges, and the FTC has suggested invalidating such laws in all 20 states that have them. Some local bar associations have already switched signals and declared that member law firms may advertise for clients.

GOOD TASTE

Morals and customs are changing, and what constitutes good taste in many instances has become an open question. Most problems arise from advertising of feminine hygiene products, illustrations containing nude or nearly nude persons, words or pictures with implied sexual overtones, and ads for movies and literature considered offensive or pornographic. No nationwide standards in this area exist, and the U.S. Supreme Court has ruled that each locality must establish what is generally acceptable within the context of its own population's constantly changing standards.

SOME ADVICE FOR ADVERTISERS

Dr. Fred S. Siebert, dean emeritus of the College of Communication Arts of Michigan State University and a member of the bar with an international reputation in communications law, offers these words of advice for advertisers:

1. *Lotteries* may not be advertised under certain federal laws and the laws of many states. What constitutes a lottery is usually the problem. To be a lottery in the legal sense, a retail promotion scheme must have all three of these elements: (a) *chance* (winners must be decided by pure chance, not by a demonstrated skill or some other means); (b) a *prize* (there must be a worthwhile reward for winners—something of value); and (c) *consideration* (something the participants buy, give, pay, or do to become eligible to compete—by chance—for the prize—something valuable). It is the question of consideration and its definition that causes most of the trouble. If you must pay $1 (or donate a bushel of corn!) to compete, the lottery is obvious. But courts have held, in many decisions over the years, that entering a store to deposit a coupon, buying a newspaper which contains the required entry blank, or even being present in a crowd on the village square when the drawing takes place, is consideration. Therefore, technically, most of the prize schemes commonly used to generate customer interest do turn out to be violations of law when tested. In practice, [the] definition by the courts [of what constitutes a lottery] varies, and so does the aggressiveness with which local officials seek to enforce the existing law. [Recent legislation exempts lotteries operated by *units of government* from federal antilottery laws.]

2. *Errors in ads* which were the fault of the medium and might embarrass the advertiser bring us to an area of many questions and inclusive principles. Court decisions have varied

widely here. It has, however, been established that *obvious* errors (which any reasonable person can clearly see are mistakes, like Cadillac cars advertised for $80.00 instead of $8,000.00) are generally *not* considered cause for legal action against the medium. In practice, when mistakes occur (usually in price figures), the medium provides the merchant with a letter of explanation which customers usually accept in good faith. . . .

3. [The *copying*] *of advertising* by one print medium out of another print medium places the advertiser in the midst of an internecine battle between competing media (often a paid newspaper and a shoppers' guide printed by offset lithography, which makes copying whole ads a quick, easy and inexpensive process). Since most newspapers are not copyrighted, the question is up in the air, to a degree. It depends on *who constructed* the ad: If the retailer does it in his own advertising department, *he owns the ad,* say the courts; but if the *newspaper's* art and copy department did it, this becomes dirty pool when the competitor copies it by photography. Sometimes the artwork used in the ad bears the copyright of the syndicate that sells it to the medium, strengthening the case against copying.

4. *Libel* can be present either in news columns or ads, and in such cases both the medium *and* the advertiser are responsible for any damage done the injured party. Truth is a generally accepted defense, so if the allegedly libelous matter can be proven as true, the complainant usually gets nowhere. If the libel was *unintentional* (not malicious) and it can be proven that neither the medium nor

the advertiser *intended* to injure anyone's reputation or prestige . . . , it may reduce the penalty. Comments about your competitor's merchandise are not cause for action against you, even if you say it's of poor quality or low value and the competitor believes otherwise. Both the degrading remarks you make in your ads and the enthusiastic boasting the other merchant puts in his are considered, legally, to be matters of *opinion*.

5. *The right of privacy* is guaranteed by law to everyone—including customers or passersby whose likenesses may appear in photos taken in or near your store, or those who write letters to you as testimonials without expecting [that] you will make them public through advertising. Get a *release* from the person involved, before putting such matters into ads.[3]

A POSITIVE APPROACH FOR STORES

Much of this chapter has been negative in tone, listing the things retailers should not do. But the best response to many situations is a positive one, and big and small stores everywhere are meeting the consumerist challenge positively. Since 1967 Carson's of Chicago has had an ordained clergyman as vice president of civic affairs, dubbed "the conscience of Carson's," who oversees a $250,000 annual program supporting educational, health, cultural, and social welfare activities in the communities Carson's serves. Alexander's Markets in Los Angeles has a seven-point ecology program to improve the environment of its community. The Revco discount drug chain in the Midwest stations "consumer affairs counsellors" in its stores. Hecht's, a Washington, D.C., department store,

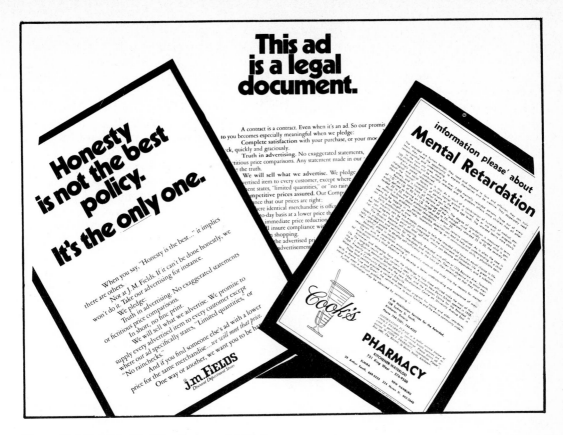

Figure 16–2 Retailers Meet the Consumerist Challenge

Ethical businesses, large and small, have turned to institutional advertising as one means of counteracting the "antibusiness" prejudice stirred up by the actions of their unethical associates. Here, at left and center, a discount department store tells the public about its own impeccable standards of advertising: "We pledge: Truth in advertising. . . . no fine print. We will sell what we advertise. . . ." And at right, a pharmacy uses its advertising space for a series of public service messages, written by medical service associations and doctors, about various diseases and physical and mental disorders.

Source: By courtesy of the International Newspaper Advertising Executives' *Sales and Idea Book,* September 1971, p. 53 (left and center) and August 1973, p. 54 (right).

pays for a series of "How to Buy" ads telling people how to get more and better merchandise for their money (in whatever store they shop), with copy written by the Better Business Bureau. The 7-Eleven Food Stores, a franchised chain, have spent $2 million (half in media ads) to promote a refuge for the bald eagle, the national symbol and an endangered species.

In Cleveland, Higbee's has a three-pronged program including consumer redress, consumer protection, and consumer information projects; Woodward & Lothrop, in the nation's capital city, operates a home furnishings service center where 15 employees help nearly 100,000 customers a year with their problems. The Giant Food chain hired Mrs. Esther Peterson, the first White House consumer advisor, to head its consumer advisory program. Sears offers a comprehensive set of teaching aids to home economics classes, 4-H clubs, extension programs, and distributive education, social studies, and business classes.

These programs and scores like them place retailing in the forefront of the consumerism movement in a practical, useful way; and all call for tasteful institutional advertising to explain and promote them.

Questions for Discussion

1. What are the major criticisms of advertising today? How would you answer them?

2. How does the Federal Trade Commission police advertising? What penalties may it impose on deceptive advertisers?

3. What federal agencies other than the FTC have an interest in regulating advertising? What other kinds of governmental bodies, not in Washington, may also regulate retail advertising?

4. What is the function of local advertising review boards? What authority do they have?

5. Why is it difficult to determine what "good taste" in advertising really is? Do you think that your own community is more or less conservative or liberal in matters of "taste" than the country as a whole? Why?

Suggested Projects

1. Find out from your chamber of commerce or local advertising professionals if there is an advertising review board in your community or in a nearby larger city. If there is, find out the names and occupations of its members. If there is not, check to see if there is a local Better Business Bureau. Visit the bureau and learn whether it performs some of the same functions as a review board. Also find out from the nearest Better Business Bureau or the chamber of commerce (if it handles consumer complaints as a service to the community) what kinds of complaints and problems are most common in your area.

2. Examine a few dozen retail ads in local advertising media, and see if you can find any potentially misleading or questionable statements. If you do, go to the advertisers and check matters out. Ask for proof that every statement is correct. Then think about the merchants' reactions. Were they cooperative? Or did they resent your inquiries? Which would you buy from yourself, and why?

3. Examine a few dozen local ads carefully, to see if any of them reflect a positive effort by business people to educate the public about products or to call attention to store policies aimed at improving the community or assisting the consumer. If you find little of this sort of advertising locally, obtain some newspapers or attend to broadcast media from a neighboring larger city, and see if some of the advertisers there are engaging in consumer education or public-service activities that they advertise. Do ads of this type ring true to you? Do you believe the merchants are sincere? Discuss.

Notes

1. "In the Matter of Pfizer, Inc." *Federal Trade Commission Decision,* Volume

81, Document No. 8819 (Washington, D.C.: Federal Trade Commission, 1972), p. 23.

2. Federal Trade Commission, *Guides* *for the Household Furniture Industry,* 1974.

3. Personal interview with the author, August 1974.

Preview

Complete storewide follow-through is essential to ensure the most results from advertising. Displays must be coordinated, merchandise stocks set in place, and sales personnel made aware of the advertising and the advertised merchandise or services. The advertising staff must maintain a scrapbook of all advertising for future reference and make appropriate notations on sales and traffic results and on conditions that may have affected those results (other than the advertising itself).

All stores should conduct continuous research to verify the profitability of their advertising and to isolate the different factors affecting advertising results. Accurate monitoring and continuous evaluation of advertising-sales and advertising-traffic relationships can make the retailer's promotion increasingly profitable over time. Techniques for gathering data and methods of arriving at conclusions need not be complex, but enough tests must be made to weed out the influence of unpredictable variables.

Learning Goals

Chapter 17 should give students an appreciation of the need for close coordination between advertising and other sales-producing activities, in particular displays and personal selling. They should also learn the importance of keeping track of advertising results for future reference and how to set up simple testing programs to provide a basis for evaluating those results and improving advertising concepts and techniques as time goes on.

17

Advertising Follow-Through

For even the best ads to produce maximum results, some critical details must be attended to during the crucial period after final approval has been given to the ads and they have gone to the media to be printed, broadcast, or mailed. And there are still further details to attend to after the advertised event or sale is over, to wrap up loose ends and help the store do a better job next time.

1 Before the Ads Appear

No matter who is responsible for integrating advertising with other sales-stimulating activities, those who prepared the advertising should be eager to meet their store colleagues more than halfway by volunteering to help coordinate the actions needed to make things happen all along the line.

Displays featuring the advertised items and related merchandise or promoting the common theme of a special event must be in place in both windows and the store interior just as the ads break. Signs must be in place on advertised items, to identify them, give their price, and perhaps suggest an added selling feature there was not room for in the ad. Crisp reproduction proofs of print ads on bright enameled paper should be neatly mounted on easels placed around the store, rather than dull tear sheets tacked or taped here and there. Blowups of dramatic scenes from television commercials can be similarly displayed, and the current ad campaign's musical theme is easily transcribed from broadcast commercials onto tapes for the in-store audio system to include in its background music.

Store operations people must make sure that adequate quantities of the advertised merchandise are on the sales floor and that a reserve stock is ready to move out quickly if the ad is a real bellringer.

Salespersons must see proofs of the newspaper ads, copies of the scripts for broadcast commercials, and copies of mailing pieces before the customers see them. Buyers and department managers must brief the sales staff on the demonstration of advertised selling features and on extra sales points not included in the ads. Substitute items, similar but not identical to those advertised, should be available, so that shoppers who seem disappointed with the advertised product can be shown an alternative. Salespersons should also have at their fingertips data on related items. *Telephone personnel* must be equally well informed, able to give particulars of advertised items when inquiries come in and perhaps to close sales to charge customers over the phone. *Clerical personnel* must be alerted if mail-order forms, perhaps on coupons, are included in advertising.

Preparations should be made to collect and tabulate data on sales and traffic (transaction counts) quickly after any major advertising campaign or the appearance of key individual ads. In stores using point-of-purchase terminals or other methods of feeding inventory-movement data through computers, the equipment must be programmed before selling begins to provide special reports on featured items.

2 After the Ads Appear

CLERICAL CHORES

Certain clerical chores remain to be completed after any advertising has been used. Someone should see to it that each ad is checked to determine whether its physical dimensions were as specified on the layout and whether the insertion date was correct. If ads appeared in big newspapers with "split" editions, someone should check that they appeared in the right edition. In the case of broadcast ads, someone must check whether they were aired during the time periods paid for, whether any were preempted, and whether any audio or video portion of a commercial was lost due to a technical failure. In the case of co-op ads, someone must see that all the forms required to secure rebates are promptly sent to the appropriate party.

THE ADVERTISING SCRAPBOOK

An advertising scrapbook is a very important tool for evaluating and improving advertising. Keeping it up to date daily is a key job for the ad department. Every newspaper ad the store runs must be clipped and pasted in the book; likewise, the script for every broadcast commercial and a copy of each mailing piece. The *date* of each ad should be noted, the *medium* through which it was delivered, and also the *weather* on the day it was run (so that the circumstances affecting the response to the ad can be evaluated at a future date). Later, notations should be made beside each ad indicating how well the featured items sold. This will help the store gauge how successful each ad was.

Competitor's ads should also be preserved. This is easy to do in the case of newspaper ads and perhaps direct-mail or magazine ads; it is more difficult in the case of broadcast ads. Nevertheless, being able to compare the store's ads with those of other stores, date for date, item for item, and price for price, will be helpful in planning future advertising.

A conference between the advertising people, merchandise managers, and others with a voice in the store's ad policy should be held following each major campaign, each important series of ads, or every major, extra-large "key" advertisement to determine how well the advertising worked, why, and how performance might be improved in the future.

3 Testing Advertising Results

By systematically studying their various ads and the sales, traffic, or inquiries that can be traced directly or indirectly to them, retailers can continually sharpen their promotional skills. Their ads will produce better and better results as they become more knowledgeable about selecting media, choosing items to advertise, designing ads, writing copy and headlines, using art, and timing ads and ad campaigns. A professional research expert can be retained to offer counsel and advice from time to time, to establish a framework for testing advertising results by the store's own personnel, or to conduct research for the store.

Whether a program of *post-testing* advertising effectiveness is handled internally or by outsiders, the first thing to be considered must always be the *purposes* of the advertising. A useful testing plan starts all the way back with the store's overall objectives, its broad promotional goals, the missions assigned each advertising campaign, and finally the specific tasks each ad was expected to accomplish. Testing can be meaningful only when these things are sharply defined and reviewed after the ads have appeared, as a basis for their evaluation. Was the purpose of a particular ad to sell the merchandise it mentioned, to generate traffic that would result in the sale of that merchandise and other products, or to build consumer awareness and inclinations to buy from the store over a long period of time? Beyond these considerations, there are additional specifics that must be determined before a reasonable testing plan can be set in motion. Is the store testing copy or media? In some cases the purpose of a test will be to determine whether factual copy or emotional copy worked best to either sell items or build image; in another, it will be to find out whether newspapers, radio, TV, or mailed ads were most effective in attracting a target customer group. Other tests will be to determine if Tuesday advertising is more profitable than Friday advertising, or whether national brands mentioned in ads generate more sales and/or traffic than private brands or promotion of unbranded merchandise. When questions like these have been answered, the testing of advertising results can begin.

TEST ONE FACTOR AT A TIME, AND
CONSIDER EXTRANEOUS VARIABLES

After accumulating records of the sales attributable to various ads, the store should divide them into two groups: those that produced a *high response* and those that produced a *low response*. To increase the probability of valid results, it may be wise to eliminate a middle group of ads that produced

medium results and focus on the *very best* and *very worst*. The next step is to check out *each factor* that may have affected an ad's success or failure. If *most* of the successful ads had headlines that attracted particular target groups ("selective" heads) and *most* of the unsuccessful ones had "label" headlines, perhaps future ads should have more of one type of head and less of the other. If most of the broadcast commercials that pulled were aired during morning hours and most of the duds were broadcast in the evening, then the store should think about scheduling its future commercials for the early part of the day. If photographs were used in many of the high-response ads and pencil sketches predominated in the low-response ones, perhaps more emphasis should be placed on photography. The effectiveness of heavy and light typefaces, musical commercials and ones that are all talk, and black-and-white and color ads can also be checked from time to time.

In evaluating any ads, another factor to bear in mind is their cost. A weak response to evening radio ads may be more than compensated for by lower rates for time, and spectacular results from two-color ads may be less than sufficient to offset the color premium.

Facts should first be assembled that indicate the apparent sales results that can be attributed to specific variables in the store's ads—copy appeal, timing, size, art, sound effects, media, or other factors. Then, it will often be best to organize the resulting comparative data in a graphic form. Turn back to Chapter 5 and reexamine Figure 5–1, "How the Most Profitable Advertising Level for a Small Store Is Determined." A similar set of charts might be constructed to facilitate quick and easy evaluation of sales and profits resulting from changing any specified variable in the store's advertising, and to relate the effectiveness of that variable to its cost.

Another necessity in post-testing the effectiveness of advertising is to strain out of the data the effects of variables *other* than advertising. Sales in a particular period may have been affected by a spell of unusual weather or by national advertising that coincided with the store's advertising. Or the store's top salesperson could have been on vacation and the next-best salesperson could have stayed home with the flu.

A competitor may have run a bigger ad offering the same merchandise at a lower price, or a big store in a neighboring metropolis may have promoted the same merchandise at the same time. Its newspaper spreads (perhaps large and in brilliant colors) and television commercials (probably professionally designed and produced) may have penetrated surrounding trading areas. This high-impact advertising either could have produced business for the smaller store that was attributed to the smaller store's own ads or, conversely, could have drawn so many shoppers away from the smaller community as to have depressed local business. Two very fundamental considerations, of course, are whether the state of the local economy favored heavy spending by consumers at the time the ad appeared (was it a pay-day week, a layoff week, or an overtime week for industrial workers?), and whether the merchandise in the ad was well chosen and in harmony with consumer demand for it at that particular time. All these extraneous variables must be taken into account in evaluating the effectiveness of ads.

In many cases, of course, it may be next to impossible to segregate the effects of different variables. For example, if ads were run simultaneously in two media, it may be impossible to decide which one had the greatest effect. To compensate for the many variables that can affect sales, a store should build up as large a file of test ads as possible. It should eliminate entirely those whose apparent results it knows were probably affected, positively or negatively, by extraneous influences like those cited above. And it should focus on ads directly responsible for known sales results. Then, if the total number of ads whose effects are measured is large enough, the differences will, in effect, average out, and the store's conclusions will be reasonably valid. Examining the effects of one or two or even half a dozen ads will probably not prove anything; examining the effects of fifty or a hundred will.

COLLECTING DATA TO TEST ADS' RESULTS

Sophisticated means of testing advertising's specific results are sometimes available or can be devised with effort and a large-enough budget. Some newspapers offer *split-run testing*, whereby advertisers can run two or three ads (of the same size and in the same position, but containing different art, headlines, and copy and featuring different items) on the same day. Afterwards, the papers will supply delivery lists of the two or three different editions to help trace sales to persons who saw ad A as opposed to ad B. A Richmond, Virginia, store used this split-run technique to test two small ads for Easter dresses, one containing bold prices and a heavy, black headline, and the other, delicate type and a subdued listing of prices. Returns from a mail-order coupon in each ad (one designated "Return to Department X" and the other "Return to Department Y") demonstrated that the soft-sell approach produced 17 orders in a week, while the hard-sell ad brought in only 10.

Customer questionnaires can be used to determine how many persons responded to particular ads, but not all types of customers respond equally well to such inquiries, so that there is likely to be a statistical bias in the results. Questionnaires can be filled in by store personnel as sales are made, they can be mailed to customers' homes with return postcards, or they can be completed by special interviewers at the store, on the street, or in the mall.

Another useful method of testing ads, despite its nonrandom choice of respondents, is the *group focus session.* Sometimes as part of their public relations and promotional activities, stores have college fashion advisory boards of young women, or homemakers' groups that meet in the store, or groups of officers of civic and social clubs that use the store's public-service rooms for meetings. These groups can be asked which of the store's recent ads they remembered and which of them they liked. They can even be shown some finished layouts of ads not yet published and be invited to express opinions about them (a technique known as *pre-testing* that national advertisers often use, but which is seldom practicable for retailers). At the same session, competitor's key ads can also be discussed and reactions noted. Broadcast commercials can be played or projected for their evaluation, as well as print ads. A very sophisticated version of the group session can be arranged to test image-building ads when two stores in different cities cooperate by showing each other's ads to their customer panels. In this way it can be determined if people who are unfamiliar with a store correctly perceive its image when they are exposed only to its ads.

Coupons are a testing device much used in the food industry. Simply counting the number of them turned in for "cents-off" promotions, the supermarket operator does a form of research on ad results. Stores that do not customarily use coupons, however, should beware of doing so only to test ad readership. By doing something *out of character,* something contrary to their normal procedure, they are creating a new variable. Coupons should be used a number of times, if at all, and the apparent results averaged. Moreover, the "test item" must be very carefully chosen, the coupon carefully designed, and the results considered merely tentative until and unless they are verified by other testing techniques.

As the *Universal Product Code* spreads to merchandise lines other than food, stores using EDP inventory-movement data collected at point-of-sale terminals can have current, accurate sales information on specific advertised items on which to base their evaluation of advertising results.

HOW SOME STORES, BIG AND SMALL, CHECK ADVERTISING RESULTS EFFECTIVELY

Sometimes one stumbles upon an advertising "test" quite by accident. A Wisconsin department store always ran its ads to promote Friday-evening shopping in the Thursday-evening paper. One week, an ad for one of the store's many departments was omitted from the Thursday edition by mistake, an error the paper "made good" by running the ad on Friday. To the store management's amazement, the department whose ad appeared on Friday enjoyed spectacular sales. The featured item sold out early in the evening, in many cases to customers who actually mentioned the ad.

A successful independent food retailer in a small Michigan town tested the effectiveness of ads in a free shopping guide and a paid-circulation weekly by counting coupon returns from identical ads in both publications. While 120 customers had clipped coupons from the newspaper (a remarkable rate of return, since it had but 1,800 subscribers), only 80 had clipped them from the "shopper" (which was delivered to over 4,000 homes). He therefore concluded that most of his customers were in the area where the newspaper's circulation was heaviest (i.e., in the town's natural trading area), and that the paper was his best bet for steady advertising. But he also concluded that since the free publication did draw some extra business, and since it had very low rates, it was a worthwhile medium for advertising periodic special promotions.

TESTING THE RESULTS
OF IMAGE–BUILDING CAMPAIGNS

Testing *institutional,* or "attitude-changing," ads is obviously much more difficult than testing item-price promotional ads. Long-range changes in customer attitudes toward a store may be the result of institutional ads, better sales personnel, better public relations,

and other factors. Generally, a professional research firm should be retained to test institutional advertising. Dealing with intangible factors that change slowly over a long period is beyond the ability of most retailers to handle by themselves.

One of the country's largest department stores invested several hundred thousand dollars in a sustained campaign whose primary goal was to make women, especially younger women, in the local metropolitan area more conscious of the store's *fashion leadership.* It then employed the market-research affiliate of a famous ad agency to test the results of the campaign.

The study was conducted in two parts. Six hundred area women were selected at random and interviewed by telephone before the campaign started. Immediately after the campaign, another 600 women were interviewed by telephone. By comparing the women's responses before and after the campaign, the researchers were able to determine what changes, if any, had occurred in the local female population's awareness of and attitudes toward the store as a fashion leader. The results of this test are presented here as an example of the kind of work being done in this area by large retailers.

1. The campaign achieved important increases in *penetration* of the store's advertising.

   Interviewees were asked to name stores in the area that they had heard or seen advertising for in the past month.

   Responses: Pre-test 70% mentioned this store.
   Post-test 86% mentioned it.

This is an increase of 16%.

Pre-test 36% mentioned it as the first store they could think of.

Post-test 58% mentioned this store as the first store they could think of.

This is an increase of 22%.

These figures show a dramatic change in top-of-the-mind awareness (instant recall).

When asked, "Do you remember seeing or hearing any advertising from this store in the past month?" 90% of the women replied yes. This This was a 20% increase.

The recall of the campaign slogan was also very high. 80% of the women were aware that the store had a special advertising campaign during the two-month period of the all-out special advertising effort.

The research indicated that the special slogan communicated an image of this store as "new/modern/youthful" to 59% of the women tested in the post-study.

2. The campaign created further increases in the already high level of *awareness* of this store as a department store.

Women were asked to list all the department stores they could think of.

Responses: Pre-test 57% mentioned this store first.
Post-test 65% mentioned it first.
This is an 8% increase.

Pre-test 89% mentioned the store in their list.

Post-test 94% mentioned it in their list.
This is a 5% increase.

3. The campaign generated across-the-board improvements in the store's *image* for all merchandise areas by from 2 to 5 percent and in all store characteristics measured.

In the women's merchandise area, the store was compared to the high specialty and moderate specialty shops. While this store increased 5% as the preferred store, the high specialty stores decreased 2%, the moderate specialties decreased 1% and the other department stores decreased 2%.

Such testing of the effectiveness of advertising clearly shows what results a campaign had had. No chance to thus evaluate a store's advertising should be neglected, for the time and money the research requires will be more than compensated for by the money saved in the future by knowing what kinds of advertising are useful and productive and what kinds are wasteful.

Questions for Discussion

1. If you were the advertising manager of a medium-sized store, what other members of the store's staff would you check with to coordinate the overall promotional effort *after* sending material to the media for a very important ad? How could a failure to coordinate the advertising with other sales-stimulating activities at this stage reduce its effectiveness?

2. What should go into a store's advertising scrapbook? How can such

records be used to improve the store's advertising in the long run?

3. What are some of the methods a smaller store could use to test the effectiveness of its advertising? Which methods do you think would be easiest to use and still produce useful results?

Suggested Projects

1. Pick out eight or ten items prominently advertised by retailers in the local newspaper or on local broadcasting stations today or this week. Go to the stores that did this advertising and check their window displays to see how many of the advertised items are featured. Go inside and examine interior displays to ascertain how many of the advertised items are conspicuously shown. Then ask salespersons to show you some items and explain their benefits. Note how many can do so effectively. How good, do you think, is the stores' advertising follow-through? To what extent did displays and personal selling back up the ads?

2. Collect all the print ads by one store in your area for a period of several weeks. Get a notebook and paste in these ads, day by day. Make a note of the date each appeared, the publication it appeared in and the weather that day. Also clip and paste, on facing pages for each date, ads by the store's most important direct competitor. Since you have no record of the traffic and sales related to each ad and no record of the store's broadcast ads (if they used broadcast media), your advertising scrapbook is not as complete as an actual retailer's. You can, however, compare the ads you have collected. Whose, on the whole, do you think are more effective? Which elements do you especially like? Which do you especially dislike? Do you find any instance where the competitor's ad for the same date might well have had a bad influence on sales results for the store?

Epilogue

Epilogue

In a nutshell, in Part 1 we focused on understanding what the vast, rapidly changing markets are that retailers serve, how stores themselves are changing, how they operate and employ research to pinpoint target markets in this era of diverse lifestyles and attitudes and varying wants and needs. In Part 2 we examined the preliminary management steps necessary to successful retail advertising: establishing a budget, setting goals, and distributing ad funds prudently among departments, merchandise lines, and services each month or each week. And we investigated how manufacturers' national advertising, advertising agencies, and cooperative advertising programs could be used to increase the power of local advertising.

In Part 3 we turned to the various advertising media, the channels through which advertising messages reach customers (and those a store hopes to turn into customers).

Both general guidelines for media selection and the special advantages, limitations, and technical characteristics of each medium were explored. Part 4 brought us to the creation and production of specific advertisements. We studied how to write copy for newspaper ads and to design and illustrate them; how to write broadcast commercials and use sound, sight, and motion to magnify impact; and how to use other media effectively. And we discussed why all advertising today must be done within the context of a new awareness of the social responsibilities of businesses, a new emphasis on consumer needs, and new laws and codes that define what is ethical and what is not.

We might conclude with a bit of history, advice given more than a century ago in the 1871 edition of the *Strickland Almanac* (a farmers' almanac), in an era when the only available advertising medium was the news-

498

paper. The references to newspapers can today be taken to mean all the mass media. Otherwise, Strickland's admonitions are as sound today as they were over a hundred years ago:

> Advertisers will do well to ponder the following sensible remarks, contained in a little book entitled *How to Get Money:* "Whatever your occupation or calling may be, if it needs support from the public, advertise it thoroughly and efficiently in some shape or other that will arrest public attention. It has been observed by those who have tried advertising, that it did not pay; this is only when advertising has been done sparingly and grudgingly. Homeopathic doses of advertising may perhaps not pay—it is like half a potion of physic—making the patient sick, but effecting nothing. Administer liberally, and the cure will be sure and permanent. Some say they cannot afford to advertise; they mistake—they cannot afford *not* to advertise. In a country where everybody reads the newspapers, the man must be blind who does not see that these are the cheapest media through which he can speak to the public, among whom he must find his customers. Put on the appearance of business and, generally, the reality will follow. The farmer plants his seed, and while he is sleeping his corn and potatoes are growing. So with advertising. While you are sleeping or eating, or conversing with one set of customers, your advertisement is being read by hundreds and thousands of persons who never saw you, nor heard of your business, and never would, had it not been for your advertisement in the newspapers."

Glossary

Account Executive An advertising agency official who represents the agency in its dealings with a client, and in turn represents that client in coordinating the work of other agency personnel. Also, in some cases, the sales-service representative of an advertising medium.

Adjacencies In radio and television, commercials or programs that immediately precede or immediately follow one another on the same station.

Advertising Paid-for communication, directed at a mass audience, that seeks to impart information, develop attitudes, or sell goods, services, or ideas to the benefit of the advertiser.

Advertising Agency An organization that develops and prepares advertising for its clients and places that advertising in various media.

Advertising Appropriation Funds earmarked by a firm's management for advertising over a given period (often loosely called an ad "budget").

Advertising Budget An outline of planned advertising expenditures over a period of time. Specific amounts are generally budgeted each month or each week for advertising in various media and for each department or merchandise line.

Advertising Campaign A series of advertising messages devoted to the same theme, based on the same concept or idea, and designed to achieve some specific objective.

Advertising Request A department store buyer's request to advertise designated items, directed to the store's advertising department for execution.

Agate Line A unit of measure of printed advertising space used by magazines and large newspapers. A "line" is one column wide and one-fourteenth of an inch deep (regardless of the width of the column).

Air Brushing In commercial art, blowing a fine spray containing a liquid pigment to retouch photographs or produce tonal gradations in wash drawings.

AM (Amplitude Modulation) A form of radio transmission that carries long distances, achieved by varying the amplitude (size) of the electromagnetic wave transmitted. (See also **FM.**)

Animation In television and films, an illusion of motion created using a series of drawings that are arranged in sequential order.

Announcement A radio or TV commercial, usually 10, 20, 30, 40, or 60 seconds long. Also called a *spot*.

Artwork An illustration other than a photograph. Line and wash drawings are among the most common kinds of artwork used in retail advertising.

Atmospherics The conscious effort to design buying environments in a retail store to produce emotional effects in the shopper that enhance his or her purchase probability.

Audience The people reached by an advertising medium.

Audience Composition The number and kinds of people listening to a broadcast program, classified according to their age, sex, income, or some other characteristic. A study of audience composition produces what is often called an *audience profile*.

Audience, Cumulative ("Cume") For radio and TV, the total number of different people reached by a station in two or more time periods, or simply the net (unduplicated) viewing audience delivered by the medium in a given span of time, such as a week. For newspapers, usually the number of different people reached by a paper in a week (or during the five weekdays). Also known as *reach*.

Audience Rating The proportion of total homes in a market equipped with TV or radio receivers that are tuned in to a given station at a given time. The degree of penetration of a total market achieved by a station at a particular time. (See also **Audience Survey.**)

Audience Survey A market study that measures the number of homes or individuals in a radio or television station's audience. Such studies are used to produce audience rating figures and can be done by aided recall, coincidental interview, diary, or meter techniques.

Audio   In television, the sound portion of a commercial.

Availability   In radio and TV, a time slot for a commercial that has not yet been sold and is, therefore, "available" for purchase.

Background   In radio and TV, a sound effect, musical or otherwise, used in addition to dialogue or other elements to enhance the realism or emotional effect of a presentation.

Bait-and-Switch Advertising   Attracting customers to a store by advertising a well-known product at exceptionally attractive prices or on alluringly easy terms when the merchant has no sincere intention to sell that product but rather intends to switch the customers to more profitable items.

Balance   In advertising design, the artistic relationship between the elements in the two vertical halves of a display space. Balance may be formal (static) or informal (dynamic).

Balance Sheet   A statement of the assets and liabilities of a business, such as a store, as of a given date.

Benday (or Ben Day)   A screen of dots or lines placed over any part of a piece of artwork to soften the tones; named for its inventor, Benjamin Day.

Billings   The amount of business done by an advertising agency.

Body Copy   The main paragraph(s) of copy in an advertisement.

Body Type   The type normally used for body copy, as distinguished from the display type used for headlines; generally 14-point or smaller type.

Boldface   A darker, heavier typeface whose letters are composed of bolder, thicker strokes than regular type.

Box   A drawn or printed frame enclosing a unit of type or an illustration.

Break-even Point (BEP)   The point at which the total income of a business will cover all its expenses. An increase in sales revenue beyond that point, without a commensurate increase in costs, produces a profit.

Bridge   Music or sound effects at the opening and closing of a broadcast commercial that link the parts of the ad together. The material in between may be changed frequently, often by the local announcer.

Broadside   A large circular, resembling a newspaper page or section in format, delivered by mail or door-to-door messengers.

Brochure   An elaborate booklet or folder.

Buyer   A store employee who purchases the merchandise offered for resale to customers. In traditionally organized stores, a buyer also supervises the selling force on the floor of his or her department and initiates advertising requests to promote the department's merchandise.

Camera-Ready Copy   A paste-up of an advertisement or a piece of copy, from which the final negative will be shot. Used in offset lithography and/or cold-type composition.

Caption   The headline of an advertisement or the descriptive matter accompanying an illustration.

CATV (Community Antenna Television)   A TV system in which signals picked up by a single high antenna are relayed by cable to many homes in a community, to give viewers access to a greater variety of television channels. Some CATV systems also transmit local programs, news, and advertising.

Chain (Store)   A group of essentially similar stores, centrally owned and managed, selling essentially the same type of merchandise. In the past, two or more such stores were considered a chain; increasingly, as local stores increase their branch operations, true retail chains are considered to be those with more than ten units.

Checking Copy A copy of a publication sent to an advertiser or its agency to show that a scheduled ad appeared as directed.

Circulation The number of copies distributed per issue of a publication.

Classified Advertising In newspapers, shopping guides, and some magazines, advertisements grouped together by classifications under particular headings, generally in a separate "classified" section. Includes "liner" ads in small type without illustrations and "display classifieds," in larger type, more white space, and, possibly, limited illustrative material.

Closing Date (or Hour) The deadline for acceptance of an advertisement for publication or broadcast in a given issue or at a stated time.

Cold Type Type set by typewriter or by some photographic or electronic means that does not involve the use of molten metal. Especially associated with lithographic (offset) printing, but also increasingly used by letterpress printers.

Column-Inch A space one column wide and one inch deep. The most common unit of measuring and pricing retail newspaper display advertising space. A "ten (column) inch ad," for example, might be one column wide by 10 inches deep or two columns wide by 5 inches deep.

Combination Rate A special rate for placing the same advertisement in two or more papers owned by the same publisher, such as a morning and an evening daily, or two or more weeklies serving different (usually adjacent) communities.

Commercial An advertising message on radio or television. Also called an *announcement* or *spot*.

Composition The setting and arranging of copy in type.

Condensed Type Type in which the letters are narrower than letters in ordinary type.

Continuity Scripts for radio or television programs or commercials.

Controlled Circulation The circulation of printed advertising media, such as neighborhood shopping guides, free newspapers, or magazines, by the publisher to selected homes or areas.

Convenience Goods Products people need and usually buy frequently in small quantities, often at the stores nearest to their homes.

Cooperative Advertising Most often, in retailing, advertising mutually sponsored by a manufacturer and a retailer and placed locally by the retailer. Cooperative advertising is used to sell branded products to local consumers. The term also refers to any advertising jointly conducted by two or more advertisers, such as "horizontal" cooperative advertising by two or more local retail or service businesses for the benefit of their segment of the industry or joint promotions by members of the same trade association or tenants in the same shopping center.

Copy Strictly speaking, the written material or text for a printed advertisement. Also, more broadly, any material (including photographs, artwork, rules, and designs) used in print ads. Sometimes, in broadcast advertising, a synonym for continuity or scripts.

Copy Platform A statement of basic ideas for an advertisement or campaign, ranking in order of importance the several selling points to be included. It may also include instructions regarding advertising policy.

Coverage The number of homes or individuals exposed to a given advertising medium within a specified period or to a stated issue of a print medium. Also, the percentage of a specified area, community, or group that may be reached by a medium.

CPM (Cost per Thousand) A method of analyzing advertising costs, useful in comparing similar media. Can mean cost per 1,000 *readers, viewers, listeners,* or *prospects* reached.

Crop To cut off or trim an illustration to make it fit a space, eliminate undesirable portions, or change its proportions.

Cume Abbreviation for "Cumulative Audience." (See **Audience, Cumulative.**)

Customer Profile A statement of the estimated demographic characteristics of the people most likely to buy a given product or shop at a specific store and of the purchase patterns they habitually follow.

Cut In print media, an engraving or a plate of a pictorial or illustrative element in an advertisement (derived from *woodcut* in past centuries). In broadcast advertising, an abrupt switch from one scene to another. Also used to indicate the elimination of any portion of an advertisement, printed or broadcast.

Dealer Imprint A retailer's name, address, etc., imprinted, stamped, or pasted in a designated space, as on direct-mail literature printed by a manufacturer or voluntary chain.

Dealer Tie-in A local retailer's ad that "ties in" with a national ad from a manufacturer whose products it sells. Also, promotional materials supplied by a manufacturer to a retailer and related to a national advertising campaign.

Demographics The vital statistics of a population sample. For example, data on the age, sex, income, race, size of family, type of residence, and geographical location of the sample.

Direct Advertising Any form of printed advertising issued to specific prospects through the mail, canvassers, salespeople, or dealers or by other means. Popular types of direct advertising include leaflets, letters, cards, folders, booklets, and catalogs.

Direct-Mail Advertising Direct advertising sent through the mail.

Direct Copy Advertising copy dealing primarily with facts about the merchandise, services, or stores, and appealing to the customer's logical faculties. Also termed factual or rational copy.

Direct Voice (DV) Television script spoken on screen by announcers or actors.

Directory Advertising Advertising in directories, such as the telephone *Yellow Pages,* city directories, and other alphabetical lists of people.

Display On-site advertising, such as window or in-store displays (including point-of-purchase displays).

Display Advertising Printed advertising containing headlines, illustrations, and other display elements as well as text, or "body" copy.

Display Type Fourteen-point or larger type, used for headlines.

Dissolve In television production, a shift in a scene or an image effected by superimposing one picture on another; one fades out as the other comes in.

Down and Under A technique used in broadcast advertising wherein the opening music becomes gradually lower in volume as the announcer's voice comes on; as the announcer nears the end of the spoken message, the music may gradually become louder again.

Em A printer's unit of measure: the square of any given typeface. Called an "em" because the letter "m" is as wide as it is high. A pica "em" in 12-point type is one-sixth of an inch square.

Endorsement Advertising Advertising in which a well-known personality endorses, or says something good about, a product, service, or store. Also termed *personality advertising.*

ET (Electrical Transcription) A radio commercial recorded on tape. In some cases, music and sound effects may be ET while the announcement is "live."

Extended Type Type whose horizontal dimension is exaggerated; hence a given letter or word occupies more space along the line than regular type of the same vertical size.

Fact Sheet A form used for information supplied by a buyer to a store's advertising department about an item to be promoted.

Fade In TV or radio production, to gradually change the intensity of image or sound. To *fade-in* is to increase the intensity of the video picture as the scene comes into vision from total black, or of the audio as the sound grows out of total silence. To *fade-out* is to cause the picture to recede gradually into total black, or to decrease the sound level to silence.

Fair Trade Retail price maintenance imposed by manufacturers of branded products. This practice was greatly weakened after repeal of federal and many state fair trade laws in 1975.

FIFO (First In, First Out) The traditional method of keeping retail inventory accounts, wherein an item sold is assumed to be drawn from the oldest stocks of goods. In times of rapid price inflation, this tends to give a falsely optimistic tinge to net profit figures. (See also **LIFO.**)

Flat Rate A *per unit* rate for space or time that does not vary with the volume or frequency of advertising. Typically, national advertisers are charged flat rates, but local (retail) advertisers have opportunities to secure discounts for volume and/or frequency, especially from newspapers.

Flight The period of an advertiser's campaign or the period in which a series of related ads in the same medium are run —for example, during a specific selling season.

Flyer An announcement or a circular in which copy is printed on one side of a sheet of paper.

FM (Frequency Modulation) A technique for transmitting radio signals by varying the frequency of electromagnetic waves. FM broadcasts reach relatively short distances, but eliminate static and deliver superior sound reproduction. (See also **AM.**)

Folder A printed circular, folded and used as a mailing piece.

Format The size, shape, style, and appearance of a publication, such as a newspaper or magazine. Also, the sort of programming a radio station offers, such as all news, classical music, country and western, all talk, or ethnic programming.

Freeze Frame One of a series of television scenes that continues to be projected when the action is stopped.

Frequency In media exposure, the number of times a person or household is exposed to a medium or to an advertiser's message within a given period. In broadcasting, also the number of waves per second a transmitter radiates, which determines where that station will come in on the receivers' dials.

Frequency Rate A special rate for frequent advertisers in a medium.

Gross Impressions The total number of times a commercial is heard or seen during a specified period. Frequency × cume = gross impressions. (See **Frequency** and **Cume.**)

Gross (Profit) Margin The difference between the total cost of goods sold and net sales.

Gross Rating Points (GRP) A rating point indicates the number of listeners or viewers in a radio or TV station's audience during a specified time segment, expressed as a proportion of all the potential listeners or viewers in the market. The gross rating points are the total number of rating points delivered by an advertiser's radio or television schedule.

Halftone   A printing plate used to reproduce illustrations other than line drawings by a screening process that produces fine dots of varying size. The resulting tonal variations range from almost pure white through nearly total black. The coarseness or fineness of the screen determines the clarity of the printed illustration.

Head(line)   The major caption set above a printed advertisement or advertising text. The most important element in most printed ads, it serves to summarize the contents and/or gain the reader's attention.

Hot Type   Metal printing type and materials produced by the use of molten lead alloys that, when cooled, become hard and are used for letterpress printing. (See **Cold Type,** a more modern and increasingly used method.)

House Brand   Merchandise bearing a retailer's brand name, rather than that of its manufacturer. It may be identical in all other respects to a national brand made by the same manufacturer, or it may be constructed according to retailer specifications that make it different from any other product on the market. (Also known as a *store brand* or a *private brand.*)

I. D. ("Idee")   Identification of an advertiser in a broadcast commercial. Usually, a 10-second unit.

Image   The qualities, real or imaginary, that the public attributes to a product, brand, company, or store.

Indirect Copy   Imaginative copy that focuses on the user's feelings, emotions, and senses rather than on product facts.

Insert   A page or a section preprinted by or for an advertiser, then shipped to a publisher for inclusion in a publication on a specified date.

Institutional Advertising   Advertising intended to enhance the public relations of the advertiser as an institution by emphasizing its services, reputation, class, support of worthy civic activities, etc. No immediate sale of tangible products or services is expected as a result of such advertising, though the advertiser hopes to benefit by increased traffic and sales in the long run.

Italic Type   Type on which the letters slant to the right.

Jingle   A musical accompaniment to an advertising message. In time, the advertiser tends to be associated with the tune, as it is with a printed logotype in newspaper ads; hence jingles are sometimes known as *sound logos.*

Justify   In printing, to space out letters within words or add spaces between words so that all lines appear to be of equal length.

Layout   A working drawing that shows what a printed ad will look like in its final form.

Legend   The title or description under an illustration; also called a *caption* or *cut line.*

Letterpress   Printing from a raised surface that, when inked, transfers an image to paper against which it is pressed.

LIFO (Last In, First Out)   A method of keeping retail inventory accounts which assumes that items sold are taken from the freshest stocks. The LIFO method of inventory accounting tends to produce a more realistic report of profits in periods of rapid price inflation than the **FIFO** method.

Linage   The number of agate lines of space occupied by an advertisement, a series of advertisements, or all the advertising of a given advertiser during a specified period (such as that covered by a space contract with a printed medium). Also spelled "lineage."

Lip Sync (Lip Synchronization) In TV production, the coordination of an actor's lip movements and the words spoken. It can be achieved by recording the video and audio portions of the ad simultaneously, or by adding the words later.

Lithography Printing from a plate on which the nonprinting area is chemically treated to repel ink and attract water. Both ink and water are spread on the plate out of their respective "fountains" as the press runs. In modern high-speed rotary applications, the image is first transferred from the plate cylinder to an offset cylinder wrapped in a rubber blanket, and from that to the paper that runs around the impression cylinder. It is from this process that the term *offset lithography* derives.

Live (Commercial or Copy) A broadcast commercial, or portions of a broadcast commercial, delivered directly over the air and received by the audience at the same time it is being produced at the station (as opposed to commercials on tape, records, or film).

Local Rate The advertising rate paid by most retail stores and local service firms, as opposed to the "national" rate of an advertising medium, paid by out-of-town advertisers and their agencies. Since the local "open rate" is often the same as the national rate, in practice the local rate usually implies a contract between the advertiser and the medium guaranteeing a specified minimum volume or frequency.

Logotype ("Logo") A piece of type bearing the name of a store or company, or any name or trademark, with or without a distinctive design as a symbol. Also, in broadcasting, a "musical signature."

Loss Leader An item sold at a loss to build store traffic.

Mail-Order Advertising Advertising to obtain orders directly from consumers, without using retail stores or salespersons as intermediaries.

Make-Good A free republication or rebroadcast of a scheduled ad that was omitted or garbled or whose impact was seriously weakened by a technical malfunction for which the medium was responsible.

Management Information System A formal means by which information about company operations is collected, analyzed, and reported to management.

Marginal Analysis An analysis of the costs of additional (marginal) increments of advertising expenditures in relation to additional (marginal) units of profit produced by those expenditures, in order to determine the optimum advertising appropriation for a business. The optimum (most profitable) appropriation is reached when the marginal cost of advertising equals the marginal net revenue it produces.

Mark-down A reduction from the original selling price of an item.

Market A group of people who are able to buy a product or service should they desire it. Also, the geographical area from which a seller, such as a retail merchant, draws its customers.

Market Profile A demographic description of the people or households in a market.

Marketing The sum total of the planning, pricing, promotional, and distribution activities involved in getting goods or services from producers to consumers or users.

Marketing Strategy The plan adopted and followed by a seller to speed up the sale of the goods and services it offers.

Mark-on The difference between the cost of merchandise and the original retail value assigned to it.

Mark-up The difference between the cost of merchandise and its actual selling price.

Mass Medium An advertising medium that delivers a message to masses of readers, listeners, or viewers, as opposed to a medium beamed at a selected audience.

Matrix ("Mat") A mold made of pulp or a similar substance from an original illustration or ad that can be used to provide an exact duplicate for letterpress printing.

Media Plan The portion of an advertising budget that lists the media to be used, their costs, the reasons for their selection, the amount to be invested in each, etc.

Medium (*plural—Media*) A vehicle, such as a newspaper or broadcasting station, through which an advertiser delivers its message. Also, the material used by an artist in creating illustrations, such as pen and ink, pencil, crayons, or water colors.

Merchandising The buying and selling functions of a retail operation.

Mood Copy Advertising copy with a strongly emotional appeal.

Motivational Research Psychological studies to probe fundamental, underlying conscious and unconscious reasons for consumers' purchasing behavior.

National Advertising The advertising of a manufacturer or producer, as opposed to that of a local retailer or service firm. Usually the same national advertisement appears in two or more markets, while a retail ad supports one store or a group of stores in the same or neighboring communities.

Negative Film used for making offset lithographic printing plates.

Net Paid Circulation The total number of copies of a given issue of a printed advertising medium actually sold or the average number of copies per issue sold over a stated period (often audited and certified by an outside authority, such as the Audit Bureau of Circulations).

Net Profit The gross margin of a business minus its expenses.

Net Sales The gross sales of a business minus returns and adjustments.

Net Worth The amount by which the total assets of a business exceeds its total liabilities at any given moment.

Objective-and-Task Budgeting A method of establishing the amount of a firm's advertising appropriation by defining its goals and estimating the probable cost of the advertising needed to achieve those goals.

Off-Camera Voice In TV production, the voice of an actor who does not appear in the visual scenes of the commercial. (Also termed *off-screen* voice.)

Offset (Lithography) (See **Lithography**.)

On Location Commercial In TV production, a commercial shot away from the studio (for example, at a store).

Open Rate The basic advertising rate of a medium, charged to the occasional or very small advertiser who does not qualify for a contract rate or discount. The same as a *one-time, transient,* or *noncontract* rate.

Open to Buy A retail expression indicating that the buyer for a store or department has not used all of the merchandise budget allotted for a given period and is in a position to buy additional stock. Sometimes used by advertising managers to signify that they have the authority to commit additional funds for advertising within a budgetary period.

Operating Statement A summary of the financial results of the operations of a business for a stated period, such as a month or a year. It shows the relationship between the firm's sales, its cost of goods sold, and its expenses, and indicates the resulting profit or loss. Also called an *Income Statement* or a *Profit-and-Loss Statement*.

Outdoor Advertising Advertising on signs of various kinds, such as posters and painted bulletins.

Participation Program (or Show) A broadcast program in which two or more advertisers' messages are included.

Paste-up A sheet of paper on which all the finished elements of an ad have been pasted in proper sequence so that it may be photographed and the resulting image transferred to a plate for printing by offset lithography.

Penetration In broadcasting, the size of a station's audience as measured by the percentage of households with receivers, the percentage of color TV sets in a market, the percentage of multi-set households, or the percentage equipped to receive UHF television or FM radio.

Percentage-of-Sales Budgeting A method of establishing an advertising appropriation (or controlling any other variable expenses of a business) based on the relationship of the expense to the sales volume of a past period or the projected sales volume of a future period.

Photocomposition A method of setting type, using taped instructions from a typewriter or computer, by means of photography. Photocomposition is widely used, especially in offset lithographic printing. (See also **Cold Type.**)

Pica A unit of measure of linear distances equal to 12 printer's "points," or one-sixth of an inch. A *pica em* is the square of the letter *m* in 12-point type.

Plant In outdoor advertising, a company that leases land, erects signs, prepares the advertisers' copy, and places the paper sheets on signs.

Plate The metal or plastic form from which impressions are made in a printing operation.

Point In printing and typography, a unit of measure 1/72nd of an inch in size. Hence "36-point type" is on a half-inch base, "18-point" is on a quarter-inch base, etc.

Point-of-Purchase Advertising Advertising and promotional material in a store, at or near the place where the sale of merchandise takes place. Point-of-purchase ads are prepared by the manufacturer for the retailer's use and incorporated into the merchant's interior display scheme.

Poster An outdoor sign whose structure is permanent but upon which sheets of paper are "posted" to change the advertising message at intervals.

Preempt To shift a scheduled broadcast commercial to another time slot to make room for one paying a higher rate. The most desirable (and expensive) kind of commercial is "nonpreemptible" and cannot be "bumped" at the option of the station.

Preferred Position An especially desirable position in a printed publication, for which the advertiser pays a premium rate.

Premium (Rate) An extra charge for advertising that is to receive some special treatment—for example, printed in color or positioned on the front page of a newspaper section. The premium is added to whatever space rate the advertiser is paying on a flat-rate basis.

Preprint A previously printed page or section to be inserted in a publication. (See also **Insert.**)

Primary Research Original research conducted by or for the user, as opposed to the compilation of data from "secondary" sources such as those available in reference libraries or census reports.

Private Brand (See **House Brand.**)

Process Printing The reproduction of printed advertisements in full color by overprinting from a series of plates each carrying a different color ink (usually the three primary colors, red, blue, and yellow, plus black).

Profit-and-Loss Statement (See **Operating Statement.**)

Projection In sampling for a research study, the extension of the sample data to the limits of the total "population" or "universe." Theoretically, projections are valid if a *probability* sample is accurately drawn and large enough.

Promotion Broadly speaking, everything done to "promote" sales, including advertising itself, special events, displays, and sometimes personal selling. More narrowly, a particular sales-stimulating event or series of events that will draw crowds to a store and sell merchandise, either immediately or in the long run.

Promotional Advertising The advertising of specific items, as opposed to **institutional advertising.**

Promotional Mix The assortment of activities designed to persuade customers to buy a product or service, including advertising, sales promotion, displays, public relations, and personal selling.

Proof A copy of an advertisement or a portion of an advertisement provided before it is printed in quantity so that its final appearance can be checked, errors can be corrected, and the store personnel can see what the ad will look like.

Psychographics The measurement and evaluation, for marketing purposes, of consumers' lifestyles, motivations, attitudes, unfulfilled psychic needs, and personality traits. (See footnote 4, page 22.)

Publicity Broadly, a term often used in the past to indicate promotion and/or advertising in retail stores. More narrowly, news about an organization printed or broadcast free of charge.

Rate Card A card issued by an advertising medium showing its advertising rates and perhaps other information, such as technical requirements and deadlines.

Rate-Holder A small advertisement run by an advertiser who has a frequency contract with a medium when the advertiser does not really want or need an ad.

Rating In broadcast advertising, a measure of the popularity of a station or program period. Determined by ascertaining the proportion of total receivers in use tuned to a given station at a stated time.

Rating Points An index of the number of viewers or listeners in a broadcasting station's audience in relation to the total potential audience in the market.

Reach The total actual coverage of an advertising medium.

Rebate A special discount sometimes given to an advertiser by a medium when the former has used enough time or space over and above the amount contracted for to have qualified for a lower rate.

Registration The proper alignment of printed matter on a page. Multicolor printing is marred by an overlapping of colors or gaps between them when the color plates are "out of register."

Regular-Price-Line Copy Advertising copy pertaining to merchandise at normal retail prices—that is, goods not marked down or on sale.

Reminder Advertising Simple, brief advertisements that merely remind prospects about a store, a product, or a service without elaborating on reasons for making a purchase.

Remote Pick-Up A broadcast (other than a network show) that originates outside a station's studio, such as a radio broadcast from a shopping center or a store's parking lot.

Respondent In a research study, the person from whom information is sought.

Retail Advertising Advertising for goods and/or services sponsored by a local retailer or dealer, and not by a manufacturer or producer. Major retail chains do "national" advertising, in addition to retail advertising, in localities where they have stores. When manufacturers participate in cooperative advertising, it is still termed retail advertising.

Retail Method of Inventory Accounting The commonly used system of inventory accounting in retail companies, in which merchandise is valued at its retail, or selling, price rather than its cost, or wholesale price.

Retail Rate (See **Local Rate.**)

Resource A retailer's term for the company from which it obtains goods for resale, such as a manufacturer, wholesaler, or jobber.

Reverse (Plate or Type) Printed material in which the line copy and/or type is reversed, with the background black (or dark) and the image white (or light).

Roll Time In television, the first few seconds (usually two) of a commercial, which contain video but no audio effects.

R.O.P. (Run of Paper) Ad In newspaper advertising, an advertisement that may be run anywhere in the paper at the option of the newspaper (as opposed to in a "preferred position").

R.O.S. (Run of Schedule) Commercial A broadcast commercial the station may air at any time it chooses.

Rough A crude, preliminary sketch of an advertising layout, requiring further editing and refinement before it is ready for production (also called a *rough draft* or *rough layout*).

Rule In printing, a line that divides a space horizontally or vertically.

Sale Copy Copy that advertises merchandise at temporarily reduced prices.

Sales Promotion Loosely, the combination of advertising, personal selling, and all other sales-producing activities of a business. Narrowly, those sales-stimulating activities that supplement both advertising and personal selling, such as displays and special selling events.

Sample In research, a representative selection of a total group of people or things, chosen so as to permit conclusions applicable to the total. There are cluster samples, judgment samples, probability samples, quota samples, random samples, nonprobability samples, stratified samples, and systematic samples, varying in cost and accuracy. Each has its uses for specific purposes.

Sandwich In broadcast commercials, live copy inserted between a recorded opening and closing.

Saturation Advertising A pattern of advertising messages at frequent intervals over a limited period, for example, during a major selling event. Saturation advertising achieves maximum impact and coverage for that time period, reaching many people frequently.

Schedule An advertiser's media time and space plan for a series of messages during a campaign, a season, a month, etc.

Screening The dividing up of the image of a photograph into a mass of fine dots of unequal size so that it can be reproduced in printed matter. (See **Halftone.**)

Script The written form of a broadcast commercial, indicating the words to be spoken and probably technical instructions for the music or video part of the ad.

Secondary Research Research that draws on data already collected and tabulated rather than on original material produced exclusively for the project at hand.

Self-Mailer A folder, circular, or other direct-mail advertising piece on which the address is printed directly, so that no envelope is needed for mailing it.

Shopping Goods Merchandise consumers usually buy infrequently, often at stores distant from their homes, after comparing the prices, quality, and service offered by various retailers. Such purchases usually involve substantial sums of money. Cars, furniture, appliances, jewelry, and musical instruments are generally considered shopping goods. (See also **Convenience Goods.**)

Shopping Guide   A controlled-circulation paper containing little or no news or feature material. Also called a *shopper, free sheet, pennysaver,* or *advertiser.*

Short Rate   The difference between the discount rate (contract rate) an advertiser agreed to for a given period and the rate it actually earned based on the volume and/or frequency of its ads.

Showing   In outdoor advertising, the number of posters offered as a unit, based on the intensity of the impact desired.

Signature   The name of an advertiser as it appears in an ad, usually in special type and often accompanied by an identifying symbol. In broadcasting, the music or sound effect that identifies a given program or advertiser. In printing, a group of pages that are printed together, then folded, cut, and perhaps stitched to form part of a book or booklet.

Silver Print   In offset lithography, a brown-line image on a white background used for studying the accuracy of the finished ad before a printing plate is made.

Single Rate System   A system in which national advertisers pay the same rate as local advertisers. More often found in large cities than small ones, and more often in television than in newspapers or radio. Federal authorities tend to favor this system, and it may become more common in the future.

Slide Commercial   One of the least expensive forms of television commercials, produced by showing a series of still pictures synchronized with "voice-over" spoken announcements.

Sound Effects (SFX)   Sounds other than music or words in broadcast commercials.

Space Discount   A discount granted by a medium to an advertiser for buying and using a stated volume of advertising space within a given period.

Specialty Advertising   Imprinting useful articles, usually low-cost items, with an advertiser's name and a brief message and distributing them free to potential customers.

Specialty Store   A store that handles an assortment of specialty merchandise such as women's apparel, men's clothing, shoes, or jewelry. Also refers to a departmentalized apparel store, to distinguish it from a full-line department store.

Split Run   A method of testing two ads against each other by exposing half the subscribers to a publication to one version of the ad and the other half to a different version.

Spot Announcement (or "Spot")   A broadcast commercial of from 10 to 60 seconds not directly related to the accompanying program; hence, in effect, almost any local radio or TV commercial. Should not be confused with a *"spot" campaign* by a *national* advertiser focused on specific markets instead of nationwide network audiences.

Spot Color   The use of color in a specific portion of an ad, perhaps to emphasize a specific feature of a product in an illustration; usually a "solid" or "flat" color is used, with no screening to soften the tones.

Spread   A double-page advertisement on two facing pages; also called a *double spread.* When it appears on the center pages of a section and occupies the same continuous sheet of paper, the ad may include the "gutter" down the middle; it is then called a *center spread.*

Stereotype   A duplicate printing plate made by pouring molten metal into a matrix.

Stock Cut   A duplicate of a printing plate for an illustration, an ornament, or a design kept "in stock" by a printer for immediate use at little or no cost.

Stock Music Music already available on tape or records in a broadcasting station's sound library for use in local commercials.

Stock Turnover Rate (Stockturn) The number of times per year a store's average inventory is sold and replaced; the higher the stock turnover rate, the more profitable the store, other things being equal. A primary purpose of retail advertising is to accelerate a store's stock turnover.

Stop Motion A television technique like animation, in which the appearance of movement is achieved by photographing a series of sequential scenes, with the subject in a slightly different pose in each scene.

Storyboard A series of drawings outlining the sequence of scenes for a television commercial; accompanied by an audio script and scene-by-scene instructions.

Straight Announcement A broadcast commercial delivered by a single voice with no embellishments.

Stripping In lithographic printing, cutting out all the components of a negative and pasting them into position on sheets of transparent film, for making a printing plate.

Subhead (-line) A small-scale headline that either follows and elaborates on a larger main headline or introduces additional selling points in the body of an ad.

Super In television production, to impose one picture (often a title or caption) over another scene as both are seen simultaneously. An abbreviation for "superimposition."

Tabloid A newspaper or newspaper section with pages about half the size of regular newspaper pages. Often the format of an advertising insert for larger stores or a special feature supplement containing "targeted" editorial matter and advertisements.

Tag A local retailer's brief message at the end of a manufacturer's broadcast commercial.

Talent Actors and musicians employed to produce broadcast commercials.

Target Market A defined segment of a larger market, to which a store directs its merchandising and advertising appeals.

Target Audience A special group within the audience of a mass advertising medium, or the small but select audience of a highly specialized medium, which certain advertisers especially seek to reach and motivate.

Tear Sheet A page or an advertisement cut out from a publication for the advertiser's internal use or to send to an agency or a cooperating manufacturer as proof of publication.

Testimonial Copy An endorsement of a product or service by a satisfied user, used as part of an advertisement.

Theme The main selling idea of an advertising campaign or program.

Time Classifications Periods of a broadcast day in which the size and nature of the audience habitually attending to a station varies. Though classifications are not necessarily uniform from station to station, Class A time offers the largest audience, Class B next largest, etc. *Drive time* refers to periods when commuter traffic is heaviest and many people are listening to car radios, *prime time* to the evening hours when TV audiences are largest, and *fringe time* to periods just before and just after "prime" periods.

Time Discount A reduced rate allowed a broadcast advertiser based on the number of times its commercial is aired.

Tint Block In printed advertising that employs color, a rectangle within an ad that allows a color to be printed beneath a portion of the copy. Usually the color is a light shade or "tint," and it often contains fine shading produced by "Ben Day" dots or lines.

Trade Advertising   Advertising by a manufacturer, directed at wholesalers or retailers rather than ultimate consumers.

Trade Area   The area from which a given store (or a given group of stores such as those in a shopping center or a central business district) derives most of its business.

Trademark   A distinctive symbol affixed to merchandise or its package to identify the brand and its maker or seller; it can be registered and then becomes legally defensible against imitators.

Transient Rate   An advertising rate paid by an occasional or irregular advertiser. (See also **Open Rate.**)

Transit Advertising   Poster advertising in or on vehicles of a mass-transit system or on its station platforms.

Typeface   The style and design of a type letter.

Type Family   A group of typefaces having similar characteristics and often bearing the name of the original designer.

Type Font   A complete set of type, including the 26 capital letters, the 26 small letters, numerals, punctuation marks, and special symbols.

Type Series   A group of typefaces in the same family, but of different sizes (and also perhaps in different postures).

Type Race   A broad subdivision of styles of type, such as roman, modern, sans serif, script, gothic, or square serif type.

Typo   A typographical error; a mistake in setting type.

Universe   The total "population" involved in a research study, from which a sample is drawn to predict characteristics of the whole.

UHF   In television, an ultra high frequency station, with a shorter range than the more numerous VHF stations.

Vendor   A seller of merchandise; often, in retailing, one who sells to retail outlets.

VHF   In television, a very high frequency station, the most common kind, whose signal carries farther than that of a UHF station.

Video   The visual elements of a television commercial.

Videotape   In TV production, a system of recording a commercial or program on magnetic tape. Both visual and sound elements are recorded and can be played back instantly.

Visual Continuity   The integration, coordination, and harmonizing of pictures, designs, artwork, symbols, colors, and typefaces in all visual elements of a promotional program or advertising campaign. This continuity may extend through all visual mass media (newspaper, television, direct-mail, and sign advertising) to other promotional devices such as store displays, shopping bags, delivery trucks, the store's letterheads and envelopes, menus in its lunchroom, and employees' name tags.

VO (Voice-Over)   Television copy read by an announcer who does not appear "on screen."

White Space   The blank area of a printed ad; one of the basic elements of design.

Zoom   A technique in television production that makes a subject suddenly grow larger on the screen.

Suggested Readings

Suggested Readings

The purpose of this bibliography is to suggest additional readings for the serious student who wishes to explore certain topics in the field of retail advertising in greater depth. However, the works listed here are by no means the only ones available, and those who peruse the card indexes of major libraries or the periodic book lists of leading publishers will find many other excellent volumes. In some cases, several editions of a particular book may have been published. If possible, the most recent edition of each work should be used.

A. A General Bibliography

Other Retail Advertising Texts

Each of these books has its own unique virtues to delight students who wish to choose one or more as collateral reading, to broaden and deepen their understanding of the various phases of retail advertising (or simply to see how various authors say essentially the same thing).

BURKE, John D., *Advertising in the Marketplace.* New York: McGraw-Hill Book Company, 1973. (This is the one introductory advertising text that emphasizes both "national" agency-oriented advertising and "local" store-and-media-centered advertising. It is authoritative, easy to read, and profusely illustrated.)

EDWARDS, Charles M., Jr., and Russell A. Brown, *Retail Advertising and Sales Promotion,* 3rd ed. Englewood Cliffs, N.J.: Prentice-Hall, Inc., 1959. (The great, all-time classic of retail advertising, which has inspired students, teachers, and authors ever since the first edition appeared in 1936. It is very comprehensive, authoritative, profusely illustrated, and scholarly. It vigorously expounds the timeless fundamentals of the field.)

JACOBS, Lawrence W., *Advertising and Promotion for Retailing: Text and Cases.* Glenview, Ill.: Scott, Foresman and Company, 1972. (The one retail advertising book expressly designed for teaching by the case-study method. It is crisp and concise, yet covers all the high points well. It contains some thought-provoking discussions of management concepts.)

MILTON, Shirley F., *Advertising for Modern Retailers: Making It Work in a Consumer World*. New York: Fairchild Publications, 1974. (The newest book on this list, Ms. Milton's volume has an origin unlike the others: questionnaire interviews with a large number of leading retailers in all parts of the country. It reflects the current thinking of those who are active in the field of retail advertising.)

General Advertising Texts

These books focus primarily on national advertising and agencies, but each also includes a chapter or unit on retail advertising. One or more should be read by any student of retail advertising who has not had a thorough grounding in advertising as a whole. Much of the material on advertising management and techniques is applicable to (or can be readily adapted to be applicable to) local or retail advertising—especially by larger stores, those using a complex mix of media, and those employing advertising agencies.

COHEN, Dorothy, *Advertising*. New York: John Wiley and Sons, Inc., 1972.

DUNN, Watson S., and A. M. Barban, *Advertising: Its Role in Modern Marketing*. New York: Holt, Rinehart & Winston, 1974.

FREY, Albert W., and Jean C. Halterman, *Advertising*. New York: Ronald Press, 1970.

KLEPPNER, Otto, and Stephen Greyser, *Advertising Procedure*, 6th ed. Englewood Cliffs, N.J.: Prentice-Hall, Inc., 1973.

MANDELL, Maurice I., *Advertising*, 2nd ed. Englewood Cliffs, N.J.: Prentice-Hall, Inc., 1974.

WRIGHT, John S., D. S. Warner, and W. L. Winter, *Advertising*, 3rd ed. New York: McGraw-Hill Book Company, 1971.

B. A Special Bibliography

The special course and curriculum needs of particular educational institutions and the individual preferences of teachers may dictate further coverage of certain topics covered by the text. Individual students may also have a special interest in certain subjects. The following list of books is a guide to supplementary readings on the material presented in various chapters.

A few of these books deserve special attention because of their treatment of certain areas of crucial importance in retail advertising or the unusual credentials of their authors. These "key books," most of them of very recent date, are indicated by an asterisk (*).

Chapter 1

BELL, Daniel, *Toward the Year 2000*. Boston: Houghton Mifflin Company, 1973.

BENNETT, Peter D., and Harold H. Kassarjian, *Consumer Behavior*. Englewood Cliffs, N.J.: Prentice-Hall, Inc., 1972. (Also related to Chap. 4.)

CLARKE, Arthur C., *Profiles of the Future*. New York: Harper & Row, Inc., 1973.

The U.S. Economy in 1990. New York: The Conference Board (No. 535), 1972.

GERSUNY, Carl, and William Rosengren, *The Service Society*. Cambridge, Mass.: Schenkman Publishing, 1974.

JAFFE, Eugene D., *Social, Cultural and Economic Change in the '70's: Interpreting the Trends*. Rochelle Park, N.J.: Edward E. Emmanuel and Company, 1972.

KAHN, E. J., Jr., *The American People*. New York: Weybright and Talley, 1974.

KAHN, Herman, and A. J. Wiener, *The Year 2000*. New York: The Macmillan Company, 1973.

KURTZ, David L., *Marketing Concepts, Issues and Viewpoints*. Morristown, N.J.: General Learning Press, 1972.

LEVITT, Theodore, *Marketing for Business Growth*. New York: McGraw-Hill Book Company, 1974.

LIPSON, Harry A., and John R. Darling, *Marketing Fundamentals: Text and Cases*. New York: John Wiley & Sons, Inc., 1974.

MAYER, Albert, *The Urgent Future*. New York: McGraw-Hill Book Company, 1967.

* MOTT, Vincent V., *The American Consumer: A Sociological Analysis*. Florham Park, N.J.: Florham Park Press, 1972. (New edition in production. Provides exceptionally useful background facts for understanding modern markets. From the pen of a foremost marketing sociologist, this concise volume is packed with pertinent statistics on which the author makes astute observations. Reads easily.)

RATHMELL, John M., *Marketing in the Service Sector*. Cambridge, Mass.: Winthrop Publishers, Inc., 1974.

TALARZYK, W. Wayne, *Contemporary Cases in Marketing*. New York: Holt, Rinehart & Winston, Inc., 1974.

TOFFLER, Alvin, *Future Shock*, 1970; and *The Futurists* (readings), 1972. New York: Random House.

* WATTENBERG, Ben J., *The Real America: A Surprising Examination of the State of the Union*. New York: Doubleday and Company, 1974. (A magnificent blend of data gleaned from the latest U.S. census and attitudinal research studies by the leading pollsters, this volume is essentially optimistic in tone. Its prolific and keen-minded author opens up a luscious panorama of vast markets to be cultivated in the years ahead—an effective counterbalance to the many gloom and doom prophets of the mid-1970s.)

WEISS, E. B., *How Marketing Will Change: From Growthmanship to Shrinkmanship*, 1972; and *Marketing to the New Society*, 1973. Chicago: Crain Books.

WELLS, William D., *Life Style and Psycho-*

graphics. Chicago: American Marketing Association, 1974. (Also related to Chap. 4.)

Chapter 2

de BERNARDI, J. M., *The Catalog Showroom Formula.* New York: Chain Store Publishing Corp., 1974.

HERNDON, Booton, *Satisfaction Guaranteed: An Unconventional Report to Today's Consumers.* New York: McGraw-Hill Book Company, 1972.

JARNOW, Jeannette A., and Beatrice Judelle, *Inside the Fashion Business: Text and Readings,* 2nd ed. New York: John Wiley & Sons, Inc., 1974.

MARCUS, Stanley, *Minding the Store.* Boston: Little, Brown and Company, 1974.

MARQUARDT, Raymond A., James C. Makens, and Robert G. Roe, *Retail Management: Satisfaction of Consumer Needs.* Hinsdale, Ill.: The Dryden Press, 1975. (Also related to material in Chapters 1, 3, and 4 and Parts 2 and 3.)

WALKER, Bruce J., and Joel B. Haynes (Eds.), *Marketing Channels and Institutions: Readings on Distribution Concepts and Practices.* Columbus, Ohio: Grid, Inc., 1973.

Chapter 3

DICKINSON, Roger A., *Retail Management: A Channels Approach.* Belmont, Calif.: Wadsworth Publishing Co., 1974.

* DUNCAN, Delbert J., Charles F. Phillips, and Stanley C. Hollander, *Modern Retailing Management—Basic Concepts and Practices,* 8th ed. Homewood, Ill.: Richard D. Irwin, Inc., 1972. (A classic since its first edition in 1941. Comprehensive, thorough, and authoritative, this is the ideal basic reference work for those who need to fill in the gaps in their understanding of retail management.)

LANDOW, Melvin S., *How to Make a Million in Retailing.* Hallandale, Fla.: Kennedy and Cohen, 1970 (out of print); or *Your People Are Your Business.* Jericho, N.Y.: Exposition Press, 1973. (The latter is essentially a new edition of the original volume. This is a brief, breezy, easily read "Manager's Manual for Making Millions in Merchandising." A young, vigorous, and brilliantly successful retailer shares his experiences, methods, and reasoning with his readers. A perfect background book for everyone who seeks an overall view of practical merchandising, it is especially appealing to those who are easily bored with the "heavy" and theoretical approaches often found in purely academic writings.)

RACHMAN, David J., *Retail Management Strategy* (readings), 1970; and *Retail Strategy and Structure: A Management Approach,* 1975. Englewood Cliffs, N.J.: Prentice-Hall, Inc. (Choice selections from many of the most brilliant retail executives on fundamental concepts in modern retail management and a text that is especially provocative about social pressures on store managements.)

Retailing With EDP. New York: National Retail Merchants Association, 1975.

WILL, R. Ted, and Ronald W. Hasty, *Retailing: A Mid-Management Approach.* San Francisco: Canfield Press div. of Harper and Row, 1973.

Chapter 4

GOVONI, Norman A. P., *Contemporary Marketing Research.* Morristown, N.J.: General Learning Press, 1972. (Readings.)

MAURO, John (Ed.), *Newspaper Research Primer.* Reston, Va.: International Newspaper Promotion Association, 1974. (Focused on local market research—sources of secondary data and primary field research.)

WALTERS, C. Glenn, *Consumer Behavior*. Homewood, Ill.: Richard D. Irwin, Inc., 1974.

(Note: The material in Chapters 5 through 16 can be effectively reinforced by selective readings from any of the general advertising texts listed in the general bibliography.)

Chapter 6

* OCKO, Judy Young, and M. L. Rosenblum, *The Secret Ingredient of Good Retail Ads: A Handbook for Buyers and Their Bosses*. New York: National Retail Merchants Association, 1974. (Two of the nation's foremost retail advertising experts combined forces to produce this unique volume. It focuses on the all-important relationship between merchants and their advertising staffs, in particular the vital role of buyers and merchandise managers in the planning and execution of the store's advertising program.)

Chapter 7

BRESNEHEN, C. M., Howard Nicks, and Charles E. Treat, *The Cooperative Advertising Concept and Use*. Oklahoma City, Okla.: C. M. Bresnehen, 1971.

Chapter 10

* ABRAHAMS, Howard P., *Making Television Pay Off: A Retailer's Guide to Television Advertising*. New York: Fairchild Publication, 1975. (A step-by-step workbook; also related to material in Chap. 15. The author is preeminently qualified, having served as head of the sales promotion division of the National Retail Merchants Association and as the retail specialist on the staff of the Television Bureau of Advertising.)

How to Profit from Retail Radio Advertising. New York: National Retail Merchants Association, 1975. (Ten retail radio professionals contributed chapters to the comprehensive new book.)

Chapter 11

BRANDSBERG, George, *The Free Papers*. Omaha, Neb.: Wordsmith Books, 1970.

FRESON, Jeannette, *Fairchild's Book of Window Displays*. New York: Fairchild Publications, 1972.

Display Manual. New York: National Retail Merchants Association, 1975.

Visual Merchandising. New York: National Retail Merchants Association, 1976. (Chapters by 24 display and store planning professionals.)

Chapter 12

* YOUNG, James Webb, *A Technique for Producing Ideas*. Chicago: Crain Books, 1975. (A classic, this little gem concentrates on the starting point for all successful advertising writing and production: getting the basic *idea*.)

Chapter 13

* BURTON, Philip Ward, *Advertising Copywriting*, 3rd ed. Columbus, Ohio: Grid, Inc., 1974. (A truly outstanding book for beginners and experts alike. It shows exactly how to write copy for all forms of advertising, with substantial emphasis on *retail* copy throughout. It offers exhaustive coverage of all facets of newspaper copy, as well as excellent guidance on copy for the broadcast media, direct mail, and even the various minor media.)

FLESCH, Rudolf, *The Art of Readable Writing* (1962) and *Say What You Mean* (1972). New York: Harper & Row, Inc.

MILTON, Shirley, *Advertising Copywriting*. Dobbs Ferry, N.Y.: Oceana Publications, 1969.

* OCKO, Judy Young, *Retail Advertising Copy: The How, the What, the Why*. New York: National Retail Merchants Association, 1971. (This easy to read little book

has become a best seller among retail copywriters and students of the art. It insures a firm grounding in the fundamentals and is based on years of practical experience. Since it too covers both newspaper copy and copy for other media, it is related to the material in Chapter 15 as well.)

Chapter 14

* ARNOLD, Edmund, *Ink on Paper.* New York: Harper & Row, Inc., 1972. (A splendid volume by a leading authority on advertising design, typography, and technical production for print media.)

* HIRT, Paul S. *Designing Retail Ads for Profit.* Reston, Va.: International Newspaper Promotion Association, 1968. (A stimulating, heavily pictorial book based on experience in the practical, real-life world of metropolitan daily newspaper retail advertising.)

IRELAND, Patrick John, *Fashion Drawing in Advertising.* New York: John Wiley & Sons, Inc., 1974.

NELSON, Roy P., *The Design of Advertising,* 2nd ed. Dubuque, Iowa: W. C. Brown Company, 1973.

* ROSENBLUM, M. L., *How to Design Effective Store Advertising,* rev. ed. New York: National Retail Merchants Association, 1974. (This exquisitely illustrated book is a "must" for the serious student of layout, illustration, and typography for retail advertising. Written by the nationally renowned former creative vice president of America's largest retail store, who shares with the reader his lifetime of experience and expertise, it is perhaps the most important book in this bibliography.)

Chapter 15

BOOK, Albert C., and Norman D. Cary, *The Television Commercial.* Chicago: Crain Books, 1970.

MILLERSON, George, *The Technique of Television Production.* New York: Focal Press, 1972.

MONOGHAN, Patrick, *Writing Letters That Sell.* New York: Fairchild Publications, 1968.

ROBINSON, Sol, *Radio Advertising—How to Sell and Write It.* Blue Ridge Summit, Pa.: Tab Books, No. 565, 1974.

STONE, Bob, *Successful Direct Marketing Methods.* Chicago: Crain Books, 1974.

WAINWRIGHT, Charles Anthony, *The Television Copywriter.* New York: Hastings House, 1966.

(Also see Chapter 10 listing, ABRAHAMS; Chapter 13 listings, BURTON and OCKO.)

Chapter 16

BERENSON, Conrad, and Henry Eilbert, *The Social Dynamics of Marketing.* New York: Random House, 1972.

BROZEN, Yale, ed., *Advertising and Society.* New York: New York University Press, 1974.

KELLEY, William T., *New Consumerism: Selected Readings.* Columbus, Ohio: Grid, Inc., 1973.

NICOSIA, Francesco M., *Advertising, Management and Society.* New York: McGraw-Hill Book Company, 1974.

PETERSON, Mary B., *The Regulated Consumer.* Los Angeles: Nash Publishing Company, 1972.

WEBSTER, Frederick E., Jr., *The Social Aspects of Marketing.* Englewood Cliffs, N.J.: Prentice-Hall, Inc., 1974.

Chapter 17

Measuring Payout. New York: Advertising Research Foundation, 1973. (Annotated bibliography of 143 books, articles, and speeches on sales effectiveness of advertising.)

Index

1 2 3 4 5 6 7 8 9–KP–82 81 80 79 78 77 76